Peter Norton's

Windows 3.1
Power
Programming
Techniques

SECOND EDITION

Peter Norton's
Windows 3.1
Power
Programming
Techniques

SECOND EDITION

Peter Norton
Paul L. Yao

BANTAM BOOKS

NEW YORK · TORONTO · LONDON · SYDNEY · AUCKLAND

PETER NORTON'S WINDOWS 3.1 POWER PROGRAMMING TECHNIQUES,
Second Edition
A Bantam Book / June 1992

Produced by MicroText
Composed in Ventura Publisher by Context Publishing Services

Throughout this book, tradenames and trademarks of some companies
and products have been used, and no such uses are intended to convey
endorsement of or other affiliations with the book.

ISBN 0-553-37062-6

Published simultaneously in the United States and Canada

Bantam Books are published by Bantam Books, a division of Bantam
Doubleday Dell Publishing Group Inc. Its trademark, consisting of the words
"Bantam Books" and the portrayal of a rooster, is registered in the U.S. Patent
and Trademark Office and in other countries. Marca Registrada, Bantam Books,
Inc., 666 Fifth Avenue, New York, New York 10103.

PRINTED IN THE UNITED STATES OF AMERICA

0 9 8 7 6 5 4 3 2 1

Preface to the Second Edition

Much has happened in the two years since the first edition of this book was published. The IBM-PC celebrated its tenth anniversary. Microsoft started shipping version 3.1 of Windows and IBM started shipping version 2.0 of OS/2. Peter Norton Computing started shipping its first Windows product, the *Norton Desktop*. And International Systems Design started shipping Paul Yao around the world to teach his *Windows Power Programming Techniques* class. It's been a busy two years.

So what's new with Windows 3.1? Windows' three main libraries (KERNEL, USER, and GDI) have gained a few new functions. But most new features are provided in dynamic link libraries. Microsoft will grant you a license to distribute these DLLs so that your users don't need a new version of Windows to access the new features. Features provided in redistributable DLLs include:

- Object Linking and Embedding (OLECLI.DLL, OLESVR.DLL, and SHELL.DLL)

- The Dynamic Data Exchange Management Library (DDEML.DLL)

- A set of common dialog boxes (COMMDLG.DLL)

- Tool Development support (TOOLHELP.DLL)

- Data Compression support (LZEXPAND.DLL)

- Drag and Drop support (SHELL.DLL)

- Pen Extensions (PENWIN.DLL)

To gain the benefit of some features, users must upgrade to Windows 3.1. For example, these enhancements are available only as part of a full upgrade to Windows 3.1:

- Performance enhancements: In particular, printing and file I/O are faster than in previous versions.

- Enhanced Stability: Microsoft has worked hard to prevent UAE (Unexpected Application Errors) errors. In many cases, the user can decide whether to allow a program to continue or whether it should be terminated. Also, Windows' local reboot facility lets users terminate a single misbehaved application without rebooting the entire system.

- TrueType fonts: These device-independent fonts can be scaled and rotated.

- Support for installable device drivers

- Multimedia Extensions

Among the most important "new" features of Windows 3.1 are additions to the API in anticipation of WIN32. WIN32 describes a 32-bit programming interface that Microsoft is positioning as the portable Windows interface. It will have many incarnations and run on non-Intel processors (including the MIPS R4000 and the DEC Alpha). Microsoft first plans to provide WIN32s ("s" stands for "subset"), a 32-bit programming interface for Windows 3.1. Windows NT, which Microsoft plans to ship by the end of 1992, will provide a complete implementation of WIN32.

This book has been completely rewritten to take into account the subtle changes that you must make to your code in preparation for WIN32. The good news is that very little changes between WIN16 (the Windows 3.x API) and WIN32. But we believe there are enough subtle "gotchas" to warrant a completely new edition of this book. You'll find, for example, that every program has been rewritten from the first edition.

We're excited because the success of Windows guarantees that the power of this graphical user interface is fast becoming available to everyone. As IBM-PC compatible computers enter their second decade, we think it is destined to become the "decade of Windows."

Preface

In the spring of 1989, we got word that Microsoft was planning to create its third major revision to Windows. The more we learned about it, the more we became convinced that this would be the version that would attract the critical mass of developers and users to turn it into a hit. Events have proved that our hunch was correct: Microsoft shipped more than one million copies of Windows in the first three months after its announcement on May 22, 1990. Sales of the software development kit are said to be five times what had been expected.

This book was written to help experienced C programmers learn to program in Windows. There are a couple of resources that are invaluable when learning about a new environment. One is sample code that shows the basic techniques necessary to take advantage of the features of the environment. Another is the help of a guru who knows the ins and outs of the environment. This book provides you both.

We have written dozens of programs to demonstrate the use of different features in Windows. We have provided a complete listing of these programs, to give you a complete picture of the pieces that you must work with. Someone once said that only one Windows program has ever been written. Every other Windows program has been cut and paste from the very first one. Feel free to use any of the code in your Windows development projects. (These programs are available in machine-readable form. For more details, please see the inside back cover.)

To get started in programming for Windows, you're going to need the following:

- The Microsoft Software Development Kit (SDK)

- A Windows compatible C compiler (see the list in Chapter 2)

- Windows version 3

Although it's not a requirement, if you plan to run the Codeview debugger, you'll also want the following hardware, which will give Codeview its own output device:

- On computer equipped with an AT-style bus, an MDA card and a monochrome monitor. A Hercules-compatible graphics card can often be used in the place of an MDA card.

- On computers equipped with an MCA bus, you'll want to have an 8514/a adapter and a compatible display, in addition to a VGA-style monitor.

Intertwined with the discussion of Windows programming, this book describes the architecture and inner-workings of Windows. We've worked closely with the Windows development teams—both past and present—to create a picture that we hope you'll find complete and accurate. One thing is for certain: the more we learn about Windows, the more impressed we have become with the ingenuity with which the product has been created.

This book is divided into seven sections. In Section I, we provide a brief history of Windows, and describe the three challenges that new programmers face: message-driven programming, creating and controlling graphical output, and learning how to use the various user-interface objects.

Section II dissects a minimum Windows program, and explores several fundamental topics in Windows programming. The focus of this section is understanding the basic structure that all Windows programs share. A Windows program is made up of at least two subroutines: its entry point, WinMain, and a window procedure.

Section III introduces topics relating to creating graphical output. Output is the domain of Windows' Graphic Device Interface (GDI), which provides device-independent graphic output on displays, printers and plotters. Chapter 6 describes basic concepts in graphic programming, such as drawing coordinates, GDI's device context, and clipping. From there, subsequent chapters cover the output of pixels, lines, filled areas, and text.

In Section IV, we cover three key user-interface objects: menus, windows, and dialog boxes. We describe the inner-workings of each type of object and all of the basics in making them operational.

Section V is dedicated to getting user input. Windows is a message driven operating environment, and so it is not surprising to find that keyboard and mouse input arrives in the form of messages. We describe the flow of data from the physical hardware, through the system buffers and into a Windows program.

We cover operating system considerations in Section VI. This covers two basic areas: memory and dynamic linking. One of the big news items of Windows 3 involves the improvements that have been made in memory use. To help you understand exactly what this means, we describe the inner workings of each of Windows' operating modes.

And finally, in Section VII, we return to topics in GDI programming. Chapter 20 describes scrolling and coordinate transformation. Scrolling describes the way a program helps the user to view a data object that is larger than a window. Coordinate transformation is a service provided by GDI to let you choose the type of coordinates that you wish to use. The default is pixels, but GDI also lets you draw using inches, millimeters, or your own, custom scaling factors. Chapter 21 introduces topics that relate to printing. To help in the creation of full-blown Windows programs, we provided complete source code to a printer configuration dialog box.

Acknowledgments

Researching and organizing the amount of information required for a book like this is impossible without the help of a lot of people. We are fortunate to be associated with a group of individuals who share an incredible commitment to the success of Windows.

We'd like to start off by thanking the development teams of Windows 1.x, 2.x and 3.0. In particular, we want to thank the developers and marketeers who gave of their time and energies to help us understand the subtle nuances of the way Windows works: Peter Belew, John Butler, Mark Cligget, Clark Cyr, Rick Dill, Marlin Eller, Ron Gery, Bob Gunderson, Paul Klinger, Scott MacGregor, Ed Mills, Walt Moore, Gabe Newell, Chris Peters, John Pollock, Rao Remala, Lin Shaw, Charles Simonyi, Tandy Trower, Manny Vellon, David Weise, and Steve Wood.

Within other divisions at Microsoft, thanks to the individuals who helped us and supported us in the creation of this book. At Microsoft University, we'd like to thank Kim Crouse, Mel Kanner, Sheila Keane, Bruce King, Janet Shepardigian, John Thorsen, Mark Ursino, and Ceil Wallick. A special word of thanks goes to David Durant, who is and always will be our first Windows programming instructor. Within the Application's Development Division, thanks to Jim Cash, for helping us solve the puzzle of making Windows programming comprehensible, and to Paul Klemond, a cracker-jack Windows application developer who helped us solve a few Windows programming riddles.

At Bantam Electronic Publishing, we'd like to thank our publisher, and the vice-president of publishing, Kenzi Sugihara. Thanks go to Stephen Guty, our editor, for his long hours and painstaking efforts. And thanks are also due to Lauralee Reinke, Janice Borzendowski, and Randall Pink, who handled the production of the book itself.

Thanks to Kevin Goldstein at Peter Norton Computing, who helped give the manuscript its cohesive direction.

Finally, we'd like to thank the staff at Waterside Productions, and especially their chief, Bill Gladstone, the literary agent for both Peter Norton and to Paul Yao.

Contents

PART I   AN INTRODUCTION TO WINDOWS   1

1   An Introduction to Windows   3

PART II   A MINIMUM WINDOWS PROGRAM   25

2   A Minimum Windows Program   27

P A R T I

AN INTRODUCTION TO WINDOWS

1

An Introduction to Windows

Microsoft Windows is a graphical extension to the MS-DOS operating system. Windows extends DOS in several ways. DOS is built to support a single program at a time; Windows runs multiple programs concurrently. DOS has limited support for graphical output; Windows supports sophisticated, high-level graphics. DOS requires each program to provide its own user interface, which means that users must learn a different set of commands for every DOS program they use. A different command structure in different programs is like having a different steering mechanism and gear shift in different cars: Variety is nice, but a standard interface allows the user to operate any Windows program with a minimum of training. Windows provides a standard set of user-interface objects like windows, menus, and icons. A common set of user-interface objects means a consistent "look and feel" for all Windows programs, which helps make Windows programs easy to learn and easy to use.

Windows provides a multitasking, graphical user interface, or **GUI**, that fosters the creation of interactive programs. Windows represents a relatively new type of operating environment that is optimized for the interaction between human beings and computer programs. Windows programs have a different structure from programs in more traditional environments. This structure has a lot in common with programs written for other GUI systems, like the Apple Macintosh and the OS/2 Presentation Manager. Programs that run in these environments are **event-driven**. That is to say, the structure and operation of these types of programs centers around user-generated events (like keystrokes and mouse clicks). The architecture of such programs has more in common with operating-system software and interrupt-management routines than with traditional application software.

Traditionally, application programs have been sequence-driven and not event-driven. That is to say, *the program* dictates the sequence that the user must follow to accomplish the goal of the program. Event-driven programs, on the other hand, allow the *user* to dictate the steps required to complete a given task. The change from sequence-driven programming to event-driven programming requires a new way of thinking. Helping you learn this new way of thinking is what this book is all about.

A History of Windows

All GUI systems trace their roots back to the work done at Xerox. In 1970, Xerox created the Palo Alto Research Center. Its charter was to create a new architecture for the way information is handled. Among its other accomplishments, PARC is credited with the development of laser printing, local area networks, graphical user interfaces, and object-oriented programming.

The researchers at PARC built several versions of a machine they dubbed "Alto." Over the years, several hundred of these internal research machines were built and were in widespread use. Built on the research of Alto, Xerox created a commercial GUI system: the Star 8010 workstation. Xerox introduced the Star in April 1981, four months before the IBM PC was made public. This multitasking system came equipped with a mouse and a bitmapped graphical display on which were displayed icons, windows, and proportionally spaced text. Although its high price kept it from becoming a commercial success, the Star marks an important milestone as the first commercially available GUI system.

The story is told that Steve Jobs, a co-founder of Apple Computer, was taken on a tour of Xerox PARC sometime around 1979. He was so impressed by the various Alto systems on view that he returned to Apple and pushed for research in the development of a similar system. Apple introduced its first GUI system in 1983: the Apple Lisa. Apple followed the Lisa with its second GUI system, the Apple Macintosh. For its announcement, Apple bought time during the Super Bowl in January 1984 and aired a commercial that introduced the Macintosh as the computer to save the world from the nightmare of Big Brother described in George Orwell's novel *1984*. Although it took a few years to achieve success in the market, the Apple Macintosh was the first commercially successful GUI system.

Microsoft started working on Windows in the spring of 1983. Eight years had passed since Microsoft's founders, Bill Gates and Paul Allen, wrote a BASIC interpreter for the world's first computer kit, the MITS Altair. And two years had passed since IBM introduced its personal computer, which came bundled with two Microsoft products: DOS and BASIC. Microsoft was just getting ready to ship version 2.0 of DOS, with its support for a hierarchical file system to support the hard disk of another new product, IBM's PC/XT computer.

At that time, there was talk at Microsoft of building a GUI system for the IBM personal computers, but no firm plans had been put in place. The primary reason was that the typical PC in those days had two floppy drives, 64K of RAM, and an 8088 CPU. For a GUI system to have acceptable performance, it was felt that more powerful hardware was needed. Hard disks would have to be available to provide fast access, and more memory would be needed to accommodate both the sophisticated code and the memory-hungry graphic data that such systems require. But something happened to spur Microsoft into GUI development.

In February 1983, VisiCorp, makers of the then-popular spreadsheet VisiCalc, announced a GUI product for the IBM PC. Dubbed "VisiOn," it provided the motivation for Microsoft to begin working on its own GUI system. After all, if VisiOn caught on, it presented the possibility of taking software developers off the MS-DOS standard. And one thing was clear very early on at Microsoft: Software standards and compatibility would always be critical to the success of the microcomputer industry.

A team of developers that became known as the "Interactive Systems Group," or ISG, was assembled at Microsoft. Among the members of the team was a Xerox PARC alumnus, Scott MacGregor. Another Windows developer, Neil Konzen, had worked on porting Microsoft's spreadsheet, Multiplan, to the Macintosh. When the first version of Windows was introduced in November 1985, it had features that reflected the influence of Xerox PARC and the Apple Macintosh. But Windows itself was home-grown Microsoft, with features that anticipated the power of an operating system yet to be born: OS/2.

Version 1.01 of Windows started shipping in November 1985. As depicted in Figure 1.1, the first version of Windows provided automatic tiling of program windows. It was felt that the automatic arrangement of windows minimized the amount of work required of the user. This first version also supported overlapping or "popup" windows, which served primarily for the creation of dialog boxes. Windows 1 sported a "three-slice toaster," which provided access to the system menu. Some of the developers joked that this was actually a tiny vent that served to cool the screen lest it become overheated from the speed of the graphics.

The first version of Windows was built to run on a two-floppy drive IBM PC with 256K RAM and an Intel 8088 CPU. This, incidentally, was the configuration used by

Figure 1.1 Windows version 1.01

ISG team members themselves during the earliest days of Windows development. Only later were tools available that developers today take for granted: hard disks and high-speed local area networks with file servers and print servers. While this slowed development somewhat, Microsoft knew that this was the equipment that application developers would someday use to create software that would run under Windows. Developing in this environment, then, helped to stress test its suitability for application development.

The next major revision of Windows was version 2, which started shipping in September 1987. Windows 2, shown in Figure 1.2, featured overlapping Windows. The primary reason for the change from automatic tiling was that Microsoft had received feedback from end users who did not appreciate the benefits of tiled windows, and felt that tiling got in the way. The move away from automatic tiling was also part of an effort to make Windows consistent with another graphical environment that had been announced in April of that year: the OS/2 Presentation Manager.

The similarity between the Windows and the OS/2 user interface was intended to help users move easily from one environment to the other. In fact, the user interface shared by these two environments is part of a much larger IBM strategy to create software consistency that extends from the smallest personal computer to the largest mainframe. This strategy is called **Systems Application Architecture**, or **SAA**. A primary goal of SAA is to allow a program written on one platform to be easily ported to another environment. For example, if SAA comes to complete fruition, you will someday see OS/2 Presentation Manager programs running on IBM mainframes, minicomputers, and, of course, on personal computers. The part of SAA that addresses user-interface issues is known as **Common User Access**, or **CUA**.

One of the other key improvements introduced in Windows 2 was better use of memory in the form of support for expanded memory—memory made available according to the **Expanded Memory Specification (EMS)**. EMS describes a bank-switching technique that makes additional memory available, although bank-switched memory is

Figure 1.2   Windows version 2

not *simultaneously* available. EMS under Windows 2 allowed more Windows programs to reside in memory at the same time, since each program was given a private EMS bank. Although EMS helped relieve the memory crunch that Windows 1 users had experienced, it didn't completely solve the memory shortage problem because Windows 2 only ran in the Real Mode. For compatibility reasons, Intel gave the powerful Intel 80286 and 80386 chips the same one megabyte address space as its less powerful siblings, the 8088 and 8086.

With much fanfare, Microsoft announced version 3 of Windows on May 22, 1990 and started shipping shrink-wrapped packages immediately. Within six weeks, Microsoft had shipped 500,000 copies of the new version, breaking every record for sales of any software product in a six-week period. From a sales standpoint, industry watchers worldwide have found Windows 3 to be a smashing success.

Figure 1.3 shows the new Windows 3 user interface, created to give Windows a new look for the 90s. It features a proportional system font which gives Windows a more refined look and makes text easier to read. Three-dimensional shadowing, color icons, and redesigned applications combine to make Windows more appealing to the average user. Windows 3 also has better support for running DOS applications, which has prompted many to use it as the primary user interface for DOS-based computers.

From a programming point of view, Microsoft has brought an even richer set of capabilities into the user interface: Support for owner-draw menus, owner-draw listboxes, and owner-draw buttons gives programmers the capability to customize Win-

Figure 1.3 Windows version 3

dows more than ever before. Menus in the new Windows can be nested as deeply as programmers can make them, and tear-off menus give programmers the freedom to place menus anywhere they please. The MS-DOS Executive, which was familiar to users of earlier versions, has been fired and replaced by a set of programs that manage programs and files: the **Program Manager**, the **Task List**, and the **File Manager**.

Internally, the most significant feature of Windows 3 is support for extended memory. Under Windows 3, Windows programs can access up to 16 megabytes of RAM. (Windows 3.1 raises the maximum to 256M of RAM.) When an 80386 or higher CPU is present, Windows uses the memory management features of these chips to provide virtual memory. In its 386-Enhanced mode, virtual memory up to four times (or more) the installed physical memory is available. For example, with 16 megabytes of physical memory (and enough room on the swap disk) Windows provides a 64-megabyte address space!

Windows 3 also has better network support than earlier versions, making it easy to connect network file servers and print servers. It supports a device-independent bitmap format that provides a standard for sharing color bitmaps among devices; on devices that support more than 256 colors, applications are even given access to the hardware color palette. This means picture-perfect images, such as those that a multimedia system might use, can now be supported in Windows. Another new feature is a built-in, sophisticated help facility that can be used to provide hyper text help to the program users.

At the second annual Windows World conference in April 1992, Microsoft launched Windows version 3.1, which features a host of improvements. Overall, Windows 3.1 provides better performance and more stable operation than earlier versions. For example, in earlier versions a single application could hang the system. With 3.1, a feature known as "local reboot" allows a user to terminate a single application with a minimum of disruption to other applications.

On the performance end, Windows 3.1 features faster printing, thanks in part to a new approach to printing embodied in the universal printer driver. While making it easier for hardware manufacturers to create printer drivers, the universal driver also uses more efficient printing algorithms than earlier Windows printer drivers.

Windows 3.1 also incorporates a technology called FASTDISK that improves file i/o operations by eliminating some of the overhead that was incurred in earlier versions of Windows. In particular, FASTDISK runs in protected mode—unlike the DOS file i/o of Windows 3.0 which required the processor to briefly switch to real mode.

Another enhancement in Windows 3.1 is the font technology, TrueType, developed by Apple Computer and licensed to Microsoft. One benefit of TrueType fonts is that they are truly device-independent, so that once you purchase a TrueType font face, you can use it on any display or printer that you own. Windows 3.1 itself ships with five TrueType faces: Arial, Courier New, Symbol, Times New Roman, and WingDings. Every major font vendor has already announced support for TrueType, so that users can standardize on a single font format.

Along with Windows 3.1, Microsoft is also making public two important enhancements: the Multimedia and Pen extensions. The Multimedia extensions provide a standard device driver interface and programming interface for a host of new devices. Included is support for sophisticated sound adapters, CD-ROM drives, animation, real-time interrupt services, joysticks, and MIDI support. Individually, these represent fairly simple additions to the Windows API. Together, they allow the development of highly interactive software with the ability to engage the user in ways previously not possible.

Windows' Pen Extensions bring the rich base of Windows software to the new generation of portable, notebook computers. The idea behind pen computing is that people learn to write using a stylus-type writing implement—either a pencil or a pen—long before they learn to use a keyboard. Pen computing incorporates handwriting recognition technology to allow users to replace keyboard input with handwritten data. In addition, Windows' mouse-based pointing operations can easily be performed using a pen. Thus, pen computing offers a unique new way to attract users who have previously avoided computers.

As this book was going to press, Microsoft started to make public a new operating system that it plans to ship in 1992: Windows NT (New Technology). This operating system will support quite a few different types of programs: 16-bit Windows 3.x programs, MS-DOS programs, and POSIX-compliant programs (a UNIX-like API). It will also provide a 32-bit version of the Windows API. Programs written to the Windows 32-Bit API will have a host of new features available to them, including access to a flat address space, semaphores, threads, and a more powerful GDI. Let's consider some of the implications of this new operating system.

Windows NT

It seems that every company that develops a GUI system has gone on to build "new and improved" versions. Xerox first built the Alto, then created the Star. Apple started with its Lisa and later built the Macintosh. After Windows, Microsoft joined forces with IBM to create the OS/2 Presentation Manager.

One goal of OS/2 was to provide a migration path for existing Windows applications. While some Windows applications *did* make the move to OS/2, many did not. The reason for this is simple. Although the Presentation Manager is architecturally very similar to Windows, it provides a completely new API. Every function name is different. For example, Presentation Manager has **WinCreateWindow** to replace Windows' **CreateWindow**. Parameters to similar functions are in a different order or are missing. Presentation Manager introduced a completely new set of symbolic constants. If a Windows developer was thinking of porting code to a new operating system, the work required to move to OS/2 was about the same as moving to any other GUI environment, such as Macintosh or X-Windows.

Windows NT represents Microsoft's admission that it made a mistake with OS/2. Although there are warts on the Windows API, enough application software has been written to make them *our* warts. While the Windows 32-Bit API cures some of the ills of Windows, in general it represents an API that is based on and derived from the Windows 16-Bit API of Windows 3.0. The new API was created with portability in mind, and retains the same function names, symbolic constants, and data structures as the old API.

One change that did occur between the two APIs is that every 16-bit element has been made 32-bits wide. While this may sound like a radical change, it's not. As you'll see, every Windows data type is defined using portable types. In other words, instead of using **short int** or **long int**, there are uppercase types like **HWND** and **HDC**. When you compile a program for either of the APIs, it's a simple matter to select the correct include file for the target API. The compiler then sorts out the differences between 16-bit and 32-bit values.

What does all this mean to you as a Windows programmer? As you begin to create Windows programs, you can feel confident that your software will have a long life. After all, the programs you write for Windows 3.x will be binary compatible with Windows NT, even when Windows NT is running on non-Intel processors. At present, Windows NT is being co-developed on Intel-based computers, as well as computers built using the MIPS RISC processors. In addition, you will be able to recompile 32-bit Windows programs for each host CPU to get the best performance.

Now that you know where Windows has come from, and have an idea about where it's going, the time has come to discuss the major obstacles that you will encounter as you learn to program in Windows. It is important to be aware of the effort required, because it is easy to look at Windows' flexible user interface and conclude (incorrectly) that the programming interface is just as easy to work with.

In fact, the challenge to Windows programmers is to understand the fundamental principles and models embodied in its architecture. Once you understand the "Windows way of thinking," you'll find that Windows programming is as easy to tackle as any other type of programming that you have done. Incidentally, if you have programmed with any other GUI system, such as the Apple Macintosh, the OS/2 Presentation Manager, or the various X-Windows systems, you'll find much that is familiar in Windows. Let's consider the challenges that lie ahead.

The Windows Programming Challenges

Consider the following scenario. It is Friday afternoon, and on your way out of the office you run into your boss. He has good news: The proposal that you made for the Windows development project has been approved. This means that you, and the crack team of programmers who work for you, are going to get to build your company's first Windows program. One of the first things you'll have to do is make sure that everyone on your team is up to speed on Windows. What challenges will be faced by the programmers who work for you who have no previous Windows programming experience?

Assuming that a programmer is proficient in C, the three primary challenges are understanding message-driven programming, controlling graphical output, and using the various user-interface objects like windows, menus, and dialog boxes. Incidentally, if a programmer has been exposed to one or more of these areas, learning Windows programming will be easier.

Before we discuss each of these areas in detail, one suggestion we'd like to make is that you become a full-time Windows user. There are subtleties in the Windows user interface that only become evident when you have spent time as an *end user*. For example, there are the ways the keyboard and mouse work together, the ways that menus and accelerator keys operate, and the operation of the various types of dialog box controls. If you become a full-time Windows user, it will help you to become a better

Windows programmer. At the very least, try to find one Windows program that you use on a daily basis: It might be a word processing program, a drawing package, terminal emulation software, or even a game.

Let's take a look at the three challenges that every new Windows programmer faces, starting with message-driven programming.

Challenge 1: Message-Driven Programming

Most programmers are used to writing code that runs in a sequential, procedure-driven manner. Such a program has a well-defined beginning, middle, and end. Consider, for example, a program that displays a series of data entry screens for the creation of some written document, which might be an airplane ticket or a company purchase order. The flowchart in Figure 1.4 depicts the strict sequence in which such a program might operate.

For the sake of this discussion, let's say that this flowchart represents a program used by travel agents to issue airplane tickets. The first entry screen accepts passenger information, such as name and address. The second screen allows the input of flight information and provides fares and scheduling information. Finally, the third screen accepts payment information based on the fares in the previous screen. Each data entry screen must be correctly filled in before the travel agent can proceed to the next step, and all three screens must have correct information to issue a ticket.

At first glance, this seems like a reasonable way for such a program to proceed. After all, the job of the computer program is not only to issue tickets, but also to make sure that correct passenger information has been received and that the payment provided agrees with the currently available fares. There are limitations to this approach, however, that are a direct result of this sequence-driven orientation.

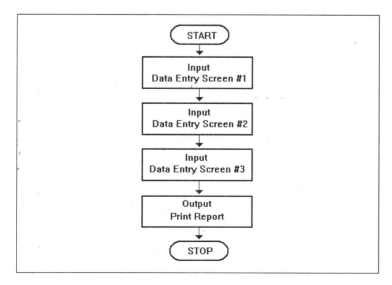

Figure 1.4 A sequence-driven program

For example, since the program dictates the sequence of operation, a travel agent cannot get to the second screen—for fare and flight information—without first entering complete passenger information. While a travel agency might like this feature, since it allows them to avoid giving away free information, the net result is unnecessary steps.

While the program insures that all required information has been entered, it doesn't take into account real-world exceptions. For example, if a travel agent were to sell a group of tickets—perhaps to a family that is going on vacation—the travel agent must traverse all three screens for every ticket that is issued. Once again, the program does its job of insuring that all the necessary information has been collected, but at a cost to the travel agent in the form of the additional work required.

An event-driven program, on the other hand, allows a travel agent to enter the data in whatever order seems appropriate. Perhaps an agent would choose the same order that the sequence-driven program dictated. However, an agent would be free to perform the necessary tasks in a sequence that fits the requirements of different customers. Figure 1.5 gives a rough idea of how an event-driven approach might change the traditional, sequence-driven program that we described earlier.

This is only one aspect of the way that an event-driven program differs from a sequence-driven program. An event-driven operating system like Windows goes even further; for example, within the data entry screens, the travel agent would have a tremendous amount of flexibility with the order in which fields were entered.

A sequence-driven program is built on an awkwardly arranged set of **modes**. A mode is a state of a program in which user actions are interpreted in a specific way and produce a specific set of results. In a reaction against sequence-driven programs, some GUI programmers may tell you that modes are bad. Unfortunately, this is a bit of an oversimplification.

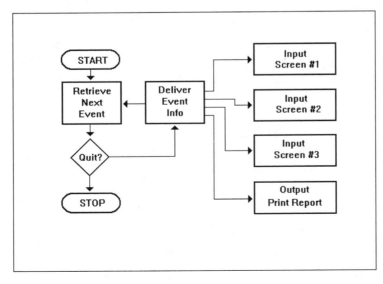

Figure 1.5 An event-driven program

A primary problem having to do with modes is when the user cannot easily move from one mode to another. In our sequence-driven ticketing program, for example, each of the four steps is a mode. But since the program dictates that the user traverse the modes in a strict sequence, the user is prevented from structuring his use of the program to meet the various demands that are made.

Another problem with modes occurs in programs that rely on the user to remember the current mode. A program should provide visual clues to help the user identify the program's current mode. In Windows, there are many user-interface objects that support this. The shape of the mouse cursor, for example, can indicate when a drawing package is in rectangle drawing mode or when it is in text drawing mode. You will see that modal dialog boxes are a very common way to retrieve input from the user that is required to complete a command.

The modes in a program should be carefully designed to prevent data loss when the user accidentally stumbles into a mode. A story often told about modes involves a text editor called Bravo, which was built at Xerox PARC in the 1970s. In this editor, regular keyboard keys are used for commands. For example, the letter "i" puts the program into insert mode, "d" is used for delete mode, and so forth. One user wanted to place the word "edit" in a document, but forgot to first enter insert mode. The editor interpreted these keystrokes as

E (verything) — select everything in the document.

D (elete)   — delete it.

I (nsert)   — enter insert mode.

T   — type the letter 't'.

Oops, the entire contents of the document were replaced by the letter "T." When designing the user interface of a program, you should be aware of the modes that are created and build in the necessary safeguards to help users avoid such unpleasant surprises.

From a programming point of view, modal programs are easier to implement than modeless programs. The code that supports each mode can be written and debugged in relative isolation from the other parts of the program. And yet, Windows makes it easier to create modeless programs because all interaction with the outside world—all events—is funneled to a program in a modeless manner. All events of interest generate messages.

What is a message? It is information about some change in the user interface, such as a window getting moved, or a keyboard key being pressed. Messages notify a program that a timer has gone off. Messages are used for data-sharing operations.

From a programming point of view, a message is a 16-bit unsigned value that, for ease of reading, is assigned a symbolic constant that starts with the letters "WM_". For example, the WM_LBUTTONDOWN message tells a program that the user has pushed the left mouse button. Another message, which gets sent after the left mouse button has been released, is WM_LBUTTONUP. Throughout this book, we'll introduce messages in the context of the different topics that are covered. But if you're impatient to see all the different types of messages in the system, you may want to skip ahead to Appendix A which summarizes the various types of Windows messages.

Messages are very important to a Windows programmer. Most of the work that you will do as a Windows programmer involves deciding which messages to process and which messages to ignore. Keep in mind that messages do not appear in any predefined order. If you are used to a sequentially oriented program, things may seem disorganized and chaotic at first. It may seem that messages fly at you like bullets. To help you understand the flow of messages in the system, Microsoft provides a utility called SPY in the Windows SDK. Figure 1.6 shows SPY listening to the messages of the Windows Program Manager. As you progress in your Windows programming efforts, you will learn which messages to pay attention to and which ones you can safely ignore.

Windows' message orientation is best suited for programs that require a high level of interaction with the user. Therefore, language compilers, which tend to have very little interaction with the user, gain little from running as Windows programs. But games and word processing programs are well suited for Windows, since both require a high level of user interaction. Spreadsheets and data entry programs are also good candidates for interactive, event-driven applications.

A message-driven operating system like Windows puts a high priority on allowing the user to intervene at any point in a process. A sequence-driven program, on the other hand, puts a high priority on dictating the sequence in which a job must be performed. In a sequence-driven program, it is all too tempting for the programmer to create arbitrary rules about the order in which steps should be taken. In such cases, the programmer puts artificial and unnecessary limits on what can and cannot be done by the user. While it is possible to create sequence-driven programs in Windows, the extra effort it requires virtually guarantees that such restrictions will only be put in place where they are actually needed.

Figure 1.6 SPY listening to messages belonging to the Program Manager

MESSAGES AND PROGRAM SCHEDULING

Windows is a multitasking system. To a user, this means that several programs can run "at the same time." Of course, with a single CPU, programs do not run at the same time. Instead, each is scheduled and runs one at a time. In traditional operating systems, this scheduling is done by the clock. Each program is allotted a "time-slice" during which it can run. When its time is up, one program is interrupted, and another program is allowed to run. This is called preemptive scheduling, a process whereby programs are interrupted by the operating system.

Windows does not schedule programs preemptively. Instead, Windows has a non-preemptive scheduling system. Windows programs are not interrupted by the operating system; instead, each program voluntarily interrupts its own operation to let other programs run.

Windows' scheduling system is built into its message delivery mechanism. When a program has finished processing a message, it asks for another message. A message-based scheduling system means that the user is the ultimate source of scheduling decisions. When the user wishes to work with a program, he focuses his attention on one of the program's windows, perhaps by clicking the mouse, or by selecting a window from the keyboard. Each of these actions causes messages to flow to a program, which gives it the "time-slices" that it needs to run.

Messages provide a program with input, but that's only half the story. The other half involves the output that a program produces. Output in Windows means just one thing: graphical output. This is the second challenge that new Windows programmers must face, and our next topic of discussion.

Challenge 2: Graphical Output

All output created by Windows programs is graphical. Figure 1.7 shows a sample of some of the lines, filled figures, and text that GDI can draw. Programmers who are used to working in a character-oriented environment will find that graphical output requires a new way of thinking. As you might expect, graphical output means that geometric figures such as lines, circles, and boxes, can be drawn. In addition, text itself is treated as a graphical object. This makes it easier, for example, to freely mix text and geometric figures. Paradoxically, while graphical output systems make the output of geometric shapes easier, they also tend to make the output of text harder.

Geometric shapes are easier because your program does not have to calculate each pixel. For example, by simply calling the **Rectangle** routine, GDI draws a filled rectangle for you. Text output is harder because GDI's graphical orientation requires that you deal with text as a graphical object. Text is positioned using pixel coordinates rather than by character cell position.

DEVICE-INDEPENDENT GRAPHICS

GDI provides device-independent graphics. This means a Windows program can draw on any device using the same set of calls. For example, the Rectangle routine is called to draw rectangles on the display screen as well as on printers. GDI works hard so that,

Figure 1.7   A sample of GDI's lines, filled figures, and text

from the point of view of a program, all devices look similar. This includes devices that only know how to turn pixels on and off—like the CGA display card—as well as very smart devices that know how to do complex graphics, like Postscript printers. Each device has a device driver that is responsible for doing the actual drawing. For devices that require assistance, GDI provides *software simulations* that use the low-level capabilities of a device to provide high-level functionality.

GDI knows about four types of devices: the display screen, hard-copy devices (like printers and plotters), bitmaps, and metafiles. Two of these are physical devices: the display screen and hard-copy devices. The other two, bitmaps and metafiles, are pseudo-devices. A pseudo-device provides a means to store a picture in RAM or on disk, as well as a standard way to share graphical images between applications.

When displaying information on the display screen, GDI provides window-oriented graphics which involve several things. First, each window is treated like a separate drawing surface. When a program draws in a window, the default drawing coordinates are set up so that the origin (0,0) is in the upper-left corner of the window's client area (see Figure 1.8).

Window-oriented graphics also means that drawings are automatically clipped to a window. Clipping restricts the drawing done for each window to that window's border. Even if a window tried to draw beyond its own border, it would not be able to. Each window is automatically protected from the wayward pixels that other windows might send its way. This protection mechanism works both ways, so that when you draw, you don't have to worry about accidentally overwriting another program's window.

Challenge 3: User-Interface Objects

Windows has built-in support for a number of user-interface objects, such as windows, icons, menus, and dialog boxes. Built-in support means that the amount of effort required to create and maintain these objects is fairly minimal. In particular, if you were to

Figure 1.8 Default origin in Client Area Coordinates

write your own code to support these objects, it would require a vast amount of effort, and the results would probably not be as flexible or robust as the user-interface objects that Windows provides.

Taking advantage of what these user-interface objects can provide requires you to understand how each is implemented. As we look at the different types of user-interface objects, we'll provide some insights into the design and implementation of each. In many cases, this will mean a discussion of the messages that are associated with a given user-interface object. In other cases, this means delving into the various Windows library routines that control each type of object. For now, we're going to introduce you to the user-interface objects and describe the role of each in the user interface.

Among user-interface objects, the most important is the window. Any program that wishes to interact with the user must have a window, since a window receives mouse and keyboard input and displays a program's output. All other user-interface objects, like menus, scroll bars, and cursors, play supporting roles for the leading character: the window.

THE WINDOW

From the perspective of a user, a window provides a view of some data object inside the computer. But it is more than that, since to a user, a window *is* an application. When the user starts to run an application, a window is expected to appear. A user closes a window to shut down an application. To decide the specific application to be worked with, a user selects the application's window. Figure 1.9 shows the standard parts of a typical program's main window.

To programmers, a window represents several things. It serves to organize the other user-interface objects and directs the flow of messages in the system. A window provides a display area that can be used to communicate with the user. Input is channeled to a window and thereby directed to the program. Applications also use windows to subdi-

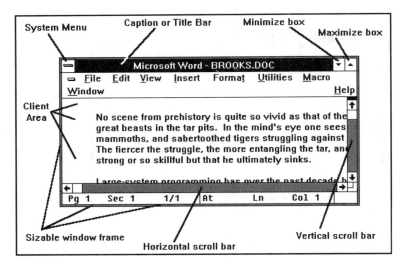

Figure 1.9 The standard parts of a window

vide other windows. For example, dialog boxes are implemented as a collection of small windows inside a larger window.

Every window is created from a **window class** that provides a template from which to create windows. Associated with every window class—and therefore with every window—is a special type of subroutine called a **window procedure**. The job of a window procedure is to process messages. In a message-oriented operating system like Windows, this is an important task. In fact, most of the work that you will do as a Windows programmer will involve deciding how to handle one message or another that is received in a window procedure. It receives the mouse and keyboard input that is directed to a window, which arrives in the form of messages. It receives notifications about other events of interest, such as changes in the size and location of a window. Starting with the next few chapters, one of the first areas that we're going to explore is the way that messages arrive at and are processed by window procedures.

ICONS

An icon is a symbol that serves as a reminder to the user. GUI systems are built on the principle that what is concrete and visible is more easily understood than what is abstract and invisible. Icons provide a concrete, visible symbol of a command, a program, or some data. By making such things visible, a Windows program makes them accessible. By making all of a user's choices visible, Windows programs lessen the user's dependence on memorized information.

Examples of icons include standard window ornaments: the system menu box, the minimize box, and the maximize box. As depicted in Figure 1.10, one of the most

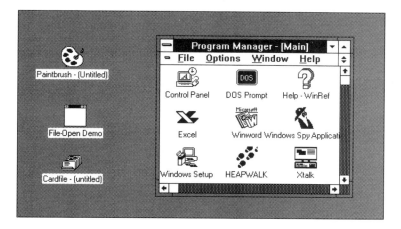

Figure 1.10   Icons in the Program Manager and on the desktop

common uses of an icon is to represent a program. In the Program Manager's window, an icon reminds the user of the programs that are available to be run. On the desktop, an icon serves to remind the user of the programs that are currently running, but whose windows have been closed. Icons can also be used to represent commands. For example, Figure 1.11 shows icons displayed by the Paintbrush program to show users the set of drawing operations available in this program, as well as the available fill patterns.

Figure 1.11   Icons as commands in the Paintbrush program

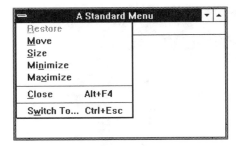

Figure 1.12   The system menu

MENUS

A menu is a list of commands and program options. Windows has five types of menus: system menus, menu-bar menus, pull-down menus, nested menus, and tear-off menus. The system menu, shown in Figure 1.12, provides a standard set of operations that can be performed on a window. These operations are referred to as "system commands." Users expect to find a system menu on the top-level window of every program they run. System commands require very little work on the part of a program, since Windows itself does everything to make system commands operational and uniform throughout the system.

Figure 1.13 shows the three types of menus that are connected together. The menu-bar menu connects to the top of a window, popup menus appear when a menu bar item is selected, and nested menus are displayed when a popup menu item that has an arrow is

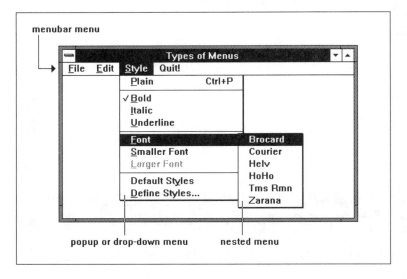

Figure 1.13   Three Types of Menus

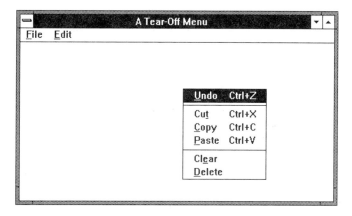

Figure 1.14 A Tear-Off Menu

selected. Applications can nest menus as far as they'd like; however, in general, programmers should avoid nesting too deeply, since this can disorient the user.

Figure 1.14 shows a tear-off menu positioned in the middle of a window. Tear-off menus can be made to appear anywhere in a window, and in fact anywhere on the display screen. They provide another alternative for programs that do not wish to rely solely on menus that descend from the menu-bar menu. Thus, a menu can be made to appear when a specific object is clicked, or in response to a hot key struck by the user on the keyboard.

SCROLL BARS

When a scroll bar is shown in a window, the user knows that the data object is larger than the window. Scroll bars provide a means by which the user can control the display of such objects and also can see at a glance the relative location of an object that is being viewed. Scrolling, and the use of scroll bars, is described in detail in Chapter 20. Figure 1.15 shows the two types of scroll bars: vertical and horizontal.

CURSORS

A cursor is a bitmap that floats on the display screen in response to the movement of a mouse or other pointing device. Programs can change the shape of the cursor to indicate a change in the system. For example, programs often display an hourglass cursor to let the user know that some lengthy operation is taking place. Programs can also change the cursor to let the user know that a program has entered a specific mode. For example, drawing programs often change the cursor to reflect the type of object that can be drawn.

Using the Image Editor utility, which Microsoft includes with the Windows software development kit, programmers can create custom cursors. Cursors can also be created "on the fly," a process that we'll describe in Chapter 16. Of course, you may not need to

Figure 1.15 Vertical and horizontal scroll bars

create your own cursors, if the ones that Windows provides will serve your needs. All of Windows' built-in cursors are shown in Figure 1.16.

CARETS

A caret is a tiny bitmap that blinks and serves as a pointer for keyboard control. The window that has control of the keyboard (also known as the focus) may wish to create a caret to notify the user of this fact. Carets are quirky in two ways: the name and the

Figure 1.16 Windows Predefined Cursors

control. The name is quirky because most other environments use the term "cursor" for the keyboard pointer. But in Windows, "cursor" is already used for the mouse pointer.

The control is quirky because programs must maintain carets. The Windows user interface only supports a single caret at a time. Therefore, programs that wish to use a caret must create one on receiving the keyboard focus and must destroy it on losing the keyboard focus. In Chapter 15, we'll look at what a program must do to properly maintain a caret when we describe keyboard input.

DIALOG BOXES

Dialog boxes, also known as dialogs, provide a standard way to receive input from users. In particular, when a user has entered a command for which additional information is required, dialog boxes are the standard way to retrieve that input. While browsing through a Windows program, you often see an ellipsis (...) as part of a menu name. This indicates that a dialog box will appear when the menu item is selected.

One dialog box that is quite common is displayed whenever the user asks for a file to be opened. It is the file-open dialog box, shown in Figure 1.17. This dialog box provides the user with the opportunity to type in a filename. It also shows two lists: one of file names and the other of directory names and disk drives. If the users are unable to remember a specific filename, they can browse the directories until the desired file is found.

Notice that this dialog box has two pushbuttons: one marked "Ok" and the other marked "Cancel." In general, pushbuttons in dialog boxes are used to request an action. For this dialog box, there are two possible actions. The Ok pushbutton tells the program to accept the values that the user has entered. The Cancel pushbutton tells the program to ignore the results that have been entered in the dialog box. Wherever possible, programs should allow a user to withdraw a request without incurring any damage to files or data.

Figure 1.17   An Open dialog box

DIALOG BOX CONTROLS

Like all dialog boxes, the file-open dialog is a window that holds individual windows that either display information or accept input from the user. Each of these tiny windows is called a dialog box control. For example, the file-open dialog contains thirteen dialog box controls: three pushbuttons (Ok, Cancel and Help), two listboxes, two comboboxes, an edit control, and five static text controls. Windows has six predefined window classes from which dialog box controls are created: button, combo-box, edit, listbox, scrollbar, and static.

In Chapter 14, we're going to investigate the creation of dialog boxes. You will see that dialog box controls do a lot of the work of interacting with the user. Edit controls, for example, handle all of the keyboard input without your having to intercede. Once a listbox has received its list of items, it will happily display and scroll the items in a list without your having to intervene to assist it. You will see that, like many other parts of Windows, dialog boxes and dialog box controls are primarily message-driven.

The first step in learning to program in Windows involves understanding the structure of a Windows program. Windows programs are structured around Windows' event-driven nature. As events occur, they cause messages to be generated. Certain messages are stored in system buffers until your program is ready to receive them. Other messages force their way into your program in a manner that is similar to the way in which hardware interrupts force interrupt-handling code to respond.

The next few chapters discuss Windows' event-driven nature in the context of a minimum Windows program. You may be surprised at the size of this program, but it represents the *minimum* required to respond both to messages that are buffered and to messages that don't wait to be invited in. The minimum Windows program creates a single window and demonstrates how message traffic must be handled in a Windows program. As we look at each piece in the program, we'll describe how it fits into the overall architecture of Windows itself.

P A R T II

A MINIMUM WINDOWS PROGRAM

2

A Minimum
Windows Program

This chapter introduces a minimum Windows program. Figure 2.1 shows the window that our program creates. The window can be moved, resized, closed, **minimized** (made into an icon), or **maximized** (enlarged to fill the screen). In other words, to an experienced Windows user, the window created by this program does all of the "right" things.

Figure 2.1 The window created by our minimum Windows program

Table 2.1 Files That Make Up the Minimum Windows Program

min.c	C source code.
min.def	Module definition file, used by the linker.
min.lnk	Linker command line file.
min.mak	Make file, automates program build process.
min.rc	Resource file, for user-interface data objects.
min.ico	Icon file, a resource.
min.cur	Cursor file, another resource.

The seven files that make up our minimum Windows program are listed in Table 2.1. Five are text files (min.c, min.def, min.lnk, min.mak, and min.rc) and appear in the accompanying listing. The other two files (min.cur and min.ico) contain graphic images, as depicted in Figure 2.2. Min.cur is a mouse cursor in the shape of a hand. Min.ico is the icon displayed when our program is minimized.

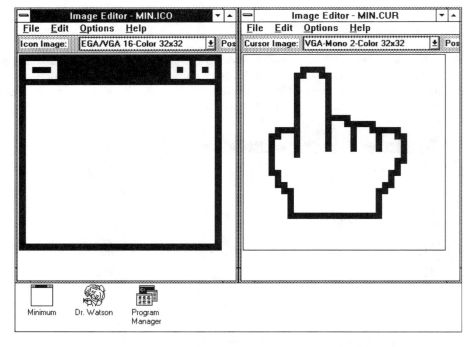

Figure 2.2 The icon and cursor for the minimum Windows program

MIN.C: A Minimum Windows Program

```
/*------------------------------------------------------------*\
 |   MIN.C   A Minimum Windows Program that displays a window. |
 |           The window can be moved, sized, minimized and     |
 |           maximized.  The WM_QUIT message is correctly      |
 |           handled so that the program terminates properly.  |
 \*------------------------------------------------------------*/
#define STRICT
#include <Windows.H>


/*------------------------------------------------------------*\
 |                    Function Prototypes.                     |
 \*------------------------------------------------------------*/
LRESULT CALLBACK MinWndProc (HWND, UINT, WPARAM, LPARAM);


/*------------------------------------------------------------*\
 |                    Global Variables.                       |
 \*------------------------------------------------------------*/
char achWndClass[] = "MIN:MAIN";
char achAppName[]  = "Minimum";


/*------------------------------------------------------------*\
 |                  Main Function:  WinMain.                  |
 \*------------------------------------------------------------*/
int PASCAL
WinMain (HINSTANCE hInstance,       // Who am I?
         HINSTANCE hPrevInstance,   // Any older siblings?
         LPSTR     lpszCmdLine,     // Ptr to command line.
         int       cmdShow)         // How to open my window?
    {
    HWND      hwnd;
    MSG       msg;
    WNDCLASS  wndclass;

    if (!hPrevInstance)
        {
        wndclass.lpszClassName = achWndClass;
        wndclass.hInstance     = hInstance;
        wndclass.lpfnWndProc   = MinWndProc;
        wndclass.hCursor       = LoadCursor (hInstance, "hand");
        wndclass.hIcon         = LoadIcon (hInstance,"snapshot");
        wndclass.lpszMenuName  = NULL;
        wndclass.hbrBackground = (HBRUSH)(COLOR_WINDOW+1);
        wndclass.style         = NULL;
        wndclass.cbClsExtra    = 0;
        wndclass.cbWndExtra    = 0;

        RegisterClass( &wndclass);
        }
```

```
hwnd = CreateWindowEx(0L,                         // Extra style.
                      achWndClass,                // Class name.
                      achAppName,                 // Title.
                      WS_OVERLAPPEDWINDOW,        // Style bits.
                      CW_USEDEFAULT,              // x - default.
                      0,                          // y - default.
                      CW_USEDEFAULT,              // cx - default.
                      0,                          // cy - default.
                      NULL,                       // No parent.
                      NULL,                       // Class menu.
                      hInstance,                  // Creator.
                      NULL);                      // Params.
ShowWindow (hwnd, cmdShow);

while (GetMessage(&msg, 0, 0, 0))
    {
    TranslateMessage(&msg); // Convert KEYDOWNs to CHARs
    DispatchMessage(&msg);  // Transmit message to WndProc
    }
return 0;
}

/*------------------------------------------------------------*\
|                 Window Procedure:  MinWndProc.               |
\*------------------------------------------------------------*/
LRESULT CALLBACK
MinWndProc (HWND    hwnd,      // For whom is message sent?
            UINT    mMsg,      // What is exact message?
            WPARAM  wParam,    // ...message details.
            LPARAM  lParam)    // ...message details.
    {
    switch (mMsg)
        {
        case WM_DESTROY:
            PostQuitMessage(0);  // Handle application shutdown.
            break;

        default:
            return(DefWindowProc(hwnd,mMsg,wParam,lParam));
            break;
        }
    return 0L;
    }
```

MIN.DEF: Module Definition File

```
NAME    MIN

EXETYPE WINDOWS

DESCRIPTION 'Minimum Windows Program (c) 1992 By Paul Yao'
```

```
CODE      MOVEABLE PRELOAD
DATA      MOVEABLE MULTIPLE PRELOAD

HEAPSIZE    512
STACKSIZE   5120

SEGMENTS
    MIN_TEXT MOVEABLE PRELOAD

EXPORTS
    MinWndProc
```

MIN.LNK: The Linker Command File

```
Min.obj
Min.exe/align:16/map/nod/noe/CO
nul
mlibcew libw
Min.def
```

MIN.MAK: The MAKE File

```
# Directory search paths.

INCDIR = \WINDEV\INCLUDE

# Windows version to support
# Valid pairs include:
#     (0x0300, 30)
#     (0x0310, 31)

CLVER = WINVER=0x0300
RCVER = 30

# Compiler switches for applications.

CL_APP_SHIP_ALL = -AM -c -D$(CLVER) -Gsw -I$(INCDIR) -Ow -W3 -Zp
CL_APP_DEBG_ALL = -AM -c -D$(CLVER) -Gsw -I$(INCDIR) -Od -W3 -Zpi

CL_APP_SHIP_31  = -AM -c -G2s  -I$(INCDIR) -Ow -W3 -Zp
CL_APP_DEBG_31  = -AM -c -G2s  -I$(INCDIR) -Od -W3 -Zpi

# Compiler switches for DLLs.

CL_DLL_SHIP_ALL = -AMw -c -D$(CLVER) -Gsw -I$(INCDIR) -Ow -W3 -Zp
CL_DLL_DEBG_ALL = -AMw -c -D$(CLVER) -Gsw -I$(INCDIR) -Od -W3 -Zpi
```

```
CL_DLL_SHIP_31  = -AMw -c -G2s  -I$(INCDIR) -Ow -W3 -Zp
CL_DLL_DEBG_31  = -AMw -c -G2s  -I$(INCDIR) -Od -W3 -Zpi


# Make file primary target.

all: Min.exe

# Make file dependency targets.

Min.res: Min.rc Min.cur Min.ico
    rc -r -i$(INCDIR) Min.rc

Min.obj: Min.c
    cl $(CL_APP_SHIP_ALL) Min.c

Min.exe: Min.obj Min.def Min.res
    link @Min.lnk
    rc -$(RCVER) Min.res

Min.exe: Min.res
    rc -$(RCVER) Min.res
```

MIN.RC: The Resource File

```
snapshot icon Min.ico

hand   cursor Min.cur
```

You may be surprised at the size of our minimum program. With about 90 lines of source code, MIN.C may be the longest *minimum* program you have ever encountered. The size reflects the amount of work that a program must do to tap into the Windows' user interface. But, once a program has made the necessary connections, Windows does a substantial amount of work for you.

For example, Windows provides default support for the different parts of our window. Consider the system menu, with its seven commands: *Restore*, *Move*, *Size*, *Minimize*, *Maximize*, *Close*, and *Switch To*. The structure of our minimum program allows these commands to be operational.

Let's consider just one of the system menu commands. In response to the *Move* command, Windows directly interacts with the user to find a new home for our window. Windows also makes the other parts of our window, such as the sizing border, the title bar, minimize icon, and maximize icon, work.

All of the *parts* of this minimum program are required to allow Windows to do this work for us. The *structure* of this program supports the flow of information from the user, through the user interface, into our program. The structure of this program is important because it embodies the structure of every Windows program. In fact, we'll use this program to build every other program you encounter in this book.

Because you may be eager to compile and run this program, we'll start by talking about the tools that you'll need to build Windows programs. Some tools will already be familiar to you, such as the Microsoft C Compiler and the Linker. You'll need to pay special attention to the compiler switches in order to generate Windows-compatible code. As for the linker, it needs a special input file: the **module definition file**. Other tools that we'll describe are specific to the Windows development environment, such as the Resource Compiler and the Image Editor.

After we describe the development tools, we're going to take a minor detour in the next chapter to talk about some of the conventions that have been adopted for Windows programming. This includes the **Hungarian Naming Convention**, which is used to name data structures and variables. And, we'll introduce the Windows include file, **Windows.h**, that contains symbolic constants and data structures needed in Windows programming. Windows 3.1 introduces a related include file, **WindowsX.h**, which contains a set of quite useful C macros.

Subsequent chapters look at the code from our minimum Windows program. In Chapter 4, we discuss the `WinMain` function, the entry point for every Windows program. `WinMain` typically creates one or more windows and then enters an (almost) endless loop to retrieve hardware-related **messages**. A message is a unit of input to a Windows program, as well as the "time-slice" that makes Windows' nonpreemptive multitasking system work.

In Chapter 5, we're going to review the second function in our program, the window procedure. Our tiny window procedure seems to do very little, yet it plays an important role in every Windows program. We'll use our minimum window procedure to learn about the structure of a typical window procedure, including the function declaration and use of the **default window procedure**. The default window procedure is often overlooked in most discussions of Windows programming; yet, it provides the minimum heartbeat required to bring this user interface to life. In brief, it processes messages that make most of the standard parts of a window, such as the system menu and sizing border, work.

We'll conclude this section of the book with an in-depth look at the different types of messages that you'll encounter in your Windows programming career. There are more than 250 different messages defined in Windows.h and in other include files. We've divided these messages into different categories to provide a framework to begin to understand all of the different types.

Let's begin with a look at the development tools that are used to build our minimum Windows program.

The Mechanics of Compiling and Linking MIN.EXE

When you write Windows programs, you'll use some development tools that you may already be pretty familiar with: a language compiler and a linker. If you don't use the Microsoft C Compiler, you should double-check to make sure that the compiler you do use generates Windows-compatible code. Table 2.2 provides a list of compilers and linkers that, as of this writing, provide the necessary support. We use the Microsoft C Compiler, version 6.0.

Table 2.2 Compilers That Generate Windows-Compatible Code

Manufacturer	Compiler	Version Required
Borland	C++	2.0 and later
Jensen & Partners, International	C, C++	1.05b and later
MetaWare	C	1.61 and later
Microsoft	C	4.0 and later
Microsoft	Quick-C for Windows	1.0 and later
Watcom Products, Inc.	C	8.0 and later
Zortech, Inc.	C, C++	2.1 and later

Some tools, like the **Resource Compiler**, are specific to the Windows environment. This tool serves two purposes: version control and resource binding. By version control, we mean that it defines the version of Windows for which a program or DLL is created. For example, the following command to the resource compiler will allow an executable program to run in both Windows 3.0 as well as in Windows 3.1:

```
rc -30 min.res min.exe
```

Resource binding involves attaching resources to an executable (.EXE or .DLL) file. Generally speaking, a **resource** is a read-only data object which is read into memory by Windows when it's needed and discarded from memory when it's not. In Chapters 11 and 14, you'll use the resource compiler to attach menu and dialog box definitions to executable program files. For now, we'll use the resource compiler to connect our two graphic objects, the cursor and the icon, to MIN.EXE.

> ***Note to Apple Macintosh programmers:*** Windows resources are similar to Macintosh resources. Unlike a Macintosh program, however, a Windows program *cannot* alter the disk-image of its resources. In other words, Windows resources contain *read-only data.*

To coordinate the use of the development tools, programmers often use a utility called **MAKE**, or an enhanced version called **NMAKE**, which stands for "New Make."

The NMAKE and NMK Utilities

Every language compiler provides an automated program creation tool called "make." Such tools are descended from a Unix utility of the same name. A make utility manages the program creation process to eliminate redundant processing: Only updated files are recompiled or relinked. To be this smart, these utilities use an input file (called a **make file**) that describes the relationship of each source file to the output file.

Prior to version 6.0, the Microsoft compiler came equipped with MAKE.EXE. This was a functional, but underpowered, tool. Starting with version 6.0, the Microsoft C compiler featured two new make utilities called NMAKE.EXE and NMK.COM. The "N" stands for "New", to distinguish this newer version from the older version.

NMAKE.EXE is the primary make utility. However, when compiling large source files or when using large include files, NMK.COM can be very useful. This utility calls NMAKE to check for changed files and to build a batch file. NMK then executes the commands, one at a time. Because the Windows include files are so large, we find that we use NMK.COM most of the time.

The make file for our minimum Windows program, MIN.MAK, may seem like a very long file, particularly since it is supposed to represent a minimum of some sort. We wrote the make file the way we did to make it flexible enough to cover the wide range of situations that we feel most Windows programmers will encounter. Let's review the contents of our minimum make file, one line at a time.

The first line is a macro definition:

```
INCDIR = \WINDEV\INCLUDE
```

It defines INCDIR, which identifies the location of the needed include files. As an alternative, we could provide this path in an environment variable named INCLUDE. But we like to save our environment space for other uses.

These two macros:

```
CLVER = WINVER=0x0300
RCVER = 30
```

allow our programs to run in the version 3.0 of Windows. The first variable, CLVER, causes the symbol WINVER to be defined to the C compiler. When set equal to 0x0300, this symbol hides Windows 3.1 features from the preprocessor. The compiler responds with a somewhat confusing message: It provides a warning that a particular function has no prototype. When you see this message, you should realize that you're asking for Windows features that are specific to Windows 3.1 and unavailable in Windows 3.0. To enable the features that are new with Windows 3.1, you'll set this macro equal to 0x0310.

The second macro, RCVER, is a switch that gets passed to the resource compiler when it's binding the compiled resources in min.res to our executable file. This switch overrides the default behaviour which is to mark an executable file as dependent on Windows 3.1.

This set of macros provide a wide set of choices for C compiler switches:

```
# Compiler switches for applications.

CL_APP_SHIP_ALL = -AM -c -D$(CLVER) -Gsw -I$(INCDIR) -Ow -W3 -Zp
CL_APP_DEBG_ALL = -AM -c -D$(CLVER) -Gsw -I$(INCDIR) -Od -W3 -Zpi

CL_APP_SHIP_31  = -AM -c -G2s  -I$(INCDIR) -Ow -W3 -Zp
CL_APP_DEBG_31  = -AM -c -G2s  -I$(INCDIR) -Od -W3 -Zpi
```

```
# Compiler switches for DLLs.

CL_DLL_SHIP_ALL = -AMw -c -D$(CLVER) -Gsw -I$(INCDIR) -Ow -W3 -Zp
CL_DLL_DEBG_ALL = -AMw -c -D$(CLVER) -Gsw -I$(INCDIR) -Od -W3 -Zpi

CL_DLL_SHIP_31  = -AMw -c -G2s  -I$(INCDIR) -Ow -W3 -Zp
CL_DLL_DEBG_31  = -AMw -c -G2s  -I$(INCDIR) -Od -W3 -Zpi
```

Whether building an application or a DLL, pick your switches from the correct set. The macros which contain DEBG will set up to debug with Codeview, while the ones containing SHIP enable optimizations for shipping a production product. The macros containing ALL will run in Windows 3.0 or Windows 3.1. The inclusion of 31, on the other hand, compiles a program to run in Windows version 3.1 or later versions. A little later, we'll discuss the meaning of each of these compiler switches.

The heart of a make file consists of command groups. Notice that our make file consists of five command groups, with a blank line between each. To understand the operation of NMAKE, look at this command group:

```
Min.obj: Min.c
    cl $(CL_APP_SHIP_ALL) Min.c
```

There are three parts to this (and every) command group: a **target file**, one or more **input files**, and one or more **commands** to be executed. The target file is min.obj. The date and time stamps on the target file are compared with the date and time stamps on all input file(s). In this case, there is only one input file: min.c. If min.obj is *older* than min.c, the command line is run. In the example, the command line runs the C Compiler. If min.obj is *younger* than min.c, the command line is ignored. Command lines are any program names (or DOS commands) that can be run from the DOS command prompt. Before the command line is run, the macro

```
$(CL_APP_SHIP_ALL)
```

is first expanded to the set of compiler switches shown earlier in the make file:

```
-AM -c -D$(CLVER) -Gsw -I$(INCDIR) -Ow -W3 -Zp
```

The two macros, **$(CLVER)** and **$(INCDIR)**, are expanded to produce this compiler command line:

```
cl -AM -c -DWINVER=0x0300 -Gsw -I\WINDEV\INCLUDE -Ow -W3 -Zp Min.c
```

The first command group in MIN.MAK defines a pseudo-target, all. In general, NMAKE builds a dependency tree based on the implicit relationships between the source files. The top of this tree is determined by the first command group you define (even though this command group contains no commands!). NMAKE also works properly if the first command block builds your make file's final target, or MIN.EXE in our example.

Run NMAKE to rebuild an .EXE file after changing a source file. For example, after changing MIN.C, we recreate MIN.EXE by running NMAKE like this:

```
C> NMAKE MIN.MAK
```

We also like using a batch file, MK.BAT, to call NMAKE and redirect the output to an error log file:

```
del z.msg
nmk /C Min.mak > z.msg
```

The /C switch prevents NMAKE from complaining about minor irritations that are not interesting to us. For example, it complains that our target file—MIN.EXE—has 'too many rules.' We need two rules to create MIN.EXE, however, because of the way the resource compiler binds resources into an .EXE file.

Microsoft C Compiler Switches

Table 2.3 shows our favorite compiler switches for use with Microsoft C. Eight sets are shown; your choice depends on whether you wish to create a Windows program or a Windows dynamic link library, whether you wish to create an optimized production version or an unoptimized version for debugging, and whether your program will be marked to run only in version 3.1 or whether it will also run in Windows 3.0.

The name of the compiler program is "cl." Each switch or set of switches is preceded by a hyphen (-), although a slash (/) can also be used.

The **-A** switch is for *addressing.* The letters after -A set the compiler defaults for accessing both code and data. The most generally useful type of addressing for Windows programs is the **medium memory model**, which you request with the -AM switch. The medium memory model means that *far* code pointers are used, to allow multiple code

Table 2.3 Microsoft C Compiler Switches

Type of Module	*Switches*
Windows 3.0, 3.1 or higher:	
Program—production	`cl -AM -c -DWINVER=0x0300 -Gsw -Ows -W3 -Zp <file.c>`
Program—debugging	`cl -AM -c -DWINVER=0x0300 -Gw -Od -W3 -Zip <file.c>`
DLL—production	`cl -AMw -c -DWINVER=0x0300 -Gsw -Ows -W3 -Zp <file.c>`
DLL—debugging	`cl -AMw -c -DWINVER=0x0300 -Gw -Od -W3 -Zip <file.c>`
Requires Windows 3.1 or higher:	
Program—production	`cl -AM -c -G2s -Ows -W3 -Zp <file.c>`
Program—debugging	`cl -AM -c -G2 -Od -W3 -Zip <file.c>`
DLL—production	`cl -AMw -c -G2sw -Ows -W3 -Zp <file.c>`
DLL—debugging	`cl -AMw -c -G2w -Od -W3 -Zip <file.c>`

segments. It also means that *near* data pointers are used, with the result that our program is limited to a single data segment. Dynamic link libraries require the "w" option to let the compiler know that some of the assumptions made for the medium memory model do not apply. To use a term that is familiar to many experienced Windows programmers, dynamic link libraries run with "SS != DS."

Although you might be tempted to use the large memory model (the -AL compiler switch), you'd be asking for trouble. With the Microsoft compiler, two or more data segments are automatically created. This causes Windows to only allow a single copy (or instance) of your application to run at a time. It also awakens a nasty bug in Windows 3.0: With more than one data segment, the segments are fixed and page-locked. This causes a disruption in the Windows global heap and prevents the virtual memory manager from doing its job. The easy way to avoid these problems is to use the medium memory model.

The **-c** switch tells the C Compiler to compile but not to link. You'll want to use this switch to override the C Compiler's default behavior, which is to call to the linker when compilation is done.

The **-D** switch creates a symbol to the compiler's preprocessor. The −DWINVER=0x0300 compiler switch, in other words, provides the same result as adding the following line to a C source file:

```
#define WINVER 0x0300
```

The Windows.h file was built to include or exclude various definitions based on the value of this symbolic constant.

The **-Gs** switch tells the C compiler not to call a tiny subroutine that checks for stack overflows. We recommend that you disable stack checking because it requires a special version of Windows to be installed on your computer: the **debug version**. It is a good idea to test your programs against the debug version of Windows in order to locate stack overflows and other hidden bugs inside a Windows program. For more information on creating a debug version of Windows, see the Windows SDK.

The **-Gw** switch tells the C compiler to generate special support for Windows programs. This support consists of adding a tiny prolog and epilog to every far function. While this causes some additional overhead to be incurred, it is necessary for the magic of dynamic linking to occur. A complete discussion of the Windows dynamic link mechanism is provided in Chapter 21.

The **-G2** switch tells the compiler to use native 80286 instructions, which are recognized by all Intel processors above the 80286. The benefit is faster operation. If you're writing code to run on machines with the Intel 8088 or 8086 processors, you must avoid this switch. But if Microsoft's market research is correct, the vast majority of Windows users have an 80286 processor or better. Therefore, this compiler is safe to use in most cases.

The **-O** switches control optimization. **-Ow** instructs the compiler to optimize in a way that is compatible with Windows programs. **-Os** tells the compiler to favor smaller code size over speed of execution. **-Od** disables optimization. We use this last switch to prepare for the use of a debugger with a Windows program. Since optimization can change the relationship between source code and machine code, the -Od switch helps the debugger to correctly connect source code and machine code.

The **-W3** switch sets the compiler warning level. Some people call this the "whine-level." While this switch is not required to create correct code, it lets the compiler help you find **type-mismatch errors,** among others. Given the complexity of Windows programming, it makes sense to get as much help as the compiler is willing to offer.

The **-Zi** switch tells the compiler to generate symbol information. This is required if you wish to use Microsoft's Codeview debugger with your program.

The **-Zp** switch sets data structure packing level. By default, the C Compiler packs data structures to word (even-byte) boundaries. This generates code that runs a little faster on the Intel family of CPUs, which can take twice as long to access data on odd-byte boundaries. However, since memory is the most severely constrained resource in Windows, Microsoft packs all data structures to the byte boundary to save memory, even though it does require a little more processing time.

The Resource File

MIN.RC lists the resources that are to be merged into MIN.EXE. To the Windows memory manager, a resource is a read-only data object. By separating a program's read-only data from its read-write data, a Windows program helps the Windows memory manager optimize the way memory is used. Since almost all of the definitions for user-interface objects are stored as resources, every Windows program (knowingly or not) is built to help make the best use of memory. Table 2.4 lists the eight types of predefined resources. By "predefined," we mean that there are Windows library routines for the creation and control of these objects. If your program requires you to use a large block of read-only data, you can create your own custom resource types to further optimize your program's use of memory.

Resources are normally read into memory as they are needed, although you can mark a resource as PRELOAD to make it resident when your program starts running. When read into memory, a resource usually resides in a memory block that is marked as

Table 2.4 Windows' Predefined Resources

Resource Type	Covered in Depth
Acclerator table	Chapter 11
Bitmaps	
Cursors	Chapter 16
Dialog box template	Chapter 14
Fonts	Chapter 10
Icons	
Menu template	Chapter 11
String table	Chapter 18

DISCARDABLE. This means that it can be purged from memory if the Windows memory manager needs to reuse the memory for some other data object (perhaps another resource). When the resource is needed again, it is reloaded into memory from the program's executable file.

Our minimum Windows program has two types of resources: an icon and a cursor. To create your own icons and cursors, you'll need a tool called the Image Editor. Microsoft supplies this graphic editor as a part of the Windows Software Development Kit. One very useful feature of this program is that it can read the Windows Clipboard. This means you can use other, more sophisticated drawing tools to create pictures, and then use the Clipboard to move these pictures to the Image Editor.

Cursors are bitmaps that respond to the movement of the mouse and allow the user to "point to" different objects on the display screen. For our minimum Windows program, we created a pointer in the image of the human hand. We used **PaintBrush** (bundled with Windows) to create the picture. Figure 2.3 shows the PaintBrush drawing next to the cursor we created with the Image Editor. Once we transferred the image into the Image Editor, we had to do a little bit of cleanup, which accounts for the difference between the original drawing and the final cursor image. This cleanup is necessary because, at 32 by 32 pixels, the cursor bitmap is quite a bit smaller than the original drawing.

In creating MIN's icon, we took a slightly different approach. Since an icon reminds the user that a program exists, we created our icon from a snapshot taken of MIN while it was running. The snapshot was created using a built-in capability of Windows. When

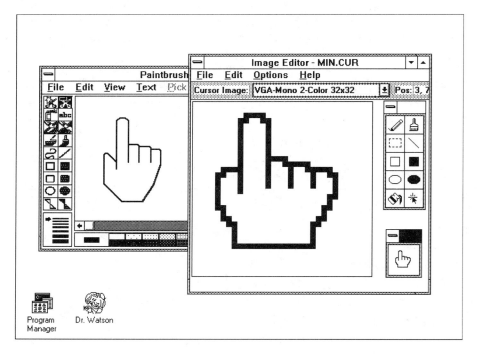

Figure 2.3 Paintbrush drawing next to cursor image

you strike the **[PrtSc]** (print screen) key, Windows puts a snapshot of the *entire screen* onto the Clipboard. When you strike **[Alt]** + **[PrtSc]**, Windows limits the snapshot to the currently active window.

We used the **[Alt]** + **[PrtSc]** combination to capture a snapshot of MIN.EXE. We then pasted this into the Image Editor. After a little bit of cleanup, we had an icon that was ready to use. After saving the icon and cursor into their own files, we made entries into our resource file, MIN.RC, indicating our name for the resource, the resource type, and the file where the resource data was to be found:

```
snapshot icon min.ico

hand cursor min.cur
```

When our program was built, a copy of each resource was merged into our program's executable file. This means that every Windows program can be built as a stand-alone file, with a minimum requirement for external files.

> **HINT:** The Windows screen-capture capability will be very useful in creating documentation for your Windows programs. In fact, we used this method to create all of the screen shots for this book. We used a monochrome VGA display driver and an HP Laserjet II printer. We then pasted the screen shots into Microsoft Word for Windows, which allowed us to print the final results.

Linking and the Module Definition File

A linker builds executable (.EXE) programs from object (.OBJ) and library (.LIB) files. When building Windows programs, the Microsoft linker also reads a **module definition file** (.DEF), that describes the structure and organization of a program. Think of the DEF file as a set of linker switches. To help you understand the role of this important file, let's review each statement in our module definition file, MIN.DEF.

The first line in MIN.DEF is

```
NAME MIN
```

In the Windows world, all code and data is organized into "modules." There are two types of modules: **executable programs** and **dynamic link libraries** (**DLLs**). The **NAME** keyword designates an executable program. (When creating a DLL, use the **LIBRARY** keyword.) For this program, the module name is "MIN." Although previous versions of Windows used the module name to differentiate one module from another, in Windows 3.0 the filename has priority in how Windows distinguishes one module from another.

The second statement in MIN.DEF tells the linker the type of program to create:

```
EXETYPE WINDOWS
```

This is necessary since the Microsoft linker creates both Windows and OS/2 program files.

The DESCRIPTION statement inserts text into our executable file:

```
DESCRIPTION 'Minimum Windows Program (c) 1992 By Paul Yao'
```

This statement is ordinarily used for a program's copyright or version information. To see the description of a Windows program (or dynamic link library), run the EXEHDR utility.

The CODE statement sets the default memory disposition for the code segments in a Windows program:

```
CODE MOVEABLE PRELOAD
```

MOVEABLE means the memory manager can move the segment in the physical address space. Because of the magic of protected mode, the logical address of the segment stays the same. PRELOAD causes code segments to be loaded into memory before the first program instruction is executed. As you'll see in Chapter 18, the SEGMENTS statement lets you take complete control over the memory attributes of each of your program's code segments.

The DATA statement is similar to the CODE statement, except that it sets the memory disposition of a program's automatic data segment:

```
DATA MOVEABLE MULTIPLE PRELOAD
```

MOVEABLE allows the data segment to move in memory. Unless you're creating an application to run in the Real Mode of Windows 3.0, you won't have to worry about this movement. It is hidden from your application in the memory management of the processor's protected mode. MULTIPLE means that copies of your default data segment should be made if a second instance of your program is started.

STACKSIZE sets the a program's stack size:

```
STACKSIZE 5120
```

The stack has three uses: storing of local variables, passing parameters to called functions, and saving return addresses to allow "anonymous calling." Windows programs must have a minimum stack size of 5K. (If a smaller amount is specified, the Windows loader automatically allocates a 5K stack.) Of this, 2K is meant for your program's use; the other 3K is for Windows' use. The reason for this is that the arguments to the routine are passed on the program's stack when a program calls a Windows library routine. Use a higher value for programs with a lot of local variables or for recursive operations.

The HEAPSIZE statement sets the initial size of a program's local heap. Our minimum programs use the following value:

```
HEAPSIZE 512
```

The local heap is one of two places from which dynamic memory allocation can occur. (The other place is the system's global heap.) The local heap is private to a program and resides in the program's data segment. Figure 2.4 shows the layout of a program's data segment. The HEAPSIZE statement sets the initial size of the local heap. A heap can grow beyond its initial size, limited only by the restriction that a segment cannot be larger than 64 kilobytes.

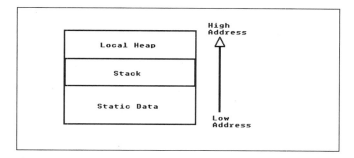

Figure 2.4 The layout of a program's data segment

The SEGMENTS statement lets you assign memory attributes for individual code segments:

```
SEGMENTS
    _TEXT_MIN MOVEABLE PRELOAD
```

We'll explore this in greater detail in Chapter 18.

The EXPORTS statement lists all the functions in MIN that are accessible from outside MIN, sometimes referred to as "exported entry points":

```
EXPORTS
    MinWndProc
```

MIN has one exported function: the procedure for the main window, MinWndProc. As we'll discuss in Chapter 19, the EXPORT is necessary to properly set up our program's data segment when Windows calls our window procedure in Windows 3.0. If you're writing a program which will only run in Windows 3.1, you can disregard the EXPORTS—but it will be some time before everyone can ignore the EXPORTS statement.

> **HINT:** A common programming error involves forgetting to export a window procedure or dialog box procedure. Part of the problem is simply that neither the compiler nor the linker is able to detect a missing export declaration. The problem is compounded since a program will run without the required **EXPORT** declarations. Things seem normal, except that the program develops a "minor" case of amnesia: It forgets all its global variables!

At this point, you should have enough information to type in and create the minimum Windows program. We suggest that you pause now and do this. It will give you a good opportunity to be sure that your development environment has been properly set up. It will also give you the chance to become familiar with this program before we delve into its inner workings. In the next chapter, we're going to address some of the coding conventions of the Windows programming world.

3

Windows Programming Conventions

Among a programmer's concerns, the creation of variables names would probably rate as a low priority. Yet, this task occupies every programmer's time. Once created, a variable name in a program often outlives its creator and gets passed on to successive generations of code maintainers. While most programmers give little thought to the manner in which they create variable names, it's clearly an important task.

In this chapter, we introduce **Hungarian Naming**, a practice that permeates Windows programs. If you're like many people, you will be puzzled by your first encounter with this variable naming convention. Over time, however, you'll find that it has a much greater value than is first apparent.

We'll discuss **handles**, a data type you will encounter often while programming Windows. Handles are often referred to as "magic-numbers," "magic cookies," and "claim check numbers." Regardless of the term you prefer to use, a handle identifies an object created by one part of the system or another. A handle is a number, the meaning of which is known only to the part of the system that created the object and issued the handle.

Next, we talk about the Windows include file. You may have already noticed that one of the first lines in every Windows program is:

```
#include <Windows.h>
```

We'll describe the contents of this file to help you appreciate its importance, and also tell you about some of the other include files that you may need. By the way, as you peruse these include files, you'll find that the symbolic names and data structures are named according to the Hungarian Naming convention.

Finally, we'll touch on an issue that will concern you when you look at older Windows code: **casting**. While it used to be required in the earliest days of Windows programming, developments in language compilers have made this an obsolete practice. In fact, the use of casts can be downright dangerous and can introduce hard-to-find errors into your code.

Let's get started with a look at Hungarian Naming.

Hungarian Naming

Hungarian Naming is a convention for creating names of variables and functions. It is widely used by Windows programmers because it makes code easier to read and maintain. Hungarian Naming, or Hungarian for short, gets its name from the nationality of the original developer, Charles Simonyi. The name is also a tongue-in-cheek description for the convention because programmers often find Hungarian to be confusing initially. For years, new programmers at Microsoft were given documentation for Hungarian that had a picture of Simonyi next to the words "Blame This Guy!" In spite of this ribbing, Hungarian is both highly regarded and widely used inside Microsoft for application programs as well as for operating system software.

Creating *useful* variable names can be a real challenge. Should they be short and sweet? Short variable names are easy to type, but they make code hard to understand. You know what we mean if you've tried reading BASIC programs with very short variable names. What can you tell about the variables "A" and "B" in these lines of BASIC code?

```
20    LET B=10
30    FOR A=1 to 10
40    LET B=B+A
50    NEXT A
```

If short names are cryptic, perhaps we can create useful variable names by making them long and descriptive. Is there any doubt about how a variable called `loopindex` is used? And yet, this approach can lead to variable names that are too long and unwieldy. Consider these names:

```
countofcharacters
numberoffiles
temporaryfilename
windowhandle
pointertoarrayofcharacters
```

While such names may make code more readable, they put a burden on the programmer who has to type them. The use of long names also increases the chance that one will be mistyped.

Hungarian takes a middle road between these two extremes in which variable names are created by putting a short prefix in front of a longer, more descriptive name. The prefix describes the *type of data* referenced by the variable. In some cases, a prefix also describes the *way a variable is used*. For convenience, a prefix can be used alone as a variable name. Here are some examples of Hungarian:

```
char        ch;
char        achFile[128];
char far *  lpszName;
int         cbName;
```

Note that prefixes are lowercase, and long names combine upper- and lowercase. The first variable, ch, is the prefix for character data. It is an example of a prefix used as a variable name. The prefix for achFile has two parts: "a" means this is an array, and "ch" tells us the type of data in the array, characters. The prefix for lpszFirstName also has two parts: "lp" means long-pointer, and "sz" describes the data pointed to, a NULL-terminated string. The variable cbName, contains the prefix "cb" to tell us that the variable contains a count of bytes.

Understanding Hungarian helps us read and understand these otherwise convoluted lines of code:

```
LPSTR  lpszName;
LPSTR  lpsz;
int    cbName;

for (lpsz = lpszName, cbName=0;
     *lpsz != '\0';
     lpsz++, cbName++);
```

The prefix "cb" tells us that the variable cbName *must* contain a count of bytes. Since that's the case, it is pretty clear that the purpose of this code is to calculate the number of characters in the null-terminated string referenced by the pointer lpszName. Incidentally, the use of a Hungarian prefix by itself is quite common for "temporary" variables, which is what lpsz is used for.

In addition to helping you read code, Hungarian helps you avoid silly (but very common) programming errors. As you become familiar with Hungarian, you will come to recognize that

```
lpszName = achFile;
```

is a valid statement, while the following is not:

```
lpszName = cbName;
```

After all, it makes sense to assign the address of an array to a pointer. But, it does not make sense to assign a count of bytes to a pointer.

The trick to mastering Hungarian is to learn the prefixes. Here is a list of the more common prefixes used in Windows programming:

Prefix	*Data Type*
a	Array (compound type)
ch	Character
cb	Count of bytes

Prefix	Data Type
dw	Unsigned long (Windows.h typedef: DWORD)
h	Handle-16 bit identifier
hdc	Handle to a device context
hwnd	Handle to a window
i	Index (compound)
l	Long integer (Windows.h typedef: LONG)
lp	Long (or far) pointer (compound type)
n	Integer
np	Near (or short) pointer (compound type)
pt	An x,y point (Windows.h typedef: POINT)
r	A Rectangle structure (Windows.h typedef: RECT)
sz	Null-terminated string
w	Unsigned integer (Windows.h typedef: WORD)

Notice that some of these prefixes are "compound types" which means they are used as prefixes to other prefixes. The following code fragment shows how two compound prefixes, "a" and "i" define variables that can be used together.

```
char    ch;
int     ich;            /* Index a character array. */
char    achName[64];    /*  Character array. */
...
ch = achName[ich];
```

It is worth noting that there is no "official" list of prefixes. Since any given programming project is bound to have its own unique data types, prefixes will have to be created to reflect those types. In general, however, the usefulness of Hungarian comes from a relatively small number of types and from agreement by all members of a project on the definition of each type.

Hungarian naming is also used for function names. There are several "dialects" that we have encountered. One common use combines a verb and a noun to describe the action of a function. For example, three Windows library routines are CreateWindow, DrawText, and LoadIcon. Within the Windows' libraries you can see other dialects: Some library routines consist of a noun by itself, such as DialogBox. For routines that convert from one type to another, the form X to Y is common. For example, the Windows library routine DPtoLP converts device points into logical points. Two special types of routines, window procedures and dialog box procedures, seem to have their own rules for names: You'll often see the letters "WndProc" embedded into a window procedure, and "DlgProc" embedded into the name of a dialog box procedure.

With a few exceptions, this book uses the noun-verb convention. To help you distinguish our code from Windows library routines, we use a short prefix for function names which reflect the name of the program. For example, the window procedure in MIN.EXE is called MinWndProc.

If you choose to adopt Hungarian naming, it will help you write code that is easier to read and maintain. Even if you don't adopt this convention, a familiarity with Hungarian will help you read sample code from this book and from the Windows Software Development Kit. It will also help you read and make sense of definitions that you encounter in the Windows include file, Windows.h. Let's take a look at some of the definitions from Windows.h.

Handles

A handle is a number. In the same way that MS-DOS issues file handles when a file is opened, Windows issues handles to identify objects. Keep in mind that the only use of a handle is as an identifier. It is just a number that has no meaning outside the context for which it was issued. You cannot, for example, cast a handle to a pointer and do any useful work with it. Quite a few Windows library routines return handles. When such routines fail, they return a "null handle" (that is, `handle == NULL`).

▢ *Warning!*

Be careful—while a NULL value indicates an invalid handle from Windows, an invalid *file* handle has a value of -1. This is because file handles are issued by MS-DOS and not by Windows.

To a Windows programmer, the three most important types of handles are *window handles*, *device context handles*, and *memory handles*. It's more than a coincidence that each of these handles is managed by the three main components of Windows. The user-interface module, USER.EXE, manages windows. The graphics output engine, GDI.EXE, manages device connections. The core operating system module, KERNEL.EXE, manages memory. (With the advent of protected mode, Microsoft has actually split the Windows Kernel into two parts: KRNL286.EXE is the 286-specific version, and KRNL386.EXE is the 386-specific version. The Real-Mode kernel, KERNEL.EXE, has been retired from Windows). Let's take a moment to look at each type of object.

The user-interface module handles many types of objects, such as menus, cursors, and icons. The premier object is the window. When you create these other objects, you make them available in the system by attaching them to a window. As you may recall from the minimum Windows program, Windows programs have a special function which manages the operation of a window: the window procedure.

Each window in the system has a unique handle. When a window procedure is called, the window handle is passed as the first parameter. Once you have a handle to a window, you can completely control the window: show it, hide it, move it, size it, minimize it to an icon, or maximize it to fill the display screen.

Windows' graphic output engine is the **Graphics Device Interface** (**GDI**). Anytime a pixel gets lit on a display screen or a line gets drawn on a printer, you know that GDI is involved. Even Windows' user-interface system relies on GDI to draw windows, menus, and dialogs. When the mouse cursor floats on the display screen, it is GDI's display driver which makes this happen.

To use GDI's services, a program must obtain a handle to a **device context** (**DC**). A DC represents a connection to a particular device. Thus, you'll have one DC to draw on the display and another one to draw on a printer. In addition to providing a device connection, a DC controls the appearance of graphic output. The importance of a DC handle is reflected by the fact that every GDI drawing routine accepts a DC handle as its first parameter.

When the Windows KERNEL allocates memory for an application, it provides a memory handle which identifies the memory object. To access a memory object, an application must *lock* the object. When a memory object is locked, the KERNEL provides a pointer to let you access the object's contents. Although this may seem like a lot of overhead, it allows for the creation of discardable objects. A discardable object is one that the memory manager can purge from system memory when the object is unlocked. This allocation and locking semantic was critical in Real Mode Windows, which—as you may recall—was the only mode available for the early versions of Windows (version 1.x and 2.x). Even today, this mechanism will help you create a single body of source code that can be compiled both for the 16-bit programming environment of Windows 3.x and for the 32-bit environment of Windows NT.

As you begin your trek into Windows, your main task is to understand the operation of these three key objects. After all, they serve as the foundation for the way Windows operates. Keep in mind, though, that there are many other types of objects for which Window issues a handle.

The Windows Include File

While C-language libraries are provided with many small include files (stdio.h, string.h, etc.), the Windows libraries have come equipped with a single, large include file: Windows.h. In the earliest days of Windows (circa 1984), this file was a paltry 20K. For Windows 1.x, it grew to 80K. Windows 3.1 features a Windows.h that's about 150K. Clearly, the system has grown!

As shown in Table 3.1, Microsoft has created other include files. Altogether, 22 include files provide the basic definitions for accessing the Windows API. Even with these new include files, however, Windows' core functionality is described in the oldest of these, Windows.h. You'll reference this file in every Windows source file you write.

You may have noticed that our minimum Windows program has the following line before the line which includes Windows.h:

```
#define STRICT
```

This definition enables strict type checking for the data types defined in Windows.h. Strict type checking forces the compiler to warn you when you assign an inappropriate value to a variable. In particular, STRICT causes each object type to have a unique handle type. This prevents a problem that occurred in earlier versions of the SDK in which a program could get confused when it assigned a memory handle value to a window handle variable, for example.

Table 3.1 Include Files for Windows 3.1

File Name	Description
WINDOWS.H	Primary include file.
CDERR.H	Common dialog's error codes.
COLORDLG.H	Common dialog's color picker defines.
COMMDLG.H	Common dialogs.
CPL.H	Control panel extensions.
CUSTCNTL.H	Custom control interface.
DDE.H	Low-level DDE definitions.
DDEML.H	DDE Management library.
DLGS.H	Common dialogs.
LZEXPAND.H	Compression API.
MMSYSTEM.H	Multimedia APIs.
OLE.H	Object Linking & Embedding.
PENWIN.H	Pen Windows.
PRINT.H	Printing helper functions.
SCRNSAVE.H	Screen saver definitions.
SHELLAPI.H	Shell functions.
STRESS.H	System stress functions.
TOOLHELP.H	The ToolHelp library.
VER.H	Version management functions.
WFEXT.H	File Manager extensions.
WINDOWSX.H	Macro APIs, message crackers, & control APIs.
WINMEM32.H	WinMem32.Dll.

Windows.h contains three types of definitions: symbolic constants, data types, and library function prototypes. Let's look at them one at a time.

Symbolic Constants. In general, it's a bad practice to place "magic numbers" like 15 and 400 into a program because it makes your code hard to read. You should use symbolic constants instead. By convention, symbolic constants are written in uppercase to distinguish them from variable names. In C, the #define preprocessor statement creates symbolic constants:

```
#define MAXOPENFILES 15
```

In addition to improving the readability of a program, the use of symbolic constants makes program maintenance easier. Instead of hunting through a mountain of source

Table 3.2 Symbolic Constants Used in MIN.C

Symbolic Constant	Value	Description
CW_USEDEFAULT	0x8000	CreateWindow constant for default location and/or size of a window being created.
COLOR_WINDOW	5	Identifies a user-defined system color, specifically, the default window color. The user defines system colors with the Control Panel.
NULL	0	Value of zero.
WM_DESTROY	0x0002	This window message is sent to a program to tell it that a window has been destroyed.

code when a numeric value changes, you need only find the single line of code that defines the value.

Windows.h contains more than 1900 symbolic constants. To help you sort them out, Hungarian naming is used. For example, the symbols for window messages start with the prefix WM_ (as in WM_CREATE and WM_DESTROY). If a constant is only used with a single library function, the Hungarian prefix is derived from the function name. For example, you use CW_USEDEFAULT with the CreateWindow function.

Table 3.2 lists the symbolic constants that are used in MIN.C.

Data Type Definitions. Windows.h contains quite a few data type definitions. Some are little more than a convenient way to refer to commonly used C types. For example, here's how Windows.h defines a far character pointer:

```
typedef char far * LPSTR;
```

This typedef statement makes it easy to define a pointer without the need for an asterisk ('*'), since:

```
LPSTR lpszName;
```

is equivalent to:

```
char far * lpszName;
```

Here is a list of commonly used data types:

Windows.H Name	C Definition
BOOL	int
BYTE	unsigned char
DWORD	unsigned long
HANDLE	unsigned int
HDC	unsigned int

Windows.H Name	*C Definition*
HGLOBAL	unsigned int
HINSTANCE	unsigned int
HWND	unsigned int
LONG	long
LPSTR	char far *
NPSTR	char near *
UINT	unsigned int
WORD	unsigned int

Notice that quite a few of these data types are defined *unsigned int*. While you might be tempted to use the regular 'C' designation instead of the uppercase replacements, don't! There are two basic reasons for not using this designation: type-checking and portability. The compiler will provide type-checking to insure that you're using every type in its intended way. If you break a rule, there's a good chance you're introducing errors in your code. When this happens, the compiler issues a warning ("indirection to different types") to indicate that you have a potential problem.

Portability has to do with compiling your source code for the various 32-bit Windows APIs that Microsoft plans to ship. By using the uppercase types, you simplify the porting process: Compiling for the new API will simply involve using a new set of include files. If you use native 'C' types, on the other hand, you'll have to rewrite your code in order to compile properly. Microsoft plans to make the 32-bit Windows API (also known as WIN32) in a variety of forms: as the WIN32 extensions to Windows 3.1, as part of Windows 4.0, and as part of Windows NT. Therefore, writing code with the uppercase types will help you move to all the future 32-bit implementations of the Windows API.

In addition to these basic data types, Windows.h defines quite a few structures. If you imagine that a rectangle structure would be useful in an environment that creates rectangular windows, you'd be right. Here is the rectangle data structure from Windows.h:

```
typedef struct tagRECT
    {
        int     left;
        int     top;
        int     right;
        int     bottom;
    } RECT;
```

Since Windows allows the user to select objects with a mouse pointer, you might expect to find a data structure to record the location of the mouse pointer. Again, you'd be right on target. Here's the POINT data structure:

```
typedef struct tagPOINT
    {
        int     x;
        int     y;
    } POINT;
```

Function Prototypes. An important feature of the Microsoft C Compiler (and part of ANSI-Standard C) is the ability to create *function prototypes*. Prototypes provide a means by which the C Compiler can perform some critical error checking for you. A function prototype tells the C Compiler how a routine should be called. Consider this protype from Windows.h:

```
BOOL   FAR PASCAL TextOut(HDC, int, int, LPSTR, int);
```

This declaration tells the C Compiler that the routine *must* be called with five parameters. A compiler error is generated if the function is called with too few (or too many) parameters. If you think about it, this capability alone makes the use of prototypes a recommended practice. How many times have you written a function, later added a parameter to the function definition, and then forgotten to change a line of code that calls the function? By doing so, you introduced a bug into your program. (Of course, this type of bug waits to appear until you demo your work to your boss . . .) A prototype lets the C Compiler complain about this type of problem so that you can find and correct it early.

A prototype tells the C Compiler about the expected *type* of each argument. When a type mismatch is encountered, a compiler error is generated. Consider this call to `TextOut`. It is clear that the fourth parameter is incorrect.

```
TextOut (hDC, 10, 20, 30, 2);
```

Based on the prototype from Windows.h, the fourth parameter should be a far pointer to a character string (`LPSTR` or `char far *`). When the C Compiler encounters the value of 30, it complains because the type is incorrect. Correcting this particular problem might require placing quotes around the number, as in

```
TextOut (hDC, 10, 20, "30", 2);
```

The C Compiler will also check for the correct use of a function's return value. That is, it checks for type-mismatch errors. The prototype for `TextOut`, for example, defines the return value as BOOL (`int` in Windows.h). This code causes the C Compiler to complain:

```
char far * lpch;
lpch = TextOut (hDC, 10, 10, "Hello", 5);
```

Every Windows function has a prototype in Windows.h, so that the C Compiler can check your calls. Prototyping is useful for Windows library functions; therefore, we recommend that you create a prototype for every function you write. You can use the -Zg switch with the Microsoft C Compiler to request the automatic generation of prototype declarations for your existing C code.

> **HINT:** Be sure to prototype all routines in your Windows code. Prototypes let the C compiler check for errors resulting from calling a routine with the wrong *number* of parameters, the wrong *type* of parameters, or incorrect use of return values.

The availability of function prototypes has made casting obsolete, but a lot of code was written before function prototypes were available. For this reason, you need to be on the lookout for older Windows programs that may reflect an overuse of explicit casting.

Casting: An Outdated Practice

One of the best ways to learn any new programming environment is to look at someone else's code. However, be careful not to be misled by a practice that you might come across in some older Windows programming: *casting of pointers*. It is outdated because newer compilers support function prototypes, which allow the compiler to automatically generate the correct code.

A moment ago, we looked at the function prototype for the `TextOut` function:

```
BOOL  FAR PASCAL TextOut(HDC, int, int, LPSTR, int);
```

The earliest Windows programmers had to write code like the following:

```
TextOut (hDC, 10, 10, (LPSTR)"Hello World", 12);
```

Notice the cast to `LPSTR`. This forces the creation of a *far pointer*. In a small-model or medium-model program, it used to be that the expression "Hello World" would cause a near pointer to be generated. But the function requires a far pointer, so a cast was required.

At first glance, this casting seems harmless enough. The only problem seems to be that a lot of extra keystrokes are wasted. However, there is a real danger to casting. If you were to follow the old-fashioned practice of casting every pointer, you might hide certain problems that the compiler would otherwise detect for you. Consider the following line of code:

```
TextOut (hDC, 10, 10, (LPSTR)30, 2);
```

Perhaps the programmer meant to use the string "30" as the fourth parameter. Without the cast, the compiler notifies us of the type-mismatch error. But a cast forces the value to the correct type, hiding the error from the compiler. In effect, the cast tells the compiler "I know what I'm doing. Please don't ask any questions."

The message is clear: Avoid casting. It negates the compiler's automatic checking, and can hide problems from you.

This is not to say that casts are never needed. For example, they are often needed when working with Windows' dynamic memory allocation routines. These routines are prototyped to return character pointers. If you assign the return value to any other type, the compiler complains. The `GlobalLock` routine, for example, is defined as returning a LPSTR (char far *):

```
LPSTR  FAR PASCAL GlobalLock(HANDLE);
```

The following lines of code cause the compiler to complain:

```
int far * lpint;  /* Define an integer pointer. */
lpint = GlobalLock(hMem);  /* Compiler whines.  */
```

The second line of code would be required if we had stored an array of integers in the block of memory referenced by the handle hMem. Even though the compiler complains, this line of code creates a correct result. However, it's a good practice to reserve compiler complaints for things that really matter. The cast in the following line of code produces the same result, except that the compiler is now happy that there is no type-mismatch error:

```
lpint = (int far *)GlobalLock(hMem);
```

So you see, there are times when casting is necessary. In general, however, the compiler will let you know when the time is right. The rule still stands: Avoid casting. Then, when the compiler complains, you can look at the offending code and determine whether or not a cast will fix your problem.

Messages

Most programmers are used to writing code that runs in a sequential, procedure-driven manner. In Windows, programmers work with a nonsequential, message-driven programming model in which programs are structured around messages and not around a program-defined sequence.

What is a message? It is information about some change in the user interface, such as a window being moved or the user striking a key on the keyboard. Messages are used to notify a program that a timer has gone off. Messages are also used for data sharing operations, which means the **Clipboard**, **Dynamic Data Exchange** (**DDE**), and **Object Linking and Embedding** (**OLE**).

From a programming point of view, a message is an unsigned integer value (UINT) that, for ease of reading, is given a parameter name that starts with a WM_, like WM_LBUTTONDOWN. The WM_LBUTTONDOWN message means that the left button on the mouse has been pushed down. Another message gets sent when the left mouse button is released: WM_LBUTTONUP.

Messages are very important to a Windows programmer. Most of the work that you do as a Windows programmer will involve deciding which messages to process and which to ignore. Keep in mind that there is no predefined order to messages. For this reason, if you are used to a procedural orientation, things may seem disorganized and chaotic at first. Messages will seem to fly at you like bullets. To help you understand the flow of messages in the system, Microsoft includes a utility called SPY with the Windows SDK. Figure 3.1 shows SPY listening to the messages created by the Program Manager. As you progress in your Windows programming efforts, you will learn which messages should be processed. To help you get started, all different types of messages that occur in Windows are organized at the end of Chapter 5 into a "Taxonomy of Messages." For your covenience, this list also appears in Appendix A.

Message Crackers in WindowsX.h

Earlier, we talked about the main include file, Windows.h. All of the core components of Windows are defined in this one file, which you'll include in every Windows source

Figure 3.1 SPY listening to the Program Manager's messages

file that you create. There is another include file, WindowsX.h, that Microsoft is shipping for the first time with Windows 3.1. Among other things, this file defines a set of macros which have come to be known as **message crackers**.

A message cracker is a C macro that parses the wParam and lParam parameters for specific messages. As you recall from our earlier discussion, the contents of these two message parameters depends entirely on the type of message. By parsing the values for you, message crackers make it easy to access the unique values of a particular message.

Each macro assumes the existence of a message processing function that will receive the macro's parsed parameters. For example, every mouse message puts keyboard state information into wParam and cursor location data into lParam. Here is the message cracker for the WM_LBUTTONDOWN message as defined in WindowsX.h:

```
#define HANDLE_WM_LBUTTONDOWN(hwnd, wParam, lParam, fn) \
        ((fn))((hwnd), \
                FALSE, \
                (int)LOWORD(lParam), \
                (int)HIWORD(lParam), \
                (UINT)(wParam)), \
                OL)
```

To use this macro, your window procedure will contain code like this:

```
case WM_LBUTTONDOWN:
    HANDLE_WM_LBUTTONDOWN(hwnd, wParam, lParam, OnLeftButtonDown);
```

This macro constructs a call to a function named OnLeftButtonDown. This function is defined like this:

```
void
OnLeftButtonDown(HWND hwnd,         // Which window is calling
                 BOOL fDoubleClick // Whether double-click
                 int x,            // X-location of mouse
                 int y,            // Y-location of mouse
                 UINT keyFlags)    // Shift-key states
```

A benefit of the message cracker macros is easier source code portability to the 32-bit API of Windows NT. Microsoft will provide a set of macros with the 32-bit development tools, to smooth the few bumps in an otherwise painless porting process. Another benefit is that you won't have to worry about parsing message prameters, since the message crackers do that for you.

When you use these macros, your chief concern will be defining message processing functions that match the one expected by each macro. We simply open the WindowsX.h include file, which—in addition to the message cracker macros—contains sample function prototypes that we cut and paste into our source files.

Now that we've reviewed some of the basic conventions of Windows programming, it's time to look at the source code for our sample program. We'll take it from the top with a look at `WinMain`, our program's main entry point.

4

Understanding the WINMAIN Function

One of the first things you might have noticed about our minimum Windows program is that it has two functions: `WinMain` and `MinWndProc`. Every Windows program needs a `WinMain` function because it is the entry point. The other routine, `MinWndProc`, is a "window procedure," although the name "message processing procedure" is probably a more accurate description. We'll look at our window procedure in the next chapter. For now, we're going to examine the `WinMain` function to find out what it can tell us about Windows programming.

`WinMain` is divided into three parts: procedure declaration, program initialization, and a message loop. Most of the complexity of `WinMain` lies in its initialization. The message loop is an (almost) endless loop that continually reads a message queue and sends messages to the right place for processing.

Procedure Declaration

Let's start our look at `WinMain` by considering the procedure declaration. `WinMain` takes four parameters, as follows:

```
int PASCAL
WinMain (HINSTANCE hInstance,       // Who am I?
         HINSTANCE hPrevInstance,   // Any older siblings?
         LPSTR     lpszCmdLine,     // Ptr to command line.
         int       cmdShow)         // How to open my window?
```

When a program starts running, Windows gives it some information about who it is and to whom it is related. The `hInstance` parameter says who a program is; think of it as a program's name, if you'd like. Windows gives each program in the system a unique name. Of course, the name is not "Joe" or "Fred," but an unsigned integer (the type for which `HINSTANCE` is defined in Windows.h).

Windows tells a program its name because certain Windows library routines require this as a parameter. This allows Windows to know who is calling. Our program calls two routines that take `hInstance` as a parameter: `RegisterClass` and `CreateWindowEx`.

The second parameter, `hPrevInstance`, tells a program to whom it is related. If it isn't related to any currently running program, the value of `hPrevInstance` is `NULL`. How does Windows decide if two programs are related? By name. In the same way that two people with the same last name are (often) related, two programs with the same **module name** are related. Recall that the following entry in our module definition file defines the module name in our minimum Windows program:

```
NAME MIN
```

When a user selects a program to run, Windows looks at the module name hidden in the executable file (and readable by you using the EXEHDR utility). If it finds the name of a module that is already running, it starts up a second instance. It lets the program know that it has a relative already present by passing the name of the relative in the `hPrevInstance` parameter.

Figure 4.1 shows four instances of MIN, three instances of CLOCK, two instances of REVERSI, and a single instance of PAINTBRUSH with a drawing of a partridge in a pear tree. When each subsequent instance of each program starts running, `hPrevInstance` has the name of the previous family member.

Why does a program want to know if it has relatives in town? One thing you should know about instances is that, like real-life relations, they share a lot of things. For example, to conserve memory, all instances of a program share code and resources. The only thing that is not shared, in fact, is the instance's data. The reason a Windows program is notified about its relatives is so that it can call them (that is, send them messages) to share even more things! Of course, you don't have to share. But if you want to share with your cousin Jim, you've got his number.

You should be aware that in the 32-bit API of Windows NT, the `hPrevInstance` parameter is always NULL. For the sake of system security, each copy of every program runs in its own address space and will not share anything with other instances. At least the sharing will be hidden in the NT Executive, which uses a "copy on write" scheme to allow sharing as long as code (and resources) are shared on a read-only basis. As soon as any process writes into a shared resource, the system responds by creating a private copy for the process.

Most likely this change will only affect you if you're writing an application that just allows one copy of itself to run. In Win16 (that is, in the Windows 16-Bit API), this is accomplished by writing code like the following:

```
if (hPrevInstance)
    {
    ...
    // Switch to previous version...
    }
```

Since `hPrevInstance` is always `NULL` in the Windows 32-Bit API, you'll accomplish the same thing with the following code fragment:

```
HWND hwndPrev;
...
hwndPrev = FindWindow ("MIN:MAIN", 0);
if (hwndPrev)
    {
    ...
    // Switch to previous version...
    }
```

In other words, we call `FindWindow` to see if there exists a window with the class name of our application's main window. If so, that most likely means that we're not the first copy; therefore, we respond by passing control to the previous copy, then exiting.

Figure 4.1 Four instances of MIN, three of CLOCK, two of REVERSI and one of Paintbrush

The third parameter to `WinMain`, `lpszCmdLine`, gives us the command line arguments for our program. There are a number of ways that command line arguments get created. The simplest involves putting the arguments after the program name in the Program Manager's File Properties... dialog box. Like the `argv` parameter in the standard C program entry point:

```
main (int argc, char **argv)
```

the `lpszCmdLine` parameter is used to pass parameters such as filenames and option switches. Unlike `argv`, however, `lpszCmdLine` points to a single character string and *not* an array of character pointers.

The final parameter, `cmdShow`, tells a program what to do with its main window when it first starts. Should it be minimized? Should it be displayed full screen? Notice that we later pass this value as the second parameter to the `ShowWindow` routine.

With this basic understanding of the four `WinMain` parameters, we're ready to look at the initialization of our minimum Windows program. This involves creating a window for our program to use.

Program Initialization

This is how MIN's `WinMain` function performs its initialization:

```
if (!hPrevInstance)
    {
    wndclass.lpszClassName = achWndClass;
    wndclass.hInstance     = hInstance;
    wndclass.lpfnWndProc   = MinWndProc;
    wndclass.hCursor       = LoadCursor (hInstance, "hand");
    wndclass.hIcon         = LoadIcon (hInstance,"snapshot");
    wndclass.lpszMenuName  = NULL;
    wndclass.hbrBackground = (HBRUSH)(COLOR_WINDOW+1);
    wndclass.style         = NULL;
    wndclass.cbClsExtra    = 0;
    wndclass.cbWndExtra    = 0;

    RegisterClass( &wndclass);
    }
hwnd = CreateWindowEx(0L,                  // Extra style.
                   achWndClass,            // Class name.
                   achAppName,             // Title.
                   WS_OVERLAPPEDWINDOW,    // Style bits.
                   CW_USEDEFAULT,          // x - default.
                   0,                      // y - default.
                   CW_USEDEFAULT,          // cx - default.
                   0,                      // cy - default.
                   NULL,                   // No parent.
                   NULL,                   // Class menu.
                   hInstance,              // Creator.
                   NULL);                  // Params.
ShowWindow (hwnd, cmdShow);
```

Initialization involves calling three Windows library routines: `RegisterClass`, `CreateWindowEx`, and `ShowWindow`.

Recall that earlier we said `hPrevInstance` would be `NULL` when the first copy of a program is run. For subsequent copies, it contains the instance handle for the previous instance of a program (in the Win16 API, that is). This means that `RegisterClass` is only called for a program's first instance. Whatever `RegisterClass` does (we'll see in a moment), the results are shared by every other instance. In addition to sharing code and resources, instances share the results of `RegisterClass`.

Window Class Registration

`RegisterClass` takes a single parameter: a pointer to a structure of type `WNDCLASS`. Since this structure contains 10 values, it would be more accurate to say that `RegisterClass` takes 10 parameters.

`RegisterClass` defines a window class. Windows copies the elements from this data structure into a place that might be called the **Class Database**. When a program wants to create a window, it references an entry in the Class Database. Windows then uses that information to create the window. The key point to remember about a window class is that a single class definition can support multiple windows. In other words, a window class is a template from which windows are created.

What are the advantages of a class definition? A moment ago we said that instances of a program shares the results of `RegisterClass`. Since `RegisterClass` creates a class definition, it follows that every instance of a program shares the class definition. One of the benefits this brings is better memory use. Let's look at each element in `WNDCLASS` to better understand what a class definition provides.

Every class has a name. You create the name, place it in a character string, and put a pointer to the string in the `lpszClasssName` element of the `WNDCLASS` structure. This is the key, or lookup value, that identifies a class database entry.

The `hInstance` value tells Windows *who* created the class definition. This is needed for Windows' internal housekeeping. When the last instance of a program terminates, Windows removes all class definitions created by that family.

The `lpfnWndProc` value gives Windows the address of a function to associate with a window class. This function is called a **window procedure**. The role of a window procedure can be simply stated: A window procedure processes messages. This sounds rather bland; but you will see that almost all of the pizazz and sparkle in a Windows program comes from the way messages are handled by its window procedure(s) when we describe our window procedure a little later.

The `hCursor` value identifies the default mouse cursor for our window class. Every time the cursor moves across our window, its shape will change to the one defined here. As you may recall, our MIN program has a cursor that we created using the Image Editor. The file that contains the cursor definition, MIN.CUR, is referenced in our resource file, MIN.RC, with the line:

```
hand cursor min.cur
```

To load this cursor definition into memory, we must ask for it. We do so by calling the Windows `LoadCursor` function. It returns a handle that identifies the cursor, which we assign to the corresponding member of the `WNDCLASS` structure:

```
wndclass.hCursor = LoadCursor (hInstance, "hand");
```

Notice that `LoadCursor`'s second parameter is `hand`, the name we gave the cursor's resource in MIN.RC.

The `hIcon` element of `WNDCLASS` is handled in a similar manner. We create an icon using the Image Editor, store it in the file MIN.ICO, and make the following entry into MIN.RC:

```
snapshot icon min.ico
```

Like the cursor definition, the icon data is bound into MIN.EXE at program creation time. Also like cursors (and other resources), the icon is accessed by making a call to a special routine:

```
wndclass.hIcon = LoadIcon (hInstance,"snapshot");
```

The class definition provides a place to define a menu for our window. But MIN doesn't have a menu; so we assign `NULL` to so inform Windows:

```
wndclass.lpszMenuName = NULL;
```

The `hbrBackground` field of `WNDCLASS` asks us for one thing, and we give it something else! This requires a little explanation. This field defines the background color for a window. If we were to define a background color for this printed page, we would select white (since the book is printed black text on white paper). Before any drawing is done in a window, we often paint a window with the background color. This gives us a clean surface on which to draw.

The Hungarian prefix "hbr" tells us that this element is a "handle to a brush." We'll talk about brushes when we talk about using the Graphics Device Interface (GDI) to fill areas in Chapter 9. In brief, a Windows programs defines how an area should be filled by defining a brush. Although MIN could use a brush to describe how its background is to be filled, it doesn't.

Instead, MIN uses a magic number that lets Windows know it wants to use the system's default background color. A user can select the system wide background color using the Control Panel program. By selecting the following value, MIN tells Windows to use the color selected by the user. To make the default background color a part of our window class definition, we use the special `COLOR_WINDOW+1` value:

```
wndclass.hbrBackground = (HBRUSH)(COLOR_WINDOW+1);
```

The definition that appears in Windows.h is

```
#define COLOR_WINDOW        5
```

which is one of 19 system color constants that are defined. You might be wondering why we add one to this constant. It turns out that the first value in this group has the value zero. But zero is an invalid value for a brush handle (or any other handle, for that matter). So, to use these constants in place of a handle, we add one to make the entire range of system colors valid.

You might also wonder why the value is cast to HBRUSH. In particular, you may recall that we warned you to avoid casting in the last chapter because it can hide certain types of problems. There are times, however, when casting is perfectly reasonable. As you must have guessed by now, this is one of those times.

The next WNDCLASS structure member that we're going to look at is the **style** field. In the world of Windows programming, the term style refers to a collection of options each of which is controlled by one or two bits. To conserve space, style fields combine these options into a two-byte (or four-byte) field. We'll delve into the meaning of each style bit in Chapter 13, where we'll cover all the aspects of creating windows. For now, MIN doesn't use any style bits:

```
wndclass.style         = NULL;
```

The last two fields in WNDCLASS, cbClsExtra, and cbWndExtra, are used to request that extra space be allocated in the class database (cbClsExtra) and in a related database, the **window database** (cbWndExtra), which contains an entry for every window in the system. This allows you to attach your own, private data to a class or a window. Right now, it may seem like a strange thing to do, but window extra bytes provide one of the most convenient ways for making a connection between a user-interface object and your program's data. In a sense, it provides a form of built-in data encapsulation.

After the first instance of our program calls RegisterClass, an entry is made into Window's class database. With an entry in the database, every instance of MIN can create its own private window. We could even modify MIN to create multiple copies of a MIN:MAIN window, if desired. But RegisterClass doesn't create windows. That job falls to the next routine we're going to discuss: CreateWindowEx.

Window Creation

Once a window class has been registered, we can begin creating windows. Here is the call we make to CreateWindowEx. As you might expect, one of the first parameters to CreateWindowEx specifies the class of window that we wish to create:

```
hwnd = CreateWindowEx(0L,                   // Extra style.
                      achWndClass,          // Class name.
                      achAppName,           // Title.
                      WS_OVERLAPPEDWINDOW,  // Style bits.
                      CW_USEDEFAULT,        // x - default.
                      0,                    // y - default.
                      CW_USEDEFAULT,        // cx - default.
                      0,                    // cy - default.
                      NULL,                 // No parent.
                      NULL,                 // Class menu.
                      hInstance,            // Creator.
                      NULL);                // Params.
```

The `CreateWindowEx` function is the offspring of an older Windows function, `CreateWindow`. This new routine had to be added for one reason: The Windows development team ran out of unique bit positions in the style parameter (the fourth parameter to `CreateWindowEx`). Since `CreateWindow` simply calls `CreateWindowEx`, we prefer directly calling this newer routine.

The third parameter is the window title which appears in the titlebar when a window is opened, and next to the window's icon when a window is minimized. This is a good place to put a program's name. After a window has been created, your program can call `SetWindowText` to change the title.

The fourth parameter is for style bits. As we mentioned in our discussion of class-style bits, a style field combines several one- and two-bit wide fields into a single two- or four-byte value. For your convenience, top-level windows can use the `WS_OVER-LAPPEDWINDOW` definition. This combines six simpler style bits together. Here is the definition from Windows.h:

```
#define WS_OVERLAPPEDWINDOW (WS_OVERLAPPED | WS_CAPTION |
WS_SYSMENU | WS_THICKFRAME |  WS_MINIMIZEBOX | WS_MAXIMIZEBOX)
```

The C-language bitwise OR operator, |, packs together these simpler bit-definitions:

```
#define WS_OVERLAPPED       0x00000000L
#define WS_CAPTION          0x00C00000L
#define WS_SYSMENU          0x00080000L
#define WS_THICKFRAME       0x00040000L
#define WS_MINIMIZEBOX      0x00020000L
#define WS_MAXIMIZEBOX      0x00010000L
```

The definition of `WS_OVERLAPPED` has no bits turned on, which means this field has no effect when ORed with the other style values. This flag is defined to help distinguish the three types of windows. The other two types are created using the following style-flags:

```
#define WS_POPUP       0x80000000L
#define WS_CHILD       0x40000000L
```

WS_OVERLAPPED is simply a place holder so that at a glance you can tell what type of window is being created.

The other style bits that are part of the `WS_OVERLAPPEDWINDOW` definition serve to create the different parts of the window. Figure 4.2 shows the relationship of window-style bits to the parts of a window. For a complete discussion of the different window-style bits, refer to Chapter 13.

The fifth, sixth, seventh, and eighth parameters determine the starting size and location of a window. The X and Y values describe the location of the upper-left corner of our window relative to the upper-left corner of the display screen. The units for all four parameters are pixels. MIN takes the easy way out by asking Windows to create an appropriate size and location for our window with the `CW_USEDEFAULT` flag. This flag must be set in the X and CX fields of `CreateWindowEx`. When it is used, the Y and CY values are ignored.

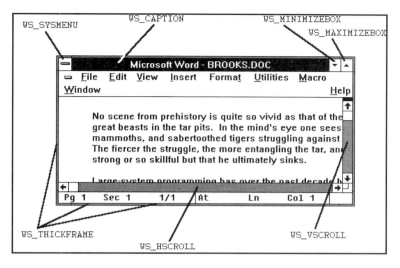

Figure 4.2 Style bits and the parts of a window

The ninth parameter defines a window's parent. While the term "parent" has lots of connotations, both in the real world and in the world of object-oriented programming, the meaning here is much simpler. It describes lifetime and visibility: A window's life ends when its parent is destroyed, and it is hidden and displayed when its parent window is hidden or displayed. (There is a third meaning for WS_CHILD windows: They must reside in the pixels of their parent. More on that meaning will be covered in Chapter 13). Like the main window in most programs, the main window in MIN has no parent. We declare this with a value of NULL in this parameter.

The tenth parameter allows us to attach a menu to a window. This is the second chance we have to specify a menu—the first was in the class definition. The WNDCLASS data structure lets us define a menu to be shared by every member of a class. If our class definition had a menu name, we would automatically get the class menu by specifying NULL in this parameter. If a window has a private menu, it can use this field to establish that fact. Our window has no menu because we set the class menu name to NULL, and set the ninth parameter to CreateWindowEx to NULL as well.

The eleventh parameter, an instance handle, identifies the window owner. This lets Windows know which instance of our program has created the window. The reason for this parameter is subtle, but essentially it allows Windows to set up the data segment register correctly when it calls our window procedure. (See the box on page 72 for more details on this mechanism, and Chapter 19 for an in-depth discussion of the data-segment side of dynamic linking.)

The twelfth parameter lets us pass a data pointer to our window procedure. The pointer is passed to our window procedure with the very first message, WM_CREATE. This is used for providing window initialization data. Since MIN doesn't have any initialization data to pass, we set this parameter to NULL.

Once we return from this call to CreateWindowEx, Windows has created all the internal information needed to support a window. That is, it has created an entry in the window database. But our window hasn't appeared on the screen yet. For this, we must call the `ShowWindow` function.

The `ShowWindow` routine opens our window in a way that the user has requested. Our program receives the user's request in `WinMain`'s `cmdShow` parameter, which serves as the second parameter in our call:

```
ShowWindow (hwnd, cmdShow);
```

Depending on the value of `cmdShow`, a program's main window might be minimized, appear as a regular open window, or it might even get maximized.

With the call to `ShowWindow`, MIN's initialization is complete, and a window is visible on the screen. This initialization is typical for a Windows program: The first instance registers the window class. Then the first instance, and all subsequent instances, create and display a window of this class.

But there is more to Windows programming than making a window appear. Once a window is born, it is starved for attention from the user. The user can type on the keyboard or click with the mouse to interact with a window. In response, a flood of messages are generated. These messages let your program know how the user is interacting with a window. Your program, in turn, responds to the messages by making changes appear in a window. The cycle starts again when the user responds to the new contents of a window.

Clearly, then, once a window has been created, there needs to be a mechanism for the program to retrieve messages. As you will see, Windows has not one but *two* message delivery mechanisms.

As we begin our investigation of Windows' message delivery mechanism, we're going to introduce a topic that may at first seem strangely out of place: Windows' multitasking capability. But we're going to address both topics simultaneously because Windows' multitasking is tightly interwoven into the fabric of the message delivery mechanism. Let's begin our study of messages with the relationship between messages and multitasking.

Messages: Input Mechanism and Multitasking Time Slice

In Chapter 1, we introduced the idea that Windows is a multitasking operating system. Unlike other multitasking systems, however, it does not interrupt one program to allow another to run. An interrupt-based approach to multitasking is sometimes called **preemptive multitasking**, since the operating system preempts one program to allow another to run (Windows NT is an example of such an operative system). Windows 3.x, on the other hand, is a **nonpreemptive** system. This means that programs are not interrupted by the operating system, but interrupt themselves to allow other programs to run. How can such a cooperative system be made to work?

Windows' multitasking switcher is embedded into Windows' message delivery system. Windows programs rely on messages to receive input from the user and from user-interface objects. Some messages are hardware related, and tell a program that the user has pointed with the mouse or typed a keystroke. Other messages come from user-interface objects like windows, menus, and scroll bars. To access the flow of messages, a program calls the message delivery system. It gets one message per call. If a program has no more messages, the message delivery system will start delivering messages to a program that *does* have messages to be delivered.

From this discussion, it should be clear that a message serves a larger purpose than its namesake in the real world; that is, it does more than just communicate something. To a Windows program, messages are the unit of processing. They have the effect of creating time-slices during which a program runs. To get a clearer understanding about the dual role that messages play, let's take a closer look at the message delivery system.

A Windows program receives messages in two ways. The first way is by reading message buffers. Windows doesn't allow us direct access to its internal buffers, but rather reads a buffer for us when our program calls a Windows library routine: `GetMessage`.

There are two system buffers that `GetMessage` reads. One is the **hardware event queue**, which holds system-wide mouse and keyboard events. The other buffer is an **application message queue**, used for an application's private messages. Every program has its own message queue. In fact, every *instance* of every program has its own message queue. If it finds a message for a program, `GetMessage` retrieves the message.

If `GetMessage` doesn't find messages for a program, it puts the program to sleep. At such times, the Windows switcher takes over and transfers control to another program that *does*, in fact, have messages waiting for it. The `GetMessage` routine, then, serves to make Windows' message-driven multitasking system work.

The second way that our program can receive messages is by a direct call to one of our window procedures. Our window procedure is called as if it were a subroutine that was a part of Windows. In fact, think of a window procedure as an *installable extension to Windows*. Messages delivered by this mechanism don't wait in a message queue, but are processed immediately when a call is received.

Let's pause to consider the implications of these two approaches. The first method, in which `GetMessage` reads message buffers for us, is called **pull-model processing**. The name describes the active role our program plays in pulling a message from a queue. The second method is called **push-model processing**. The name describes the passive role our program plays in waiting to be called and letting Windows *push* a message into our window procedure.

It may strike you as odd that Windows has *two* mechanisms for delivering messages. After all, other systems have been written that are strictly pull-model (the Apple Macintosh) or push-model (like the Xerox Star). Why does Windows have two mechanisms? A little bit of history may make this clear.

Before Microsoft started shipping Windows in November 1985, it spent two years building the system. The earliest internal versions of Windows (1983–1984) were entirely push-model. In those days, a Windows program was just a subroutine package. For each window class, 10 subroutines were defined, with a subroutine for each of 10 different types of user-interface events. For example, one routine was called when a window was created, another to deliver mouse and keyboard input, and still another when it was time to draw in a window.

Things worked well, with the exception of mouse and keyboard input. The Microsoft engineers had trouble incorporating interrupt-driven hardware into push-model processing. After all, push-model processing does its work in a very orderly, synchronized manner. Interrupt-driven hardware, on the other hand, is quite chaotic. Depending on whether the user is typing at 60 words per minute, punching the function keys, or torturing the mouse, input arrives in a random order and at unpredictable times.

In a purely push-model system, each application requires time-critical interrupt handling code. Otherwise, if an application took too long processing a mouse or keyboard event, other mouse or keyboard events could be lost. Or, they might interrupt the application with a new hardware event before the previous hardware event has been handled. In either case, mouse and keyboard events aren't handled properly. The solution? Windows uses both push-model processing and pull-model processing.

The advantage of push-model processing is that it allows user-interface objects that are part of the operating system to directly interact with application programs. Can you think of a more direct way to be connected to an operating system than to be a *subroutine* to the operating system?

Pull-model processing, on the other hand, lets us buffer unpredictable hardware input. It also allows the creation of *modal* loops, during which time a program filters out all messages except for a specified few. A simple example of a modal loop occurs in non-Windows programs when a message like the following is displayed:

```
Strike Any Key When Ready...
```

and suspends all processing until the user has typed a key on the keyboard.

Used together, pull-model and push-model processing create a unique, hybrid system in Windows. Let's go back to the source code from MIN.C in order to understand the implementation details of this hybrid approach.

The Message Loop

Every Windows program has a message loop to allow it to continuously poll for messages. In this way, every Windows program is able to stay in touch with the supply of messages that are vital to the proper operation of a Windows program. Here is the message loop from MIN.C:

```
while (GetMessage(&msg, 0, 0, 0))
    {
    TranslateMessage(&msg); // Convert KEYDOWNs to CHARs
    DispatchMessage(&msg);  // Transmit message to WndProc
    }
```

This loop runs continuously for as long as a Windows program is running. Each iteration through the loop represents the receipt of a single message from the hardware event queue or from the application message queue. With the exception of the WM_QUIT message, every message causes GetMessage to return a value of TRUE. On receipt of the WM_QUIT message, a program drops out of its message loop and terminates. When we discuss the window procedure in Chapter 5, you'll see that it's the job of a top level window to send the WM_QUIT message when it is destroyed. Otherwise, a program will not terminate properly and will remain in memory, taking up space that could be used by other programs.

Let's look at each routine in this tiny message loop. A moment ago, we introduced the idea that GetMessage pulls messages into our program from system buffers. We can request `GetMessage` to filter messages by providing filter information in the second, third, and fourth parameters. Since we're interested in *all* messages, however, filtering is disabled by setting these to zero.

The most interesting parameter to us is the first parameter, which is a pointer to a structure that `GetMessage` fills with message data. Notice that a pointer to this structure is the sole parameter to the other routines in our message loop.

Our program defines this structure as

```
MSG msg;
```

For the definition of `MSG`, we can look in Windows.h where we find the following:

```
typedef struct tagMSG
{
    HWND      hwnd;
    UINT      message;
    WPARAM    wParam;
    LPARAM    lParam;
    DWORD     time;
    POINT     pt;
} MSG;
```

Let's look at each of the six elements in this structure.

- `hwnd` contains a window handle. Every window in the system is given a unique handle. Like the instance handle, a window handle uniquely identifies a particular object in the system—a window. A window handle is associated with a message because every message is directed at one window or another.

- `message`, an unsigned integer, contains the *type* of message, encoded as a 16-bit value in Win16 or as a 32-bit value in Win32. In the next chapter, we'll take a look at all the different types of messages in Windows.

- `wParam` and `lParam` contain message data. The meaning depends on the type of message. For example, the menu command message uses `wParam` to identify the particular menu item that has been selected. Mouse messages pack the location of the mouse pointer into `lParam`. Notice the `WPARAM` and `LPARAM` data types. In the Win16 API, `wParam` is a 16-bit value and `lParam` is a 32-bit value. In the Win32 API, both are 32-bit values.

- The last two items, `time` and `pt`, are rarely used by Windows programs. Both describe the state of the system when the message was put into the message queue: `time` holds the time, and `pt` holds the location of the mouse pointer.

As you'll see in Chapter 5, the first four members of this data structure get passed to a program's window procedure. It's in the window procedure, after all, that messages are processed. With a few exceptions, most message loops are as short and simple as the one you see in MIN. Let's look at the other two routines in our message loop.

The second routine in our message loop is a call to `TranslateMessage`. This routine calls the Windows keyboard device driver to convert raw keystroke messages (`WM_KEYDOWN`) into cooked character values, which are placed in the application's private message queue as WM_CHAR messages. This makes it easy for our program to tell the difference between "A" and "a" without knowing the state of the shift key.

TranslateMessage also provides support for international keyboards. A British shopkeeper, for example, would probably use the £ symbol to quote you the special price of £35. If the shopkeeper used a Windows word processor to send you a note with this information, the word processor would call TranslateMessage to convert the keystroke to the proper symbol. As part of this translation process, TranslateMessage makes diacritic marks available; It allows Windows programs to display French words like *Voilá*, Spanish phrases like *¿Hablo Español?* and German city names like *München*.

The final routine in this loop, DispatchMessage, takes message data from the MSG structure and calls the correct window procedure. It *pushes* the message into the window procedure for processing. A program's window procedure, after all, is a piece of code that represents a pure push-model design. Pull-model processing is incorporated in the message loop's call to GetMessage.

⃞ *Warning!*

You might wonder if you could speed things up by calling a window procedure directly rather than by calling DispatchMessage. The answer is "no." Windows must make all calls to a window procedure.

The reason has to do with the way data is addressed. A windows program usually has its own data segment. The dynamic link library that controls the Windows user interface, USER, also has its own data segment. When USER calls a window procedure, it places the window procedure's data segment identifier into a special place: the AX register of the CPU.

The Compiler generates the following code at the beginning of our window procedures:

```
PUSH DS          ; Save USER's data segment value
MOV  DS, AX      ; Install our data segment value
```

At the very end of the window procedure, right before we return, we restore the USER module's data segment by saying:

```
POP  DS          ; Restore USER's data segment
```

For a Windows program to directly call into a window procedure, it would have to set up the AX register with the proper data segment value. Otherwise, the window procedure would not be able to access its data.

At this point, our walk through WinMain is complete. Along the way, we have explored some of the fundamentals of the Windows architecture. But our journey is not over yet. We still have one more routine to explore: our program's window procedure. This is the subject of our next chapter.

5

Understanding
Window Procedures

Until now, the only thing that we have said about window procedures is that they process messages. But what does it mean to *process* a message? We have already explored how messages serve as the time-slice for Windows' multitasking. As we discuss the window procedure, we'll emphasize the other role of messages: communication.

When a window is created, moved, sized, minimized, or closed, messages are generated. When the user types at the keyboard, clicks with the mouse, selects a menu item, or cancels a dialog box, one or more messages are generated to communicate these events. Messages are the lifeblood of this operating system, as well as the time-slice that allocates processor use.

The centerpiece of every Windows program is one (or more) functions that receive and process messages. These functions are called **window procedures**. The user creates a flood of messages to a window procedure when interacting with a Windows program. From this flood, a window procedure scoops up the messages that it needs to do its work. Exactly what this means depends on the message. A window procedure might respond to a message by drawing a pie chart, closing a window, or turning the mouse cursor into a pumpkin. The personality of a Windows program comes from the way it handles the messages it decides to use. In other words, a spreadsheet program, a game, and a word processor each get their unique qualities by the response each makes to the stream of messages that ultimately starts with the user.

From a coding point of view, the structure of a window procedure usually is a switch statement, with a different case for each message. Our minimum window procedure processes only one message, but you can see how the switch structure can easily be expanded to include other messages we might want to process:

```
LRESULT CALLBACK
MinWndProc (HWND    hwnd,      // For whom is message sent?
            UINT    mMsg,      // What is exact message?
            WPARAM  wParam,    // ...message details.
            LPARAM  lParam)    // ...message details.
    {
    switch (mMsg)
        {
        case WM_DESTROY:
            PostQuitMessage(0); // Handle application shutdown.
            break;

        default:
            return(DefWindowProc(hwnd,mMsg,wParam,lParam));
            break;
        }
    return 0L;
    }
```

Our window procedure is small, but it has a big brother that helps it quite a bit—the default window procedure: `DefWindowProc`. Notice that every message we don't want is routed to this procedure. This routine takes on the burden of performing all of the default actions required to make each window work. The default window procedure is provided by Microsoft in the Windows software development kit. For your convenience, we have listed it in Appendix B.

Let's dissect our window procedure, starting with the procedure definition. We'll take a look at the single message we process, `WM_DESTROY`, and a closer look at the workhorse for our program, the default window procedure. Finally, since messages are such an important part of a Windows programmer's life, we're going to examine the major categories of messages in Windows.

The Window Procedure Declaration

Every window procedure must be defined exactly like the window procedure in our minimum window procedure. Of course, the name of the procedure and the name of each parameter is up to you. But the number and type of parameters as well as the procedure declaration must appear as shown here. This is important because you don't write the code that calls this routine. As the push-model part of our program, this routine is always called directly by Windows.

The return value for every window procedure is an `LRESULT` value. This is defined in Windows.h as a `long` value. As with other uppercase definitions, the goal is to allow portability to the Win32 API. The meaning of the return value depends on the message. For example, the `WM_QUERYENDSESSION` message expects a `TRUE` (nonzero) or `FALSE` (zero) value. This particular message lets programs vote on whether Windows should honor the user's request to shut down the system (Windows can be very democratic). The `WM_GETTEXT` message, on the other hand, expects a far pointer to a string (`char far *`) as a return value.

The name of the window procedure, `MinWndProc`, must be specified in the module definition file, MIN.DEF, under the `EXPORTS` statement. This is important in order to make dynamic linking work properly (and, more specifically, to give the window procedure access to your program's automatic data segment), as further detailed in Chapter 19.

Every window procedure has exactly four parameters: a window handle (`hwnd`), a message identifier (`mMsg`), and two parameter values (`wParam` and `lParam`). The window handle, `hwnd`, identifies the window associated with a message. This is a necessary parameter because a single window procedure can support several different windows on the display screen at the same time. The window handle identifies the window that is calling our window procedure. This is very convenient, because most of the Windows library routines that act on a window take this handle as a parameter.

The second parameter, `mMsg`, is the window message. If the window handle tells us who is calling, then the message value tells us what they want. Perhaps it is to announce that a window has been born (`WM_CREATE`), lives in a new location (`WM_MOVE`), has grown up (or shrunk) (`WM_SIZE`), needs a facelift (`WM_PAINT`), or has passed away (`WM_DESTROY`).

The `wParam` and `lParam` parameters give some more information about a given message. `wParam` is defined as a `WPARAM` value, which in Windows.h is defined as a 16-bit unsigned integer. `lParam` is an `LPARAM` value, which is a 32-bit unsigned value. The meaning of `wParam` and `lParam` depend on the message type. For example, the `WM_COMMAND` message, which is sent when a menu item is selected, uses `wParam` to identify the specific menu item that was selected. Mouse messages, like `WM_LBUTTONDOWN` and `WM_MOUSEMOVE`, use the `lParam` to store the location of the mouse cursor in the window's client area.

You'll notice that the window procedure is defined using `CALLBACK`. This combines two extensions that Microsoft has made to ANSI standard C: `_far` and `_pascal`. Not surprisingly, Windows.h has an uppercase equivalent for these two: `FAR` and `PASCAL`. Let's roll up our sleeves and dig into the reasons for the `FAR` and `PASCAL` keywords.

The PASCAL Calling Convention

The `PASCAL` keyword causes a function to use the Pascal Calling Convention. This keyword is not part of ANSI Standard C, but an extension that Microsoft made to their C language compiler. This keyword takes advantage of a quirk in the Intel architecture to generate code that is smaller and faster than the C Compiler's default calling convention. Several years ago, Microsoft converted Windows itself from the C Convention to the Pascal Convention. Afterwards, the code to Windows itself was nine percent smaller.

If the Pascal Convention generates better code, you might wonder why anyone would want to use the C Convention. The C Convention allows functions to accept a variable number of parameters. C library functions like `sprintf()` and `scanf()` *must* be written with the C convention. For a function with a fixed number of parameters, though, the PASCAL Convention can be used. This is the reason it is a part of every window procedure declaration.

Windows takes advantage of the PASCAL calling convention in every possible way. For example, every Windows library function (except one) is declared this way. In this book, we use the PASCAL Convention for all of our functions. Because it results in better code, we recommend that you do the same for all of your functions that use a fixed number of parameters.

The other keyword that we need to explore is the FAR keyword. We'll take this opportunity to explore a related keyword: NEAR.

The NEAR and FAR Keywords

To understand the NEAR and FAR keywords, you need to know something about the architecture of the processors that run Windows. Windows runs on the Intel family of CPUs, which includes the 8088, 8086, 80186, 80286, 80386, and 80486. One characteristic of this family is a segmented memory addressing scheme. The NEAR and FAR keywords give you the ability to control the way a program interacts with the memory architecture.

The key to understanding segmented addressing is to realize that every memory reference is made up of two parts: a **segment identifier** and an **offset** into the segment. A two-part address is somewhat unusual in computer architecture. Yet, in everyday life addresses with two (or more) parts are quite common. If you write a letter to the President of the United States, you would address it to 1600 Pennsylvania Avenue. If you wanted to drop a note to Bill Gates, the CEO of Microsoft Corporation, you would send it to One Microsoft Way. In Intel addressing, the segment identifier corresponds to the street name, and the offset to the building number.

The origin of this addressing scheme goes back to the first member of this family, the 8086. When Intel was designing this chip in the mid-1970s, the goal was to create a CPU that would allow compatibility with Intel's earlier CPUs, the 16-bit 8080 and 8085. Both chips had 16-bit address registers. The 8086-family has 16-bit address registers as well; but to overcome the 64K boundary, two registers instead of one are used to reference memory.

This approach has proven to be quite flexible. In the *real mode* of the Intel processors, the two registers are combined to create a 20-bit address. This allows a one-megabyte address space. In the *protected modes* of the higher end processors (80286, 80386, and 80486), the segment identifier references into special tables, called the local and global descriptor tables (LDT and GDT). These tables allow even more memory to be addressable: On the 80286, 16 megabytes of physical memory can be addressed. On the other high-end chips, up to four gigabytes (four billion bytes) of physical memory can be addressed. Since Windows 3.1 runs in protected mode, a Windows programs can access gobs and gobs of memory. This segmented addressing scheme has allowed Intel to create a compatibility path for their CPUs that has lasted three decades!

Of course, this flexibility has not come without a price. The primary disadvantage of segmentation is that programmers must pay attention to segmented addressing when

Figure 5.1 The Intel-86 family registers and flags

writing software. If you are not used to working with the segmented addressing, it takes some time to adjust.

Figure 5.1 shows the 14 registers shared by every member of this family. To reference a memory location, we use a segment register for our street name and an offset or scratch register to hold the house number. In real life, if we're going to visit the houses of several friends, it is easier to visit houses on the same street than to visit houses that are all on different streets. The same holds true for addressing memory. In other words, it is more efficient to address several memory locations in the same segment than to address the same number of memory locations if they are all in different segments.

For example, consider Figure 5.2. There are two segments, which we label 1000 and 2000. To reference a specific location in either segment, we need to specify a segment register and an offset value. If we start at offset 6 in segment 1000, as pointed to by the DS:BX register pair, we only need to change the BX register in order to access offset 2 in the same segment. At least three times the work is required if we wish to access offset 4 in segment 2000, since we need to change the DS register to 2000 and the BX register to 4. It is even more costly in protect mode, since loading a segment register requires the segment protection information to be loaded by the CPU as well.

To get the best performance from this architecture, you need to pay attention to the way your programs use memory. The NEAR keyword specifies a reference in the same segment. The FAR keyword specifies an intersegment reference.

If NEAR addressing provides better performance, why use FAR addressing? FAR addressing is required in certain situations. The first involves calls to the Windows library routines. Since Windows routines reside in their own code segments, programs must use FAR calls to access them. Also, when we pass data pointers as parameters to Windows routines, they must be FAR data pointers.

Figure 5.2 FAR references require twice the work of a NEAR reference

FAR references are also needed because the maximum size of a segment is 64K. This size limitation comes from the fact that, with the exception of the 80386 and 80486, offsets are 16 bits in the Intel 86 family of processors. A 16-bit offset means we can address no more than two to the sixteenth power, 64 kilobytes (65535).

Programs with more than 64K of code require multiple code segments. Likewise, programs with more than 64K of data require multiple data segments. Even if a program has less than 64K of code, there are still good reasons to use multiple code segments, as we'll discuss in Chapter 18.

Of course, segmented addressing is an integral part of the 16-bit API of Windows 3.0 and 3.1. With the introduction of the 32-bit API of Windows-NT, Microsoft lets you break your ties to segmented memory. The 32-bit API supports a flat, linear address space. Microsoft has announced that this API will be supported in their new operating system, Windows NT, as well as in upgrades to the MS-DOS based versions of Windows. At some point in the future, the only time you'll need to worry about segmented addressing is if you're writing programs that must run in Windows' (80286-based) Standard Mode.

After this in-depth look at our window procedure's declaration, it's time to move on to look at the message processing performed by our window procedure. The creator of a window procedure will decide the specific messages to process in order to give each window in a Windows program the desired behavior. However, one bit of processing must be performed by a window in every Windows program: that is, the termination processing. The proper termination of a Windows program is a task that usually falls to the window procedure for the top-level window in a program. The message that triggers this is one of the last messages that a window procedure sees when a window is destroyed: WM_DESTROY.

Program Termination and the WM_DESTROY Message

An important issue for every Windows program is proper termination. Proper termination is necessary to allow the cleanup and reclamation of memory and other resources used by your program. In our discussion of `WinMain`, we introduced the `WM_QUIT` message. When the `GetMessage` routine reads this message from our message queue, it returns `FALSE`, which causes our infinite message loop (and our program) to terminate. Let's see how the `WM_QUIT` message gets into our message queue.

Program termination usually occurs when a program's main window is closed. A user can close a window in any number of ways. Two of the more common ways are by selecting the [System Menu] Close item and by striking the [Alt] + [F4] key combination. Each of these user actions causes a stream of messages to be sent to our window procedure. Here is a list of messages that are sent to our window procedure when MIN's window is closed using the [Alt] + [F4] key combination:

Message	*Comment*
WM_SYSKEYDOWN	[Alt] key was struck
WM_SYSKEYDOWN	[F4] key was struck
WM_SYSCOMMAND	System Command generated
WM_CLOSE	Window is told to close
WM_NCACTIVATE	Turn off titlebar (non-client area) highlight
WM_ACTIVATE	Window is becoming inactive
WM_ACTIVATEAPP	Application is becoming inactive
WM_KILLFOCUS	Window is losing the keyboard
WM_DESTROY	Window has been destroyed
WM_NCDESTROY	Time to clean up non-client area data

The first thing to be said about this stream of messages is that the default window procedure handles the bulk of the work to make the right things happen. For example, it takes the first two messages, which are raw keystroke messages, and translates them into the third message: a system command. The system command message is handled by the default window procedure to implement system level commands.

A system command is a generic request for some action to occur such as move a window or size a window. Your window procedures won't usually process these messages. Instead, you'll look for a more specific message to elicit a response. In this case, that message is `WM_CLOSE`, a request to close our window.

A typical response to `WM_CLOSE` message is to check whether there are unsaved files in our window. If there are, we display a message box like that shown in Figure 5.3 to warn the user of the possible loss of data.

Figure 5.3 Protecting the user from loss of data

When we are sure it is safe to close a window, our window procedure destroys our window with a call to the `DestroyWindow` function. This, in fact, is what the default window procedure will do for us. For this reason, our minimum window procedure does not respond to `WM_CLOSE`, but passes it on to the default window procedure.

As you can tell, a long stream of messages is usually generated when a window is destroyed. Even though the window is being destroyed, Windows continues to communicate with a window procedure until the window destruction process is complete. Each of the remaining messages, after the `WM_CLOSE`, notifies us about a change in the state of our window.

The message of particular interest to us is `WM_DESTROY`. This message, which is ignored by the default window procedure, belongs to our program. In response to `WM_DESTROY`, our program generates a `WM_QUIT` message to cause our `GetMessage` loop to exit. This is done by making a call to `PostQuitMessage`.

Of all the work that is required for a minimum Windows program, program termination is the only task that falls to our window procedure. Every other task is taken up by the Windows library routine that translates all the important messages into the proper actions for the maintenance of the Windows user interface. That library routine is the default window procedure, `DefWindowProc`. Let's focus our attention on this workhorse.

Default Message Handling

As we discussed in Chapter 1, the chief reason for the attractiveness of Windows comes from the consistent look and feel of the Windows user interface. Even the most casual Windows user notices the remarkable uniformity between programs. For example, menus work the same between two otherwise unrelated programs, and windows in different programs respond in the same way to the same actions.

It is the work of the default window handler deep in the bowels of Windows that accounts for this high degree of uniformity. The flood of messages that our window procedure diverts to the default handler is the cause of the similarities between programs. A moment ago, for example, we described the role of the default window procedure in closing a window. The default window procedure performs the same services for all Windows programs.

While all this work is being done for us, there is still something that we must do. Our window procedure plays the role of traffic cop for messages. After all, the default message handler is never called directly by Windows. Instead, our window procedure always receives messages first. To keep the user interface working properly, our program must pass messages on to the default window procedure.

There may, in fact, be times when we wish to vary the behavior of a window away from the default behavior. For example, we might wish to prevent the user from picking up a window by the titlebar. (This is a typical way for a user to move a window.) It is a simple matter to trap the messages associated with this action, and prevent them from arriving at the default window handler. For the most part, however, we'll allow the default window procedure to do its work for us, so that our program can participate in the consistency that makes Windows so usable.

In looking at the different parts of our minimum Windows program, we have talked a lot about the flow of messages through the system. We have also identified a few messages that are important. In order for you to fully understand how the message pipeline can work to your advantage, it will help you to know the types of messages that flow through these pipes. For this reason, we're going to conclude this chapter with an in-depth look at the types of messages in Windows.

A Taxonomy of Messages

There are over 250 predefined messages in Windows. Fortunately, you do not have to be familiar with every one of them, because most have very specialized uses. For example, a large number of messages are specific to one type of window. Other messages are used for very special purposes, like sharing data or implementing the **multiple-document interface** (**MDI**) standard. Still other messages float through our message pipeline, but are never documented for our use. These are internal messages that Windows creates for its own purposes.

To help you come to terms with messages, we'll divide the messages into eight categories. These categories are intended as a framework in which to begin understanding messages. But this won't be the last time you will hear about messages. Almost every chapter in this book will provide details on the messages that apply to the different parts of Windows. So let's get started on our look at Windows messages.

Messages have names. Message names are defined in Windows.h like this:

```
#define WM_COMMAND 0X0111
```

The WM Hungarian prefix tells us that a symbol is a window message. In spoken language, the prefix is ignored, so that programmers often refer to WM_COMMAND as a "command message." These symbolic names stand in for the raw numeric value of a message: a 16-bit unsigned integer (in the Win16 API—and 32-bits wide in the Win32

API). Besides the WM prefix, there are other Hungarian prefixes for messages: EM_, BM_, DM_, LB_, and CB_ (like EM_GETSEL, BM_GETCHECK, etc.). These are private messages which don't concern us at this moment, except that they show that you can create your *own* private messages as you need them.

A useful tool for learning about messages is the SPY program, which Microsoft provides with the Windows Software Development Kit. We like SPY because it lets you eavesdrop on the message traffic for a window—even if you didn't write the program! When you use SPY, you will probably be surprised at the number of messages encountered. For example, Figure 5.4 shows the messages generated by the simple action of making a menu selection. Even without knowing what specific messages do, you can tell that this is a lot of messages. A little experimentation with SPY will demonstrate that this is typical for other user actions as well.

Why are there so many messages? Some messages are for Windows' internal use, to synchronize events in different parts of the system. These messages are passed along to the default window procedure, which we introduced a short time ago. Other messages notify a window procedure of actions taken by the user. Messages guarantee that a window procedure will always have the latest information about what the user is doing. Once you understand the type of messages that are generated, messages ultimately mean less work on your part to keep in touch with a lot of information. It's like having a daily paper delivered to your door: "All the Messages Fit to Print."

Figure 5.4 SPY showing messages generated by making a menu selection

Table 5.1 The Eight Types of Messages

Type	*Description*
Hardware	Mouse, Keyboard, Pen & Timer Input
Window Maintenance	Notification, Request for action, Query
User-Interface Maintenance	Menu, mouse pointer, scroll bar, dialog boxes, MDI
Termination	Application or system shutdown
Private	Dialog box controls: edit, button, list box, combobox
System Resource Notification	Color Changes, fonts, spooler, device modes
Data Sharing	Clipboard and Dynamic Data Exchange (DDE)
Internal System	Undocumented Messages

Table 5.1 shows the eight categories of messages. As we review each category, we'll list the specific messages that are in the category. Since some of the categories are quite specialized, we'll limit our discussion to a brief introduction and omit a list of specific messages. All messages from all categories are listed in Appendix A, in case you're curious about what it is that we're omitting. Let's start with our first message category: hardware messages.

Hardware Messages

A window procedure receives messages generated by three (and possibly four) different pieces of hardware: the keyboard, the mouse, a pen, and the system timer. Each of these generates hardware interrupts. Since Windows' scheduling is not interrupt-oriented, hardware events have to be buffered. This insures that hardware events are processed in the order in which they occur.

For example, when you strike the "H" key, an interrupt notifies the system that keyboard input is ready. The Windows keyboard device driver retrieves this input and creates an entry into the **hardware event queue**. When its turn comes, messages bearing "H" key information are delivered to the proper window procedure. The mouse and timer messages are handled in a similar fashion. Table 5.2 shows the 29 messages that are generated in response to hardware activity.

> ***Caution:*** Like mouse and keyboard messages, timer messages are queued, which means that Windows timers are not exact. This is necessary since an interrupt-driven timer message would conflict with the nonpreemptive nature of Windows. The usefulness of a timer is that it lets you know that a minimum amount of time has passed.

Table 5.2 Hardware Messages

Mouse Messages: In a window's client area

WM_LBUTTONDBLCLK	Left button double-click.
WM_LBUTTONDOWN	Left button down.
WM_LBUTTONUP	Left button up.
WM_MBUTTONDBLCLK	Middle button double-click.
WM_MBUTTONDOWN	Middle button down.
WM_MBUTTONUP	Middle button up.
WM_MOUSEMOVE	Mouse move.
WM_RBUTTONDBLCLK	Right button double-click.
WM_RBUTTONDOWN	Right button down.
WM_RBUTTONUP	Right button up.

Mouse Messages: In a window's non-client area

WM_NCLBUTTONDBLCLK	Left button double-click.
WM_NCLBUTTONDOWN	Left button down.
WM_NCLBUTTONUP	Left button up.
WM_NCMBUTTONDBLCLK	Middle button double-click.
WM_NCMBUTTONDOWN	Middle button down.
WM_NCMBUTTONUP	Middle button up.
WM_NCMOUSEMOVE	Mouse move.
WM_NCRBUTTONDBLCLK	Right button double-click.
WM_NCRBUTTONDOWN	Right button down.
WM_NCRBUTTONUP	Right button up.

Keyboard Messages

WM_CHAR	Character input.
WM_DEADCHAR	Dead-character (umlaut, accent, etc.).
WM_KEYDOWN	Key has been depressed.
WM_KEYUP	Key has been released.
WM_SYSCHAR	System character input.
WM_SYSDEADCHAR	System dead-character.
WM_SYSKEYDOWN	System key has been depressed.
WM_SYSKEYUP	System key has been released.

(continued)

Table 5.2 Hardware Messages

Pen Messages (only systems with Pen for Windows installed)

WM_GLOBALRCCHANGE	The global recognition context has changed.
WM_HEDITCTL	Private message for the handwriting edit controls.
WM_HOOKRCRESULT	Message reporting the results of the handwriting recognition hook.
WM_RCRESULT	Message from the handwriting recognizer with the results of a recognition.
WM_SKB	Message used by on-screen keyboard.

Timer Message

WM_TIMER	Timer has gone off.

With mouse messages, a distinction is made between the mouse messages generated in a window's client area and those generated in the non-client area. (Remember: The non-client area of a window includes such items as its border, system menu, title bar, and menu.) In general, an application only pays attention to client-area mouse messages and lets the default window procedure process non-client area mouse messages.

While we're on the subject of mouse messages, the WM_MOUSEMOVE message deserves some special attention. The WM_MOUSEMOVE message is handled in a special way to keep the hardware event queue from overflowing. After all, if you move the mouse quickly, you can easily create hundreds of mouse interrupts. To minimize the disruption this might cause, Windows keeps only *one* mouse move message at a time. When a new mouse move message arrives, Windows checks whether the previous message in the queue is a mouse move message. If so, the old message is updated with the new location information. A new entry is made only if a mouse move message isn't already present.

There are two basic types of keyboard messages: regular and system. In general, you can ignore system keyboard messages, which have names like WM_SYSCHAR and WM_SYSKEYDOWN. The default window procedure turns these into the proper system commands. The regular keyboard messages are intended for application use. We'll discuss the details of the keyboard messages in Chapter 15, when we talk about getting keyboard input from the user.

Window Maintenance Messages

This group has 27 messages. This is the trickiest group of messages, mostly because it takes a long time to learn the subtle nuances of each. Unfortunately, the names of the messages do not help very much.

To begin with, there are three types of window maintenance messages: notification, request for action, and queries. Table 5.3 lists all the window maintenance messages, sorted into these three types.

Table 5.3 Window Maintenance Messages

Window Messages: Notification

WM_ACTIVATE	Window is active.
WM_ACTIVATEAPP	Application is active.
WM_CREATE	Window has been created.
WM_DESTROY	Window has been destroyed.
WM_ENABLE	Input to the window has been enabled.
WM_KILLFOCUS	Window has lost keyboard control.
WM_MOUSEACTIVATE	Notifies a window that it is going to become active because of a mouse click.
WM_MOVE	Window has been moved.
WM_PARENTNOTIFY	The child of a window has been created, destroyed, or been clicked by the mouse.
WM_SETFOCUS	Window has gained keyboard control.
WM_SIZE	Window's client area has changed size.
WM_WINDOWPOSCHANGING	Window is about to be moved, resized, or relocated in the system's Z-ordering.
WM_WINDOWPOSCHANGED	Window has just been moved, resized, or relocated in the system's Z-ordering.

Window Messages: Request for Action

WM_CANCELMODE	Send to inform a window to cancel any internal modes, such as mouse capture. The default window procedure responds to this message by finishing any modal scroll bar or menu activity.
WM_CLOSE	Close (destroy) window.
WM_ERASEBKGND	Erase background.
WM_ICONERASEBKGND	Erase background of iconic window.
WM_NCACTIVATE	Change title bar to show active state.
WM_NCCREATE	Create non-client area data.
WM_NCDESTROY	Destroy non-client area data
WM_NCPAINT	Redraw non-client area.
WM_PAINT	Redraw client area.
WM_SETREDRAW	Inhibit redrawing of window.

(continued)

Table 5.3 Window Maintenance Messages

Window Messages: Request for Action *(continued)*

WM_SETTEXT	Change window text.
WM_SHOWWINDOW	Change window visibility.

Window Messages: Query

WM_GETMINMAXINFO	What is min/max sizes for window?
WM_GETTEXT	What is the window text?
WM_GETTEXTLENGTH	What is the length of the window text?
WM_NCCALCSIZE	How big should the client area be?
WM_QUERYDRAGICON	Send to a minimized window which doesn't have a class icon to retrieve the icon to display for the window.
WM_QUERYNEWPALETTE	Do you have a new palette?
WM_QUERYOPEN	Can iconic window be opened?

A notification message tells a window procedure that the state of a window has changed. Nothing is required from the window procedure to perform the action implied by the message name. The WM_MOVE message, for example, is *not* a request for your program to move anything. Instead, it is an after-the-fact message to tell you that your window has already been moved. It is worth noting that nothing in the message tells us *how* our window was moved. Maybe the user moved a window with the mouse. Perhaps another program moved our window. Whatever the case, notification messages are a one-way communication path to a window procedure, and require neither a reply nor any action.

By contrast, our second type of window message—a request for action—is sent when some response is necessary. Without the action, a hole is created in the user interface. For example, the WM_PAINT message is sent to a window procedure when a window has been damaged and needs to be redrawn. If the window procedure doesn't repair the window, it stays broken. For the most part, the default window procedure provides the needed minimum action. There are times, however, when you must intercept and process one of these messages yourself, as is the case with the WM_PAINT message. When you do, be sure that you mimic the actions of the default handler. Finding out what this means is simpler than you might think: Just look at the source code to **DefWindowProc**.

Because this is an important piece of code, Microsoft provides the source to the default window procedure in the Windows Software Development Kit. For your convenience, we have duplicated a listing in Appendix B of this book for version 3.0 of the Software Development Kit (SDK). Check with your software dealer for the latest version of the SDK, since the listing in this book is subject to change.

A Query message requires an answer. This is used for two-way communication between Windows and your program. Like the Request for Action messages, you can rely on the default window procedure to give a reasonable answer for most cases. You may decide to intercept one if you want to change the default answer. For example, you will get a WM_QUERYOPEN message when the user tries to open a minimized window. If you want a program to run only in an iconic state, you return FALSE instead of the default answer of TRUE.

User-Interface Messages

This group contains messages for the other user-interface objects, including the application menu, mouse pointer, scroll bar, dialog boxes, and dialog box controls. It also includes a group of messages used to support the Multiple Document Interface (MDI) as shown in Table 5.4. This is a user-interface convention that was first seen in Microsoft's EXCEL spreadsheet program. Since then, it has become something of a standard, so that Windows now includes built-in support for MDI. The use of MDI is beyond the scope of this book, but we'll cover the other types of messages elsewhere: menu messages in Chapter 11, mouse pointer messages in Chapter 16, scroll bar messages in Chapter 20, and dialog box messages in Chapter 14.

Table 5.4 User-Interface Messages

Dialog Box and Dialog Box Control Messages

WM_CHARTOITEM	Listbox w/LBS_WANTKEYBOARDINPUT style has received a WM_CHAR message.
WM_COMMAND	Dialog box control is sending a notification code to its parent.
WM_COMPAREITEM	Sent to the parent of an owner draw dialog box control, asking to compare two items for the purpose of sorting.
WM_CTLCOLOR	Control asking for colors to be set.
WM_DELETEITEM	Notification to an owner-draw listbox or an owner-draw combobox that an item has been deleted.
WM_DRAWITEM	Request to the parent of an owner-draw control, or owner-draw menu, to draw.
WM_GETDLGCODE	Query control: want keyboard input?
WM_GETFONT	Query control: what font are you using?
WM_INITDIALOG	Initialize dialog.
WM_MEASUREITEM	Request to the parent of an owner-draw control or an owner-draw item to provide the dimensions of the item that is going to be drawn.
WM_SETFONT	Request to control: use this font.
WM_VKEYTOITEM	Listbox w/LBS_WANTKEYBOARDINPUT style has received a WM_KEYDOWN message.

(continued)

Table 5.4 User-Interface Messages

Drag and Drop API Messages

WM_DROPFILES	Notifies an application that the user has dropped a file. This message is only sent if the application is registered as a draw & drop recipient.

Menu Messages

WM_COMMAND	Menu item has been selected.
WM_INITMENU	Initialize menu bar menu.
WM_INITMENUPOPUP	Initialize popup menu.
WM_MENUCHAR	Mneumonic key used to select menu.
WM_MENUSELECT	User is browsing through menus.

Mouse Pointer Messages

WM_NCHITTEST	Query: where is mouse on the window?
WM_SETCURSOR	Request: Change pointer to correct shape.

Multiple Document Interface Messages

WM_CHILDACTIVATE	Notifies a parent window that a child is active.
WM_MDIACTIVATE	Notifies an MDI child window that it is either gaining or losing activation.
WM_MDICASCADE	Request to arrange the open MDI child windows in a cascading, stair-step fashion.
WM_MDICREATE	Requests an MDI client window to create an MDI child window.
WM_MDIDESTROY	Requests to an MDI client window to destroy an MDI child window.
WM_MDIGETACTIVE	Query an MDI client window for the currently active MDI child window.
WM_MDIICONARRANGE	Request to arrange the iconic MDI child windows in an orderly fashion.
WM_MDIMAXIMIZE	Request to maximize, or zoom, an MDI child window so that it occupies all of its parent's client area.
WM_MDINEXT	Request to activate the next MDI child window.
WM_MDIRESTORE	Request to restore an MDI child window to its previous state—iconic, normal or zoomed.
WM_MDISETMENU	Adjusts the menu on an MDI frame window.
WM_MDITILE	Request to arrange the open MDI child windows in a tiled fashion in the MDI parent's client window.

(continued)

Table 5.4 User-Interface Messages

Scroll Bar Messages

WM_HSCROLL	Horizontal scrollbar has been clicked.
WM_VSCROLL	Vertical scrollbar has been clicked.

System Commands: System Menu, Min/Max Buttons, Titlebar, etc.

WM_SYSCOMMAND	A system command has been selected.

Termination Messages

This is the smallest group of messages, as shown in Table 5.5. These messages are very important, since they are used to control the termination of a Windows program (WM_QUIT), as well as the termination processing for the system (WM_QUERYENDSESSION and WM_ENDSESSION). We covered the WM_QUIT message earlier.

Private Messages

Private window messages are for use with a specific window class. The predefined private messages in Windows.h are used with the following window classes: edit, button, listbox, and combobox.

The use of private messages by predefined window types is a pretty good clue that we can use this technique for our own windows. Why would you want to do this? You might find that existing messages do not provide the required functionality. It is a simple matter to define your own private message types and use them for communicating between different windows that you create. Even though 250 message types have already been defined, message variables are unsigned integers, which means that there is

Table 5.5 Termination Messages

Application and System Termination

WM_QUIT	Request that a program should terminate.
WM_QUERYENDSESSION	Queries whether application will allow system to shutdown.
WM_ENDSESSION	Notification of results of shutdown query.

---

room for 65535 different message types. When you define a private message, you should use the range starting at WM_USER, which is defined in Windows.h as follows:

```
#define WM_USER      0x0400
```

If we wrote a window procedure for windows that displays numbers, we might control how numbers appear with the following private messages (PM is Hungarian for "Private message"):

```
#define PM_DECIMAL      WM_USER + 0
#define PM_BINARY       WM_USER + 1
#define PM_HEX          WM_USER + 2
#define PM_OCTAL        WM_USER + 3
#define PM_NODECIMAL    WM_USER + 4
#define PM_DOLLARS      WM_USER + 5
#define PM_WITHCOMMAS   WM_USER + 6
```

Other parts of our program (or other programs that we write) can control the number display window simply by sending messages.

System Resource Notification

There are fifteen system resource notification messages, as shown in Table 5.6. These are sent to the top-level window of every program when a change has been made to a system resource. For example, when fonts are added or removed from the system, a WM_FONTCHANGE message is distributed. When the user changes the system colors or the system time from the Control Panel program, the WM_SYSCOLORCHANGE or WM_TIMECHANGE messages are sent out. The typical response to a notification is to record the change.

Of course, not every change is of interest to every program. For example, a clock program would probably check the new time when it receives a WM_TIMECHANGE message. But if it didn't use different fonts, it would probably ignore the WM_FONTCHANGE message.

Because most programs use the system colors, just about every program will respond to the WM_SYSCOLORCHANGE message. This is a notification that one or more system colors have changed. Ordinarily, system colors are changed by the Control Panel program under the direction of the user. When a change has been made, the Control Panel sends WM_SYSCOLORCHANGE. On receipt of this message, programs that use system colors respond by redrawing with the new colors.

Data Sharing Messages

Data sharing plays an important role in Windows. So it's not surprising that there are messages that are used in data sharing. Both data sharing mechanisms, the Clipboard and Dynamic Data Exchange (DDE), make extensive use of messages. A full discussion

Table 5.6 System Resource Notification Messages

System Resources Notification Messages

WM_COMMNOTIFY	An event has occured with a communication's device.
WM_COMPACTING	Notification that system memory is low, and that the Memory Manager is trying to free up some memory.
WM_DEVMODECHANGE	Printer setup has changed.
WM_ENTERIDLE	A menu or modal dialog box has entered an idle state.
WM_FONTCHANGE	Installed fonts in the system have changed.
WM_PALETTECHANGED	Hardware color palette has changed.
WM_PALETTEISCHANGING	Notification that the hardware palette is going to change.
WM_POWER	Sent to notify applications that the system is either entering or leaving power-down suspended mode. This message is used to support the battery-saving feature on battery-powered computers.
WM_QUERYNEWPALETTE	Notifies an application that it can install a new logical palette.
WM_QUEUESYNC	Notifies a CBT application of the start and end of journal playback operations.
WM_SPOOLERSTATUS	A job has been removed from the spooler queue.
WM_SYSCOLORCHANGE	One or more system colors has changed.
WM_SYSTEMERROR	Sent by the Windows KERNEL when a critical system error has occured during task or DLL startup or termination.
WM_TIMECHANGE	System time has changed.
WM_WININICHANGE	Initialization file, WIN.INI, changed.

of data sharing is beyond the scope of this book; however, Windows' data sharing messages are listed in Table 5.7.

Internal System Messages

A large group of messages are defined in Windows.h, but not described in any documentation. These are internal system messages, the last group of messages we are going to discuss. Windows uses these messages for its own purposes. This is the same idea as private messages, with the exception that private messages are meant for only one class of window. Internal messages are encountered in the context of every window class.

If Microsoft hasn't told us the reason for these messages, why are they sent to a window procedure? Like other message types, if a window procedure does not process it, the message is passed on to the default message handler. The default message handler does the right thing with this group of messages.

Table 5.7 Data Sharing Messages

Clipboard Messages

WM_ASKCBFORMATNAME	Asks for the name of a Clipboard format.
WM_CHANGECBCHAIN	Notification of a change in the viewing chain.
WM_CLEAR	Delete the currently selected item.
WM_COPY	Copy the currently selected item to the clipboard.
WM_CUT	Delete the currently selected item and place it on the clipboard.
WM_DESTROYCLIPBOARD	Clipboard contents are being destroyed.
WM_DRAWCLIPBOARD	Clipboard contents have changed.
WM_HSCROLLCLIPBOARD	Horizonal scrolling of owner draw clipboard item.
WM_PASTE	Copy the current contents of the clipboard to the current location.
WM_PAINTCLIPBOARD	Requests drawing of an owner draw clipboard item.
WM_RENDERALLFORMATS	Request to provide the data for all clipboard formats that have been promised.
WM_RENDERFORMAT	Request to provide data for a single clipboard format that has been promised.
WM_UNDO	Undo previous action.
WM_SIZECLIPBOARD	Notification to the owner of owner draw clipboard data that the size of the Clipboard viewer window has changed.
WM_VSCROLLCLIPBOARD	Vertical scrolling of an owner draw clipboard item.

Dynamic Data Exchange (DDE) Messages

WM_DDE_ACK	Acknowledgement.
WM_DDE_ADVISE	Request from a DDE client to establish a permanent data link.
WM_DDE_DATA	Send a data item from a DDE server to a DDE client.
WM_DDE_EXECUTE	Request a DDE server to execute a series of commands.
WM_DDE_INITIATE	Logon to a DDE server.
WM_DDE_POKE	Request by a client for a server to update a specific data item.
WM_DDE_REQUEST	One-time request by a DDE client for a piece of information.
WM_DDE_TERMINATE	Logoff from a DDE server.
WM_DDE_UNADVISE	Terminate a permanent data link that was initiated with the WM_DDE_ADVISE message.

Since you have the source code to the default message handler, you might think that you could reverse-engineer some of these messages and use them for your own purpose. You can do this, but be careful. In a future version of Windows, Microsoft may decide to change the way an internal message is used, or eliminate it altogether! It has been our experience that undocumented "goodies" are interesting to look at, but dangerous to include in software that is intended for general distribution.

P A R T **III**

INTRODUCTION TO THE GRAPHICS DEVICE INTERFACE

6

Overview of GDI

In the next few chapters, we will focus on issues relating to the creation of graphical output, and discuss the various types of drawing that can be done using Windows' **Graphic Device Interface** (**GDI**). In this chapter, we will look at some of the basic concepts and capabilities of GDI. Succeeding chapters will build on this beginning by looking at pixels, lines, filled areas, and text. But GDI is much too big a topic to digest at one time, so we will postpone a discussion of certain topics until the last section of the book. Let's roll up our sleeves, then, and take a look at Windows' pixel-powered graphic output engine.

An Overview of the Graphics Device Interface

GDI is Windows' graphic output library, which handles graphic output for the display screen as well as hardcopy devices like printers and plotters. GDI creates every line, letter, and mark displayed by a Windows program. Windows itself uses GDI to assemble the pieces which make up the user interface, such as windows, icons, menus, and dialog boxes. Figure 6.1 shows some of the types of graphic objects that GDI can draw: lines, filled figures, and text of different shapes and sizes.

Figure 6.1   A sample of GDI lines, filled figures, and text

GDI Devices

GDI can draw on many different types of devices, such as display screens, laser printers, dot-matrix printers, and plotters. For GDI to work with a specific device, it depends on a special piece of software: a **device driver**. A GDI device driver converts drawing requests into the specific actions needed to draw on a specific device. For example, when a Windows program draws a picture of the space shuttle on an EGA display, GDI calls the EGA device driver to turn on the correct pixels. And when a program generates output on an HP Laserjet printer, GDI calls another device driver for help: the HP printer driver.

In addition to performing this work, a device driver provides GDI with a set of **device capability bits**. These are flags that let GDI know about a device's built-in drawing ability. There are five sets of flags: one each for curves, lines, polygons, bitmaps, and text. These flags tell GDI when to give a high-level drawing request directly to a device and when it must convert such requests into an equivalent set of low-level drawing requests.

At a minimum, a GDI device must be able to do two things: turn on pixels and draw solid lines. For a device with these minimum capabilities, GDI (with the help of a device driver) is able to do the rest. GDI has a set of built-in software simulations which take a high-level drawing request, like "draw a filled polygon," and convert it into a series of line and pixel operations. The software simulations are one reason that GDI is referred to as a **device-independent** graphics library. For devices with capabilities beyond the minimum, such as a Postscript printer, GDI uses the capability bits to determine when to send a high-level drawing request directly to the device driver.

In addition to physical devices like video screens and printers, GDI supports logical or **pseudo-devices**. Pseudo-devices are used for picture storage. Unlike physical devices, which display pictures using dedicated hardware, pseudo-devices capture a picture in RAM or on disk. GDI supports two types of pseudo devices: **bitmaps** and **metafiles**.

In Windows, bitmaps are always rectangular. A bitmap stores a picture in memory in the same way that a display adapter uses memory to hold graphic images. For this reason, bitmaps provide a fast way to make a copy of a picture. Bitmaps are also used to store images that must be drawn quickly onto the screen. For example, Windows itself uses bitmaps to store icons and cursors, as well as the tiny symbols used to draw system menus, minimize/maximize icons, and the parts of a scroll bar.

Another use of bitmaps is to store scanned images, such as company logos. A scanned image is created by running a paper copy of a logo through a device called a **scanner**. A scanner digitizes an image, making it suitable for storage in a bitmap. Figure 6.2 shows a logo bitmap that was created using a hand-held scanner, and placed into a PageMaker document.

Metafiles are created by GDI's record-and-playback facility. A metafile is cheaper than a bitmap in terms of memory use, but is slower in terms of drawing time. A metafile is like a cassette tape. To create a metafile, you place the tape into GDI's cassette deck and push the "Record" button. GDI calls are recorded onto the metafile until you press the "Stop" button. Once a metafile has been created, it can be stored on disk or passed to another program. For example, the Clipboard is often used to pass GDI metafiles between programs. To recreate the drawing, GDI is given the metafile "tape" and told to replay its contents.

As you get started with GDI programming, you'll probably concentrate most of your efforts on learning to draw on physical devices. After all, there are a number of subtle issues that you need to learn about before you can make effective use of display screens and printers. When you are comfortable drawing on these devices, you will then be ready to begin exploring how the pseudo-devices can be used to enhance your program's graphic output.

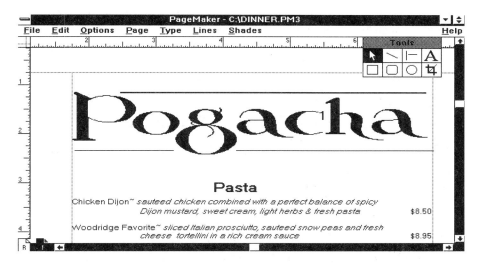

Figure 6.2 A scanned image in a PageMaker document

The Programming Interface

With the variety of devices and pseudo-devices that GDI supports, you might be concerned that this somehow translates into a complicated and hard-to-use graphics library. After all, some graphics libraries provide two sets of routines: one for display screens and one for printers. If GDI were like that, you might have *four* different sets of drawing routines to worry about: one each for displays, printers, bitmaps, and metafiles.

However, GDI has one set of routines for all devices. The `SetPixel` routine, for example, draws a single pixel on all devices that GDI supports. The `Polyline` routine draws a series of connected lines on any GDI-supported device or pseudo-device. Although we will focus our attention on writing output to the display screen in this chapter, the material covered applies to all of the different devices that GDI supports.

Drawing Coordinates

Before using GDI to create any output, you need to understand how GDI interprets drawing coordinates. GDI gives you quite a bit of control over drawing coordinates. For example, you can request that GDI use inches, millimeters, or hybrid units that you specify. For the most control over your drawing, GDI lets you specify units which correspond to a device's native pixels. GDI uses the term **mapping mode** to refer to the different coordinate systems which it supports. Table 6.1 shows the eight mapping modes available in GDI.

For now, we will limit discussion to GDI's default mapping mode: MM_TEXT. In this mapping mode, a unit refers to a pixel—that is, to the smallest "picture element" which a device can draw. This mapping mode gives us the greatest control over graphic output and avoids rounding errors that other mapping modes can create. It is often used for programs requiring absolute precision. For example, Aldus PageMaker, a page layout program, uses the MM_TEXT mapping mode to insure that objects aligned on the display screen match the alignment on the printer.

Table 6.1   GDI Mapping Modes

Mapping Mode Name	1 Logical Unit	Inches	Millimeters
MM_TEXT	1 pixel	—	—
MM_HIMETRIC	0.01 mm	0.000394	0.01
MM_TWIPS	1/1440 inches	0.000694	0.0176
MM_HIENGLISH	0.001 inches	0.001	0.0254
MM_LOMETRIC	0.1 mm	0.00394	0.1
MM_LOENGLISH	0.01 inches	0.01	0.254
MM_ISOTROPIC	} Scaling based on ratio between two DC		
MM_ANISOTROPIC	} attribute values: window and viewport extents.		

Figure 6.3 GDI's default coordinate system

One drawback to MM_TEXT, however, is that it requires additional effort to avoid writing device-specific programs. That's the key advantage to the other mapping modes: They provide a way to draw in a device-independent manner. In Chapter 20, we'll discuss the other mapping modes when we address the theory underlying coordinate systems and coordinate transformations.

An advantage of MM_TEXT coordinates is that they are identical to the coordinates that are used for mouse input. This coordinate system is called **client area coordinates**. In client area coordinates, the origin (0,0) is located at the upper-left corner of the client area. Unlike the Cartesian coordinate system you may remember from your high school days, the value of Y increases as we move downward. Figure 6.3 shows the location of the origin and the directions in which X and Y values increase.

Logical Drawing Objects

One of the means that GDI uses to achieve device independence is logical drawing objects. A logical drawing object describes how output should appear: It is a high-level, device-independent request. GDI supports the following logical drawing objects: pens (to draw lines), brushes (to fill areas), fonts (to display text), and logical colors (to describe color).

When a logical drawing object is created, it can be used on any device. However, the results may differ from one device to another, since devices have different capabilities. For example, a red pen might draw a red line on a 16-color EGA display, but draw a black line on a monochrome dot-matrix printer. It's the device driver's job to interpret a logical drawing object in a way that makes sense given a specific device's capabilities.

As we introduce each type of GDI drawing primitive, we'll describe the use of different logical drawing objects, and provide sample code to show how to use them.

The Device Context

To get an idea how GDI works with different types of devices, let's take a look at a GDI drawing routine: `TextOut`. The routine displays a single line of text on any GDI-supported device. This line of code writes the word "Hello":

```
TextOut (hdc, 10, 10, "Hello", 5);
```

Notice the first parameter: `hdc`. This is a commonly used Hungarian prefix for an important GDI data type: a *handle to a device context*. Recall what we have already said about handles: They are unsigned integers used to identify objects. The object identified by this particular handle plays a key role whenever a Windows program wishes to draw on any device.

A device context is a combination of several things rolled into one. It is a toolbox full of drawing tools, a connection to a specific device, and a permission slip to help GDI control the use of different devices by different programs. GDI never gives a program direct access to a device context. Instead, it provides a handle to identify a specific DC. Like the `TextOut` routine, every GDI drawing routine takes a DC handle as its first parameter.

As a toolbox, the DC is a set of **drawing attributes** which include one pen to draw lines, one brush to fill areas, and one font to display text. Therefore, at any time while drawing, you can change the tools in a DC to give you, for example, red lines, green areas, and bold text. Put together, drawing attributes give you total control over the appearance and location of your program's output.

Every DC is a toolbox with 20 drawing attributes. By storing these in the DC, GDI hides complexity from you. There is a slight drawback to this approach, but we think you'll agree that it makes GDI easier to work with in the long run. The drawback is that hidden attributes can be confusing, until you become familiar with what they do for you. For example, consider the `TextOut` routine. We'll add some comments to explain the parameters:

```
TextOut (hdc,      // Handle to a DC.
         10,       // X-location of text.
         10,       // Y-location of text.
         "Hello",  // Text to display.
         5);       // Text length.
```

From this code, can you tell what color the letters will be—will they be red, blue, or black? What type of font will be used—will it be 14-point bold Times Roman, or 24-point italicized Helvetica? Because this information is part of the DC, you can't answer these questions by reading this one line of code.

When `TextOut` draws, it uses the current drawing attributes in the DC. These attributes determine the appearance and location of the displayed text (including text color and font). As we introduce the different GDI drawing routines, we'll describe the DC attributes that each set of routines depends upon.

By hiding drawing attributes in a DC, Microsoft was able to define library routines with a minimum number of parameters. In practical terms, this means less typing for you when you write code that calls GDI. After all, drawing attributes tend to stay the same from one call to the next. To get an idea of the work that might be required in a world without a DC, consider what the TextOut function might look like:

```
/* Mythical TextOut in a world without DCs. */

TextOut (10,      //  X-location of text.
10,               //  Y-location of text.
"Hello",          //  Text to display.
5,                //  Length of text.
coFore,           //  Foreground text color.
coBack,           //  Background text color.
hClip,            //  Clipping Region.
hPalette,         //  Color Palette.
hFont,            //  Text Font.
iSpace,           //  Intercharacter spacing.
mmMapMode,        //  Mapping mode.
xyViewExt,        //  Viewport extent.
xyViewOrg,        //  Viewport origin.
xyWinExt,         //  Window extent.
xyWinOrg);        //  Window origin.
```

Even without knowing the meaning of each drawing attribute, you can tell that 15 is a lot more than the five parameters that TextOut actually needs. In a world without DCs, you'd have a lot of work to do just to say "Hello."

What's in a DC? Here is a list of all the drawing attributes in a DC. For your convenience, we have indicated the type of primitive used by each attribute.

Drawing Attribute	Default Value	Lines	Filled Areas	Text	Raster	Comments
Background Color	White	X	X	X		Styled pen, hatch brush, text background
Background Mode	OPAQUE	X	X	X		On/Off switch
Brush Handle	White Brush		X		X	Filled areas
Brush Origin	(0,0)		X		X	Hatch and dithered brushes
Clipping Region Handle	Entire Surface	X	X	X	X	
Color Palette Handle	Default Palette	X	X	X		
Current Pen Position	(0,0)	X				For LineTo routine
Drawing Mode	R2_COPYPEN	X	X			Boolean mixing

Drawing Attribute	*Default Value*	*Lines*	*Filled Areas*	*Text*	*Raster*	*Comments*
Font Handle	System Font			X		
Intercharacter Spacing	0			X		
Mapping Mode	MM_TEXT	X	X	X	X	One unit = 1 pixel
Pen Handle	Black Pen	X	X			
Polygon-Filling Mode	Alternate		X			For Polygon routine
Stretching Mode	Black on White				X	For StretchBlt routine
Text Alignment	Left & Top		X			
Text Color	Black		X	X		Foreground color for monochrome pattern brushes
Text justification	(0,0)			X		Break extra and character extra
Viewport Extent	(1 , 1)	X	X	X	X	Coordinate mapping
Viewport Origin	(0 , 0)	X	X	X	X	Coordinate mapping
Window Extent	(1 , 1)	X	X	X	X	Coordinate mapping
Window Origin	(0 , 0)	X	X	X	X	Coordinate mapping

Not every drawing attribute in the DC is used by every drawing routine. For example, the text color is never used to draw lines. Instead, each drawing routine takes the attributes it needs from the DC. Let's look at the other roles played by the DC.

The second role of a DC is that it connects a program to a specific drawing surface. For example, a program that wants to draw on the system display must gain access to a DC for the system display (we'll describe how this is done in a moment). To draw on a printer, or on a pseudo-device like a bitmap, a program obtains a DC to connect to each of these drawing surfaces.

The connection that the DC provides is a logical connection, not a physical one. Windows, after all, is a multitasking system. If programs had direct access to the physical device, it would cause confusion both for the user and for the Windows programs. As each program fought to maintain control of a given device, the result would be mixed up graphical nonsense.

To understand what we mean by a physical connection, consider the way an MS-DOS program like LOTUS 1-2-3 works. When it draws on the display, it writes directly to the memory buffers on the video adapter board. It directly manipulates the hardware registers to cause the hardware to perform the necessary tricks to display the desired spreadsheet or graph. To support this capability, it requires a private device driver so that it can tell the difference between the CGA, VGA, and 8514/a display cards. LOTUS 1-2-3 is able to do this because MS-DOS is a single-tasking operating system. There isn't any danger that other programs might be disrupted.

But Windows is multitasking, so programs cannot access a physical output device without disrupting other programs. Instead, a Windows program must use the logical connection represented by the DC. All Windows programs use this approach, so that GDI resolves the conflicts that might otherwise disrupt the system when two programs access the same device. This introduces the third role of a DC: its role as a permission slip.

To avoid conflicts on shared devices, a DC is a permission slip that a program must have before it can draw on any device. The permission system works in one of two ways, depending on the type of device. On hardcopy devices, the process is known as **spooling**. On video display devices, the permission system is called **clipping**.

On printers and plotters, GDI borrows a technique from mainframe computers: Output is spooled to disk. The Windows Spooler, also known as the Print Manager, plays the role of a traffic cop to direct the flow of output to hardcopy devices. Otherwise, the output of one program might get mixed in with the pages of another. For spooled output, the DC helps GDI keep different print jobs separate.

On the display screen, Windows takes a different approach to separate the output from different programs. The method, called **clipping**, involves the creation of imaginary fences around a program's drawing area. To paraphrase an old saying: "Good fences make good Windows programs."

My next-door neighbor has a fence around his yard that prevents his dog from running away. The dog can roam where he'd like inside the yard, but cannot stray into my yard. The fences that GDI creates provide the same type of boundary enforcement. When a program wants to draw in a window, it gets a DC with a built-in fence around the window's client area from the Window Manager. Inside the fence, a program is free to draw what it likes. But the fence prevents the program from letting its drawing stray.

An example might clarify exactly what we mean by clipping. Figure 6.4 shows two programs sharing the display screen: NOTEPAD and CLOCK. Before either program draws, a fence is built to prevent either program from drawing outside its client area.

NOTEPAD's fence forms a rectangle. Notice that the fence prevents NOTEPAD from drawing on the face of the clock. It also prevents NOTEPAD from drawing on the non-client area of its own window. Like most Windows programs, NOTEPAD doesn't maintain the non-client area of its window; it leaves that work to Windows.

The clipping for CLOCK is a little more complex. We know that the clipping works because CLOCK's sweeping second hand doesn't brush NOTEPAD away. Instead, the clock hands appear to go "behind" the NOTEPAD window. Figure 6.5 shows the shape of the fence that prevents NOTEPAD from drawing outside its client area.

You might imagine that CLOCK has its work cut out for it to avoid drawing on NOTEPAD. In fact, CLOCK doesn't even "know" that NOTEPAD is present. The DC that CLOCK gets from the Window Manager is the key to this magic. When CLOCK

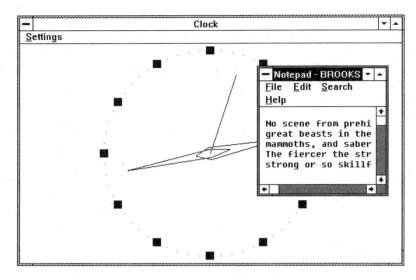

Figure 6.4   Output from Clock and Notepad are kept separate through clipping

calls different GDI drawing routines, the DC handle lets GDI check the location of the fence to make sure that no drawing is done out of bounds. Hence, CLOCK must do very little work; GDI does it all.

How does GDI perform boundary checking? Let's look at the simpler case: the way GDI clips NOTEPAD's output to NOTEPAD's client area. GDI works with the device driver to establish a rectangular fence, which is defined in terms of four coordinates: top side, left side, bottom side, and right side. The boundaries of this fence are part of a

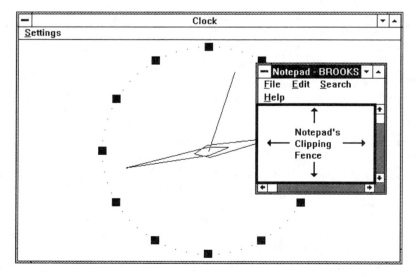

Figure 6.5   The shape of the clipping fence around Notepad

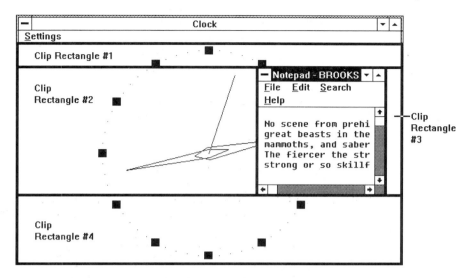

Figure 6.6   The four clip rectangles for Clock

drawing attribute in the DC: the **clipping region**. Every GDI drawing routine checks these boundaries when it draws. As a result, letters and graphic output might get chopped in half, but this is necessary to make windowing a reality.

The more complex clipping we observe in CLOCK can be understood in terms of this simpler case. Namely, GDI defines clipping for CLOCK in terms of the four rectangles shown in Figure 6.6. Now, instead of the four boundaries for one rectangle, GDI works with 16 boundaries for four rectangles. The principle is the same, even though GDI does four times as much work. To handle this kind of clipping, GDI treats each drawing operation like four separate drawing operations, with one for each clipping rectangle.

This complex clipping gives us a clue as to how GDI stores clipping information. A set of one or more rectangles is combined into a data structure called a clipping region which is an attribute that is part of the DC, we mentioned earlier. This means that clipping can be performed on any GDI device. A clipping region might contain the entire drawing surface, or it might contain a set of one or more rectangles.

While clipping can be done on any device, clipping on the display screen is special because Windows provides the clipping information to keep one program from accidentally overwriting another program's output. The part of Windows that takes care of display screen clipping is that part responsible for creating windows: the Window Manager.

Clipping and the Window Manager

From our discussion of the interaction between NOTEPAD and CLOCK, it is clear that GDI's ability to perform clipping is what makes windowing possible. It lets programs share the display screen without requiring programs to worry about stepping on each other's toes.

Table 6.2 Routines to Borrow and Return System Display DCs

Borrowing Routine	Returning Routine	Description
BeginPaint	EndPaint	Clip to invalid part of client area
GetDC	ReleaseDC	Clip to entire client area
GetWindowDC	ReleaseDC	Clip to entire window (client and non-client areas)

Although GDI routines provide the clipping service, GDI itself does not set window boundaries. That job belongs to the Window Manager. When we introduced the Window Manager in Chapter 1, we said it was responsible for the user interface. Since the user interface resides on the display screen, the Window Manager builds and maintains all the display screen "fences."

The Window Manager owns a set of DCs for drawing on the system display. When a program wants to draw in a window, it borrows one of these DCs. Before it lends a DC to a program, the Window Manager installs a clipping region. There are three different Window Manager routines that a program can use to borrow a DC. For each of them, a different clipping region is installed in the DC. These routines are shown in Table 6.2, along with the routine used to return the DC to the Window Manager. When a program borrows a DC from the Window Manager, it must be careful to return the DC when it is finished. As you'll see shortly, this is the role of the "Sandwich" code construction.

Figure 6.7 shows how clipping is set for each of these three routines. The first routine, `BeginPaint`, allows a program to respond to requests by the Window Manager to draw in a window or repair damage that has been done to part of a window. The Window Manager sends the `WM_PAINT` message to let a program know that a window needs to be repaired. As you'll see in the next chapter, the `WM_PAINT` message plays a central role in the maintenance of a window's client area.

Figure 6.7 Three ways that the Window Manager sets clipping

The second routine, `GetDC`, allows a program to draw in the client area of a window. The clipping fence keeps output in the client area, even if another program's window is lying on top of the client area, as we saw in the CLOCK-NOTEPAD example. This routine is used for most drawing *outside* the `WM_PAINT` message. For example, in response to a `WM_CHAR` message, we might wish to echo the character typed.

The third routine, `GetWindowDC`, sets clipping to allow drawing anywhere in a window, including the non-client area. The Window Manager itself calls this routine to get a DC for drawing a window's non-client areas.

This introduction to GDI may have left you hungering for some sample code to provide a framework for understanding all the concepts that we've introduced. In our next chapter, we will examine a program that illuminates a single pixel, and introduce you to one of the most important messages that Windows programs work with: `WM_PAINT`. We'll also discuss how Windows handles color, and we'll enhance GDI's drawing primitives by creating one of our own to draw markers.

7

Pixels and Markers

The first program that we're going to look at lights up a single pixel. In doing so, it introduces you to the most important message for any program that draws on the display: WM_PAINT. Figure 7.1 shows three instances of PIXEL running. As you can see, the program illuminates a pixel in the very center of the client area.

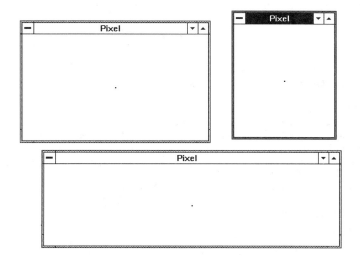

Figure 7.1 Three instances of PIXEL

Like other programs in this book, MIN serves as a starting point for the program. Here is the source listing for the files that make up PIXEL.

PIXEL.C

```c
/*----------------------------------------------------------------*\
|    PIXEL.C - Illuminate a pixel in the center of the client    |
|              area.                                             |
\*----------------------------------------------------------------*/
#define STRICT
#include <Windows.H>


/*----------------------------------------------------------------*\
|                     Function Prototypes.                        |
\*----------------------------------------------------------------*/
LRESULT CALLBACK PixelWndProc (HWND, UINT, WPARAM, LPARAM);


/*----------------------------------------------------------------*\
|                     Global Variables.                           |
\*----------------------------------------------------------------*/
char achWndClass[] = "Pixel:MAIN";
char achAppName[]  = "Pixel";


/*----------------------------------------------------------------*\
|                   Main Function:  WinMain.                      |
\*----------------------------------------------------------------*/
int PASCAL
WinMain (HINSTANCE hInstance,      // Who am I?
         HINSTANCE hPrevInstance,  // Any older siblings?
         LPSTR     lpszCmdLine,    // Ptr to command line.
         int       cmdShow)        // How to open my window?
    {
    HWND     hwnd;
    MSG      msg;
    WNDCLASS wndclass;

    if (!hPrevInstance)
        {
        wndclass.lpszClassName = achWndClass;
        wndclass.hInstance     = hInstance;
        wndclass.lpfnWndProc   = PixelWndProc;
        wndclass.hCursor       = LoadCursor (hInstance, "hand");
        wndclass.hIcon         = LoadIcon (hInstance,"snapshot");
        wndclass.lpszMenuName  = NULL;
        wndclass.hbrBackground = (HBRUSH)(COLOR_WINDOW+1);
        wndclass.style         = CS_HREDRAW | CS_VREDRAW;
        wndclass.cbClsExtra    = 0;
        wndclass.cbWndExtra    = 0;

        RegisterClass( &wndclass);
        }
```

```
        hwnd = CreateWindowEx(0L,              // Extra style.
                        achWndClass,           // Class name.
                        achAppName,            // Title.
                        WS_OVERLAPPEDWINDOW,   // Style bits.
                        CW_USEDEFAULT,         // x - default.
                        0,                     // y - default.
                        CW_USEDEFAULT,         // cx - default.
                        0,                     // cy - default.
                        NULL,                  // No parent.
                        NULL,                  // Class menu.
                        hInstance,             // Creator.
                        NULL);                 // Params.
        ShowWindow (hwnd, cmdShow);

        while (GetMessage(&msg, 0, 0, 0))
            {
            TranslateMessage(&msg); // Convert KEYDOWNs to CHARs
            DispatchMessage(&msg);  // Transmit message to WndProc
            }
        return 0;
        }


/*--------------------------------------------------------------*\
|               Window Procedure:  PixelWndProc.                 |
\*--------------------------------------------------------------*/
LRESULT CALLBACK
PixelWndProc (HWND    hwnd,       // For whom is message sent?
              UINT    mMsg,       // What is exact message?
              WPARAM  wParam,     // ...message details.
              LPARAM  lParam)     // ...message details.
    {
    switch (mMsg)
        {
        case WM_DESTROY:
            PostQuitMessage(0);  // Handle application shutdown.
            break;

        case WM_PAINT:
            {
            int x, y;
            PAINTSTRUCT ps;
            RECT r;

            BeginPaint (hwnd, &ps);
            GetClientRect (hwnd, &r);
            x = r.right/2;
            y = r.bottom/2;
            SetPixel (ps.hdc, x, y, RGB (0, 0, 0));
            EndPaint (hwnd, &ps);
            }
            break;

        default:
```

```
                    return(DefWindowProc(hwnd,mMsg,wParam,lParam));
                    break;
            }
        return 0L;
        }
```

PIXEL.DEF

```
NAME    PIXEL

EXETYPE WINDOWS

DESCRIPTION 'SetPixel Demo Program (c) 1992 By Paul Yao'

CODE    MOVEABLE PRELOAD
DATA    MOVEABLE MULTIPLE PRELOAD

HEAPSIZE    512
STACKSIZE   5120

SEGMENTS
    PIXEL_TEXT MOVEABLE PRELOAD

EXPORTS
    PixelWndProc
```

PIXEL.LNK

```
Pixel.obj
Pixel.exe/align:16/map/nod/noe/CO
nul
mlibcew libw
Pixel.def
```

PIXEL.MAK

```
# Directory search paths.

INCDIR = \WINDEV\INCLUDE

# Windows version to support
# Valid pairs include:
#     (0x0300, 30)
#     (0x0310, 31)

CLVER = WINVER=0x0300
```

```
RCVER = 30

# Compiler switches for applications.

CL_APP_SHIP_ALL = -AM -c -D$(CLVER) -Gsw -I$(INCDIR) -Ow -W3 -Zp
CL_APP_DEBG_ALL = -AM -c -D$(CLVER) -Gsw -I$(INCDIR) -Od -W3 -Zpi

CL_APP_SHIP_31 = -AM -c -G2s  -I$(INCDIR) -Ow -W3 -Zp
CL_APP_DEBG_31 = -AM -c -G2s  -I$(INCDIR) -Od -W3 -Zpi

# Compiler switches for DLLs.

CL_DLL_SHIP_ALL = -AMw -c -D$(CLVER) -Gsw -I$(INCDIR) -Ow -W3 -Zp
CL_DLL_DEBG_ALL = -AMw -c -D$(CLVER) -Gsw -I$(INCDIR) -Od -W3 -Zpi

CL_DLL_SHIP_31 = -AMw -c -G2s  -I$(INCDIR) -Ow -W3 -Zp
CL_DLL_DEBG_31 = -AMw -c -G2s  -I$(INCDIR) -Od -W3 -Zpi

# Make file primary target.

all: Pixel.exe

# Make file dependency targets.

Pixel.res: Pixel.rc Pixel.cur Pixel.ico
    rc -r -i$(INCDIR) Pixel.rc

Pixel.obj: Pixel.c
    cl $(CL_APP_SHIP_ALL) Pixel.c

Pixel.exe: Pixel.obj Pixel.def Pixel.res
    link @Pixel.lnk
    rc -$(RCVER) Pixel.res

Pixel.exe: Pixel.res
    rc -$(RCVER) Pixel.res
```

PIXEL.RC

```
snapshot icon Pixel.ico

hand  cursor Pixel.cur
```

Although PIXEL's `WinMain` function is essentially the same as MIN's, there is one change worth mentioning. We have added two new style bits to the window class definition:

```
wndclass.style          = CS_HREDRAW | CS_VREDRAW;
```

These style bits direct the Window Manager to generate a WM_PAINT message when the size of the window changes, in either the vertical direction (CS_VREDRAW) or the horizontal direction (CS_HREDRAW). PIXEL redraws the contents of its window whenever the size changes to insure that the pixel is always at the center of the window.

The WM_PAINT message is the most important message for any program that draws in a window. Like a bull in a china shop, the user can cause quite a bit of damage as he charges across the display screen: Windows are moved, resized, opened, and closed. Dialog boxes are brought up and dismissed, and data is scrolled inside various windows.

Each of these actions can cause holes to appear in the user interface. Windows does its best to patch these holes, but in many cases can't do it alone. In particular, when the client area of a window has been overwritten, Windows has a limited ability to repair the damage.

There are occasions when Windows is able to anticipate that an object (like a dialog box or a menu) will overwrite a window for a very short period of time. In such cases, Windows takes a snapshot of the area before it is overwritten. When the short-term guest disappears, Windows restores the screen without any outside help.

Such snapshots are quite memory intensive, so Windows only does this when it is critical to the performance of the user interface. Clearly, peak performance of the system's menus is important to encourage users to browse menu items. Without such performance boosts, the entire system would appear sluggish to the user.

Most of the time, Windows calls on your program to help repair a hole in the user interface. The request arrives as a WM_PAINT message. In response to WM_PAINT, a window procedure repairs the damaged window by redrawing its contents. This requires the window procedure to obtain a DC, which gives it the drawing tools, device access, and permission slip required to draw in a window.

The BeginPaint Routine

As shown in our PIXEL program, the BeginPaint routine provides a DC handle that a program uses in responding to the WM_PAINT message. BeginPaint borrows a DC from the supply maintained by the Window Manager. The routine is specially designed to work with the WM_PAINT message, because it installs a clipping region in the DC that corresponds to the damaged part of our window. This area is sometimes referred to as a window's **invalid region**, or **invalid rectangle** if the region is defined in terms of a simple rectangle.

The invalid region might consist of the entire client area of our window, but in many cases includes only a portion of the client area. For example, Figure 7.2 shows CLOCK and PIXEL sharing the display screen, with part of CLOCK's window covering a portion of PIXEL's client area. When we click on PIXEL to activate its window, the covered part of PIXEL's client area must be redrawn. That's the job of the WM_PAINT message. The dotted lines in the figure show the shape of the clipping region installed in the DC that BeginPaint returns. By making the invalid region a subset of the total client area, the Window Manager helps minimize the amount of effort that is required to repair a damaged window.

From our earlier discussion on clipping, you may recall that the clipping rectangle shown in Figure 7.2 only allows drawing inside the boundaries of the clipping fence. Outside the fence, no drawing is allowed. Why is clipping set in this manner?

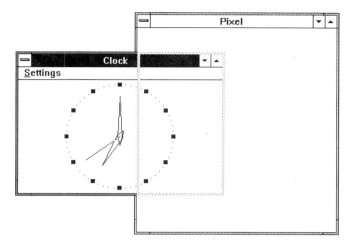

Figure 7.2 CLOCK covering part of PIXEL's client area

Since the purpose of a `WM_PAINT` message is to repair damage to a window, the clipping fence surrounds the *exact* part of the window which has been damaged, as shown in the example. On the one hand, this is the only area in which our program will be allowed to draw. On the other hand, this is the only part into which we *need* to draw. By definition we don't need to repair the undamaged part of a window for a `WM_PAINT` message.

Let's take a closer look at the code involved with handling the `WM_PAINT` message, to get a better idea of what is involved. `BeginPaint` takes two parameters: a window handle and a pointer to a **PAINTSTRUCT** data structure. The window handle identifies the window whose client area is to be repaired.

The `PAINTSTRUCT` data structure is defined in Windows.h as follows:

```
typedef struct tagPAINTSTRUCT
        {
            HDC    hdc;
            BOOL   fErase;
            RECT   rcPaint;
            BOOL   fRestore;
            BOOL   fIncUpdate;
            BYTE   rgbReserved[16];
        } PAINTSTRUCT;
```

Of the six fields in this data structure, only the first and third are really useful. The first field, `hdc`, is a DC handle that we'll pass to GDI drawing routines. According to the Windows Development Kit documentation, the second field, `fErase`, is a flag designed to tell us if our window needs erasing. In fact, this field always has the value of zero. The fourth, fifth, and sixth fields are all used internally by Windows.

The `rcPaint` field describes a rectangle surrounding the damaged area of our window—that is, the invalid region of our window. While most programs ignore this field, it serves as a hint that a program can use to minimize the amount of work it forces

GDI to do. For example, if a program did a lot of drawing in a window, it might use this rectangle to decide exactly what needs repairing. By preclipping to this rectangle, drawing-intensive programs can get a substantial performance improvement.

BeginPaint gives us a handle to a DC, which is all we need to draw our pixel. Let's look at the other routines called by our window procedure in response to the WM_PAINT message.

GetClientRect Routine

Earlier, we compared a window to a canvas on which an artist draws. Unlike an artist's canvas, however, a window can change size. To help you cope with that change, the GetClientRect routine allows you to determine the size of a window's client area (saving this information from the WM_SIZE message also does the trick). GetClientRect takes two parameters:

- **A window handle**. We use the window handle that was passed to our window procedure.

- **A pointer to a rectangle (RECT) data structure**. The size of the client area, in pixels, is returned in this structure.

The RECT structure is defined in Windows.h as shown here:

```
typedef struct tagRECT
    {
        int    left;
        int    top;
        int    right;
        int    bottom;
    } RECT;
```

One aspect of the GetClientRect routine is that it always returns zero in two of these fields: left and top—so they can be safely ignored. To determine the client area size, we rely on the right and bottom fields. We position the pixel in the middle of the client area using the values r.right/2 and r.bottom/2 as x and y coordinates.

SetPixel Routine

The SetPixel routine takes four parameters:

```
SetPixel (hDC, X, Y, crColor);
```

- **Handle to a device context**. We use the handle provided by BeginPaint.

- **x and y Coordinates**. We positioned the pixel in the middle of the client area by dividing the values returned in GetClientRect by two.

- **Color**. GDI provides three ways to specify color: an RGB triplet, a palette index, and a palette relative RGB triplet.

An RGB triplet gets its name from its three parts: a red value, a green value, and a blue value. An RGB triplet is always an unsigned long integer; that is, a four-byte-wide, 32-bit value. Three of the bytes are used to store the red, green, and blue intensity of the color for which you are looking. With one byte per color, that means there are 256 intensities for each color, and over 16 million unique combinations.

The RGB macro in Windows.h provides the easiest means for creating an RGB triplet. The syntax for this macro is

```
rgbColor = RGB (bRed, bGreen, bBlue)
```

where bRed, bGreen, and bBlue are integers between 0 and 255. The RGB macro packs the intensity of all three colors into a single unsigned long integer.

Although you can specify over 16 million different RGB combinations, the actual color which is produced will depend on the device. For example, the 16-color EGA adapter will map the RGB values to the nearest available **physical color**. When we talk about pens, we'll talk about how GDI **dithers** to simulate many more colors on a device. But for pixels, the only colors that are available are the physical, or "pure," colors. Two RGB triplets have guaranteed results: RGB(0,0,0) is always black, and RGB(255,255,255) is always white.

A second way to specify color is with a palette index. A Palette is a table of RBG triplets. Therefore, at first glance, a palette index is another way to specify an RGB triplet. But, unlike RGB triplets, palettes allow a program to specify the exact physical color that should be represented. For example, the VGA and 8514/a display adapters have hardware that supports 262,144 different colors, but only 256 of these colors are available at any one moment. The device driver selects a palette that is distributed evenly across the color range. But this isn't good enough for some uses. Palettes allow a program to select the exact colors to be used in the 256 available slots.

On devices that support GDI palettes, a program can actually change the hardware registers of a device to represent the exact set of colors required. For example, if a program wants to display a color bitmap of a woodland scene, it might need 150 shades of green to show all the subtle nuances in the grasses, trees, and shrubs. Or a color bitmap of skiers on a snow-covered mountain might require 100 shades of white, 50 shades of hot-pink and orange, and 10 shades of blue. Palettes allow a program to show images like these on a display screen with near picture-perfect representation.

Like RGB triplets, palette indices are unsigned long integers. The only difference is that a flag is set in the fourth, unused byte to indicate that the value is a palette index and not an actual RGB triplet. The PALETTEINDEX macro selects a palette index value. For example, to select color number 137, you would use the following:

```
PALETTEINDEX (137);
```

The third and final way to specify color is with a palette-relative RGB index. Like an RGB triplet, this allows you to specify a red, green, and blue portion of a color. But a PALETTEINDEX color is never dithered. Instead, GDI finds the nearest pure color in the existing palette, and uses it. The PALETTERGB macro creates this type of color reference:

```
PALETTERGB (0, 128, 255);
```

EndPaint Routine

After all the drawing for the WM_PAINT message is done, a program calls the End-Paint routine to return the display DC to the Window Manager. When the Window Manager receives the DC, it restores all the drawing attributes to the default state so that the DC is ready to be loaned to the next program that needs to draw in a window.

The EndPaint routine also notifies the Window Manager that the damaged window has been repaired. In Windows' terms, the *invalid* part of a window has been made *valid*. Later in this chapter, you'll see that a program can call the InvalidateRect routine to declare a client area damaged, which causes a WM_PAINT message to be generated. The EndPaint routine calls another Windows library routine, ValidateRect, which tells the Window Manager to recognize that the window has been repaired.

If a program does not call EndPaint in response to a WM_PAINT message, the Window Manager will send a constant stream of WM_PAINT messages. Until the Window Manager is told that a window has been repaired, it will continue to ask you to repair it, which it does via the WM_PAINT message.

The use of the BeginPaint/EndPaint pair is the standard way that programs respond to WM_PAINT. As you'll see, the use of a pair of routines like this is common in other parts of Windows programming: for locking memory, reading files, and accessing the Clipboard. We call this construction the *Windows sandwich*. Let's take a moment to describe this construction in more detail.

The Windows Sandwich

A construction that you will encounter often in your Windows programming career is something we call the **Windows sandwich**. While this term is not something you will read about in any book on structured programming, it is important in Windows programming.

Like its culinary counterpart, the Windows sandwich has three parts: two outside pieces (the bread) which serve to hold the third part: the filling. When I was a child, my mother made sandwiches with two pieces of wheat bread and a filling of peanut butter and jelly. All three ingredients were important to the proper creation of my lunchtime meal. When making a sandwich, it's important to remember all three ingredients, but it is also important to arrange the three ingredients in the proper order.

Figure 7.3 shows the three parts of the Windows programming sandwich. The first piece of bread represents a line of code which grabs a resource. The second piece of bread is the final line of code which returns the resource. In between, the filling is made up of one or more lines of code.

This construction is important because there are certain resources that must be shared with every other program that's running. Since Windows is a multitasking system, programs must cooperate with each other to share the scarce resources of the system. The sandwich represents the most common way that this is done.

The resource we borrow might be a connection to a graphics output device, a disk file, or the Windows clipboard. In general, a sandwich holds the resource for the duration of a single message, like the DC that we borrow in response to the WM_PAINT message.

Figure 7.3 The Windows programming sandwich

```
case WM_PAINT:
    {
    PAINTSTRUCT ps;

    BeginPaint (hwnd, &ps);     // Top slice...
    ...                         // ...Filling...
    EndPaint (hwnd, &ps);       // ...Bottom Slice.
    }
```

The BeginPaint call borrows the DC from the Window Manager. A handle to that resource is stored in the hdc field of the PAINTSTRUCT structure. From that line until the EndPaint line, the program has complete use of the DC. The filling of this sandwich in our PIXEL program drew a single pixel on the display. Once the End-Paint routine returns the DC, we no longer have access to it. Therefore, our program should not try to draw in the window after the second slice of bread.

▼ **TIPS:**

You don't have to be a chef at a four-star restaurant to tell that the following sandwiches have been made incorrectly. The problem with this first sandwich is that the filling is outside the bread. You have jelly on your fingers:

```
case WM_PAINT:
    {
    PAINTSTRUCT ps;

    BeginPaint (hwnd, &ps);                 // Top slice...
    EndPaint (hwnd, &ps);                   // ...Bottom Slice.
    SetPixel (ps.hdc, x, y, RGB (0, 0, 0)); // ...Filling...
    }
```

This second sandwich is only made from a single slice of bread: The bottom slice of bread is missing. Again, you have jelly on your fingers:

```
case WM_PAINT:
    {
    PAINTSTRUCT ps;

    BeginPaint (hwnd, &ps);                    // Top slice...
    SetPixel (ps.hdc, x, y, RGB (0, 0, 0)); // ...Filling...
    }
```

This third sandwich is made without any bread at all. Peanut butter and jelly is everywhere. Yuk!

```
case WM_PAINT:
    {
    PAINTSTRUCT ps;

    SetPixel (ps.hdc, x, y, RGB (0, 0, 0)); // ...Filling...
    }
```

A few sandwich constructions span multiple messages. You might call this a double-decker sandwich, or a Dagwood Sandwich (named for the cartoon character who liked to make huge sandwiches). An example involves the capture of the mouse pointer. Sometimes, it is advantageous for a program to request exclusive use of the mouse pointer. Here is the code structure for such a sandwich:

```
case WM_LBUTTONDOWN:
    SetCapture (hwnd);        // Top slice...
    ...
    break;
case WM_MOUSEMOVE:
    ...                       // ...Filling...
    break;
case WM_LBUTTONUP:
    ReleaseCapture();         // ...Bottom Slice.
    ...
    break;
```

We'll take a closer look at this double-decker sandwich in Chapter 16, when we discuss mouse input. Let's move on to our next drawing primitive. This is not actually a GDI primitive, but one that we're going to build on top of the `SetPixel` routine.

Creating Markers

Our second GDI program introduces a type of drawing primitive which is not native to GDI: **markers**. The most obvious use of a marker is on a graph, like the one in Figure 7.4. Each "+" symbol is a marker. In this example, each marker represents a population value for a given year.

At first glance, you might wonder why markers are special. After all, from the chart it is clear that GDI can display text. What's the difference between a marker and a text character?

Figure 7.4 Markers highlight points on a graph

As you'll see in Chapter 10, GDI text routines make it easy to work with different sizes and styles of text on a variety of devices. This very flexibility makes it difficult to guarantee that a specific letter will be centered on a specific location. For example, if you used GDI letters to mark the location of buried treasure on a map, you introduce a margin of error. The location of the cross-hairs on the letter X, for example, will move depending on the font you are using.

Markers overcome this limitation since a marker is guaranteed to be centered over an exact location. That's the reason that markers are used for graphs. In the chapters that follow, you'll see that we use markers to help explain all of the GDI drawing routines.

One way to mark a location is with the `SetPixel` routine that we introduced in the preceding section. But a single pixel is often hard to see. For this reason, we create our "+" marker by grouping several pixels together.

When we introduce other GDI drawing primitives, we're going to use markers to show the relationship between the coordinates we specify when we call a drawing primitive and the resulting output. This will help clarify GDI's "inclusive-exclusive" drawing approach, and help you see how GDI creates lines, filled areas, and text output.

Figure 7.5 shows a sample of the output produced by our marker program, MARKER.C. This program uses mouse input to place markers.

Figure 7.5 Sample output of MARKER

Here are the source files to MARKER:

MARKER.C

```
/*--------------------------------------------------------------*\
| MARKER.C  Draws markers in response to mouse clicks.          |
\*--------------------------------------------------------------*/
#define STRICT
#include <Windows.H>
#define MAXPOINTS 12


/*--------------------------------------------------------------*\
|                     Function Prototypes.                       |
\*--------------------------------------------------------------*/
LRESULT CALLBACK MarkerWndProc (HWND, UINT, WPARAM, LPARAM);
VOID NEAR PASCAL DrawMarker (HDC hdc, int x, int y);


/*--------------------------------------------------------------*\
|                      Global Variables.                         |
\*--------------------------------------------------------------*/
char achWndClass[] = "Marker:MAIN";
char achAppName[]  = "Marker";


/*--------------------------------------------------------------*\
|                  Main Function:  WinMain.                      |
\*--------------------------------------------------------------*/
int PASCAL
WinMain (HINSTANCE hInstance,      // Who am I?
         HINSTANCE hPrevInstance,  // Any older siblings?
         LPSTR     lpszCmdLine,    // Ptr to command line.
         int       cmdShow)        // How to open my window?
    {
    HWND      hwnd;
    MSG       msg;
    WNDCLASS wndclass;

    if (!hPrevInstance)
        {
        wndclass.lpszClassName = achWndClass;
        wndclass.hInstance     = hInstance;
        wndclass.lpfnWndProc   = MarkerWndProc;
        wndclass.hCursor       = LoadCursor (hInstance, "hand");
        wndclass.hIcon         = LoadIcon (hInstance,"snapshot");
        wndclass.lpszMenuName  = NULL;
        wndclass.hbrBackground = (HBRUSH)(COLOR_WINDOW+1);
        wndclass.style         = NULL;
        wndclass.cbClsExtra    = 0;
        wndclass.cbWndExtra    = 0;

        RegisterClass( &wndclass);
        }
```

```
    hwnd = CreateWindowEx(0L,                   // Extra style.
                    achWndClass,                // Class name.
                    achAppName,                 // Title.
                    WS_OVERLAPPEDWINDOW,        // Style bits.
                    CW_USEDEFAULT,              // x - default.
                    0,                          // y - default.
                    CW_USEDEFAULT,              // cx - default.
                    0,                          // cy - default.
                    NULL,                       // No parent.
                    NULL,                       // Class menu.
                    hInstance,                  // Creator.
                    NULL);                      // Params.
    ShowWindow (hwnd, cmdShow);

    while (GetMessage(&msg, 0, 0, 0))
        {
        TranslateMessage(&msg); // Convert KEYDOWNs to CHARs
        DispatchMessage(&msg);  // Transmit message to WndProc
        }
    return 0;
    }

/*-------------------------------------------------------------*\
|               Window Procedure:  MarkerWndProc.               |
\*-------------------------------------------------------------*/
LRESULT CALLBACK
MarkerWndProc (HWND   hwnd,      // For whom is message sent?
               UINT   mMsg,      // What is exact message?
               WPARAM wParam,    // ...message details.
               LPARAM lParam)    // ...message details.
    {
    static POINT pt[MAXPOINTS];
    static int   cpt = 0;

    switch (mMsg)
        {
        case WM_DESTROY:
            PostQuitMessage(0);  // Handle application shutdown.
            break;

        case WM_LBUTTONDOWN:
            if (cpt < MAXPOINTS)
                {
                pt[cpt] = MAKEPOINT (lParam);
                cpt++;
                InvalidateRect (hwnd, NULL, TRUE);
                }
            break;

        case WM_PAINT:
            {
            PAINTSTRUCT ps;
            int i;
```

```
                    BeginPaint (hwnd, &ps);

                    for (i=0; i< cpt; i++)
                        DrawMarker (ps.hdc, pt[i].x, pt[i].y);

                    EndPaint (hwnd, &ps);
                    }
                    break;

            default:
                return(DefWindowProc(hwnd,mMsg,wParam,lParam));
                break;
        }
    return 0L;
    }

/*-------------------------------------------------------------*\
|                Marker Drawing Function: DrawMarker.           |
\*-------------------------------------------------------------*/
#define MARKERSIZE 3
void NEAR PASCAL
DrawMarker (HDC hdc,   //  DC for drawing.
            int x,     //  X coordinate for marker.
            int y)     //  Y coordinate for marker.
    {
    DWORD dwColor;
    int i;

    dwColor = GetPixel (hdc, x, y);
    dwColor = ~dwColor;
    SetPixel (hdc, x, y, dwColor);

    for (i=1;i<=MARKERSIZE; i++)
        {
        dwColor = GetPixel (hdc, x+i, y);
        dwColor = ~dwColor;
        SetPixel (hdc, x+i, y, dwColor);

        dwColor = GetPixel (hdc, x-i, y);
        dwColor = ~dwColor;
        SetPixel (hdc, x-i, y, dwColor);

        dwColor = GetPixel (hdc, x, y+i);
        dwColor = ~dwColor;
        SetPixel (hdc, x, y+i, dwColor);

        dwColor = GetPixel (hdc, x, y-i);
        dwColor = ~dwColor;
        SetPixel (hdc, x, y-i, dwColor);
        }
    }
```

MARKER.DEF

```
NAME    MARKER

EXETYPE WINDOWS

DESCRIPTION 'Marker Demo (c) 1992 By Paul Yao'

CODE    MOVEABLE PRELOAD
DATA    MOVEABLE MULTIPLE PRELOAD

HEAPSIZE    512
STACKSIZE   5120

SEGMENTS
    MARKER_TEXT MOVEABLE PRELOAD

EXPORTS
    MarkerWndProc
```

MARKER.LNK

```
Marker.obj
Marker.exe/align:16/map/nod/noe/CO
nul
mlibcew libw
Marker.def
```

MARKER.MAK

```
# Directory search paths.

INCDIR = \WINDEV\INCLUDE

# Windows version to support
# Valid pairs include:
#     (0x0300, 30)
#     (0x0310, 31)

CLVER = WINVER=0x0300
RCVER = 30

# Compiler switches for applications.
```

```
CL_APP_SHIP_ALL = -AM -c -D$(CLVER) -Gsw -I$(INCDIR) -Ow -W3 -Zp
CL_APP_DEBG_ALL = -AM -c -D$(CLVER) -Gsw -I$(INCDIR) -Od -W3 -Zpi

CL_APP_SHIP_31  = -AM -c -G2s  -I$(INCDIR) -Ow -W3 -Zp
CL_APP_DEBG_31  = -AM -c -G2s  -I$(INCDIR) -Od -W3 -Zpi

# Compiler switches for DLLs.

CL_DLL_SHIP_ALL = -AMw -c -D$(CLVER) -Gsw -I$(INCDIR) -Ow -W3 -Zp
CL_DLL_DEBG_ALL = -AMw -c -D$(CLVER) -Gsw -I$(INCDIR) -Od -W3 -Zpi

CL_DLL_SHIP_31  = -AMw -c -G2s  -I$(INCDIR) -Ow -W3 -Zp
CL_DLL_DEBG_31  = -AMw -c -G2s  -I$(INCDIR) -Od -W3 -Zpi

# Make file primary target.

all: Marker.exe

# Make file dependency targets.

Marker.res: Marker.rc Marker.cur Marker.ico
    rc -r -i$(INCDIR) Marker.rc

Marker.obj: Marker.c
    cl $(CL_APP_SHIP_ALL) Marker.c

Marker.exe: Marker.obj Marker.def Marker.res
    link @Marker.lnk
    rc -$(RCVER) Marker.res

Marker.exe: Marker.res
    rc -$(RCVER) Marker.res
```

MARKER.RC

```
snapshot icon Marker.ico

hand   cursor Marker.cur
```

The window procedure in our program, MarkerWndProc, processes three messages: WM_DESTROY, WM_LBUTTONDOWN, and WM_PAINT. We respond to WM_DESTROY in the same way that all top-level window procedures do: We post a WM_QUIT message to cause our GetMessage loop to terminate.

The WM_LBUTTONDOWN is a mouse message. Our window procedure receives a WM_LBUTTONDOWN message when two things happen at the same time: the mouse cursor is in our client area, and the user pushes the left mouse button. Every time the window procedure receives this mouse message, it records the X and Y location of the mouse cursor. For all mouse messages, the cursor location is provided in the lParam parameter, in client area coordinates. As you may recall, this coordinate system has its origin (0,0) at the upper-left corner of the client area.

In response to the WM_LBUTTONDOWN message, we store the X and Y location of the mouse cursor in an array of POINT structures. The POINT data type is defined in Windows.h as

```
typedef struct tagPOINT
      {
            int    x;
            int    y;
      } POINT;
```

The line:

```
pt[cpt] = MAKEPOINT (lParam);
```

uses the MAKEPOINT macro to move the four-byte lParam value into the four-byte point structure.

Once a new point has been added to the array, our program forces the window to be redrawn:

```
InvalidateRect (hwnd, NULL, TRUE);
```

This routine causes a WM_PAINT message to be generated by telling Windows that "the window is completely damaged." InvalidateRect takes three parameters:

• Handle of the window to be redrawn.

• A far pointer to a rectangle that is being declared damaged. NULL means that the entire window is to be redrawn.

• An "erase first" flag. TRUE means erase the background before redrawing; FALSE means do not erase first.

In response to the WM_PAINT message, our MARKER program uses the BeginPaint/EndPaint sandwich to borrow a DC from the Window Manager. The filling of the sandwich is a loop that calls our marker routine, DrawMarker, giving the X and Y location of every point in the array pt.

The marker routine, DrawMarker, is built using two GDI routines: GetPixel and SetPixel. In general, if you don't find a GDI drawing routine that creates the exact output that you need, it is often a simple matter to write a routine that builds on top of existing GDI routines, as we've done here.

One word of caution is needed. GetPixel and SetPixel are not supported on a few devices (in particular, on some plotters), so you may wish to rewrite this routine using a line drawing primitive from the next chapter.

Our last program, PIXEL, wrote a single black pixel with the following call:

```
SetPixel (hdc, r.right/2, r.bottom/2, RGB (0,0,0));
```

We could draw a black marker by simply making several calls like this. But what happens when we try to draw a marker on an area that is already black? The marker disappears. Our marker routine solves this problem with Boolean algebra. Before we write a pixel, we read a pixel with the GetPixel routine. GetPixel returns an RGB triplet that lets us know the color of the pixel. We perform a bit-wise negation of the

RGB value to invert the color, and write a pixel with a call to `SetPixel`. Here is a code fragment to show what we mean:

```
dwColor = GetPixel (hdc, x, y);
dwColor = ~dwColor;
SetPixel (hdc, x, y, dwColor);
```

By making a series of calls like this, we draw a marker that will show up on just about any surface, regardless of its original color.

The ~ operator performs a one's complement on the operand, which in this case is an RGB triplet value. All of the zeros are turned into ones, and all of the ones into zeros. While this might seem strange, in fact this type of Boolean arithmetic is very useful in the world of graphics. Later on, we'll describe how **drawing modes** let us perform a logical operation when we draw lines, fill areas, or copy bitmaps.

For now, though, you can rest assured that this approach will be effective in making a mark on a display surface. This approach has one shortcoming: two markers placed at the same location have the effect of negating each other. The markers disappear! Can you think of a way to solve this problem?

One way around this problem would require your program to walk the list of points every time it draws. If it finds a duplicate point, it simply ignores it instead of drawing it. Another way to avoid this problem might involve walking the list of points every time the user clicks the mouse. If a point has already been highlighted, a program could beep at the user to announce that such a point is invalid.

We introduced the marker routine to help describe how native GDI routines work. Let's use our markers to learn about GDI's line draw capabilities, the subject of the next chapter.

8

Drawing Lines

Before we begin to draw lines with GDI routines, let's stop to consider: *What exactly is a line, anyway?* A line is a geometric figure created by joining a set of points. Lines are considered **open figures**, meaning that our interest is in the line itself, and not on the area around the line. In the next chapter, we will examine **closed figures**, in which a line plus the area it surrounds make up a single geometric figure.

A GDI line is a geometric figure drawn by a GDI line drawing routine. Every GDI line has a starting point and an ending point. GDI draws lines using what graphics programmers refer to as an **inclusive/exclusive algorithm**. That is, the starting point is *included* in the line, but the ending point is *excluded*.

Let's use the ZoomIn tool from the Software Development Kit to convince ourselves that this is the case. ZoomIn lets you magnify the pixels on any part of the display screen. Figure 8.1 shows a GDI line with markers to highlight the end points and the ZoomIn utility to show the inclusive/exclusive drawing.

The white pixel in the center of the marker at the starting point shows that the starting point is *included* in the line. The marker, after all, is drawn by inverting the existing pixels: The inverse of black gives us white. However, the center of the marker at the ending point is black, indicating that the ending point has been *excluded* from the line.

Although inclusive/exclusive drawing may seem odd at first, it lets you draw complex figures by making many simple line drawing calls. Each new figure picks up where the other left off. As we'll see in Chapter 16, this process is especially important when using different drawing modes and when creating draggable objects for the mouse pointer.

Inclusive/exclusive drawing is used by all of GDI's line drawing routines. Let's take a brief tour through the available routines to see what GDI can do for us. After that, we'll

Figure 8.1 ZoomIn shows GDI's inclusive/ exclusive line drawing

review the DC attributes that affect line drawing, concentrating our attention on the most important line drawing attribute: pens.

Line Drawing Primitives

GDI has four line drawing routines: `MoveTo`, `LineTo`, `Polyline`, and `Arc`. We'll consider each in turn. Let's start with the first two routines, `MoveTo` and `LineTo`, which are always used together.

MoveTo and LineTo

Our first routine, `MoveTo`, doesn't actually draw lines. Instead, it stores a pair of X and Y values in a DC attribute called the **current position**. The second routine, `LineTo`, uses this value as a starting point for a line. The `LineTo` function itself provides the ending point as a parameter. Here is how you use these routines to draw a line from point X1,Y1 to point X2, Y2:

```
MoveTo (hdc, X1, Y1);
LineTo (hdc, X2, Y2);
```

After the `LineTo` function has drawn a line, it updates the value of the current position in the DC to reflect the end point of the line. You can connect a series of points by making calls like the following:

```
MoveTo (hdc, X1, Y1);
LineTo (hdc, X2, Y2);
LineTo (hdc, X3, Y3);
LineTo (hdc, X4, Y4);
```

When these routines are called in this way, they produce the same result as our next routine, the `Polyline` function. You might wonder why GDI has this kind of redundancy. It is partly a question of convenience. You will find that `MoveTo/LineTo` requires less work, since each takes an X,Y value as a parameter. The `Polyline` function, on the other hand, requires the X,Y values to be stored in an array of `POINTS`.

Although it requires its parameters in a special format, the `Polyline` routine is the obvious choice when performance is important. The speed advantage is a direct result of the overhead incurred when a function is called. One `Polyline` call will draw many lines. With `MoveTo/LineTo`, many calls would be required to draw the same lines.

Like the `MoveTo/LineTo` pair, `Polyline` draws straight lines. Unlike this pair, however, `Polyline` does not use the current position value in the DC. It relies solely on an array of `POINTS` that are passed as a parameter. If we store the points (x1, y1), (x2, y2), (x3, y3), and (x4, y4) in an array like this:

```
POINTS pt[] = {x1, y1, x2, y2, x3, y3, x4, y4};
```

the following call to `Polyline` connects the points:

```
Polyline (hdc, pt, 4);
```

The `Arc` function draws a curved line. The parameters to `Arc` define three boundaries: a bounding box, a starting point, and an ending point (see Figure 8.2). If the starting point and the ending point are the same, the `Arc` function draws a complete ellipse (or a circle, if the bounding box is a square). Otherwise, `Arc` draws a portion of an ellipse.

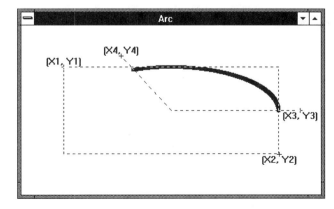

Figure 8.2 The ARC function

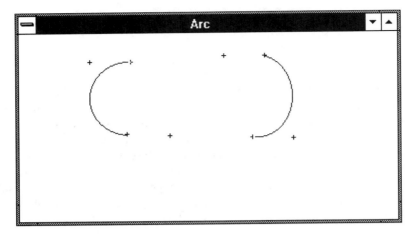

Figure 8.3 Arcs are drawn counterclockwise

The relationship of starting point to ending point was important with the other line-drawing functions, since GDI uses inclusive/exclusive drawing. This is also true for arcs. In addition, arcs are always drawn in a counterclockwise direction. Figure 8.3 shows how two different curves are drawn if the starting and ending points are swapped.

Our line drawing program uses all three types of line drawing primitives. You enter points by clicking the left mouse button in the client area. The first four points are used to draw two lines using `MoveTo`/`LineTo`; the second four points are used to draw a set of lines using `Polyline`. Finally, the last four points are used as input to the `Arc` function.

Figure 8.4 shows the output created by LINES. A complete listing of LINES follows.

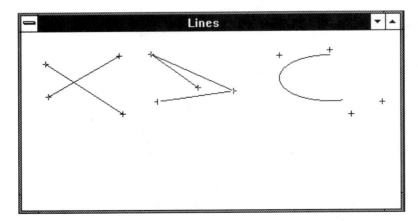

Figure 8.4 The three primitives that LINES can draw

LINES.C

```c
/*-------------------------------------------------------------*\
| LINES.C:  Draw lines using MoveTo/LineTo, Polyline and Arc. |
\*-------------------------------------------------------------*/
#define STRICT
#include <Windows.H>
#define MAXPOINTS 12


/*-------------------------------------------------------------*\
|                    Function Prototypes.                      |
\*-------------------------------------------------------------*/
LRESULT CALLBACK LinesWndProc (HWND, UINT, WPARAM, LPARAM);
VOID NEAR PASCAL DrawMarker (HDC hdc, int x, int y);


/*-------------------------------------------------------------*\
|                    Global Variables.                        |
\*-------------------------------------------------------------*/
char achWndClass[] = "Lines:MAIN";
char achAppName[]  = "Lines";


/*-------------------------------------------------------------*\
|                 Main Function:  WinMain.                     |
\*-------------------------------------------------------------*/
int PASCAL
WinMain (HINSTANCE hInstance,      // Who am I?
         HINSTANCE hPrevInstance, // Any older siblings?
         LPSTR     lpszCmdLine,    // Ptr to command line.
         int       cmdShow)        // How to open my window?
    {
    HWND      hwnd;
    MSG       msg;
    WNDCLASS wndclass;

    if (!hPrevInstance)
        {
        wndclass.lpszClassName = achWndClass;
        wndclass.hInstance     = hInstance;
        wndclass.lpfnWndProc   = LinesWndProc;
        wndclass.hCursor       = LoadCursor (hInstance, "hand");
        wndclass.hIcon         = LoadIcon (hInstance,"snapshot");
        wndclass.lpszMenuName  = NULL;
        wndclass.hbrBackground = (HBRUSH)(COLOR_WINDOW+1);
        wndclass.style         = NULL;
        wndclass.cbClsExtra    = 0;
        wndclass.cbWndExtra    = 0;

        RegisterClass( &wndclass);
        }

    hwnd = CreateWindowEx(0L,                     // Extra style.
                    achWndClass,                   // Class name.
                    achAppName,                    // Title.
                    WS_OVERLAPPEDWINDOW,           // Style bits.
```

```
                            CW_USEDEFAULT,     // x - default.
                            0,                 // y - default.
                            CW_USEDEFAULT,     // cx - default.
                            0,                 // cy - default.
                            NULL,              // No parent.
                            NULL,              // Class menu.
                            hInstance,         // Creator.
                            NULL);             // Params.
        ShowWindow (hwnd, cmdShow);

        while (GetMessage(&msg, 0, 0, 0))
            {
            TranslateMessage(&msg); // Convert KEYDOWNs to CHARs
            DispatchMessage(&msg);  // Transmit message to WndProc
            }
        return 0;
        }

/*-------------------------------------------------------------*\
|               Window Procedure:  LinesWndProc.                |
\*-------------------------------------------------------------*/
LRESULT CALLBACK
LinesWndProc (HWND   hwnd,      // For whom is message sent?
              UINT   mMsg,      // What is exact message?
              WPARAM wParam,    // ...message details.
              LPARAM lParam)    // ...message details.
    {
    static POINT pt[MAXPOINTS];
    static int   cpt = 0;

    switch (mMsg)
        {
        case WM_DESTROY:
            PostQuitMessage(0);  // Handle application shutdown.
            break;

        case WM_LBUTTONDOWN:
            if (cpt < MAXPOINTS)
                {
                pt[cpt] = MAKEPOINT (lParam);
                cpt++;
                InvalidateRect (hwnd, NULL, TRUE);
                }
            break;

        case WM_RBUTTONDOWN:
            cpt = 0;
            InvalidateRect (hwnd, NULL, TRUE);
            break;

        case WM_PAINT:
            {
            PAINTSTRUCT ps;
            int i;
```

```
                BeginPaint (hwnd, &ps);

                // Draw lines with MoveTo / LineTo.
                if (cpt > 1)
                    {
                    MoveTo (ps.hdc, pt[0].x, pt[0].y);
                    LineTo (ps.hdc, pt[1].x, pt[1].y);
                    }
                if (cpt > 3)
                    {
                    MoveTo (ps.hdc, pt[2].x, pt[2].y);
                    LineTo (ps.hdc, pt[3].x, pt[3].y);
                    }

                // Draw lines using Polyline.
                if (cpt > 7)
                    Polyline (ps.hdc, &pt[4], 4);

                // Draw an arc.
                if (cpt == 12)
                    Arc (ps.hdc, pt[8].x,  pt[8].y,
                                 pt[9].x,  pt[9].y,
                                 pt[10].x, pt[10].y,
                                 pt[11].x, pt[11].y);


                // Highlight control points with markers.
                for (i=0; i< cpt; i++)
                    DrawMarker (ps.hdc, pt[i].x, pt[i].y);

                EndPaint (hwnd, &ps);
                }
                break;

        default:
                return(DefWindowProc(hwnd,mMsg,wParam,lParam));
                break;
        }
    return 0L;
    }

/*-------------------------------------------------------------*\
|               Marker Drawing Function: DrawMarker.            |
\*-------------------------------------------------------------*/
#define MARKERSIZE 3
void NEAR PASCAL
DrawMarker (HDC hdc, //  DC for drawing.
            int x,   //  X coordinate for marker.
            int y)   //  Y coordinate for marker.
    {
    DWORD dwColor;
    int i;

    dwColor = GetPixel (hdc, x, y);
```

```
        dwColor = ~dwColor;
        SetPixel (hdc, x, y, dwColor);

        for (i=1;i<=MARKERSIZE; i++)
            {
            dwColor = GetPixel (hdc, x+i, y);
            dwColor = ~dwColor;
            SetPixel (hdc, x+i, y, dwColor);

            dwColor = GetPixel (hdc, x-i, y);
            dwColor = ~dwColor;
            SetPixel (hdc, x-i, y, dwColor);

            dwColor = GetPixel (hdc, x, y+i);
            dwColor = ~dwColor;
            SetPixel (hdc, x, y+i, dwColor);

            dwColor = GetPixel (hdc, x, y-i);
            dwColor = ~dwColor;
            SetPixel (hdc, x, y-i, dwColor);
            }
        }
```

LINES.DEF

```
NAME    LINES

EXETYPE WINDOWS

DESCRIPTION 'Line Drawing Program (c) 1992 By Paul Yao'

CODE    MOVEABLE PRELOAD
DATA    MOVEABLE MULTIPLE PRELOAD

HEAPSIZE    512
STACKSIZE   5120

SEGMENTS
    LINES_TEXT MOVEABLE PRELOAD

EXPORTS
    LinesWndProc
```

LINES.LNK

```
Lines.obj
Lines.exe/align:16/map/nod/noe/CO
nul
```

```
mlibcew libw
Lines.def
```

LINES.MAK

```
# Directory search paths.

INCDIR = \WINDEV\INCLUDE

# Windows version to support
# Valid pairs include:
#     (0x0300, 30)
#     (0x0310, 31)

CLVER = WINVER=0x0300
RCVER = 30

# Compiler switches for applications.

CL_APP_SHIP_ALL = -AM -c -D$(CLVER) -Gsw -I$(INCDIR) -Ow -W3 -Zp
CL_APP_DEBG_ALL = -AM -c -D$(CLVER) -Gsw -I$(INCDIR) -Od -W3 -Zpi

CL_APP_SHIP_31  = -AM -c -G2s  -I$(INCDIR) -Ow -W3 -Zp
CL_APP_DEBG_31  = -AM -c -G2s  -I$(INCDIR) -Od -W3 -Zpi

# Compiler switches for DLLs.

CL_DLL_SHIP_ALL = -AMw -c -D$(CLVER) -Gsw -I$(INCDIR) -Ow -W3 -Zp
CL_DLL_DEBG_ALL = -AMw -c -D$(CLVER) -Gsw -I$(INCDIR) -Od -W3 -Zpi

CL_DLL_SHIP_31  = -AMw -c -G2s  -I$(INCDIR) -Ow -W3 -Zp
CL_DLL_DEBG_31  = -AMw -c -G2s  -I$(INCDIR) -Od -W3 -Zpi

# Make file primary target.

all: Lines.exe

# Make file dependency targets.

Lines.res: Lines.rc Lines.cur Lines.ico
    rc -r -i$(INCDIR) Lines.rc

Lines.obj: Lines.c
    cl $(CL_APP_SHIP_ALL) Lines.c

Lines.exe: Lines.obj Lines.def Lines.res
    link @Lines.lnk
    rc -$(RCVER) Lines.res

Lines.exe: Lines.res
    rc -$(RCVER) Lines.res
```

LINES.RC

```
snapshot icon Lines.ico

hand   cursor Lines.cur
```

Now that we've looked at GDI's line drawing routines, let's examine the DC drawing attributes that affect lines.

DC Attributes

Five DC attributes are used by the GDI to draw lines:

Drawing attribute	*Comments*
Background Color	second color for non-solid pens
Background Mode	turns on/off background color
Current Position	(x,y) position for `LineTo` routine
Drawing Mode	Boolean drawing operation
Pen	line color, width, and style

Without a doubt, the most important attribute is the pen, which determines the appearance of the line in terms of color, width, and style (or pattern, such as solid or dotted). The term **styled lines** is often used for lines with a non-solid style, such as dotted and dashed.

The second most important attribute is the drawing mode, which lets us specify a Boolean operator to use in a drawing operation. More on that later.

Of the other three attributes, two affect *styled* lines, but not solid lines: background color and background mode. GDI uses the background color for the spaces between the lines—that is, between the foreground dashes or dots. The background mode toggles whether the background part of a styled line should be filled in or left alone. Keep in mind while using these two attributes that they also affect filled areas—when a hatched brush is used—and text.

The background color is set using the `SetBkColor` routine, defined as follows:

```
SetBkColor (hDC, crColor)
```

- `hDC` is a handle to a DC.

- `crColor` is a color reference value, using either (a) an RGB triplet, (b) a palette index, or (c) a palette relative RGB value.

The following line of code sets the background color to blue:

```
SetBkColor (hDC, RGB(0, 0, 0xFF));
```

To set the background mode, you call the `SetBkMode` routine, whose syntax is

```
SetBkMode (hDC, nBkMode)
```

- `hDC` is a handle to a DC.

- `nBkMode` is the on/off switch: Set to `OPAQUE` to enable background color, and to `TRANSPARENT` to disable background color.

The final attribute, the current position, is a DC attribute that we discussed in relation to the `MoveTo`/`LineTo` routines. It is an X,Y value which is used by these routines as part of their drawing: `MoveTo` sets the current position, `LineTo` uses it as the starting point for the line to draw. `LineTo` updates the current position to the end point of the line it draws.

Let's turn our attention to pens, and the way they are created and manipulated.

Pens

A pen is a DC drawing attribute that describes how lines are drawn. Pens have three qualities: color, width, and style. If you'd like, you can think of each of these qualities as a drawing attribute in its own right. In the world of graphics programming, when drawing attributes are grouped in this way, the group is called an **attribute bundle**. Attribute bundles are convenient because they let you refer to several drawing attributes at the same time.

GDI is very flexible in the way it lets you share pens: Pens can be shared between programs and between devices. GDI has a set of stock pens that any program can use, or a program can create a set of custom pens and let different devices share them. The net effect of this sharing is that GDI minimizes the amount of memory needed to store drawing attributes. GDI is thrifty with memory because earlier versions of Windows had to run in only 640K of RAM.

Since Windows started running in protected mode, GDI has much less need to be thrifty. Of greater concern is for each application to operate in ways that don't interfere with other applications. For this reason, Microsoft has adopted the position that GDI objects should not be shared. For compatibility reasons, sharing of GDI objects will still be allowed in the Win16 API of Windows 3.1. But the 32-Bit Windows API of Windows NT will not allow GDI objects to be shared. Since this is the future of Windows, your best strategy is to adopt a non-sharing policy of GDI drawing objects in the applications which you're writing today.

Pens and Device Independence

How can pens be used for different devices? The term **logical pen** describes how this is possible. A pen is a request to a device to create lines with a particular appearance. When GDI is ready to draw on a specific device, it makes a request to the device to **realize** a pen. Only at this time does the device driver create the data structures needed to draw lines with the desired qualities. This aspect is hidden in the GDI device-driver interface, but it allows a program to share pens between devices.

Creating and Using Pens

When Windows starts up, GDI creates a set of pens, known as **stock pens**, which can be shared by all programs. GDI has three stock pens: one black, one white, and one null (invisible ink) pen. The null pen is a placeholder, since every DC must contain a valid pen. The other two pens draw solid lines with a width of one pixel.

Pens are identified by a handle. To get the handle of a stock pen, you call the `GetStockObject` routine, as shown here:

```
HPEN hpen;

hpen = GetStockObject (BLACK_PEN);   /* or */
hpen = GetStockObject (WHITE_PEN);   /* or */
hpen = GetStockObject (NULL_PEN);
```

Once you have a pen handle, you call another GDI routine to install the pen into a DC:

```
SelectObject (hdc, hpen);
```

After a pen has been selected into a DC, it is used for all subsequently drawn lines. This includes lines drawn with `MoveTo/LineTo`, `Polyline`, and `Arc`.

One thing about a DC is that it only has room for a single pen at any point in time. Therefore, by selecting one pen into a DC, you automatically remove the old pen. For your convenience, the `SelectObject` routine returns the handle of the pen being removed. For example, the following leaves the DC unchanged:

```
/* No Change to DC.  */
hpenOld = SelectObject (hdc, hpenNew);
SelectObject (hdc, hpenOld);
```

If the three stock pens do not provide you with all the line drawing capability that you need, GDI has two routines for creating pens: `CreatePen` and `CreatePenIndirect`. The only difference between these two routines is in the way parameters are specified. The syntax for `CreatePen` is

```
hpen = CreatePen (nPenStyle, nWidth, crColor);
```

- `nPenStyle` selects a pen style from the flags shown in Figure 8.5.

- `nWidth` sets the width in the X direction. Since we're limiting ourselves to pixels, the units are in pixels. But when we discuss coordinate transformations, you'll see that the width value reflects the coordinate system installed in the DC into which the pen is installed.

- `crColor` is a color reference; as before, it can be either (a) an RGB triplet, (b) a color palette index, or (c) a palette relative RGB value.

So, to create a black pen with a width of 1 logical unit, you say:

```
hpen = CreatePen (PS_SOLID, 1, RGB(0,0,0));
```

The syntax for `CreatePenIndirect`, on the other hand, is

```
LOGPEN logpen;
hpen = CreatePenIndirect (&logpen)
```

LOGPEN is defined in Windows.h as

```
typedef struct tagLOGPEN
    {
    WORD  lopnStyle;
    POINT lopnWidth;
    DWORD lopnColor;
    } LOGPEN;
```

One difference between `CreatePen` and `CreatePenIndirect` is that LOGPEN uses a `POINT` structure for the pen width. As you may recall, the `POINT` structure has two integer members, one for an X value and one for a Y value. To create the same black pen as above, you say:

```
LOGPEN logpen;
logpen.lopnStyle = PS_SOLID;
logpen.lopnWidth.x = 1;
logpen.lopnColor = RGB (0, 0, 0));
hpen = CreatePenIndirect (&logpen)
```

GDI supports seven pen **styles**, as illustrated in Figure 8.5. The last style, `PS_IN-SIDEFRAME`, provides the same results as the `PS_SOLID` style with two important differences: color and use in filled figures. This is the only line style that uses dithered colors. All other pens are only available in solid colors.

In the context of filled figures, the `PS_INSIDEFRAME` style has some unique features. A pen with the style `PS_INSIDEFRAME` draws on the inside of the boundaries, while other pens are centered on the boundary so that half is inside the border and half is outside. If this seems confusing, it will be made clearer when we talk about filled figures in Chapter 9.

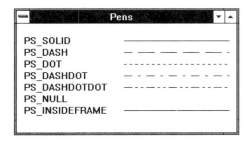

Figure 8.5 GDI's seven pen styles

The width of a pen is specified in logical units, which corresponds to the units of the current mapping mode in the x-axis. Since we have limited ourselves to the MM_TEXT mapping mode, this means that our units are pixels. If you specify a pen width of zero, then regardless of the mapping mode, you will get a pen that is exactly 1 pixel wide.

Most GDI devices currently do not support *wide styled lines*—that is, styled lines with a width greater than 1. For this reason, if you ask for a six-unit wide *dotted* pen, you will most likely get a six-unit wide *solid* pen. As hardware gets smarter, however, you'll see wide-styled lines on more devices. Until then, you should assume that if you want a non-solid pen, you'll have to settle for those that are 1 pixel wide.

Like pixel colors, pen colors are defined using one of three methods: an RGB triplet, a palette index value, or a palette relative RGB triplet. Whichever method you choose, pens are ordinarily created from solid colors. The exception is pens with the PS_IN-SIDEFRAME style. The color of such a pen can include dithered colors.

Dithered colors are created by combining two or more colors. In the real-world, color mixing is nothing new. If you buy paint, for example, the store clerk might mix some black paint into a can of white paint to create a shade of gray.

GDI creates dithered colors by combining two (or more) colors in a regular pattern to create the illusion of hundreds of colors on 16-color devices, like EGA and VGA display adapters. On monochrome devices, like the Hercules and CGA display adapters, dozens of shades of gray can be created using this technique. Dithering works so well that, without the aid of a special program like ZoomIn, it is often hard to tell a dithered color from a pure color.

Because dithered colors require a little more work for a device driver, only one pen style supports dithering: PS_INSIDEFRAME. Usually, dithering is reserved for brushes—a subject we'll cover when we discuss the creation of filled figures (see Chapter 9).

Figure 8.6 shows the output of our PENS program. Eleven lines are drawn using all the pen styles, and each line has a marker to highlight the end points. Notice that the

Figure 8.6 Lines drawn using GDI pens

markers appear in the middle of each line for the wide lines. In addition, notice that the end of each line is rounded. To GDI, a pen is a round drawing object.

Another imprtant fact is that, with the exception of PS_INSIDEFRAME pens, pens are limited to solid (nondithered) colors. With the help of ZoomIn, you can see that the line in our figure that was drawn with the PS_INSIDEFRAME pen is, in fact, dithered. Here is the listing of our PENS program:

PENS.C

```
/*-------------------------------------------------------------*\
|    PENS.C - Show different GDI pens.                         |
\*-------------------------------------------------------------*/
#include <Windows.H>

typedef struct tagPENDATA {
    WORD     wStyle;
    int      iWidth;
    COLORREF crColor;
    char *   pchName;
    } PENDATA;

/*-------------------------------------------------------------*\
|                    Function Prototypes.                      |
\*-------------------------------------------------------------*/
LRESULT CALLBACK PensWndProc (HWND, UINT, WPARAM, LPARAM);
VOID NEAR PASCAL DrawMarker (HDC hdc, int x, int y);

/*-------------------------------------------------------------*\
|                     Global Variables.                       |
\*-------------------------------------------------------------*/
char achWndClass[] = "Pens:MAIN";
char achAppName[]  = "Pens";

/*-------------------------------------------------------------*\
|                  Main Function:  WinMain.                    |
\*-------------------------------------------------------------*/
int PASCAL
WinMain (HINSTANCE hInstance,       // Who am I?
         HINSTANCE hPrevInstance,  // Any older siblings?
         LPSTR     lpszCmdLine,    // Ptr to command line.
         int       cmdShow)        // How to open my window?
    {
    HWND     hwnd;
    MSG      msg;
    WNDCLASS wndclass;

    if (!hPrevInstance)
        {
        wndclass.lpszClassName = achWndClass;
        wndclass.hInstance     = hInstance;
        wndclass.lpfnWndProc   = PensWndProc;
```

```
    wndclass.hCursor        = LoadCursor (hInstance, "hand");
    wndclass.hIcon          = LoadIcon (hInstance,"snapshot");
    wndclass.lpszMenuName   = NULL;
    wndclass.hbrBackground  = (HBRUSH)(COLOR_WINDOW+1);
    wndclass.style          = NULL;
    wndclass.cbClsExtra     = 0;
    wndclass.cbWndExtra     = 0;

    RegisterClass( &wndclass);
    }

hwnd = CreateWindowEx(0L,                 // Extra style.
                achWndClass,              // Class name.
                achAppName,               // Title.
                WS_OVERLAPPEDWINDOW,      // Style bits.
                CW_USEDEFAULT,            // x - default.
                0,                        // y - default.
                CW_USEDEFAULT,            // cx - default.
                0,                        // cy - default.
                NULL,                     // No parent.
                NULL,                     // Class menu.
                hInstance,                // Creator.
                NULL);                    // Params.
ShowWindow (hwnd, cmdShow);

while (GetMessage(&msg, 0, 0, 0))
    {
    TranslateMessage(&msg); // Convert KEYDOWNs to CHARs
    DispatchMessage(&msg);  // Transmit message to WndProc
    }
return 0;
}

/*-------------------------------------------------------------*\
|              Window Procedure:  PensWndProc.                 |
\*-------------------------------------------------------------*/
LRESULT CALLBACK
PensWndProc (HWND    hwnd,       // For whom is message sent?
             UINT    mMsg,       // What is exact message?
             WPARAM  wParam,     // ...message details.
             LPARAM  lParam)     // ...message details.
    {
#define PENCOUNT 11
    static HPEN hpen[PENCOUNT];
    static PENDATA pendata[PENCOUNT] = {
        PS_SOLID, 1, RGB (0,0,0), "PS_SOLID",
        PS_SOLID, 2, RGB (0,0,0), "PS_SOLID, 2 wide",
        PS_SOLID, 4, RGB (0,0,0), "PS_SOLID, 4 wide",
        PS_DASH, 1, RGB (0,0,0), "PS_DASH",
        PS_DOT, 1, RGB (0,0,0), "PS_DOT",
        PS_DASHDOT, 1, RGB (0,0,0), "PS_DASHDOT",
        PS_DASHDOTDOT, 1, RGB (0,0,0), "PS_DASHDOTDOT",
        PS_NULL, 1, RGB (0,0,0), "PS_NULL",
        PS_INSIDEFRAME, 1, RGB (0,0,0), "PS_INSIDEFRAME",
        PS_INSIDEFRAME, 3, RGB (0,0,0),
                        "PS_INSIDEFRAME, 3 wide",
```

```
                    PS_INSIDEFRAME, 11, RGB (180,180,180),
                            "PS_INSIDEFRAME, Gray, 11 wide    "};

switch (mMsg)
    {
    case WM_CREATE:
        {
        int  i;

        for (i=0;i<PENCOUNT; i++)
            {
            hpen[i] = CreatePen (pendata[i].wStyle,
                                 pendata[i].iWidth,
                                 pendata[i].crColor);
            }
        }
        break;

    case WM_DESTROY:
        {
        int i;
        for (i=0;i<PENCOUNT; i++)
            DeleteObject (hpen[i]);
        PostQuitMessage(0);
        }
        break;

    case WM_PAINT:
        {
        DWORD dw;
        int i;
        int xEnd, xStart, xText;
        int yIncr, yLine, yText;
        PAINTSTRUCT ps;
        RECT r;

        BeginPaint (hwnd, &ps);

        GetClientRect (hwnd, &r);
        yIncr = r.bottom/ (PENCOUNT+2);
        yText = yIncr;
        xText = 10;
        dw = GetTextExtent (ps.hdc, pendata[10].pchName,
                            lstrlen(pendata[10].pchName));

        for (i=0;i<PENCOUNT; i++)
            {
            TextOut (ps.hdc, xText, yText,
                     pendata[i].pchName,
                     lstrlen(pendata[i].pchName));

            xStart = xText + LOWORD(dw);
            xEnd   = r.right - 10;
            yLine  = yText + HIWORD(dw)/2;
            SelectObject (ps.hdc, hpen[i]);
```

```
            MoveTo (ps.hdc, xStart, yLine);
            LineTo (ps.hdc, xEnd, yLine);

            /* Draw Markers.  */
            DrawMarker (ps.hdc, xStart, yLine);
            DrawMarker (ps.hdc, xEnd, yLine);
            yText += yIncr;
            }

        EndPaint (hwnd, &ps);
        }
        break;

    default:
        return(DefWindowProc(hwnd,mMsg,wParam,lParam));
        break;
    }
    return 0L;
    }

/*------------------------------------------------------------*\
|                Marker Drawing Function: DrawMarker.          |
\*------------------------------------------------------------*/
#define MARKERSIZE 3
void NEAR PASCAL
DrawMarker (HDC hdc,   //  DC for drawing.
            int x,     //  X coordinate for marker.
            int y)     //  Y coordinate for marker.
    {
    DWORD dwColor;
    int i;

    dwColor = GetPixel (hdc, x, y);
    dwColor = ~dwColor;
    SetPixel (hdc, x, y, dwColor);

    for (i=1;i<=MARKERSIZE; i++)
        {
        dwColor = GetPixel (hdc, x+i, y);
        dwColor = ~dwColor;
        SetPixel (hdc, x+i, y, dwColor);

        dwColor = GetPixel (hdc, x-i, y);
        dwColor = ~dwColor;
        SetPixel (hdc, x-i, y, dwColor);

        dwColor = GetPixel (hdc, x, y+i);
        dwColor = ~dwColor;
        SetPixel (hdc, x, y+i, dwColor);

        dwColor = GetPixel (hdc, x, y-i);
        dwColor = ~dwColor;
        SetPixel (hdc, x, y-i, dwColor);
        }
    }
```

PENS.DEF

```
NAME     PENS

EXETYPE WINDOWS

DESCRIPTION 'Sample GDI Pens (c) 1992 By Paul Yao'

CODE     MOVEABLE PRELOAD
DATA     MOVEABLE MULTIPLE PRELOAD

HEAPSIZE     512
STACKSIZE    5120

SEGMENTS
    PENS_TEXT MOVEABLE PRELOAD

EXPORTS
    PensWndProc
```

PENS.LNK

```
Pens.obj
Pens.exe/align:16/map/nod/noe/CO
nul
mlibcew libw
Pens.def
```

PENS.MAK

```
# Directory search paths.

INCDIR = \WINDEV\INCLUDE

# Windows version to support
# Valid pairs include:
#     (0x0300, 30)
#     (0x0310, 31)

CLVER = WINVER=0x0300
RCVER = 30

# Compiler switches for applications.

CL_APP_SHIP_ALL = -AM -c -D$(CLVER) -Gsw -I$(INCDIR) -Ow -W3 -Zp
CL_APP_DEBG_ALL = -AM -c -D$(CLVER) -Gsw -I$(INCDIR) -Od -W3 -Zpi
```

```
CL_APP_SHIP_31  = -AM -c -G2s  -I$(INCDIR) -Ow -W3 -Zp
CL_APP_DEBG_31  = -AM -c -G2s  -I$(INCDIR) -Od -W3 -Zpi

# Compiler switches for DLLs.

CL_DLL_SHIP_ALL = -AMw -c -D$(CLVER) -Gsw -I$(INCDIR) -Ow -W3 -Zp
CL_DLL_DEBG_ALL = -AMw -c -D$(CLVER) -Gsw -I$(INCDIR) -Od -W3 -Zpi

CL_DLL_SHIP_31  = -AMw -c -G2s  -I$(INCDIR) -Ow -W3 -Zp
CL_DLL_DEBG_31  = -AMw -c -G2s  -I$(INCDIR) -Od -W3 -Zpi

# Make file primary target.

all: Pens.exe

# Make file dependency targets.

Pens.res: Pens.rc Pens.cur Pens.ico
    rc -r -i$(INCDIR) Pens.rc

Pens.obj: Pens.c
    cl $(CL_APP_SHIP_ALL) Pens.c

Pens.exe: Pens.obj Pens.def Pens.res
    link @Pens.lnk
    rc -$(RCVER) Pens.res

Pens.exe: Pens.res
    rc -$(RCVER) Pens.res
```

PENS.RC

```
snapshot icon Pens.ico

hand   cursor Pens.cur
```

This program creates 10 pens in response to the WM_CREATE message and destroys them in response to WM_DESTROY. This is important; every Windows program must take care to dispose of its pens (and other drawing objects) properly. The problem actually results from one of the nice features of pens: They can be shared.

To allow GDI objects to be shared, Windows doesn't clean up leftover objects. If a program terminates without cleaning up its pens, that memory is lost forever (at least until the computer is turned off). So, always take care to destroy your pens when you no longer need them.

We're now going to investigate the last DC drawing attribute that affects lines: the drawing mode. In the process, we'll give you a preview of our mouse input program from Chapter 16.

Drawing Modes and Lines

A **drawing mode** is a Boolean operation that directs GDI how to draws pixels, lines, and filled figures. The drawing mode, sometimes called a raster operation or 'ROP' for short, determines how the source and destination interact.

In the context of lines, the drawing mode describes how a pen interacts with the pixels already on the display surface. In the physical world, pens ordinarily overwrite what is already on the drawing surface. You'll get a better idea about drawing modes if you imagine drawing with a fountain pen onto a wet colored surface: Some mixing takes place.

In an earlier chapter, the MARKER program used the NOT operator to insure that a marker is visible. A drawing mode provides a faster, more convenient way to get the same effect. It is faster since the Boolean logic is built in at the device driver layer.

One context in which drawing modes play a key role involves drawing shapes that seem to "float" on the display screen. This is the technique used for the mouse cursor, which wanders everywhere without leaving a trail of dirty pixels. In Chapter 16, we'll write a program that uses drawing modes to drag objects across the display. Figure 8.7 gives you an idea of why this object dragging is useful.

It may seem strange that we want to perform Boolean algebra on graphic output. Yet, in a digital computer, every piece of data is encoded as a number. For example, RGB triplets are numbers that describe colors. In the depths of graphic devices like the EGA display, numbers make up the pixels of a graphic image.

Drawing modes take advantage of this to allow the application of Boolean operations. Since a computer's CPU uses Boolean algebra as part of its day-to-day operation, it is a simple matter to apply Boolean operations to graphic images.

[a] Click to start dragging.

[b] Dragging over other rectangles.

[c] Still dragging.

[d] Release to place rectangle.

Figure 8.7 One use of drawing modes: draggable objects

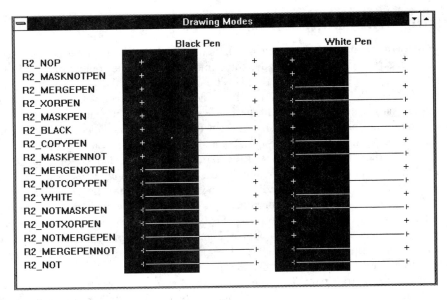

Figure 8.8 GDI's sixteen drawing modes

Figure 8.8 shows the 16 raster operations that GDI supports, along with the lines that are created with a white and with a black pen. Notice how every drawing mode is different. If you'd like, you can inhibit output with the R2_NOP mode, or guarantee that something will be drawn using the R2_NOT mode. Two of the modes, R2_BLACK and R2_WHITE, ignore the pen color.

One thing to keep in mind about drawing modes is that they affect more than just lines: They affect the output of pixels (SetPixel routine) and filled geometric figures (which we'll discuss in the next chapter). GDI doesn't use drawing modes when drawing text, however. The reason primarily has to do with performance. Even though raster operations are implemented at the level of the device driver and are quite fast, they nevertheless slow down the output of text; therefore, they are not used by GDI's text drawing routines.

To find out the current setting of the drawing mode, you call the GetROP2 routine. To set a new drawing mode value in the DC, you call the SetROP2 routine, as in:

```
SetROP2 (hdc, R2_XORPEN);
```

Here is a newer, faster version of our marker drawing routine, which we've rewritten to use ROP codes:

```
/*-------------------------------------------------------------*\
|            Marker Drawing Function: DrawMarker.               |
\*-------------------------------------------------------------*/
#define MARKERSIZE 3
void NEAR PASCAL
```

```
DrawMarker (HDC hdc,    //  DC for drawing.
            int x,      //  X coordinate for marker.
            int y)      //  Y coordinate for marker.
    {
    int i;
    int rop;

    rop = SetROP2 (hdc, R2_NOT);
    SetPixel (hdc, x, y, RGB(0, 0, 0));

    for (i=1;i<=MARKERSIZE; i++)
        {
        SetPixel (hdc, x+i, y, RGB(0, 0, 0));
        SetPixel (hdc, x-i, y, RGB(0, 0, 0));
        SetPixel (hdc, x, y+i, RGB(0, 0, 0));
        SetPixel (hdc, x, y-i, RGB(0, 0, 0));
        }

    SetROP2 (hdc, rop);
    }
```

This version is faster because the Boolean operation isn't performed in our application code. Instead, it's done in the more specialized, performance-tuned device driver.

As you recall, the SetPixel routine illuminates a pixel with the color specified by the last parameter. In this routine, RGB(0,0,0) selects black. But since we're using the R2_NOT drawing mode, GDI ignores the color we specify and inverts the destination pixel.

In the next chapter, we're going to discuss filled figures. Every filled figure has a border, which is simply a line drawn as an outline. As you will see, everything dealing with line drawing that we have discussed thus far applies equally well to the creation of GDI filled figures.

9

Drawing Filled Figures

The next set of GDI drawing routines to be examined are those that create filled figures. A filled figure has two parts: an area and a border around the area. Filled figures are sometimes referred to as **closed figures** because the border closes in on itself. In line drawing terms, the starting and ending points are the same.

Figure 9.1 shows some examples of the types of filled figures that GDI can draw. Notice the variation in the thickness and style of different borders. These are the result of different pens. After all, a border is simply a line, and GDI uses pens to draw lines.

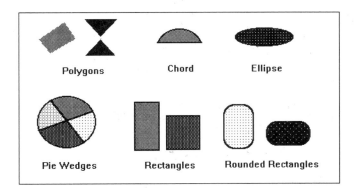

Figure 9.1 Examples of GDI filled figures

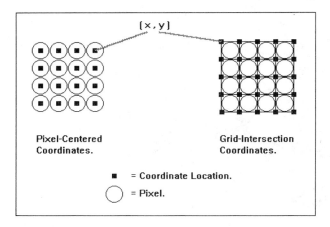

Figure 9.2 Pixel-centered and grid-intersection coordinates

Notice also the variation in the interior area of the figures in the illustration. This is the result of another GDI drawing object: a *brush*. In the same way that you use different pens to draw different types of lines, you use different brushes for different filled areas.

To understand the way that GDI draws filled figures, it is important to understand how coordinates are interpreted. Filled-figure coordinates are slightly different from those used in line drawing. If you draw both types of figures, you will need to make adjustments to insure that objects line up the way you expect them to.

In the world of graphics programming, there are two primary ways to interpret a coordinate. Put simply, the issue is: Do coordinates lie in the center of pixels or at the intersections of a grid surrounding the pixels? Figure 9.2 illustrates pixel-centered and grid-intersection coordinates.

All of GDI's line-drawing primitives use pixel-centered coordinates. Of GDI's seven area-filling primitives, two use pixel-centered coordinates and five use grid-intersection coordinates. While this may seem odd, each type of coordinate has its own uses that makes sense in its own right. Table 9.1 shows GDI's seven area-filling primitives, and the type of coordinates that each uses.

Notice that two of the filled-figure routines, `Polygon` and `PolyPolygon`, use pixel-centered coordinates. You can think of these routines as extensions to `Polyline`, one of GDI's line primitives. It's easy to use these routines with line-drawing routines, since both sets use pixel-centered coordinates.

The other five routines use grid-intersection coordinates. These are the coordinates that GDI uses to define clipping regions. This makes it easy to use these routines with GDI's clipping routines.

GDI uses pixel-centered coordinates when the emphasis of a routine is line-drawing, and grid-intersection coordinates when the emphasis is a two-dimensional area. However, if you wish to use both types of routines, it's usually a simple matter to modify the coordinates of one type of routine to fit in with the other type of routine.

The visible effect of grid-intersection coordinates is that filled figures seem to be one pixel smaller than expected. With the help of ZoomIn, you can see this in Figure 9.3.

Table 9.1 GDI's Area-Filling Routines

Routine	Coordinates	Description
Polygon	pixel-centered	A filled Polyline
PolyPolygon	pixel-centered	Multiple Polygons
Chord	grid-intersection	Partial arc joined by a straight line
Ellipse	grid-intersection	Full arc
Pie	grid-intersection	Pie wedge
Rectangle	grid-intersection	Rectangle
RoundRect	grid-intersection	Rectangle with rounded corners

The program that created this output is RECT. The source code to RECT is in the accompanying listing. This program uses two mouse messages to draw a rectangle: `WM_LBUTTONDOWN` and `WM_LBUTTONUP`. Each message provides one of the two pairs of points that are required by the `Rectangle` routine. `Rectangle` takes five parameters:

```
Rectangle (hdc, X1, Y1, X2, Y2);
```

The points (`X1, Y1`) and (`X2, Y2`) identify opposite corners of a rectangle to be drawn.

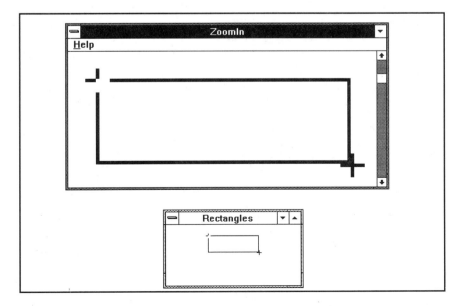

Figure 9.3 Grid-intersection coordinates seem to be one pixel off

RECT.C

```
/*-------------------------------------------------------------*\
| RECT.C - Draws rectangles in response to mouse messages       |
|          generated by the left mouse button.                  |
\*-------------------------------------------------------------*/
#define STRICT
#include <Windows.H>


/*-------------------------------------------------------------*\
|                     Function Prototypes.                       |
\*-------------------------------------------------------------*/
LRESULT CALLBACK RectWndProc (HWND, UINT, WPARAM, LPARAM);
VOID NEAR PASCAL DrawMarker (HDC hdc, int x, int y);


/*-------------------------------------------------------------*\
|                     Global Variables.                         |
\*-------------------------------------------------------------*/
char achWndClass[] = "Rect:MAIN";
char achAppName[]  = "Rectangles";


/*-------------------------------------------------------------*\
|                  Main Function:  WinMain.                      |
\*-------------------------------------------------------------*/
int PASCAL
WinMain (HINSTANCE hInstance,      // Who am I?
         HINSTANCE hPrevInstance,  // Any older siblings?
         LPSTR     lpszCmdLine,    // Ptr to command line.
         int       cmdShow)        // How to open my window?
    {
    HWND     hwnd;
    MSG      msg;
    WNDCLASS wndclass;

    if (!hPrevInstance)
        {
        wndclass.lpszClassName = achWndClass;
        wndclass.hInstance     = hInstance;
        wndclass.lpfnWndProc   = RectWndProc;
        wndclass.hCursor       = LoadCursor (hInstance, "hand");
        wndclass.hIcon         = LoadIcon (hInstance,"snapshot");
        wndclass.lpszMenuName  = NULL;
        wndclass.hbrBackground = (HBRUSH)(COLOR_WINDOW+1);
        wndclass.style         = NULL;
        wndclass.cbClsExtra    = 0;
        wndclass.cbWndExtra    = 0;

        RegisterClass( &wndclass);
        }

    hwnd = CreateWindowEx(0L,                   // Extra style.
                    achWndClass,                // Class name.
                    achAppName,                 // Title.
                    WS_OVERLAPPEDWINDOW,        // Style bits.
```

```
                         CW_USEDEFAULT,          // x - default.
                         0,                      // y - default.
                         CW_USEDEFAULT,          // cx - default.
                         0,                      // cy - default.
                         NULL,                   // No parent.
                         NULL,                   // Class menu.
                         hInstance,              // Creator.
                         NULL);                  // Params.
        ShowWindow (hwnd, cmdShow);

        while (GetMessage(&msg, 0, 0, 0))
            {
            TranslateMessage(&msg); // Convert KEYDOWNs to CHARs
            DispatchMessage(&msg);  // Transmit message to WndProc
            }
        return 0;
        }

/*--------------------------------------------------------------*\
|                 Window Procedure:  RectWndProc.                |
\*--------------------------------------------------------------*/
LRESULT CALLBACK
RectWndProc (HWND    hwnd,      // For whom is message sent?
             UINT    mMsg,      // What is exact message?
             WPARAM wParam,     // ...message details.
             LPARAM lParam)     // ...message details.
    {
    static RECT    arRectangles[50]; /*  array of rectangles.  */
    static int     cRects = 0;       /*  count of rectangles.  */

    switch (mMsg)
        {
        case WM_DESTROY:
            PostQuitMessage(0);  // Handle application shutdown.
            break;

        case WM_LBUTTONDOWN:
            {
            POINT pt;

            pt = MAKEPOINT (lParam);
            arRectangles[cRects].left = pt.x;
            arRectangles[cRects].top  = pt.y;
            }
            break;

        case WM_LBUTTONUP:
            {
            POINT pt;

            pt = MAKEPOINT (lParam);
            arRectangles[cRects].right  = pt.x;
            arRectangles[cRects].bottom = pt.y;
            cRects++;
            if (cRects == 50)
```

```
                    cRects = 0;
            InvalidateRect (hwnd, NULL, TRUE);
            }
            break;

        case WM_PAINT:
            {
            PAINTSTRUCT ps;
            int i;

            BeginPaint (hwnd, &ps);

            for (i = 0; i < cRects ; i++ )
                {
                Rectangle (ps.hdc, arRectangles[i].left,
                                   arRectangles[i].top,
                                   arRectangles[i].right,
                                   arRectangles[i].bottom);

                DrawMarker (ps.hdc, arRectangles[i].left,
                                        arRectangles[i].top);
                DrawMarker (ps.hdc, arRectangles[i].right,
                                        arRectangles[i].bottom);
                }

            EndPaint (hwnd, &ps);
            }
            break;

        default:
            return(DefWindowProc(hwnd,mMsg,wParam,lParam));
            break;
        }
    return 0L;
    }

/*------------------------------------------------------------*\
|              Marker Drawing Function: DrawMarker.            |
\*------------------------------------------------------------*/
#define MARKERSIZE 3
void NEAR PASCAL
DrawMarker (HDC hdc,   //  DC for drawing.
            int x,     //  X coordinate for marker.
            int y)     //  Y coordinate for marker.
    {
    int i;
    int rop;

    rop = SetROP2 (hdc, R2_NOT);
    SetPixel (hdc, x, y, RGB(0, 0, 0));

    for (i=1;i<=MARKERSIZE; i++)
        {
        SetPixel (hdc, x+i, y, RGB(0, 0, 0));
```

```
        SetPixel (hdc, x-i, y, RGB(0, 0, 0));
        SetPixel (hdc, x, y+i, RGB(0, 0, 0));
        SetPixel (hdc, x, y-i, RGB(0, 0, 0));
        }

    SetROP2 (hdc, rop);
    }
```

RECT.DEF

```
NAME    RECT

EXETYPE WINDOWS

DESCRIPTION 'Rectangle Drawing (c) 1992 By Paul Yao'

CODE    MOVEABLE PRELOAD
DATA    MOVEABLE MULTIPLE PRELOAD

HEAPSIZE    512
STACKSIZE   5120

SEGMENTS
    RECT_TEXT MOVEABLE PRELOAD

EXPORTS
    RectWndProc
```

RECT.LNK

```
Rect.obj
Rect.exe/align:16/map/nod/noe/CO
nul
mlibcew libw
Rect.def
```

RECT.MAK

```
# Directory search paths.

INCDIR = \WINDEV\INCLUDE

# Windows version to support
# Valid pairs include:
```

```
#      (0x0300, 30)
#      (0x0310, 31)

CLVER = WINVER=0x0300
RCVER = 30

# Compiler switches for applications.

CL_APP_SHIP_ALL = -AM -c -D$(CLVER) -Gsw -I$(INCDIR) -Ow -W3 -Zp
CL_APP_DEBG_ALL = -AM -c -D$(CLVER) -Gsw -I$(INCDIR) -Od -W3 -Zpi

CL_APP_SHIP_31  = -AM -c -G2s  -I$(INCDIR) -Ow -W3 -Zp
CL_APP_DEBG_31  = -AM -c -G2s  -I$(INCDIR) -Od -W3 -Zpi

# Compiler switches for DLLs.

CL_DLL_SHIP_ALL = -AMw -c -D$(CLVER) -Gsw -I$(INCDIR) -Ow -W3 -Zp
CL_DLL_DEBG_ALL = -AMw -c -D$(CLVER) -Gsw -I$(INCDIR) -Od -W3 -Zpi

CL_DLL_SHIP_31  = -AMw -c -G2s  -I$(INCDIR) -Ow -W3 -Zp
CL_DLL_DEBG_31  = -AMw -c -G2s  -I$(INCDIR) -Od -W3 -Zpi

# Make file primary target.

all: Rect.exe

# Make file dependency targets.

Rect.res: Rect.rc Rect.cur Rect.ico
    rc -r -i$(INCDIR) Rect.rc

Rect.obj: Rect.c
    cl $(CL_APP_SHIP_ALL) Rect.c

Rect.exe: Rect.obj Rect.def Rect.res
    link @Rect.lnk
    rc -$(RCVER) Rect.res

Rect.exe: Rect.res
    rc -$(RCVER) Rect.res
```

RECT.RC

```
snapshot icon Rect.ico

hand   cursor Rect.cur
```

To store the points that describe each rectangle, we allocate an array of type RECT:

```
static RECT arRectangles [50]
```

This structure is defined in Windows.h as:

```
typedef struct tagRECT
{
    int left;
    int top;
    int right;
    int bottom;
} RECT;
```

The elements of this array are named in a somewhat odd fashion, reflecting the use of this structure for clipping rectangles. In general, you can assume that left and right are X values, and that top and bottom are Y values.

We use the MAKEPOINT macro to copy the mouse location from the lParam parameter of a mouse message to a POINT variable. For the WM_BUTTONDOWN message, we store the mouse location in the left and top portions of arRectangles. We get an X,Y pair from the WM_LBUTTONUP routine and store the values in the right and bottom parts of arRectangles.

The last thing that we do in response to WM_LBUTTONUP is to declare the entire window to be damaged with the InvalidateRect routine. As you recall, this causes a WM_PAINT message to be generated. This allows us to put all our rectangle drawing code in one place.

In response to the WM_PAINT message, we run through the entire array of rectangles drawing each in turn. After each rectangle has been drawn, a marker is placed at the two points which defined the rectangle.

This brief introduction to the Rectangle routine, and GDI's two different types of coordinates, has gotten us ready to look at the rest of GDI's filled-figure routines.

GDI Filled-Figure Routines

Let's take a close look at each of GDI's seven filled-figure routines: Polygon, Poly-Polygon, Chord, Ellipse, Pie, Rectangle, and RoundRect. Let's start our examination with the two routines which use pixel-centered coordinates.

Polygon and PolyPolygon

The Polygon routine is defined:

```
Polygon (hDC, lpPoints, nCount)
```

- hDC is a handle to a device context.

- lpPoints is a pointer to an array of type POINT. It is the points to connect.

- nCount is the number of points to connect.

Like the Polyline routine encountered in the last chapter, this routine connects a series of points using the pen that is currently installed in the DC. In addition, if the first

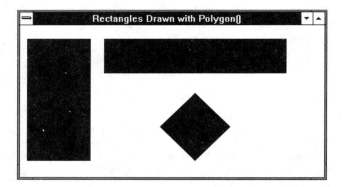

Figure 9.4 Rectangles drawn with the Polygon routine

and last points are not the same, a line is drawn to close the figure, and the area inside
the figure is filled using the brush that is currently installed in the DC.

Polygon is GDI's most flexible filled-area routine, since you can use it to draw any
filled figure. As a simple example, Figure 9.4 shows rectangles drawn using Polygon.
Unlike the normal Rectangle routine, Polygon can draw *rotated* rectangles.

Here is the code fragment that created this illustration:

```
case WM_PAINT:
    {
    PAINTSTRUCT ps;
    POINT apt[4];

    BeginPaint (hwnd, &ps);
    SelectObject (ps.hdc, GetStockObject (BLACK_BRUSH));

    apt[0].x =  10;   apt[0].y =  20;
    apt[1].x = 100;   apt[1].y =  20;
    apt[2].x = 100;   apt[2].y = 200;
    apt[3].x =  10;   apt[3].y = 200;
    Polygon (ps.hdc, apt, 4);

    apt[0].x = 120;   apt[0].y =  20;
    apt[1].x = 380;   apt[1].y =  20;
    apt[2].x = 380;   apt[2].y =  70;
    apt[3].x = 120;   apt[3].y =  70;
    Polygon (ps.hdc, apt, 4);

    apt[0].x = 200;   apt[0].y = 150;
    apt[1].x = 250;   apt[1].y = 100;
    apt[2].x = 300;   apt[2].y = 150;
    apt[3].x = 250;   apt[3].y = 200;
    Polygon (ps.hdc, apt, 4);

    EndPaint (hwnd, &ps);
    }
    break;
```

The `PolyPolygon` routine lets us draw many polygons with a single call. This routine is an extension of the `Polygon` routine. Programs that draw many polygons will run faster if they call `PolyPolygon` than if they make many separate calls to `Polygon`. The speed advantage is a direct result of the overhead involved with making a function call. `PolyPolygon` is defined as follows:

```
PolyPolygon (hDC, lpPoints, lpPolyCount, nCount);
```

- `hDC` is a handle to a device context.

- `lpPoints` is a pointer to an array of type `POINT`. It is the points to connect to create the various polygons.

- `lpPolyCount` is a pointer to an array of type `INT`. The elements of this array indicate the number of points in each polygon.

- `nCount` is an integer for the number of points in the `lpPolyCount` array. In other words, it is the number of polygons to draw.

Here is the code that draws the previous figure using a single call to `PolyPolygon`:

```
case WM_PAINT:
    {
    PAINTSTRUCT ps;
    POINT apt[15];
    int   ai[3];

    hdc = BeginPaint (hwnd, &ps);
    SelectObject (ps.hdc, GetStockObject (BLACK_BRUSH));

    /*  First Rectangle.  */
    apt[0].x =  10;  apt[0].y =   20;
    apt[1].x = 100;  apt[1].y =   20;
    apt[2].x = 100;  apt[2].y =  200;
    apt[3].x =  10;  apt[3].y =  200;
    apt[4].x =  10;  apt[4].y =   20;
    ai[0] = 5;

    /*  Second Rectangle.  */
    apt[5].x = 120;  apt[5].y =  20;
    apt[6].x = 380;  apt[6].y =  20;
    apt[7].x = 380;  apt[7].y =  70;
    apt[8].x = 120;  apt[8].y =  70;
    apt[9].x = 120;  apt[9].y =  20;
    ai[1] = 5;

    /*  Third Rectangle.  */
    apt[10].x = 200;  apt[10].y = 150;
    apt[11].x = 250;  apt[11].y = 100;
    apt[12].x = 300;  apt[12].y = 150;
    apt[13].x = 250;  apt[13].y = 200;
    apt[14].x = 200;  apt[14].y = 150;
    ai[2] = 5;
```

```
    PolyPolygon (ps.hdc, apt, ai, 3);

    EndPaint (hwnd, &ps);
    }
    break;
```

When we talk about `Polygons`, we normally think of figures with flat sides—like the rectangles we drew in our sample code. But we can also use the `Polygon` routines to draw curves, as long as we provide enough points. In fact, that's how GDI simulates curves—with a series of short lines. Of course, if we want to draw curves in this way, we have our work cut out for us, because we would have to calculate all of the points along the curve.

GDI has a set of routines that do this work for us and make it easy to draw filled figures with curved sides. Let's take a look at those routines.

Ellipse, Chord, and Pie

GDI has three routines that create filled figures with curved sides. You can think of these routines as extensions of the `Arc` routine covered in the last chapter. Each routine uses a bounding rectangle to draw a curve.

Here is the definition of the `Ellipse` function:

```
Ellipse (hDC, X1, Y1, X2, Y2)
```

- `hDC` is a handle to a device context.

- (`X1, Y1`) is a corner of the bounding rectangle.

- (`X2, Y2`) is the opposite corner of the bounding rectangle.

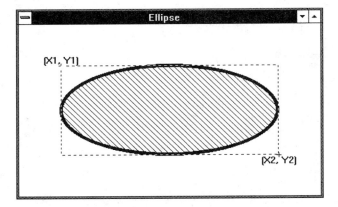

Figure 9.5 A figure drawn with the Ellipse function

Figure 9.6   A figure drawn with the Chord function

The `Ellipse` function creates an ellipse whose perimeter is tangent to the sides of the bounding rectangle, as illustrated in Figure 9.5.

The `Chord` function also makes use of a bounding rectangle to draw a partial arc connected with a line segment. This function is defined as follows:

```
Chord (hDC, X1, Y1, X2, Y2, X3, Y3, X4, Y4)
```

- `hDC` is a handle to a device context.
- (`X1,  Y1`) and (`X2,  Y2`) define the bounding rectangle.
- (`X3,  Y3`) is the starting point of the line segment.
- (`X4,  Y4`) is the ending point of the line segment.

Figure 9.6 shows a chord drawn with this function, with notation to show the bounding box and the line segment coordinates.

The `Pie` function takes the same parameters as the `Chord` function. This function draws a wedge of a pie instead of a chord. The function is defined as follows:

```
Pie (hDC, X1, Y1, X2, Y2, X3, Y3, X4, Y4)
```

- `hDC` is a handle to a device context.
- (`X1,  Y1`) and (`X2,  Y2`) define the bounding rectangle.
- (`X3,  Y3`) is the starting point of the wedge.
- (`X4,  Y4`) is the ending point of the wedge.

Figure 9.7 shows a pie wedge, with the bounding box, starting point, and ending point shown.

Figure 9.7 Figure drawn with the Pie function

Rectangle and RoundRect

We have seen the `Rectangle` function before, but for completeness sake, here is the function definition:

```
Rectangle (hDC, X1, Y1, X2, Y2)
```

- `hDC` is a device context handle.
- `(X1, Y1)` is one corner of the rectangle.
- `(X2, Y2)` is the opposite corner of the rectangle.

Like other GDI filled-figure routines, `Rectangle` uses the pen from the DC to draw the rectangle border and the brush to fill the interior. This routine only draws rectangles with sides that are parallel with the X and Y axes. For rotated rectangles, you must use either the `Polygon` function or the `PolyPolygon` function. Figure 9.8 illustrates the relationship of the two control points to the rectangle that is drawn.

Figure 9.8 Figure drawn with the Rectangle function

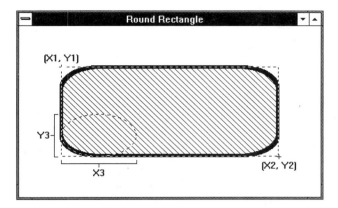

Figure 9.9 Sample of RoundRect output

The `RoundRect` routine draws a rectangle with rounded corners. It is defined as follows:

```
RoundRect (hDC, X1, Y1, X2, Y2, X3, Y3)
```

- `hDC` is a device context handle.
- (`X1,  Y1`) is one corner of the rectangle.
- (`X2,  Y2`) is the opposite corner of the rectangle.
- (`X3,  Y3`) define a bounding box for an ellipse that is used to draw the rounded corners.

Figure 9.9 shows an example of the type of output that `RoundRect` can be used to create.

DC Attributes

As with other GDI drawing primitives, we must visit the device context to fully understand how much control GDI gives us over filled figures. The attributes that affect filled figures are shown in this table:

Drawing Attribute	*Comments*
Background Color	Second color for hatched brushes and non-solid pens
Background Mode	Turns on/off background color
Brush	Color for filling interior
Brush Origin	Alignment of hatched brushes
Drawing Mode	Boolean drawing operation
Pen	Border color, width, and style
Polygon Filling Mode	For `Polygon` and `PolyPolygon` routines

Figure 9.10 Polygon Filling Modes only affect complex Polygons

Since the border of every filled area is simply a line, all of the DC attributes that affect lines also affect filled areas: background color, background mode, drawing mode, and pen. An important point to note about pens is, that when used to draw a filled figure, a pen is always centered on the border. For example, a nine-pixel-wide pen will draw a border with four pixels inside the figure, four pixels outside the figure, and one pixel on the border itself.

The exception to this involves the PS_INSIDEFRAME style. Pens created with this style never draw borders that extend beyond the border of the figure. A nine-pixel-wide PS_INSIDEFRAME pen, for example, will draw a border that has one pixel on the exact border and eight pixels inside the figure.

Three attributes are specific to filled areas: Brush, Brush Origin, and Polygon Filling Mode. Before we discuss GDI brushes, we're going to briefly discuss Polygon Filling Mode and Drawing Mode.

The names of drawing modes seem to imply that they only affect lines. For example, the default drawing mode, R2_COPYPEN, includes the word "pen," the line drawing attribute. In spite of this unfortunate choice of names, drawing modes affect both the inside area and the border of filled figures. Drawing modes affect pens and brushes equally.

The Polygon Filling Mode determines how to fill complex figures created by two routines: Polygon and PolyPolygon. For simple figures, like squares and rectangles, the Polygon Filling Mode has no effect. For complex figures, like the star in Figure 9.10, the Polygon Filling Mode determines which areas to fill.

The WINDING mode fills all areas inside the border. The ALTERNATE mode, on the other hand, fills only the odd areas. That is, if you were to draw a line segment through a figure, filling is turned *on* after odd boundary crossings (1, 3, 5, etc.), and turned *off* after even boundary crossings (2, 4, 6).

The SetPolyFillMode routine, which sets this drawing attribute, is defined as follows:

```
SetPolyFillMode (hDC, nPolyFillMode)
```

- hDC is a handle to a device context.

- nPolyFillMode is either ALTERNATE or WINDING.

Now let's turn our attention to the attribute that has the most effect on the appearance of filled figures: GDI brushes.

About Brushes

A brush is a DC drawing attribute for filling areas. Three qualities make up a brush: a style, a color, and a pattern. The size of a brush is 8 pixels by 8 pixels. When we discussed GDI pens, we mentioned that attribute bundles allow a convenient way for a program to refer to several attributes at the same time. The convenience factor is certainly one of the reasons for brushes.

Brushes, like pens, can be shared between programs and between devices. Just as there are stock pens, there are stock brushes. That is, GDI creates a set of brushes for use by any program. If stock brushes don't provide what you need, it is a simple matter to create your own brushes. Finally, like pens, you must be sure to clean up all of the brushes that you create. Otherwise, the memory is lost from the system. Let's look at some of the details surrounding the creation and use of brushes.

Creating and Using Brushes

At system start-up time, GDI creates the following stock brushes: black, dark gray, gray, light gray, white, and null (or hollow). Like the null pen, a null brush is a place holder. You can think of a null brush as one having a transparent color.

The GetStockObject routine provides a handle to stock brushes. To use a brush, install it into a DC with the SelectObject routine. Here is one way to draw a rectangle with a gray interior:

```
hpen = GetStockObject (GRAY_BRUSH);
SelectObject (hdc, hpen);
Rectangle (hdc, X1, Y1, X2, Y2);
```

To supplement the stock brushes, you can create custom brushes. There are three types of custom brushes: solid, hatched, and pattern. Figure 9.11 shows examples of each type. GDI provides five routines to create brushes: CreateBrushIndirect, CreateDIBPatternBrush, CreateHatchBrush, CreatePatternBrush, and CreateSolidBrush.

Let's take a closer look at the last three routines in this list. The first, CreateBrushIndirect, is able to do the job of any of the other routines. It is unique in that it takes as a parameter a pointer to a data structure that can describe any brush: a LOGBRUSH (logical brush).

The second routine in this list, CreateDIBPatternBrush, creates a brush from a device-independent bitmap, also known as a 'DIB.' DIBs are bitmaps whose color

Figure 9.11 Eleven different brushes

information is stored in a standard format. The colors in a DIB can be correctly interpreted on any GDI device.

Let's now turn our attention to the three types of bitmaps: solid, hatched, and pattern. As we examine each, we'll look at the three routines that we use in our sample program to create these types of brushes: `CreateSolidBrush`, `CreateHatchBrush`, and `CreatePatternBrush`.

A **solid brush** is created from either a pure or a dithered color. We introduced dithered colors in the last chapter in our discussion of dithered pens. Dithered colors are created by arranging two or more pure colors in a checker-board fashion.

For example, the device that created Figure 9.11 has just two colors: black and white. By dithering, we can create many different shades of gray, like the one used to draw the rectangle labeled 'Solid Gray Brush' in our figure.

The `CreateSolidBrush` routine, which lets you create these brushes is defined as

```
HBRUSH CreateSolidBrush (crColor)
```

- `crColor` is a color reference. This can be an RGB triplet, a palette index, or a palette relative RGB value.

For example, here's how to create a white brush:

```
hbr = CreateSolidBrush (RGB(255,255,255));
```

A **hatch brush** fills areas with a pattern created with hatch marks. GDI provides six built-in hatch patterns, all of which are shown in Figure 9.11. The `CreateHatchBrush` routine is the easiest way to create a hatch brush (although the `CreateBrushIndirect` routine can be used as well).

The syntax of `CreateHatchBrush` is as follows:

```
HBRUSH CreateSolidBrush (nIndex, crColor)
```

- `nIndex` can be any one of six values:

```
HS_BDIAGONAL
HS_CROSS
HS_DIAGCROSS
HS_FDIAGONAL
HS_HORIZONTAL
HS_VERTICAL
```

- `crColor` is a color reference. This can be an RGB triplet, a palette index, or a palette relative RGB value.

A **pattern brush** is a brush created from a bitmap pattern. If the six styles of hatch brushes aren't enough for you, a pattern brush can be created with just about any hatch pattern you'd like to use. A pattern brush can also be made to resemble a solid brush, although this is usually more work than it's worth.

To create a pattern brush, you use the `CreatePatternBrush` routine. Its syntax is as follows:

```
HBRUSH CreatePatternBrush (hBitmap)
```

- `hBitmap` is a handle to a bitmap.

To create a pattern brush, you first need a bitmap. There are quite a few ways to create a bitmap. We're going to look at the two methods used by BRUSHES, which is our next sample program: We use a bitmap resource and create a bitmap on the fly.

One way to incorporate a bitmap into a program involves creating the bitmap ahead of time and storing it as a bitmap resource. This involves using a graphic editor, like Microsoft SDK Image Editor. As shown in figure 9.12, this utility can be used to draw a bitmap. We save this bitmap to a file, `SQUARE.BMP`. To incorporate this bitmap into our program as a resource, we make an entry in the resource file, BRUSHES.RC, like this:

```
square bitmap square.bmp
```

Like other resources, the bitmap resource is attached to BRUSHES.EXE as a resource segment. While BRUSHES is running, it accesses the bitmap resource by calling `LoadBitmap` like this:

```
hbm = LoadBitmap (hInst, "square");
```

This routine loads the bitmap resource from BRUSHES.EXE, and calls GDI to create a RAM-resident GDI bitmap. The next step involves calling `CreatePatternBrush` to use the bitmap pattern to create an actual GDI brush:

```
hbr[9] = CreatePatternBrush (hbm);
```

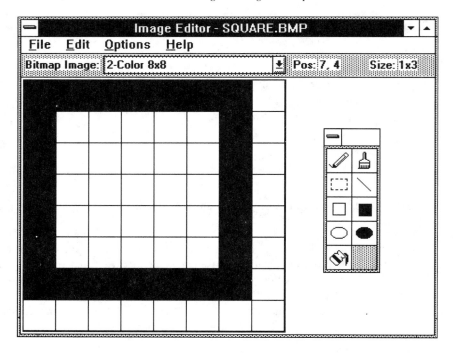

Figure 9.12   Microsoft SDK Image Editor used to create a bitmap

This brush is now ready to be selected into a DC for use in filling the inside of a GDI filled figure.

Another way to create a bitmap involves calling GDI directly with a routine like CreateBitmap. Once a bitmap is created, we can call the various GDI drawing routines and create a picture that suits our need. BRUSHES shows a simple way to initialize a GDI bitmap: It passes a predefined pixel array at bitmap creation time.

The routine that BRUSHES uses to create a bitmap, CreateBitmap, is defined:

```
HBITMAP CreateBitmap (nWidth, nHeight, nPlanes, nBitCount, lpBits)
```

- nWidth and nHeight are the width and height of the bitmap in pixels. Since all GDI brushes are 8 pixels wide by 8 pixels high, the value of both fields must be set to 8.

- nPlanes is the number of planes in the bitmap. Planes provide one means to store color information (for example, the EGA display adapter uses this method). We're going to create a monochrome bitmap, so we'll use the value 1 here.

- nBitCount is the number of bits per color. Packed pixels provide a second way to store color information (some modes of the CGA display adapter use this method). Since we are creating a monochrome bitmap, we set this to 1.

- lpBits is a pointer to the bits to use to initialize the bitmap.

Our program creates its second pattern bitmap by making the following calls:

```
hbm = CreateBitmap (8, 8, 1, 1, acPattern);
hbr[10] = CreatePatternBrush (hbm);
```

The last parameter of the CreateBitmap call is a pointer to an array of character values. Our program's predefined pixel array is defined as follows:

```
static unsigned char acPattern[] =
{0xFF, 0,    /*  1 1 1 1 1 1 1 1  */
 0xE7, 0,    /*  1 1 1 0 0 1 1 1  */
 0xC3, 0,    /*  1 1 0 0 0 0 1 1  */
 0x99, 0,    /*  1 0 0 1 1 0 0 1  */
 0x3C, 0,    /*  0 0 1 1 1 1 0 0  */
 0x7E, 0,    /*  0 1 1 1 1 1 1 0  */
 0xFF, 0,    /*  1 1 1 1 1 1 1 1  */
 0xFF, 0};   /*  1 1 1 1 1 1 1 1  */
```

Our array is defined with hexadecimal values, but for your convenience the comment shows the values in binary. The 1's represent white pixels and the 0's represent black pixels. Bitmap data is expected to be aligned on 16-bit boundaries; therefore, we have an additional zero byte between the bitmap byte values.

Each routine creates a **logical brush**. Like logical pens, logical brushes are requests that can be passed to any device. When asked to use a brush, the device driver *realizes* the brush; that is, it converts the logical request to a form that matches the capabilities of the specific device.

All the source code to our brush creation program, BRUSHES, is shown here:

BRUSHES.C

```c
/*------------------------------------------------------------*\
| BRUSHES.C - Show different types of GDI brushes.            |
\*------------------------------------------------------------*/
#include <Windows.H>

#define BRUSHCOUNT 11

/*------------------------------------------------------------*\
|                     Function Prototypes.                    |
\*------------------------------------------------------------*/
LRESULT CALLBACK BrushesWndProc (HWND, UINT, WPARAM, LPARAM);


/*------------------------------------------------------------*\
|                     Global Variables.                       |
\*------------------------------------------------------------*/
char achWndClass[] = "Brushes:MAIN";
char achAppName[]  = "Brushes";
```

```
HANDLE hInst;

/*---------------------------------------------------------------*\
|                    Main Function:  WinMain.                     |
\*---------------------------------------------------------------*/
int PASCAL
WinMain (HINSTANCE hInstance,      // Who am I?
         HINSTANCE hPrevInstance,  // Any older siblings?
         LPSTR     lpszCmdLine,    // Ptr to command line.
         int       cmdShow)        // How to open my window?
   {
   HWND      hwnd;
   MSG       msg;
   WNDCLASS  wndclass;

   if (!hPrevInstance)
       {
       wndclass.lpszClassName = achWndClass;
       wndclass.hInstance     = hInstance;
       wndclass.lpfnWndProc   = BrushesWndProc;
       wndclass.hCursor       = LoadCursor (hInstance, "hand");
       wndclass.hIcon         = LoadIcon (hInstance,"snapshot");
       wndclass.lpszMenuName  = NULL;
       wndclass.hbrBackground = (HBRUSH)(COLOR_WINDOW+1);
       wndclass.style         = CS_HREDRAW | CS_VREDRAW;
       wndclass.cbClsExtra    = 0;
       wndclass.cbWndExtra    = 0;

       RegisterClass( &wndclass);
       }

   hInst = hInstance;

   hwnd = CreateWindowEx(0L,                      // Extra style.
                    achWndClass,            // Class name.
                    achAppName,             // Title.
                    WS_OVERLAPPEDWINDOW,    // Style bits.
                    CW_USEDEFAULT,          // x - default.
                    0,                      // y - default.
                    CW_USEDEFAULT,          // cx - default.
                    0,                      // cy - default.
                    NULL,                   // No parent.
                    NULL,                   // Class menu.
                    hInstance,              // Creator.
                    NULL);                  // Params.
   ShowWindow (hwnd, cmdShow);

   while (GetMessage(&msg, 0, 0, 0))
       {
       TranslateMessage(&msg); // Convert KEYDOWNs to CHARs
       DispatchMessage(&msg);  // Transmit message to WndProc
       }
   return 0;
   }
```

```
/*--------------------------------------------------------------*\
|                Window Procedure:  BrushesWndProc.              |
\*--------------------------------------------------------------*/
LRESULT CALLBACK
BrushesWndProc (HWND     hwnd,    // For whom is message sent?
                UINT     mMsg,    // What is exact message?
                WPARAM   wParam,  // ...message details.
                LPARAM   lParam)  // ...message details.
    {
    static HBRUSH hbr[BRUSHCOUNT];
    static char * apszDesc[BRUSHCOUNT];
    static unsigned char acPattern[] =
            {0xFF, 0,   /*  1 1 1 1 1 1 1 1  */
             0xE7, 0,   /*  1 1 1 0 0 1 1 1  */
             0xC3, 0,   /*  1 1 0 0 0 0 1 1  */
             0x99, 0,   /*  1 0 0 1 1 0 0 1  */
             0x3C, 0,   /*  0 0 1 1 1 1 0 0  */
             0x7E, 0,   /*  0 1 1 1 1 1 1 0  */
             0xFF, 0,   /*  1 1 1 1 1 1 1 1  */
             0xFF, 0};  /*  1 1 1 1 1 1 1 1  */

    switch (mMsg)
        {
        case WM_CREATE:
            {
            HBITMAP hbm;

            apszDesc[0] = "Solid Black Brush";
            hbr[0]  = CreateSolidBrush (RGB (0, 0, 0));

            apszDesc[1] = "Solid Gray Brush";
            hbr[1]  = CreateSolidBrush (RGB (64, 64, 64));

            apszDesc[2] = "Solid White Brush";
            hbr[2]  = CreateSolidBrush (RGB (255, 255, 255));

            apszDesc[3] = "Hatch - Horizontal";
            hbr[3]  = CreateHatchBrush (HS_HORIZONTAL , RGB(0, 0, 0));

            apszDesc[4] = "Hatch - Vertical";
            hbr[4]  = CreateHatchBrush (HS_VERTICAL , RGB(0, 0, 0));

            apszDesc[5] = "Hatch - Forward Diagonal";
            hbr[5]  = CreateHatchBrush (HS_FDIAGONAL , RGB(0, 0, 0));

            apszDesc[6] = "Hatch - Backward Diagonal    ";
            hbr[6]  = CreateHatchBrush (HS_BDIAGONAL, RGB(0, 0, 0));

            apszDesc[7] = "Hatch - Cross";
            hbr[7]  = CreateHatchBrush (HS_CROSS , RGB(0, 0, 0));

            apszDesc[8] = "Hatch - Diagonal Cross";
            hbr[8]  = CreateHatchBrush (HS_DIAGCROSS , RGB(0, 0, 0));
```

```
        apszDesc[9] = "Pattern Brush #1";
        hbm = LoadBitmap (hInst, "square");
        hbr[9]  = CreatePatternBrush (hbm);
        DeleteObject (hbm);

        apszDesc[10] = "Pattern Brush #2";
        hbm = CreateBitmap (8, 8, 1, 1, acPattern);
        hbr[10] = CreatePatternBrush (hbm);
        DeleteObject (hbm);
        }
        break;

case WM_DESTROY:
        {
        int i;
        for (i=0;i<BRUSHCOUNT; i++)
            DeleteObject (hbr[i]);
        PostQuitMessage(0);
        }
        break;

case WM_PAINT:
        {
        DWORD dw;
        int i;
        int xStart, xEnd, xText;
        int yIncr, yLine, yText;
        int cxWidth, cyHeight;
        PAINTSTRUCT ps;
        RECT r;
        TEXTMETRIC tm;

        BeginPaint (hwnd, &ps);

        /*  Divide available client area.  */
        GetClientRect (hwnd, &r);
        yIncr = r.bottom/ (BRUSHCOUNT+2);
        yText = yIncr;

        /*  Get measurements to indent text 4 spaces.  */
        GetTextMetrics (ps.hdc, &tm);
        xText = tm.tmAveCharWidth * 4;

        /*  Get measurements of longest text string.  */
        dw = GetTextExtent (ps.hdc, apszDesc[6],
                            lstrlen(apszDesc[6]));
        cxWidth = LOWORD(dw);
        cyHeight = HIWORD (dw);

        /*  Calculate width of rectangles.  */
        xStart = xText + cxWidth;
        xEnd   = r.right - 10;

        /*  Loop through all brushes.  */
        for (i=0;i<BRUSHCOUNT; i++, yText += yIncr)
```

```
                    {
                    TextOut (ps.hdc, xText, yText,apszDesc[i],
                            lstrlen(apszDesc[i]));

                    SelectObject (ps.hdc, hbr[i]);
                    yLine  = yText + yIncr - tm.tmHeight/4;
                    Rectangle (ps.hdc, xStart, yText, xEnd, yLine);
                    }

            EndPaint (hwnd, &ps);
            }
            break;

        default:
            return(DefWindowProc(hwnd,mMsg,wParam,lParam));
            break;
        }
    return 0L;
    }
```

BRUSHES.DEF

```
NAME    BRUSHES

EXETYPE WINDOWS

DESCRIPTION 'Sample GDI Brushes (c) 1992 By Paul Yao'

CODE    MOVEABLE PRELOAD
DATA    MOVEABLE MULTIPLE PRELOAD

HEAPSIZE    512
STACKSIZE   5120

SEGMENTS
    BRUSHES_TEXT MOVEABLE PRELOAD

EXPORTS
    BrushesWndProc
```

BRUSHES.LNK

```
Brushes.obj
Brushes.exe/align:16/map/nod/noe/CO
nul
mlibcew libw
Brushes.def
```

BRUSHES.MAK

```
# Directory search paths.

INCDIR = \WINDEV\INCLUDE

# Windows version to support
# Valid pairs include:
#     (0x0300, 30)
#     (0x0310, 31)

CLVER = WINVER=0x0300
RCVER = 30

# Compiler switches for applications.

CL_APP_SHIP_ALL = -AM -c -D$(CLVER) -Gsw -I$(INCDIR) -Ow -W3 -Zp
CL_APP_DEBG_ALL = -AM -c -D$(CLVER) -Gsw -I$(INCDIR) -Od -W3 -Zpi

CL_APP_SHIP_31  = -AM -c -G2s  -I$(INCDIR) -Ow -W3 -Zp
CL_APP_DEBG_31  = -AM -c -G2s  -I$(INCDIR) -Od -W3 -Zpi

# Compiler switches for DLLs.

CL_DLL_SHIP_ALL = -AMw -c -D$(CLVER) -Gsw -I$(INCDIR) -Ow -W3 -Zp
CL_DLL_DEBG_ALL = -AMw -c -D$(CLVER) -Gsw -I$(INCDIR) -Od -W3 -Zpi

CL_DLL_SHIP_31  = -AMw -c -G2s  -I$(INCDIR) -Ow -W3 -Zp
CL_DLL_DEBG_31  = -AMw -c -G2s  -I$(INCDIR) -Od -W3 -Zpi

# Make file primary target.

all: Brushes.exe

# Make file dependency targets.

Brushes.res: Brushes.rc Brushes.cur Brushes.ico
    rc -r -i$(INCDIR) Brushes.rc

Brushes.obj: Brushes.c
    cl $(CL_APP_SHIP_ALL) Brushes.c

Brushes.exe: Brushes.obj Brushes.def Brushes.res
    link @Brushes.lnk
    rc -$(RCVER) Brushes.res

Brushes.exe: Brushes.res
    rc -$(RCVER) Brushes.res
```

BRUSH.RC

```
snapshot icon Brushes.ico

hand   cursor Brushes.cur

square bitmap square.bmp
```

BRUSHES does its work in response to three messages: WM_CREATE, WM_DE-STROY, and WM_PAINT. The WM_CREATE message is received when the window is created. It is a very useful time to perform whatever initialization a window requires. In this case, we create all the GDI brushes that our program uses and the GDI bitmaps needed to create these brushes.

When our window procedure receives the WM_DESTROY message, it knows that a window has been closed. That's the time to destroy all GDI objects, to avoid losing valuable pieces of system memory.

In response to the WM_PAINT message, our program divides up the available client area to display 11 rectangles using the 11 brushes that we've created. For easy identification, each of these rectangles is labeled with the brush type.

In the course of this program, we call three GDI text routines: GetTextMetrics, GetTextExtent, and TextOut. GetTextMetrics provides measurement information for the current font or text pattern table. GetTextExtent is used to determine the width and height of a specific line of text, while TextOut displays a line of text.

In the next chapter, we're going to take a closer look at these routines and all of the other facilities that GDI provides for the creation of text output.

10

Drawing Text

In most programs, text serves as the primary output media. Yet, we have postponed a discussion of text until now because text output in GDI is quite different from text output in traditional programming environments. GDI treats text as a type of graphic object.

You may have written programs with **line-oriented output**. This method was used on the earliest interactive computer systems, which used typewriters to display output and receive input. With today's display screens, this type of output causes lines of text to roll off the top of a screen into an imaginary "bit-bucket." Interaction is simple: The computer displays a request, the user responds. Beginning C programmers always start with this type of output because it is part of the standard C library. Here is an example:

```
printf ("Enter first number:");
scanf ("%i", &iValue);
```

The next step up is **screen-oriented output**, which treats the display screen as a grid of character cells. Programs like word processors and full screen editors typically use this method. One popular MS-DOS database language, dBASE, uses commands like these to write text and receive input on the display screen:

```
@ 10, 25 SAY "Please Enter Your Name:"
@ 10, 49 GET NAME
```

GDI's approach to text can be described as **pixel-oriented**, since GDI has no built-in idea of the size of a character cell. Instead, GDI lets you position text using the same

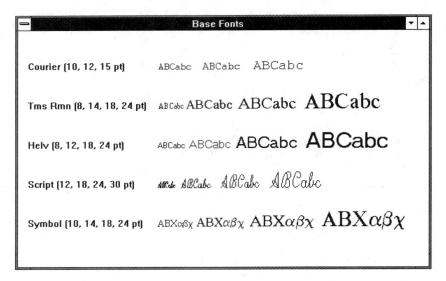

Figure 10.1 A sampling of VGA base fonts

pixel grid that you use for lines, rectangles, and other geometric shapes. This gives you a great deal of control over text placement and makes it easy to mix text with geometric figures. You can even mix different sizes and styles of text with a minimum of effort.

Unlike other graphic objects, text is not drawn using simple geometric equations. Instead, **fonts** are required to create text output. A font is a database of patterns that describe the shape and size of every letter, number, and punctuation mark. Each GDI device supports one or more fonts. Figure 10.1 shows some of the VGA display adapter's base fonts. The accompanying box discusses GDI's base fonts.

▼ **GDI Base Fonts**

Display Fonts

Every GDI display driver is equipped with a set of base fonts, like those shown in Figure 10.1. A common set of base fonts insures a minimum level of support will be available on all video displays. Microsoft carefully chose the following fonts as part of the base set. All of these fonts are bitmap fonts, which means they are stored on disk as bitmap images. This allows them to be drawn quickly, but also makes them dependent on a particular device.

Courier—provides a serifed, fixed-pitch font for typewriter-like output.

MS Serif (also known as **Tms Rmn**)—a set of proportional, serif fonts available in a fairly wide range of sizes. This set can be used as a "stand-in" for other serif fonts for programs that wish to mimic a printer's output on a display screen.

MS Sans Serif (also known as **Helv**)—a set of proportional, sans serif Helvetica-like fonts, also available in a wide range of sizes. Like Tms Rmn, they are meant for use in programs that mimic a printer's output on a display screen.

Symbol—shows that an alternative character set can be used in a font; this font uses Greek letters.

Vector Fonts

Any GDI device can draw using these vector fonts. This type of font is defined as a series of vectors—that is, as a series of line segments. Although more flexible than bitmap fonts, vector fonts are much slower and are also not as attractive as other types of fonts.

Roman—Provides serif letterforms in a proportional font.

Modern—Provides sans serif letterforms in a proportional font.

Script—Provides cursive letters to create a handwriting-like appearance.

TrueType Fonts

TrueType fonts are new with Windows 3.1. They provide the device-independence of vector fonts with the high quality and speed of bitmap fonts. On disk, a TrueType font is stored in a special font-hinting assembly-language like code. When brought into memory, the TrueType font engine rasterizes the fonts—that is, converts them into bitmap patterns. TrueType's device-independent nature allows a single font to be used on many different devices—both displays and printers of differing resolutions. TrueType promises to ease the creation of WYSIWYG applications.

Arial—Replacement for the MS Sans Serif font. A proportionally-spaced font which features sans serif letterforms.

Courier New—Replacement for the Courier font. Provides a fixed-pitch font with serif, typewriter-like letterforms.

Symbol—Replacement for the bitmap Symbol font. Provides support for non-standard characters.

Times New Roman—Replacement for the MS Serif font. A proportionally-spaced font with serif letterforms.

WingDings—Provides a set of non-alphabetic graphic images, including text bullets, page symbols, and other useful general purpose pictograms.

The available fonts can be extended beyond this base set. An end user can purchase fonts and install them using the Windows Control Panel. Programmers can create custom fonts and incorporate them into Windows programs. Starting with Windows 3.1, Microsoft is making their *TrueType* font technology available. Developed in conjunction with Apple Computer, *TrueType* fonts provide a device-independent way to use the same set of fonts on both display screens and printers.

Placing text often involves determining the **font metrics**, which is a table of values that tells you height and width information for a specific font.

If you wish to think in terms of a 25-line, 80-column output area, GDI gives you the tools to do so. You will find, however, that there are a few more things that you have to keep in mind, such as the size of your output area (windows can shrink or grow) and the size of your text (every display has over 20 sizes and styles to choose from). You'll want to do all of this in a way that allows your program to run on any display or printer— you'll want to do this in a device-independent manner.

Although it may seem strange at first to position text in a framework of pixels, this is necessary to allow you to freely mix text with other types of graphic objects. In GDI, text is positioned using the same pixel-oriented grid that we used to draw markers, lines, and rectangles.

We will start by reviewing the available text routines. Then we'll examine the DC attributes that affect text giving special attention to the most important attribute: the font. The chapter will conclude with a discussion of text metrics, which is important to create device-independent text output.

Text Drawing Primitives

There are five routines for outputting text: `DrawText`, `ExtTextOut`, `GrayString`, `TabbedTextOut`, and `TextOut`. Strictly speaking, three of these, `DrawText`, `GrayString`, and `TabbedTextOut`, are not part of GDI, but are part of the Window Manager instead. Even though these routines are not GDI routines, they provide some useful enhancements to GDI and are worth considering in our discussion.

Let's begin by looking at `TextOut`, probably the most widely used GDI text routine.

TextOut

`TextOut` is GDI's simplest text routine: It draws a single line of text. We used this routine to write labels in some of our earlier programs, but now it's time to give it a closer look. `TextOut` is defined as

```
TextOut (hDC, x, y, lpString, nCount)
```

- `hDC` is a DC handle. It tells GDI the device to draw on, and the drawing attributes to use.

- `x` and `y` are integers that specify a **control point** used to position the text. The control point is a location in the coordinate system as defined in the DC. Since we're limiting ourselves to the `MM_TEXT` coordinate system, our units are pixels.

- `lpString` is a far pointer to a character string. This does not have to be a null-terminated string, since `TextOut` gets the string size from the `nCount` parameter.

- `nCount` is the number of characters in the text string.

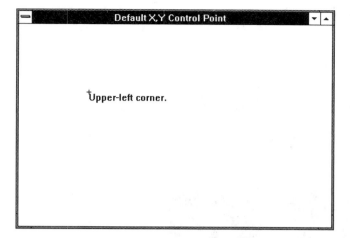

Figure 10.2 Default relationship of control point to text

By default, GDI positions a line of text with the upper-left corner at the control point. Figure 10.2 demonstrates this with a marker. Later in this chapter, when we talk about DC attributes, we'll describe how other text alignment choices can be selected.

It is often convenient to call `TextOut` like this:

```
static char ac[] = "Display This Text.";

BeginPaint (hwnd, &ps);
TextOut (ps.hdc, X, Y, ac, lstrlen(ac));
EndPaint (hwnd, &ps);
```

This code calculates string length "on the fly" using `lstrlen`, a Windows routine that mimics the standard *strlen* function.

Some programmers prefer to split length calculation from drawing, as in

```
static char ac[] = "Display This Text.";
static int  cb = sizeof(ac) - 1;

BeginPaint (hwnd, &ps);
TextOut (ps.hdc, X, Y, ac, cb);
EndPaint (hwnd, &ps);
```

so that text length is calculated at compile time and not at run time. The result is faster drawing. In many cases, the time saved is hardly noticed. But when performance is critical, every little bit helps.

The next text routine is similar to `TextOut`, but provides some extra features.

ExtTextOut

Like `TextOut`, `ExtTextOut` draws a single line of text, but adds three options: character width control, clipping, and an opaque rectangle. You can mix and match

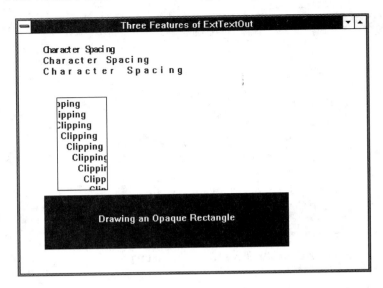

Figure 10.3 ExtTextOut

these options as your needs require. Figure 10.3 shows text drawn with each of these options.

ExtTextOut is defined as follows:

```
ExtTextOut (hDC, X, Y, wOptions, lpRect, lpString, nCount, lpDx);
```

- hDC is a DC handle. It tells GDI the device to draw on and the drawing attributes to use.

- x and y are integers that specify a *control point* used to position the text. The control point is a location in the coordinate system as defined in the DC. Since we're limiting ourselves to the MM_TEXT coordinate system, our units are pixels.

- wOptions is a flag for two of the three extras that this routine provides. It can be 0, ETO_CLIPPED, ETO_OPAQUE, or a combination: ETO_CLIPPED | ETO_OPAQUE. We'll explain these options in a moment.

- lpRect is a pointer to a rectangle. Depending on the value of wOptions, lpRect points to a clip rectangle, an opaque rectangle, or both.

- lpString is a far pointer to a character string. This does not have to be a null-terminated string, since this function gets the string size from the nCount parameter.

- nCount is the number of characters in the text string.

- lpDx points to an array of character width values.

The first option that we're going to discuss is character spacing, which gives you total control over the amount of space between characters. Unlike TextOut, which uses the default spacing defined in a font, `ExtTextOut` lets you specify your own width values for each character by passing an array of integers. The last parameter, `lpDx`, points to this array.

Here is source code to our sample program, **EXTTEXT**:

EXTTEXT.C

```
/*----------------------------------------------------------------*\
 | EXTEXT.C - Program to show capabilities of ExtTextOut.         |
 \*----------------------------------------------------------------*/
#define STRICT
#include <Windows.H>


/*----------------------------------------------------------------*\
 |                     Function Prototypes.                        |
 \*----------------------------------------------------------------*/
LRESULT CALLBACK ExtTextWndProc (HWND, UINT, WPARAM, LPARAM);
void NEAR PASCAL ExtTextClipping (HDC hdc, HWND hwnd);
void NEAR PASCAL ExtTextOpaqueRect (HDC hdc, HWND hwnd);
void NEAR PASCAL ExtTextSpacing (HDC hdc, HWND hwnd);


/*----------------------------------------------------------------*\
 |                     Global Variables.                          |
 \*----------------------------------------------------------------*/
char achWndClass[] = "ExtText:MAIN";
char achAppName[]  = "Three Features of ExtTextOut";


/*----------------------------------------------------------------*\
 |                   Main Function:  WinMain.                      |
 \*----------------------------------------------------------------*/
int PASCAL
WinMain (HINSTANCE hInstance,        // Who am I?
         HINSTANCE hPrevInstance,    // Any older siblings?
         LPSTR     lpszCmdLine,      // Ptr to command line.
         int       cmdShow)          // How to open my window?
    {
    HWND      hwnd;
    MSG       msg;
    WNDCLASS  wndclass;

    if (!hPrevInstance)
        {
        wndclass.lpszClassName  = achWndClass;
        wndclass.hInstance      = hInstance;
        wndclass.lpfnWndProc    = ExtTextWndProc;
        wndclass.hCursor        = LoadCursor (hInstance, "hand");
        wndclass.hIcon          = LoadIcon (hInstance, "snapshot");
        wndclass.lpszMenuName   = NULL;
        wndclass.hbrBackground  = (HBRUSH)(COLOR_WINDOW+1);
        wndclass.style          = CS_HREDRAW | CS_VREDRAW;
        wndclass.cbClsExtra     = 0;
```

```
        wndclass.cbWndExtra    = 0;

        RegisterClass( &wndclass);
        }

    hwnd = CreateWindowEx(0L,                    // Extra style.
                       achWndClass,              // Class name.
                       achAppName,               // Title.
                       WS_OVERLAPPEDWINDOW,      // Style bits.
                       CW_USEDEFAULT,            // x - default.
                       0,                        // y - default.
                       CW_USEDEFAULT,            // cx - default.
                       0,                        // cy - default.
                       NULL,                     // No parent.
                       NULL,                     // Class menu.
                       hInstance,                // Creator.
                       NULL);                    // Params.
    ShowWindow (hwnd, cmdShow);

    while (GetMessage(&msg, 0, 0, 0))
        {
        TranslateMessage(&msg); // Convert KEYDOWNs to CHARs
        DispatchMessage(&msg);  // Transmit message to WndProc
        }
    return 0;
    }

/*------------------------------------------------------------*\
|            Window Procedure:  ExtTextWndProc.                |
\*------------------------------------------------------------*/
LRESULT CALLBACK
ExtTextWndProc (HWND    hwnd,    // For whom is message sent?
                UINT    mMsg,    // What is exact message?
                WPARAM  wParam,  // ...message details.
                LPARAM  lParam)  // ...message details.
    {
    switch (mMsg)
        {
        case WM_DESTROY:
            PostQuitMessage(0);  // Handle application shutdown.
            break;

        case WM_PAINT:
            {
            PAINTSTRUCT ps;

            BeginPaint (hwnd, &ps);

            ExtTextSpacing(ps.hdc, hwnd);
            ExtTextClipping(ps.hdc, hwnd);
            ExtTextOpaqueRect(ps.hdc, hwnd);

            EndPaint (hwnd, &ps);
```

```
                  }
              break;

          default:
              return(DefWindowProc(hwnd,mMsg,wParam,lParam));
              break;
          }
      return 0L;
      }


/*-----------------------------------------------------------*\
 | ExtTextSpacing: Demonstrate ExtTextOut character          |
 |                 spacing.                                  |
 \*-----------------------------------------------------------*/
void NEAR PASCAL ExtTextSpacing(HDC hdc, HWND hwnd)
    {
    static char ac1[] = "Character Spacing";
    static int  cb1   = sizeof (ac1) - 1;
    static int  ai1[] = {6, 6, 6, 6, 6, 6, 6, 6,
                         6, 6, 6, 6, 6, 6, 6, 6};
    static int  ai2[] = {9, 9, 9, 9, 9, 9, 9, 9,
                         9, 9, 9, 9, 9, 9, 9, 9};
    static int  ai3[] = {12, 12, 12, 12, 12, 12, 12, 12,
                         12, 12, 12, 12, 12, 12, 12, 12};
    int        x;
    int        y;
    int        yHeight;
    TEXTMETRIC tm;

    GetTextMetrics (hdc, &tm);
    yHeight = tm.tmHeight + tm.tmExternalLeading;
    x = tm.tmAveCharWidth * 5;
    y = yHeight;

    ExtTextOut (hdc, x, y, 0, NULL, ac1, cb1, ai1);
    y += yHeight;
    ExtTextOut (hdc, x, y, 0, NULL, ac1, cb1, ai2);
    y += yHeight;
    ExtTextOut (hdc, x, y, 0, NULL, ac1, cb1, ai3);
    y += yHeight;
    }


/*-----------------------------------------------------------*\
 |    ExtTextClipping: Demonstrate ExtTextOut Clipping.      |
 \*-----------------------------------------------------------*/
void NEAR PASCAL ExtTextClipping(HDC hdc, HWND hwnd)
    {
    static char ach[] = "Clipping";
    static int  cch   = sizeof (ach) - 1;
    int x;
    int y;
```

```
    int yHeight;
    RECT r;
    TEXTMETRIC tm;

    GetTextMetrics (hdc, &tm);
    yHeight = tm.tmHeight + tm.tmExternalLeading;
    x = tm.tmAveCharWidth * 5;
    y = yHeight * 6;

    r.top = y;
    r.left  = x + 20;
    r.right = x + 90;
    r.bottom = y + tm.tmHeight * 8 + tm.tmHeight/2;
    Rectangle (hdc, r.left-1, r.top-1,
                r.right+1, r.bottom+1);
    while (y< r.bottom)
        {
        ExtTextOut (hdc, x, y, ETO_CLIPPED, &r, ach, cch, NULL);
        y += yHeight;
        x += 8;
        }
    }

/*-----------------------------------------------------------*\
 |  ExtTextOpaqueRect: Demonstrate ExtTextOut opaque         |
 |                      rectangle.                           |
 \*-----------------------------------------------------------*/
void NEAR PASCAL ExtTextOpaqueRect(HDC hdc, HWND hwnd)
    {
    static char ach[] = "Drawing an Opaque Rectangle";
    static int  cch  = sizeof (ach) - 1;
    int x;
    int y;
    int yHeight;
    RECT r;
    TEXTMETRIC tm;

    GetTextMetrics (hdc, &tm);
    yHeight = tm.tmHeight + tm.tmExternalLeading;
    x = tm.tmAveCharWidth * 5;
    y = yHeight * 15;

    GetClientRect (hwnd, &r);
    r.top = y;
    r.bottom = r.top + (5 * tm.tmHeight);
    r.left = x;
    r.right = x + tm.tmAveCharWidth * 50;
    SetBkColor (hdc, RGB (0, 0, 0));
    SetTextColor (hdc, RGB (255, 255, 255));
    SetTextAlign (hdc, TA_CENTER | TA_BASELINE);
    x = (r.left + r.right) / 2;
    y = (r.top  + r.bottom) / 2;
    ExtTextOut (hdc, x, y, ETO_OPAQUE, &r, ach, cch, NULL);
    }
```

EXTTEXT.DEF

```
NAME      EXTTEXT

EXETYPE WINDOWS

DESCRIPTION 'Features of ExtTextOut function (c) 1992 By Paul Yao'

CODE      MOVEABLE PRELOAD
DATA      MOVEABLE MULTIPLE PRELOAD

HEAPSIZE      512
STACKSIZE   5120

SEGMENTS
    EXTTEXT_TEXT MOVEABLE PRELOAD

EXPORTS
    ExtTextWndProc
```

EXTTEXT.LNK

```
ExtText.obj
ExtText.exe/align:16/map/nod/noe/CO
nul
mlibcew libw
ExtText.def
```

EXTTEXT.MAK

```
# Directory search paths.

INCDIR = \WINDEV\INCLUDE

# Windows version to support
# Valid pairs include:
#     (0x0300, 30)
#     (0x0310, 31)

CLVER = WINVER=0x0300
RCVER = 30

# Compiler switches for applications.

CL_APP_SHIP_ALL = -AM -c -D$(CLVER) -Gsw -I$(INCDIR) -Ow -W3 -Zp
CL_APP_DEBG_ALL = -AM -c -D$(CLVER) -Gsw -I$(INCDIR) -Od -W3 -Zpi
```

```
CL_APP_SHIP_31  = -AM -c -G2s  -I$(INCDIR) -Ow -W3 -Zp
CL_APP_DEBG_31  = -AM -c -G2s  -I$(INCDIR) -Od -W3 -Zpi

# Compiler switches for DLLs.

CL_DLL_SHIP_ALL = -AMw -c -D$(CLVER) -Gsw -I$(INCDIR) -Ow -W3 -Zp
CL_DLL_DEBG_ALL = -AMw -c -D$(CLVER) -Gsw -I$(INCDIR) -Od -W3 -Zpi

CL_DLL_SHIP_31  = -AMw -c -G2s  -I$(INCDIR) -Ow -W3 -Zp
CL_DLL_DEBG_31  = -AMw -c -G2s  -I$(INCDIR) -Od -W3 -Zpi

# Make file primary target.

all: ExtText.exe

# Make file dependency targets.

ExtText.res: ExtText.rc ExtText.cur ExtText.ico
    rc -r -i$(INCDIR) ExtText.rc

ExtText.obj: ExtText.c
    cl $(CL_APP_SHIP_ALL) ExtText.c

ExtText.exe: ExtText.obj ExtText.def ExtText.res
    link @ExtText.lnk
    rc -$(RCVER) ExtText.res

ExtText.exe: ExtText.res
    rc -$(RCVER) ExtText.res
```

EXTTEXT.RC

```
snapshot icon ExtText.ico

hand   cursor ExtText.cur
```

Each of the subroutines, `ExtTxtSpacing`, `ExtTxtClipping` and `Ext-TxtOpaqueRect`, demonstrates a different feature of `ExtTextOut`.

In our example, we display "Character Spacing" using arrays with three different widths: 6, 9, and 12 pixels. Notice that the third line is twice as wide as the first line. This option is used to justify text. Text justification lets us expand lines of text to the left and right margins. For example, the text on the page of this book is *justified* text. Depending on how we fill the character width array, we could fit a line of text into just about any margin. The `ExtTxtSpacing` function in our sample program gives you an idea of how this character spacing can be performed.

Our character array has 17 characters, which means there are 16 spaces between letters. For this reason, our character width array has 16 values. Each value defines the width of one character cell. While it requires some extra work to maintain a character width array, it also means that you have a tremendous amount of control over the placement of each letter in a line of text.

Notice the call to GetTextMetrics. This provides measurement information for the current font. We use the values returned by this routine to position our first line of text one line from the top of the window, and five spaces from the left side of the window. We'll explore this routine more fully later in the chapter.

The second option available with ExtTextOut lets you specify a clip rectangle for text. When we introduced the DC, we said that every DC comes equipped with a clipping region. With the ETO_CLIPPED option, ExtTextOut lets you specify an *additional* clipping rectangle. This option provides a way to create a window of text without incurring the overhead of creating an actual window. In our sample program, the ExtTxtClipping routine drew the various lines of clipped text.

Once again, we rely on the GetTextMetrics routine to help us decide where to draw lines of text. In this case, we start six lines from the top of the window and five spaces from the left side of the window.

We have arbitrarily made our clip rectangle 70 pixels wide and eight and one-half lines high. The coordinates used in a clip rectangle are *grid-intersection coordinates*, which we first encountered in the context of drawing filled areas in Chapter 9. To make the clip rectangle more readily apparent, we draw a rectangle just outside its border.

ExtTextOut's third option creates an opaque rectangle; it is like having a free call to the Rectangle routine. It's useful for drawing many lines of unequal length to insure that the background is the correct color. Incidentally, as indicated in our sample code, the background color is selected by making a call to the SetBkColor routine, which sets a DC attribute value that is used by all text drawing routines. In our sample program, it is the ExtTxtOpaqueRect routine which draws the opaque rectangle around the text.

Once again, we rely on the GetTextMetrics routine to help us place the text and its black opaque background. In this case, the top of the rectangle is situated 15 lines from the top of the window and five spaces from the left side.

We set the size of our rectangle to be five character cells high and 50 character cells wide. To make the opaque rectangle visible, we changed two DC attributes: the text color (set to white) and the background color (set to black). We used a third DC attribute, text alignment, to center the text inside the rectangle.

TabbedTextOut

Our third text-drawing primitive draws a single line of text, but expands tabs to tab stops. This provides a convenient way to align columns of data. Microsoft included this routine in the Windows library for listboxes to make it easy to create lists of column-oriented data. But it's a simple matter to use this routine in your programs to achieve the same benefit.

Figure 10.4 shows an example of text drawn with this routine. Here is the window procedure to the code that created the sample output:

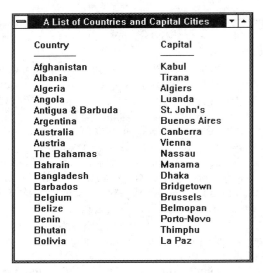

Figure 10.4 TabbedTextOut

```
/*-------------------------------------------------------*\
|              Window Procedure:  TxtTabWndProc.          |
\*-------------------------------------------------------*/
LRESULT CALLBACK
TxtTabWndProc (HWND    hwnd,
               UINT    mMsg,
               WPARAM  wParam,
               LPARAM  lParam)
    {
#define COUNT 19
    static char *apch[]= {"Country \tCapital",
                          "-------------- \t-----------",
                          "Afghanistan \tKabul",
                          "Albania \tTirana",
                          "Algeria \tAlgiers",
                          "Angola \tLuanda",
                          "Antigua & Barbuda \tSt. John's",
                          "Argentina \tBuenos Aires",
                          "Australia \tCanberra",
                          "Austria \tVienna",
                          "The Bahamas \tNassau",
                          "Bahrain \tManama",
                          "Bangladesh \tDhaka",
                          "Barbados \tBridgetown",
                          "Belgium \tBrussels",
                          "Belize \tBelmopan",
                          "Benin \tPorto-Novo",
                          "Bhutan \tThimphu",
                          "Bolivia \tLa Paz"};
```

```
switch (mMsg)
    {
    case WM_DESTROY:
        PostQuitMessage(0);
        break;

    case WM_PAINT:
        {
        DWORD dwSize;
        int i;
        int xTab;
        int xText;
        int yText;
        int yHeight;
        PAINTSTRUCT ps;

        BeginPaint (hwnd, &ps);
        dwSize = GetTextExtent (ps.hdc, "X", 1);
        yHeight = yText = HIWORD(dwSize);
        xText = 3 * LOWORD (dwSize);
        xTab  = 20 * LOWORD (dwSize);

        for (i=0;i<COUNT;i++, yText += yHeight)
            {
            TabbedTextOut (ps.hdc, xText, yText,
                           apch[i], lstrlen(apch[i]),
                           1, &xTab, xText);
            }
        EndPaint (hwnd, &ps);
        }

        break;

    default:
        return(DefWindowProc(hwnd,mMsg,wParam,lParam));
        break;
    }
return 0L;
}
```

This code calls GetTextExtent to determine the width and height of the letter X in the current (system) font. In previous examples, we've used the GetTextMetrics routine to determine this information, but for the sake of variety we have chosen this alternative method. Notice the use of the HIWORD and LOWORD macros, which filter out the desired part of this routine's return value.

We use the results to calculate three values: the X and Y starting position of the text (one line from the top and three characters from the left), and the location of the tab-stop. In this case, we have placed the tab-stop at approximately 20 spaces from the X and Y starting point. If there had been more than a single tab-stop, we would have had to allocate an array to hold them. As it is, we get by with allocating a single integer value and then passing this value to our routine.

Figure 10.5 DrawText

DrawText

Like `TabbedTextOut`, `DrawText` provides some formatting capability. In our opinion, the most useful option is the ability to perform word wrapping for multiple lines of text (although this is just one of several things that `DrawText` will do for you).

Figure 10.5 shows three instances of a sample program that uses `DrawText` to display a long line of text in an area of different sizes and shapes. Here is the code to our sample program:

```
/*------------------------------------------------------------*\
|               Window Procedure:  DrwTxtWndProc.              |
\*------------------------------------------------------------*/
LRESULT CALLBACK
DrwTxtWndProc (HWND    hwnd,
              UINT    mMsg,
              WPARAM  wParam,
              LPARAM  lParam)
    {
    static char *apchDesc = "The DT_WORDBREAK flag makes "
                            "DrawText split a long string "
                            "into several lines of text.  "
                            "As you can tell, the split is "
                            "only performed at normal word "
                            "breaks.";
```

```
switch (mMsg)
    {
    case WM_DESTROY:
        PostQuitMessage(0);
        break;

    case WM_PAINT:
        {
        DWORD dwSize;
        PAINTSTRUCT ps;
        RECT r;

        BeginPaint (hwnd, &ps);
        dwSize = GetTextExtent(ps.hdc, "X", 1);

        GetClientRect (hwnd, &r);
        r.top    += HIWORD (dwSize);
        r.bottom -= HIWORD (dwSize);
        r.left   += LOWORD (dwSize) * 2;
        r.right  -= LOWORD (dwSize) * 2;

        DrawText (ps.hdc, apchDesc, lstrlen (apchDesc),
                  &r, DT_WORDBREAK);

        EndPaint (hwnd, &ps);
        }
        break;

    default:
        return(DefWindowProc(hwnd,mMsg,wParam,lParam));
        break;
    }
return 0L;
}
```

Once more, we use `GetTextExtent` to determine the width and height of the letter X. We use these values to offset the dimensions of our client area so that there is a margin around our text.

The `GetClientRect` routine gets the dimensions of the client area into a `RECT` variable. We then modify the values in this structure to create margins on all four sides of the text. The resulting rectangle is passed to `DrawText`, which uses the values to determine where to position the text.

GrayString

The text produced by this routine is best described as checkered. But the name of the routine describes the primary reason that Microsoft created this routine: to create text with a gray appearance.

The Window Manager uses this routine for disabled menu items and disabled dialog box controls. If you write your own custom dialog box controls (discussed in Chapter

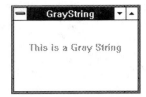

Figure 10.6 GrayString

14), or create owner-drawn menu items (discussed in Chapter 12), then this routine may
be quite useful to you. Figure 10.6 shows an example of a gray string.

Here is the code that created this output:

```
/*------------------------------------------------------------*\
|               Window Procedure:  TxtGryWndProc.            |
\*------------------------------------------------------------*/
LRESULT CALLBACK
TxtGryWndProc (HWND    hwnd,
              UINT    mMsg,
              WPARAM  wParam,
              LPARAM  lParam)
    {
    static char acString[] = "This is a Gray String";
    static int  cb = sizeof (acString) - 1;

    switch (mMsg)
        {
        case WM_DESTROY:
            PostQuitMessage(0);
            break;

        case WM_PAINT:
            {
            DWORD dwSize;
            int xText, yText;
            PAINTSTRUCT ps;
            TEXTMETRIC tm;

            BeginPaint (hwnd, &ps);
            GetTextMetrics (ps.hdc, &tm);
            xText = tm.tmAveCharWidth * 3;
            yText = tm.tmHeight * 2;

            GrayString (ps.hdc, GetStockObject (BLACK_BRUSH),
                        NULL, (DWORD)(LPSTR)acString, cb,
                        xText, yText, 0, 0);

            EndPaint (hwnd, &ps);
            }
            break;
```

```
    default:
        return(DefWindowProc(hwnd,mMsg,wParam,lParam));
        break;
    }
return 0L;
}
```

As in earlier examples, we depend on the results of `GetTextMetrics` to give us some size information to help us position lines of text. Here, we place the gray string two lines from the top of the window and three character widths from the left margin.

This is the only text-drawing routine that uses a brush. The color of the brush determines the foreground color of the checkered text. In this case we use a black brush, which gives the text a grayed appearance. If we had chosen a red brush, it would give the appearance of red and white checkered text.

This concludes our tour of the different GDI text-drawing routines. As you can see, there are quite a few different effects that you can achieve by making a single call to one of these routines. But the library routines are only half the story. To get the complete picture of the amount of control that GDI allows you over text drawing, we need to address the issue of DC attributes that affect text appearance.

DC Attributes for Text Drawing

Six attributes affect the appearance and positioning of text:

Attribute	Description
Background Color	Color of "empty space" in text
Background Mode	Turns on/off background color
Font	Text style and size
Intercharacter Spacing	Extra pixels between characters for text justification
Text Alignment	Relationship of text to control point
Text Color	Color of letters themselves

The most important of these attributes is the font, which determines the shape and size of the individual characters. Before we delve into the way GDI handles fonts, let's explore some of the other text attributes, starting with those that control color.

Color

Three different DC attributes deal with the color of text: text color, background color, and background mode. Text can only be drawn with *pure* colors, and not dithered colors like those available for filled areas. As with pixel, pen, and brush colors, you can use any of three methods to define colors: an RGB triplet, a palette index, or an RGB palette relative value.

The text color attribute determines the actual color of the letters. If GDI had been used to create the letters on this page, it would have been with text color set to black. To set the text color, you must call the `SetTextColor` routine. Its parameters are

```
SetTextColor (hDC, crColor);
```

where `crColor` is a color reference value, using one of the three methods. Here is how to set text color to blue, using an RGB triplet:

```
SetTextColor (hDC, RGB(0,0,0xFF));
```

The background color attribute determines the color of the areas inside character cells not touched by the text color. From GDI's point of view, the text on this page has a white background, since that's the color of the space between letters and the area inside hollow letters like O and Q.

As you may have noticed, the background color attribute is also used for hatched brushes and styled lines to set, respectively, the color *between* the hatches and the blank area *inside* the pattern of a style line.

To set the background color, call the `SetBkColor` routine, which takes the same two parameters as `SetTextColor`:

```
SetBkColor (hDC, crColor);
```

For example, here is how to request a green background:

```
SetBkColor (hDC, RGB(0,0xFF,0));
```

Our third color attribute, background mode, is a toggle switch for the background color. The routine that controls this attribute, `SetBkMode`, takes two parameters:

```
SetBkMode (hDC, nBkMode);
```

When `nBkMode` is `OPAQUE`, the background color is turned *on*. When set to `TRANS-PARENT`, the background color is turned *off*.

Figure 10.7 draws three lines of text, using different foreground and background colors. Notice that the second line of text is unreadable, because we set both foreground and background colors to black.

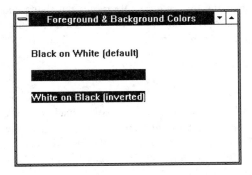

Figure 10.7   Three lines showing different foreground/background colors

Here is the windows procedure that created this figure:

```
/*----------------------------------------------------------*\
 |              Window Procedure:  TxtClrWndProc.           |
 \*----------------------------------------------------------*/
LRESULT CALLBACK
TxtClrWndProc (HWND   hwnd,
               UINT   mMsg,
               WPARAM wParam,
               LPARAM lParam)
    {
    static char acFirst[]  = "Black on White (default)";
    static char acSecond[] = "Black on Black (invisible)";
    static char acThird[]  = "White on Black (inverted)";

    switch (mMsg)
        {
        case WM_DESTROY:
            PostQuitMessage(0);
            break;

        case WM_PAINT:
            {
            int X;
            int Y;
            PAINTSTRUCT ps;
            TEXTMETRIC tm;

            BeginPaint (hwnd, &ps);
            GetTextMetrics (ps.hdc, &tm);
            X = tm.tmAveCharWidth * 3;
            Y = tm.tmHeight * 2;

            TextOut (ps.hdc, X, Y, acFirst, lstrlen (acFirst));
            Y += tm.tmHeight * 2;

            SetBkColor (ps.hdc, RGB (0, 0, 0));
            TextOut (ps.hdc, X, Y, acSecond,
                     lstrlen (acSecond));
            Y += tm.tmHeight * 2;

            SetTextColor (ps.hdc, RGB (255, 255, 255));
            TextOut (ps.hdc, X, Y, acThird, lstrlen (acThird));

            EndPaint (hwnd, &ps);
            }
            break;

        default:
            return(DefWindowProc(hwnd,mMsg,wParam,lParam));
            break;
        }
    return 0L;
    }
```

Although our example is in black and white, it is a simple matter to create red or green text on devices that support color: Supply the appropriate color reference, and GDI does the rest.

Text Alignment

The text alignment attribute lets you change the relationship between the control point, which is the (X,Y) pair that is passed to each routine, and the text to be displayed. Figure 10.8 shows the nine possible ways to align text, with a marker at each control point to emphasize the alignment.

To set text alignment, you call the `SetTextAlign` routine, which has the following syntax:

```
SetTextAlign (hDC, wFlags);
```

As indicated in the example, there are nine possible alignments. Select an alignment by combining two flags from the following table, with one flag taken from each of the two categories.

Horizontal Flag	*Vertical Flag*
TA_LEFT	TA_TOP
TA_CENTER	TA_BASELINE
TA_RIGHT	TA_BOTTOM

The default alignment is `TA_LEFT | TA_TOP`. To set alignment to the bottom right, you say

```
SetTextAlign (hDC, TA_BOTTOM | TA_RIGHT);
```

Figure 10.8 Nine different text alignments

Here is the code for our example:

```
/*-----------------------------------------------------------*\
|                 Window Procedure:   TxtAlnWndProc.          |
\*-----------------------------------------------------------*/
LRESULT CALLBACK
TxtAlnWndProc (HWND    hwnd,
               UINT    mMsg,
               WPARAM wParam,
               LPARAM lParam)
    {
#define LINECOUNT 9
    static char * apchDesc[LINECOUNT] =
            { "Top Left Corner",
              "Top Center",
              "Top Right Corner",
              "Baseline Left",
              "Baseline Center",
              "Baseline Right",
              "Bottom Left Corner",
              "Bottom Center",
              "Bottom Right Corner"};
    static int  fAlign [LINECOUNT] =
            {
            TA_LEFT   | TA_TOP ,
            TA_CENTER | TA_TOP ,
            TA_RIGHT  | TA_TOP ,
            TA_LEFT   | TA_BASELINE ,
            TA_CENTER | TA_BASELINE,
            TA_RIGHT  | TA_BASELINE ,
            TA_LEFT   | TA_BOTTOM ,
            TA_CENTER | TA_BOTTOM ,
            TA_RIGHT  | TA_BOTTOM };

    switch (mMsg)
        {
        case WM_DESTROY:
            PostQuitMessage(0);
            break;

        case WM_PAINT:
            {
            int i;
            int xText;
            int yText;
            int yLineHeight;
            PAINTSTRUCT ps;
            RECT r;

            BeginPaint (hwnd, &ps);
            GetClientRect (hwnd, &r);
            xText = r.right/2;
            yLineHeight = r.bottom/ (LINECOUNT+1);
            yText = yLineHeight;
```

```
                    for (i = 0; i < LINECOUNT; i++)
                        {
                        SetTextAlign (ps.hdc, fAlign[i]);

                        TextOut (ps.hdc, xText, yText, apchDesc[i],
                                lstrlen(apchDesc[i]));
                        MrkDrawMarker (ps.hdc, xText, yText);
                        yText += yLineHeight;


                        }
                    EndPaint (hwnd, &ps);
                    }
                    break;

            default:
                    return(DefWindowProc(hwnd,mMsg,wParam,lParam));
                    break;
            }
        return 0L;
        }
```

In this code, we have departed from our usual practice of spacing lines. Instead of using the `GetTextMetrics` or `GetTextExtent` routines, we have split the available space in the window into ten areas, with one line per area. Since GDI treats text as a graphic object, there is nothing to stop you from devising interesting and useful methods like this to take advantage of available screen real estate when you draw text.

Intercharacter Spacing

This attribute allows you to insert extra pixels between characters. It provides another option (besides the `ExtTextOut` routine) to expand a line of text to fit an arbitrary margin. Figure 10.9 shows six lines of text, with extra spacing varying from zero to five pixels. It is difficult to detect the difference from one line to the next, but between the top and bottom lines the difference is quite apparent.

Figure 10.9 Intercharacter spacing (also known as character extra spacing)

Here is the code we used to generate the example:

```
/*----------------------------------------------------------*\
|                 Window Procedure:  ExtWndProc.             |
\*----------------------------------------------------------*/
LRESULT CALLBACK
ExtWndProc (HWND    hwnd,
            UINT    mMsg,
            WPARAM  wParam,
            LPARAM  lParam)
    {
#define COUNT 6
    static char acLine[] = "AaBbCcDdEeFfGgHhIiJjKkLlMm"
                           "NnOoPpQqRrSsTtUuVvWwXxYyZz";
    static char *apch[] = {"0", "1", "2", "3", "4", "5"};
    static int  cbLine = sizeof (acLine) - 1;

    switch (mMsg)
        {
        case WM_DESTROY:
            PostQuitMessage(0);
            break;

        case WM_PAINT:
            {
            int i;
            int xText;
            int xText2;
            int yText;
            PAINTSTRUCT ps;
            TEXTMETRIC tm;

            BeginPaint (hwnd, &ps);
            GetTextMetrics (ps.hdc, &tm);
            xText  = tm.tmAveCharWidth * 3;
            xText2 = tm.tmAveCharWidth * 6;
            yText = tm.tmHeight * 2;
            for (i=0;i<COUNT;i++)
                {
                SetTextCharacterExtra (ps.hdc, i);
                TextOut (ps.hdc, xText, yText,
                         apch[i], lstrlen (apch[i]));
                TextOut (ps.hdc, xText2, yText,
                         acLine, cbLine);
                yText += tm.tmHeight;
                }

            EndPaint (hwnd, &ps);
            }
            break;

        default:
            return(DefWindowProc(hwnd,mMsg,wParam,lParam));
```

```
            break;
        }
    return 0L;
    }
```

We have one more DC attribute to describe, the one that plays the most important role in determining the shape and size of letters that GDI draws: the font.

About Fonts

A font is a collection of patterns used to create text output. Fonts come in all shapes, sizes, and styles, and have a lot in common with other GDI drawing objects, like pens and brushes. Fonts can be shared between programs, and, like these other GDI objects, they are referenced using a handle. When a program is ready to use a specific font, it selects the font handle into a DC using the `SelectObject` routine:

```
SelectObject (hDC, hFont);
```

Internally, GDI recognizes two types of fonts: **logical fonts** and **physical fonts**. A logical font describes text in a standard, device-independent manner. As we'll see in a moment, a logical font consists of the set of values in the data structure `LOGFONT`. By itself, a logical font isn't enough information to draw text on a device. Instead, like other logical drawing objects, a logical font is a *request* for text with a specific appearance.

The GDI **font mapper** selects a physical font from the description contained in a logical font. The mapping is done when a logical font handle is selected into a DC. A physical font is a device-*dependent* set of patterns. These patterns are used to create the letters, numbers, and punctuation marks that we normally associate with text. A physical font might live in the device hardware, which is typical for printer fonts, or it may be kept in memory by GDI.

Physical fonts are device-dependent because every font is created with a specific type of device in mind. Two measurements are used to match fonts to devices: resolution (pixels per inch) and aspect ratio (the *squareness* of the pixels). By default, the GDI mapper only selects physical fonts that match the metrics of a given device. Otherwise, the results might be very odd.

For example, a VGA display has approximately 72 pixels per inch. Today's typical laser printer has 300 pixels per inch. If you tried to mix fonts between these two devices, the results would be strange: VGA fonts on a laser printer would create text that is too small to be readable. Going the other way, if you used laser printer fonts to create text on a VGA, the resulting text would be too large.

If a program needs precise control over its text selection, it can ask for a list of available physical fonts that a device can support. This process is called **font enumeration**. When a device driver enumerates fonts, it provides a logical font description for each physical font. When a program wishes to use a specific font, it turns the process around: It gives the logical font description to GDI, which in turn makes the connection to the physical font.

Many programs don't need a lot of control over the appearance of text. Such programs can use the default fonts. Every device has a default font. Not surprisingly, the default font is the default selection in the DC.

On a video display, the default font is also called the **system** font. Windows 1.x and 2.x used a fixed-pitch system font—that is, a font in which every character is the same width. Starting with Windows 3.0, the system font is proportionally spaced; therefore, some characters are wider than others. For example, W is given more room than i. Microsoft made this change because proportionally spaced text is easier to read than fixed-pitch text and gives a better overall appearance.

Windows uses the system font for menus, title bars, dialog box controls, and, of course, as the default font in any DC that a program gets its hands on. Microsoft has decreed that every Windows display driver must provide a system font that allows a minimum of 25 lines and 80 columns of text to be displayed. This guarantees that Windows programs will be able to display at least as much text as their MS-DOS counterparts.

To maintain compatibility with programs written for earlier versions of Windows (versions 1.x and 2.x), every display driver also maintains a fixed-pitch system font. When GDI detects that a program was written for an older version of Windows, it provides a system font that these programs expect.

Here is a list showing the characteristics of the default font on four popular displays and four popular printers:

Device	*Size of Drawing Surface*	*Height*	*Width (avg)*
CGA Display	640 x 200	8	7
EGA Display	640 x 350	12	7
VGA Display	640 x 480	16	7
8514/a Display	1024 x 768	20	9
Apple Imagewriter II Printer	2550 x 3300	42	25
Epson LQ-1050 (24 pin) Printer	3060 x 1980	25	36
HP Laserjet II Printer	2550 x 3300	50	30
Okidata ML 320 (9 pin) Printer	1020 x 792	10	12

As shown, the size of the default font can vary substantially from one device to another. To make sure the text created by your program looks good on every device, it's important to ask GDI about the size of a font before you start drawing. GDI provides two routines for this purpose: `GetTextExtent` and `GetTextMetrics`.

GetTextExtent

The `GetTextExtent` routine calculates the size of a line of text using the font currently selected in a DC. Here is how to calculate the width and height of the phrase "Device Independent":

```
DWORD dwSize;
WORD  yHeight, xWidth;

dwSize = GetTextExtent (hDC, "Device Independent", 18);
yHeight = HIWORD (dwSize);
xWidth  = LOWORD (dwSize);
```

This routine takes three parameters: a DC handle, a long pointer to a string, and the count of characters. The return value is a single DWORD (unsigned long) value, in which are packed the height and width of the text. The HIWORD and LOWORD macros separate these two values.

GetTextMetrics

A more complete set of font measurements are provided by the GetTextMetrics routine. Every physical font has a header record that includes font metric information. There are 20 fields, defined by the data structure TEXTMETRIC. Here is a call that retrieves the metrics of the font currently selected in a DC:

```
TEXTMETRIC tm;

GetTextMetrics (hDC, &tm);
```

Figure 10.10 shows five of the key fields in this data structure. The **tmHeight** field defines the size of the characters in the font in pixels (since we're using the MM_TEXT mapping mode) or in the units of the currently selected mapping mode. Notice that this

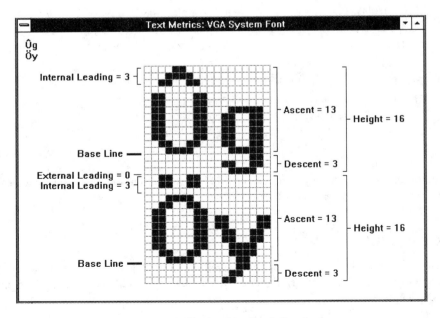

Figure 10.10 Key TextMetric fields visually defined

field has two components: `tmAscent`, which is the height above the baseline, and **tmDescent**, which is the height below the baseline for characters like "g" and "y."

The `tmInternalLeading` field describes the size of the area for diacritic marks, such as accents and umlauts. With two lines of text, the top of the diacritic marks can touch the bottom of descenders. This is normal for many fonts.

If, however, a font designer wants to avoid this situation, he does so with the `tmExternalLeading` field. The value in this field is the suggested width to place between lines of text. In our example, this field is zero. The term "leading" comes from the days when type was cast in lead and set by hand. To separate lines of text, typesetters would add a thin bar of lead between rows of type.

You may have noticed that many of our sample programs combine `tmHeight` and `tmExternalLeading` for the height of a line, as in

```
int yLineHeight;
TEXTMETRIC tm;

GetTextMetrics (hDC, &tm);
yLineHeight = tm.tmHeight + tm.tmExternalLeading;
```

This is a very common method for spacing lines of text.

All this theory about fonts is well and good, but now it's time to do something practical. We're going to explore the use of different fonts and the display of multiple lines of text.

Creating and Using Logical Fonts

As discussed earlier, a logical font is a request, which provides a way for a program to describe the physical font it wants to use. Two routines create logical fonts: `Create-Font` and `CreateFontIndirect`. The results of both are the same: The difference is in the way parameters are passed. `CreateFont` takes 14 parameters, while `CreateFontIndirect` takes a single parameter: a pointer to a structure filled with the same 14 values. Our discussion will be limited to `CreateFontIndirect`, since it is somewhat easier to use.

`CreateFontIndirect` takes one parameter: a pointer to a `LOGFONT` structure. `LOGFONT` is defined in Windows.H as

```
typedef struct tagLOGFONT
{
    int     lfHeight;
    int     lfWidth;
    int     lfEscapement;
    int     lfOrientation;
    int     lfWeight;
    BYTE    lfItalic;
    BYTE    lfUnderline;
    BYTE    lfStrikeOut;
    BYTE    lfCharSet;
    BYTE    lfOutPrecision;
```

```
        BYTE      lfClipPrecision;
        BYTE      lfQuality;
        BYTE      lfPitchAndFamily;
        char      lfFaceName[LF_FACESIZE];
} LOGFONT;
```

We're not going to get into all the details of this data structure. Instead, we will examine the fields to be used in our sample program: `lfFaceName`, `lfHeight`, `lfWidth`, `lfItalic`, and `lfUnderline`.

lfFaceName is a 32-character-wide field for the font name. A program can use font names to tell users about available fonts. In this way, a user can select fonts by name. Here is a list of the face names for the Windows base fonts:

Courier	Helv	Modern	Roman
Script	Symbol	System	Terminal
Tms Rmn			

Each font is available in different sizes and styles.

The **lfHeight** field is identical to the tmHeight field in the `TEXTMETRIC` data structure. Since we're dealing with the `MM_TEXT` mapping mode, the units are pixels. When another coordinate system is used, GDI converts the values to the mapping mode currently selected in the DC.

The **lfWidth** field is the average width of characters in the font. There is also a field in the `TEXTMETRIC` data structure that contains the identical information, `tmAveCharWidth`.

The **lfItalic** field is a flag: A nonzero value requests an italic font.

The **lfUnderline** field is also a flag: A nonzero value requests an underlined font.

Our next program displays text using three different fonts. The first font is the system font, which is already installed in the DC for us. The other two are fonts, a Times Roman (Tms Rmn) and a Helvetica font (Helv), which we request by defining a logical font.

The program displays the first eight `TEXTMETRIC` fields for each of the fonts, as shown in Figure 10.11. The name of each font is also included, for ease of reference.

Three Fonts

System		Tms Rmn		Helv	
Height	16	Height	16	Height	16
Ascent	13	Ascent	13	Ascent	13
Descent	3	Descent	3	Descent	3
Internal Leading	3	Internal Leading	3	Internal Leading	3
External Leading	0	External Leading	0	External Leading	0
Ave Char Width	7	Ave Char Width	6	Ave Char Width	7
Max Char Width	14	Max Char Width	14	Max Char Width	14
Weight	700	Weight	400	Weight	400

Figure 10.11   Three fonts

Here is the code to our program:

TXTLINES.C

```
/*-----------------------------------------------------------*\
| TXTLINES.C  - Text showing three fonts.                     |
\*-----------------------------------------------------------*/
#define STRICT
#include <Windows.H>
#include <memory.H>


/*-----------------------------------------------------------*\
|                    Function Prototypes.                     |
\*-----------------------------------------------------------*/
LRESULT CALLBACK TxtLinesWndProc (HWND, UINT, WPARAM, LPARAM);
void NEAR PASCAL TxtWriteTextMetrics (HDC, int, int);


/*-----------------------------------------------------------*\
|                     Global Variables.                       |
\*-----------------------------------------------------------*/
char achWndClass[] = "TxtLines:MAIN";
char achAppName[]  = "Three Fonts";


/*-----------------------------------------------------------*\
|                  Main Function:  WinMain.                   |
\*-----------------------------------------------------------*/
int PASCAL
WinMain (HINSTANCE hInstance,       // Who am I?
         HINSTANCE hPrevInstance,   // Any older siblings?
         LPSTR     lpszCmdLine,     // Ptr to command line.
         int       cmdShow)         // How to open my window?
    {
    HWND     hwnd;
    MSG      msg;
    WNDCLASS wndclass;

    if (!hPrevInstance)
        {
        wndclass.lpszClassName = achWndClass;
        wndclass.hInstance     = hInstance;
        wndclass.lpfnWndProc   = TxtLinesWndProc;
        wndclass.hCursor       = LoadCursor (hInstance, "hand");
        wndclass.hIcon         = LoadIcon (hInstance,"snapshot");
        wndclass.lpszMenuName  = NULL;
        wndclass.hbrBackground = (HBRUSH)(COLOR_WINDOW+1);
        wndclass.style         = CS_HREDRAW | CS_VREDRAW;
        wndclass.cbClsExtra    = 0;
        wndclass.cbWndExtra    = 0;

        RegisterClass( &wndclass);
        }
```

```
    hwnd = CreateWindowEx(0L,                    // Extra style.
                          achWndClass,            // Class name.
                          achAppName,             // Title.
                          WS_OVERLAPPEDWINDOW,    // Style bits.
                          CW_USEDEFAULT,          // x - default.
                          0,                      // y - default.
                          CW_USEDEFAULT,          // cx - default.
                          0,                      // cy - default.
                          NULL,                   // No parent.
                          NULL,                   // Class menu.
                          hInstance,              // Creator.
                          NULL);                  // Params.
    ShowWindow (hwnd, cmdShow);

    while (GetMessage(&msg, 0, 0, 0))
        {
        TranslateMessage(&msg); // Convert KEYDOWNs to CHARs
        DispatchMessage(&msg);  // Transmit message to WndProc
        }
    return 0;
    }


/*-------------------------------------------------------------*\
|            Window Procedure:  TxtLinesWndProc.              |
\*-------------------------------------------------------------*/
LRESULT CALLBACK
TxtLinesWndProc (HWND    hwnd,     // For whom is message sent?
                 UINT    mMsg,     // What is exact message?
                 WPARAM  wParam,   // ...message details.
                 LPARAM  lParam)   // ...message details.

    {
    static HANDLE hfontTmsRmn;
    static HANDLE hfontHelv;

    switch (mMsg)
        {
        case WM_CREATE:
            {
            LOGFONT lf;

            memset (&lf, 0, sizeof (LOGFONT));
            lf.lfHeight = 16;
            lf.lfWidth = 6;
            lf.lfUnderline = 1;
            lstrcpy (lf.lfFaceName, "Tms Rmn");
            hfontTmsRmn = CreateFontIndirect (&lf);

            memset (&lf, 0, sizeof (LOGFONT));
            lf.lfHeight = 16;
            lf.lfWidth = 7;
            lf.lfItalic = 1;
            lstrcpy (lf.lfFaceName, "Helv");
            hfontHelv  = CreateFontIndirect (&lf);
            }
            break;
```

```
                case WM_DESTROY:
                    DeleteObject (hfontTmsRmn);
                    DeleteObject (hfontHelv);
                    PostQuitMessage(0);
                    break;

                case WM_PAINT:
                    {
                    DWORD dwSize;
                    int xText;
                    int yText;
                    PAINTSTRUCT ps;
                    RECT r;

                    BeginPaint (hwnd, &ps);
                    GetClientRect (hwnd, &r);

                    dwSize = GetTextExtent (ps.hdc, "X", 1);
                    yText = HIWORD (dwSize) * 2;
                    xText = LOWORD (dwSize) * 2;
                    TxtWriteTextMetrics (ps.hdc, xText, yText);

                    SelectObject (ps.hdc, hfontTmsRmn);
                    xText += r.right/3;
                    TxtWriteTextMetrics (ps.hdc, xText, yText);

                    SelectObject (ps.hdc, hfontHelv);
                    xText += r.right/3;
                    TxtWriteTextMetrics (ps.hdc, xText, yText);

                    EndPaint (hwnd, &ps);
                    }
                    break;

            default:
                return(DefWindowProc(hwnd,mMsg,wParam,lParam));
                break;
            }
        return 0L;
        }

/*------------------------------------------------------------*\
 |  TxtWriteTextMetrics - Writes metrics of currently selected |
 |                        font.                                |
 \*------------------------------------------------------------*/
void NEAR PASCAL TxtWriteTextMetrics (HDC hdc,
                                      int xText,
                                      int yText)
    {

    char buffer[80];
    DWORD dwSize;
    int   nLength;
    int   yLineHeight;
    int   xIndent;
```

```
TEXTMETRIC tm;
static char *apchLabel[] =
                { "Height",                /* [0] */
                  "Ascent",                /* [1] */
                  "Descent",               /* [2] */
                  "Internal Leading",      /* [3] */
                  "External Leading",      /* [4] */
                  "Ave Char Width",        /* [5] */
                  "Max Char Width",        /* [6] */
                  "Weight"};               /* [7] */

GetTextMetrics (hdc, &tm);
yLineHeight = tm.tmHeight + tm.tmExternalLeading;

nLength = GetTextFace (hdc, sizeof(buffer) - 1, buffer);
TextOut (hdc, xText, yText, buffer, nLength);
yText += yLineHeight * 2;

dwSize = GetTextExtent (hdc, apchLabel[4],
                        lstrlen (apchLabel[4]));
xIndent = LOWORD (dwSize);
dwSize = GetTextExtent (hdc, "XXXX", 4);
xIndent += LOWORD (dwSize);

/* Height. */
TextOut (hdc, xText, yText, apchLabel[0],
        lstrlen (apchLabel[0]));
nLength = wsprintf (buffer, "%d", tm.tmHeight);
SetTextAlign (hdc, TA_RIGHT);
TextOut (hdc, xText + xIndent, yText, buffer, nLength);
SetTextAlign (hdc, TA_LEFT);
yText += yLineHeight;

/* Ascent. */
TextOut (hdc, xText, yText, apchLabel[1],
        lstrlen (apchLabel[1]));
nLength = wsprintf (buffer, "%d", tm.tmAscent);
SetTextAlign (hdc, TA_RIGHT);
TextOut (hdc, xText + xIndent, yText, buffer, nLength);
SetTextAlign (hdc, TA_LEFT);
yText += yLineHeight;

/* Descent. */
TextOut (hdc, xText, yText, apchLabel[2],
        lstrlen (apchLabel[2]));
nLength = wsprintf (buffer, "%d", tm.tmDescent);
SetTextAlign (hdc, TA_RIGHT);
TextOut (hdc, xText + xIndent, yText, buffer, nLength);
SetTextAlign (hdc, TA_LEFT);
yText += yLineHeight;

/* Internal Leading. */
TextOut (hdc, xText, yText, apchLabel[3],
        lstrlen (apchLabel[3]));
nLength = wsprintf (buffer, "%d", tm.tmInternalLeading);
```

```
SetTextAlign (hdc, TA_RIGHT);
TextOut (hdc, xText + xIndent, yText, buffer, nLength);
SetTextAlign (hdc, TA_LEFT);
yText += yLineHeight;

/*  External Leading.  */
TextOut (hdc, xText, yText, apchLabel[4],
        lstrlen (apchLabel[4]));
nLength = wsprintf (buffer, "%d", tm.tmExternalLeading);
SetTextAlign (hdc, TA_RIGHT);
TextOut (hdc, xText + xIndent, yText, buffer, nLength);
SetTextAlign (hdc, TA_LEFT);
yText += yLineHeight;

/*  Average Character Width.  */
TextOut (hdc, xText, yText, apchLabel[5],
        lstrlen (apchLabel[5]));
nLength = wsprintf (buffer, "%d", tm.tmAveCharWidth);
SetTextAlign (hdc, TA_RIGHT);
TextOut (hdc, xText + xIndent, yText, buffer, nLength);
SetTextAlign (hdc, TA_LEFT);
yText += yLineHeight;

/*  Max Character Width.  */
TextOut (hdc, xText, yText, apchLabel[6],
        lstrlen (apchLabel[6]));
nLength = wsprintf (buffer, "%d", tm.tmMaxCharWidth);
SetTextAlign (hdc, TA_RIGHT);
TextOut (hdc, xText + xIndent, yText, buffer, nLength);
SetTextAlign (hdc, TA_LEFT);
yText += yLineHeight;

/*  Weight.  */
TextOut (hdc, xText, yText, apchLabel[7],
        lstrlen (apchLabel[7]));
nLength = wsprintf (buffer, "%d", tm.tmWeight);
SetTextAlign (hdc, TA_RIGHT);
TextOut (hdc, xText + xIndent, yText, buffer, nLength);
SetTextAlign (hdc, TA_LEFT);

    }
```

TXTLINES.DEF

```
NAME    TXTLINES

EXETYPE WINDOWS

DESCRIPTION 'Sample Lines of Text (c) 1992 By Paul Yao'

CODE    MOVEABLE PRELOAD
DATA    MOVEABLE MULTIPLE PRELOAD
```

```
HEAPSIZE      512
STACKSIZE    5120

SEGMENTS
    TXTLINES_TEXT MOVEABLE PRELOAD

EXPORTS
    TxtLinesWndProc
```

TXTLINES.LNK

```
TxtLines.obj
TxtLines.exe/align:16/map/nod/noe/CO
nul
mlibcew libw
TxtLines.def
```

TXTLINES.MAK

```
# Directory search paths.

INCDIR = \WINDEV\INCLUDE

# Windows version to support
# Valid pairs include:
#    (0x0300, 30)
#    (0x0310, 31)

CLVER = WINVER=0x0300
RCVER = 30

# Compiler switches for applications.

CL_APP_SHIP_ALL = -AM -c -D$(CLVER) -Gsw -I$(INCDIR) -Ow -W3 -Zp
CL_APP_DEBG_ALL = -AM -c -D$(CLVER) -Gsw -I$(INCDIR) -Od -W3 -Zpi

CL_APP_SHIP_31  = -AM -c -G2s  -I$(INCDIR) -Ow -W3 -Zp
CL_APP_DEBG_31  = -AM -c -G2s  -I$(INCDIR) -Od -W3 -Zpi

# Compiler switches for DLLs.

CL_DLL_SHIP_ALL = -AMw -c -D$(CLVER) -Gsw -I$(INCDIR) -Ow -W3 -Zp
CL_DLL_DEBG_ALL = -AMw -c -D$(CLVER) -Gsw -I$(INCDIR) -Od -W3 -Zpi

CL_DLL_SHIP_31  = -AMw -c -G2s  -I$(INCDIR) -Ow -W3 -Zp
CL_DLL_DEBG_31  = -AMw -c -G2s  -I$(INCDIR) -Od -W3 -Zpi

# Make file primary target.
```

```
all: TxtLines.exe

# Make file dependency targets.

TxtLines.res: TxtLines.rc TxtLines.cur TxtLines.ico
    rc -r -i$(INCDIR) TxtLines.rc

TxtLines.obj: TxtLines.c
    cl $(CL_APP_SHIP_ALL) TxtLines.c

TxtLines.exe: TxtLines.obj TxtLines.def TxtLines.res
    link @TxtLines.lnk
    rc -$(RCVER) TxtLines.res

TxtLines.exe: TxtLines.res
    rc -$(RCVER) TxtLines.res
```

TXTLINES.RC

```
snapshot icon TxtLines.ico

hand   cursor TxtLines.cur
```

To create a logical font, this program sets the desired fields in a `LOGFONT` structure and calls `CreateFontIndirect`. The routine ignores zero values and creates a font request using the fields we have explicitly set. That is the reason we call the C-library routine, `memset`, to initialize all fields to zero.

Like other GDI objects, logical fonts take up memory, which must be explicitly freed to avoid depleting system memory from other uses. In response to the `WM_DESTROY` message, the program removes the logical fonts with calls to `DeleteObject`.

Most of the work in our program is done in response to the `WM_PAINT` message. It starts by getting the width of the window, using `GetClientRect`, and splitting the window into three columns. We first display the metric information for the system font before proceeding to the Times Roman and Helvetica fonts. It is worth noting that, although the logical font has already been created, the physical font is not determined until the logical font handle is selected into the DC, as in

```
SelectObject (hDC, hfontTmsRmn);
```

Our routine, `TxtWriteTextMetrics`, displays the first eight fields in the `TEXTMETRIC` data structure for each of the fonts. To obtain the name of each font face, we call the `GetTextFace` routine, which is defined as

```
GetTextFace (hDC, nCount, lpFaceName);
```

in which `hDC` is a handle to a device context, `nCount` is the size of the buffer to receive the font face name, and `lpFaceName` is a long pointer to a character buffer.

We call `GetTextExtent` twice, to determine the width of the widest field name, "External Leading," and then again to determine the width of "XXXX." The variable `xIndex` holds the sum of these two widths and is used as a margin between the field names and the value.

Notice that for each `TEXTMETRIC` field, we display the field name then call on the `wsprintf` routine to convert the numeric value into a text string suitable for display with the `TextOut` routine. `wsprintf` behaves in the same way as the C-library `sprintf` routine, except that it overcomes some of the incompatibilities of that routine in the Windows environment.

Notice also that we use the text alignment attribute (via `SetTextAlign`) to create a table with neatly left-justified text, and right-justified numeric values.

Since GDI treats text as a graphic object, you get a great deal of control over the placement, sizing, and color of text. You can freely mix text and geometric shapes, and combine text of different sizes and styles onto the same page. We think you'll find that the extra effort required is well worth the device-independent punch that GDI packs in text creation.

For programmers who don't need a lot of variety in text, GDI guarantees that you will find a default font for every GDI device. This will provide reasonable-looking text output with a minimum of effort on your part.

P A R T IV

USER-INTERFACE OBJECTS

11

Commands: Menu and Accelerator Basics

Windows has built-in support for two user-interface objects that retrieve command input from users: menus and accelerators. Menus allow a program to show users available actions and options, and encourage users to explore the capabilities of a program. Menus help beginners by eliminating the need to memorize commands. More advanced users can take advantage of accelerators, which translate keystrokes into program commands. To bridge the gap between menus and accelerators, programs often list accelerator keys inside menus. As an example, the menu in Figure 11.1 indicates that the **Edit.Select All** command would result from the [Ctrl] + [NumPad-5] keystrokes.

Programs that adhere to the Windows standards for accelerators and menus are easier for users to learn than those that do not. Therefore, it's important for programmers who plan to design menus to first learn these standards. There are two things you can do that will help you become familiar with these standards: You can use Windows and you can read the style guidelines that Microsoft includes with the software development kit. Learning the standards is time well spent, since it will minimize the time required for a user to become comfortable with your program. Users who are familiar with the "look and feel" pervading Windows programs will be put off by programs that ignore widely accepted standards.

Let's start with a quick look at some of the things that users expect to find in menus.

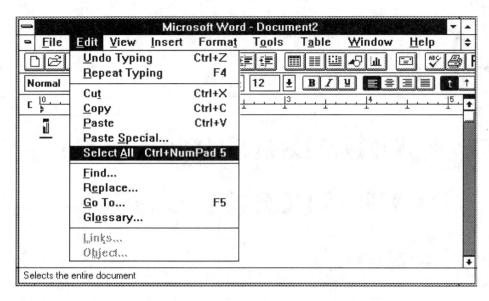

Figure 11.1 A menu with accelerator key entries

User Interface Standards

Users expect to find two types of items in a menu: **actions** and **options**. A menu action is usually expressed as a verb or as a noun-verb combination. For example, many programs have an "Open" menu item inside a "File" menu. Menu actions usually act on a specific object selected by the user. But menu actions can also cause a change that will affect an entire program. The *Close* item in a system menu, for example, can cause a program to terminate when the window being closed is the program's main, top-level window.

Options are toggle switches. Unlike menu actions, which create a short-lived response, options have a more long-lasting effect that is usually reversible. Programs often display check marks in menus to indicate whether an option is active. For example, the **Program Manager** has an *Options* menu that lets the user enable and disable several features, including "Auto Arrange" and "Minimize on Use." While certain important options are set inside menus, most large programs make use of dialog boxes to allow the user to control a program's settable options. In other words, you don't need to put every available option inside menus. The less frequently required options can be placed into dialog boxes, which we'll discuss in more detail in Chapter 14.

Users expect menus to contain **visual clues**. A visual clue can be subtle, like the appearance of ellipses (...) when a menu item selection causes a dialog box to appear, or it can be as obvious as the way menu items are grouped. Here is a list of some of the different visual clues that can be incorporated into menus to indicate special handling of menu items:

- *Accelerator keystrokes* tell the user the accelerator key that matches the menu selection.

- An *arrow* indicates that a menu item is a doorway to a nested menu. The nested menu appears when the user touches the menu item, either by dragging the mouse or moving the menu selection using keyboard cursor keys.

- A *separator* divides longer menus into smaller groups of menu items.

- A *check mark* next to a menu item indicates that that option has been turned on.

- An *ellipsis* (...) after a menu item tells the user to expect a dialog box when the menu item is selected.

- An *exclamation point* at the end of a menu item in a top-level menu indicates that the menu item causes an action and will not cause a popup menu to appear.

- A *grayed* menu item is unavailable. In the system menu, for example, several menu items are grayed when a window is maximized.

- An *underlined letter* in the menu item text indicates the letter can be used to select the menu item. Such a letter is called a **mnemonic**. To make a popup menu appear, the Alt key is pressed with the mnemonic of the popup menu. Once a popup has appeared, menu items can be selected by pressing the mnemonic corresponding to the desired menu item.

Figure 11.2 shows a menu with an example of each of these different visual clues.

Users expect every program to have a **system menu**. From a programming point of view, this is easily accomplished since Windows creates and maintains the system menu for you. In general, programs should not alter the contents of the system menu without a very good reason. A program may *add* certain items to the system menu. In particular, programs which only run in a minimized (or iconic) state can add private menu items to the system menu. The system menu, after all, is the only menu to appear when a program is iconic. Tiny utility and toy applications can add items to the system menu as well, to avoid the fuss of creating private menus. It's not something you'll do often, but it makes sense to add items under certain conditions. Figure 11.3 shows a standard system menu.

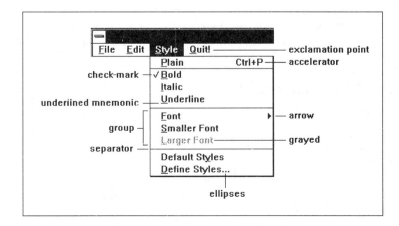

Figure 11.2 Menu showing various visual clues

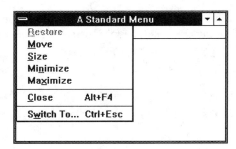

Figure 11.3 The standard system menu

In programs that work with data files, users expect to find a **File** popup menu. This menu provides access to the commands involved with opening, closing, and printing files. As shown in Figure 11.4, the *Exit* menu item is a standard part of the File menu. When selected, this item causes the program to terminate. While this duplicates the *Close* menu item in the system menu of a top-level window, it is a standard that users have come to expect. If you write a program without a File menu, you'll still want to put an *Exit* menu item at the bottom of your first popup menu.

Another standard menu that users expect is the **Edit** popup menu. This menu lists general purpose editing actions, including clipboard control, search and replace, undo previous actions, and repeat previous actions. A program can add other items to the standard Edit menu to allow an application-specific object to be manipulated. For example, a word processing program might list an action in its Edit menu to allow a user to edit the header or footer of a document. Figure 11.5 shows a typical Edit menu, which is part of the first program we're going to write.

Menus can be accessed using any combination of mouse and keyboard input. For example, after a mouse click makes a popup menu appear, users can browse through menu items by pressing arrow keys and can select a menu item by pressing the return key. As an alternative, users can activate a popup menu from the keyboard by pressing the Alt or the F10 key. Menu browsing and selection can then be done with the mouse.

This ability to choose between the mouse and the keyboard for menu operations is part of a larger plan to allow these devices to be used interchangeably in other actions as well. Of course, there are limits—entering characters with the mouse is difficult. But

Figure 11.4 A typical File menu

Figure 11.5   A typical Edit menu

aside from such extremes, a program designer should insure that users can freely choose between the mouse and the keyboard. Some users will rely solely on the keyboard, either because they don't have a mouse or simply out of habit. Other users will switch between the two input methods, depending on the operation and their personal preference.

Now that you've got a general understanding of user-interface issues as they relate to menus, let's get into programming menus.

Menu Programming Issues

Windows has a very robust, flexible menuing system that is, at the same time, quite easy to work with. While menus are easy to create for Windows programmers, the creation of the menuing system proved one of the most challenging tasks in the creation of Windows. The code that supports menuing has been reworked, tuned, and rewritten more than any other part of the system. One reason has to do with performance: From the beginning, menus had to be snappy. Otherwise, the system itself would risk appearing sluggish. To help menus disappear quickly with minimum performance impact, a bitmap "snapshot" is taken of the screen where a menu is going to be drawn. When a user has finished using a menu, the snapshot is used to restore the area where the menu had been.

After all of Microsoft's efforts to make menus work quickly and efficiently, you'll be happy to know that menu creation is easy. As we'll see shortly, the quickest way to create a menu involves writing a short menu description in a program's resource file. When a window class is registered, a WNDCLASS parameter accepts a menu name. When a window of that class is created, a menu is created as well. The only other step for a programmer is to process the WM_COMMAND messages that the menu sends to the window procedure.

Since we're working with a message-driven system, it probably won't surprise you to learn that menus created in Windows use messages to communicate with your program. Or, more precisely, messages are used to communicate with your *window procedure*. The most important menu message is the WM_COMMAND message, which is sent to notify you that a menu item has been selected.

Table 11.1 shows the different steps in the operation of a menu, the mouse and keyboard actions that lead to each step, and the associated messages. Identical message

Table 11.1 Menu Operation and Menu Messages

Menu Operation	Mouse Action	Keyboard Action	Message
Initiate menu use	n/a	F10 or Alt key	WM_INITMENU
Display a popup	n/a	arrow or mnemonic keys	WM_INITMENUPOPUP
Initiate and display popup	\<Click\>	Alt + mnemonic key	WM_INITMENU and WM_INITMENUPOPUP
Browse a menu item	\<Drag\>	arrow keys	WM_MENUSELECT
Select a menu item	\<Release\>	Enter key or mnemonic key	WM_COMMAND

traffic occurs whether the mouse or the keyboard is used. The details of the interaction between the user and your menus are hidden in the menu system, so your program can simply respond to the messages with complete trust that the menuing system is taking care of the rest.

While the WM_COMMAND message is the most useful, you'll want to understand the role of the other messages since there are times when they can be useful as well. For example, if a program wishes to initialize a top-level menu before the user makes a selection, it would respond to the WM_INITMENU message. To initialize a popup menu before it appears, a program would respond to WM_INITMENUPOPUP. Programs that use the clipboard often respond to one of these initialization messages to let the user know, for example, whether there is data on the clipboard that can be pasted. If there is, the Paste item in the Edit menu is enabled. Otherwise, it is grayed.

As the user browses through the items in a menu, the WM_MENUSELECT message tells a program the specific menu item that the user is highlighting at every moment. This information can be used to support an "information area" to display hints about the meaning of each menu item. Quite a few commercial Windows programs provide this feature to assist in the selection of menu items. In Chapter 13, where we discuss issues relating to windowing, we'll create a status line window that shows how WM_MENUSELECT messages can be useful in this way.

Menu Template

The simplest menus start with a menu template, which defines the popup menus and menu items that make up a menu. A menu template is a hierarchical data structure, like the DOS file system with its root directory and subdirectories. At the top of the hierarchy—the root directory—are the items for the menu bar, also known as the **action bar**. At this top level, items can be either menu items, which send command messages when selected, or the doorway to a popup menu. As a side note, it's something of a curiosity that popup menus are also referred to as **pull-down menus**.

Popup menus are like subdirectories that are one level below the root directory in the DOS file hierarchy. In the same way that subdirectories can themselves contain *other* subdirectories, popup menus can contain other popup menus. There isn't any limit to the number of nested menu levels that the menu subsystem will provide. However, common sense would indicate that three levels of menus—the main menu bar and two levels of popup menus—is the deepest you will most likely want to go. Otherwise, you risk losing your user in a sea of menus.

A resource file menu template has the following form:

```
menuID MENU [load option] [memory option]
BEGIN
    {
    MENUITEM or POPUP statement
    MENUITEM or POPUP statement
    ...
    }
END
```

The [load option] can be either PRELOAD or LOADONCALL, and the [memory option] can be either FIXED, MOVEABLE, or DISCARDABLE. These describe how the menu data itself is handled as a memory object. PRELOAD causes a menu resource to be loaded into memory before a program starts running. LOADONCALL causes the menu item to be loaded only when it is needed. The other three options, FIXED, MOVEABLE, and DISCARDABLE, describe how the memory object should behave once it has been loaded into memory. In Chapter 17, we'll describe in detail the meaning of these three options. Since the default behavior of LOADONCALL and the memory option of DISCARDABLE are good enough for now, we won't bother specifying these options in our menu examples.

Each MENUITEM statement defines a menu item that, when selected, causes a WM_COMMAND message to be sent. Each POPUP statement starts the definition of a popup menu, with a BEGIN and an END statement to bracket other MENUITEM or POPUP statements. Incidentally, if you want to save yourself some typing, you can use the C language braces, "{" and "}", in place of the BEGIN and END statements. Here is the menu definition for the File and Edit menus discussed earlier in this chapter:

```
7 MENU
    {
    POPUP "&File"
        {
        MENUITEM "&New",        1
        MENUITEM "&Open...",    2
        MENUITEM "&Save",       3
        MENUITEM "Save &As...",     4
        MENUITEM SEPARATOR
        MENUITEM "&Print",      5
        MENUITEM SEPARATOR
        MENUITEM "E&xit",       6
        }
```

```
POPUP "&Edit"
    {
    MENUITEM "&Undo\tCtrl+Z, 7
    MENUITEM SEPARATOR
    MENUITEM "Cu&t\tCtrl+X",      8
    MENUITEM "&Copy\tCtrl+C",     9
    MENUITEM "&Paste\tCtrl+V",    10
    MENUITEM SEPARATOR
    MENUITEM "Cl&ear",       11
    MENUITEM "&Delete",      12
    }
}
```

The menu identifier is the number 7. Although we could have specified an ASCII text string, using a number is more efficient. This identifier is our name for the menu; it is how we'll identify this menu definition to Windows. Each ampersand (&) defines a **mnemonic**, which is a letter used in the keyboard interface to menus. The \t causes a tab character to be generated, to separate an accelerator keystroke name from a menu item name.

Perhaps the most important value in the definition of each menu item is the command result code. This is the number at the end of each of these MENUITEM statements that distinguishes one menu item from another. The menu system uses the result code to identify menu items for the WM_COMMAND and WM_MENUSELECT messages.

The general syntax of the POPUP statement is

```
POPUP text [,optionlist]
```

and the MENUITEM statement has the following syntax:

```
MENUITEM text, result-code [,optionlist]
```

The big difference between the two statements is that a MENUITEM statement has a result code and the POPUP statement does not. As far as the [optionlist] goes, there are five options that can be selected. The first three select the initial state of the menu item:

CHECKED Places a check mark next to the popup or menu item name. This only affects items inside a popup menu, and not items in the top level menu.

GRAYED Item is initially grayed and inactive.

INACTIVE Item appears normally, but cannot be selected. The GRAYED option is better, since it provides the user with visual feedback indicating that a menu item isn't available.

The other two options change the physical layout of the menu itself:

MENUBREAK Causes a menu break. For horizontal (top-level) menus, this means a break in the vertical direction. For vertical (popup) menus, this means a break in the horizontal direction. If used with wild abandon, you could have vertical top-level and horizontal popup menus.

MENUBARBREAK Causes a menu break. In popup menus, the break is accompanied by a vertical bar.

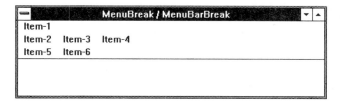

**Figure 11.6 Results of a MENUBREAK and
MENUBARBREAK option on a top-level menu**

In a top-level menu, these last two options have the same effect: to cause a menu item to start on a new line. For example, consider the following menu definition:

```
7 MENU
    {
    MENUITEM "Item-1", 1
    MENUITEM "Item-2", 2, MENUBREAK
    MENUITEM "Item-3", 3
    MENUITEM "Item-4", 4
    MENUITEM "Item-5", 5, MENUBARBREAK
    MENUITEM "Item-6", 6
    }
```

As depicted in Figure 11.6, the two break statements, MENUBREAK and MENUBARBREAK, cause the menu to wrap on the second and the fifth menu items. Windows itself will break top-level menus when the window is too narrow. But if you want to control when and how this occurs, these options are what you'll need.

To see the effect of these two options in a popup menu, consider the following menu template:

```
7 MENU
    {
    POPUP "Popup"
        {
        MENUITEM "Item-1", 1
        MENUITEM "Item-2", 2, MENUBREAK
        MENUITEM "Item-3", 3
        MENUITEM "Item-4", 4
        MENUITEM "Item-5", 5, MENUBARBREAK
        MENUITEM "Item-6", 6
        }
    }
```

Figure 11.7 shows the resulting popup menu. Notice that both options cause the menus to begin a new column, but that the MENUBARBREAK option adds a vertical bar to separate the different columns of menu items that are created.

Although an additional option, HELP, is listed in the Microsoft documentation, it no longer applies to the current standard for menus, so it has no effect. The old standard put the Help menu on the far right side of the top-level menu, with a vertical bar separating it from the other menu items. The current standard simply calls for making the Help

Figure 11.7 Results of a MENUBREAK and MENUBARBREAK option in a popup menu

menu the last item on the top-level menu. If you experiment with this option, you'll see that the menu system simply ignores it. (Although the HELP resource option has been disabled, a corresponding menu style bit—MF_HELP—is still active. If you specify this style bit when adding a popup menu to the main menu bar—which, as you'll see, you can do by calling AppendMenu—you'll get a popup menu on the far right side of the main menu bar.)

Let's take a look at a full-blown program that incorporates a menu. The menus we'll use are the standard File and Edit menus looked at earlier.

A Sample Program: STANMENU

This program shows all of the pieces that must be put together to get a working menu. The menu itself is defined in the resource file, STANMENU.RC. But a resource by itself is just a data definition. To bring it into a program and make it work requires some code. There is room in the window class data structure, WNDCLASS, for a menu name. So, we add one as follows:

```
wndclass.lpszMenuName = "#7";
```

The number sign indicates that we've used a numeric value in our menu definition. This is one of the easiest and most efficient ways to reference a menu. A regular ASCII name could have been used, but this would waste memory and take more time to use.

If we do not want to associate this menu with our window class, we can connect a menu to a window at creation time by referencing our menu as the tenth parameter in the call to CreateWindowEx. In this way, a single window class can be associated with several different menus. Here is an example of calling CreateWindowEx to add the same menu:

```
hmenu = LoadMenu (hInstance, "#7");
hwnd = CreateWindowEx(0L,                    // Extra style.
                achWndClass,                 // Class name.
                achAppName,                  // Title.
                WS_OVERLAPPEDWINDOW,         // Style bits.
                CW_USEDEFAULT,               // x - default.
                0,                           // y - default.
                CW_USEDEFAULT,               // cx - default.
                0,                           // cy - default.
```

```
        NULL,                           // No parent.
        hmenu,                          // Private menu.
        hInstance,                      // Creator.
        NULL);                          // Params.
```

The call to `LoadMenu` retrieves a menu handle, which is what `CreateWindowEx` expects to find.

A third alternative to connecting the menu to the window is to call `SetMenu` anytime after the window is created. Like `CreateWindowEx`, `SetMenu` takes a handle to a menu as a parameter. Here is another way we could have created the same menu:

```
hmenu = LoadMenu (hInstance, "#7");
SetMenu (hwnd, hmenu);
```

Here is the code to our first sample menu creation program.

STANMENU.C

```
/*-------------------------------------------------------------*\
 |   STANMENU.C  -  Program showing standard items in File and  |
 |                  Edit menus.                                 |
\*-------------------------------------------------------------*/
#define STRICT
#include <Windows.H>


/*-------------------------------------------------------------*\
 |                    Function Prototypes.                      |
\*-------------------------------------------------------------*/
LRESULT CALLBACK StanMenuWndProc (HWND, UINT, WPARAM, LPARAM);


/*-------------------------------------------------------------*\
 |                     Global Variables.                        |
\*-------------------------------------------------------------*/
char achWndClass[] = "StanMenu:MAIN";
char achAppName[]  = "A Standard Menu";


/*-------------------------------------------------------------*\
 |                  Main Function:  WinMain.                     |
\*-------------------------------------------------------------*/
int PASCAL
WinMain (HINSTANCE hInstance,      // Who am I?
         HINSTANCE hPrevInstance,  // Any older siblings?
         LPSTR     lpszCmdLine,    // Ptr to command line.
         int       cmdShow)        // How to open my window?
    {
    HWND     hwnd;
    MSG      msg;
    WNDCLASS wndclass;

    if (!hPrevInstance)
```

```
        {
        wndclass.lpszClassName = achWndClass;
        wndclass.hInstance     = hInstance;
        wndclass.lpfnWndProc   = StanMenuWndProc;
        wndclass.hCursor       = LoadCursor (hInstance, "hand");
        wndclass.hIcon         = LoadIcon (hInstance,"snapshot");
        wndclass.lpszMenuName  = "#1";
        wndclass.hbrBackground = (HBRUSH)(COLOR_WINDOW+1);
        wndclass.style         = NULL;
        wndclass.cbClsExtra    = 0;
        wndclass.cbWndExtra    = 0;

        RegisterClass( &wndclass);
        }

    hwnd = CreateWindowEx(0L,                  // Extra style.
                    achWndClass,               // Class name.
                    achAppName,                // Title.
                    WS_OVERLAPPEDWINDOW,       // Style bits.
                    CW_USEDEFAULT,             // x - default.
                    0,                         // y - default.
                    CW_USEDEFAULT,             // cx - default.
                    0,                         // cy - default.
                    NULL,                      // No parent.
                    NULL,                      // Class menu.
                    hInstance,                 // Creator.
                    NULL);                     // Params.
    ShowWindow (hwnd, cmdShow);

    while (GetMessage(&msg, 0, 0, 0))
        {
        TranslateMessage(&msg); // Convert KEYDOWNs to CHARs
        DispatchMessage(&msg);  // Transmit message to WndProc
        }
    return 0;
    }

/*-------------------------------------------------------------*\
|            Window Procedure:  StanMenuWndProc.               |
\*-------------------------------------------------------------*/
LRESULT CALLBACK
StanMenuWndProc (HWND   hwnd,     // For whom is message sent?
                UINT   mMsg,      // What is exact message?
                WPARAM wParam,    // ...message details.
                LPARAM lParam)    // ...message details.
    {
    switch (mMsg)
        {
        case WM_COMMAND:
            {
            char buffer[80];
            char *npch;

            switch (wParam)
                {
```

```
        case 1:
            npch = "File.New";
            break;
        case 2:
            npch = "File.Open...";
            break;
        case 3:
            npch = "File.Save";
            break;
        case 4:
            npch = "File.Save As...";
            break;
        case 5:
            npch = "File.Print";
            break;
        case 6:
            npch = "File.Exit";
            break;
        case 7:
            npch = "Edit.Undo";
            break;
        case 8:
            npch = "Edit.Cut";
            break;
        case 9:
            npch = "Edit.Copy";
            break;
        case 10:
            npch = "Edit.Paste";
            break;
        case 11:
            npch = "Edit.Clear";
            break;
        case 12:
            npch = "Edit.Delete";
            break;
        }

    // Display message box with
    // name of selected menu item.
    wsprintf (buffer, "%s command selected.", (LPSTR)npch);
    MessageBox (hwnd, buffer, achAppName, MB_OK);

    // If user selected File.Exit,
    // simulate {-}.Close menu selection.
    if (wParam == 6)
        {
        SendMessage (hwnd, WM_SYSCOMMAND, SC_CLOSE, 0L);
        }
    }
    break;

case WM_DESTROY:
    PostQuitMessage(0);  // Handle application shutdown.
    break;
```

```
        default:
            return(DefWindowProc(hwnd,mMsg,wParam,lParam));
            break;
        }
    return 0L;
    }
```

STANMENU.DEF

```
NAME    STANMENU

EXETYPE WINDOWS

DESCRIPTION 'Some Standard Menu Items (c) 1992 By Paul Yao'

CODE    MOVEABLE PRELOAD
DATA    MOVEABLE MULTIPLE PRELOAD

HEAPSIZE    512
STACKSIZE   5120

SEGMENTS
    STANMENU_TEXT MOVEABLE PRELOAD

EXPORTS
    StanMenuWndProc
```

STANMENU.LNK

```
StanMenu.obj
StanMenu.exe/align:16/map/nod/noe/CO
nul
mlibcew libw
StanMenu.def
```

STANMENU.MAK

```
# Directory search paths.

INCDIR = \WINDEV\INCLUDE

# Windows version to support
# Valid pairs include:
#    (0x0300, 30)
```

```
#     (0x0310, 31)

CLVER = WINVER=0x0300
RCVER = 30

# Compiler switches for applications.

CL_APP_SHIP_ALL = -AM -c -D$(CLVER) -Gsw -I$(INCDIR) -Ow -W3 -Zp
CL_APP_DEBG_ALL = -AM -c -D$(CLVER) -Gsw -I$(INCDIR) -Od -W3 -Zpi

CL_APP_SHIP_31  = -AM -c -G2s  -I$(INCDIR) -Ow -W3 -Zp
CL_APP_DEBG_31  = -AM -c -G2s  -I$(INCDIR) -Od -W3 -Zpi

# Compiler switches for DLLs.

CL_DLL_SHIP_ALL = -AMw -c -D$(CLVER) -Gsw -I$(INCDIR) -Ow -W3 -Zp
CL_DLL_DEBG_ALL = -AMw -c -D$(CLVER) -Gsw -I$(INCDIR) -Od -W3 -Zpi

CL_DLL_SHIP_31  = -AMw -c -G2s  -I$(INCDIR) -Ow -W3 -Zp
CL_DLL_DEBG_31  = -AMw -c -G2s  -I$(INCDIR) -Od -W3 -Zpi

# Make file primary target.

all: StanMenu.exe

# Make file dependency targets.

StanMenu.res: StanMenu.rc StanMenu.cur StanMenu.ico
    rc -r -i$(INCDIR) StanMenu.rc

StanMenu.obj: StanMenu.c
    cl $(CL_APP_SHIP_ALL) StanMenu.c

StanMenu.exe: StanMenu.obj StanMenu.def StanMenu.res
    link @StanMenu.lnk
    rc -$(RCVER) StanMenu.res

StanMenu.exe: StanMenu.res
    rc -$(RCVER) StanMenu.res
```

STANMENU.RC

```
snapshot icon StanMenu.ico

hand  cursor StanMenu.cur

1 MENU
    {
    POPUP "&File"
        {
```

```
            MENUITEM "&New",          1
            MENUITEM "&Open...",      2
            MENUITEM "&Save",         3
            MENUITEM "Save &As...",   4
            MENUITEM SEPARATOR
            MENUITEM "&Print",        5
            MENUITEM SEPARATOR
            MENUITEM "E&xit",         6
            }
        POPUP "&Edit"
            {
            MENUITEM "&Undo\tCtrl+Z",    7
            MENUITEM SEPARATOR
            MENUITEM "Cu&t\tCtrl+X",     8
            MENUITEM "&Copy\tCtrl+C",    9
            MENUITEM "&Paste\tCtrl+V",  10
            MENUITEM SEPARATOR
            MENUITEM "Cl&ear",          11
            MENUITEM "&Delete",         12
            }
        }
```

As menu items are selected, a WM_COMMAND message is sent to our program to let us know. When a WM_COMMAND message arrives, the wParam parameter contains a result code indicating exactly which menu item has been selected. Each value should be unique so you can tell the difference between different menu selections. In STANMENU, we don't do very much when a WM_COMMAND message arrives. We simply display a message box with the name of the command that was selected. When the user selects the **File.Exit** menu item, a WM_COMMAND message is sent with a command result code of 6. At this time, our program simulates the user clicking on the **Close** item of the system menu by sending ourselves a WM_SYSCOMMAND message, like this:

```
SendMessage (hwnd, WM_SYSCOMMAND, SC_CLOSE, 0L);
```

Typically, a switch statement is used to sort out the different command result codes that result from having more than one menu item. As STANMENU shows, there is a different case for each different command result code.

Most programs get along quite nicely using the approach taken by STANMENU. A menu resource defines a menu. The menu is defined as part of the window class. The application receives WM_COMMAND messages as menu items are selected. For programs (and programmers) that demand more, Windows has 27 menu support routines that you can use. To help you grasp them, we're going to divide these routines into six main types and discuss each type in turn.

Menu Support Routines

Windows has 27 menu support routines, which we divide into six categories. Each category describes a different type of activity that can be performed on a menu. The categories are creation, connect to a window, destruction, modification, query, and tracking. When you need more than just the simplest menu operations, you can go to each group of routines and find one or more of them to help you with whatever problem you have. Table 11.2 summarizes the various categories of menu functions.

Let's look at each type of menu routine, starting with the menu creation routines.

Table 11.2 A Summary of Menu Functions

Category	Routine	Description
Creation (4)	CreateMenu	Creates an empty menu in memory.
	CreatePopupMenu	Creates an empty popup menu in memory.
	LoadMenu	Creates a menu from a disk-based (.EXE or .DLL file) menu resource.
	LoadMenuIndirect	Creates a menu from a memory-based menu resource.
Connect to a Window (1)	SetMenu	Attaches a top-level menu to a window.
Destruction (2)	DeleteMenu	Removes a menu item from a top-level or popup menu, and destroys any associated popup menus.
	DestroyMenu	Destroys a specific top-level or popup menu, and all the menus below it.
Modification (10)	AppendMenu	Adds items to the end of a top-level or popup menu.
	ChangeMenu	Old Windows 1.x and 2.x menu modification function.
	CheckMenuItem	Toggles a check mark inside a popup menu.
	DrawMenuBar	Forces the top-level menu to be redrawn after it has been changed.
	EnableMenuItem	Enables, disables, and grays menu items.
	HiliteMenuItem	Toggles highlighting of an item in a top-level menu.
	InsertMenu	Puts a new item into a menu.
	ModifyMenu	Changes an item in a menu.
	RemoveMenu	Removes a menu item or a popup menu. After a popup menu is removed, it is not destroyed, which means it can be reused.

(continued)

Table 11.2 A Summary of Menu Functions

Category	*Routine*	*Description*
	SetMenuItemBitmaps	Defines two bitmaps to be used in place of the default checked and unchecked display.
Query (9)	GetMenu	Retrieves the menu handle for a window's top-level menu.
	GetMenuCheckMarkDimensions	Gets the size of the default menu check mark, as set by the display driver.
	GetMenuItemCount	Returns the number of items in a top-level or popup menu.
	GetMenuItemID	Finds the menu ID for a given menu item.
	GetMenuState	Returns the flags that are set for a given menu item.
	GetMenuString	Returns the label of a menu item.
	GetSubMenu	Retrieves the menu handle of a popup menu.
	GetSystemMenu	Retrieves a handle to a system menu.
	IsMenu	Returns whether a menu handle is valid or not.
Tracking (1)	TrackPopupMenu	Creates a floating popup menu to appear anywhere on the display screen.

Menu Creation

To the user, menus are user-interface objects that sit inside windows. All of the work that Windows does to support a menu remains hidden behind the scenes. It's the programmer's job, however, to understand what goes on behind the scenes, to make sure that things operate smoothly and efficiently. From a programmer's point of view, menu support requires that certain data structures that define the shape and behavior of a menu be created. We have already seen that a program can call LoadMenu to request that a menu resource be loaded. This is one way to tell Windows to build the required internal data structures. Let's see what other possibilities are available.

Using the CreateMenu and CreatePopup routines, a program can build empty menus, which can then be filled with menu command items and connected to other popup menus. Adding a menu item can involve any of several of the menu modification routines. In the following example, we've decided to use `AppendMenu`. This code fragment creates from scratch a menu like the one that STANMENU built using a menu resource:

```
{
HMENU hSub;
HMENU hTop;

hTop = CreateMenu ();

hSub = CreatePopupMenu ();
AppendMenu (hSub, MF_STRING, 1, "&New");
AppendMenu (hSub, MF_STRING, 2, "&Open...");
AppendMenu (hSub, MF_STRING, 3, "&Save");
AppendMenu (hSub, MF_STRING, 4, "Save &As...");
AppendMenu (hSub, MF_SEPARATOR, 0, 0);
AppendMenu (hSub, MF_STRING, 5, "&Print");
AppendMenu (hSub, MF_SEPARATOR, 0, 0);
AppendMenu (hSub, MF_STRING, 6, "E&xit");

AppendMenu (hTop, MF_POPUP, (UINT)hSub, "&File");

hSub = CreatePopupMenu ();
AppendMenu (hSub, MF_STRING, 7, "&Undo\tAlt+Backspace");
AppendMenu (hSub, MF_SEPARATOR, 0, 0);
AppendMenu (hSub, MF_STRING, 8, "Cu&t\tShift+Del");
AppendMenu (hSub, MF_STRING, 9, "&Copy\tCtrl+Ins");
AppendMenu (hSub, MF_STRING,10, "&Paste\tShift+Ins");
AppendMenu (hSub, MF_SEPARATOR, 0, 0);
AppendMenu (hSub, MF_STRING,11, "Cl&ear");
AppendMenu (hSub, MF_STRING,12, "&Delete");

AppendMenu (hTop, MF_POPUP, (UINT)hSub, "&Edit");
SetMenu (hwnd, hTop);
}
```

The `AppendMenu` routine provides the glue to put the different menu pieces together. It attaches menu items to menus and connects popup menus to top level menus. `AppendMenu` is defined as

```
BOOL AppendMenu (hMenu, wFlags, wIDNewItem, lpNewItem)
```

- `hMenu` is a handle to a menu, either a popup or a top-level menu.

- `wFlags` is a combination of one or more of the MF_ flags, as described below.

- `wIDNewItem` is the result code delivered with the WM_COMMAND message, or a handle to a popup menu when a popup menu is being appended. In the latter case, be sure to use the (UINT) cast to prevent the compiler from complaining (particularly when compiling with the STRICT flag set).

- lpNewItem is a long value that can contain three different types of values. When inserting a string, it is a long pointer to a text string. When inserting a bitmap, it is a bitmap handle. Otherwise, if you are creating an "owner-draw" menu item, it identifies the specific item that you wish to draw.

AppendMenu has several different uses, depending on whether you are attaching a regular menu item or a popup menu, and whether the new item will display a string, a bitmap, or an owner-draw menu item. To put a new string item in a menu for a regular command item, you can call AppendMenu like this:

```
AppendMenu (hMenu, MF_STRING, wID, "Open...");
```

The value of wID is the command result code that will be sent with the WM_COMMAND message when the user selects the menu item identified by the label "Open..."

Alternatively, AppendMenu can be used to attach a popup menu to a top-level menu (or a popup menu to another popup menu). In such cases, it could be called like this:

```
AppendMenu (hMenuTop, MF_POPUP, (UINT)hMenuPopup,"File");
```

In this case, the value of the third parameter, hMenuPopup, is not a command result code, but it is a handle to a popup menu that is to be appended to the end of the menu identified by the hMenuTop menu handle. We cast the handle to a UINT; otherwise, the compiler will complain about a type-mismatch. When the popup is added, it will be identified with the string "File".

AppendMenu can also be used to install a bitmap in place of a string as the label that is displayed for a menu item. When a bitmap is used, the last parameter is used to hold the bitmap handle, instead of a long pointer to a string. In the following example, the variable hbm is a bitmap handle, and is packed into the last parameter using the MAKE-LONG macro:

```
AppendMenu (hMenu, MF_BITMAP, wID, MAKELONG(hbm, 0));
```

There are 13 menu flags that can be placed in the wFlags field. Table 11.3 lists and describes each menu flag. Table 11.4 shows how these flags can be divided into four categories in which the top line in each category identifies the default value. Of these 13 flags, 10 describe features that have a corresponding resource file flag. The other three are MF_HELP, MF_BITMAP, and MF_OWNERDRAW. The last two are used for placing a bitmap into a menu and for defining an owner-draw menu item. These methods for putting graphic objects inside a menu will be covered in detail in Chapter 12.

The only menu creation routine we have not investigated is LoadMenuIndirect, which builds a menu from a memory-resident menu template. This routine is just like LoadMenu, except that LoadMenu creates a menu from a disk-based menu template. LoadMenuIndirect creates a menu using data that is memory-resident. Thus, you can create a menu template "on the fly" and give it to the menu system for use in creating a menu. Doing this requires that you duplicate what the resource compiler does in creating a memory object that describes a menu. The data structures in Windows.h that

Table 11.3 The **MF_** Menu Creation Flags

Menu Flag	Available in a Resource	Description
MF_BITMAP	No	Displays a GDI bitmap instead of a text string for a menu item. It provides one way that graphic images can be displayed in a menu. The other way involves an MF_OWNERDRAW menu item.
MF_CHECKED	Yes	Puts a check mark next to a menu item.
MF_DISABLED	Yes	Disables a menu item. Use the MF_GRAYED flag instead, since it provides the user with visual feedback.
MF_ENABLED	Yes	Enables a menu item.
MF_GRAYED	Yes	Disables and grays a menu item.
MF_HELP	No	This flag right-justifies menu items on the top-level menu bar. Although now obsolete, this was at one time a user-interface standard in Windows.
MF_MENUBARBREAK	Yes	Creates a menu break, and a vertical bar for items inside a popup menu.
MF_MENUBREAK	Yes	Creates a menu break.
MF_OWNERDRAW	No	The creator of the menu is sent a message, WM_DRAWITEM, which includes a handle to a device context to be used for drawing custom menu labels using GDI drawing calls. It cannot be used for top-level menu items.
MF_POPUP	Yes	A popup menu is being attached to a top-level menu, or to another popup.
MF_SEPARATOR	Yes	A horizontal separator should be created in a menu item.
MF_STRING	Yes	A text string is being supplied for a menu item label.
MF_UNCHECKED	Yes	Menu item should be drawn without a check mark.

have been defined for this purpose include the MENUITEMTEMPLATEHEADER and MENUITEMTEMPLATE.

The next routine that we're going to cover is SetMenu. This routine provides the one and only way to attach a menu to a window.

Table 11.4 Four Categories of Menu Flags

Type of Object	Checked	Enabled	Menu Break
MF_STRING	MF_UNCHECKED	MF_ENABLED	\<none\>
MF_POPUP	MF_CHECKED	MF_GRAYED	MF_MENUBARBREAK
MF_BITMAP		MF_DISABLED	MF_MENUBREAK
MF_SEPARATOR			
MF_OWNERDRAW			

Connect to a Window

A single Windows function supports the placement of a menu in a window: `SetMenu`. This single function gets its own category because it provides the only way to replace a top-level menu. In addition, there are some system memory cleanup issues raised by this routine, which we'll describe in a moment. The syntax of this routine is

```
BOOL SetMenu (hWnd, hMenu)
```

- `hWnd` is a window handle to a `WS_OVERLAPPED` or `WS_POPUP` window. A menu cannot be attached to a `WS_CHILD` window.

- `hMenu` is the handle of a top-level menu to be attached to a window.

A program can create several menus and make a different menu available to the user at different times during the operation of a program. There are several reasons why this might be useful. One has to do with supporting different levels of users. A beginner might only want to see short menus, with a program's most basic commands. More advanced users can set a program option to allow them to view a program's longer, more complete menus.

Another reason for a program to have multiple menus involves program security. Different menus can be used to enforce privilege levels in a program. For example, a program might ask for a password at program startup time, which dictates the menu to be installed. A regular user might get an abbreviated set of menus, while more privileged users receive a more complete set of menus, giving them the ability to engage in more privileged operations.

Yet another reason for a program to have different menus is to support the **multiple-document interface (MDI)** standard, which opens a new document window for each new document requested by the user. Different types of documents may need different menus. For example, Microsoft's Excel spreadsheet has two types of documents: worksheets and charts. There are two menus, one for each type of document. Excel switches between the two menus, depending on the type of document with which the user is working.

Whatever the reason for having different menus, `SetMenu` lets you quickly switch from one menu to another. When you do this, be sure to call `DrawMenuBar` to force Windows to draw your new menu. Otherwise, your application's top-level menu will develop some odd quirks.

Also, if you decide to create several menus and switch between them, you'll have some housekeeping issues to handle. In particular, Windows 3.0 only cleans up menu items which are connected to a window. If you have menus which are disconnected from any window, you'll want to be sure that you destroy the menu yourself. If a program terminates without explicitly destroying such menus, the memory taken up by the menu is lost forever (or until the user exits Windows). In Windows 3.1, on the other hand, the system properly handles the clean up of detached menus. The next section discusses destroying menus.

> **HINT:** If you replace a menu by calling `SetMenu`, be sure to hold onto the handle of the old menu. Then, when your program exits, destroy the menu. This is necessary because in Windows 3.0 menus that aren't attached to windows are not cleaned up automatically.

Menu Destruction

Windows has two routines that destroy menus and free the memory associated with them: `DestroyMenu` and `DeleteMenu`. `DestroyMenu` destroys menus that are *not* connected to any window. If you pass it the menu handle for a menu connected to a window, you'll get strange results. In Windows 3.0, your program will crash. Windows 3.1 behaves a little better: It removes the menu before destroying it. `DestroyMenu` is defined as follows:

```
BOOL DestroyMenu (hmenu)
```

- `hmenu` is the handle of a top-level or popup menu that is to be destroyed. The menu specified, and all associated popup menus, are destroyed.

Here is code that will determine the currently installed menu; remove it from the window, and destroy it:

```
HMENU hmenu;

hmenu = GetMenu(hwnd);    /* Find out menu handle. */
SetMenu (hwnd, NULL);     /* Remove menu.          */
DestroyMenu (hmenu);      /* Destroy the menu.     */
```

You don't have to do this for every menu you create, though, because a menu that is attached to a window is automatically destroyed when the window is destroyed.

The second menu destruction routine, `DeleteMenu`, actually does two things: It removes a menu item from a menu and destroys whatever popup menus are associated with the menu item. This routine frees the memory used by the menu in the same way that `DestroyMenu` does.

`DeleteMenu` is defined as

```
BOOL DeleteMenu (hMenu, nPosition, wFlags)
```

- `hMenu` is a handle to either a top-level or a popup menu.
- `nPosition` identifies the menu item of interest. The meaning of this field depends on the value of the last parameter, `wFlags`.
- `wFlags` is either `MF_BYPOSITION` or `MF_BYCOMMAND`.

If `wFlags` is `MF_BYPOSITION`, then the menu item is selected by its relative position in the menu: The first item in a menu has an offset of zero, the next has an offset of one, and so forth. This is necessary to reference popup menus that don't have an associated result code. Here is one way to remove the Edit popup menu from the top-level menu in the STANMENU program:

```
HMENU hmenu;

hmenu = GetMenu (hwnd);
DeleteMenu (hmenu, 1, MF_BYPOSITION);
DrawMenuBar (hwnd);
```

The call to `DrawMenuBar` is necessary whenever the top-level menu changes, to request that it be completely redrawn. (We discuss this routine in more detail later in this chapter.)

The `MF_BYPOSITION` flag also can be used to remove an item in a popup menu. But you must first get a handle to the popup menu that contains the item by calling `GetSubMenu`. For example, here is how to delete the *Copy* command, which is the fourth item in our standard menu:

```
HMENU hmenu;
HMENU hmenuEdit;
hmenu = GetMenu (hwnd);
hmenuEdit = GetSubMenu (hMenu, 1);
DeleteMenu (hmenuEdit, 3, MF_BYPOSITION);
```

Menu items can also be deleted via the command result code, by using the `MF_BY-COMMAND` flag in `DeleteMenu`'s last parameter. For deleting items in popup menus, using the command result code is faster than using the relative position, since the command result code lets you reference any item in the menu hierarchy by referencing the handle to the top-level menu. For example, here is another way to remove the *Copy* command from the Edit menu in STANMENU:

```
HMENU hmenu;

hmenu = GetMenu (hwnd);
DeleteMenu (hmenu, 9, MF_BYCOMMAND);
```

Our discussion of `DeleteMenu` has introduced two more menu flags: `MF_BY-COMMAND` and `MF_BYPOSITION`. These two plus the 13 flags that were introduced in the discussion of the `AppendMenu` routine bring to 15 the total number of menu flags presented. You'll use these 15 flags in just about all of the work you do with menus.

The next set of routines modify a menu once it has been created.

Menu Modification

Once a program has created a menu and attached it to a window, there is no reason for the menu to remain unchanged. In fact, Windows provides 10 routines that let you fiddle with menus as much as you'd like. We've looked at one of them already, `AppendMenu`. Four other routines change the structure of an existing menu: `ChangeMenu`, `InsertMenu`, `ModifyMenu`, and `RemoveMenu`. In general, the `ChangeMenu` routine should be avoided since it was created for an earlier version of Windows and is somewhat clumsy and complicated to use. More to the point, its capabilities are replaced by the other three menu modification routines.

`InsertMenu` installs a new menu item or popup menu into an existing menu. Unlike `AppendMenu`, which can only create new items at the *end* of a menu, `InsertMenu` creates new items anywhere. The `ModifyMenu` routine *changes* an existing menu item. For example, it can be used to change the menu string or the command result code, to enable a grayed menu item, or to gray and disable a menu item. The `RemoveMenu` routine detaches a popup menu from a top-level or other popup menus. This routine leaves the internal menu structure intact, so that a menu can be reused later. Of course, if you remove a menu item from a menu, you must remember to destroy the menu item before your program exits; otherwise, the memory will be lost to the system.

Our first routine, `InsertMenu`, is defined as follows:

```
BOOL InsertMenu( hMenu, nPosition, wFlags, wID, lpNew)
```

- `hMenu` is a handle to a popup or top-level menu.

- `nPosition` indicates the menu item before which the new item is to be created. This value can be either the relative position of a menu item or the result code of a menu item, depending on whether the `MF_BYPOSITION` or `MF_BYCOMMAND` flag is selected.

- `wFlags` is a combination of the 12 menu flags that were described earlier with the AppendMenu routine. Two other flags indicate how the new item location is selected: `MF_BYPOSITION` and `MF_BYCOMMAND`.

- `wID` is the result code for a new menu item and is the value delivered with the `WM_COMMAND` message. Or, when a popup menu is being inserted, it is a popup menu handle. Remember to cast such menu handles to `UINT` to keep the compiler happy.

- `lpNew` is a long value that can contain three different types of values. When inserting a string, it is a long pointer to a text string. When inserting a bitmap, it is a bitmap handle. Otherwise, if you are creating an "owner-draw" menu item, it identifies the specific item that you wish to draw.

Here is one way to add a *Close* command to the File menu, underneath the *Open...* menu item:

```
HMENU hmenu;
HMENU hmenuFile;

hmenu = GetMenu (hwnd);
hmenuFile = GetSubMenu (hmenu, 0);
InsertMenu (hmenuFile, 2, MF_BYPOSITION, 13, "&Close");
```

This code fragment uses the `MF_BYPOSITION` method to specify the location of the new menu item. Since we're inserting a menu item in a popup menu, this approach requires us to get a handle to the popup menu. The `GetMenu` routine gets a handle to the top-level menu. The `GetSubMenu` routine gets a handle to the File menu, since it's the first (zeroth) item in the top-level menu. Once we have a handle to the correct popup menu, the `InsertMenu` routine embeds a new menu command having a result code of 13. The second parameter, 2, specifies that the menu item is to be inserted *before* menu item 2. In zero-based counting, that means before the *third* item. Figure 11.8 shows the File menu with the newly added *Close* menu item.

Here's another slightly simpler approach which involves no call to `GetSubMenu`:

```
HMENU hmenu;

hmenu = GetMenu (hwnd);
InsertMenu (hmenu, 3, MF_BYCOMMAND, 13, "&Close");
```

The `MF_BYCOMMAND` parameter lets us specify the location using a command result code. In this case, the value of 3 is chosen since this is the result code for the **File.Save** menu item, before which we wish to have a menu item inserted.

The `ModifyMenu` routine, which can change any aspect of a menu item, takes the same parameters and flags as `InsertMenu`. This routine uses the same two methods

Figure 11.8 File menu with newly added Close menu item

for specifying a specific menu item: MF_BYPOSITION and MF_BYCOMMAND. Of course, since this routine modifies existing menu items instead of inserting new menu items, the way an item is specified is a little different. With InsertMenu, we point to the item that will follow the new menu item. ModifyMenu, on the other hand, requires us to point to the item itself.

ModifyMenu can put a new label on a menu item, gray a regular menu item, or enable a grayed menu item. It can be used to change a regular menu item into a bitmap or into an owner-draw menu item. In brief, anything that can be added to a menu with InsertMenu or AppendMenu can be changed using ModifyMenu. For example, here is how ModifyMenu can be used to change the labels on a menu item. We're going to change the Edit menu's Cut, Copy, and Paste menu items so that each menu item displays the equivalent French phrase instead. Using the MF_BYPOSITION option, we would say:

```
HMENU hmenu;
HMENU hmenuEdit;

hmenu = GetMenu (hwnd);
hmenuEdit = GetSubMenu (hmenu, 1);
ModifyMenu (hmenuEdit, 2, MF_BYPOSITION, 8,  "Couper");
ModifyMenu (hmenuEdit, 3, MF_BYPOSITION, 9,  "Copier");
ModifyMenu (hmenuEdit, 4, MF_BYPOSITION, 10, "Coller");
```

As we saw in earlier examples, the MF_BYPOSITION option requires us to get the handle of the specific menu or submenu that contains the item of interest. A simpler approach involves using the MF_BYCOMMAND option. Here is how to use the MF_BY-COMMAND option to achieve the same results as in our previous example, except it requires no call to GetSubMenu:

```
HMENU hmenu;

hmenu = GetMenu (hwnd);
ModifyMenu (hmenu,  8, MF_BYCOMMAND,  8, "Couper");
ModifyMenu (hmenu,  9, MF_BYCOMMAND,  9, "Copier");
ModifyMenu (hmenu, 10, MF_BYCOMMAND, 10, "Coller");
```

Our next menu modification function, RemoveMenu, removes items from a menu. If an item is a command, it is removed and the memory associated with it is freed. However, if an item is a popup menu, it is not destroyed so that it can be used again. RemoveMenu is defined as

```
BOOL RemoveMenu (hMenu, nPosition, wFlags)
```

- hMenu is a handle to a popup or top-level menu.

- nPosition indicates the menu item to be removed. This value is either the relative position of a menu item, or the result code of a menu item, depending on whether the MF_BYPOSITION or MF_BYCOMMAND flag is selected.

- wFlags is either MF_BYPOSITION or MF_BYCOMMAND.

Using the `MF_BYCOMMAND` flag, we could delete the *Clear* menu item with

```
HMENU hmenu;

hmenu = GetMenu (hwnd);
RemoveMenu (hmenu, 11, MF_BYCOMMAND);
```

To remove the entire Edit menu, we use the `MF_BYPOSITION` flag as shown here:

```
HMENU hmenu;

hmenu = GetMenu (hwnd);
hmenuEdit = GetSubMenu (hmenu, 1);
RemoveMenu (hmenu, 1, MF_BYPOSITION);
DrawMenuBar (hwnd);
```

Since we are removing a popup menu from the menu hierarchy, unless we attach it later on, we're going to have to be sure to destroy the menu before our program terminates:

```
DestroyMenu (hmenuEdit);
```

so that the memory associated with the Edit menu is freed.

You may have noticed the call to `DrawMenuBar` after the popup menu is removed. Whenever a change is made to a top-level menu, `DrawMenuBar` should be called. The reason is that the menu modification routines *only* change the internal data structures that support a menu. For the user to see the change, `DrawMenuBar` must be called to redraw the newly modified menu. Otherwise, the change does not appear to the user, which is sure to result in some confusion.

All of the remaining routines in this group are used to change the state of existing menu items. `CheckMenuItem`, for example, is used to place a check mark next to a menu item or to remove a check mark. Incidentally, if you don't like the shape of the default check mark, you can create a bitmap with an image that you do like and associate it with a menu item by calling `SetMenuItemBitmaps`. This routine also lets you select the bitmap to be displayed when a menu item is not checked. In Chapter 12, we'll show you exactly how this is done, when we discuss how to enhance menu items using graphics.

The `EnableMenuItem` routine lets you pick one of three enable states for a menu item: enabled, disabled, and grayed. Because the disabled state provides no visual feedback to the user, it is probably best to avoid using it. *Enabled* is the default state of a menu in which it can be selected and manipulated in a normal manner. A *grayed* menu item, on the other hand, is displayed in a grayed text and cannot be selected by the user.

A final routine, `HiliteMenuItem`, lights up items in the top-level menu. This routine is used by the keyboard accelerator support code when a keyboard accelerator is pressed. The top-level menu item that is associated with the selected menu item is highlighted for a moment. Unless you plan to simulate this functionality yourself, you probably won't ever use this routine.

Our next set of routines perform a query—that is, they ask the menu system for some information.

Query

The Query routines let you ask for information about menus. There are two types of routines: One set returns a handle to a menu, and the other provides menu attribute information. In general, if you can set a value or a flag, there is a query routine to let you know the currently selected value or flag associated with a menu item.

Three query routines give you menu handle information: `GetMenu`, `GetSubMenu`, and `GetSystemMenu`. Figure 11.9 gives a graphic depiction of the menu handles returned by these three routines. `GetMenu` gives you a handle to the top-level menu that is attached to a window. Here is how it is called:

```
hmenuTop = GetMenu (hwnd);
```

Once you have the handle to a top-level menu, you get a handle to one of its popups by calling:

```
hmenu = GetSubMenu (hmenuTop, nPosition);
```

where `nPosition` is the zero-based index of the popup in the top-level menu, or the index of a popup within another popup menu. Once you have a popup menu handle, it can be used with any of the menu modification routines to add, remove, or modify any item in the menu.

The `GetSystemMenu` routine has two uses, to handle the special nature of the system menu. Most programs will use the default system menu, so Windows only maintains a single copy. However, a copy is automatically created for a window if it calls `GetSystemMenu` like this:

```
hmenuSys = GetSystemMenu (hwnd, 0);
```

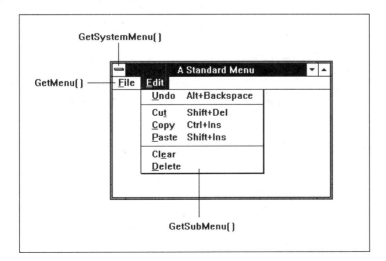

Figure 11.9 Three query routines return menu handles

The zero in the second parameter tells the menu system to give you a handle to a private system menu that you can modify. If, after changing the system menu, you decide that you want to return to the original system menu, you make a call like this:

```
hmenuSys = GetSystemMenu (hwnd, 1);
```

A nonzero value in the second parameter attaches the default system menu to your window, which cannot be modified.

If you have a handle, but are not sure whether it connects to a valid menu handle, you can call `IsMenu`. It takes a single parameter, a menu handle, and returns `TRUE` or `FALSE` depending on whether the menu handle is valid:

```
BOOL hValid;

hValid = IsMenu (hmenu);
```

The other five query routines return menu attribute information. Figure 11.10 shows the specific attribute for four of the routines. To find out the number of items in a menu, you call:

```
w = GetMenuItemCount (hMenu);
```

where `hMenu` is either a top-level menu handle or a popup menu handle. The number of items includes the vertical separators appearing in the menu. If you need to find out the result code for a menu item command, you can call:

```
w = GetMenuItemID (hMenu, nPosition);
```

This routine can't tell you about a popup menu item, since they don't have result codes. If you ask for the result code for a popup menu, you get a -1. To find out the handle of a popup menu, you need to call `GetSubMenu`.

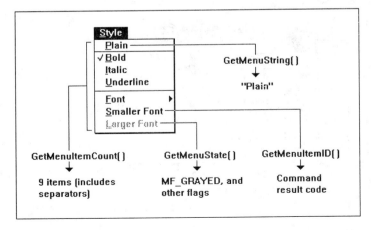

Figure 11.10 Menu attributes that a program can query

Another menu query routine is `GetMenuState`, which tells you the current settings for various menu flags. If you want to test for a specific menu flag, use the logical AND function. For example, this code fragment produces the flags for the menu command item that has a result code of 38, then checks to see if the menu item is grayed or not:

```
WORD wFlags;

wFlags = GetMenuState (hmenu, 38, MF_BYCOMMAND);
if (wFlags & MF_GRAYED)
  {
  . . .
```

Be careful when using this routine, however. All of the default flags (`MF_STRING`, `MF_UNHILITE`, `MF_ENABLED`, and `MF_UNCHECKED`) have a value of zero. You really can't test for them with the logical AND, since ANDing with zero always gives a result of zero. Instead, to test for any of the default flags, you need to check whether the flags that represent the *opposite* are present. For example, here is how to check whether a menu is enabled:

```
WORD wFlags

wFlags = GetMenuState (hmenu, 38, MF_BYCOMMAND);
if (!(wFlags & (MF_DISABLED | MF_GRAYED))
      {
      . . .
```

If the disabled and grayed flags are not set, this conditional statement returns a value of true. While it may seem like an odd way to test for the presence of a flag, it is necessary because of the way in which the default flag information is stored. Notice that the `GetMenuState` routine lets you choose between the `MF_BYCOMMAND` and `MF_BYPOSITION` flags for picking a specific menu item.

If you have a menu item that displays a string (as opposed to a separator, a bitmap, or an owner-draw item), you can retrieve a copy of the string by calling:

```
cbSize = GetMenuString (hmenu, wID, lpBuff, bufsize, wFlag);
```

where `hmenu` is a menu handle, `wID` is either a command result code or the relative position of an item, `lpBuff` is a long pointer to a character buffer, `bufsize` is the buffer size, and `wFlag` is either `MF_BYCOMMAND` or `MF_BYPOSITION`. The return value, `cbSize`, is the number of bytes that were copied.

Our last menu query routine has perhaps the longest routine name in Windows: `GetMenuCheckMarkDimensions`. As indicated in Figure 11.11, this routine returns the width and height of a default menu check mark. This is a useful way for programs to install custom check marks to replace the default check mark. In addition, a program can install a mark that is displayed when the menu item is *not* checked. This routine returns a four-byte value that must be split apart to yield the two size values:

Figure 11.11   Check mark dimensions returned by GetMenuCheckMarkDimensions( )

```
DWORD dwCheck;
int cxWidth;
int cyHeight;
dwCheck  = GetMenuCheckMarkDimensions();
cxWidth  = LOWORD (dwCheck);
cyHeight = HIWORD (dwCheck);
```

As indicated in the code example, this routine takes no parameters.

There is one more category that deals with tracking, which is the support of a popup menu outside a window's regular menu.

Tracking

Our final category of menu routines is made up of a single routine that is used for menu tracking. This routine, `TrackPopupMenu`, allows a program to create a popup menu anywhere on the display screen. Menus that are not attached to a top-level menu are sometimes referred to as **tear-off** menus, since they look like regular popup menus, except they can appear anywhere. `TrackPopupMenu` is defined as

```
BOOL TrackPopupMenu (hMenu, 0, x, y, 0, hwnd, 0L)
```

- `hMenu` is a handle to a popup menu.
- `x` is the X value of the upper-left corner of the menu, in screen coordinates.
- `y` is the Y value of the upper-left corner of the menu, in screen coordinates.
- `hwnd` is a handle of the window to which the `WM_COMMAND` and other menu messages are sent.
- The second, fifth, and seventh parameters are reserved values and must be zero, as shown here.

An important point to keep in mind with this routine is that the popup menu is *not* positioned in client area coordinates but in **screen coordinates**. Like client area coordinates, screen coordinates are a pixel-based coordinate system. However, the origin (0,0) in screen coordinates is the upper-left corner of the *display screen*. If you wish to put a popup menu in your client area, you must convert client area coordinates to screen coordinates. The `ClientToScreen` routine does this conversion for you. Here is how a left button up mouse message can be used to trigger a tear-off menu at the point where the user clicks the mouse:

```
case WM_LBUTTONUP:
    {
    HMENU hmenu;
    HMENU hmenuEdit;
    POINT pt;
    hmenu = GetMenu (hwnd);
    hmenuEdit = GetSubMenu (hmenu, 1);
    pt = MAKEPOINT (lParam);
    ClientToScreen(hwnd, &pt);
    TrackPopupMenu (hmenuEdit,  // Popup menu handle.
        0,                      // Reserved.
        pt.x,                   // X-coordinate.
        pt.y,                   // Y-coordinate.
        0,                      // Reserved.
        hwnd,                   // Hwnd to send msgs.
        0L);                    // Reserved.
    }
    break;
```

This code fragment makes the Edit menu from STANMENU appear anywhere in the client area.

The popup menu created by the `TrackPopupMenu` routine is just like a regular popup menu. An important difference, however, is that a `WM_INITMENUPOPUP` message is *not* sent before this menu is displayed. Instead, the only menu initialization message that you receive is the `WM_INITMENU` message.

The reason is that a tear-off menu created by `TrackPopupMenu` is treated as a top menu in a menu hierarchy. From the point of view of the menu system, then, it has equal status with the menu-bar menu displayed under a window's caption bar. The `WM_INITMENU` message is reserved for the initialization of all top-level menus, including the popup menu displayed by `TrackPopupMenu`. But if a tear-off menu created by `TrackPopupMenu` were to have any nested popup menus, a `WM_INIT-MENUPOPUP` message is sent to tell you to perform whatever initialization is required for these lower level, nested menus.

Although menus allow a program to show the user the available commands, some users prefer to enter keyboard commands. To help you give these users what they want, Windows supports the creation of keyboard accelerators. Keyboard accelerators provide a virtually seamless connection between keyboard input and menu commands. The connection is so good that accelerator commands even cause a menu item to be illuminated briefly to let the user know that a command has been selected. Let's take a look at the capabilities available with keyboard accelerators and see how they can be incorporated into a Windows program.

Keyboard Accelerators

Keyboard accelerator support was one of the last pieces to be put in place when Microsoft was getting ready to ship the first version of Windows in 1985. Windows' original design called for a user interface that relied primarily on the mouse for command input. But after taking a second look at the existing base of computers—most of which didn't have a mouse—Microsoft had second thoughts. Another major influence on their decision to put accelerator support into Windows was feedback from software developers who were considering the use of Windows for their applications. Since some of the software developers had successful DOS programs that relied heavily on a keyboard interface, they were concerned about the suitability of Windows for their products. Microsoft's response was to provide keyboard accelerators.

Keyboard accelerators tie together keyboard input and menu command selection. For users who don't have a mouse or who prefer to use the keyboard to enter commands, accelerators link keystrokes with the creation of messages that match the menu messages described earlier in this chapter. For programmers, this means that a minimum amount of effort is required to incorporate accelerator support in a Windows program.

Microsoft did such a good job of creating accelerator support that programmers usually think of accelerators as little more than an extension to the menu system. In fact, accelerators are a separate part of Windows that can support commands with no menu equivalent. Carried to an extreme, you could even write programs that rely *solely* on accelerator keystrokes for command input and make no use of menus. Of course, you probably won't want to do this since the presence of both menus *and* accelerators makes for a very flexible user interface.

In Chapter 15, you'll see that keyboard input goes through a *two-step* translation process. Keyboard hardware generates **scan codes** to report keyboard activity. In fact, every key on the keyboard has *two* scan codes: one that says the key is being pressed and another which says the key is being released. A scan code lets the keyboard hardware report that a change has taken place. In general, scan codes are not interesting to most programs since they are too low-level to work with, and because Windows' keyboard driver translates scan codes into more useful information.

The first translation process converts scan codes into **virtual key codes**. While these codes bring us one step closer to character information, they don't distinguish between a capital "A" and a lowercase "a," for example. This is because virtual key codes represent keyboard keys, not characters. From the point of view of accelerators, virtual key codes are the most useful way to think about keyboard input. After all, when a user enters a keyboard command such as Ctrl+A, it should have the same effect whether or not the Caps Lock key is active. In other words, there shouldn't be a difference between Ctrl+A (capital A) and Ctrl+a (lowercase a).

The second translation process converts virtual key codes into the extended **ASCII** character set that Windows supports. Programs designed to receive character input—such as a word processor—are most interested in ASCII characters and ignore scan codes and virtual key codes. From the point of view of accelerators, a program *can* incorporate ASCII characters as accelerators. But this could be very limiting, for example, to a word processing program if certain letters were command keys and not interpreted as data. Of course, if you're writing a program that uses keyboard input *only* for command input, there is no reason not to use ASCII characters.

Windows lets you define accelerator keys using either virtual key code information or ASCII characters. Virtual keys are the more common type of accelerator because they do not rely on the state of the shift keys and, in particular, because they let the user ignore the state of the Caps Lock key. To create case-sensitive command keys, on the other hand, you are required to use ASCII character accelerators.

For a program to get access to accelerators, an accelerator table must be created. Programs can have more than one accelerator table, but will (usually) only access one at a time. Acclerator tables are created by making an entry in a program's resource file using the `ACCELERATORS` keyword. This template shows the two basic types of accelerator table entries. Each line in the table represents a different keyboard accelerator:

```
table-name ACCELERATORS
    {
    <key>,<cmd>,VIRTKEY [,NOINVERT][,ALT][,SHIFT][,CONTROL]
    <key>,<cmd>,ASCII   [,NOINVERT][,ALT][,SHIFT][,CONTROL]
    }
```

- `<key>` is the key, either text in quotes, "A", or a virtual key constant from Windows.h, like `VK_F1`. It can also be a numeric value, like `58` or `0x6C`.

- `<cmd>` is the command result code to be included with the `WM_COMMAND` message to notify a program that an accelerator key combination has been pressed.

- `VIRTKEY` specifies that the value of `<key>` represents a virtual key code.

- `ASCII` specifies that `<key>` is an ASCII key code.

- `NOINVERT` inhibits the automatic highlighting of the related menu command.

- `ALT` indicates that an accelerator uses the Alt key.

- `SHIFT` indicates that an accelerator uses the Shift key.

- `CONTROL` indicates that an accelerator uses the Ctrl key.

Here is an example of an accelerator table containing only ASCII values:

```
AscKeys ACCELERATORS
    {
    "A", 25, ASCII
    "a", 26, ASCII
    "1", 27, ASCII
    }
```

The command result code is the value sent to the window procedure in the `wParam` parameter as part of the `WM_COMMAND` message. For example, here is code that would trap and process the keystrokes for the `AscKeys` accelerator table:

```
LRESULT CALLBACK WindowProc (...)
    {
    switch (msg)
        {
        case WM_COMMAND:
```

```
switch (wParam)
    {
    case 25:
        ...
    case 26:
        ...
    case 27:
        ...
    }
}
}
```

This approach would allow you to write a program that uses regular character values as commands. Notice, though, that the use of ASCII makes your commands case-sensitive. The capital-A command is created when either the Shift key is pressed *or* Caps-Lock is on. As you're probably aware, when both keys are active, they cancel each other out to create lowercase letters.

Instead of using ASCII accelerators, most programs use virtual key code accelerators. Virtual key codes let you define accelerators in a case-insensitive fashion. They also allow you to combine keys with any combination of the Alt, Shift, and Control keys. Here is another accelerator table showing how virtual key accelerators can be defined:

```
VirtKeys ACCELERATORS
    {
    "A",   35, VIRTKEY, CONTROL
    VK_F1, 36, VIRTKEY
    VK_F8, 37, VIRTKEY, ALT, CONTROL, SHIFT
    }
```

This table defines three virtual key accelerators: Control+A, F1, and Alt+Control+Shift+F8. Because virtual key codes are tied to keyboard *keys* and not ASCII code values, the Control+A accelerator ignores the state of the Caps-Lock key. For this reason, virtual key accelerators are less confusing to the user. The second accelerator in this table causes the F1 function key to send a WM_COMMAND message with a value of 36 in the wParam parameter. The last accelerator in this table shows that an accelerator can be defined using all three shift keys: Alt, Control, and Shift. Of course, it's probably *not* a good idea to use all three shift keys in a single accelerator, since you'd be asking your user to press four keys simultaneously just to make a command selection. Of course, if you *do* need this capability, you will sleep better at night knowing that it's available.

Certain key combinations should not be used as accelerator keys. Some of them are shown in this accelerator table:

```
AvoidThese ACCELERATORS
    {
    VK_TAB,    99, VIRTKEY, ALT      ; switch programs
    VK_SPACE, 100, VIRTKEY, ALT      ; system menu
    VK_F10,   101, VIRTKEY           ; menu hot key
    VK_F4,    102, VIRTKEY, ALT      ; close window
```

```
VK_ESCAPE, 103, VIRTKEY, CONTROL ; get task list
VK_ESCAPE, 104, VIRTKEY, ALT     ; switch programs

VK_MENU,   105, VIRTKEY         ; Alt key
VK_SHIFT,  106, VIRTKEY         ; Shift key
VK_CONTROL,107, VIRTKEY         ; Control key

VK_DELETE, 108, VIRTKEY,CONTROL,ALT  ; Reboot!
}
```

The first set of accelerator definitions are key combinations reserved for Windows' use. If you create an accelerator key for one of them, you will prevent that key combination from playing its standard role in the user interface. The second set of accelerator keys involves the use of the Alt, Shift, and Control keys alone. The keyboard accelerator system ignores these keys when used alone, since they are reserved for use with other keys. The very last accelerator key in this table needs no further explanation other than to say that you will never use it as an accelerator key command.

You'll want to avoid another set of accelerator key combinations, except when you need them for the actions for which they are reserved. Ctrl+X, for example, is reserved for the **Edit.Cut** menu item, a standard menu item for programs that use the Clipboard. Table 11.5 summarizes these reserved accelerator keys and describes the use of each. From this set, you can see that the number of reserved accelerator keys is small and that you are left with a very wide range of keyboard combinations from which to choose.

If you are creating a Windows program that may someday be translated for use in a different language, you will probably want to avoid creating any accelerators that com-

Table 11.5 Reserved Accelerator Key Combinations

Key Combination	Description
Ctrl + Z	Edit.Undo menu item.
Alt + Backspace	Old-style Edit.Undo menu item.
Ctrl + X	Edit.Cut menu item to remove an item to the clipboard.
Shift + Del	Old-style Edit.Cut menu item.
Ctrl + C	Edit.Copy to place a copy of an item on the clipboard.
Ctrl + Ins	Old-style Edit.Copy.
Ctrl + V	Edit.Paste to copy the contents of the clipboard into a document.
Shift + Ins	Old-style Edit.Paste.
Del	Edit.Clear or Edit.Delete to remove data without affecting the contents of the clipboard.
F1	Help.
F6	Switch to a different panel in a split window.
Ctrl + F6	Switch to a different window under the multiple document interface.

Figure 11.12 A sample Finnish program

bine Alt with a letter key, for example Alt+A. Such accelerators create the possibility of a conflict with mnemonic keystrokes. As we discussed earlier, a mnemonic keystroke lets the user strike Alt + letter to call up a popup menu. If an accelerator is defined for such a keystroke, like Alt + A, and a popup menu uses the letter as a mnemonic, the mnemonic is disabled because accelerator key combinations have a higher priority.

At first glance, you might think that the solution would be simply to avoid creating accelerators that conflict with mnemonic letters. Consider a program with two popups: File and Edit. If Alt-F and Alt-E are the only two mnemonic keystrokes used by the program, you might think that you can use Alt-T without any problem. But when the time comes for you to convert your product for use in Finland, where the word for file is "Tiedosto," you will find that your accelerator, Alt-T, has collided with the most obvious mnemonic for this menu. See Figure 11.12 for an example of how a Finnish program might appear.

As this program reveals, either an Alt+T or Alt+M accelerator would collide with the mnemonics in the Finnish version of our program for the File (Tiedosto) or Edit (Muokkaus) menus. The easiest way to avoid this problem is simply to avoid creating accelerator keys consisting of Alt and a letter key alone.

Once an accelerator table has been defined in the resource file, bringing it into a program requires a call to the `LoadAccelerators` routine:

```
HANDLE LoadAccelerators (hInstance, lpTableName)
```

- `hInstance` is an instance handle passed to a program as a parameter to `WinMain`.

- `lpTableName` is a long pointer to a character string containing the name of an accelerator table in the program's resource file.

The return value is a handle to an accelerator table, which identifies the specific set of accelerator keystrokes to be used. Load an accelerator table named `VIRTKEYS` like this:

```
HANDLE hAccel;

hAccel = LoadAccelerators (hInstance, "VIRTKEYS");
```

Like other resources (such as menus), a numeric value can identify an accelerator table:

```
23 ACCELERATORS
    {
    "A",   35, VIRTKEY, CONTROL
    ...
    }
```

To load this accelerator table into memory, make a call like this:

```
hAccel = LoadAccelerators (hInstance, "#23");
```

Or, the MAKEINTRESOURCE macro can be used to package the value in another way so that it is recognized as a numeric identifier:

```
hAccel=LoadAccelerators(hInstance,MAKEINTRESOURCE(23));
```

Once an accelerator table has been loaded, you'll call TranslateAccelerator inside your program's message loop to make it active. This routine is defined:

```
int TranslateAccelerator (hWnd, haccTable, lpMsg)
```

- hWnd is a handle of the window that receives the command and menu control messages created by keyboard accelerators. This window will normally have a menu attached, so that menu and accelerator support can be seamlessly integrated.

- haccTable is a handle to an accelerator table loaded with the LoadAccelerators routine.

- lpMsg is a long pointer to an MSG data structure.

The most common way to use accelerators is to modify the standard GetMessage loop in your WinMain function. TranslateAccelerator checks the message traffic received by GetMessage and converts it to the appropriate menu messages. If it performs a translation, it provides a return code of TRUE. Otherwise, the return code is FALSE. Here is the most common way to incorporate this routine into a standard message loop:

```
while (GetMessage(&msg, 0, 0, 0))
    {
    if (!TranslateAccelerator (hwnd, hAccel, &msg))
        {
        TranslateMessage(&msg);
        DispatchMessage(&msg);
        }
    }
```

If TranslateAccelerator does not find an accelerator, it returns a value of FALSE. This causes the message to be handled by TranslateMessage and DispatchMessage. If, on the other hand, an accelerator *was* found, then no other steps are required by the GetMessage loop, since the accelerator is handled entirely by TranslateAccelerator.

Here is a complete program that shows how an accelerator table can be implemented. It is built on the standard menu program introduced at the beginning of this chapter, STANMENU. We have added the four standard accelerators, which support the standard clipboard operations: undo, cut, copy, and paste.

ACCEL.C

```
/*----------------------------------------------------------------*\
|   Accel.C - Demo showing creation and use of keyboard           |
|             accelerators.                                       |
\*----------------------------------------------------------------*/
#define STRICT
#include <Windows.H>
#include "Accel.H"


/*----------------------------------------------------------------*\
|                     Function Prototypes.                        |
\*----------------------------------------------------------------*/
LRESULT CALLBACK AccelWndProc (HWND, UINT, WPARAM, LPARAM);

/*----------------------------------------------------------------*\
|                     Global Variables.                           |
\*----------------------------------------------------------------*/
char achWndClass[] = "Accel:MAIN";
char achAppName[]  = "Accelerators";


/*----------------------------------------------------------------*\
|                     Main Function:  WinMain.                     |
\*----------------------------------------------------------------*/
int PASCAL
WinMain (HINSTANCE hInstance,       // Who am I?
         HINSTANCE hPrevInstance,  // Any older siblings?
         LPSTR     lpszCmdLine,    // Ptr to command line.
         int       cmdShow)        // How to open my window?
    {
    HACCEL   hAccel;
    HWND     hwnd;
    MSG      msg;
    WNDCLASS wndclass;

    if (!hPrevInstance)
        {
        wndclass.lpszClassName  = achWndClass;
        wndclass.hInstance      = hInstance;
        wndclass.lpfnWndProc    = AccelWndProc;
        wndclass.hCursor        = LoadCursor (hInstance, "hand");
        wndclass.hIcon          = LoadIcon (hInstance,"snapshot");
        wndclass.lpszMenuName   = "#1";
        wndclass.hbrBackground  = (HBRUSH)(COLOR_WINDOW+1);
        wndclass.style          = NULL;
        wndclass.cbClsExtra     = 0;
        wndclass.cbWndExtra     = 0;
```

```
        RegisterClass ( &wndclass);
        }

    hwnd = CreateWindowEx(0L,              // Extra style.
                    achWndClass,           // Class name.
                    achAppName,            // Title.
                    WS_OVERLAPPEDWINDOW,   // Style bits.
                    CW_USEDEFAULT,         // x - default.
                    0,                     // y - default.
                    CW_USEDEFAULT,         // cx - default.
                    0,                     // cy - default.
                    NULL,                  // No parent.
                    NULL,                  // Class menu.
                    hInstance,             // Creator.
                    NULL);                 // Params.
    ShowWindow (hwnd, cmdShow);

    hAccel = LoadAccelerators (hInstance, "#1");

    while (GetMessage(&msg, 0, 0, 0))
        {
        if (!TranslateAccelerator (hwnd, hAccel, &msg))
            {
            TranslateMessage(&msg); // Convert KEYDOWNs to CHARs
            DispatchMessage(&msg);  // Transmit message to WndProc
            }
        }

    return 0;
    }


    /*-------------------------------------------------------------*\
    |               Window Procedure:  AccelWndProc.               |
    \*-------------------------------------------------------------*/
LRESULT CALLBACK
AccelWndProc (HWND   hwnd,      // For whom is message sent?
              UINT   mMsg,      // What is exact message?
              WPARAM wParam,    // ...message details.
              LPARAM lParam)    // ...message details.
    {
    switch (mMsg)
        {
        case WM_COMMAND:
            {
            char buffer[80];
            char *npch;

            switch (wParam)
                {
                case IDM_FILE_NEW:
                    npch = "File.New";
                    break;
                case IDM_FILE_OPEN:
                    npch = "File.Open...";
                    break;
```

```
                case IDM_FILE_SAVE:
                    npch = "File.Save";
                    break;
                case IDM_FILE_SAVEAS:
                    npch = "File.Save As...";
                    break;
                case IDM_FILE_PRINT:
                    npch = "File.Print";
                    break;
                case IDM_FILE_EXIT:
                    npch = "File.Exit";
                    break;
                case IDM_EDIT_UNDO:
                    npch = "Edit.Undo";
                    break;
                case IDM_EDIT_CUT:
                    npch = "Edit.Cut";
                    break;
                case IDM_EDIT_COPY:
                    npch = "Edit.Copy";
                    break;
                case IDM_EDIT_PASTE:
                    npch = "Edit.Paste";
                    break;
                case IDM_EDIT_CLEAR:
                    npch = "Edit.Clear";
                    break;
                case IDM_EDIT_DELETE:
                    npch = "Edit.Delete";
                    break;
                }

            // Display message box with
            // name of selected menu item.
            wsprintf (buffer, "%s command selected.", (LPSTR)npch);
            MessageBox (hwnd, buffer, achAppName, MB_OK);

            // If user selected File.Exit,
            // simulate {-}.Close menu selection.
            if (wParam == 6)
                {
                SendMessage (hwnd, WM_SYSCOMMAND, SC_CLOSE, 0L);
                }
            }
            break;

        case WM_DESTROY:
            PostQuitMessage(0);   // Handle application shutdown.
            break;

        default:
            return(DefWindowProc(hwnd,mMsg,wParam,lParam));
            break;
        }
    return 0L;
    }
```

ACCEL.DEF

```
NAME     ACCEL

EXETYPE WINDOWS

DESCRIPTION 'Accelerators (c) 1992 By Paul Yao'

CODE     MOVEABLE PRELOAD
DATA     MOVEABLE MULTIPLE PRELOAD

HEAPSIZE    512
STACKSIZE   5120

SEGMENTS
    ACCEL_TEXT MOVEABLE PRELOAD

EXPORTS
    AccelWndProc
```

ACCEL.H

```
/*-------------------------------------------------------------*\
|  Accel.h  - Include file for Accel.c.                       |
\*-------------------------------------------------------------*/

#define IDM_FILE_NEW      101
#define IDM_FILE_OPEN     102
#define IDM_FILE_SAVE     103
#define IDM_FILE_SAVEAS   104
#define IDM_FILE_PRINT    105
#define IDM_FILE_EXIT     106

#define IDM_EDIT_UNDO     201
#define IDM_EDIT_CUT      202
#define IDM_EDIT_COPY     203
#define IDM_EDIT_PASTE    204
#define IDM_EDIT_CLEAR    205
#define IDM_EDIT_DELETE   206
```

ACCEL.LNK

```
Accel.obj
Accel.exe/align:16/map/nod/noe/CO
nul
mlibcew libw
Accel.def
```

ACCEL.MAK

```
# Directory search paths.

INCDIR = \WINDEV\INCLUDE

# Windows version to support
# Valid pairs include:
#     (0x0300, 30)
#     (0x0310, 31)

CLVER = WINVER=0x0300
RCVER = 30

# Compiler switches for applications.

CL_APP_SHIP_ALL = -AM -c -D$(CLVER) -Gsw -I$(INCDIR) -Ow -W3 -Zp
CL_APP_DEBG_ALL = -AM -c -D$(CLVER) -Gsw -I$(INCDIR) -Od -W3 -Zpi

CL_APP_SHIP_31  = -AM -c -G2s  -I$(INCDIR) -Ow -W3 -Zp
CL_APP_DEBG_31  = -AM -c -G2s  -I$(INCDIR) -Od -W3 -Zpi

# Compiler switches for DLLs.

CL_DLL_SHIP_ALL = -AMw -c -D$(CLVER) -Gsw -I$(INCDIR) -Ow -W3 -Zp
CL_DLL_DEBG_ALL = -AMw -c -D$(CLVER) -Gsw -I$(INCDIR) -Od -W3 -Zpi

CL_DLL_SHIP_31  = -AMw -c -G2s  -I$(INCDIR) -Ow -W3 -Zp
CL_DLL_DEBG_31  = -AMw -c -G2s  -I$(INCDIR) -Od -W3 -Zpi

# Make file primary target.

all: Accel.exe

# Make file dependency targets.

Accel.res: Accel.rc Accel.cur Accel.ico
    rc -r -i$(INCDIR) Accel.rc

Accel.obj: Accel.c Accel.h
    cl $(CL_APP_SHIP_ALL) Accel.c

Accel.exe: Accel.obj Accel.def Accel.res
    link @Accel.lnk
    rc -$(RCVER) Accel.res

Accel.exe: Accel.res
    rc -$(RCVER) Accel.res
```

ACCEL.RC

```
#include <Windows.h>
#include "Accel.h"

snapshot icon Accel.ico

hand   cursor Accel.cur

1 MENU
    {
    POPUP "&File"
        {
        MENUITEM "&New",          IDM_FILE_NEW
        MENUITEM "&Open...",      IDM_FILE_OPEN
        MENUITEM "&Save",         IDM_FILE_SAVE
        MENUITEM "Save &As...",   IDM_FILE_SAVEAS
        MENUITEM SEPARATOR
        MENUITEM "&Print",        IDM_FILE_PRINT
        MENUITEM SEPARATOR
        MENUITEM "E&xit",         IDM_FILE_EXIT
        }
    POPUP "&Edit"
        {
        MENUITEM "&Undo\tCtrl+Z",   IDM_EDIT_UNDO
        MENUITEM SEPARATOR
        MENUITEM "Cu&t\tCtrl+X",    IDM_EDIT_CUT
        MENUITEM "&Copy\tCtrl+C",   IDM_EDIT_COPY
        MENUITEM "&Paste\tCtrl+V",  IDM_EDIT_PASTE
        MENUITEM SEPARATOR
        MENUITEM "Cl&ear",          IDM_EDIT_CLEAR
        MENUITEM "&Delete",         IDM_EDIT_DELETE
        }
    }


1 ACCELERATORS
    {
    ;  New Windows 3.1 clipboard accelerators.
    "Z",       IDM_EDIT_UNDO,   VIRTKEY, CONTROL
    "X",       IDM_EDIT_CUT,    VIRTKEY, CONTROL
    "C",       IDM_EDIT_COPY,   VIRTKEY, CONTROL
    "V",       IDM_EDIT_PASTE,  VIRTKEY, CONTROL

    ;  Maintain support for older clipboard accelerators.
    VK_BACK,   IDM_EDIT_UNDO,   VIRTKEY, ALT
    VK_DELETE, IDM_EDIT_CUT,    VIRTKEY, SHIFT
    VK_INSERT, IDM_EDIT_COPY,   VIRTKEY, CONTROL
    VK_INSERT, IDM_EDIT_PASTE,  VIRTKEY, SHIFT
    }
```

All of the accelerator processing in our code is done in the `WinMain` function, which loads the accelerator table into memory. It contains a modified message loop that scans for accelerator key combinations and diverts the flow of messages as appropriate.

Instead of using numeric constants in our resource file, we have defined a set of symbolic constants in an include file, ACCEL.H. This allows you to use a more meaningful value, like `IDM_FILE_NEW`, instead of "magic numbers" that don't explain their function. With the set of values defined in the include file, both the resource file and our C source files can access this file with the familiar include statement:

```
#include "Accel.H"
```

Windows gives you a comprehensive set of menu creation and management routines and lets you create accelerator keystrokes to define keyboard commands. It communicates via messages each action taken by the user with menus. The menu system is robust, fast, and flexible. You can create static menu templates, build menus on the fly, or change any part of an existing menu.

In the next chapter, we will see how we can get a little more sparkle out of our menus by adding graphics, and we will explore three techniques that allow us to use GDI drawing routines to change the appearance of menu items: owner draw menu items, bitmaps in menus, and custom check marks.

12

Enhancing Menus with Graphics

Windows uses the System Font, a bold, Helvetica-like proportionally spaced font, to draw the text inside menus. This default font was chosen because it is easy to read and has a slick, modern look. However, there may be times when you'd like to use another font inside a menu, or to create a menu that contains geometric figures or graphic images. On these occasions, Windows lets you hook into its menu creation mechanism so that you can enhance the look of your menus with graphical objects. In this chapter, we will examine the three methods that are available to you: owner-draw menu items, bitmaps in menus, and custom check marks.

Owner-Draw Menu Items

All of the menus that we've created thus far have used a text label drawn with the system font. For most applications, this is a reasonable approach. However, for those times when you want to replace the text with a graphic object, or change the font, the **Owner-draw** menu items give you the ability to create graphical menu images using GDI drawing calls. Instead of just *telling* users what a menu item will produce, you can *show* them. A drawing program might use this capability to show the user the different lines, shapes, and fonts that are available. A flowchart program might put different flowchart elements into menus to provide instant feedback concerning available flowchart elements.

Because the resource compiler does not provide any support for owner-draw menu items, you have to dynamically create the menu items by calling one of the menu modification routines we discussed in the last chapter. If you want an owner-draw menu item to appear in your menu the first time your window appears, you'll probably want to add the menu item in response to the `WM_CREATE` message.

After an owner-draw menu item has been inserted into a menu, two messages will be sent to the window procedure to measure and draw the menu item: `WM_MEASUREITEM` and `WM_DRAWITEM`. The `WM_MEASUREITEM` message arrives before the menu item is ever drawn. Your program must respond to this message by filling in a data structure that describes the width and height of your menu item in pixels. The second message, `WM_DRAWITEM`, is sent whenever drawing is needed for the menu item—when a menu is displayed and when the menu item is highlighted to provide the user with visual feedback while menu items are browsed.

These two messages are also sent for the other types of owner-draw objects: buttons, comboboxes, and listboxes. As you'll see, there are elements of the owner-draw mechanism, intended for use with the other owner-draw objects, that can be safely ignored when dealing with owner-draw menu items. As we look at each part of this mechanism, we'll be sure to identify these elements for you.

The WM_MEASUREITEM Message

An owner-draw item can be as small or as large as you would like to make it. The `WM_MEASUREITEM` message provides a way for you to let the menu system know the exact size needed to draw the menu item. Although the units are in pixels, you will use GDI routines to draw; therefore, you can use GDI's coordinate mapping system, described in more detail in Chapter 20.

When calculating the size of the area needed in an owner-draw menu item, you should consider space for a margin around the menu item. For one thing, you'll want to allow enough space between your menu item and other menu items. It's also a good idea to reserve space for a check mark on the left side of your menu. You can call the `GetMenuCheckMarkDimensions` routine for information about the default width and height of a check mark. Even if you don't use a check mark for your owner-draw menu item, you'll still want to do this. The width of a check mark defines the left and right margins of a menu item; using this value will help give your owner-draw menu items a consistent look with normal menu items.

To accommodate the higher resolution of devices that we may see some day, it's a good idea to avoid hard-coding any specific sizes for owner-draw menu items. Instead, you should make your drawing relative to the size of system objects, because they are automatically scaled for different device resolutions. Icons are a type of system object that can serve as a good reference point for owner-draw menu items. Icon dimensions are determined by the system display device driver. To determine the dimensions of an icon, call `GetSystemMetrics`. If you want to make your menu items the same size as an icon, here's how to do it:

```
DWORD dwCheckMark;
int cxWidth, cyHeight;

cxWidth  = GetSystemMetrics (SM_CXICON); // Width.
cyHeight = GetSystemMetrics (SM_CYICON); // Height.
```

```
// Adjust for check mark.          •
dwCheckMark = GetMenuCheckMarkDimensions ();
cxWidth += LOWORD (dwCheckMark);
cyHeight = max (HIWORD (dwCheckMark), cyHeight);
```

We add a value for the width of the check mark, and we also update `cyHeight` to make sure that it can accommodate the height of a check mark.

As an alternative, you can base the size of your owner-draw items on the metrics of the system font. When we discuss dialog boxes in Chapter 14, you'll see that the dialog box manager uses this approach to provide device-independent **dialog box coordinates**. To calculate the dimensions of an owner-draw menu item that is twice as tall as the system font, with a width equal to that of 15 characters, you can say:

```
DWORD dwCheckMark;
HDC hdc
int cxWidth, cyHeight;
TEXTMETRIC tm;

hdc = GetDC (hwnd);
GetTextMetrics (hdc, &tm);
ReleaseDC (hwnd, hdc);

cxWidth  = tm.tmMaxCharWidth * 15;
cyHeight = tm.tmHeight * 2;

// Adjust for check mark.
dwCheckMark = GetMenuCheckMarkDimensions ();
 cxWidth +=       LOWORD (dwCheckMark);
 cyHeight = max (HIWORD (dwCheckMark), cyHeight);
```

The `GetTextMetrics` routine (discussed in Chapter 10) gets the metrics of the font that is currently installed in a DC. In the absence of special window class styles (discussed in Chapter 13), `GetDC` returns a DC with the a system font installed. As in the earlier example, this code includes the dimensions of a menu check mark in the overall dimensions of the owner-draw item.

Whichever method you choose, one `WM_MEASUREITEM` message is sent for each owner-draw menu item. When it arrives, the `lParam` parameter contains a long pointer to a structure of type `MEASUREITEMSTRUCT`. This structure is defined in Windows.h as

```
typedef struct tagMEASUREITEMSTRUCT
     {
     WORD    CtlType;    // ODT_MENU
     WORD    CtlID;      // Ignore for menus.
     WORD    itemID;
     WORD    itemWidth;  // Return width.
     WORD    itemHeight; // Return height.
     DWORD   itemData;
     } MEASUREITEMSTRUCT;
```

When you get a WM_MEASUREITEM message, the two fields that you use to return the width and height of your owner-draw item are itemWidth and itemHeight. The other fields in this data structure help you identify a specific owner-draw item, since you will have one WM_MEASUREITEM message for each owner-draw menu item. When working with owner-draw menu items, one of these fields can be ignored since it's only used for owner-draw dialog box controls: CtlID.

The CtlType field describes the type of owner-draw item. It is set to ODT_MENU for menus. The presence of this field means a single body of code can support owner-draw objects in menus, listboxes, or comboboxes.

itemID is the command result code for a menu item. It is the value that gets sent in the wParam parameter of a WM_COMMAND message. As we'll see in a moment, this value is set when a menu item is created.

The itemData field provides another way to identify an owner-draw menu item. It is a 32-bit field that you create and provide when you create an owner-draw menu item. When you create an owner-draw popup menu (as opposed to a regular command menu item), this field provides the only way to distinguish one owner-draw popup menu from another, since popup menu items do not have a command result code.

If you create an owner-draw menu item by calling AppendMenu like this:

```
AppendMenu (hmenu, MF_OWNERDRAW, 38, (LPSTR)200);
```

it creates a menu item with an itemID of 38 and an itemData value of 200. The last parameter is cast as an LPSTR because that is how this routine is prototyped. Otherwise, the compiler issues an unnecessary warning message. If the variables cxWidth and cyHeight contained the desired dimensions of this menu item, we could respond to the WM_MEASUREITEM message like this:

```
case WM_MEASUREITEM:
    {
    LPMEASUREITEMSTRUCT lpmi;

    lpmi = (LPMEASUREITEMSTRUCT)lParam;

    if (lpmi-> itemID == 38)
        {
        lpmi-> itemWidth  = cxWidth;
        lpmi-> itemHeight = cyHeight;
        }
    }
```

Another approach involves checking itemData for the specific owner-draw menu item:

```
case WM_MEASUREITEM:
    {
    LPMEASUREITEMSTRUCT lpmi;

    lpmi = (LPMEASUREITEMSTRUCT)lParam;
```

```
if (lpmi->itemData == 200)
    {
    lpmi->itemWidth  = cxWidth;
    lpmi->itemHeight = cyHeight;
    }
}
```

A program receives a single WM_MEASUREITEM message for each owner-draw menu item. After that, the menu system remembers the dimensions of the menu item and sends a WM_DRAWITEM message whenever it needs a menu item to be drawn.

The WM_DRAWITEM Message

A WM_DRAWITEM message is sent to your window procedure when a popup menu that contains an owner-draw menu item is opened. Then, as the user browses through a menu, this message is sent to toggle menu highlighting. As you'll see in a moment, the WM_DRAWITEM message provides flags indicating the effect that the menu system requires.

When the WM_DRAWITEM message is sent, the window procedure's lParam parameter contains a long pointer to a structure of type DRAWITEMSTRUCT, defined in Windows.h as follows:

```
typedef struct tagDRAWITEMSTRUCT
    {
    WORD    CtlType;     // ODT_MENU.
    WORD    CtlID;       // Ignore for menus.
    WORD    itemID;
    WORD    itemAction;  // Ignore for menus.
    WORD    itemState;   // Selected,grayed,checked.
    HWND    hwndItem;    // Handle to popup menu.
    HDC     hDC;
    RECT    rcItem;      // Bounding rectangle.
    DWORD   itemData;
    } DRAWITEMSTRUCT;
```

Four of the items in this data structure, CtlType, CtlID, itemID, and itemData, are identical to items in the data structure that are sent with the WM_MEASUREITEM message. The CtlType field describes the type of owner-draw item, and is set to ODT_MENU for menus. The CtlID field can be ignored for owner-draw menu items, since it is only used for owner-draw dialog box controls. itemID is the command result code for a menu item, which is the value sent to a window procedure in the wParam parameter of a WM_COMMAND message. The itemData field provides another way to identify an owner-draw menu item and is the only way to distinguish one owner-draw popup menu from another.

The itemAction field describes the action the menu system wants you to perform. However, since menu items are drawn to reflect the menu item state, you can usually ignore this field and determine the menu state from the next field.

The `itemState` field defines the current state of the menu item, as shown in the following list:

Value	Menu Item State
ODS_CHECKED	Check mark is to appear in the menu.
ODS_DISABLED	Menu to be drawn disabled.
ODS_FOCUS	Ignore—not used for menus.
ODS_GRAYED	Menu to be drawn grayed.
ODS_SELECTED	Menu to be drawn selected.

The most important flag is `ODS_SELECTED`. When this bit is set, it indicates that the menu item needs to be highlighted. A highlighted menu item is drawn in a different color from a regular menu item to provide visual feedback while the user is browsing a menu. You should draw highlighted menu items using two system colors that are defined for this purpose. To obtain the RGB values of the required system colors, call the `GetSysColor` routine. Here are the color indices that you should use for menu highlights:

Value	Description
COLOR_HIGHLIGHT	Background color of the highlighted object.
COLOR_HIGHLIGHTTEXT	Foreground color of the highlighted object.

If you plan to set the state of an owner-draw menu item to checked, or if you plan to gray the menu item, your response to the `WM_DRAWITEM` message must provide for this. You will need to test the value in the `itemState` field and change the way you draw your menu item according to the desired effect. For example, you might use a shade of gray in your drawing to indicate a grayed menu item. You can draw a check mark using a bitmap that is built into the display driver. Here is one way to obtain a handle to that bitmap, and draw with it:

```
hbm = LoadBitmap (NULL,MAKEINTRESOURCE(OBM_CHECK));
hdcBitmap = CreateCompatibleDC (hDC);
hbmOld = SelectObject (hdcBitmap, hbm);

dwDimensions = GetMenuCheckMarkDimensions();
cxWidth  = LOWORD(dwDimensions);
cyHeight = HIWORD(dwDimensions);

BitBlt (ps.hdc, 0, 0, cxWidth, cyHeight,
        hdcBitmap, 0, 0, SRCCOPY);

SelectObject (hdcBitmap, hbmOld);
DeleteDC (hdcBitmap);
```

In spite of its name, the `hwndItem` field is not a window handle but a popup menu handle for the menu that contains the owner-draw item. Its name comes from its use with owner-draw dialog box controls, when it does contain a window handle. When a program receives a `WM_DRAWITEM` message, it might use the popup menu handle to call a menu query routine to find out, for example, the number of items in the current menu or the state of other menu items.

The `hDC` field is a handle to a device context for drawing in the menu. Be sure to restore the DC to its initial state when you are done; otherwise, you risk causing problems for the menu system when it draws other parts of your menu.

The `rcItem` field defines a rectangle within which you can draw your menu item. You should not go beyond this rectangle, since doing so risks overwriting other menu items.

The owner-draw items supported by these messages and data structures give a program a remarkable amount of flexibility in deciding how a menu item should appear. Let's look at a sample program that shows how to put these messages and data structures to work for you.

A Sample Program: OWNDRAW

Our sample program, **OWNDRAW**, shows how owner-draw menu items can be used to display different fonts in a menu. The menu from OWNDRAW is shown in Figure 12.1. Not only is the user provided with the *name* of the font, but also with the *image* of the font itself. This would be a useful technique in any program that lets the user select a font. If you do this, keep in mind the fact that only display fonts can be used to draw in menus. Therefore, if you wish to show a user the available printer fonts, you would be limited in some cases to the name of the font. Of course, with TrueType fonts, the differences between display and printer fonts is going to be substantially reduced.

Here is the source listing of OWNDRAW. To write this program, we used the STANMENU program as a base and added the items needed for our owner-draw items.

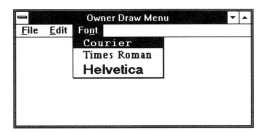

Figure 12.1 An Owner-Draw Menu showing three fonts

OWNDRAW.C

```
/*-------------------------------------------------------------*\
 |  Owndraw.C  -  A sample owner-draw menu.                    |
\*-------------------------------------------------------------*/
#define STRICT
#include <Windows.H>
#include <memory.h>
#include "OwnDraw.H"


/*-------------------------------------------------------------*\
 |                   Function Prototypes.                      |
\*-------------------------------------------------------------*/
LRESULT CALLBACK OwnDrawWndProc (HWND, UINT, WPARAM, LPARAM);


/*-------------------------------------------------------------*\
 |                   Global Variables.                        |
\*-------------------------------------------------------------*/
char achWndClass[] = "OwnDraw:MAIN";
char achAppName[]  = "Owner Draw Menu";
HFONT hfontTmsRmn;
HFONT hfontHelv;
HFONT hfontCour;


/*-------------------------------------------------------------*\
 |                 Main Function:  WinMain.                    |
\*-------------------------------------------------------------*/
int PASCAL
WinMain (HINSTANCE hInstance,        // Who am I?
         HINSTANCE hPrevInstance,    // Any older siblings?
         LPSTR     lpszCmdLine,      // Ptr to command line.
         int       cmdShow)          // How to open my window?
    {
    HACCEL    hAccel;
    HWND      hwnd;
    MSG       msg;
    WNDCLASS wndclass;

    if (!hPrevInstance)
        {
        wndclass.lpszClassName = achWndClass;
        wndclass.hInstance     = hInstance;
        wndclass.lpfnWndProc   = OwnDrawWndProc;
        wndclass.hCursor       = LoadCursor (hInstance, "hand");
        wndclass.hIcon         = LoadIcon (hInstance,"snapshot");
        wndclass.lpszMenuName  = "#1";
        wndclass.hbrBackground = (HBRUSH)(COLOR_WINDOW+1);
        wndclass.style         = NULL;
        wndclass.cbClsExtra    = 0;
        wndclass.cbWndExtra    = 0;

        RegisterClass( &wndclass);
        }
```

```
    hwnd = CreateWindowEx(0L,                    // Extra style.
                    achWndClass,                 // Class name.
                    achAppName,                  // Title.
                    WS_OVERLAPPEDWINDOW,         // Style bits.
                    CW_USEDEFAULT,               // x - default.
                    0,                           // y - default.
                    CW_USEDEFAULT,               // cx - default.
                    0,                           // cy - default.
                    NULL,                        // No parent.
                    NULL,                        // Class menu.
                    hInstance,                   // Creator.
                    NULL);                       // Params.
    ShowWindow (hwnd, cmdShow);

    hAccel = LoadAccelerators (hInstance, "#1");

    while (GetMessage(&msg, 0, 0, 0))
        {
        if (!TranslateAccelerator (hwnd, hAccel, &msg))
            {
            TranslateMessage(&msg); // Convert KEYDOWNs to CHARs
            DispatchMessage(&msg);  // Transmit message to WndProc
            }
        }

    return 0;
    }

/*-------------------------------------------------------------*\
|              Window Procedure:  OwnDrawWndProc.               |
\*-------------------------------------------------------------*/
LRESULT CALLBACK
OwnDrawWndProc (HWND   hwnd,      // For whom is message sent?
                UINT   mMsg,      // What is exact message?
                WPARAM wParam,    // ...message details.
                LPARAM lParam)    // ...message details.
    {
    static COLORREF crHighlight;
    static COLORREF crHighlightText;

    switch (mMsg)
        {
        case WM_COMMAND:
            {
            char buffer[80];
            char *npch;

            switch (wParam)
                {
                case IDM_FILE_NEW:
                    npch = "File.New";
                    break;
                case IDM_FILE_OPEN:
                    npch = "File.Open...";
                    break;
```

```
              case IDM_FILE_SAVE:
                  npch = "File.Save";
                  break;
              case IDM_FILE_SAVEAS:
                  npch = "File.Save As...";
                  break;
              case IDM_FILE_PRINT:
                  npch = "File.Print";
                  break;
              case IDM_FILE_EXIT:
                  npch = "File.Exit";
                  break;
              case IDM_EDIT_UNDO:
                  npch = "Edit.Undo";
                  break;
              case IDM_EDIT_CUT:
                  npch = "Edit.Cut";
                  break;
              case IDM_EDIT_COPY:
                  npch = "Edit.Copy";
                  break;
              case IDM_EDIT_PASTE:
                  npch = "Edit.Paste";
                  break;
              case IDM_EDIT_CLEAR:
                  npch = "Edit.Clear";
                  break;
              case IDM_EDIT_DELETE:
                  npch = "Edit.Delete";
                  break;
              case IDM_FONT_TMSRMN:
                  npch = "Font.Tms Rmn";
                  break;
              case IDM_FONT_HELV:
                  npch = "Font.Helv";
                  break;
              case IDM_FONT_COURIER:
                  npch = "Font.Courier";
                  break;
              }

      // Display message box with
      // name of selected menu item.
      wsprintf (buffer, "%s command selected.", (LPSTR)npch);
      MessageBox (hwnd, buffer, achAppName, MB_OK);

      // If user selected File.Exit,
      // simulate {-}.Close menu selection.
      if (wParam == 6)
          {
          SendMessage (hwnd, WM_SYSCOMMAND, SC_CLOSE, 0L);
          }
      }
      break;
```

```
case WM_CREATE:
    {
    HDC     hdc;
    HMENU   hmenu;
    HMENU   hmenuPopup;
    LOGFONT lf;
    TEXTMETRIC tm;

    /*  Create a menu with three owner-draw items    */
    /*  for the three fonts were going to create.    */

    hmenu = GetMenu (hwnd);
    hmenuPopup = CreatePopupMenu();
    AppendMenu (hmenu, MF_POPUP, (UINT)hmenuPopup, "Fo&nt");

    AppendMenu (hmenuPopup,
                MF_OWNERDRAW,
                IDM_FONT_COURIER,
                MAKEINTRESOURCE(IDM_FONT_COURIER));
    AppendMenu (hmenuPopup,
                MF_OWNERDRAW,
                IDM_FONT_TMSRMN,
                MAKEINTRESOURCE(IDM_FONT_TMSRMN));
    AppendMenu (hmenuPopup,
                MF_OWNERDRAW,
                IDM_FONT_HELV,
                MAKEINTRESOURCE(IDM_FONT_HELV));

    memset (&lf, 0, sizeof (LOGFONT));

    hdc = GetDC (hwnd);
    GetTextMetrics (hdc, &tm);
    ReleaseDC (hwnd, hdc);

    /*  Create three logical fonts, with different    */
    /*  sizes and styles.                             */

    lf.lfWeight = 700;              /*  Bold.         */

    lstrcpy (lf.lfFaceName, "Courier");
    lf.lfHeight = tm.tmHeight;      /*  Sysfont height. */
    hfontCour = CreateFontIndirect (&lf);

    lstrcpy (lf.lfFaceName, "Tms Rmn");
    lf.lfHeight = tm.tmHeight + tm.tmHeight/4; /* 125% */
    hfontTmsRmn = CreateFontIndirect (&lf);

    lstrcpy (lf.lfFaceName, "Helv");
    lf.lfHeight = tm.tmHeight + tm.tmHeight/2; /* 150% */
    hfontHelv = CreateFontIndirect (&lf);

    /*  Get system colors for our owner draw items.   */
    crHighlight = GetSysColor (COLOR_HIGHLIGHT);
    crHighlightText = GetSysColor (COLOR_HIGHLIGHTTEXT);
```

```
            }
        break;

    case WM_DESTROY:
        DeleteObject (hfontTmsRmn);
        DeleteObject (hfontHelv);
        DeleteObject (hfontCour);
        PostQuitMessage(0);   // Handle application shutdown.
        break;

    case WM_DRAWITEM:
        {
        char buff[80];
        COLORREF crFore;
        COLORREF crBack;
        DWORD dwCheckMark;
        HFONT hfontOld;
        HFONT hfont;
        int fSwapColors;
        int xText,yText;
        int cxCheck;
        LPDRAWITEMSTRUCT lpdi;

        lpdi = (LPDRAWITEMSTRUCT)lParam;

        switch (lpdi->itemID)
            {
            case IDM_FONT_COURIER:
                lstrcpy (buff, "Courier");
                hfont = hfontCour;
                break;
            case IDM_FONT_TMSRMN:
                lstrcpy (buff, "Tms Rmn");
                hfont = hfontTmsRmn;
                break;
            case IDM_FONT_HELV:
                lstrcpy (buff, "Helv");
                hfont = hfontHelv;
                break;
            }
        hfontOld = SelectObject (lpdi->hDC, hfont);

        /*   If current menu item should be highlighted,    */
        /*   install the correct system colors.             */

        if (lpdi->itemState & ODS_SELECTED)
            {
            crFore = SetTextColor (lpdi->hDC,
                                    crHighlightText);
            crBack = SetBkColor (lpdi->hDC,
                                    crHighlight);
            fSwapColors= TRUE;
            }
```

```
    else
        fSwapColors= FALSE;

    /*  Get width of checkmark.                        */
    dwCheckMark = GetMenuCheckMarkDimensions();
    cxCheck = LOWORD (dwCheckMark);

    xText = lpdi->rcItem.left + cxCheck;
    yText = lpdi->rcItem.top;


    /*  Display line of text.                          */
    ExtTextOut (lpdi->hDC, xText, yText,
                ETO_OPAQUE,
                &lpdi->rcItem,
                buff,
                lstrlen(buff),
                NULL);

    /*  Restore DC before we send it home.            */

    SelectObject (lpdi->hDC, hfontOld);    /*  Font.   */
    if (fSwapColors)
        {
        SetTextColor (lpdi->hDC, crFore);  /*  Colors. */
        SetBkColor (lpdi->hDC, crBack);
        }
    }
    break;

case WM_MEASUREITEM:
    {
    char buff[80];
    DWORD dwSize;
    DWORD dwCheckMark;
    HDC hdc;
    HFONT hfont;
    int cxWidth, cyHeight;
    int cxCheck, cyCheck;
    LPMEASUREITEMSTRUCT lpmi;

    lpmi = (LPMEASUREITEMSTRUCT)lParam;
    switch (lpmi->itemID)
        {
        case IDM_FONT_COURIER:
            lstrcpy (buff, "Courier");
            hfont = hfontCour;
            break;
        case IDM_FONT_TMSRMN:
            lstrcpy (buff, "Times Roman");
            hfont = hfontTmsRmn;
            break;
```

```
            case IDM_FONT_HELV:
                lstrcpy (buff, "Helvetica");
                hfont = hfontHelv;
                break;
            }

        /*  Find size of string.                      */
        hdc = GetDC (hwnd);
        SelectObject (hdc, hfont);
        dwSize = GetTextExtent (hdc, buff, lstrlen(buff));
        ReleaseDC (hwnd, hdc);

        /*  Start with string size information.        */
        cxWidth  = LOWORD(dwSize);
        cyHeight = HIWORD(dwSize);

        /*  Add in check mark size information.        */
        dwCheckMark = GetMenuCheckMarkDimensions();
        cxCheck = LOWORD (dwCheckMark);
        cyCheck = HIWORD (dwCheckMark);

        lpmi->itemWidth  = cxWidth + cxCheck;
        lpmi->itemHeight = max (cyHeight, cyCheck);
        }
        break;

    default:
        return(DefWindowProc(hwnd,mMsg,wParam,lParam));
        break;
    }
return 0L;
}
```

OWNDRAW.DEF

```
NAME      OWNDRAW

EXETYPE WINDOWS

DESCRIPTION 'Owner-Draw Menu (c) 1992 By Paul Yao'

CODE      MOVEABLE PRELOAD
DATA      MOVEABLE MULTIPLE PRELOAD

HEAPSIZE      512
STACKSIZE     5120

SEGMENTS
    OWNDRAW_TEXT MOVEABLE PRELOAD

EXPORTS
    OwnDrawWndProc
```

OWNDRAW.H

```
/*------------------------------------------------------------*\
|  OwnDraw.h  - Include file for OwnDraw.c.                   |
\*------------------------------------------------------------*/

#define IDM_FILE_NEW      101
#define IDM_FILE_OPEN     102
#define IDM_FILE_SAVE     103
#define IDM_FILE_SAVEAS   104
#define IDM_FILE_PRINT    105
#define IDM_FILE_EXIT     106

#define IDM_EDIT_UNDO     201
#define IDM_EDIT_CUT      202
#define IDM_EDIT_COPY     203
#define IDM_EDIT_PASTE    204
#define IDM_EDIT_CLEAR    205
#define IDM_EDIT_DELETE   206

#define IDM_FONT_TMSRMN   301
#define IDM_FONT_HELV     302
#define IDM_FONT_COURIER  303
```

OWNDRAW.LNK

```
OwnDraw.obj
OwnDraw.exe/align:16/map/nod/noe/CO
nul
mlibcew libw
OwnDraw.def
```

OWNDRAW.MAK

```
# Directory search paths.

INCDIR = \WINDEV\INCLUDE

# Windows version to support
# Valid pairs include:
#     (0x0300, 30)
#     (0x0310, 31)

CLVER = WINVER=0x0300
RCVER = 30
```

```
# Compiler switches for applications.

CL_APP_SHIP_ALL = -AM -c -D$(CLVER) -Gsw -I$(INCDIR) -Ow -W3 -Zp
CL_APP_DEBG_ALL = -AM -c -D$(CLVER) -Gsw -I$(INCDIR) -Od -W3 -Zpi

CL_APP_SHIP_31  = -AM -c -G2s  -I$(INCDIR) -Ow -W3 -Zp
CL_APP_DEBG_31  = -AM -c -G2s  -I$(INCDIR) -Od -W3 -Zpi

# Compiler switches for DLLs.

CL_DLL_SHIP_ALL = -AMw -c -D$(CLVER) -Gsw -I$(INCDIR) -Ow -W3 -Zp
CL_DLL_DEBG_ALL = -AMw -c -D$(CLVER) -Gsw -I$(INCDIR) -Od -W3 -Zpi

CL_DLL_SHIP_31  = -AMw -c -G2s  -I$(INCDIR) -Ow -W3 -Zp
CL_DLL_DEBG_31  = -AMw -c -G2s  -I$(INCDIR) -Od -W3 -Zpi

# Make file primary target.

all: OwnDraw.exe

# Make file dependency targets.

OwnDraw.res: OwnDraw.rc OwnDraw.cur OwnDraw.ico
    rc -r -i$(INCDIR) OwnDraw.rc

OwnDraw.obj: OwnDraw.c OwnDraw.h
    cl $(CL_APP_SHIP_ALL) OwnDraw.c

OwnDraw.exe: OwnDraw.obj OwnDraw.def OwnDraw.res
    link @OwnDraw.lnk
    rc -$(RCVER) OwnDraw.res

OwnDraw.exe: OwnDraw.res
    rc -$(RCVER) OwnDraw.res
```

OWNDRAW.RC

```
#include <Windows.h>
#include "OwnDraw.h"

snapshot icon OwnDraw.ico

hand  cursor OwnDraw.cur

1 MENU
    {
    POPUP "&File"
        {
        MENUITEM "&New",        IDM_FILE_NEW
        MENUITEM "&Open...",    IDM_FILE_OPEN
        MENUITEM "&Save",       IDM_FILE_SAVE
```

```
            MENUITEM "Save &As...",    IDM_FILE_SAVEAS
            MENUITEM SEPARATOR
            MENUITEM "&Print",         IDM_FILE_PRINT
            MENUITEM SEPARATOR
            MENUITEM "E&xit",          IDM_FILE_EXIT
            }
    POPUP "&Edit"
        {
        MENUITEM "&Undo\tCtrl+Z",    IDM_EDIT_UNDO
        MENUITEM SEPARATOR
        MENUITEM "Cu&t\tCtrl+X",     IDM_EDIT_CUT
        MENUITEM "&Copy\tCtrl+C",    IDM_EDIT_COPY
        MENUITEM "&Paste\tCtrl+V",   IDM_EDIT_PASTE
        MENUITEM SEPARATOR
        MENUITEM "Cl&ear",           IDM_EDIT_CLEAR
        MENUITEM "&Delete",          IDM_EDIT_DELETE
        }
    }


1 ACCELERATORS
    {
    ;  New Windows 3.1 clipboard accelerators.
    "Z",        IDM_EDIT_UNDO,    VIRTKEY, CONTROL
    "X",        IDM_EDIT_CUT,     VIRTKEY, CONTROL
    "C",        IDM_EDIT_COPY,    VIRTKEY, CONTROL
    "V",        IDM_EDIT_PASTE,   VIRTKEY, CONTROL

    ;  Maintain support for older clipboard accelerators.
    VK_BACK,    IDM_EDIT_UNDO,    VIRTKEY, ALT
    VK_DELETE,  IDM_EDIT_CUT,     VIRTKEY, SHIFT
    VK_INSERT,  IDM_EDIT_COPY,    VIRTKEY, CONTROL
    VK_INSERT,  IDM_EDIT_PASTE,   VIRTKEY, SHIFT
    }
```

In response to the WM_CREATE message, **OWNDRAW** creates three owner-draw menu items and three logical fonts. It also calls GetSysColor to determine the foreground and background colors to use in our menu. In response to the WM_MEASUREITEM message, GDI is called to calculate the dimensions of each string that will appear in the menu. The size of each item is adjusted to make sure there is room for a check mark, so that menu items have a reasonable left margin.

Once the measurement information has been provided, our window procedure starts to receive WM_DRAWITEM messages. Since we're not interested in grayed or disabled items, OWNDRAW doesn't check for these flags. We also don't check whether the item should display a check mark. If we wanted a check mark, we would have to draw it ourselves in response to the WM_DRAWITEM message. That is to say, if we are going to draw *part* of a menu item, we must draw the *entire* menu item.

Keyboard mnemonics are not supported in owner-draw menu items. In general, this makes sense, since a graphic image can hardly be expected to have an associated keyboard keystroke. However, the presence of text inside these owner-draw menu items creates the paradox that, even though our owner-draw items could certainly use a mnemonic keystroke as graphic objects, Windows does not provide mnemonic keystroke support for owner-draw items. If this is important to you, there is a way for an owner-draw menu item to simulate a mnemonic. Start by underlining the mnemonic letter in each of the font names. Then, in response to the WM_MENUCHAR message, check for the mnemonic letters and indicate either an error or a menu selection in the return value. The WM_MENUCHAR message is sent when the user strikes a keystroke that doesn't correspond to any mnemonic or accelerator key. When the default window procedure receives this message, it provides a return value that tells the menu system to beep at the user. But processing this message yourself would allow you to provide the necessary return value so that the menu system would handle the keystroke as a regular mnemonic.

The fonts that were created in response to the WM_CREATE message are, of course, GDI drawing objects that take up memory in GDI's local heap. Before OWNDRAW can exit, it must destroy these objects; otherwise, the memory occupied by them will be lost and unavailable for other programs to use. OWNDRAW makes several calls to DeleteObject in response to the WM_DESTROY message:

```
case WM_DESTROY:
     DeleteObject (hfontTmsRmn);
     DeleteObject (hfontHelv);
     DeleteObject (hfontCour);
     PostQuitMessage(0);
     break;
```

The use of owner-draw items gives a program the greatest control and flexibility in the appearance of menu items. From one moment to the next, a menu item may change in response to some outside event. But you may not need this much flexibility in the graphic images you put in a menu. You have a second choice, which in some respects is easier to implement than owner-draw menu items. It involves the creation of a GDI bitmap, which can be associated with a menu item and automatically displayed by the menu system without any intervention required on your part. Let's take a look at what is involved in putting bitmaps into menu items.

Bitmaps in Menus

In our introduction to GDI, (see Chapter 6) we discussed how bitmaps are useful for storing graphic images. Once a graphic image has been created in a bitmap, it can be incorporated into a menu as an alternative to the normally displayed text in menus. Bitmaps in menus provide a somewhat easier method than owner-draw menu items for getting graphic images into menus.

To take advantage of this capability, we need to start by describing how a Windows program goes about creating and using GDI bitmaps. The clearest way to understand what GDI expects is to examine a code fragment that shows how all the pieces are brought together. Here is one way to create a GDI bitmap that can be displayed in a menu:

```
HDC     hdcScreen;
HDC     hdcBitmap;
```

```
HBITMAP        hbm;
HBITMAP        hbmOld;

hdcScreen = GetDC (hwnd);
hdcBitmap = CreateCompatibleDC (hdcScreen);
hbm = CreateCompatibleBitmap (hdc, cxWidth, cyHeight);
ReleaseDC (hwnd, hdcScreen);

hbmOld = SelectObject (hdcBitmap, hbm);
```

Using a bitmap requires that two objects be created and connected together: a bitmap and a device context. Creating a bitmap requires us to specify the size of the rectangular display image that we wish to store. GDI responds by allocating the required memory. We need a device context because every GDI drawing routine takes a handle to a DC as its first parameter. Without this special "membership card," the bitmap won't be admitted to the private club to which all GDI devices belong. But *with* the DC, a bitmap becomes a full participant in all the drawing capabilities that GDI has to offer.

The quickest and easiest way to create a DC involves asking GDI to clone an existing DC, by calling `CreateCompatibleDC`. This routine takes a single parameter, a handle to an existing DC. Since our bitmap is going to be copied to the display screen, we pass a display DC obtained by calling `GetDC`. To create a bitmap that is compatible with the display screen, we call a related routine, **CreateCompatibleBitmap**. This routine also takes a DC handle as a parameter, along with a width and a height value for the size of the drawing surface to create.

The only thing missing is a way to connect the bitmap and the DC. The routine we use is a familiar one:

```
hbmOld = SelectObject (hdcBitmap, hbm);
```

You probably remember that we use this routine to install pens, brushes, and fonts into DCs. Here you see another use: connecting a bitmap to a device context. Once this connection has been made, we can use any GDI drawing routine to draw in our bitmap. For example, we could draw an ellipse in the bitmap with the following call:

```
Ellipse (hdcBitmap, x1, y1, x2, y2);
```

When you have finished drawing into the bitmap, place it into a menu by calling one of these routines: `AppendMenu`, `InsertMenu`, or `ModifyMenu`. Here is a call to `AppendMenu` that inserts the bitmap at the end of a popup menu, and gives the new menu item a command result code of 23:

```
HMENU hmenu;
HMENU hmenuPopup;

hmenu = GetMenu (hwnd);
hmenuPopup = GetSubMenu (hmenu, 1);
AppendMenu (hmenuPopup, MF_BITMAP, 23, MAKEINTRESOURCE(hbm));
```

Once the bitmap has been installed into the menu, our DC isn't needed anymore, so we destroy it. But first, we must remove the bitmap handle from the DC. When we installed the bitmap handle into our DC, `SelectObject` returned a value that we

**Figure 12.2 Menu containing bitmaps with
GDI brush images**

stored in hbmOld. This value represents a place-holder for a bitmap. Before we can
destroy the DC, we must first break the connection between the DC and the bitmap. This
is accomplished by another call to SelectObject:

```
SelectObject (hdcBitmap, hbmOld);
```

after which, we can destroy the DC with this call:

```
DeleteDC (hdcBitmap);
```

Figure 12.2 shows a menu that was created by attaching five bitmaps to five different
menu items. Each menu item represents a different brush that the user can select and use
to draw. This menu was created by our next sample program, BITMENU.

BITMENU.C

```
/*-------------------------------------------------------------*\
 | Bitmenu.C  -  Creation and placement of bitmaps in a menu.  |
 \*-------------------------------------------------------------*/
#include <Windows.H>
#include "BitMenu.H"

/*-------------------------------------------------------------*\
 |                      Function Prototypes.                    |
 \*-------------------------------------------------------------*/
LRESULT CALLBACK BitMenuWndProc (HWND, UINT, WPARAM, LPARAM);
VOID NEAR PASCAL BitmenuCreate (HWND);

/*-------------------------------------------------------------*\
 |                      Global Variables.                      |
 \*-------------------------------------------------------------*/
char achWndClass[] = "BitMenu:MAIN";
char achAppName[]  = "Bitmap Menu";
HBITMAP hbm[COUNT];
HBRUSH  hbr[COUNT];
```

```
/*-------------------------------------------------------------*\
|                   Main Function:  WinMain.                    |
\*-------------------------------------------------------------*/
int PASCAL
WinMain (HINSTANCE hInstance,      // Who am I?
         HINSTANCE hPrevInstance, // Any older siblings?
         LPSTR     lpszCmdLine,   // Ptr to command line.
         int       cmdShow)       // How to open my window?
    {
    HACCEL   hAccel;
    HWND     hwnd;
    MSG      msg;
    WNDCLASS wndclass;

    if (!hPrevInstance)
        {
        wndclass.lpszClassName = achWndClass;
        wndclass.hInstance     = hInstance;
        wndclass.lpfnWndProc   = BitMenuWndProc;
        wndclass.hCursor       = LoadCursor (hInstance, "hand");
        wndclass.hIcon         = LoadIcon (hInstance,"snapshot");
        wndclass.lpszMenuName  = "#1";
        wndclass.hbrBackground = (HBRUSH)(COLOR_WINDOW+1);
        wndclass.style         = NULL;
        wndclass.cbClsExtra    = 0;
        wndclass.cbWndExtra    = 0;

        RegisterClass( &wndclass);
        }

    hwnd = CreateWindowEx(0L,                 // Extra style.
                    achWndClass,              // Class name.
                    achAppName,               // Title.
                    WS_OVERLAPPEDWINDOW,      // Style bits.
                    CW_USEDEFAULT,            // x - default.
                    0,                        // y - default.
                    CW_USEDEFAULT,            // cx - default.
                    0,                        // cy - default.
                    NULL,                     // No parent.
                    NULL,                     // Class menu.
                    hInstance,                // Creator.
                    NULL);                    // Params.
    ShowWindow (hwnd, cmdShow);

    hAccel = LoadAccelerators (hInstance, "#1");

    while (GetMessage(&msg, 0, 0, 0))
        {
        if (!TranslateAccelerator (hwnd, hAccel, &msg))
            {
            TranslateMessage(&msg); // Convert KEYDOWNs to CHARs
            DispatchMessage(&msg);  // Transmit message to WndProc
            }
        }
```

```
        return 0;
        }


/*--------------------------------------------------------------*\
|               Window Procedure:  BitMenuWndProc.               |
\*--------------------------------------------------------------*/
LRESULT CALLBACK
BitMenuWndProc (HWND    hwnd,       // For whom is message sent?
                UINT    mMsg,       // What is exact message?
                WPARAM  wParam,     // ...message details.
                LPARAM  lParam)     // ...message details.
    {
    switch (mMsg)
        {
        case WM_COMMAND:
            {
            char buffer[80];
            char *npch;

            switch (wParam)
                {
                case IDM_FILE_NEW:
                    npch = "File.New";
                    break;
                case IDM_FILE_OPEN:
                    npch = "File.Open...";
                    break;
                case IDM_FILE_SAVE:
                    npch = "File.Save";
                    break;
                case IDM_FILE_SAVEAS:
                    npch = "File.Save As...";
                    break;
                case IDM_FILE_PRINT:
                    npch = "File.Print";
                    break;
                case IDM_FILE_EXIT:
                    npch = "File.Exit";
                    break;
                case IDM_EDIT_UNDO:
                    npch = "Edit.Undo";
                    break;
                case IDM_EDIT_CUT:
                    npch = "Edit.Cut";
                    break;
                case IDM_EDIT_COPY:
                    npch = "Edit.Copy";
                    break;
                case IDM_EDIT_PASTE:
                    npch = "Edit.Paste";
                    break;
                case IDM_EDIT_CLEAR:
                    npch = "Edit.Clear";
                    break;
```

```
        case IDM_EDIT_DELETE:
            npch = "Edit.Delete";
            break;
        case IDM_BRUSHES_FIRST:
            npch = "Brushes.First";
            break;
        case IDM_BRUSHES_SECOND:
            npch = "Brushes.Second";
            break;
        case IDM_BRUSHES_THIRD:
            npch = "Brushes.Third";
            break;
        case IDM_BRUSHES_FOURTH:
            npch = "Brushes.Fourth";
            break;
        case IDM_BRUSHES_FIFTH:
            npch = "Brushes.Fifth";
            break;
        default:
            npch = "Unknown";
        }

    // Display message box with
    // name of selected menu item.
    wsprintf (buffer, "%s command selected.", (LPSTR)npch);
    MessageBox (hwnd, buffer, achAppName, MB_OK);

    // If user selected File.Exit,
    // simulate {-}.Close menu selection.
    if (wParam == 6)
        {
        SendMessage (hwnd, WM_SYSCOMMAND, SC_CLOSE, 0L);
        }
    }
    break;

case WM_CREATE:
    BitmenuCreate(hwnd);
    break;

case WM_DESTROY:
    {
    int i;

    for (i=0;i<COUNT;i++)
        {
        DeleteObject (hbr[i]);
        DeleteObject (hbm[i]);
        }
    }
    PostQuitMessage(0);  // Handle application shutdown.
    break;

default:
    return(DefWindowProc(hwnd,mMsg,wParam,lParam));
```

```
                    break;
            }
        return 0L;
        }


/*-------------------------------------------------------------*\
|           BitMenuCreate:  Process WM_CREATE Messages.          |
\*-------------------------------------------------------------*/

VOID NEAR PASCAL BitMenuCreate(HWND hwnd)
    {
    COLORREF  crBackground;
    HBITMAP   hbmOld;
    HBRUSH    hbrBackground;
    HDC       hdcScreen;
    HDC       hdcBitmap;
    HMENU     hmenu;
    HMENU     hmenuPopup;
    int       i;
    int       cxWidth;
    int       cyHeight;
    int       cyOffset;

    /*  Calculate bitmap size information.                      */
    cxWidth  = GetSystemMetrics (SM_CXICON) * 3;
    cyHeight = GetSystemMetrics (SM_CYICON);
    cyOffset = cyHeight - cyHeight/5;

    /*  Create the background brush to initialize bitmaps.    */
    crBackground = GetSysColor (COLOR_MENU);
    hbrBackground = CreateSolidBrush (crBackground);

    /*  Create the needed GDI objects: DCs and bitmaps.      */
    hdcScreen = GetDC (hwnd);
    hdcBitmap = CreateCompatibleDC (hdcScreen);
    SelectObject (hdcBitmap, hbrBackground);

    for (i=0;i<COUNT;i++)
        {
        hbm[i] = CreateCompatibleBitmap (hdcScreen,
                                      cxWidth, cyHeight);
        if (i==0)
            hbmOld = SelectObject (hdcBitmap, hbm[0]);
        else
            SelectObject (hdcBitmap, hbm[i]);
        PatBlt (hdcBitmap, 0, 0, cxWidth, cyHeight, PATCOPY);
        }
    ReleaseDC (hwnd, hdcScreen);

    /*  Create an empty popup menu, and attach it to menu-bar. */
    hmenuPopup =CreatePopupMenu();
    hmenu = GetMenu (hwnd);
    AppendMenu (hmenu, MF_POPUP, (UINT)hmenuPopup, "&Brushes");
```

```
/*  Create the brushes we're going to use.                  */
hbr[0] = CreateHatchBrush (HS_DIAGCROSS , RGB(0, 0, 0));
hbr[1] = CreateSolidBrush (RGB (64, 64, 64));
hbr[2] = CreateHatchBrush (HS_CROSS , RGB(0, 0, 0));
hbr[3] = CreateSolidBrush (RGB (0, 0, 0));
hbr[4] = CreateHatchBrush (HS_VERTICAL , RGB(0, 0, 0));

/*  Put a brush into the DC, attach the DC to a bitmap,     */
/*  and then draw a rectangle into the bitmap.  Finally,    */
/*  create a new menu item using the bitmap.                */
for (i=0;i<COUNT;i++)
    {
    SelectObject (hdcBitmap, hbr[i]);
    SelectObject (hdcBitmap, hbm[i]);
    Rectangle (hdcBitmap,
               0,
               cyOffset,
               cxWidth,
               cyHeight-cyOffset);
    AppendMenu (hmenuPopup, MF_BITMAP, IDM_BRUSHES_FIRST+i,
               MAKEINTRESOURCE(hbm[i]));
    }

/*  Clean up all GDI objects we've created.                 */
SelectObject (hdcBitmap, GetStockObject(BLACK_BRUSH));
DeleteObject (hbrBackground);

SelectObject (hdcBitmap, hbmOld);
DeleteDC (hdcBitmap);
}
```

BITMENU.DEF

```
NAME    BITMENU

EXETYPE WINDOWS

DESCRIPTION 'Bitmap Menu Demo (c) 1992 By Paul Yao'

CODE    MOVEABLE PRELOAD
DATA    MOVEABLE MULTIPLE PRELOAD

HEAPSIZE     512
STACKSIZE    5120

SEGMENTS
    BITMENU_TEXT MOVEABLE PRELOAD

EXPORTS
    BitMenuWndProc
```

BITMENU.H

```
/*-------------------------------------------------------------*\
| BitMenu.h  - Include file for BitMenu.c.                      |
\*-------------------------------------------------------------*/

#define IDM_FILE_NEW          101
#define IDM_FILE_OPEN         102
#define IDM_FILE_SAVE         103
#define IDM_FILE_SAVEAS       104
#define IDM_FILE_PRINT        105
#define IDM_FILE_EXIT         106

#define IDM_EDIT_UNDO         201
#define IDM_EDIT_CUT          202
#define IDM_EDIT_COPY         203
#define IDM_EDIT_PASTE        204
#define IDM_EDIT_CLEAR        205
#define IDM_EDIT_DELETE       206

#define IDM_BRUSHES_FIRST     301
#define IDM_BRUSHES_SECOND    302
#define IDM_BRUSHES_THIRD     303
#define IDM_BRUSHES_FOURTH    304
#define IDM_BRUSHES_FIFTH     305

#define COUNT 5
```

BITMENU.LNK

```
BitMenu.obj
BitMenu.exe/align:16/map/nod/noe/CO
nul
mlibcew libw
BitMenu.def
```

BITMENU.MAK

```
# Directory search paths.

INCDIR = \WINDEV\INCLUDE

# Windows version to support
# Valid pairs include:
#    (0x0300, 30)


CLVER = WINVER=0x0300
```

```
RCVER = 30

# Compiler switches for applications.

CL_APP_SHIP_ALL = -AM -c -D$(CLVER) -Gsw -I$(INCDIR) -Ow -W3 -Zp
CL_APP_DEBG_ALL = -AM -c -D$(CLVER) -Gsw -I$(INCDIR) -Od -W3 -Zpi

CL_APP_SHIP_31  = -AM -c -G2s  -I$(INCDIR) -Ow -W3 -Zp
CL_APP_DEBG_31  = -AM -c -G2s  -I$(INCDIR) -Od -W3 -Zpi

# Compiler switches for DLLs.

CL_DLL_SHIP_ALL = -AMw -c -D$(CLVER) -Gsw -I$(INCDIR) -Ow -W3 -Zp
CL_DLL_DEBG_ALL = -AMw -c -D$(CLVER) -Gsw -I$(INCDIR) -Od -W3 -Zpi

CL_DLL_SHIP_31  = -AMw -c -G2s  -I$(INCDIR) -Ow -W3 -Zp
CL_DLL_DEBG_31  = -AMw -c -G2s  -I$(INCDIR) -Od -W3 -Zpi

# Make file primary target.

all: BitMenu.exe

# Make file dependency targets.

BitMenu.res: BitMenu.rc BitMenu.cur BitMenu.ico
    rc -r -i$(INCDIR) BitMenu.rc

BitMenu.obj: BitMenu.c BitMenu.h
    cl $(CL_APP_SHIP_ALL) BitMenu.c

BitMenu.exe: BitMenu.obj BitMenu.def BitMenu.res
    link @BitMenu.lnk
    rc -$(RCVER) BitMenu.res

BitMenu.exe: BitMenu.res
    rc -$(RCVER) BitMenu.res
```

BITMENU.RC

```
#include <Windows.h>
#include "BitMenu.h"

snapshot icon BitMenu.ico

hand  cursor BitMenu.cur

1 MENU
    {
    POPUP "&File"
        {
        MENUITEM "&New",        IDM_FILE_NEW
        MENUITEM "&Open...",    IDM_FILE_OPEN
```

```
          MENUITEM "&Save",         IDM_FILE_SAVE
          MENUITEM "Save &As...",   IDM_FILE_SAVEAS
          MENUITEM SEPARATOR
          MENUITEM "&Print",        IDM_FILE_PRINT
          MENUITEM SEPARATOR
          MENUITEM "E&xit",         IDM_FILE_EXIT
          }
     POPUP "&Edit"
          {
          MENUITEM "&Undo\tCtrl+Z", IDM_EDIT_UNDO
          MENUITEM SEPARATOR
          MENUITEM "Cu&t\tCtrl+X",  IDM_EDIT_CUT
          MENUITEM "&Copy\tCtrl+C", IDM_EDIT_COPY
          MENUITEM "&Paste\tCtrl+V", IDM_EDIT_PASTE
          MENUITEM SEPARATOR
          MENUITEM "Cl&ear",        IDM_EDIT_CLEAR
          MENUITEM "&Delete",       IDM_EDIT_DELETE
          }
     }


1 ACCELERATORS
     {
     ;  New Windows 3.1 clipboard accelerators.
     "Z",        IDM_EDIT_UNDO,   VIRTKEY, CONTROL
     "X",        IDM_EDIT_CUT,    VIRTKEY, CONTROL
     "C",        IDM_EDIT_COPY,   VIRTKEY, CONTROL
     "V",        IDM_EDIT_PASTE,  VIRTKEY, CONTROL

     ;  Maintain support for older clipboard accelerators.
     VK_BACK,    IDM_EDIT_UNDO,   VIRTKEY, ALT
     VK_DELETE,  IDM_EDIT_CUT,    VIRTKEY, SHIFT
     VK_INSERT,  IDM_EDIT_COPY,   VIRTKEY, CONTROL
     VK_INSERT,  IDM_EDIT_PASTE,  VIRTKEY, SHIFT
     }
```

BITMENU does most of its work in response to the WM_CREATE message, when it creates the five bitmaps and places them in the menu. It starts by calling GetSystemMetrics to determine the dimensions that the display device driver has set for icons. It uses these dimensions to calculate the size of the bitmap to create. As we mentioned earlier, this avoids the use of hard-coded sizes, which might produce unexpected results on display devices with very high resolutions. BITMENU sets the dimensions of the menu bitmaps in the following way:

```
cxWidth  = GetSystemMetrics (SM_CXICON) * 3;
cyHeight = GetSystemMetrics (SM_CYICON);
```

That is, the bitmaps are three times as wide as the display's standard icon and have the same height.

When a memory bitmap is created, GDI does not initialize the drawing surface to any particular color. Before we can draw on the bitmap, we need to erase the surface to avoid the appearance of random colors. In the same way that the OWNDRAW program called

GetSysColors to find the correct menu colors to use, BITMENU makes the same call and uses the resulting color to create a solid brush to erase the background of the bitmaps:

```
crBackground = GetSysColor (COLOR_MENU);
hbrBackground = CreateSolidBrush (crBackground);
```

As you may recall from our discussion of the OWNDRAW program, GDI can be called to draw on a bitmap only when a DC has been created and connected to the bitmap. We call CreateCompatibleDC to ask GDI to clone a display DC for us, then install the background brush into the DC so it is ready to help us initialize each of the bitmaps:

```
hdcBitmap = CreateCompatibleDC (hdcScreen);
SelectObject (hdcBitmap, hbrBackground);
```

The next step for BITMENU is to create the bitmaps and initialize them to the menu background color. As each bitmap is created, BITMENU calls the PatBlt routine to fill each newly created bitmap with the color of the brush that is currently installed in the DC, that is, with the color of our background brush:

```
for (i=0;i<COUNT;i++)
    {
    hbm[i]= CreateCompatibleBitmap (hdcScreen,
            cxWidth, cyHeight);
    if (i==0)
        hbmOld = SelectObject (hdcBitmap, hbm[0]);
    else
        SelectObject (hdcBitmap, hbm[i]);
    PatBlt (hdcBitmap,0,0, cxWidth, cyHeight, PATCOPY);
    }
```

BITMENU then creates an empty popup menu and attaches it to the top-level menu:

```
hmenuPopup = CreatePopupMenu ();
hmenu = GetMenu (hwnd);
AppendMenu (hmenu, MF_POPUP, hmenuPopup, "&Brushes");
```

It then creates a set of brushes to be used to create the bitmaps that are going to be installed in the menu:

```
hbr[0] = CreateHatchBrush (HS_DIAGCROSS, RGB(0,0,0));
hbr[1] = CreateSolidBrush (RGB(64, 64, 64));
hbr[2] = CreateHatchBrush (HS_CROSS, RGB(0, 0, 0));
hbr[3] = CreateSolidBrush (RGB(0, 0, 0));
hbr[4] = CreateHatchBrush (HS_VERTICAL, RGB(0, 0, 0));
```

Next, BITMENU enters a loop that calls SelectObject to connect each bitmap in turn to the bitmap DC. SelectObject is called a second time to install one of our brushes into the DC. With that done, we are ready to draw an image of the brush in the bitmap. We do this by calling the Rectangle routine, which draws a rectangle using the currently installed pen for the border and the currently installed brush for the inside area. Once this is done, the bitmap is ready to be added to the menu, which is accomplished by calling `AppendMenu`:

```
for (i=0;i<COUNT;i++)
    {
    SelectObject (hdcBitmap, hbr[i]);
    SelectObject (hdcBitmap, hbm[i]);
    Rectangle (hdcBitmap,
                0,
                cyOffset,
                cxWidth,
                cyHeight-cyOffset);
    AppendMenu (hmenuPopup, MF_BITMAP, IDM_FIRST+i,
                    MAKEINTRESOURCE(hbm[i]));
    }
```

Once all the bitmaps have been created and attached to a menu, the last thing we have to deal with is cleanup of the GDI objects that were created. Before a GDI object can be destroyed, it must be free of connection to any other object. Prior to destroying our background brush, we select one of the stock brushes into the DC, which causes the background brush to be de-selected:

```
SelectObject (hdcBitmap, GetStockObject(BLACK_BRUSH));
DeleteObject (hbrBackground);
```

Then we detach the last menu bitmap from the bitmap DC by calling `SelectObject`. When we do this, we install the bitmap handle that was returned when we installed our *first* bitmap handle. Pushing this handle into our DC causes the last of our bitmaps to pop out:

```
SelectObject (hdcBitmap, hbmOld);
DeleteDC (hdcBitmap);
```

This leaves two sets of GDI objects to be cleaned up. However, we can't destroy the bitmaps until the menu that uses them is destroyed. In addition, we aren't going to destroy the brushes that we created, since our program may want to use them to draw the objects the user has selected from our bitmap menu items. For both sets of GDI objects, BITMENU waits until our window is destroyed; in other words, we wait for the WM_DESTROY message to do the rest of our cleanup:

```
case WM_DESTROY:
    {
    int i;

    for (i=0;i<COUNT;i++)
        {
        DeleteObject (hbr[i]);
        DeleteObject (hbm[i]);
        }
    }
```

```
PostQuitMessage(0);
break;
```

Bitmaps in menus and owner-draw menu items are just two ways to incorporate graphical objects in your menus. We're going to look at the third type now: custom check marks.

Creating Custom Menu Check Marks

In the last chapter, we mentioned that check marks provide one type of visual clue in menus. Although the standard check mark is useful in many situations, you may want to use a different symbol in your menus. You can call GDI routines to create your own custom check marks and install them into menus. When you do this, the menu system lets you attach *two* different bitmaps to every menu item. One bitmap is displayed when the menu item is in a *checked* state, the other is for the *unchecked* state.

Creating a check-mark bitmap starts with the creation of a regular GDI bitmap (discussed earlier in this chapter). You must create a bitmap and a DC, then connect the two. From there, you use GDI routines to draw the desired figure to reflect the checked and unchecked states. Be careful, though, because your drawing has to be small enough to fit in the space that the menu system has set aside for check marks.

To determine the proper size to use, you call `GetMenuCheckMarkDimensions`. This routine takes no parameters, but returns a `DWORD` (`unsigned long`) value into which is packed the required dimensions of a check-mark bitmap. Here is how to extract the dimension information from the return value:

```
DWORD dwCheck;
int cxWidth, cyHeight;

dwCheck  = GetMenuCheckMarkDimension();
cxWidth  = LOWORD (dwCheck);
cyHeight = HIWORD (dwCheck);
```

Using the size information provided by this routine, you can create a pair of bitmaps, draw checked and unchecked images that you wish to use, and attach the bitmap to the specific menu items designated to use the check marks. Since bitmaps are shared GDI objects, you can create a single pair of check-mark bitmaps and use them in many different menu items. To attach a bitmap to a menu item, call the `Set-MenuItemBitmaps` routine, which is defined:

```
BOOL SetMenuItemBitmaps (hMenu, nPosition, wFlags,
    hbmUnchecked, hbmChecked)
```

- `hMenu` is a menu handle.

- `nPosition` identifies the menu item to which the pair of bitmaps are to be attached. If the next parameter, `wFlags`, is `MF_BYCOMMAND`, then `nPosition` is a command result code. If it is `MF_BYPOSITION`, `nPosition` is the relative position of the menu item in the menu identified by `hMenu`.

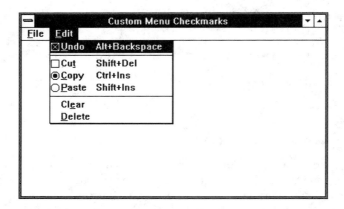

Figure 12.3 Two pairs of Custom Menu Check marks

- `wFlags` is either `MF_BYCOMMAND` or `MF_BYPOSITION`.

- `hbmUnchecked` is a handle of a GDI bitmap to be displayed when the menu is not checked.

- `hbmChecked` is a handle of a GDI bitmap to be displayed when the menu item is checked.

Once the check-mark bitmaps are attached to a menu item, they are used automatically without requiring any additional effort from your program. All you need to do at this point is call `CheckMenuItem` to set the checked state to either `MF_CHECKED` or `MF_UNCHECKED`.

If, at any time, you wish to remove a custom check mark, call `Set-MenuItemBitmaps` with a `NULL` value in the bitmap handle parameter corresponding to the bitmap to be removed. Figure 12.3 shows two sets of custom check marks created by **CHEKMENU**, our sample program.

CHEKMENU creates two pairs of custom menu check marks. One pair uses a square box with an X in the box for the checked state and an empty box for the unchecked state. The second pair is a circle check mark with a filled interior for the checked state and an empty interior for the unchecked state. Having created these two pairs of check-mark bitmaps, we could then use them for any or all of the menu items in our menu. CHEKMENU uses the standard menu that we created in the last chapter as illustrated in Figure 12.3.

CHEKMENU.C

```
/*--------------------------------------------------------------*\
 |  ChekMenu.C  -  A standard File and Edit menu, to show the  |
 |                 use of custom menu check-mark bitmaps.       |
 \*--------------------------------------------------------------*/
```

```
#include <Windows.H>
#include "ChekMenu.H"

/*-------------------------------------------------------------*\
|                     Function Prototypes.                      |
\*-------------------------------------------------------------*/
LRESULT CALLBACK ChekMenuWndProc (HWND, UINT, WPARAM, LPARAM);
VOID NEAR PASCAL ChekMenuCreate (HWND);

/*-------------------------------------------------------------*\
|                      Global Variables.                        |
\*-------------------------------------------------------------*/
char achWndClass[] = "ChekMenu:MAIN";
char achAppName[]  = "Custom Menu Checkmarks";
HANDLE hbmCheck[BITMAP_COUNT];
HMENU  hmenuMain;

/*-------------------------------------------------------------*\
|                  Main Function:  WinMain.                     |
\*-------------------------------------------------------------*/
int PASCAL
WinMain (HINSTANCE hInstance,      // Who am I?
         HINSTANCE hPrevInstance,  // Any older siblings?
         LPSTR     lpszCmdLine,    // Ptr to command line.
         int       cmdShow)        // How to open my window?
    {
    HACCEL   hAccel;
    HWND     hwnd;
    MSG      msg;
    WNDCLASS wndclass;

    if (!hPrevInstance)
        {
        wndclass.lpszClassName = achWndClass;
        wndclass.hInstance     = hInstance;
        wndclass.lpfnWndProc   = ChekMenuWndProc;
        wndclass.hCursor       = LoadCursor (hInstance, "hand");
        wndclass.hIcon         = LoadIcon (hInstance,"snapshot");
        wndclass.lpszMenuName  = "#1";
        wndclass.hbrBackground = (HBRUSH)(COLOR_WINDOW+1);
        wndclass.style         = NULL;
        wndclass.cbClsExtra    = 0;
        wndclass.cbWndExtra    = 0;

        RegisterClass( &wndclass);
        }

    hwnd = CreateWindowEx(0L,                    // Extra style.
                    achWndClass,                 // Class name.
                    achAppName,                  // Title.
                    WS_OVERLAPPEDWINDOW,         // Style bits.
                    CW_USEDEFAULT,               // x - default.
                    0,                           // y - default.
                    CW_USEDEFAULT,               // cx - default.
                    0,                           // cy - default.
```

```
                        NULL,                   // No parent.
                        NULL,                   // Class menu.
                        hInstance,              // Creator.
                        NULL);                  // Params.
        ShowWindow (hwnd, cmdShow);

        hAccel = LoadAccelerators (hInstance, "#1");

        while (GetMessage(&msg, 0, 0, 0))
            {
            if (!TranslateAccelerator (hwnd, hAccel, &msg))
                {
                TranslateMessage(&msg); // Convert KEYDOWNs to CHARs
                DispatchMessage(&msg);  // Transmit message to WndProc
                }
            }

        return 0;
        }

/*--------------------------------------------------------------*\
|              Window Procedure:  ChekMenuWndProc.               |
\*--------------------------------------------------------------*/
LRESULT CALLBACK
ChekMenuWndProc (HWND    hwnd,      // For whom is message sent?
                 UINT    mMsg,      // What is exact message?
                 WPARAM  wParam,    // ...message details.
                 LPARAM  lParam)    // ...message details.
    {
    switch (mMsg)
        {
        case WM_COMMAND:
            {
            BOOL bFlipCheckState;
            char buffer[80];
            char *npch;
            UINT uiMenuState;
            UINT uiNewCheckState;

            bFlipCheckState = FALSE;

            switch (wParam)
                {
                case IDM_FILE_NEW:
                    npch = "File.New";
                    break;
                case IDM_FILE_OPEN:
                    npch = "File.Open...";
                    break;
                case IDM_FILE_SAVE:
                    npch = "File.Save";
                    break;
                case IDM_FILE_SAVEAS:
                    npch = "File.Save As...";
                    break;
```

```
        case IDM_FILE_PRINT:
            npch = "File.Print";
            break;
        case IDM_FILE_EXIT:
            npch = "File.Exit";
            break;
        case IDM_EDIT_UNDO:
            bFlipCheckState = TRUE;
            npch = "Edit.Undo";
            break;
        case IDM_EDIT_CUT:
            bFlipCheckState = TRUE;
            npch = "Edit.Cut";
            break;
        case IDM_EDIT_COPY:
            bFlipCheckState = TRUE;
            npch = "Edit.Copy";
            break;
        case IDM_EDIT_PASTE:
            bFlipCheckState = TRUE;
            npch = "Edit.Paste";
            break;
        case IDM_EDIT_CLEAR:
            npch = "Edit.Clear";
            break;
        case IDM_EDIT_DELETE:
            npch = "Edit.Delete";
            break;
        }

// Flip check state.
if (bFlipCheckState)
    {
    uiMenuState = GetMenuState (hmenuMain, wParam,
                            MF_BYCOMMAND);
    uiNewCheckState = (uiMenuState & MF_CHECKED) ?
                    MF_UNCHECKED : MF_CHECKED;
    CheckMenuItem (hmenuMain, wParam, uiNewCheckState);
    }

// Display message box with
// name of selected menu item.
wsprintf (buffer, "%s command selected.", (LPSTR)npch);
MessageBox (hwnd, buffer, achAppName, MB_OK);

// If user selected File.Exit,
// simulate {-}.Close menu selection.
if (wParam == 6)
    {
    SendMessage (hwnd, WM_SYSCOMMAND, SC_CLOSE, 0L);
    }
}
break;
```

```
            case WM_CREATE:
                ChekMenuCreate(hwnd);
                break;

            case WM_DESTROY:
                {
                int i;

                for (i=0;i<BITMAP_COUNT;i++)
                    DeleteObject (hbmCheck[i]);
                }
                PostQuitMessage(0);  // Handle application shutdown.
                break;

            default:
                return(DefWindowProc(hwnd,mMsg,wParam,lParam));
                break;
            }
        return 0L;
        }


/*------------------------------------------------------------*\
|          ChekMenuCreate:  Process WM_CREATE Messages.        |
\*------------------------------------------------------------*/

VOID NEAR PASCAL ChekMenuCreate (HWND hwnd)
    {
    COLORREF crBackground;
    DWORD    dwCheck;
    HBITMAP  hbmOld;
    HBRUSH   hbrBackground;
    HDC      hdcScreen;
    HDC      hdcBitmap;
    HMENU    hmenu;
    int      cxWidth;
    int      cyHeight;
    int      xMin, xMax;
    int      yMin, yMax;
    int      cxFourth;
    int      cyFourth;
    int      cxMargin;
    int      i;

    /*  Get checkmark dimension information.                */
    dwCheck  = GetMenuCheckMarkDimensions();
    cyHeight = HIWORD (dwCheck);
    cxWidth  = LOWORD (dwCheck);

    /*  Calculate a margin based on border widths.          */
    cxMargin = GetSystemMetrics (SM_CXBORDER);
    xMin = cxMargin;
    xMax = cxWidth - cxMargin;
    yMin = cxMargin;
    yMax = cyHeight - cxMargin;
```

```
cxFourth = cxWidth/4;
cyFourth = cyHeight/4;

/*  Create the background brush to initialize bitmaps.     */
crBackground = GetSysColor (COLOR_MENU);
hbrBackground = CreateSolidBrush (crBackground);

/*  Create a DC and a set of bitmaps.                      */
hdcScreen = GetDC (hwnd);
hdcBitmap = CreateCompatibleDC (hdcScreen);
SelectObject (hdcBitmap, hbrBackground);

for (i=0;i<BITMAP_COUNT;i++)
    {
    hbmCheck[i] = CreateCompatibleBitmap (hdcScreen,
                                    cxWidth, cyHeight);
    if (i==0)
        hbmOld = SelectObject (hdcBitmap, hbmCheck[0]);
    else
        SelectObject (hdcBitmap, hbmCheck[i]);
    PatBlt (hdcBitmap, 0, 0, cxWidth, cyHeight, PATCOPY);
    }
ReleaseDC (hwnd, hdcScreen);


/*  Draw first unchecked menu item.                        */
SelectObject (hdcBitmap, hbmCheck[0]);
Rectangle (hdcBitmap, xMin, yMin,
                    xMax, yMax);

/*  Draw first checked menu item.                          */
SelectObject (hdcBitmap, hbmCheck[1]);
Rectangle (hdcBitmap, xMin, yMin,
                    xMax, yMax);

MoveTo (hdcBitmap, xMin, yMin);
LineTo (hdcBitmap, xMax, yMax);
MoveTo (hdcBitmap, xMin, yMax-1);
LineTo (hdcBitmap, xMax-1, yMin);

/*  Draw second unchecked menu item.                       */
SelectObject (hdcBitmap, hbmCheck[2]);
Ellipse (hdcBitmap, xMin, yMin,
                    xMax, yMax);

/*  Draw second checked menu item.                         */
SelectObject (hdcBitmap, hbmCheck[3]);
Ellipse (hdcBitmap, xMin, yMin,
                    xMax, yMax);
SelectObject (hdcBitmap, GetStockObject (BLACK_BRUSH));

Ellipse (hdcBitmap, xMin+cxFourth, yMin+cyFourth,
                    xMax-cxFourth, yMax-cyFourth);
```

```
/*  Get handle to top-level menu.                         */
hmenuMain =
hmenu = GetMenu (hwnd);

/*  Attach check marks to four menu items.                */

/*  (1) Edit-Undo, and set it to checked.                 */
SetMenuItemBitmaps (hmenu, IDM_EDIT_UNDO, MF_BYCOMMAND,
                    hbmCheck[0], hbmCheck[1]);
CheckMenuItem. (hmenu, IDM_EDIT_UNDO, MF_BYCOMMAND | MF_CHECKED);

/*  (2) Edit-Cut, and leave it unchecked.                 */
SetMenuItemBitmaps (hmenu, IDM_EDIT_CUT, MF_BYCOMMAND,
                    hbmCheck[0], hbmCheck[1]);

/*  (3) Edit-Copy, and set it to checked.                 */
SetMenuItemBitmaps (hmenu, IDM_EDIT_COPY, MF_BYCOMMAND,
                    hbmCheck[2], hbmCheck[3]);
CheckMenuItem (hmenu, IDM_EDIT_COPY, MF_BYCOMMAND | MF_CHECKED);

/*  (4) Edit-Paste, and leave it unchecked.               */
SetMenuItemBitmaps (hmenu, IDM_EDIT_PASTE, MF_BYCOMMAND,
                    hbmCheck[2], hbmCheck[3]);

/*  Clean up the GDI objects we've created.               */
SelectObject (hdcBitmap, GetStockObject(BLACK_BRUSH));
DeleteObject (hbrBackground);

SelectObject (hdcBitmap, hbmOld);
DeleteDC (hdcBitmap);
}
```

CHEKMENU.DEF

```
NAME    CHEKMENU

EXETYPE WINDOWS

DESCRIPTION 'Custom Menu Checkmarks (c) 1992 By Paul Yao'

CODE    MOVEABLE PRELOAD
DATA    MOVEABLE MULTIPLE PRELOAD

HEAPSIZE    512
STACKSIZE   5120

SEGMENTS
    CHEKMENU_TEXT MOVEABLE PRELOAD

EXPORTS
    ChekMenuWndProc
```

CHEKMENU.H

```
/*-------------------------------------------------------------*\
 | ChekMenu.h - Include file for ChekMenu.c.                   |
 \*-------------------------------------------------------------*/

#define IDM_FILE_NEW        101
#define IDM_FILE_OPEN       102
#define IDM_FILE_SAVE       103
#define IDM_FILE_SAVEAS     104
#define IDM_FILE_PRINT      105
#define IDM_FILE_EXIT       106

#define IDM_EDIT_UNDO       201
#define IDM_EDIT_CUT        202
#define IDM_EDIT_COPY       203
#define IDM_EDIT_PASTE      204
#define IDM_EDIT_CLEAR      205
#define IDM_EDIT_DELETE     206

#define BITMAP_COUNT        4
```

CHEKMENU.LNK

```
ChekMenu.obj
ChekMenu.exe/align:16/map/nod/noe/CO
nul
mlibcew libw
ChekMenu.def
```

CHEKMENU.MAK

```
# Directory search paths.

INCDIR = \WINDEV\INCLUDE

# Windows version to support
# Valid pairs include:
#     (0x0300, 30)
#     (0x0310, 31)

CLVER = WINVER=0x0300
RCVER = 30
```

```
# Compiler switches for applications.

CL_APP_SHIP_ALL = -AM -c -D$(CLVER) -Gsw -I$(INCDIR) -Ow -W3 -Zp
CL_APP_DEBG_ALL = -AM -c -D$(CLVER) -Gsw -I$(INCDIR) -Od -W3 -Zpi

CL_APP_SHIP_31  = -AM -c -G2s  -I$(INCDIR) -Ow -W3 -Zp
CL_APP_DEBG_31  = -AM -c -G2s  -I$(INCDIR) -Od -W3 -Zpi

# Compiler switches for DLLs.

CL_DLL_SHIP_ALL = -AMw -c -D$(CLVER) -Gsw -I$(INCDIR) -Ow -W3 -Zp
CL_DLL_DEBG_ALL = -AMw -c -D$(CLVER) -Gsw -I$(INCDIR) -Od -W3 -Zpi

CL_DLL_SHIP_31  = -AMw -c -G2s  -I$(INCDIR) -Ow -W3 -Zp
CL_DLL_DEBG_31  = -AMw -c -G2s  -I$(INCDIR) -Od -W3 -Zpi

# Make file primary target.

all: ChekMenu.exe

# Make file dependency targets.

ChekMenu.res: ChekMenu.rc ChekMenu.cur ChekMenu.ico
    rc -r -i$(INCDIR) ChekMenu.rc

ChekMenu.obj: ChekMenu.c ChekMenu.h
    cl $(CL_APP_DEBG_ALL) ChekMenu.c

ChekMenu.exe: ChekMenu.obj ChekMenu.def ChekMenu.res
    link @ChekMenu.lnk
    rc -$(RCVER) ChekMenu.res

ChekMenu.exe: ChekMenu.res
    rc -$(RCVER) ChekMenu.res
```

CHEKMENU.RC

```
#include <Windows.h>
#include "ChekMenu.h"

snapshot icon ChekMenu.ico

hand  cursor ChekMenu.cur

1 MENU
    {
    POPUP "&File"
        {
        MENUITEM "&New",         IDM_FILE_NEW
        MENUITEM "&Open...",     IDM_FILE_OPEN
        MENUITEM "&Save",        IDM_FILE_SAVE
        MENUITEM "Save &As...",  IDM_FILE_SAVEAS
```

```
         MENUITEM SEPARATOR
         MENUITEM "&Print",          IDM_FILE_PRINT
         MENUITEM SEPARATOR
         MENUITEM "E&xit",           IDM_FILE_EXIT
         }
     POPUP "&Edit"
         {
         MENUITEM "&Undo\tCtrl+Z",   IDM_EDIT_UNDO
         MENUITEM SEPARATOR
         MENUITEM "Cu&t\tCtrl+X",     IDM_EDIT_CUT
         MENUITEM "&Copy\tCtrl+C",   IDM_EDIT_COPY
         MENUITEM "&Paste\tCtrl+V",  IDM_EDIT_PASTE
         MENUITEM SEPARATOR
         MENUITEM "Cl&ear",          IDM_EDIT_CLEAR
         MENUITEM "&Delete",         IDM_EDIT_DELETE
         }
     }


1 ACCELERATORS
     {
     ;  New Windows 3.1 clipboard accelerators.
     "Z",        IDM_EDIT_UNDO,   VIRTKEY, CONTROL
     "X",        IDM_EDIT_CUT,    VIRTKEY, CONTROL
     "C",        IDM_EDIT_COPY,   VIRTKEY, CONTROL
     "V",        IDM_EDIT_PASTE,  VIRTKEY, CONTROL

     ;  Maintain support for older clipboard accelerators.
     VK_BACK,    IDM_EDIT_UNDO,   VIRTKEY, ALT
     VK_DELETE,  IDM_EDIT_CUT,    VIRTKEY, SHIFT
     VK_INSERT,  IDM_EDIT_COPY,   VIRTKEY, CONTROL
     VK_INSERT,  IDM_EDIT_PASTE,  VIRTKEY, SHIFT
     }
```

The creation of custom check marks starts by asking the menu system for the expected size of a check mark:

```
//  Get checkmark dimension information.
dwCheck   = GetMenuCheckMarkDimensions();
cyHeight = HIWORD (dwCheck);
cxWidth  = LOWORD (dwCheck);
```

With this information in hand, CHEKMENU calculates a border around the edges of our check mark. This is necessary because the given area actually touches the left border of a menu. The creation of a margin avoids the crowded appearance this might cause. We calculate our border by calling GetSystemMetrics with the SM_CXBORDER parameter, to get the width of a thin window border to use as a check-mark margin:

```
//  Calculate a margin based on border widths.
cxMargin = GetSystemMetrics (SM_CXBORDER);
xMin = cxMargin;
xMax = cxWidth - cxMargin;
yMin = cxMargin;
```

```
yMax = cyHeight - cxMargin;
cxFourth = cxWidth/4;
cyFourth = cyHeight/4;
```

Since we're going to create a bitmap, we will want to initialize the background of the bitmap. We call GetSysColor to determine the menu background color and create a brush to use to fill our check-mark background before we draw into it:

```
// Create the background brush to initialize bitmaps.
crBackground = GetSysColor (COLOR_MENU);
hbrBackground = CreateSolidBrush (crBackground);
```

As we saw in the BITMENU program, to draw in a bitmap you must have a DC. Here is how CHEKMENU creates a DC and a set of bitmaps, and uses the background brush to initialize our bitmaps to the menu background color:

```
//  Create a DC and a set of bitmaps.
hdcScreen = GetDC (hwnd);
hdcBitmap = CreateCompatibleDC (hdcScreen);
SelectObject (hdcBitmap, hbrBackground);

for (i=0;i<COUNT;i++)
    {
    hbmCheck[i] = CreateCompatibleBitmap (hdcScreen,
                    cxWidth, cyHeight);
    if (i==0)
        hbmOld = SelectObject (hdcBitmap, hbmCheck[0]);
    else
        SelectObject (hdcBitmap, hbmCheck[i]);
    PatBlt (hdcBitmap, 0, 0, cxWidth, cyHeight, PATCOPY);
    }
ReleaseDC (hwnd, hdcScreen);
```

Drawing the four check-mark images is as simple as calling a few GDI routines. Of course, since our four bitmaps are sharing a DC, we use the SelectObject routine to create the connection, which allows us to draw in each bitmap in turn:

```
//  Draw first unchecked menu item.
SelectObject (hdcBitmap, hbmCheck[0]);
Rectangle (hdcBitmap, xMin, yMin, xMax, yMax);

//  Draw first checked menu item.
SelectObject (hdcBitmap, hbmCheck[1]);
Rectangle (hdcBitmap, xMin, yMin, xMax, yMax);

MoveTo (hdcBitmap, xMin, yMin);
LineTo (hdcBitmap, xMax, yMax);
MoveTo (hdcBitmap, xMin, yMax-1);
LineTo (hdcBitmap, xMax-1, yMin);
```

```
//  Draw second unchecked menu item.
SelectObject (hdcBitmap, hbmCheck[2]);
Ellipse (hdcBitmap, xMin, yMin, xMax, yMax);

//  Draw second checked menu item.
SelectObject (hdcBitmap, hbmCheck[3]);
Ellipse (hdcBitmap, xMin, yMin, xMax, yMax);
SelectObject (hdcBitmap, GetStockObject (BLACK_BRUSH));

Ellipse (hdcBitmap, xMin+cxFourth, yMin+cyFourth,
         xMax-cxFourth, yMax-cyFourth);
```

Attaching the four check marks to our four menu items involves first getting a handle to our window's top-level menu, then making four calls to SetMenuItemBitmaps:

```
//  Get handle to top-level menu.
hmenu = GetMenu (hwnd);

//  Attach check marks to four menu items.

//  (1) Edit-Undo, and set it to checked.
SetMenuItemBitmaps (hmenu, IDM_UNDO, MF_BYCOMMAND,
                    hbmCheck[0], hbmCheck[1]);
CheckMenuItem (hmenu, IDM_UNDO, MF_BYCOMMAND | MF_CHECKED);

//  (2) Edit-Cut, and leave it unchecked.
SetMenuItemBitmaps (hmenu, IDM_CUT, MF_BYCOMMAND,
                    hbmCheck[0], hbmCheck[1]);

//  (3) Edit-Copy, and set it to checked.
SetMenuItemBitmaps (hmenu, IDM_COPY, MF_BYCOMMAND,
                    hbmCheck[2], hbmCheck[3]);
CheckMenuItem (hmenu, IDM_COPY, MF_BYCOMMAND | MF_CHECKED);

//  (4) Edit-Paste, and leave it unchecked.
SetMenuItemBitmaps (hmenu, IDM_PASTE, MF_BYCOMMAND,
                    hbmCheck[2], hbmCheck[3]);
```

Of course, whenever GDI objects are created, they must be destroyed before your program terminates. CHEKMENU takes care of some of these objects right after the menu check marks have been set:

```
//  Clean up the GDI objects we've created.
SelectObject (hdcBitmap, GetStockObject(BLACK_BRUSH));
DeleteObject (hbrBackground);

SelectObject (hdcBitmap, hbmOld);
DeleteDC (hdcBitmap);
```

But the final cleanup of the check-mark bitmaps must wait until the menu itself has been destroyed. Since this is part of the window destruction process, we just have to wait for the WM_DESTROY message:

```
case WM_DESTROY:
    {
    int i;

    for (i=0;i<COUNT;i++)
        DeleteObject (hbmCheck[i]);
    }
    PostQuitMessage(0);
    break;
```

The creation of custom check marks is straightforward, although it requires an understanding of how to create and manipulate GDI bitmaps. Once a bitmap has been created and attached to a DC, drawing in the bitmap only requires you to call the various GDI drawing routines. PatBlt is first called to erase the bitmap background. Then Rectangle, Ellipse, MoveTo, and LineTo draw the actual check-mark images. As shown in our other sample programs, it is important to clean up whatever GDI drawing objects you have created or used.

Our next chapter returns to a subject that was first touched on in Chapter 2 when we introduced our minimum Windows program. The issue is that of window creation. While a program doesn't have to create more than a single window to be useful, there are times when it is indispensable for providing a good user interface. Even if you never create more than one window in your windows programs, some of Windows' special capabilities are hidden in the window creation process. Let's take a look at what those capabilities are.

13

Windowing

Up till now, every program in this book has had a single top-level window. While you might use this approach for all of your Windows programs, there are times when it makes sense for a program to have more than a single window. For example, programs that use the **multiple document interface** (**MDI**) standard create a new window for every new document. Programs that use dialog boxes also use multiple windows, since dialog boxes themselves are windows, as are the pushbuttons, listboxes, and other controls living inside dialog boxes. We'll describe dialog boxes further in Chapter 14.

A program might create multiple windows to divide a single window into smaller work areas. For example, programs often place scroll bars, which are windows, inside other windows so the user can control the portion of the data that is visible. Consider a terminal emulation program, which might use a tiny text window to display communication status information. Another type of application, such as a word processing program, might show a document's margin and tab settings inside a small window resting next to a larger document window. There are as many possibilities as there are different kinds of applications.

To help you understand how to use multiple windows effectively, we will discuss the implementation details that make Windows' windows unique. Let's start by looking at the two-step process for creating a window: window class registration and window creation. Then the issue of how big to make an application's top-level window will be examined. Finally, we'll discuss the creation of a child window to output menu information to help users browse through a program's menu. In keeping with the spirit of this book, we'll provide working samples to help you with your own programming projects.

The Window Creation Process

When we introduced the minimum Windows program, in Chapter 2, we said that window creation was a two-step process. Then we introduced the two routines that control the operation of each of those steps, `RegisterClass` and `CreateWindow`. Now, we will present the details of the window creation process, which is quite involved and gives you several choices as to the shape, size, style, and behavior of a window. The sheer number of fields in the `WNDCLASS` data structure and the number of parameters that are passed to `CreateWindow` hint at more possibilities than we told you earlier. Let's start by looking at the first part of the window creation process, which revolves around a single data structure: the window class.

Window Classes

Over the next few years, we're going to be hearing a lot about **object-oriented programming**. One of the aspects of this technology involves the creation and use of **object classes**. An object class is a template for the creation of objects. In the world of Windows programming, a window class is a template for the creation of windows.

Associated with every object class is a body of code; in Windows, we call this a window procedure. In the world of object-oriented programming, the code is a collection of **methods**. You act on an object by sending a **message**, which is the term used both in Windows and in object-oriented programming.

The more you compare Windows to object-oriented programming, the more you realize that the developers of Windows were influenced by some of the early work that was done in the field of object-oriented programming. But at the time that Windows was first being developed, object-oriented programming was little more than a collection of theories for the research lab. It certainly wasn't sufficiently evolved to support full-scale, commercial development tools. Nonetheless, Windows' early connection to object-oriented programming will help make Windows a primary environment for object-oriented development tools. In fact, there are a number of such tools available today, including a few C++ compilers, a Smalltalk implementation for Windows, and Whitewater's Actor programming language.

One reason for creating an object class is that you can make many copies of the object with a minimum of overhead. You already know, for example, that only the first instance of a program has to register its window classes. In all our sample programs, we register a window class using code like this:

```
WNDCLASS wndclass;

if (!hPrevInstance)
    {
    wndclass.lpszClassName = "MIN:MAIN";
    wndclass.hInstance      = hInstance;
    wndclass.lpfnWndProc    = MinWndProc;
    wndclass.hCursor        = LoadCursor(hInstance, "hand");
    wndclass.hIcon          = LoadIcon(hInstance, "snapshot");
    wndclass.lpszMenuName   = NULL;
```

```
        wndclass.hbrBackground = (HBRUSH)COLOR_WINDOW+1;
        wndclass.style        = NULL;
        wndclass.cbClsExtra    = 0;
        wndclass.cbWndExtra    = 0;

        RegisterClass( &wndclass);
        }
```

Since it's the WNDCLASS data structure that defines a window class, let's take a closer look at each element of this data structure.

The lpszClassName field defines an ASCII text string for the class name. Although there was a problem with creating names that were identical with existing class names in earlier versions of Windows, in Windows 3.0 and later versions all window classes are **private classes** by default. A private window class is only accessible from a single program. This means that you can use any name you'd like and know that it won't interfere with the class names of other programs. Of course, you'll probably want to avoid the predefined dialog box classes to avoid interfering with dialog boxes. The names of these classes are: **button**, **combobox**, **edit**, **listbox**, **scrollbar**, and **static**. Also, to avoid getting into the way of the built-in support that Windows provides for the multiple document interface (MDI), you'll want to avoid creating a class with the name **mdiclient**.

The hInstance field tells Windows which program created the window class. The primary reason has to do with internal housekeeping. After every instance of a program has terminated, Windows automatically unregisters the classes created by the program.

The lpfnWndProc field identifies a function—a window procedure—which processes messages for every window in the class. How can a single function support multiple windows? A window procedure can differentiate between windows because each window has a unique window handle, a signature that uniquely identifies each window in the system. When a message is delivered to a window procedure, the window handle tells the window procedure exactly *which* window is sending the message. If you want to treat different windows in a different manner, you only need to look at the window handle to know which one is calling.

The hCursor field is a handle to a cursor shared by all members of a window class. The default window procedure uses this to install the correct cursor whenever it receives a WM_SETCURSOR message. If you want a window to have its own *private* cursor, different from the class cursor, skip ahead to Chapter 16 to find out how.

The hIcon field is a handle to an icon that is displayed when a window in the class is minimized. Not every kind of window will use its icon. Icons are only displayed for top-level windows (windows that have no parents) and document windows in programs that use the multiple document interface (MDI). The typical way for a program to define the icon handle involves making a call to load the icon, as shown here:

```
        wndclass.hIcon = LoadIcon(hInstance,"snapshot");
```

A program can also draw an icon "on-the-fly" by defining a NULL icon:

```
        wndclass.hIcon = NULL;
```

When the window is iconized, it appears as a tiny, empty window. Creating a drawing for the icon is surprisingly simple: You handle the WM_PAINT message just as you would when the window is *not* iconized. The only difference is that you need to be prepared to draw into a very tiny area. Here is a sample code fragment that draws an icon when the window is minimized:

```
case WM_PAINT:
{
HBRUSH hbr;
PAINTSTRUCT ps;
POINT apt[4];
RECT r;
TEXTMETRIC tm;

BeginPaint(hwnd, &ps);

if (IsIconic (hwnd))
    {
    GetTextMetrics (ps.hdc, &tm);
    GetClientRect (hwnd, &r);
    r.bottom -= tm.tmHeight/2;

    //  Draw a rectangle.
    Rectangle (ps.hdc, 0, 0, r.right, r.bottom);

    //  Draw an ellipse.
    hbr = GetStockObject (GRAY_BRUSH);
    SelectObject (ps.hdc, hbr);
    Ellipse (ps.hdc, 0, 0, r.right, r.bottom);

    //  Draw a triangle.
    hbr = GetStockObject (BLACK_BRUSH);
    SelectObject (ps.hdc, hbr);
    apt[0].x = r.right/2;     apt[0].y = 0;
    apt[1].x = 0;       apt[1].y = r.bottom;
    apt[2].x = r.right;     apt[2].y = r.bottom;
    apt[3].x = r.right/2;     apt[3].y = 0;
    Polygon (ps.hdc, apt, 4);
    }

EndPaint (hwnd, &ps);
}
break;
```

The icon created by this code fragment is shown in Figure 13.1. It creates our "on-the-fly" icon by drawing a rectangle, an ellipse, and a triangle.

A window created from a window class with a NULL icon must handle one more issue, which involves the choice of icons to display when the user drags the iconic program. When the user drags a program that does have an icon, the mouse cursor

Figure 13.1 Drawing in a NULL icon

changes to the shape of that icon. When a program's window doesn't have an icon, it has two choices: It can let the system display a default icon, or it can provide one in response to the WM_QUERYDRAGICON message. Here, for example, is what a program without an icon might do when sent this message:

```
LRESULT CALLBACK WndProc (...)
    {
    switch (msg)
        {
        case WM_QUERYDRAGICON:
            {
            HANDLE hIcon;

            hIcon = LoadIcon (hInstance, "DRAGICON");
            return (MAKELONG(hIcon, 0));
            }
            ...
```

A top-level window without an icon will see other message traffic that is different from messages sent to windows that *do* have an icon. As our earlier code fragment indicates, a top-level window without an icon will receive a WM_PAINT message when it's time to draw its iconic image. Top-level windows *with* icons receive a WM_PAINTICON message instead. The default window procedure responds to this message by displaying the icon for the window class. A program with a class icon that wanted to draw a custom icon could respond to the WM_PAINTICON message and create an "on-the-fly" icon if desired.

The **lpszMenuName** field identifies the class menu by name. As discussed in Chapter 11 when menus were introduced, this value can take one of three forms. For a menu resource defined like this:

```
15 MENU
    {
    POPUP "File"
        {
        MENUITEM "New", IDM_NEW
        ...
```

the menu name can be a character string preceded by a # sign:

```
wndclass.lpszMenuName  = "#15";
```

Alternatively, the MAKEINTRESOURCE macro can be used to sneak an integer value in place of a long pointer to a string. Here is an example showing how the MAKEINTRESOURCE macro can be used:

```
wndclass.lpszMenuName  = MAKEINTRESOURCE(15);
```

A third choice, but a less attractive one because it consumes more memory and is slower, involves using a regular character string:

```
MyMenu MENU
    {
    POPUP "File"
        {
        MENUITEM "New", IDM_NEW
        . . .
```

To load this menu into memory, you provide the name of the menu in the WNDCLASS data structure, as shown here:

```
wndclass.lpszMenuName  = "MyMenu";
```

The disadvantage to this approach is that a string takes up more space than an integer; therefore, this approach takes more memory. When the time comes to load the menu, an integer identifier allows faster loading than a string identifier since an integer compare is faster than a string compare. From the point of view of performance and memory use, integer values are better.

The **hbrBackground** field is a handle to a brush that is used to fill the background before any drawing is done. The default window procedure fills in the background in response to the WM_ERASEBACKGROUND message. This seems like a funny name for the messages, since in fact the background is really *painted* and not erased. However, it *does* suggest the idea that whatever was in the window before is removed to provide a clean surface on which to draw. There are two types of values that can be placed in this field: a brush handle and an index to a system color. Here is how to use a stock black brush for the background:

```
wndclass.hbrBackground = GetStockObject (BLACK_BRUSH);
```

A better alternative, however, involves using a "magic number" for the background color, like this:

```
wndclass.hbrBackground = (HBRUSH)COLOR_WINDOW+1;
```

When the default window procedure sees this value, it uses the default window background color defined by the user from the Control Panel.

The **cbClsExtra** field defines the number of bytes that are added at the end of the class definition as a reserved data area. These bytes are known as **class extra bytes**. This data area can be used by a program for any purpose, but Windows does not provide a pointer to the data area itself. Instead, you must set these values using the SetClassWord and SetClassLong routines, and retrieve them using the GetClassWord and GetClassLong routines. If you don't plan to use class extra

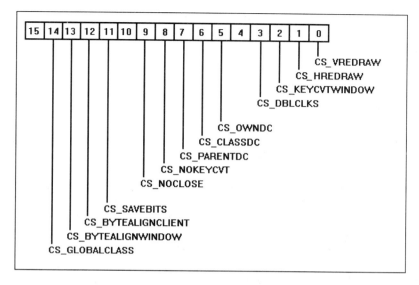

Figure 13.2 The thirteen WNDCLASS style bits

bytes, be sure to initialize `cbClsExtra` to zero. If you don't explicitly initialize this field to zero, it is possible that some random, large value will be passed as the number of bytes to be allocated. Initializing to zero avoids an accidental waste of memory.

The `cbWndExtra` field, like the `cbClsExtra` field, defines a reserved data area for the private use of your application. These bytes are referred to as **window extra bytes**. Unlike class extra bytes, which are shared by every window in a class, window extra bytes are reserved for the private use of each individual window, and provide a way for a window to have its own "bank account" for bytes that it wishes to use—like having a Swiss bank account. To read the value of the window extra bytes, a program calls either `GetWindowWord` or `GetWindowLong`. These routines take a window handle as a parameter to identify exactly whose bytes are to be accessed. To write values into the window extra bytes, a program must call the `SetWindowWord` or `SetWindowLong` routines. These routines also take a window handle, which lets the Window Manager know into whose bank account you wish to make a deposit.

The `style` field is a 16-bit field that contains a set of flags describing various features of the window class. There are 13-style flags, as shown in Figure 13.2. Let's look at each of the window class style bits in detail.

Window Class Style Bits

A lot of the subtlety in creating windows actually comes from certain class style bits that you can select. Let's take a look at all of them, to try to understand where they can be useful in a Windows program.

The `CS_VREDRAW` and `CS_HREDRAW` styles determine whether the window should be completely redrawn when the user changes the window size in either the vertical (CS_VREDRAW) or horizontal (CS_HREDRAW) direction. In other words, these styles determine whether Windows automatically makes a call like the following when a window's size changes:

```
InvalidateRect (hwnd, NULL, TRUE);
```

As you probably remember, the InvalidateRect routine is used to mark a portion of a window as damaged, which means that a WM_PAINT message will eventually be generated to repair the window. A NULL value in the second parameter declares the *entire* window to be damaged. The TRUE value in the last parameter requests that the damaged area (in this case, the entire window) be erased before being redrawn.

Two style bits are referenced in Windows.h but not mentioned in the Microsoft documentation: CS_KEYCVTWINDOW and CS_NOKEYCVT. They seem to be remnants of support for a Kanji conversion window for Japanese Windows. However, Microsoft has created a separate version of Windows for the Japanese market, which also requires its own special version of the Windows software development kit. Therefore, even though these style bits promise built-in Kanji support, you must obtain the special SDK to develop Windows programs for the Japanese market.

If you want a window to receive double-click mouse messages (WM_LBUT-TONDBLCLK, WM_MBUTTONDBLCLK, or WM_RBUTTONDBLCLK), then you must use the CS_DBLCLKS style bit. This special style bit causes a timer to be set when an initial mouse click is received. A double-click message is generated only when a second click is received before the timer runs out. The presence of this style bit helps the Window Manager to decide when to start the timer in response to a mouse click message.

Two style bits allow a window to have a private device context (DC): CS_OWNDC and CS_CLASSDC. When we introduced the device context in Chapter 6, we mentioned that most programs borrow a DC from the system DC cache. But, because of the overhead associated with checking out and returning a DC, some programs prefer to have their own. In the same way that library books require more effort than books that you own, borrowed DCs require more effort. Of course, like private book collections, private DCs cost more in terms of memory required.

How much *does* a private DC cost? Although there has been talk among Windows programmers for some years that a DC is 800 bytes, in fact the actual size is about 200 bytes, all of which is allocated from GDI's local heap. While this doesn't seem like a lot, the allocation of a private DC has to be weighed against the fact that GDI's local heap space is a shared resource for which all programs compete (see Chapter 18). Therefore, avoid allocating a private DC unless you really need it.

When is the cost of a private DC justified? In general, programs that do a lot of drawing, and programs that interact with the user *while* drawing, may run faster with a private DC. For example, a word processor program that displays text as the user types may get a performance boost by getting its own, private DC. Or a drawing package that interacts with the user to interactively draw pictures may get a slight performance benefit from a private DC. In general, you may find that a private DC is faster to work with than a shared, system DC in a program that uses keystrokes or mouse clicks to draw.

The CS_OWNDC style bit gives a private DC to *every window* in a class. This type of DC is the most expensive in terms of memory used, but gives the fastest response. It is the most expensive because one DC is allocated for each window in a class. It is fastest because you don't incur the overhead of borrowing and returning the DC every time you draw. As illustrated in the following code fragment, a window created from a class with the CS_OWNDC style bit can get a DC handle during the WM_CREATE message and use it when it needs to draw for any other message:

```
LRESULT CALLBACK WndProc (...)
    {
    static HDC hdc;
    switch(msg)
        {
        case WM_CREATE:
            hdc = GetDC (hwnd);
            break;

        case WM_CHAR:
            TextOut (hdc, ...);
            break;
        case WM_LBUTTONUP:
            Rectangle (hdc, ...);
            break;

        case WM_PAINT:
            BeginPaint (hwnd, &ps);
            ...
            EndPaint (hwnd, &ps);

        default:
            DefWindowProc (...);
        }
    }
```

Aside from the WM_CREATE message, the only other time this window procedure asks for a DC is in response to a WM_PAINT message, when a regular BeginPaint/EndPaint sandwich is used. This contrasts sharply with the approach that programs must take when they use a system DC. As shown in this code fragment, such programs must borrow and return a DC for each message:

```
LRESULT CALLBACK WndProc (...)
    {
    HDC hdc;
    switch(msg)
        {

        case WM_CHAR:
        hdc = GetDC (hwnd);
        TextOut (hdc, ...);
        ReleaseDC (hwnd, hdc);
```

```
        break;

    case WM_LBUTTONUP:
    hdc = GetDC (hwnd);
    Rectangle (hdc, ...);
    ReleaseDC (hwnd, hdc);
    break;

    case WM_PAINT:
    BeginPaint (hwnd, &ps);
    ...
    EndPaint (hwnd, &ps);
    default:
        DefWindowProc (...);
    }
}
```

From this, you can see that one advantage of a private DC is that programs don't have to borrow a DC every time they wish to draw. A second advantage is that a program can set up the DC's drawing attributes once and not have to worry about them again. In contrast with this is the way programs must work with system DCs. Every time a system DC is borrowed, its drawing attributes are reset to their initial default state. Programs that use a system DC have to set up the DC drawing attributes every time they wish to draw.

Programs with a private DC must still use a `BeginPaint`/`EndPaint` sandwich in response to a `WM_PAINT` message. This is because the `WM_PAINT` message can only be turned off by the use of these two routines. `BeginPaint` is smart enough to recognize when a window has a private DC, and it returns the correct DC handle inside the `PAINTSTRUCT` structure. The only difference is that the DC will have a clipping region installed to limit drawing to the damaged part of the window.

The `CS_CLASSDC` style provides a DC similar to a private DC except that it is shared by an entire class of Windows and not owned by a single window. Like a private DC, the drawing attributes in a class DC are not reset every time the DC is returned. This gives us a slight performance improvement over a regular system DC, in which drawing attributes *are* reset. Therefore, a class DC has some of the benefits of a private DC except that it is shared between several windows of the same class. Because it is shared between windows, a class DC must be handled like a system DC. In other words, it must be borrowed when needed—using either `GetDC` or `BeginPaint`—and returned when it is not needed—using either `ReleaseDC` or `EndPaint`.

The `CS_PARENTDC` style can also help improve performance when drawing in a window. Unlike the private DC and the class DC, however, a parent DC does not cause a new DC to be allocated in the system. Instead, a window with this style bit will receive a regular DC from the system's DC cache.

The difference lies in the way that clipping is set in the DC. Unlike a regular DC, in which clipping set is either to the visible part of the client area (by `GetDC`) or to the damaged part of a window (by `BeginPaint`), clipping in a parent DC is set to the boundaries of the parent window. Figure 13.3 compares the clipping set up in a regular system DC with clipping in a parent DC. With the parent DC, the child window can draw anywhere in the client area of its parent's window. If you have children, this may

Figure 13.3 Comparing clipping in a system cache DC and in a parent DC

sound like a familiar state of affairs. Even if your children have their own rooms, they certainly are not shy about wandering into other rooms in your home.

You might be wondering why on earth anyone would give a child window the ability to draw into its parent's client area. This is a performance optimization to help in situations when the child is drawing in a very small space and may accidentally draw outside its own border (kids will be kids). We give the child windows a little leeway so that they are not clipped in an unexpected way. After all, clipping in software is expensive (in terms of overall performance), and can cause drawings to be altered in unexpected ways.

The parent DC style bit is set for the predefined classes that create Windows' dialog box controls. As you will see when we discuss dialog boxes in Chapter 14, dialog box controls are given a size and a position using a special set of coordinates called **dialog box coordinates**. Since there can be some degree of imprecision with these coordinates, the parent DC style bit gives the dialog box controls room to maneuver. If you create your own custom dialog box controls, you may wish to use the CS_PARENTDC style bit for them as well.

The CS_PARENTDC style bit is not compatible with the WS_CLIPCHILDREN style that we'll discuss when we look at CreateWindow style bits. If the parent window has this window style bit set, then its child windows cannot draw in the parent's window. You might call this the "Aunt Edna" style bit, since the kids don't run around as much (or at all) when your Aunt Edna comes over (she has a way with kids).

The CS_NOCLOSE class style removes the **Close** item from the system menu. You use this with windows that have a system menu when you don't want the user closing the window. As we discussed in Chapter 11, another way to achieve the same result involves modifying the system menu with the various menu modification routines. This style bit provides a simpler way to achieve the same end, providing that you need this behavior for every window in the window class.

The CS_SAVEBITS class style is a performance bit that you set for windows that visit the display screen for very short periods of time. The save-bits style asks the Window Manager to take a snapshot of the bits that the window overwrites when it appears. You may recall that this is how menus are able to make a graceful exit. After a menu disappears, a window never gets a WM_PAINT message to redraw the area that the menu had occupied. Menus are very polite: They don't damage any window on the display screen.

The save-bits style asks every window in a class to behave with the same courtesy. The default dialog box class is set up this way. For the most part, when a dialog box visits your window, it can disappear quickly and easily without requiring your window to be sent a WM_PAINT message to redraw. But sometimes things happen that thwart the save-bits style. For example, if the dialog box moves, the bitmap snapshot of the area behind the dialog box can no longer be used to restore the area after the dialog box is removed. Or, if any drawing is done underneath the dialog box, then the snapshot can't be used to restore the area touched by the dialog box. In both cases, a WM_PAINT message is generated after the dialog box (or other CS_SAVEBITS window) exits.

Two class style bits are used to specify how a window should be positioned on the display screen: CS_BYTEALIGNWINDOW and CS_BYTEALIGNCLIENT. These style bits never affect the height of a window or its placement in the Y-axis. However, they *do* affect the width of a window and its placement in the X-axis. As their names suggest, these style bits force either a window or its client area to be aligned on a byte boundary. This allows a performance improvement for certain types of operations: moving the window, drawing menu items, and drawing into the window.

Byte-aligned drawing is faster on certain types of devices: monochrome displays and color displays that use multiple planes to represent color. In fact, the only kind of device that doesn't really benefit from byte-aligned drawing is a color display that uses a packed pixel approach to storing data. Since all of the most popular display devices are either monochrome or color with multiple planes (including EGA, VGA, and 8514), the byte-aligned style gives a slight performance improvement in most cases.

The CS_GLOBALCLASS class style is used for window classes that are going to be shared among different programs. For example, if you are going to create a custom dialog box control, you'll want to register the window class of your dialog box control as a global class. This allows a single window class to be shared among several programs. For example, you could use your custom dialog box control to create your spreadsheet program, your word processing program, and even for your database program.

Once a window class has been registered, you can create as many copies of the window as you like. Next, we will examine the two Windows library routines that do this for you.

Creating a Window

There are two Windows library routines that directly create a window: CreateWindow and CreateWindowEx. The "Ex" at the end of the second routine's name stands for "extended." It does all of the things that the first routine can do, plus a little more. The CreateWindowEx routine was created because Microsoft ran out of style bits in the CreateWindow routine. This being the case, we're going to start by looking at the parameters to these routines, then consider all of the available style bits—both regular and extended.

CreateWindow is defined as follows:

```
CreateWindow (lpClassName, lpWindowName, dwStyle, X, Y, nWidth,
              nHeight, hWndParent, hMenu, hInstance, lpParam)
```

The extended style bits parameter is the first one in CreateWindowEx, which is defined as:

```
CreateWindowEx (dwExStyle,
                lpClassName, lpWindowName, dwStyle, X, Y, nWidth,
                nHeight, hWndParent, hMenu, hInstance, lpParam)
```

dwExStyle is an unsigned long (DWORD) value. We'll discuss the regular and extended style bits in a moment.

The lpClassName parameter is a long pointer to a character string for the class name. This is either the class name that you define using RegisterClass, or the name of a public window class that was created by someone else. For example, Windows makes available the following public window classes: **button**, **combobox**, **edit**, **listbox**, **scrollbar**, and **static** for use as dialog box controls.

The lpWindowName parameter is a long pointer to a character string for the window text. The window text is displayed in the title bar (also known as a caption bar) for windows that have a title bar. When a window is minimized, the window text is displayed as a label for the icon. Certain types of windows without a title bar, like push buttons, use the window text for a label.

The dwStyle parameter is an unsigned long (DWORD) value that contains a set of flags to define the shape, size, and behavior of the window you wish to create. The **X** and **Y** parameters identify the X and Y coordinates of the upper-left corner of the window. For top-level windows—that is, windows without parents—this location is relative to the upper-left corner of the display screen, also known as **screen coordinates**. For child windows, this is relative to the upper-left corner of the parent window's client area, also known as client area coordinates.

The Window Manager calculates the location of a top-level window when the value of the X coordinate is set to CW_USEDEFAULT. When this option is used, each subsequent top-level window is given an initial position that cascades from the previous window. This option arranges top-level windows in an orderly fashion, like soldiers in a row. Figure 13.4 shows the cascading effect created by this flag.

The nWidth and nHeight fields allow you to define the width and height of a window. For top-level windows, you can set nWidth to CW_USEDEFAULT, which tells the Window Manager to set the size of your window for you. This feature is not available for child windows, so you will have to calculate their size yourself.

When you calculate the size of a window—whether it is a child window or a top-level window—you'll need to keep in mind that CreateWindow and CreateWindowEx expect the size of the *entire* window and not just the client area. Many programmers make the mistake of calculating the size of the client area and using

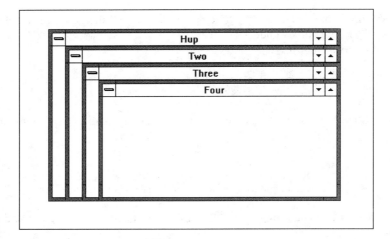

Figure 13.4 Cascading effect of the CW_USEDEFAULT flag

those dimensions. But an additional step is required: You must add in the size of the various nonclient area objects. When we discuss the issue of window metrics later in this chapter, we'll describe two different ways to calculate the size of the actual window to get a client area of the desired size.

The `hwndParent` parameter identifies the window that is to be the parent of the newborn window. Windows without a parent pass a `NULL` value in this field, which makes the window a child of the desktop window. Children of the desktop are considered **top-level windows** and are shown in the Task List that appears when the user strikes [Ctrl] + [Esc].

There are three different kinds of windows: overlapped, popup, and child. When you create a child window, it *must* have a parent window. This agrees with the way we think of human parents and children: Children depend on their parents for their well-being. The other two types of windows do not require a parent.

The `hMenu` parameter identifies the menu to be associated with a window. We have already seen that a menu name can be supplied when we register a window class. To use a different menu from the default class menu, specify a menu handle in this field. As we discussed in Chapter 11, the `LoadMenu` routine creates a menu from a resource:

```
HANDLE hMenu;
hMenu = LoadMenu (hInstance, "MENUNAME");
```

The `hInstance` parameter is an instance handle. When we discuss dynamic linking in Chapter 19, you'll see that the instance handle is a memory handle for a program's default data segment. The presence of this value in the parameter list plays a part in making sure that the window procedure is able to access its data segment correctly.

While this may seem like an odd issue when creating a window, keep in mind that a window procedure is a call-back function that is, in effect, a subroutine used exclusively by Windows. The part of Windows that calls this subroutine—Windows' USER module—has its own data segment. When a call is made into the window procedure, it goes through a gateway that uses the value of `hInstance` to store the value of our data segment in the CPU's AX register. The compiler, linker, and the Windows' loader work together to install the correct data segment selector into the CPU's DS (data segment) register (see Chapter 19).

Fortunately, this mechanism is transparent to you. Your window procedure is able to access your program's static data without having to do anything special; it only requires that you use the right compiler switches and that you list your window procedure in the EXPORTS section of the module definition (.DEF) file. The rest is taken care of for you through the magic of dynamic linking.

The lpParam parameter is an optional, four-byte long value that you can use to pass private data to your window procedure as part of the WM_CREATE message. If you translate this Hungarian notation into English, this field is intended to hold a long pointer, presumably to a private parameter block. However, if you only have two bytes of private data to pass, you don't need to use it as a long pointer but can simply pass the two bytes inside the pointer field.

If you *do* wish it to pass a parameter block, here is an example to show you how to go about it. We start by allocating a data block and passing a pointer to the block in the last parameter of CreateWindow:

```
LPSTR  lp;
RECT   rPrivate;

rPrivate.left = 10;    rPrivate.top    = 20;
rPrivate.right = 200;  rPrivate.bottom = 100;
lp = (LPSTR)&rPrivate;

hwnd = CreateWindow("MIN:MAIN",  // Class name.
    "Minimum",                   // Title.
    WS_OVERLAPPEDWINDOW,         // Style bits.
    CW_USEDEFAULT,               // x - default.
    0,                           // y - default.
    CW_USEDEFAULT,               // cx - default.
    0,                           // cy - default.
    NULL,                        // No parent.
    NULL,                        // Class menu.
    hInstance,                   // Creator.
    lp);                         // Params.
```

In this example, our data block is simply a RECT structure containing two (x,y) pairs, which are presumably of interest to our window procedure. A pointer to this structure is placed in the lParam parameter, which is the last parameter of CreateWindow.

The time to get a pointer to our data block is during the processing for the WM_CRE-ATE message. The lParam parameter of our window procedure will contain a pointer to a data structure defined in Windows.h as CREATESTRUCT. It is defined in Windows.h as

```
typedef struct tagCREATESTRUCT
    {
    LPSTR  lpCreateParams;
```

```
HANDLE  hInstance;
HANDLE  hMenu;
HWND    hwndParent;
int     cy;
int     cx;
int     y;
int     x;
LONG    style;
LPSTR   lpszName;
LPSTR   lpszClass;
DWORD   dwExStyle;
} CREATESTRUCT;
```

The first item in this structure, `lpCreateParams`, is the value that we passed as our last parameter to `CreateWindow`. Here is one way to create a pointer to our rectangle data:

```
LRESULT CALLBACK WndProc (...)
    {
    switch (msg)
        {
        case WM_CREATE:
            {
            int xTop;
            LPCREATESTRUCT lpcs;
            LPRECT lpr;

            lpcs = (LPCREATESTRUCT)lParam;
            lpr  = (LPRECT)lpcs->lpCreateParams;

            xTop = lpr -> top; /* =20    */
            break;
            ...
```

If you pass a pointer to a data block, you might want to make a private copy of the data for your window procedure, in case the creator of the window decides to free the memory or use it for other purposes.

At this point, we have discussed all of the parameters to `CreateWindow` and `CreateWindowEx`. To get a complete picture of what these routines have to offer, we need to dig a little deeper and investigate the different style bits that can be passed in the `dwExStyle` and `dwStyle` parameters.

Window Creation Style Bits

There are six categories of style bits to control window creation for `CreateWindow` and `CreateWindowEx`: type of window, window border, nonclient area components, the window's initial state, performance bits, and new Windows 3.1 style bits. These are summarized in Table 13.1.

Table 13.1 Summary of `CreateWindow` and `CreateWindowEx` Style Bits

Category	Style Bit	Description
Window Type (3)	WS_OVERLAPPED	Create an overlapped window, suitable for use as a top-level window. Overlapped windows always have a caption whether or not you specify the WS_CAPTION style, and they always have a border. A border of type WS_BORDER is used if no other type has been requested.
	WS_POPUP	Create a popup window, suitable for use as a dialog box, or secondary window.
	WS_CHILD	Create a child window, suitable for dividing up the area of overlapped, popup, and other child windows into smaller functional areas.
Border (4)	WS_BORDER	Window is to have a thin border. This is the default when a caption bar has been requested (with the WS_CAPTION style).
	WS_DLGFRAME	Window is to have a thick, solid border. In previous versions of Windows, this was the standard for dialog boxes. The WS_EX_DLGMODALFRAME style bit is used in Windows 3.0 instead.
	WS_THICKFRAME	Window is to have a thick frame. The presence of this border indicates that a window can be resized. The WS_CAPTION style must accompany this selection.
	WS_EX_DLGMODALFRAME	Window is to have an extended dialog frame, to include a system menu and caption bar, if requested. This is the standard style for dialog boxes.
Non-Client Components (6)	WS_CAPTION	Window has a caption, also known as a title bar. A caption is always accompanied by a border, with the WS_BORDER selected by default.

(continued)

Table 13.1 Summary of `CreateWindow` and `CreateWindowEx` Style Bits

Category	Style Bit	Description
	WS_HSCROLL	Window is to have a horizontal scroll bar. Scroll bars created using this style bit are always on the bottom edge of the window. To place a scroll bar in another part of a window, you must create a scroll bar control.
	WS_MAXIMIZEBOX	Window is to have a maximize box. The WS_CAPTION style must accompany this selection.
	WS_MINIMIZEBOX	Window is to have a minimize box. The WS_CAPTION style must accompany this selection.
	WS_SYSMENU	Window is to have a system menu. The WS_CAPTION style must accompany this selection.
	WS_VSCROLL	Window is to have a vertical scroll bar. Scroll bars created using this style bit are always placed on the right edge of the window. To locate a scroll bar at another location, you must create a scroll bar control.
Initial State (5)	WS_DISABLED	Window is initially disabled, which means that mouse and keyboard input is not delivered to the window. If the user tries to click on a disabled window, a warning beep is generated.
	WS_ICONIC	Window is initially iconic or minimized, which means that the window is closed, and only its icon is displayed.
	WS_MAXIMIZE	Window is initially maximized. For top-level windows, this means it occupies the complete display screen. For child windows, it means it occupies its parent's entire client area.
	WS_MINIMIZE	Window is initially iconic. This style bit is the same as the WS_ICONIC style bit.

(continued)

Table 13.1 Summary of `CreateWindow` and `CreateWindowEx` Style Bits

Category	Style Bit	Description
	WS_VISIBLE	Window is initially visible. This is a very important style bit, since without it a window will not appear.
Performance Bits (3)	WS_CLIPCHILDREN	Clipping in software is expensive; therefore, a parent window usually does not clip to avoid drawing in its children. However, if you wish a parent window to avoid overwriting its children, the parent must have this style set.
	WS_CLIPSIBLINGS	Clipping in software is expensive; therefore, sibling windows—that is, windows that have the same parent—do not make any extra effort to avoid drawing over each other. This style bit insures that siblings do not overwrite each other. It prevents what some Windows programmers refer to as "sibling rivalry."
	WS_EX_NOPARENTNOTIFY	By default, a child window sends quite a few notification messages to its parent, in the form of the WM_PARENTNOTIFY message. Notification messages are sent when the child is created, when it receives mouse click messages, and when it is destroyed. This style bit prevents a child from writing so many letters home. This decreased message traffic helps improve performance. Dialog box controls, for example, are always created with this style.
Windows 3.1 Styles (3)	WS_EX_ACCEPTFILES	A window accepts drag and drop files.
	WS_EX_TOPMOST	A top-level window, which should always stay at the top of the Z-ordering. In other words, it always appears in front of other windows.

(continued)

Table 13.1 Summary of `CreateWindow` and `CreateWindowEx` Style Bits

Category	Style Bit	Description
	WS_EX_TRANSPARENT	A window with this style bit will not paint over sibling windows. It is useful for stealing mouse events from other windows.

Type of Window

The best way to explain the three types of windows is to describe the intended use of each. The `WS_OVERLAPPED` window, for example, is meant to serve as a program's main, top-level window. A window created with the `WS_POPUP` style, which has some things in common with overlapped windows, is intended for dialog boxes and other secondary "free-floating" windows outside a program's main window. `WS_CHILD` windows are used to organize the use of overlapped, popup, and other child windows into functional areas. For example, dialog box controls are child windows used to divide a dialog box into visual and functional areas.

When you create a window with the `WS_OVERLAPPED` style, the Window Manager helps you make sure that the window meets the minimum standards required of a top-level window, such as the presence of a caption bar and a border. (You'll still need to specify `WS_CAPTION` to create system menus or other caption bar elements.) Since overlapped windows are expected to serve as top-level windows, the `CW_USE-DEFAULT` flag can be used to ask the Window Manager to automatically size and position an overlapped window. Finally, an overlapped window is positioned in **screen coordinates**. Even if an overlapped window has a parent, its positioning is independent of its parent.

The `WS_POPUP` style creates a popup window, which behaves like an overlapped window in many respects. It can reside anywhere on the display screen and is positioned in screen coordinates. Why have both styles? It's mostly an accident of history.

Version 1.x of Windows used *tiled windows* as main program windows. In those days, popup windows were provided only for dialog boxes. Starting with version 2.x of Windows, overlapping windows replaced tiled windows as the style used for main program windows. Since then, the differences between overlapped and popup windows have been mostly cosmetic, since they behave in exactly the same way.

With Windows 3.x, the differences between the two types have been reduced even further. Starting with Windows 3, a dialog box can have a title bar. As these two types of windows become more and more alike, the only reason for using both types is to prepare for the day when Windows needs to distinguish between main windows and dialogs. Presumably, if such a need should arise, your following this convention will simplify working with a future version of Windows.

A window created with the `WS_CHILD` style is a **child window**. These windows are used to divide other windows—overlapped, popup, and other child windows—into smaller functional areas. Since this is the case, a child window *must* have a parent. At window creation time, the parent is the window whose handle is passed as the `hwndParent` parameter of `CreateWindow` and `CreateWindowEx`. Like human children, *child windows* require a parent because the parent provides a place to live. A child window is only visible when positioned inside its parent's client area. Any portion outside the parent's client area is clipped—that is, is not visible.

Window Borders

Figure 13.5 shows the four available types of window borders. Among the border styles, only `WS_DLGFRAME` cannot have a caption. This outdated style has been replaced by `WS_EX_DLGMODALFRAME` for dialog boxes, but remains supported for compatibility with older Windows programs.

As mentioned earlier, a `WS_OVERLAPPED` window *must* have a border. If a border is not specified, the `WS_BORDER` style is automatically imposed. Other types of windows don't require borders, which makes it convenient to use child windows for invisibly dividing larger windows. But it doesn't make sense to create a popup window without a border, since it would get lost as windows are shuffled around the screen.

The border of a window and the caption bar change colors to let the user see a difference between active windows and inactive windows, as shown in Figure 13.5. The

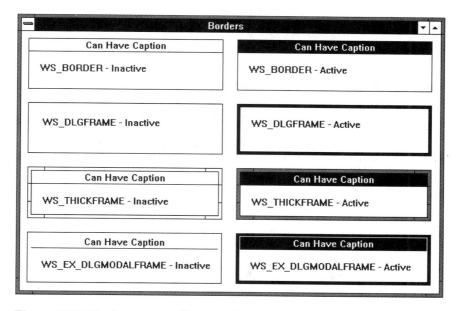

Figure 13.5 The four types of borders, in both inactive and active states

borders of top-level windows are changed automatically by the system, which sends a `WM_NCACTIVATE` message to inform a window to redraw its non-client area to reflect either an active or an inactive state. However, this message is not sent for child windows. To change a child window's border and caption to reflect an active state, you must transmit this message yourself, like this:

```
SendMessage (hwndChild, WM_NCACTIVATE, TRUE, 0L);
```

Changing the border and caption to reflect an inactive state involves the same message, with a `wParam` of `FALSE`:

```
SendMessage (hwndChild, WM_NCACTIVATE, FALSE, 0L);
```

Non-Client Area Components

Figure 13.6 shows each non-client area component and a corresponding style flag. With the exception of the two scroll bars, non-client area components are managed by the default window procedure. This means, of course, that a window procedure must forward the various non-client area messages to `DefWindowProc` for these parts to work properly. This is hardly a new requirement, since you are used to the idea that messages you don't use always get sent on for default handling.

When we cover scrolling in Chapter 22, you'll see how scroll bars send messages to let a window know what the user is doing with the scroll bar. There are two such messages: `WM_HSCROLL` is sent by horizontal scroll bars, `WM_VSCROLL` is sent by vertical scroll bars.

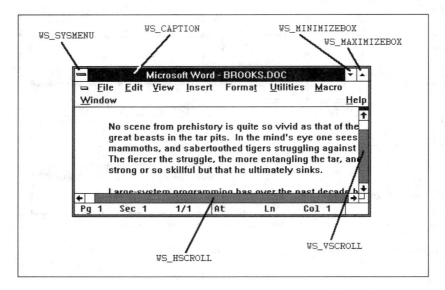

Figure 13.6 The non-client area components of a window

**Figure 13.7   A disabled push button
displays in grayed text**

Initial State

Of the four style bits that set a window's initial state, perhaps the most important is
WS_VISIBLE. Without this style bit, a window does not appear at creation time. Of
course, a window can be created without being made invisible and later made visible by
calling routines like ShowWindow and SetWindowPos, but it is often easier to
simply make a window visible at creation time.

One exception involves WS_OVERLAPPED windows. These can't be made visible
with the WS_VISIBLE style bit, but only appear when summoned by routines like
ShowWindow and SetWindowPos. We call the first of these two routines for the
top-level WS_OVERLAPPED window of every program in this book. The parameter
passed to ShowWindow for every top-level window is the cmdShow parameter provided as the last parameter to WinMain.

The WS_MINIMIZE and WS_MAXIMIZE style bits describe whether a window
should be initially minimized or maximized. You can apply these style bits to any type
of window, although WS_MAXIMIZE causes a WS_CHILD window to behave oddly.
In particular, a child window tries to occupy the full screen. Unfortunately, the visible
portion is limited to the area which lies in its parent's client area. The support routines
for the Multiple Document Interface (MDI), however, allow a maximized child window
to behave more reasonably: It expands to occupy its parent's client area. Older Windows
programs use WS_ICONIC instead of WS_MINIMIZE. If you check Windows.h,
you'll notice these two flags have identical values.

The WS_DISABLED style bit lets you create a window that might be visible, but is not
available for user interaction. Such a window is like a store that displays a "Gone to Lunch"
sign. Disabled dialog box controls are grayed when disabled; thus, not only is the user locked
out from the window, but the window provides visual feedback to make this clear. As an
example, Figure 13.7 shows two push buttons—the left one is enabled and the right one is
disabled. Plan to use the disabled state in windows that are visible, but not accessible.

Performance Bits

When we discussed window class style bits, we encountered style flags known as
performance bits. Each performance bit in a window class provides a speed boost for
certain operations.

Of the three window flags that are performance bits, only one actually improves system performance. The other two actually slow things down a bit, but provide you with some useful services. For this reason, we still call them performance bits, although perhaps a better term would be "performance *related*" style bits.

The first two styles, `WS_CLIPCHILDREN` and `WS_CLIPSIBLINGS`, control the way clipping is set up when drawing in a window. When we first discussed clipping in Chapter 6, we described how clipping is essential to allow the creation and maintenance of windows. Without clipping, one program might overwrite another program's window. Between two windows that don't belong to the same program, clipping is automatically provided.

Between windows that belong to the *same* program, clipping is not so strictly enforced. In particular, no automatic mechanism prevents a parent window from overwriting a `WS_CHILD` window. Between child windows, no automatic clipping prevents one child window from overwriting another. Clipping is turned *off* in these situations to improve system performance. Once a program places a window in a particular location, the Window Manager assumes that the program won't allow its other windows to interfere with that window. By default, the Window Manager keeps clipping—which is expensive in terms of system performance—turned off.

Things break down when the user is allowed to pick up and move windows. In this case, a program has less control over the placement of child windows. When a user might cause two windows to interfere with each other—by picking them up and moving them—the `WS_CLIPSIBLINGS` style bit should be used. This prevents "sibling rivalry," a tongue-in-cheek term we use for the border dispute between two child windows caused by the Window Manager's default settings.

The other clipping style bit, `WS_CLIPCHILDREN`, is used to prevent a parent window from overwriting its children. This is required when (a) a user can pick up a child window and move it around, and (b) the window's parent draws in its own client area. The fix involves using this style bit to force the Window Manager to do a little more work in setting up the clipping that will cause the parent window to respect the boundaries of its children.

The last performance bit is `WS_EX_NOPARENTNOTIFY`. This performance bit reduces the number of messages that a child window sends to its parent. By default, a child window lets its parent know when it is created, when it receives mouse click messages, and when it is destroyed. The child sends a `WM_PARENTNOTIFY` message to its parent, and also to all of its parent's parents. The `WS_EX_NOPARENTNOTIFY` style bit tells the child window to refrain from sending such advisory messages.

Compound Window Styles

The last three styles that we're going to look at are values that have been defined in Windows.h for the sake of convenience: `WS_OVERLAPPEDWINDOW`, `WS_POP-UPWINDOW`, and `WS_CHILDWINDOW`. These compound styles are defined as follows:

```
#define WS_OVERLAPPEDWINDOW (WS_OVERLAPPED | WS_CAPTION |
                             WS_SYSMENU | WS_THICKFRAME |
                             WS_MINIMIZEBOX | WS_MAXIMIZEBOX)
```

```
#define WS_POPUPWINDOW (WS_POPUP | WS_BORDER | WS_SYSMENU)
#define WS_CHILDWINDOW (WS_CHILD)
```

These values are available for the sake of convenience, to make it easier to select the most commonly selected style bits.

Top-Level Window Considerations

A program's top-level window is the main doorway through which users access a program. When first opened, it creates an initial impression of what to expect from a program. Many programs today allow the Windows Manager to define the initial position and size of their main window by specifying the `CW_USEDEFAULT` flag. While this provides one way to get started, we'd like to propose that you consider how your program starts out. Perhaps it makes more sense for it to run minimized, or maximized, or start in the very center of the display screen.

One approach would be to create your program's top-level window at a fixed location with a fixed size. For example, a program might create its top-level window with a location of (10, 10) and make its window 320 pixels wide and 240 pixels high. The problem with hard-coding values like this is that the effect you produce is dependent on the type of display with which the user is working. For example, a window of this size would occupy about one-half of a CGA screen, which is 640x200 pixels. But on an

Figure 13.8 A top-level window that defines its own size

8514, which has a resolution of 1024x768, this window would only occupy one-twelfth of the screen.

As an alternative, a program can call `GetSystemMetrics` to determine the size of the display screen and then set the size of the top-level window accordingly. Our next sample program, OWNSIZE, does just that. It creates a top-level window that is equal to the width of the display screen. It makes the window almost as tall as the display screen, but leaves enough room at the bottom of the display screen so that program icons resting there are visible. Figure 13.8 shows our program's top-level window when it is first created.

Here is the source code to OWNSIZE:

OWNSIZE.C

```
/*------------------------------------------------------------*\
| OwnSize.C  -  Demonstrates a self-sizing window which uses  |
|               profile files to store window size data.      |
\*------------------------------------------------------------*/
#define STRICT
#include <Windows.H>
#define REOPEN_NORMAL    0
#define REOPEN_MAXIMIZED 1
#define REOPEN_MINIMIZED 2


/*------------------------------------------------------------*\
|                    Function Prototypes.                      |
\*------------------------------------------------------------*/
LRESULT CALLBACK OwnSizeWndProc (HWND, UINT, WPARAM, LPARAM);


/*------------------------------------------------------------*\
|                     Global Variables.                       |
\*------------------------------------------------------------*/
char achWndClass[] = "OwnSize:MAIN";
char achAppName[]  = "Self-Sizing Window";
char achPr[]   = "OWNSIZE";      /* Profile file key name. */
char achFile[] = "OWNSIZE.INI"; /* Profile file name.  */


/*------------------------------------------------------------*\
|                  Main Function: WinMain.                     |
\*------------------------------------------------------------*/
int PASCAL
WinMain (HINSTANCE hInstance,      // Who am I?
         HINSTANCE hPrevInstance, // Any older siblings?
         LPSTR     lpszCmdLine,   // Ptr to command line.
         int       cmdShow)       // How to open my window?
    {
    HWND     hwnd;
    int      x, y, cx, cy;
    int      iReopen;
    MSG      msg;
    WNDCLASS wndclass;
```

```
if (!hPrevInstance)
    {
    wndclass.lpszClassName = achWndClass;
    wndclass.hInstance     = hInstance;
    wndclass.lpfnWndProc   = OwnSizeWndProc;
    wndclass.hCursor       = LoadCursor (hInstance, "hand");
    wndclass.hIcon         = LoadIcon (hInstance,"snapshot");
    wndclass.lpszMenuName  = NULL;
    wndclass.hbrBackground = (HBRUSH)(COLOR_WINDOW+1);
    wndclass.style         = NULL;
    wndclass.cbClsExtra    = 0;
    wndclass.cbWndExtra    = 0;

    RegisterClass( &wndclass);

    //  For first instance, set position & size to that
    //  of window when we last ran.
    cy = GetSystemMetrics (SM_CYSCREEN) -
         GetSystemMetrics (SM_CYICON)   -
         (GetSystemMetrics (SM_CYCAPTION) * 2);

    x = GetPrivateProfileInt (achPr, "x", 0, achFile);
    y = GetPrivateProfileInt (achPr, "y", 0, achFile);

    cx = GetSystemMetrics (SM_CXSCREEN);
    cx = GetPrivateProfileInt (achPr, "cx", cx, achFile);
    cy = GetPrivateProfileInt (achPr, "cy", cy, achFile);

    iReopen = GetPrivateProfileInt (achPr, "Reopen", 0,
                                    achFile);

    if (iReopen == REOPEN_MAXIMIZED)
        cmdShow = SW_SHOWMAXIMIZED;
    if (iReopen == REOPEN_MINIMIZED)
        {
        cmdShow = SW_SHOWMINIMIZED;
        x = cx = CW_USEDEFAULT;
        y = cy = 0;
        }
    }
else
    {
    //  Other instances, use default position & size.
    x = cx = CW_USEDEFAULT;
    y = cy = 0;
    }

hwnd = CreateWindowEx(0L,                    // Extra style.
                    achWndClass,             // Class name.
                    achAppName,              // Title.
                    WS_OVERLAPPEDWINDOW,     // Style bits.
                    x,                       // x - default.
                    y,                       // y - default.
                    cx,                      // cx - default.
                    cy,                      // cy - default.
```

```
                         NULL,                   // No parent.
                         NULL,                   // Class menu.
                         hInstance,              // Creator.
                         NULL);                  // Params.
        ShowWindow (hwnd, cmdShow);

        while (GetMessage(&msg, 0, 0, 0))
            {
            TranslateMessage(&msg); // Convert KEYDOWNs to CHARs
            DispatchMessage(&msg);  // Transmit message to WndProc
            }
        return 0;
        }


/*---------------------------------------------------------------*\
|              Window Procedure:  OwnSizeWndProc.                  |
\*---------------------------------------------------------------*/
LRESULT CALLBACK
OwnSizeWndProc (HWND   hwnd,     // For whom is message sent?
                UINT   mMsg,     // What is exact message?
                WPARAM wParam,   // ...message details.
                LPARAM lParam)   // ...message details.
        {
        static int xLeft;
        static int yTop;
        static int cxWidth;
        static int cyHeight;

        switch (mMsg)
            {
            case WM_DESTROY:
                {
                char ach[80];
                int  iReopen;

                //  Update private OwnSize entry.

                wsprintf (ach, "%d",xLeft);
                WritePrivateProfileString (achPr, "x",    //   X.
                    ach, achFile);

                wsprintf (ach, "%d",yTop);
                WritePrivateProfileString (achPr, "y",    //   Y.
                    ach, achFile);

                if (cxWidth==0) cxWidth=CW_USEDEFAULT;
                wsprintf (ach, "%u",cxWidth);
                WritePrivateProfileString (achPr, "cx",   //   CX.
                     ach, achFile);

                wsprintf (ach, "%d",cyHeight);
                WritePrivateProfileString (achPr, "cy",   //   CY.
                    ach, achFile);

                //  Write flags for iconic/maximized windows.
```

```
            iReopen = REOPEN_NORMAL;
            if (IsZoomed (hwnd))  iReopen = REOPEN_MAXIMIZED;
            if (IsIconic (hwnd))  iReopen = REOPEN_MINIMIZED;

            wsprintf (ach, "%d", iReopen);
            WritePrivateProfileString (achPr, "Reopen",
                 ach, achFile);

            PostQuitMessage(0);
            }
            break;

        case WM_MOVE:
            // Save last non-zoomed, non-iconic position.
            if (IsZoomed(hwnd) || IsIconic(hwnd))
                break;

            xLeft  = LOWORD (lParam);
            xLeft -= GetSystemMetrics (SM_CXFRAME);

            yTop   = HIWORD (lParam);
            yTop  -= (GetSystemMetrics (SM_CYFRAME) +
                    GetSystemMetrics (SM_CYCAPTION) - 1);
            break;

        case WM_SIZE:
            // Save last non-zoomed, non-iconic size.
            if (IsZoomed(hwnd) || IsIconic(hwnd))
                break;

            cxWidth  = LOWORD (lParam);
            cxWidth += 2 * GetSystemMetrics (SM_CXFRAME);

            cyHeight = HIWORD (lParam);
            cyHeight += (2 * GetSystemMetrics (SM_CYFRAME)) +
                        GetSystemMetrics (SM_CYCAPTION) - 1;
            break;

        default:
            return(DefWindowProc(hwnd,mMsg,wParam,lParam));
            break;
        }
    return 0L;
    }
```

OWNSIZE.DEF

```
NAME    OWNSIZE

EXETYPE WINDOWS

DESCRIPTION 'Self-Sizing Main Window (c) 1992 By Paul Yao'
```

```
CODE      MOVEABLE PRELOAD
DATA      MOVEABLE MULTIPLE PRELOAD

HEAPSIZE      512
STACKSIZE    5120

SEGMENTS
   OWNSIZE_TEXT MOVEABLE PRELOAD

EXPORTS
   OwnSizeWndProc
```

OWNSIZE.LNK

```
OwnSize.obj
OwnSize.exe/align:16/map/nod/noe/CO
nul
mlibcew libw
OwnSize.def
```

OWNSIZE.MAK

```
# Directory search paths.

INCDIR = \WINDEV\INCLUDE

# Windows version to support
# Valid pairs include:
#     (0x0300, 30)
#     (0x0310, 31)

CLVER = WINVER=0x0300
RCVER = 30

# Compiler switches for applications.

CL_APP_SHIP_ALL = -AM -c -D$(CLVER) -Gsw -I$(INCDIR) -Ow -W3 -Zp
CL_APP_DEBG_ALL = -AM -c -D$(CLVER) -Gsw -I$(INCDIR) -Od -W3 -Zpi

CL_APP_SHIP_31  = -AM -c -G2s  -I$(INCDIR) -Ow -W3 -Zp
CL_APP_DEBG_31  = -AM -c -G2s  -I$(INCDIR) -Od -W3 -Zpi

# Compiler switches for DLLs.

CL_DLL_SHIP_ALL = -AMw -c -D$(CLVER) -Gsw -I$(INCDIR) -Ow -W3 -Zp
CL_DLL_DEBG_ALL = -AMw -c -D$(CLVER) -Gsw -I$(INCDIR) -Od -W3 -Zpi

CL_DLL_SHIP_31  = -AMw -c -G2s  -I$(INCDIR) -Ow -W3 -Zp
CL_DLL_DEBG_31  = -AMw -c -G2s  -I$(INCDIR) -Od -W3 -Zpi
```

```
# Make file primary target.

all: OwnSize.exe

# Make file dependency targets.

OwnSize.res: OwnSize.rc OwnSize.cur OwnSize.ico
    rc -r -i$(INCDIR) OwnSize.rc

OwnSize.obj: OwnSize.c
    cl $(CL_APP_SHIP_ALL) OwnSize.c

OwnSize.exe: OwnSize.obj OwnSize.def OwnSize.res
    link @OwnSize.lnk
    rc -$(RCVER) OwnSize.res

OwnSize.exe: OwnSize.res
    rc -$(RCVER) OwnSize.res
```

OWNSIZE.RC

```
snapshot icon OwnSize.ico

hand  cursor OwnSize.cur
```

OWNSIZE retrieves the position and size of its top-level window in response to the
WM_MOVE and WM_SIZE notification messages. As is the case with almost everything
in Windows, there are other ways to accomplish this task. Another way would be with a
call to GetWindowRect, which would retrieve both location and size information.
This function gets passed a pointer to a RECT structure. The (x,y) location of the
window is simply the (left,top) members of this structure. The width and height (cx,cy)
must be calculated as follows:

```
RECT rWindow;
GetWindowRect (hwnd, &rWindow);
cx = rWindow.right - rWindow.left + 1;
cy = rWindow.bottom - rWindow.top + 1;
```

You might notice that OWNSIZE has a bit of a problem. It can restore a window to its
previous state (minimized, maximized, or normal). For a normal window, it can restore
its previous location. However, for a minimized or maximized window, the restored
location is not available. (By "restored location", we mean the normal window state
when the window is neither minimized nor maximized.) Fortunately, Windows 3.1
introduces a routine which can help: GetWindowPlacement and
SetWindowPlacement. These two routines let you query and set three different
location values: the minimized location, maximized location, and restored (or normal)
location. In fact, you could rewrite OWNSIZE with a single call to each of these routines
in place of the more complex handling of window location currently employed.

OWNSIZE demonstrates two programming techniques of general interest. First, it uses the `GetSystemMetrics` routine to determine the size of its top-level window when it is first run. When OWNSIZE is about to exit, it writes the size of its window to a private **profile file**. A profile file is an ASCII text file that a program can use to store values that it wants to remember. OWNSIZE uses a profile file to save the location and dimensions of its window, so the next time it is run it can start up with the same size. It also sets a flag if the window was zoomed; so that the next time the program is started, it can make its window zoomed as well. The profile file provides a sense of continuity for a program.

The initial window width in OWNSIZE is set to the display screen width. This is determined with a call made to `GetSystemMetrics` using the `SM_CXSCREEN` parameter:

```
cx = GetSystemMetrics (SM_CXSCREEN);
```

The initial window height in OWNSIZE leaves room to display a row of icons at the bottom of the display screen. Once again, calculating the required height involves calls to `GetSystemMetrics`. The first determines the screen height; the second determines the height of an icon; and the third determines the height of a caption, since each icon is accompanied by a caption. Here is the line of code that does this calculation:

```
cy = GetSystemMetrics (SM_CYSCREEN) -
     GetSystemMetrics (SM_CYICON)    -
    (GetSystemMetrics (SM_CYCAPTION) * 2);
```

The caption height is multiplied by two just to make sure there is enough room.

`GetSystemMetrics` provides measurement information for quite a few objects that make up the Windows user interface. Included are the size of cursors, icons, menus, and captions, as well as the widths of the different types of borders. Let's take a moment to look at some of the different measurement values that this routine can provide.

System Metrics

Table 13.2 lists all of the system metrics. To give you a better idea of what each value represents, we've also represented most of the system metrics visually in Figures 13.9, 13.10, and 13.11.

The primary reason for using these metric values is to allow an application to operate in a truly device-independent manner. Towards that end, the developer of every display driver must define the system metrics that are reasonable for a particular display device. Consider, for example, the width of a thin border. On a VGA display, borders are one pixel wide. A very high resolution display, on the other hand, might require two or three pixels to display a reasonable border.

The system metric query values shown in Table 13.2 provide your application with sizes for every user-interface object in the system. If you want to know how big icons are, call `GetSystemMetrics` with the `SM_CXICON` and `SM_CYICON` values. For

Table 13.2 Windows System Metrics

Type	Index	Description
Screen Metrics (4)	SM_CXSCREEN	Screen width in pixels.
	SM_CYSCREEN	Screen height in pixels.
	SM_CXFULLSCREEN	Screen width in pixels.
	SM_CYFULLSCREEN	Screen height in pixels minus the height of a window caption.
Border Sizes (6)	SM_CXBORDER	Width of a border created with the WS_BORDER style.
	SM_CYBORDER	Height of a border created with the WS_BORDER style.
	SM_CXFRAME	Width of a border on a window created with the WS_THICKFRAME style bit.
	SM_CYFRAME	Height of a border on a window created with the WS_THICKFRAME style bit.
	SM_CXDLGFRAME	Width of a border on a window with either a WS_EX_DLGMODALFRAME or WS_DLGFRAME style border.
	SM_CYDLGFRAME	Height of a border on a window with either a WS_EX_DLGMODALFRAME or WS_DLGFRAME style border.
Scroll Bar Metrics (6)	SM_CXVSCROLL	Width of the arrow bitmap in a vertical scroll bar.
	SM_CYHSCROLL	Height of the arrow bitmap in a horizontal scroll bar.
	SM_CYVSCROLL	Height of the arrow bitmap in a vertical scroll bar.
	SM_CXHSCROLL	Width of the arrow bitmap in a horizontal scroll bar.
	SM_CYVTHUMB	Height of the thumb in a vertical scroll bar.
	SM_CXHTHUMB	Width of the thumb in a horizontal scroll bar.
Window Components (8)	SM_CYCAPTION	Height of a caption bar.
	SM_CYMENU	Height of a single-line menu item.
	SM_CXICON	Width of an icon.
	SM_CYICON	Height of an icon.

(continued)

Table 13.3 Windows System Metrics

Type	Index	Description
	SM_CXCURSOR	Width of a cursor.
	SM_CYCURSOR	Height of a cursor.
	SM_CXSIZE	Width of the system menu, minimize and maximize icons.
	SM_CYSIZE	Height of the system menu, minimize and maximize icons.
Window Tracking (4)	SM_CXMIN	Minimum width of a window.
	SM_CYMIN	Minimum height of a window.
	SM_CXMINTRACK	Minimum tracking width of a window.
	SM_CYMINTRACK	Minimum tracking height of a window.
Miscellaneous Flags (4)	SM_DEBUG	Nonzero if the debug version of Windows is installed.
	SM_SWAPBUTTON	Nonzero if the left and right mouse buttons are swapped.
	SM_MOUSEPRESENT	Nonzero if a mouse is present.
	SM_CMETRICS	Count of the number of system metric values.

Figure 13.9 Border size system metrics

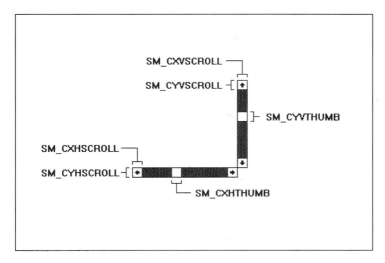

Figure 13.10 Scroll bar system metrics

the width or height of scroll bar components, borders, cursors, and caption bars, this function provides what you need.

It also provides some other, non-metric information. For example, you can find out if the debug version of Windows is present by using the SM_DEBUG flag. You can also check for the availability of a mouse, and see if the user has swapped the left and right mouse buttons from the Control Panel.

Our sample program, OWNSIZE, uses GetSystemMetrics values to position its main window the very first time the user runs this program. When it terminates, it stores

Figure 13.11 Window component system metrics

the state of its window in a private **profile file**. When it starts running again, OWNSIZE is able to position its main window at the last location it was seen by the user. Let's take a closer look at Windows' support for profile files.

Private Profile Files

One way that a program can improve its rapport with a user is to remember the user's preferences. This might mean remembering selected menu options, preferred colors, or something as simple as the position of the program's top-level window. To simplify this task, Windows has support for the creation of private profile files, also known as private initialization files. Of course, you can keep user preferences in your own format, but profile files provide a built-in, easy way to manage this type of data.

A profile file is an ASCII text file, which means that users can modify the file using a text editor. Here is an example of a profile file that OWNSIZE creates:

```
[OWNSIZE]
x=0
y=0
cx=640
cy=408
Reopen=0
```

All profile files follow the format shown here:

```
[application name]
keyname1 = value1
keyname2 = value2
keyname3 = value3
```

OWNSIZE keeps four numeric values that correspond to the location and the dimensions of the window when OWNSIZE was last run. These are associated with the keynames x, y, cx, and cy. A fifth numeric value, associated with the keyname "Reopen," is used when the window is minimized or maximized at program termination time. This flag is needed because restoring the state of a maximized or minimized window is done with a call to ShowWindow and not as a parameter to CreateWindow.

Windows provides six routines that read and write profile files. Three routines, GetProfileInt, GetProfileString, and WriteProfileString, read from and write to WIN.INI, which is the profile file used by Windows and older Windows programs. The other three, GetPrivateProfileInt, GetPrivateProfileString, and WritePrivateProfileString, read and write private initialization files.

OWNSIZE writes into its private profile file, OWNSIZE.INI, by calling WritePrivateProfileString, defined as follows:

```
WritePrivateProfileString (lpApplication, lpKey, lpString, lpFile)
```

- `lpApplication` is a long pointer to the application name. This is the name placed in square brackets in the profile file to identify a group of keyname/value pairs.

- `lpKey` is the long pointer to the name of the data identifier. That is, it is the string on the left of the equal sign in a keyname/value pair.

- `lpString` is a long pointer to the string to be placed on the right side of the equal sign in a keyname/value pair.

- `lpFile` is a long pointer to a character string for the filename to be used as a profile file. If no directory is given, the profile file is written into Windows' directory.

For example, here is how OWNSIZE writes the x location of the window:

```
wsprintf (ach, "%d",xLeft);
WritePrivateProfileString (achPr, "x",    //    X.
    ach, achFile);
```

When OWNSIZE starts up, it calls `GetPrivateProfileInt` to retrieve the various numeric values that it uses for the initial size and position of its window. This routine allows a program to establish a default value in case the requested integer value is not available. `GetPrivateProfileInt` is defined as follows:

```
WORD GetPrivateProfileInt (lpApp, lpKey, nDefault, lpFile)
```

- `lpApplication` is a long pointer to the application name. This is the name placed in square brackets in the profile file to identify a group of keyname/value pairs.

- `lpKey` is the long pointer to the name of the data identifier. That is, it is the string on the left of the equal sign in a keyname/value pair.

- `nDefault` is the value to be used if the keyname is not available in the initialization file, or if the initialization file does not exist.

- `lpFile` is a long pointer to a character string for the file name to be used as a profile file. If no directory is given, the profile file is written into Windows' directory.

It returns an unsigned integer for the value in the profile file, or the default value if an entry is not be found. Here is how OWNSIZE retrieves the (x,y) location from the private profile file:

```
x  = GetPrivateProfileInt (achPr, "x", 0, achFile);
y  = GetPrivateProfileInt (achPr, "y", 0, achFile);
```

To improve overall system performance, Windows keeps a cache of recently accessed profile information. To force a recent change to be written to disk, call

`WritePrivateProfileString` using `NULL` for every parameter except the file name. For example, OWNDRAW could flush its cache to disk with the following call:

```
WritePrivateProfileString ("OWNSIZE.INI", NULL, NULL, NULL);
```

The next topic for discussion is the use of child windows in a program's top-level window.

Creating a Child Window

In our discussion of the `CreateWindow` and `CreateWindowEx` routines, we mentioned that there are three types of windows: overlapped, popup, and child. All of the windows that we have created until now have been overlapped windows. In the next chapter, we'll create quite a few popup and child windows when we create dialog boxes. Right now, though, let's look at what is involved in creating a child window inside the client area of our program's main window.

Creating a child window involves the same two-step process already used for overlapped windows: First, a call to `RegisterClass` defines a window class; next, a window is created by calling either `CreateWindow` or `CreateWindowEx`. There are a few things to keep in mind, however, to ensure success in the creation of a child window.

When you register a class of windows that you plan to use as child windows, you'll need to define a window procedure to handle the messages to be sent to your child windows. The window procedure must be declared CALLBACK (although FAR and PASCAL can also be used); it must return an LRESULT (that is, a `long`) value, and must take the four standard window procedure parameters:

```
LRESULT CALLBACK
ChildWndProc (HWND    hwnd,
              UINT    mMsg,
              WPARAM  wParam,
              LPARAM  lParam)
```

When you create a new window procedure, be sure to list the procedure name in the EXPORTS section of your program's module definition file:

```
EXPORTS
    MinWndProc
    ChildWndProc
```

Alternatively, you could use the `_export` keyword in your function definition. Both produce the same results.

If you forget to export a call-back function, you may see some strange results when you run your program in Windows 3.0. (In Windows 3.1 this doesn't generally cause problems.) In particular, your child window won't be able to access your program's static data area. We'll cover this in more detail when we discuss dynamic linking and the module data segment in Chapter 19. Unfortunately, when you forget to export a call-back function, neither the compiler nor the linker can detect the error.

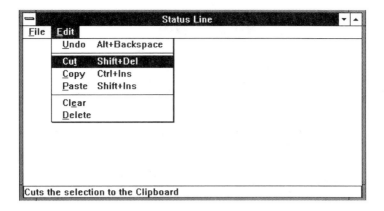

Figure 13.12 STATLINE uses a child window to display menu selection information

The next sample program that we're going to look at is STATLINE, which creates a child window to display status information about menu items as the user browses the menus.

STATLINE: Menu Status Information

In Chapter 11, when we discussed the message traffic associated with menus, we mentioned that the WM_MENUSELECT message gets sent as a user browses through menus. STATLINE responds to this message by displaying additional information about each menu item in a child window that serves as a status line. Figure 13.12 shows STATLINE and the child window that displays menu status information. Here is the source code to STATLINE:

STATLINE.C

```
/*-----------------------------------------------------------*\
| STATLINE.C  -  Creates a status line child window.          |
\*-----------------------------------------------------------*/
#define STRICT
#include <Windows.H>
#include "StatLine.H"


/*-----------------------------------------------------------*\
|                     Function Prototypes.                     |
\*-----------------------------------------------------------*/
LRESULT CALLBACK StatLineWndProc (HWND, UINT, WPARAM, LPARAM);
LRESULT CALLBACK StatLineChildWndProc (HWND, UINT, WPARAM, LPARAM);
```

```
/*-------------------------------------------------------------*\
|                      Global Variables.                        |
\*-------------------------------------------------------------*/
char achWndClass[]   = "StatLine:MAIN";
char achChildClass[] = "StatLine:CHILD";
char achAppName[]     = "Status Line";
HWND hwndChild;
int  cyChildHeight;


/*-------------------------------------------------------------*\
|                  Main Function:  WinMain.                     |
\*-------------------------------------------------------------*/
int PASCAL
WinMain (HINSTANCE hInstance,      // Who am I?
         HINSTANCE hPrevInstance,  // Any older siblings?
         LPSTR     lpszCmdLine,    // Ptr to command line.
         int       cmdShow)        // How to open my window?
    {
    HACCEL   hAccel;
    HWND     hwnd;
    MSG      msg;
    WNDCLASS wndclass;

    if (!hPrevInstance)
        {
        wndclass.lpszClassName = achWndClass;
        wndclass.hInstance     = hInstance;
        wndclass.lpfnWndProc   = StatLineWndProc;
        wndclass.hCursor       = LoadCursor (hInstance, "hand");
        wndclass.hIcon         = LoadIcon (hInstance,"snapshot");
        wndclass.lpszMenuName  = "#1";
        wndclass.hbrBackground = (HBRUSH)(COLOR_WINDOW+1);
        wndclass.style         = NULL;
        wndclass.cbClsExtra    = 0;
        wndclass.cbWndExtra    = 0;

        RegisterClass( &wndclass);

        RegisterClass( &wndclass);
        wndclass.lpszClassName = achChildClass;
        wndclass.hInstance     = hInstance;
        wndclass.lpfnWndProc   = StatLineChildWndProc;
        wndclass.hCursor       = LoadCursor (hInstance, "hand");
        wndclass.hIcon         = NULL;
        wndclass.lpszMenuName  = NULL;
        wndclass.hbrBackground = (HBRUSH)(COLOR_WINDOW+1);
        wndclass.style         = NULL;
        wndclass.cbClsExtra    = 0;
        wndclass.cbWndExtra    = 0;

        RegisterClass( &wndclass);
        }

    hwnd = CreateWindowEx(0L,                   // Extra style.
                      achWndClass,              // Class name.
```

```
                              achAppName,              // Title.
                              WS_OVERLAPPEDWINDOW |    // Style bits.
                              WS_CLIPCHILDREN,
                              CW_USEDEFAULT            // x - default.
                              0,                       // y - default.
                              CW_USEDEFAULT,           // cx - default.
                              0,                       // cy - default.
                              NULL,                    // No parent.
                              NULL,                    // Class menu.
                              hInstance,               // Creator.
                              NULL);                   // Params.

        hwndChild = CreateWindowEx(0L,                 // Extra style.
                              achChildClass,           // Class name.
                              NULL,                    // Title.
                              WS_CHILD   |             // Style bits.
                              WS_BORDER  |
                              WS_VISIBLE,
                              0, 0, 0, 0,              // x, y, cx, cy.
                              hwnd,                    // Parent window.
                              NULL,                    // No menu.
                              hInstance,               // Creator.
                              NULL);                   // Params.


        ShowWindow (hwnd, cmdShow);

        hAccel = LoadAccelerators (hInstance, "#1");

        while (GetMessage(&msg, 0, 0, 0))
            {
            if (!TranslateAccelerator (hwnd, hAccel, &msg))
                {
                TranslateMessage(&msg); // Convert KEYDOWNs to CHARs
                DispatchMessage(&msg);  // Transmit message to WndProc
                }
            }

        return 0;
        }

/*-------------------------------------------------------------*\
|              Window Procedure:  StatLineWndProc.              |
\*-------------------------------------------------------------*/
LRESULT CALLBACK
StatLineWndProc (HWND    hwnd,     // For whom is message sent?
                 UINT    mMsg,     // What is exact message?
                 WPARAM  wParam,   // ...message details.
                 LPARAM  lParam)   // ...message details.
    {
    switch (mMsg)
        {
        case WM_COMMAND:
            {
            char buffer[80];
```

```
char *npch;

switch (wParam)
    {
    case IDM_FILE_NEW:
        npch = "File.New";
        break;
    case IDM_FILE_OPEN:
        npch = "File.Open...";
        break;
    case IDM_FILE_SAVE:
        npch = "File.Save";
        break;
    case IDM_FILE_SAVEAS:
        npch = "File.Save As...";
        break;
    case IDM_FILE_PRINT:
        npch = "File.Print";
        break;
    case IDM_FILE_EXIT:
        npch = "File.Exit";
        break;
    case IDM_EDIT_UNDO:
        npch = "Edit.Undo";
        break;
    case IDM_EDIT_CUT:
        npch = "Edit.Cut";
        break;
    case IDM_EDIT_COPY:
        npch = "Edit.Copy";
        break;
    case IDM_EDIT_PASTE:
        npch = "Edit.Paste";
        break;
    case IDM_EDIT_CLEAR:
        npch = "Edit.Clear";
        break;
    case IDM_EDIT_DELETE:
        npch = "Edit.Delete";
        break;
    }

// Display message box with
// name of selected menu item.
wsprintf (buffer, "%s command selected.", (LPSTR)npch);
MessageBox (hwnd, buffer, achAppName, MB_OK);

// If user selected File.Exit,
// simulate {-}.Close menu selection.
if (wParam == 6)
    {
    SendMessage (hwnd, WM_SYSCOMMAND, SC_CLOSE, 0L);
    }
}
break;
```

```
    case WM_CREATE:
        {
        HDC hdc;
        int cyBorder;
        TEXTMETRIC tm;

        hdc = GetDC (hwnd);
        GetTextMetrics (hdc, &tm);
        ReleaseDC (hwnd, hdc);

        cyBorder = GetSystemMetrics (SM_CYBORDER);

        cyChildHeight = tm.tmHeight + cyBorder * 2;
        }
        break;

    case WM_DESTROY:
        PostQuitMessage(0);   // Handle application shutdown.
        break;

    case WM_MENUSELECT:
        SendMessage (hwndChild, mMsg, wParam, lParam);
        break;

    case WM_SIZE:
        {
        int cxWidth;
        int cyHeight;
        int xChild;
        int yChild;

        cxWidth  = LOWORD (lParam);
        cyHeight = HIWORD (lParam);

        xChild = 0;
        yChild = cyHeight - cyChildHeight + 1;

        MoveWindow (hwndChild,
                    xChild,
                    yChild,
                    cxWidth,
                    cyChildHeight,
                    TRUE);
        }
        break;

    default:
        return(DefWindowProc(hwnd,mMsg,wParam,lParam));
        break;
    }
return 0L;
}
```

```
/*------------------------------------------------------------*\
|             Window Procedure:   StatLineChildWndProc.        |
\*------------------------------------------------------------*/
LRESULT CALLBACK
StatLineChildWndProc (HWND    hwnd,    // For whom is message sent?
                      UINT    mMsg,    // What is exact message?
                      WPARAM  wParam,  // ...message details.
                      LPARAM  lParam)  // ...message details.
    {
    STATUSDATA sd[COUNT] =
        { 0xffff, "",
          IDM_POPUP_SYS,   "Move, size or close application window",
          IDM_POPUP_FILE, "Create, open, save, print, or quit",
          IDM_POPUP_EDIT, "Undo, cut, copy, paste and delete",

          IDM_FILE_NEW, "Creates a new item",
          IDM_FILE_OPEN, "Open an existing item",
          IDM_FILE_SAVE, "Save existing item",
          IDM_FILE_SAVEAS, "Save the current item with a new name",
          IDM_FILE_PRINT, "Prints the current item",
          IDM_FILE_EXIT, "Quits Statline",

          IDM_EDIT_UNDO, "Reverse the last action",
          IDM_EDIT_CUT, "Cuts the selection to the Clipboard",
          IDM_EDIT_COPY,"Copies the selection to the Clipboard",
          IDM_EDIT_PASTE, "Copies the selection from the Clipboard",
          IDM_EDIT_CLEAR, "Erases the currently selected item",
          IDM_EDIT_DELETE, "Erases the currently selected item",

          SC_SIZE, "Changes window size",
          SC_MOVE, "Changes window position",
          SC_MINIMIZE,"Reduces window to an icon",
          SC_MAXIMIZE,"Enlarges the active window to full size",
          SC_CLOSE, "Quits Statline",
          SC_RESTORE, "Restores window to normal size",
          SC_TASKLIST, "Switches to the task list"
        };

    static HMENU hmenuEdit;
    static HMENU hmenuFile;
    static HMENU hmenuSys;

    switch (mMsg)
        {
        case WM_CREATE:
            {
            HMENU hmenu;
            HWND  hwndParent;

            hwndParent = GetParent (hwnd);
            hmenu = GetMenu (hwndParent);

            hmenuFile = GetSubMenu (hmenu, 0);
            hmenuEdit = GetSubMenu (hmenu, 1);
            hmenuSys  = GetSystemMenu (hwndParent, 0);
            }
            break;
```

```
        case WM_MENUSELECT:
            {
            HDC hdc;
            int isd;
            int i;
            RECT rClient;
            WORD wFlag;

            wFlag = LOWORD (lParam);

            if (wFlag == 0xffff)
                wParam = 0xffff;
            else if (wFlag & MF_POPUP)
                {
                if ((UINT)hmenuSys == wParam)
                    wParam = IDM_POPUP_SYS;
                if ((UINT)hmenuFile == wParam)
                    wParam = IDM_POPUP_FILE;
                if ((UINT)hmenuEdit == wParam)
                    wParam = IDM_POPUP_EDIT;
                }

            // Search for a match in the string list.
            isd=0;
            for (i=0;i<COUNT;i++)
                {
                if (wParam == sd[i].wCode)
                    {
                    isd = i;
                    break;
                    }
                }

            GetClientRect (hwnd, &rClient);

            hdc = GetDC (hwnd);
            ExtTextOut (hdc,
                        0,                  /*  X.                */
                        0,                  /*  Y.                */
                        ETO_OPAQUE,         /*  Opaque rectangle. */
                        &rClient,           /*  Rectangle.        */
                        sd[isd].achMsg,     /*  String.           */
                        lstrlen(sd[isd].achMsg), /*  Length.      */
                        NULL);
            ReleaseDC (hwnd, hdc);
            }
            break;

    default:
        return(DefWindowProc(hwnd,mMsg,wParam,lParam));
        break;
    }
return 0L;
}
```

STATLINE.DEF

```
NAME      STATLINE

EXETYPE WINDOWS

DESCRIPTION 'Status Line (c) 1992 By Paul Yao'

CODE      MOVEABLE PRELOAD
DATA      MOVEABLE MULTIPLE PRELOAD

HEAPSIZE      512
STACKSIZE   5120

SEGMENTS
    STATLINE_TEXT MOVEABLE PRELOAD

EXPORTS
    StatLineWndProc
    StatLineChildWndProc
```

STATLINE.H

```
/*------------------------------------------------------------*\
| Statline.h  -- include file for Statline.C.                |
\*------------------------------------------------------------*/

#define IDM_FILE_NEW      101
#define IDM_FILE_OPEN     102
#define IDM_FILE_SAVE     103
#define IDM_FILE_SAVEAS   104
#define IDM_FILE_PRINT    105
#define IDM_FILE_EXIT     106

#define IDM_EDIT_UNDO     201
#define IDM_EDIT_CUT      202
#define IDM_EDIT_COPY     203
#define IDM_EDIT_PASTE    204
#define IDM_EDIT_CLEAR    205
#define IDM_EDIT_DELETE   206

#define IDM_POPUP_SYS     1001
#define IDM_POPUP_FILE    1002
#define IDM_POPUP_EDIT    1003

#define COUNT 23

typedef struct tagSTATUSDATA
    {
    WORD wCode;
    char achMsg[80];
    } STATUSDATA;
```

STATLINE.LNK

```
StatLine.obj
StatLine.exe/align:16/map/nod/noe/CO
nul
mlibcew libw
StatLine.def
```

STATLINE.MAK

```
# Directory search paths.

INCDIR = \WINDEV\INCLUDE

# Windows version to support
# Valid pairs include:
#     (0x0300, 30)
#     (0x0310, 31)

CLVER = WINVER=0x0300
RCVER = 30

# Compiler switches for applications.

CL_APP_SHIP_ALL = -AM -c -D$(CLVER) -Gsw -I$(INCDIR) -Ow -W3 -Zp
CL_APP_DEBG_ALL = -AM -c -D$(CLVER) -Gsw -I$(INCDIR) -Od -W3 -Zpi

CL_APP_SHIP_31  = -AM -c -G2s  -I$(INCDIR) -Ow -W3 -Zp
CL_APP_DEBG_31  = -AM -c -G2s  -I$(INCDIR) -Od -W3 -Zpi

# Compiler switches for DLLs.

CL_DLL_SHIP_ALL = -AMw -c -D$(CLVER) -Gsw -I$(INCDIR) -Ow -W3 -Zp
CL_DLL_DEBG_ALL = -AMw -c -D$(CLVER) -Gsw -I$(INCDIR) -Od -W3 -Zpi

CL_DLL_SHIP_31  = -AMw -c -G2s  -I$(INCDIR) -Ow -W3 -Zp
CL_DLL_DEBG_31  = -AMw -c -G2s  -I$(INCDIR) -Od -W3 -Zpi

# Make file primary target.

all: StatLine.exe

# Make file dependency targets.

StatLine.res: StatLine.rc StatLine.cur StatLine.ico
    rc -r -i$(INCDIR) StatLine.rc

StatLine.obj: StatLine.c StatLine.h
    cl $(CL_APP_DEBG_ALL) StatLine.c
```

```
StatLine.exe: StatLine.obj StatLine.def StatLine.res
    link @StatLine.lnk
    rc -$(RCVER) StatLine.res

StatLine.exe: StatLine.res
    rc -$(RCVER) StatLine.res
```

STATLINE.RC

```
#include <Windows.h>
#include "StatLine.h"

snapshot icon StatLine.ico

hand   cursor StatLine.cur

1 MENU
    {
    POPUP "&File"
        {
        MENUITEM "&New",          IDM_FILE_NEW
        MENUITEM "&Open...",      IDM_FILE_OPEN
        MENUITEM "&Save",         IDM_FILE_SAVE
        MENUITEM "Save &As...",   IDM_FILE_SAVEAS
        MENUITEM SEPARATOR
        MENUITEM "&Print",        IDM_FILE_PRINT
        MENUITEM SEPARATOR
        MENUITEM "E&xit",         IDM_FILE_EXIT
        }
    POPUP "&Edit"
        {
        MENUITEM "&Undo\tCtrl+Z",  IDM_EDIT_UNDO
        MENUITEM SEPARATOR
        MENUITEM "Cu&t\tCtrl+X",   IDM_EDIT_CUT
        MENUITEM "&Copy\tCtrl+C",  IDM_EDIT_COPY
        MENUITEM "&Paste\tCtrl+V", IDM_EDIT_PASTE
        MENUITEM SEPARATOR
        MENUITEM "Cl&ear",         IDM_EDIT_CLEAR
        MENUITEM "&Delete",        IDM_EDIT_DELETE
        }
    }


1 ACCELERATORS
    {
    ;   New Windows 3.1 clipboard accelerators.
    "Z",        IDM_EDIT_UNDO,    VIRTKEY, CONTROL
    "X",        IDM_EDIT_CUT,     VIRTKEY, CONTROL
    "C",        IDM_EDIT_COPY,    VIRTKEY, CONTROL
    "V",        IDM_EDIT_PASTE,   VIRTKEY, CONTROL

    ;   Maintain support for older clipboard accelerators.
```

```
VK_BACK,    IDM_EDIT_UNDO,   VIRTKEY, ALT
VK_DELETE,  IDM_EDIT_CUT,    VIRTKEY, SHIFT
VK_INSERT,  IDM_EDIT_COPY,   VIRTKEY, CONTROL
VK_INSERT,  IDM_EDIT_PASTE,  VIRTKEY, SHIFT
}
```

Creating the child window in STATLINE starts by registering the child window class, which is accomplished with a call to `RegisterClass`:

```
wndclass.lpszClassName   = "StatLine:CHILD";
wndclass.hInstance       = hInstance;
wndclass.lpfnWndProc     = StatLineChildWndProc;
wndclass.hCursor         = LoadCursor (hInstance,"hand");
wndclass.hIcon           = NULL;
wndclass.lpszMenuName    = NULL;
wndclass.hbrBackground   = (HBRUSH)COLOR_WINDOW+1;
wndclass.style           = NULL;
wndclass.cbClsExtra      = 0;
wndclass.cbWndExtra      = 0;

RegisterClass( &wndclass);
```

Once registered, the creation of a child window involves making a call to `CreateWindow` or `CreateWindowEx`. We chose `CreateWindowEx`:

```
hwndChild = CreateWindowEx(0L,              // Extra style.
                   achChildClass,           // Class name.
                   NULL,                    // Title.
                   WS_CHILD  |              // Style bits.
                   WS_BORDER  |
                   WS_VISIBLE,
                   0, 0, 0, 0,              // x, y, cx, cy.
                   hwnd,                    // Parent window.
                   NULL,                    // No menu.
                   hInstance,               // Creator.
                   NULL);                   // Params.
```

As we have discussed; a child window must have a parent. We define the parent of our status line window by using the handle of our program's top-level window as the ninth parameter in our call to `CreateWindowEx`. A child window needs a parent because it has to live in the pixels of another window. One seemingly odd thing is the initial size and location of our window. We have used all zeros for the four parameters that define a window size: `x`, `y`, `cx`, and `cy`. We select a window with no size or location because we want to postpone calculating the size and location of our child window until we know the size of the parent window. This ensures that the child window occupies the very bottom of the parent window.

To guarantee that our child window always sits on the bottom of its parent, we need to put code in the window procedure of the parent window to modify the size and location of the child window whenever the size of the parent window changes. To do this, the window procedure for our parent window responds to the WM_SIZE message as shown here:

```
case WM_SIZE:
    {
    int cxWidth;
    int cyHeight;
    int xChild;
    int yChild;

    cxWidth  = LOWORD (lParam);
    cyHeight = HIWORD (lParam);

    xChild = 0;
    yChild = cyHeight - cyChildHeight + 1;

    MoveWindow (hwndChild,
    xChild,
    yChild,
    cxWidth,
    cyChildHeight,
    TRUE);
    }
```

The MoveWindow routine changes the location of the child window to reflect the new size of the parent window. The MoveWindow routine is defined as

```
MoveWindow (hWnd, X, Y, cxWidth, cyHeight, bRepaint)
```

- hWnd identifies the window to be moved.

- X and Y are the new location of the window.

- cxWidth and cyHeight are the new width and height of the window.

- bRepaint is a Boolean flag. When set to TRUE, it causes the window to be completely redrawn in its new location. When set to FALSE, it prevents redrawing.

When the size of a window's client area changes, the window is sent a WM_SIZE message to notify it of the change.

As the user browses through a program's menus, menu messages are sent to the window procedure of the window that owns the menu. In the case of STATLINE, that means the top-level window. When the top-level window procedure receives the WM_MENUSELECT message, which is a notification that the user is browsing through a menu, it passes the message on to the window procedure of the child window by calling the SendMessage routine:

```
case WM_MENUSELECT:
    SendMessage (hwndChild, wMsg, wParam, lParam);
    break;
```

`SendMessage` delivers a message to a window procedure just as if it were directly calling the child window's window procedure. However, `SendMessage` should be used in place of a direct call, since Windows' dynamic link mechanism won't allow a direct call to a window procedure or to any other exported procedure.

In response to the `WM_MENUSELECT` message, the child window procedure checks to see what kind of menu selection is being made. The `WM_MENUSELECT` message lets you know about three types of events: browsing a regular menu item, browsing the top of a popup menu, and terminating a menu browsing. To tell the difference between these three events, you must look in the low-order word of the `lParam`. When `lParam` is equal to `0xFFFF`, browsing has terminated. When the `MF_POPUP` bit is set, the value in `wParam` is a popup menu handle. Otherwise, `wParam` is the command result code for the menu item that the user is currently viewing.

When STATLINE figures out exactly which menu is being browsed, it calls the `ExtTextOut` routine to display the description of the menu item. One of the nice features of this routine is the availability of the `ETO_OPAQUE` flag, which causes `ExtTextOut` to paint an opaque rectangle to erase whatever was drawn previously in the background.

The two sample programs in this chapter, OWNSIZE and STATLINE, provide a template that can be used to fine tune the handling of windows in your own programming projects. This is only the beginning of how you can take advantage of Windows' windows. In the next chapter, we will examine a part of the user interface that is built on top of windowing: dialog boxes.

14

Dialog Boxes

Dialog boxes are windows that provide a standard way for programs to ask users for additional information to complete a command. For example, a user may select the **File.Open...** menu item from a program's File popup menu. The ellipsis (...) at the end of the menu name indicates that a dialog box will appear. For the program to determine *which* file to open, it displays a dialog box. The user can either type the name of the file to open or select a file from a list. Figure 14.1 shows a standard file open dialog box.

Figure 14.1 A standard File-Open dialog box

A dialog box itself is a window that contains child windows. In the context of dialog boxes, these child windows are called **dialog box controls**. Windows provides six window classes to support a wide range of dialog box controls. Dialog box controls can be created using the button, combobox, edit, listbox, scrollbar, and static window classes. If these predefined window classes don't provide exactly the type of control you need, creating a custom dialog box control is as easy as creating a new window class.

Dialog boxes come in two flavors: modal and modeless. A **modal dialog box** prevents the user from interacting with other windows in a program. **System modal dialog boxes** are a special type of modal dialog boxes that prevent the user from interacting with any window in the *system*. A **modeless dialog box**, on the other hand, doesn't interfere with a user's interaction with other windows, but instead lets the user choose the window to work with.

Internally, the difference between the two has to do with the way the flow of messages is controlled. A modal dialog box cuts off the flow of mouse and keyboard messages to its parent and sibling windows by making its parent window **disabled**. If the user tries to interact with the disabled parent window by clicking the mouse in its client area, in its menu, or in any other part of its non-client area, the system responds with a warning beep. A second way in which modal dialog boxes control message flow is that each has its own message processing loop. Instead of using the `GetMessage` loop, a modal dialog box establishes its own. This means that if you have any keyboard accelerators that depend on the call to `TranslateAccelerator` in your message loop, you will find that these are disabled as well. A modal dialog box alters the flow of messages by disabling its parent window and disabling keyboard accelerators.

A modeless dialog box, on the other hand, does not alter the flow of messages to any part of your program. Once a modeless dialog box has been opened, the user is free to work with other windows in the program or to access keyboard accelerators. Modeless dialog boxes act like a set of windows that your program creates itself by calling `CreateWindow`. In fact, this is how both modeless *and* modal dialog boxes are created. The routines that create them simply make a sequence of calls to `CreateWindow` for you.

At first glance, modeless dialog boxes may seem more attractive than modal dialog boxes, since they give the user more choices over the structure of an interaction. In spite of this initial impression, you will find that most of the dialog boxes you create are *modal* dialog boxes. A modal dialog box provides an ideal way to focus the user's attention on the selected command. Once that attention is gained, the user must make a decision whether to provide the information that is required to complete the command, or to cancel the request. The ability of the user to cancel a modal dialog box is part of the reason that modal dialogs can get away with being so strict in the way they structure user interaction.

Since dialog boxes are an important part of the Windows user interface, there are a standard set of dialog box controls that users quickly learn how to manipulate. The success of your dialog box programming depends to a large degree on how well you understand these conventions. For this reason, we will start by looking at the conventions for dialog boxes and dialog box controls.

Dialog Box User Interface Standards

Perhaps the first thing to be said about interacting with a dialog box is that the user should be able to cancel a dialog box at any time without ill effects. For this reason, every dialog box will have a **push button** marked "Cancel." The user can click on this button with the mouse or use the equivalent Esc key stroke to dismiss an unwanted dialog box.

A dialog box will have other push buttons as well, to allow the user to request different types of actions. A push button marked "Ok" provides a standard way for the user to indicate that all data has been entered into the dialog box, and that the program should perform whatever requested action that first caused the dialog to be created. In the same way in which a dialog box can be canceled by either mouse or keyboard action, the user can click with the mouse on the Ok button, or use the Tab key to position the keyboard focus indicator and strike Enter to push the Ok button. At a minimum, users expect to see at least two push buttons: one to accept the changes and one to reject them.

There are other types of push buttons that a user can create, including a push button that displays a text label followed by an ellipsis (...). Like its counterpart in menus, this push button causes a dialog box to be displayed. A variation on this theme is a push button with a chevron (>>) after the button label. When such a button is pushed, it causes the dialog box to grow and reveal hidden dialog box controls. Figure 14.2 shows four types of push buttons: Ok, Cancel, ellipsis (...), and chevron (>>).

Push buttons indicate the set of actions that users can request from a dialog box. When a dialog box opens, one push button will be the default, which means it is selected when the user strikes the Enter key. Since the default push button has a thicker border than normal, the user will know it at a glance. When the user strikes the Tab key to move between dialog box controls, the push button that has the keyboard focus will always be the default push button.

Two other types of buttons are **radio buttons** and **check boxes**. Radio buttons always come in groups. A group of radio buttons is like a question in a multiple-choice test: At

**Figure 14.2 Four push button types,
from the Paintbrush program's
File Save As dialog box**

Figure 14.3   Radio buttons and check boxes

least one of the answers must be correct. A check box is like an on/off switch: When it is checked, it is turned on; when it is not checked, it is turned off. Figure 14.3 shows a dialog box containing radio buttons and check boxes.

An **edit control** lets the user enter and edit text. There are several different styles of edit controls, including single line and multi-line, automatic conversion to either upper or lower case, and character masking to hide text when entering passwords. Like most of the other standard parts of the Windows user interface, edit controls can be manipulated with the mouse or the keyboard. Either device can be used to select a character or a range of characters, or to move the insertion point. A multi-line edit control can be equipped with a scroll bar for when the text might not be able to fit into the area available in an edit control. Figure 14.4 shows a typical edit control.

The **static** window class creates controls that are used to display icons, text labels, empty and filled rectangles. Figure 14.5 shows a group of static controls in a dialog box.

A **listbox** shows the user a set of available choices. The most common type of listbox contains text, but graphic images can also be drawn into a listbox when the set of choices is best represented by a picture instead of by words. Listboxes can have scroll bars, which are necessary when the items in a list cannot all be displayed simultaneously. Figure 14.6 shows a pair of listboxes.

Figure 14.4   An edit control from the File Manager

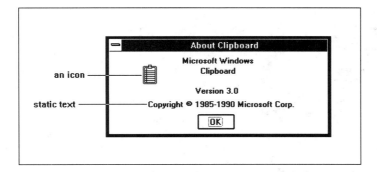

Figure 14.5 A group of static controls in a dialog box

A **combobox** combines a listbox with an edit control or a listbox with a static text control. A combobox can hide its listbox until the user clicks on an arrow icon to call up the listbox. Like regular listboxes, a combobox can have a scroll bar and can display either text or graphic images. From a user's point of view, a combobox looks and acts exactly like a listbox paired with a static or edit control. From a programming point of view, however, a combobox is much easier to support. Figure 14.7 shows an example of a combobox.

A **scroll bar** is a graphical representation of three related numbers: a minimum, a maximum, and a current value that lies between the two. You may recall that a scroll bar is installed in a regular window that was created with either the WS_HSCROLL or WS_VSCROLL style bits. Also, listboxes and edit controls can be created with a built-in scroll bar. You can also request a stand-alone scroll bar as a dialog box control. Figure 14.8 shows vertical and horizontal scroll bars in the Program Manager application.

Programs with special input requirements that cannot be met by Windows' predefined dialog box controls can provide their own. Custom dialog box controls can be incorporated into a dialog box alongside Windows' own dialog box controls.

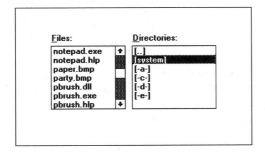

Figure 14.6 A pair of listboxes: one with and one without a scroll bar

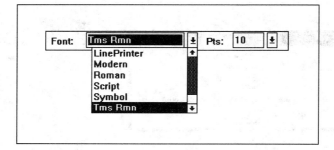

Figure 14.7   A pair of comboboxes: one showing and one hiding a listbox

Now that we've reviewed Windows' predefined dialog box controls, we're ready to examine what's involved in writing code to support a dialog box. Actually, the predefined controls do most of the work for you. All the while, they issue notification messages that help your program keep track of the user's progress in entering data. First, we will look at the creation of modal dialog boxes, because they are the more common variety. Then, we'll look at modeless dialog boxes.

Figure 14.8   Vertical and horizontal scroll bars

Modal Dialog Boxes

Creating a dialog box—whether modal or modeless—requires a combination of three ingredients: a dialog box template, code to create the dialog box, and code to maintain the dialog box. Each of these elements puts a different twist on the dialog box creation process, so we'll look at them one at a time.

Dialog Box Template

A dialog box template is a data object that defines the size of the dialog box, the type of controls in the dialog box, as well as the size and position of each dialog box control. The most common type of dialog box template is one built with a graphic editor, such as the **Dialog Box Editor**, which Microsoft provides as part of their SDK. Other dialog box tools include the Borland Resource Workshop and the Whitewater Group's Resource Toolkit. Whichever tool you use, each creates an ASCII text script that defines each element of the dialog box. Here is an example of a dialog box template created by the Microsoft SDK dialog box editor:

```
IDD_ABOUT DIALOG LOADONCALL MOVEABLE DISCARDABLE
            20, 24, 180, 84
STYLE WS_DLGFRAME | WS_POPUP
BEGIN
    CONTROL "A Sample About Box", IDD_TEXT1, "static",
            SS_CENTER | WS_CHILD,
            47, 13, 84, 8
    CONTROL "Windows 3.0 Power Programming Techniques",
            IDD_TEXT2, "static", SS_CENTER | WS_CHILD,
            0, 30, 180, 8
    CONTROL "By Peter Norton and Paul Yao", IDD_TEXT3,
            "static", SS_CENTER | WS_CHILD,
        0, 42, 180, 8
    CONTROL "Ok", IDD_OK, "button",
            BS_DEFPUSHBUTTON | WS_TABSTOP | WS_CHILD,
            70, 64, 40, 16
    CONTROL "snapshot", IDD_ICON, "static",
            SS_ICON | WS_CHILD,
            18, 8, 16, 16
END
```

The DIALOG statement is a lot like the MENU statement. The syntax of the DIALOG statement is

```
dialogID DIALOG [load option] [memory option] x, y, cx, cy
```

- dialogID identifies the dialog box resource.

- [load option] is either PRELOAD or LOADONCALL. PRELOAD causes a dialog to be loaded into memory before a program starts running. LOADONCALL causes the dialog to be loaded only when it is needed.

- [memory option] is either FIXED, MOVEABLE, or DISCARDABLE, and describes the behavior of the object once it has been loaded. For more details on these options, refer to the discussion in Chapter 18.

- x and y is the position of the dialog box window, in dialog box coordinates, relative to the client area of the dialog box's parent window.

- cx and cy is the width and height of the control, in dialog box coordinates.

Each CONTROL statement in the dialog box definition defines a different dialog box control. The general syntax of the CONTROL statement is

```
CONTROL <text>, nID, <class>, <styles>, x, y, cx, cy
```

- `<text>` is a character string in double quotes that later becomes the window text of the created window.

- `nID` is an integer value that uniquely identifies the dialog control window.

- `<class>` is the character string name of the window class from which a dialog control is to be created.

- `<styles>` are a set of generic window class styles and control-specific styles that are ORed together.

- `x` and `y` is the position of the control in the dialog box window, in dialog box coordinates.

- `cx` and `cy` is the width and height of the control, in dialog box coordinates.

The position and size of the dialog box, and of each control in the dialog box, is specified in a coordinate system called **dialog box coordinates**. This coordinate system helps a dialog box definition be somewhat device-independent, since the units are defined relative to the size of the font used in the dialog box (which, by default, is the system font). In dialog box coordinates, units in the X direction are approximately 1/4 the average width of the font. In the Y direction, they are 1/8 the height of the font. `GetDialogBoxUnits` provides the necessary base units, for converting between dialog box units and pixels using code like the following:

```
int   xBase,   yBase;
int   xDlg,    yDlg;
int   xPixel, yPixel;
LONG  lBase;

lBase = GetDialogBoxUnits();
xBase = LOWORD (lBase);
yBase = HIWORD (lBase);

xPixel = (xDlg * xBase)/4;
yPixel = (yDlg * yBase)/8;
```

The `STYLE` statement in the `DIALOG` definition lists the window styles to be included with the dialog window when it is created. From this, you may have already guessed that the dialog box template is little more than a convenient way to list the parameters of the `CreateWindow` routine. However, creating a dialog box does not require you to call `CreateWindow`, because the dialog box creation code actually calls `CreateWindow` for you: once for the dialog box frame and once for each control in the dialog box.

It's important that you understand the details of a dialog box template, since they affect the appearance and behavior of dialog boxes. However, you probably won't ever have to create these yourself, but instead will use one of the many available dialog editors. Let's take a moment to review some of the features in the Microsoft dialog box editor; these features are commonly found in just about every dialog box editor.

The Dialog Box Editor

The very first Windows programmers, had to create dialog box templates from scratch. This involved taking pencil to graph paper to create dialogs that looked somewhat reasonable. Getting a dialog box to look good required many hours of work. Fortunately, those days are long gone, and Windows programmers can take advantage of graphic tools that allow them to draw dialog boxes and to create templates from the image they draw.

Figure 14.9 shows the Microsoft Dialog Box Editor with an image of the dialog box definition examined earlier. The dialog box editor allows you to draw and manipulate a dialog box definition until you feel you have it looking just right. It supports all of the predefined type of dialog box controls and custom controls, as long as they are in a dynamic link library that has been set up correctly. The dialog box editor is fairly simple to use, although it has a few quirks that you will want to work around.

For one thing, although the dialog box editor is able to edit include (.H) files, you'll probably want to set up a separate include file for each dialog box that you define. The Microsoft Dialog Editor does not know how to interpret the syntax of normal C include files, and only understands the symbolic constants created with a #define statement. One include file for each dialog box definition is a good idea, since the editor insists that each symbolic constant have a unique value. This requirement is actually a fairly small price to pay considering the convenience provided by this tool.

To fine-tune a specific dialog box control, you can select the Edit-Styles menu item or double-click on the control. This causes a customizing dialog box to appear, which allows you to change a control's text, its ID value, and the specific style bits that will

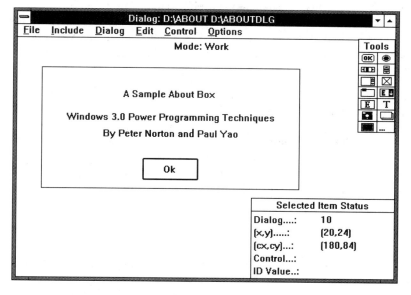

Figure 14.9 The Dialog Box Editor

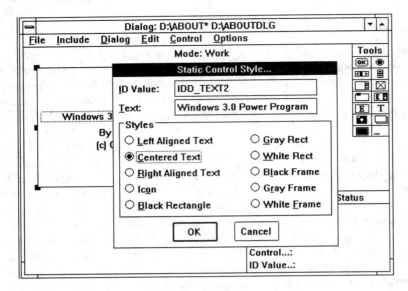

Figure 14.10 Customizing a static class dialog box control

control the appearance and behavior of the control. There is a different customizing dialog box for each class of dialog box control, since each class has its own, private style bits. Figure 14.10 shows the customizing dialog box that allows you to select the different styles available for static class dialog box controls.

Creating the dialog box template involves creating a resource object that describes the shape, size, and position of the dialog box itself and that of each control in a dialog box. This object is placed into your program's resource file, along with the icon, resource, and menu definitions that are part of your application program. With the resource defined, the next ingredient needed to create a dialog box is the actual code that triggers the dialog box creation.

Creating a Modal Dialog Box

Windows provides four routines for creating a modal dialog box: `DialogBox`, `DialogBoxIndirect`, `DialogBoxIndirectParam`, and `DialogBoxParam`. The most basic of these routines is the first one. The others simply provide some slight variations for added flexibility in the dialog box creation process. `DialogBox` is defined

```
int DialogBox (hInstance, lpszTemplate, hwndParent, lpDialogProc);
```

- `hInstance` is the instance handle of the program or dynamic link library that owns the dialog box definition.

- `lpszTemplate` is a far pointer to a character string for the name of the dialog box definition, as defined in the dialog box template. Alternatively, it can be an integer value wrapped inside the MAKEINTRESOURCE macro, when an integer is used in place of a character string to identify the dialog box template.

- hwndParent is a handle to the parent window of the dialog box. The parent window of a modal dialog box is disabled when the dialog box is displayed.

- lpDialogProc is a far pointer to a piece of code that maintains the dialog box while it is being displayed. This function is called a **dialog box procedure**. The address passed in this parameter is not the address of the routine itself, but the **instance thunk** created by the MakeProcInstance routine for the dialog box procedure.

The first and third parameters are relatively straightforward, since we have encountered instance handles and window handles previously. Let's take a closer look at the second and fourth parameters.

The second parameter to DialogBox is defined as an LPSTR value, which means it can hold a far pointer to a character string. The second parameter identifies the dialog box template from the resource file definition. This can be a regular character string for dialog box templates that are defined that way:

```
DialogBox (hInst, "MYDIALOG", hwndParent, lpproc);
```

As an alternative, an integer value can be used to define a dialog box template. When this is the case, a program can use the MAKEINTRESOURCE macro to disguise an integer value in a character string position:

```
DialogBox (hInst, MAKEINTRESOURCE(15), hwndParent, lpproc);
```

Or, instead of the MAKEINTRESOURCE macro, a pound sign can be placed in a character string to identify a dialog box template with a numeric identifier:

```
DialogBox (hInst, "#15", hwndParent, lpproc);
```

The fourth parameter to DialogBox identifies the code that will maintain the dialog box while it is opened—it will process the messages sent from the dialog box controls as notifications of the user's activity. This is a call-back procedure called a **dialog box procedure**. Dialog box procedures are similar to window procedures, which is the only other type of call-back procedure that we've encountered in this book.

A dialog box is similar to a window procedure in a number of ways, but there are differences in structure and in the messages that are received. In addition, a dialog box procedure is never directly addressed, but rather is addressed using a small piece of code called an **instance thunk**. Briefly, an instance thunk is an outgrowth of Windows' dynamic link mechanism that allows a program's code to be called by someone outside of the program itself (although it's not a critical part of the mechanism, in most cases the caller will be in a dynamic link library). An instance thunk ensures that dynamically linked code has access to the proper *data segment*. Creating an instance thunk involves making a call to MakeProcInstance, defined as:

```
FARPROC MakeProcInstance (lpProc, hInstance)
```

- lpProc is the address of a call-back procedure for which an instance thunk is to be created.

- hInstance is an instance handle.

In Chapter 19, we'll provide more detail about instance thunks.

Therefore, the creation of a dialog box involves making *two* calls: one to MakeProcInstance and one to DialogBox. Consider a dialog box procedure named AboutDlgProc, with a dialog box template defined with the symbolic constant

```
#define IDD_ABOUT 15
```

Here is the code to create a modal dialog box:

```
{
FARPROC lpitAbout;

lpitAbout = MakeProcInstance (AboutDlgProc, hInstance);
DialogBox (hInstance,
    MAKEPROCINSTANCE(IDD_ABOUT),
    hwnd,
    lpitAbout);
FreeProcInstance (lpitAbout);
}
```

The MakeProcInstance routine returns a far pointer to our instance thunk, which is stored in the lpitAbout variable (the "lpit" Hungarian stands for "long pointer to an instance thunk"). This value is passed as the fourth parameter to DialogBox, which causes the modal dialog box to appear. As mentioned earlier, modal dialog boxes have their own, private message loop. This means that control is not returned from the DialogBox routine until the dialog box has been dismissed.

Once we are finished with the dialog box, the instance thunk can be destroyed by calling FreeProcInstance. This routine forms the second slice of a sandwich, with the call to MakeProcInstance as the top slice. The sandwich construction is needed to ensure that the memory used by the MakeProcInstance routine is available for other uses. This is not the only way in which an instance thunk can be used, however. We'll see an alternative approach in our first sample program.

The first two ingredients needed to create a dialog box—the dialog box template and the code needed to create the dialog box—have been covered. There is one more important ingredient to the creation of both modal and modeless dialog boxes: the code that maintains the dialog box, the **dialog box procedure**.

Maintaining the Dialog Box

The code that maintains a dialog box is referred to as a dialog box procedure. A dialog box procedure has a role similar to that of a window procedure: It processes messages.

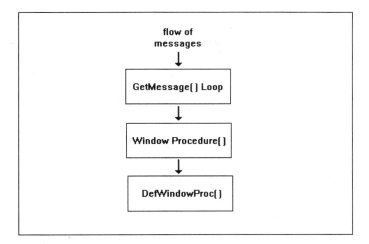

Figure 14.11 Message flow to a normal window procedure

In addition, as with a window procedure, you must list the names of every dialog box procedure in the EXPORTS section of your program's module definition file:

```
EXPORTS
    AboutDlgProc
```

Otherwise, you risk disconnecting the code in your dialog box procedure from your static data in your program's default data segment (a topic more fully explored in Chapter 19).

But a dialog box procedure is *not* itself a window procedure, but rather is called by the standard, default dialog box window procedure to customize the behavior of a specific dialog box. Figure 14.11 shows the typical message flow of a regular window procedure. By contrast, Figure 14.12 shows how this message flow is diverted from the default dialog box window procedure to a custom dialog box procedure.

A dialog box procedure returns one of two values: TRUE or FALSE. As the figure suggests, a return value of TRUE means that the dialog box procedure has processed the message, and no further processing is required. A return value of FALSE means that the dialog box procedure has not processed the message. It is up to the default dialog box procedure, DefDlgProc, to process the message if it sees fit, or to pass the message on to the default window procedure, DefWindowProc.

Since a dialog box procedure processes messages just like a regular window procedure, it takes the same four parameters as a window procedure. But, because it returns a TRUE or FALSE value, a dialog box procedure is defined with a Boolean (BOOL) return value instead of the normal long value that window procedures return. Here is a typical procedure declaration for a dialog box procedure:

```
BOOL FAR PASCAL DlgProc (HWND hdlg,      UINT wMsg,
                         WPARAM wParam, LPARAM lParam);
```

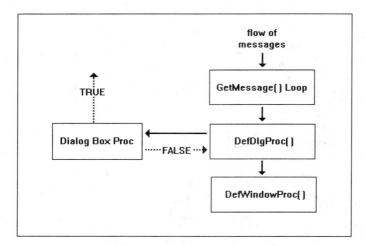

Figure 14.12 Message flow to a dialog box procedure

What types of messages is a dialog box procedure interested in? Since a dialog box procedure has a window procedure to take care of the nitty gritty issues of supporting the window, dialog box procedures mainly focus on two messages: WM_INITDIALOG and WM_COMMAND.

The WM_INITDIALOG message is sent to the dialog box procedure after all of the dialog box control windows have been created, but before they have been made visible. In response to this message, a dialog box procedure will initialize each of the dialog box controls to the correct initial state. For example, it might fill a listbox with the items to be viewed by the user, or it might set the state of radio buttons or check box buttons to a state that reflects the current settings. If there is an edit control in the dialog box, the dialog box procedure might insert a string at initialization time.

Once the dialog box controls have been given their initial settings, they work on their own to accept user input, modify the current settings, and keep out of each other's way. As they work, they send WM_COMMAND messages to the dialog box procedure to notify it of just about every action that the user takes. In some respects, dialog box controls are like children away at summer camp, who write home to tell their parents about the day's activities:

Dear Mom and Dad Window,

Camp is fun. Today we went hiking, played volleyball, received the input focus from the user, and a mouse click or two.

> Your child window control,
> Check-Box

The WM_COMMAND notification messages allow the dialog box procedure to respond to the changes that take place in a dialog box control. In some respects, the WM_COMMAND message sent from a dialog box control is just like the WM_COMMAND message

Figure 14.13 The parameters in a WM_COMMAND notification message

sent from a menu item when the user has made a menu selection. $wParam$ contains the identifier assigned to a control in the resource file, to allow your program to know the specific item with which the user is interacting. But, because a dialog box control has more to say than a menu item, $lParam$ contains some more information: The high-order word contains a notification code, and the low-order word contains the window handle of the control sending the message. Figure 14.13 graphically depicts the contents of the parameters to the $WM\_COMMAND$ message.

Since dialog box procedures are primarily interested in two messages, here is a template that you can use for just about every dialog box procedure that you create:

```
BOOL CALLBACK DlgProc (HWND hdlg,      UINT wMsg,
                       WPARAM wParam, LPARAM lParam);
{
    switch (wMsg)
        {
        case WM_INITDIALOG:
            //  Put initialization code here.
            return TRUE;

        case WM_COMMAND:
            //  Receive & process notifications.
            return TRUE;

        default:
            return FALSE;
        }
}
```

In addition to the messages that a dialog box procedure receives, there are quite a few messages that will be sent from a dialog box procedure to its dependent controls. Sending messages, in fact, provides the primary mechanism by which a dialog box procedure will communicate with its controls. Thus, at initialization time, the dialog box procedure sets the initial state of a dialog box control by sending it messages. As the dialog box procedure receives notification messages, it may send more messages to fine-tune the behavior of the dialog box controls based on the type of input that was reported in the notification messages.

One final issue is that of terminating a dialog box. In this respect, a modal dialog box is different from a modeless dialog box. We'll discuss the required termination of a modeless dialog box, after we present a sample program that shows in detail how to handle a modal dialog box. In general, modal dialog boxes are dismissed after the user has selected a push button that indicates whether to continue with the command that initially caused the dialog box to appear or whether to abandon the command. When such a push button has been clicked, a WM_COMMAND notification message is sent to the dialog box procedure. In either case, a call to EndDialog is all that is needed to dismiss the modal dialog box and return control to the calling program. EndDialog is defined

```
void EndDialog (hDlg, nResult)
```

- hDlg is a handle to the modal dialog box to be dismissed.

- nResult is a result code that is provided as the return value of the function that created the dialog box (either DialogBox, DialogBoxIndirect, DialogBoxIndirectParam, or DialogBoxParam).

Consider a dialog box with an Ok and a Cancel button. If the Ok button had a control ID equal to the symbolic constant IDD_OK, and the Cancel button had an ID equal to IDD_CANCEL, the code to dismiss the dialog box in the dialog box procedure might look like this:

```
BOOL CALLBACK DlgProc (HWND hdlg,      UINT wMsg,
                       WPARAM wParam, LPARAM lParam);
{
    switch (wMsg)
        {
        case WM_INITDIALOG:
            //  Put initialization code here.
            return TRUE;

        case WM_COMMAND:
            switch (wParam)
                {
                case IDD_OK:
                    EndDialog (hDlg, TRUE);
                    return TRUE;
                case IDD_CANCEL:
                    EndDialog (hDlg, FALSE);
                    return TRUE;
                }
            break;

        default:
```

```
                      return FALSE;
          }
    }
```

Although this example uses a result code of either TRUE or FALSE, you can return any unsigned integer value. Since the result code is the return value to the dialog box creation routine, here is how that code might be modified to respond:

```
{
BOOL     bRetVal;
FARPROC  lpitAbout;

lpitAbout = MakeProcInstance (AboutDlgProc, hInstance);
bRetVal =  DialogBox (hInstance,
                      MAKEPROCINSTANCE(IDD_ABOUT),
                      hwnd,
                      lpitAbout);
FreeProcInstance (lpitAbout);

if (bRetVal)
    {
    //  User clicked Ok.
    ...
    }
else
    {
    //  User clicked Cancel.
    ...
    }
}
```

Most of the time and energy required to fine-tune the behavior of a dialog box will be spent working on this third element, the dialog box procedure. Let's look at a sample program that brings these elements together. Our next sample program creates an About box, one of the simplest kinds of dialog boxes that a program can create. An About box provides a standard means by which programs can display copyright information, as well as other details about a program. When you see the simple dialog box procedure in this program, don't be fooled into thinking that all dialog box procedures will be as simple. As you'll see in our later programming examples, they can be quite involved.

A Simple Dialog Box: ABOUT

Our simplest dialog box, an About box, is displayed by programs to tell the user about a program: its creator, version number, and any copyright information. An About box is usually displayed by a program in response to a menu selection made from the standard Help menu, depicted in Figure 14.14. The About dialog box that our program displays is shown in Figure 14.15.

Figure 14.14 A standard Help menu

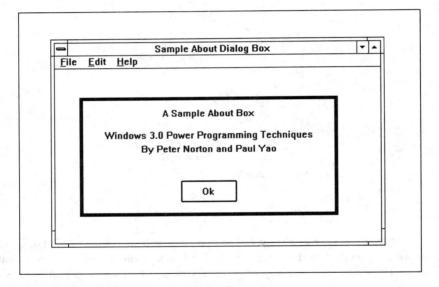

Figure 14.15 An About dialog box

Here is the source code to our program:

ABOUT.C

```
/*----------------------------------------------------------------*\
|   ABOUT.C   Sample About dialog box.                             |
\*----------------------------------------------------------------*/
#define STRICT
#include <Windows.H>
#include "About.h"
#include "Aboutdlg.h"
```

```
/*-------------------------------------------------------------*\
|                  Function Prototypes.                        |
\*-------------------------------------------------------------*/
LRESULT CALLBACK AboutWndProc (HWND, UINT, WPARAM, LPARAM);
BOOL    CALLBACK AboutDlgProc (HWND, UINT, WPARAM, LPARAM);


/*-------------------------------------------------------------*\
|                    Global Variables.                         |
\*-------------------------------------------------------------*/
char achWndClass[] = "About:MAIN";
char achAppName[]  = "Sample About Dialog Box";
FARPROC    lpitAbout;
HINSTANCE  hInst;


/*-------------------------------------------------------------*\
|                  Main Function: WinMain.                     |
\*-------------------------------------------------------------*/
int PASCAL
WinMain (HINSTANCE hInstance,      // Who am I?
         HINSTANCE hPrevInstance,  // Any older siblings?
         LPSTR     lpszCmdLine,    // Ptr to command line.
         int       cmdShow)        // How to open my window?
    {
    HACCEL    hAccel;
    HWND      hwnd;
    MSG       msg;
    WNDCLASS  wndclass;

    if (!hPrevInstance)
        {
        wndclass.lpszClassName = achWndClass;
        wndclass.hInstance     = hInstance;
        wndclass.lpfnWndProc   = AboutWndProc;
        wndclass.hCursor       = LoadCursor (hInstance, "hand");
        wndclass.hIcon         = LoadIcon (hInstance,"snapshot");
        wndclass.lpszMenuName  = "#1";
        wndclass.hbrBackground = (HBRUSH)(COLOR_WINDOW+1);
        wndclass.style         = NULL;
        wndclass.cbClsExtra    = 0;
        wndclass.cbWndExtra    = 0;

        RegisterClass( &wndclass);
        }

    hInst = hInstance;
    lpitAbout = MakeProcInstance ((FARPROC)AboutDlgProc, hInst);

    hwnd = CreateWindowEx(0L,                // Extra style.
                    achWndClass,             // Class name.
                    achAppName,              // Title.
                    WS_OVERLAPPEDWINDOW,     // Style bits.
                    CW_USEDEFAULT,           // x - default.
                    0,                       // y - default.
                    CW_USEDEFAULT,           // cx - default.
                    0,                       // cy - default.
```

```
                              NULL,                  // No parent.
                              NULL,                  // Class menu.
                              hInstance,             // Creator.
                              NULL);                 // Params.
        ShowWindow (hwnd, cmdShow);

        hAccel = LoadAccelerators (hInstance, "#1");

        while (GetMessage(&msg, 0, 0, 0))
            {
            if (!TranslateAccelerator (hwnd, hAccel, &msg))
                {
                TranslateMessage(&msg); // Convert KEYDOWNs to CHARs
                DispatchMessage(&msg);  // Transmit message to WndProc
                }
            }

        FreeProcInstance (lpitAbout);

        return 0;
        }

/*--------------------------------------------------------------*\
 |              Window Procedure:  AboutWndProc.                |
 \*--------------------------------------------------------------*/
LRESULT CALLBACK
AboutWndProc (HWND     hwnd,       // For whom is message sent?
              UINT     mMsg,       // What is exact message?
              WPARAM   wParam,     // ...message details.
              LPARAM   lParam)     // ...message details.
    {
    switch (mMsg)
        {
        case WM_COMMAND:
            {
            char buffer[80];
            char *npch;

            switch (wParam)
                {
                case IDM_FILE_NEW:
                    npch = "File.New";
                    break;
                case IDM_FILE_OPEN:
                    npch = "File.Open...";
                    break;
                case IDM_FILE_SAVE:
                    npch = "File.Save";
                    break;
                case IDM_FILE_SAVEAS:
                    npch = "File.Save As...";
                    break;
                case IDM_FILE_PRINT:
                    npch = "File.Print";
                    break;
```

```
        case IDM_FILE_EXIT:
            npch = "File.Exit";
            break;
        case IDM_EDIT_UNDO:
            npch = "Edit.Undo";
            break;
        case IDM_EDIT_CUT:
            npch = "Edit.Cut";
            break;
        case IDM_EDIT_COPY:
            npch = "Edit.Copy";
            break;
        case IDM_EDIT_PASTE:
            npch = "Edit.Paste";
            break;
        case IDM_EDIT_CLEAR:
            npch = "Edit.Clear";
            break;
        case IDM_EDIT_DELETE:
            npch = "Edit.Delete";
            break;
        case IDM_HELP_INDEX:
            npch = "Help.Index";
            break;
        case IDM_HELP_KEYS:
            npch = "Help.Keyboard";
            break;
        case IDM_HELP_USING:
            npch = "Help.Using Help";
            break;
        case IDM_HELP_ABOUT:
            DialogBox (hInst, MAKEINTRESOURCE (IDD_ABOUT),
                        hwnd, (DLGPROC)lpitAbout);
            break;
        }

    // Display message box with
    // name of selected menu item.
    if (wParam != IDM_HELP_ABOUT)
        {
        wsprintf (buffer, "%s command selected.",
                    (LPSTR)npch);
        MessageBox (hwnd, buffer, achAppName, MB_OK);
        }

    // If user selected File.Exit,
    // simulate {-}.Close menu selection.
    if (wParam == 6)
        {
        SendMessage (hwnd, WM_SYSCOMMAND, SC_CLOSE, 0L);
        }
    }
    break;
```

```
        case WM_DESTROY:
            PostQuitMessage(0);   // Handle application shutdown.
            break;

        default:
            return(DefWindowProc(hwnd,mMsg,wParam,lParam));
            break;
        }
    return 0L;
    }

/*-------------------------------------------------------------*\
  |           Dialog Box Procedure:   AboutDlgProc             |
\*-------------------------------------------------------------*/
BOOL CALLBACK AboutDlgProc (HWND    hdlg,    UINT   mMsg,
                            WPARAM wParam, LPARAM lParam)

    {
    switch (mMsg)
        {
        case WM_COMMAND:
            switch (wParam)
                {
                case IDD_OK:
                    EndDialog (hdlg, TRUE);
                }
            return TRUE;

        default:
            return FALSE;
        }
    }
```

ABOUT.DEF

```
NAME      ABOUT

EXETYPE WINDOWS

DESCRIPTION 'Sample About Dialog Box (c) 1992 By Paul Yao'

CODE      MOVEABLE PRELOAD
DATA      MOVEABLE MULTIPLE PRELOAD

HEAPSIZE     512
STACKSIZE    5120

SEGMENTS
    ABOUT_TEXT MOVEABLE PRELOAD

EXPORTS
    AboutWndProc
    AboutDlgProc
```

ABOUT.DLG

```
DLGINCLUDE RCDATA DISCARDABLE
BEGIN
    "ABOUTDLG.H\0"
END

IDD_ABOUT DIALOG 20, 24, 180, 84
STYLE DS_MODALFRAME | WS_POPUP | WS_CAPTION | WS_SYSMENU
BEGIN
    CTEXT           "A Sample About Box", -1, 47, 13, 84, 8, NOT WS_GROUP
    CTEXT           "Windows 3.0 Power Programming Techniques", -1,
                    0, 30, 180, 8, NOT WS_GROUP
    CTEXT           "By Peter Norton and Paul Yao", -1, 0, 42, 180,
                    8, NOT WS_GROUP
    CTEXT           "(c) Copyright 1992 By Paul Yao", -1, 0, 51, 180,
                    8, NOT WS_GROUP
    DEFPUSHBUTTON   "Ok", IDD_OK, 70, 64, 40, 16
    ICON            "snapshot", IDD_ICON, 18, 8, 16, 16
END
```

ABOUT.H

```
/*------------------------------------------------------------*\
|   About.h  - Include file for About.c.                       |
\*------------------------------------------------------------*/
#define IDM_FILE_NEW        101
#define IDM_FILE_OPEN       102
#define IDM_FILE_SAVE       103
#define IDM_FILE_SAVEAS     104
#define IDM_FILE_PRINT      105
#define IDM_FILE_EXIT       106

#define IDM_EDIT_UNDO       201
#define IDM_EDIT_CUT        202
#define IDM_EDIT_COPY       203
#define IDM_EDIT_PASTE      204
#define IDM_EDIT_CLEAR      205
#define IDM_EDIT_DELETE     206

#define IDM_HELP_INDEX      301
#define IDM_HELP_KEYS       302
#define IDM_HELP_USING      303
#define IDM_HELP_ABOUT      304

#define IDD_ABOUT            10
```

ABOUTDLG.H

```
#define IDD_OK      1
#define IDD_ICON    104

#define IDD_ABOUT   10
```

ABOUT.LNK

```
About.obj
About.exe/align:16/map/nod/noe/CO
nul
mlibcew libw
About.def
```

ABOUT.MAK

```
# Directory search paths.

INCDIR = \WINDEV\INCLUDE

# Windows version to support
# Valid pairs include:
#     (0x0300, 30)
#     (0x0310, 31)

CLVER = WINVER=0x0300
RCVER = 30

# Compiler switches for applications.

CL_APP_SHIP_ALL = -AM -c -D$(CLVER) -Gsw -I$(INCDIR) -Ow -W3 -Zp
CL_APP_DEBG_ALL = -AM -c -D$(CLVER) -Gsw -I$(INCDIR) -Od -W3 -Zpi

CL_APP_SHIP_31  = -AM -c -G2s  -I$(INCDIR) -Ow -W3 -Zp
CL_APP_DEBG_3.  = -AM -c -G2s  -I$(INCDIR) -Od -W3 -Zpi

# Compiler switches for DLLs.

CL_DLL_SHIP_ALL = -AMw -c -D$(CLVER) -Gsw -I$(INCDIR) -Ow -W3 -Zp
CL_DLL_DEBG_ALL = -AMw -c -D$(CLVER) -Gsw -I$(INCDIR) -Od -W3 -Zpi

CL_DLL_SHIP_31  = -AMw -c -G2s  -I$(INCDIR) -Ow -W3 -Zp
CL_DLL_DEBG_31  = -AMw -c -G2s  -I$(INCDIR) -Od -W3 -Zpi

# Make file primary target.

all: About.exe
```

```
# Make file dependency targets.

About.res: About.rc About.cur About.dlg Aboutdlg.h About.h About.ico
    rc -r -i$(INCDIR) About.rc

About.obj: About.c About.h
    cl $(CL_APP_SHIP_ALL) About.c

About.exe: About.obj About.def About.res
    link @About.lnk
    rc -$(RCVER) About.res

About.exe: About.res
    rc -$(RCVER) About.res
```

ABOUT.RC

```
#include <Windows.h>
#include "About.h"
#include "Aboutdlg.h"

snapshot icon About.ico

hand   cursor About.cur

#include "about.dlg"

1 MENU
    {
    POPUP "&File"
        {
        MENUITEM "&New",        IDM_FILE_NEW
        MENUITEM "&Open...",    IDM_FILE_OPEN
        MENUITEM "&Save",       IDM_FILE_SAVE
        MENUITEM "Save &As...", IDM_FILE_SAVEAS
        MENUITEM SEPARATOR
        MENUITEM "&Print",      IDM_FILE_PRINT
        MENUITEM SEPARATOR
        MENUITEM "E&xit",       IDM_FILE_EXIT
        }
    POPUP "&Edit"
        {
        MENUITEM "&Undo\tCtrl+Z",  IDM_EDIT_UNDO
        MENUITEM SEPARATOR
        MENUITEM "Cu&t\tCtrl+X",   IDM_EDIT_CUT
        MENUITEM "&Copy\tCtrl+C",  IDM_EDIT_COPY
        MENUITEM "&Paste\tCtrl+V", IDM_EDIT_PASTE
        MENUITEM SEPARATOR
        MENUITEM "Cl&ear",         IDM_EDIT_CLEAR
        MENUITEM "&Delete",        IDM_EDIT_DELETE
        }
```

```
        POPUP "&Help"
            {
            MENUITEM "Index",                  IDM_HELP_INDEX
            MENUITEM "Keyboard",               IDM_HELP_KEYS
            MENUITEM "Using Help",             IDM_HELP_USING
            MENUITEM SEPARATOR
            MENUITEM "About...",               IDM_HELP_ABOUT
            }
        }


1 ACCELERATORS
    {
    ;  New Windows 3.1 clipboard accelerators.
    "Z",        IDM_EDIT_UNDO,    VIRTKEY, CONTROL
    "X",        IDM_EDIT_CUT,     VIRTKEY, CONTROL
    "C",        IDM_EDIT_COPY,    VIRTKEY, CONTROL
    "V",        IDM_EDIT_PASTE,   VIRTKEY, CONTROL

    ;  Maintain support for older clipboard accelerators.
    VK_BACK,    IDM_EDIT_UNDO,    VIRTKEY, ALT
    VK_DELETE,  IDM_EDIT_CUT,     VIRTKEY, SHIFT
    VK_INSERT,  IDM_EDIT_COPY,    VIRTKEY, CONTROL
    VK_INSERT,  IDM_EDIT_PASTE,   VIRTKEY, SHIFT
    }
```

While reviewing the source code to ABOUT, you may notice that the dialog box template is in a separate file from the resource file. The resource file has a `#include` statement that causes the dialog box template to be loaded into the resource file when it is compiled. ABOUT has a separate include file that contains the symbolic constants used in the About box template definition. The primary reason for having separate files for the dialog box definition is to make it easier to work with the dialog box editor.

You may also have noticed that instead of a sandwich construction, with a call to `DialogBox` in between calls to `MakeProcInstance` and `FreeProcInstance`, the dialog box seems to be created with a single call to `DialogBox`:

```
case WM_COMMAND:
    switch (wParam)
        {
        ...
        case IDM_HELP_ABOUT:
            DialogBox (hInst, MAKEINTRESOURCE(IDD_ABOUT),
                    hwnd, lpitAboutDlgProc);
            break;
        ...
```

But if you look in ABOUT's `WinMain` function, you'll find that it creates an instance thunk during program initialization time:

```
lpitAbout = MakeProcInstance ((FARPROC)AboutDlgProc, hInst);
```

This approach helps to create dialog boxes a little more quickly because an instance thunk is created only once. Every task database has eight instance thunks preallocated for use by your program; therefore, you can create up to eight of them without requiring additional memory. If more than eight are needed, the Windows KERNEL allocates an additional set for you to use.

The dialog box procedure for the About dialog box is simple, because the dialog box doesn't do anything but wait for the user to push the push button. The dialog box doesn't need to have anything initialized, so the dialog box procedure doesn't process the WM_INITDIALOG message. When the user does push the button—either with a mouse click or by pressing the return key—a WM_COMMAND message is sent to the dialog box procedure, with a notification code of BN_CLICKED in the high-word of the lParam. Since this is the only notification code that can be sent our dialog box procedure by any control in the dialog box, ABOUT doesn't bother checking for the notification code, but simply terminates on receipt of the WM_COMMAND message by calling EndDialog:

```
BOOL CALLBACK AboutDlgProc (HWND hdlg,    UINT wMsg,
                              WPARAM wParam, LPARAM lParam)
    {
    switch (wMsg)
        {
        case WM_COMMAND:
            EndDialog (hdlg, TRUE);
            return TRUE;
        default:
            return FALSE;
        }
    }
```

Creating the modal dialog box required that three ingredients be brought together: a dialog box template, code to create the dialog box, and code to maintain the dialog box. Next, we'll see what is involved in creating a modeless dialog box. There are quite a few small differences between modal and modeless dialog boxes.

Modeless Dialog Boxes

The three elements needed to create a modeless dialog box are essentially the same as those needed for a modal dialog box. However, the differences are significant enough to warrant a separate discussion of modeless dialog box creation. Let's look at each of the three items required for modeless dialog boxes, starting with the dialog box template.

Dialog Box Template

Although the dialog box template that you create for modeless dialog boxes is almost identical with the templates used for modal dialog boxes, you'll want to change the dialog box styles to make your modeless dialog box behave properly. The easiest way to do this involves the use of the Dialog Box Editor's "Dialog Box Style..." customizing box, shown in Figure 14.16. Some additional options over and above the ones required for modal dialog boxes will be needed. Perhaps the most important is the check box marked "Initially Visible." This causes the WS_VISIBLE creation style to be added to the dialog box template's style bits. You aren't required to set this bit for a modal dialog

Figure 14.16 Dialog Box Editor's customizing options for a dialog box

box, because modal dialogs are automatically made visible. It makes sense—otherwise, a modal dialog box would disable its parent, then not be visible. Without the visible bit, however, a modeless dialog box would simply not appear.

Although it's not used in our programming example, notice that the "Dialog Box Style..." dialog box in Figure 14.16 also allows you to change the font used in a dialog box. This causes an additional statement to be added to a dialog box template, which selects the indicated font for all of the controls in a given dialog box. Each of the controls is automatically scaled to provide the same relative proportions that are provided for the system font.

Therefore, for the first element of a dialog box, the dialog box template, the only difference between a modal and a modeless dialog box is the WS_VISIBLE style flag. Let's look at the differences that modeless dialog boxes require for the second dialog box element: the code that creates a dialog box.

Creating a Modeless Dialog Box

Four routines create a modeless dialog box: CreateDialog, CreateDialogIndirect, CreateDialogIndirectParam, and CreateDialogParam. Just like the routines that create modal dialog boxes, three of these provide slight variations for added flexibility in creating a dialog box, but most programmers can get by with the first routine. For this reason, we will focus our attention on the CreateDialog routine. It is defined:

```
int CreateDialog (hInstance, lpszTemplate, hwndParent,
                  lpDialogProc);
```

- hInstance is the instance handle of the program or dynamic link library that owns the dialog box definition.

- `lpszTemplate` is a far pointer to a character string for the name of the dialog box definition, as defined in the dialog box template. Alternatively, it can be an integer value wrapped inside the `MAKEINTRESOURCE` macro, when an integer is used in place of a character string to identify the dialog box template.

- `hwndParent` is a handle to the parent window of the dialog box. The parent window of a modal dialog box is disabled when the dialog box is displayed.

- `lpDialogProc` is a far pointer to a piece of code that maintains the dialog box while it is being displayed. This is a function referred to as a dialog box procedure. The address passed in this parameter is not the actual address of the routine itself, but the instance thunk created by the `MakeProcInstance` routine for the dialog box procedure.

It's interesting to note that the parameters to `CreateDialog` are identical to those of `DialogBox`. Even though you probably will never create a dialog box that is both modal and modeless, the similarity between these two routines makes it possible. One of the reasons for the similarity is that `DialogBox` itself calls `CreateDialog` to build the actual dialog box. The difference between the two, of course, is that `DialogBox` disables its parent and has its own message loop, while `CreateDialog` simply returns when the dialog box has been built.

Just like a modal dialog box, the creation of a modeless dialog box requires an instance thunk to make sure the dialog box procedure has access to your program's data segment. This is accomplished with a call to `MakeProcInstance`:

```
lpitFind = MakeProcInstance (FindDlgProc, hInst);
```

The value returned is a far pointer to an instance thunk. This is passed as the fourth parameter to `CreateDialog`:

```
hwndFindDialog = CreateDialog (hInst,
                               MAKEINTRESOURCE (IDD_FIND),
                               hwnd,
                               lpitFind);
```

The value that `CreateDialog` returns is a window handle to the dialog box itself. A program should always save the return value from the `CreateDialog` function, because this handle is going to be needed to support the keyboard interface of the modeless dialog box.

Maintaining a Modeless Dialog Box

Maintaining a modeless dialog box requires a dialog box procedure similar to the one you'd create for a modal dialog box. Outside the dialog box procedure itself, you will probably want one additional element that provides the keyboard interface to a modeless dialog box.

The keyboard interface to a *modal* dialog box consists of support for several keys: Tab, Enter, Esc, and the arrow keys. These keys allow the user to move between controls and dismiss the dialog box. They are automatically available for modal dialog boxes because a modal dialog box has its own message loop. To get these keys to work in a *modeless* dialog box, you must modify your program's message loop to include a call to `IsDialogMessage`. This routine is defined as

```
BOOL IsDialogMessage (hDlg, lpMsg)
```

- `hDlg` is a handle to a modeless dialog box.
- `lpMsg` is a far pointer to a structure of type `MSG`.

`IsDialogMessage` returns `TRUE` when the message was for a dialog box or a dialog box control. In this case, `IsDialogMessage` makes the necessary calls to `TranslateMessage` and `DispatchMessage`. `IsDialogMessage` returns `FALSE` when the message was not for the dialog box or any of the dialog's controls. In that case, the message loop handles the message in the normal way.

Here is an example of a message loop that has been modified to correctly call `IsDialogMessage` to handle the keyboard interface for a modeless dialog box:

```
while (GetMessage(&msg, 0, 0, 0))
    {
    if (hwndFindDialog)
        if (IsDialogMessage (hwndFindDialog, &msg))
            continue;
    TranslateMessage(&msg);   //  Keyboard input.
    DispatchMessage(&msg);
    }
```

Notice that `IsDialogMessage` is only called if the value of `hwndFindDialog` is nonzero. This variable contains a valid window handle (when the modeless dialog box has been created), or zero when it is not around.

Although the dialog box procedure for a modeless dialog box is almost identical to that of a modal dialog box, a key difference is that modal dialogs are terminated with a call to `EndDialog`. Modeless dialogs, on the other hand, are terminated with a call to `DestroyWindow`:

```
DestroyWindow (hdlg);
```

Otherwise, a modeless dialog box has the same declaration as a modal dialog box, with a `CALLBACK` (`FAR` and `PASCAL`) declaration, and the four familiar parameters:

```
BOOL CALLBACK FindDlgProc (HWND hdlg,      UINT wMsg,
                           WPARAM wParam, LPARAM lParam)
```

Like any other call-back procedure, a modeless dialog box procedure must be listed in the `EXPORTS` section of the module definition file:

```
EXPORTS
    FindDlgProc
```

There are clearly enough differences between modal and modeless dialog boxes that you'll probably want to see a complete program that shows all of these elements put together. The next sample program creates and maintains a modeless dialog box, and also shows a few interesting programming techniques that can be applied to modal as well as modeless dialog boxes.

A Modeless Dialog Box: FIND

The modeless dialog box that we will create is modeled after a modeless dialog box used by a program that is bundled with Windows: Write. It creates a modeless dialog box when the user selects the *Search.Find...* menu item. This creates a modeless dialog that is left open to allow ongoing searches for strings. The user can continue working with the word processing document even while the FIND dialog remains present on the screen. Figure 14.17 shows the dialog box that our program creates.

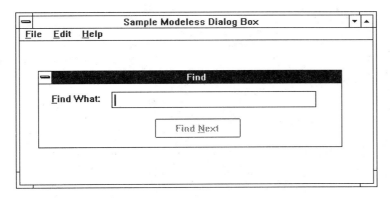

Figure 14.17 A Modeless Dialog Box

Here is the code to our modeless dialog box program:

FIND.C

```
/*-------------------------------------------------------------*\
|   FIND.C   Sample Modeless dialog box.                        |
\*-------------------------------------------------------------*/
#define STRICT
#include <Windows.H>
#include <WindowsX.H>
#include "Find.h"
#include "finddlg.h"


/*-------------------------------------------------------------*\
|                     Function Prototypes.                      |
\*-------------------------------------------------------------*/
LRESULT CALLBACK FindWndProc (HWND, UINT, WPARAM, LPARAM);
```

```
BOOL    CALLBACK FindDlgProc (HWND, UINT, WPARAM, LPARAM);
VOID NEAR PASCAL Find_OnCommand (HWND, int, HWND, UINT);


/*-------------------------------------------------------------*\
|                      Global Variables.                        |
\*-------------------------------------------------------------*/
char achWndClass[] = "Find:MAIN";
char achAppName[]  = "Sample Modeless Dialog Box";
char achFindBuffer [FINDBUFFERSIZE];
FARPROC   lpitFind;
HINSTANCE hInst;
HWND      hwndFindDialog;


/*-------------------------------------------------------------*\
|                    Main Function:  WinMain.                   |
\*-------------------------------------------------------------*/
int PASCAL
WinMain (HINSTANCE hInstance,      // Who am I?
         HINSTANCE hPrevInstance,  // Any older siblings?
         LPSTR     lpszCmdLine,    // Ptr to command line.
         int       cmdShow)        // How to open my window?
    {
    HACCEL  hAccel;
    HWND    hwnd;
    MSG     msg;
    WNDCLASS wndclass;

    if (!hPrevInstance)
        {
        wndclass.lpszClassName = achWndClass;
        wndclass.hInstance     = hInstance;
        wndclass.lpfnWndProc   = FindWndProc;
        wndclass.hCursor       = LoadCursor (hInstance, "hand");
        wndclass.hIcon         = LoadIcon (hInstance,"snapshot");
        wndclass.lpszMenuName  = "#1";
        wndclass.hbrBackground = (HBRUSH)(COLOR_WINDOW+1);
        wndclass.style         = NULL;
        wndclass.cbClsExtra    = 0;
        wndclass.cbWndExtra    = 0;

        RegisterClass( &wndclass);
        }

    hInst = hInstance;
    lpitFind  = MakeProcInstance ((FARPROC)FindDlgProc, hInst);

    hwnd = CreateWindowEx(0L,                // Extra style.
                    achWndClass,             // Class name.
                    achAppName,              // Title.
                    WS_OVERLAPPEDWINDOW,     // Style bits.
                    CW_USEDEFAULT,           // x - default.
                    0,                       // y - default.
                    CW_USEDEFAULT,           // cx - default.
                    0,                       // cy - default.
                    NULL,                    // No parent.
```

```
                            NULL,                  // Class menu.
                            hInstance,             // Creator.
                            NULL);                 // Params.
        ShowWindow (hwnd, cmdShow);

        hAccel = LoadAccelerators (hInstance, "#1");

        while (GetMessage(&msg, 0, 0, 0))
            {
            if (hwndFindDialog)
                if (IsDialogMessage (hwndFindDialog, &msg))
                    continue;

            if (!TranslateAccelerator (hwnd, hAccel, &msg))
                {
                TranslateMessage(&msg); // Convert KEYDOWNs to CHARs
                DispatchMessage(&msg);  // Transmit message to WndProc
                }
            }

        FreeProcInstance (lpitFind);

        return 0;
        }

/*--------------------------------------------------------------*\
|                 Window Procedure:  FindWndProc.                |
\*--------------------------------------------------------------*/
LRESULT CALLBACK
FindWndProc (HWND   hwnd,      // For whom is message sent?
             UINT   mMsg,      // What is exact message?
             WPARAM wParam,    // ...message details.
             LPARAM lParam)    // ...message details.
    {
    switch (mMsg)
        {
        case WM_COMMAND:
            {
            char buffer[80];
            char *npch;

            switch (wParam)
                {
                case IDM_FILE_NEW:
                    npch = "File.New";
                    break;
                case IDM_FILE_OPEN:
                    npch = "File.Open...";
                    break;
                case IDM_FILE_SAVE:
                    npch = "File.Save";
                    break;
                case IDM_FILE_SAVEAS:
                    npch = "File.Save As...";
                    break;
```

```
        case IDM_FILE_PRINT:
            npch = "File.Print";
            break;
        case IDM_FILE_EXIT:
            npch = "File.Exit";
            break;
        case IDM_EDIT_UNDO:
            npch = "Edit.Undo";
            break;
        case IDM_EDIT_CUT:
            npch = "Edit.Cut";
            break;
        case IDM_EDIT_COPY:
            npch = "Edit.Copy";
            break;
        case IDM_EDIT_PASTE:
            npch = "Edit.Paste";
            break;
        case IDM_EDIT_CLEAR:
            npch = "Edit.Clear";
            break;
        case IDM_EDIT_DELETE:
            npch = "Edit.Delete";
            break;
        case IDM_EDIT_FIND:
            if (hwndFindDialog)
                SetActiveWindow (hwndFindDialog);
            else
                hwndFindDialog = CreateDialog (hInst,
                            MAKEINTRESOURCE (IDD_FIND),
                            hwnd,
                            (DLGPROC)lpitFind);
            break;
        case IDM_HELP_INDEX:
            npch = "Help.Index";
            break;
        case IDM_HELP_KEYS:
            npch = "Help.Keyboard";
            break;
        case IDM_HELP_USING:
            npch = "Help.Using Help";
            break;
        case IDM_HELP_ABOUT:
            npch = "Help.About...";
            break;
        }

    // Display message box with
    // name of selected menu item.
    if (wParam != IDM_EDIT_FIND)
        {
        wsprintf (buffer, "%s command selected.",
                    (LPSTR)npch);
        MessageBox (hwnd, buffer, achAppName, MB_OK);
        }
```

```
                // If user selected File.Exit,
                // simulate {-}.Close menu selection.
                if (wParam == IDM_FILE_EXIT)
                    {
                    SendMessage (hwnd, WM_SYSCOMMAND, SC_CLOSE, 0L);
                    }
                }
            break;

        case WM_DESTROY:
            PostQuitMessage(0);   // Handle application shutdown.
            break;

        case PM_FIND:
            MessageBox (hwnd, achFindBuffer,
                        "Find Request Received", MB_OK);
            break;

        default:
            return(DefWindowProc(hwnd,mMsg,wParam,lParam));
            break;
        }
    return 0L;
    }

/*------------------------------------------------------------*\
|            Dialog Box Procedure:  FindDlgProc                 |
\*------------------------------------------------------------*/
BOOL CALLBACK
FindDlgProc (HWND    hdlg,     // For whom is message sent?
             UINT    wMsg,     // What is exact message?
             WPARAM  wParam,   // ...message details.
             LPARAM  lParam)   // ...message details.
    {
    switch (wMsg)
        {
        case WM_INITDIALOG:
            {
            HWND hCtl;

            hCtl = GetDlgItem (hdlg, IDD_BUTTON);
            EnableWindow (hCtl, FALSE);
            }
            break;

        case WM_COMMAND:
            HANDLE_WM_COMMAND(hdlg,wParam,lParam,Find_OnCommand);
            break;

        default:
            return FALSE;
        }
    return TRUE;
    }
```

```
/*-----------------------------------------------------------*\
|           Dialog Box Message Cracker:  Find_OnCommand.      |
\*-----------------------------------------------------------*/
VOID NEAR PASCAL
Find_OnCommand (HWND hdlg,          // Dialog window handle.
                int  id,            // ID of dialog control.
                HWND hwndCtl,       // hwnd of dialog control.
                UINT codeNotify)    // Notification code.
    {
    switch (id)
        {
        case IDD_CANCEL:
            DestroyWindow (hdlg);
            hwndFindDialog = 0;
            break;

        case IDD_BUTTON:
            {
            HWND hwndParent;

            GetDlgItemText (hdlg, IDD_EDIT, achFindBuffer,
                            FINDBUFFERSIZE);

            hwndParent = GetParent (hdlg);
            SendMessage (hwndParent, PM_FIND, 0, 0L);
            }
            break;

        case IDD_EDIT:
            {
            HWND hCtl;
            int  cc;

            if (codeNotify == EN_CHANGE)
                {
                hCtl = GetDlgItem (hdlg, IDD_BUTTON);
                cc   = GetWindowTextLength(hwndCtl);
                EnableWindow (hCtl, cc);
                }
            }
             break;

        }
    }
```

FIND.DEF

NAME   FIND

EXETYPE WINDOWS

DESCRIPTION 'Sample Modeless Dialog Box (c) 1992 By Paul Yao'

```
CODE      MOVEABLE PRELOAD
DATA      MOVEABLE MULTIPLE PRELOAD

HEAPSIZE    512
STACKSIZE   5120

SEGMENTS
    FIND_TEXT MOVEABLE PRELOAD

EXPORTS
    FindWndProc
    FindDlgProc
```

FIND.DLG

```
IDD_FIND DIALOG LOADONCALL MOVEABLE DISCARDABLE
                9, 27, 216, 47
CAPTION "Find"
STYLE WS_BORDER | WS_CAPTION | WS_DLGFRAME | WS_SYSMENU |
      WS_VISIBLE | WS_POPUP
BEGIN
    CONTROL "&Find What:", IDD_TEXT, "static",
            SS_LEFT | WS_CHILD, 9, 7, 39, 10
    CONTROL "", IDD_EDIT, "edit",
            ES_LEFT | WS_BORDER | WS_TABSTOP | WS_CHILD,
            52, 6, 146, 12
    CONTROL "Find &Next", IDD_BUTTON, "button",
            BS_DEFPUSHBUTTON | WS_TABSTOP | WS_CHILD,
            83, 26, 61, 14
END
```

FIND.H

```
/*----------------------------------------------------------*\
| Find.h  - Include file for Find.c.                        |
\*----------------------------------------------------------*/

#define IDM_FILE_NEW      101
#define IDM_FILE_OPEN     102
#define IDM_FILE_SAVE     103
#define IDM_FILE_SAVEAS   104
#define IDM_FILE_PRINT    105
#define IDM_FILE_EXIT     106

#define IDM_EDIT_UNDO     201
#define IDM_EDIT_CUT      202
#define IDM_EDIT_COPY     203
#define IDM_EDIT_PASTE    204
#define IDM_EDIT_CLEAR    205
```

```
#define IDM_EDIT_DELETE      206
#define IDM_EDIT_FIND        207

#define IDM_HELP_INDEX       301
#define IDM_HELP_KEYS        302
#define IDM_HELP_USING       303
#define IDM_HELP_ABOUT       304

#define FINDBUFFERSIZE 80

// Private message from modeless dialog to FIND's
// main window.
#define PM_FIND              WM_USER

// Dialog box keyboard interface code for
// striking the [Esc] key.
#define IDD_CANCEL        2
```

FINDDLG.H

```
#define IDD_FIND      11

#define IDD_EDIT      100
#define IDD_BUTTON    101
#define IDD_TEXT      102
```

FIND.LNK

```
Find.obj
Find.exe/align:16/map/nod/noe/CO
nul
mlibcew libw
Find.def
```

FIND.MAK

```
# Directory search paths.

INCDIR = \WINDEV\INCLUDE

# Windows version to support
# Valid pairs include:
#     (0x0300, 30)
#     (0x0310, 31)
```

```
CLVER = WINVER=0x0300
RCVER = 30

# Compiler switches for applications.

CL_APP_SHIP_ALL = -AM -c -D$(CLVER) -Gsw -I$(INCDIR) -Ow -W3 -Zp
CL_APP_DEBG_ALL = -AM -c -D$(CLVER) -Gsw -I$(INCDIR) -Od -W3 -Zpi

CL_APP_SHIP_31  = -AM -c -G2s  -I$(INCDIR) -Ow -W3 -Zp
CL_APP_DEBG_31  = -AM -c -G2s  -I$(INCDIR) -Od -W3 -Zpi

# Compiler switches for DLLs.

CL_DLL_SHIP_ALL = -AMw -c -D$(CLVER) -Gsw -I$(INCDIR) -Ow -W3 -Zp
CL_DLL_DEBG_ALL = -AMw -c -D$(CLVER) -Gsw -I$(INCDIR) -Od -W3 -Zpi

CL_DLL_SHIP_31  = -AMw -c -G2s  -I$(INCDIR) -Ow -W3 -Zp
CL_DLL_DEBG_31  = -AMw -c -G2s  -I$(INCDIR) -Od -W3 -Zpi

# Make file primary target.

all: Find.exe

# Make file dependency targets.

Find.res: Find.rc Find.cur Find.dlg Finddlg.h Find.h Find.ico
    rc -r -i$(INCDIR) Find.rc

Find.obj: Find.c Find.h
    cl $(CL_APP_SHIP_ALL) Find.c

Find.exe: Find.obj Find.def Find.res
    link @Find.lnk
    rc -$(RCVER) Find.res

Find.exe: Find.res
    rc -$(RCVER) Find.res
```

FIND.RC

```
#include <Windows.h>
#include "Find.h"
#include "Finddlg.h"

snapshot icon Find.ico

hand   cursor Find.cur

#include "find.dlg"
```

```
1 MENU
    {
    POPUP "&File"
        {
        MENUITEM "&New",          IDM_FILE_NEW
        MENUITEM "&Open...",      IDM_FILE_OPEN
        MENUITEM "&Save",         IDM_FILE_SAVE
        MENUITEM "Save &As...",   IDM_FILE_SAVEAS
        MENUITEM SEPARATOR
        MENUITEM "&Print",        IDM_FILE_PRINT
        MENUITEM SEPARATOR
        MENUITEM "E&xit",         IDM_FILE_EXIT
        }
    POPUP "&Edit"
        {
        MENUITEM "&Undo\tCtrl+Z",  IDM_EDIT_UNDO
        MENUITEM SEPARATOR
        MENUITEM "Cu&t\tCtrl+X",   IDM_EDIT_CUT
        MENUITEM "&Copy\tCtrl+C",  IDM_EDIT_COPY
        MENUITEM "&Paste\tCtrl+V", IDM_EDIT_PASTE
        MENUITEM SEPARATOR
        MENUITEM "Cl&ear",        IDM_EDIT_CLEAR
        MENUITEM "&Delete",       IDM_EDIT_DELETE
        MENUITEM SEPARATOR
        MENUITEM "&Find...",      IDM_EDIT_FIND
        }
    POPUP "&Help"
        {
        MENUITEM "Index",            IDM_HELP_INDEX
        MENUITEM "Keyboard",         IDM_HELP_KEYS
        MENUITEM "Using Help",       IDM_HELP_USING
        MENUITEM SEPARATOR
        MENUITEM "About...",         IDM_HELP_ABOUT
        }
    }

1 ACCELERATORS
    {
    ;  New Windows 3.1 clipboard accelerators.
    "Z",         IDM_EDIT_UNDO,   VIRTKEY, CONTROL
    "X",         IDM_EDIT_CUT,    VIRTKEY, CONTROL
    "C",         IDM_EDIT_COPY,   VIRTKEY, CONTROL
    "V",         IDM_EDIT_PASTE,  VIRTKEY, CONTROL

    ;  Maintain support for older clipboard accelerators.
    VK_BACK,    IDM_EDIT_UNDO,   VIRTKEY, ALT
    VK_DELETE,  IDM_EDIT_CUT,    VIRTKEY, SHIFT
    VK_INSERT,  IDM_EDIT_COPY,   VIRTKEY, CONTROL
    VK_INSERT,  IDM_EDIT_PASTE,  VIRTKEY, SHIFT
    }
```

The modeless dialog box procedure in FIND must be accessed through an instance thunk. This is created by a call to `MakeProcInstance`, which is called inside our `WinMain` function:

```
lpitFind = MakeProcInstance (FindDlgProc, hInst);
```

After this call, the value of `lpitFind` is a long pointer to an instance thunk, which provides the necessary connection between the dialog box procedure, `FindDlgProc`, and our program's data segment. We'll pass the value of `lpitFind` to `CreateDialog` as the required address of the dialog box procedure.

The modeless dialog box itself is displayed after the user selects a menu item that we added to the Edit menu, depicted in Figure 14.18. When this menu item is selected, a WM_COMMAND message is sent to the window procedure of FIND's main window, with a value of `IDM_FIND` in the `wParam`. This causes the following code to create our dialog box:

```
hwndFindDialog = CreateDialog (hInst,
                               MAKEINTRESOURCE (IDD_FIND),
                               hwnd,
                               lpitFind);
```

`CreateDialog` returns a window handle, which we store away for use in the call to `IsDialogMessage`, embedded in our message loop, to enable the modeless dialog box's keyboard interface.

Within our dialog box procedure, we use the HANDLE_WM_COMMAND macro to simplify the processing of the WM_COMMAND message. This macro is defined in the WindowsX.h include file as follows:

```
#define HANDLE_WM_COMMAND(hwnd, wParam, lParam, fn) \
        ((fn)((hwnd),(int)wParam), (HWND)LOWORD(lParam), \
        (UINT)HIWORD(lParam)), 0L)
```

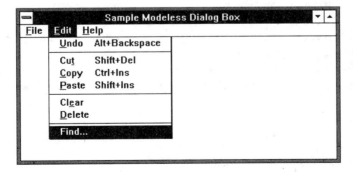

Figure 14.18 The "Find" menu item triggers the creation of the Modeless Dialog Box

This macro parses the two message parameters, `wParam` and `lParam`, and calls a function with the following prototype:

```
void func (HWND hwnd, int id, HWND hwndCtl, UINT codeNotify);
```

This macro simplifies our handling of this message, and reduces the chance of introducing errors when we parse these parameters ourself.

However, the most important reason this macro is useful is that it provides a standard portable interface with future versions of Windows. By this, of course, we mean the Win32 API, which Microsoft made public at the end of last year. In this API, almost every system value gets widened to 32-bits, which has resulted in the need to move some message parameters. The damage is not great, however, since—of the 200 or so messages in the API—only about 20 are affected by this change. Since the WM_COMMAND notification message is one of those affected, it would be a good idea for you to include this macro in all your dialog box procedures.

The "Find" push button in the modeless dialog box is initially grayed, to notify the user that it cannot be selected. Actually, we don't directly gray the dialog box control. Instead, we disable it which causes it to gray itself. We do this by calling `EnableWindow`, which is defined:

```
BOOL EnableWindow (hwnd, bEnable)
```

- `hwnd` is a handle of the window to be enabled or disabled.

- `bEnable` is TRUE (nonzero) to enable a window and FALSE (zero) to disable it.

The dialog box procedure does not enable the push button unless there are characters in the edit control.

The easiest way for a dialog box procedure to detect the presence of characters in an edit control is to wait for the edit control to send an EN_CHANGE notification. The EN_CHANGE notification is sent whenever characters are added or deleted from the edit control. Since all notifications come as WM_COMMAND messages, we rely on the HANDLE_WM_COMMAND macro to do parameter parsing for us.

To determine whether an edit control has characters or not, we send a query message to the edit control: WM_GETTEXTLENGTH. The return value is the count of characters in the edit control. We can use the count of characters as a parameter to the `EnableWindow` function, since zero will disable the push button and nonzero values will enable it:

```
hCtl = GetDlgItem (hdlg, IDD_BUTTON);
cc = GetWindowTextLength (hwndCtl);
EnableWindow (hCtl, cc);
```

The net result is that the user can only push the Find button when there is text in the edit control. At that time, the push button sends a notification to the dialog box procedure: a WM_COMMAND message. Once again, the message parsing macro grinds out the correct values from the `wParam` and `lParam` parameters. This leaves our code to retrieve the text from the edit control and notify the parent window that the user wants us to do some work.

```
GetDlgItemText (hdlg, IDD_EDIT, achFindBuffer, FINDBUFFERSIZE);
hwndParent = GetParent (hdlg);
SendMessage (hwndParent, PM_FIND, 0, 0L);
```

We don't bother checking for the BN_CLICKED notification code, since a push button can only send one other notification code, BN_DOUBLECLICKED, which always comes after a BN_CLICKED notification.

Notifying the parent window involves sending a private message, PM_FIND, that has been defined as

```
#define PM_FIND WM_USER
```

This is an example of an application-defined message. Presumably, if this were part of a full-blown program, the parent window would start a search upon receipt of this message. In this program, a message box is simply displayed to tell us that a search was requested.

You may have noticed that the dialog box procedure tests for a notification sent from a control with an ID value of IDD_CANCEL. Yet, if you look at the dialog box template, you'll see that there is no dialog box control with this identifier. Built into the dialog box handling mechanism is automatic support for sending this notification whenever the user strikes the Esc key. Also, since this dialog box has a system menu, the user may select the Close item to cause the same notification to be sent. In response to either of these actions, the modeless dialog box is dismissed with a call to DestroyWindow. This routine must be used in place of the modal dialog counterpart, EndDialog, because this latter routine performs some special termination processing that only makes sense for a modal dialog box.

This modeless dialog box has shown how two dialog box controls can be interconnected: The push button is grayed when the edit control is empty, and enabled when the edit control has character information. As you build more and more complex dialog boxes, you'll see that this is quite typical.

A File Open Dialog Box

Any program that reads and writes files to disk will need to have a dialog box to allow the user to select the file to be opened. This is such a standard that Microsoft has included a File Open dialog in the common dialog box support provided with Windows 3.1 (COMMDLG.DLL). When the time comes to create such a dialog, it makes sense to use the common dialog. Nevertheless, we've included the complete sources for our own File.Open dialog to give you a better idea for the types of interactions that are involved.

Figure 14.19 shows the standard File-Open dialog box that our program creates, and here is the source code:

Figure 14.19 A File-Open dialog box

OPEN.C

```
/*-----------------------------------------------------------*\
|   Open.C  Sample Open-File dialog box.                      |
\*-----------------------------------------------------------*/
#define STRICT
#include <Windows.H>
#include <WindowsX.H>
#include "Open.H"
#include "Opendlg.h"


/*-----------------------------------------------------------*\
|                   Function Prototypes.                      |
\*-----------------------------------------------------------*/
LRESULT CALLBACK OpenWndProc (HWND, UINT, WPARAM, LPARAM);
BOOL FAR  PASCAL OpenDlgProc (HWND, WORD, WORD, LONG);
BOOL NEAR PASCAL OpenDlg_OnInitDialog(HWND, HWND, LPARAM);
VOID NEAR PASCAL OpenDlg_OnCommand (HWND, int, HWND, UINT);


/*-----------------------------------------------------------*\
|                   Global Variables.                        |
\*-----------------------------------------------------------*/
char achWndClass[] = "Open:MAIN";
char achAppName[]  = "File-Open Dialog";

char achOpenFile[MAXFILENAMELEN];
char achWild[MAXFILENAMELEN];
char achInvalid[] = "File name or path is invalid.";
```

```
FARPROC lpitOpenDlgProc;
HANDLE  hInst;

/*-------------------------------------------------------------*\
|                   Main Function:  WinMain.                    |
\*-------------------------------------------------------------*/
int PASCAL
WinMain (HINSTANCE hInstance,       // Who am I?
         HINSTANCE hPrevInstance,   // Any older siblings?
         LPSTR     lpszCmdLine,     // Ptr to command line.
         int       cmdShow)         // How to open my window?
    {
    HACCEL    hAccel;
    HWND      hwnd;
    MSG       msg;
    WNDCLASS  wndclass;

    if (!hPrevInstance)
        {
        wndclass.lpszClassName = achWndClass;
        wndclass.hInstance     = hInstance;
        wndclass.lpfnWndProc   = OpenWndProc;
        wndclass.hCursor       = LoadCursor (hInstance, "hand");
        wndclass.hIcon         = LoadIcon (hInstance,"snapshot");
        wndclass.lpszMenuName  = "#1";
        wndclass.hbrBackground = (HBRUSH)(COLOR_WINDOW+1);
        wndclass.style         = NULL;
        wndclass.cbClsExtra    = 0;
        wndclass.cbWndExtra    = 0;

        RegisterClass( &wndclass);
        }

    hInst = hInstance;
    lpitOpenDlgProc  = MakeProcInstance ((FARPROC)OpenDlgProc,
                                          hInst);

    hwnd = CreateWindowEx(0L,                     // Extra style.
                    achWndClass,                  // Class name.
                    achAppName,                   // Title.
                    WS_OVERLAPPEDWINDOW,          // Style bits.
                    CW_USEDEFAULT,                // x - default.
                    0,                            // y - default.
                    CW_USEDEFAULT,                // cx - default.
                    0,                            // cy - default.
                    NULL,                         // No parent.
                    NULL,                         // Class menu.
                    hInstance,                    // Creator.
                    NULL);                        // Params.
    ShowWindow (hwnd, cmdShow);

    hAccel = LoadAccelerators (hInstance, "#1");
```

```
        while (GetMessage(&msg, 0, 0, 0))
            {
            if (!TranslateAccelerator (hwnd, hAccel, &msg))
                {
                TranslateMessage(&msg); // Convert KEYDOWNs to CHARs
                DispatchMessage(&msg);  // Transmit message to WndProc
                }
            }

        FreeProcInstance (lpitOpenDlgProc);

        return 0;
        }


/*-------------------------------------------------------------*\
|               Window Procedure:  OpenWndProc.                 |
\*-------------------------------------------------------------*/
LRESULT CALLBACK
OpenWndProc (HWND    hwnd,      // For whom is message sent?
             UINT    mMsg,      // What is exact message?
             WPARAM  wParam,    // ...message details.
             LPARAM  lParam)    // ...message details.
    {
    switch (mMsg)
        {
        case WM_COMMAND:
            {
            char buffer[80];
            char *npch;

            switch (wParam)
                {
                case IDM_FILE_NEW:
                    npch = "File.New";
                    break;
                case IDM_FILE_OPEN:
                    {
                    BOOL bRet;

                    bRet = DialogBox (hInst,
                                MAKEINTRESOURCE(IDD_OPEN),
                                hwnd,
                                (DLGPROC)lpitOpenDlgProc);
                    if (bRet)
                        wsprintf (buffer,
                                "User clicked Ok.  File = %s",
                                (LPSTR)achOpenFile);
                    else
                        wsprintf (buffer, "User clicked Cancel.");
                    }
                    break;
                case IDM_FILE_SAVE:
                    npch = "File.Save";
                    break;
```

```
        case IDM_FILE_SAVEAS:
            npch = "File.Save As...";
            break;
        case IDM_FILE_PRINT:
            npch = "File.Print";
            break;
        case IDM_FILE_EXIT:
            npch = "File.Exit";
            break;
        case IDM_EDIT_UNDO:
            npch = "Edit.Undo";
            break;
        case IDM_EDIT_CUT:
            npch = "Edit.Cut";
            break;
        case IDM_EDIT_COPY:
            npch = "Edit.Copy";
            break;
        case IDM_EDIT_PASTE:
            npch = "Edit.Paste";
            break;
        case IDM_EDIT_CLEAR:
            npch = "Edit.Clear";
            break;
        case IDM_EDIT_DELETE:
            npch = "Edit.Delete";
            break;
        }

    // If user didn't select File.Open, build message
    // to display.
    if (wParam != IDM_FILE_OPEN)
        {
        wsprintf (buffer, "%s command selected.",
                (LPSTR)npch);
        }

    // Display results of command selection.
    MessageBox (hwnd, buffer, achAppName, MB_OK);

    // If user selected File.Exit,
    // simulate {-}.Close menu selection.
    if (wParam == IDM_FILE_EXIT)
        {
        SendMessage (hwnd, WM_SYSCOMMAND, SC_CLOSE, 0L);
        }
    }
    break;

case WM_DESTROY:
    PostQuitMessage(0);  // Handle application shutdown.
    break;
```

```
            default:
                return(DefWindowProc(hwnd,mMsg,wParam,lParam));
                break;
            }
        return 0L;
        }


/*------------------------------------------------------------*\
|              Dialog Box Procedure:  OpenDlgProc              |
\*------------------------------------------------------------*/
BOOL FAR PASCAL
OpenDlgProc (HWND    hdlg,       // For whom is message sent?
             UINT    wMsg,       // What is exact message?
             WPARAM  wParam,     // ...message details.
             LPARAM  lParam)     // ...message details.

    {

    switch (wMsg)
        {
        case WM_INITDIALOG:
            return (BOOL)
            HANDLE_WM_INITDIALOG (hdlg, wParam, lParam,
                                  OpenDlg_OnInitDialog);
            break;

        case WM_COMMAND:
            HANDLE_WM_COMMAND (hdlg, wParam, lParam,
                               OpenDlg_OnCommand);
            break;

        default:
            return FALSE;
        }
    return TRUE;
    }


/*------------------------------------------------------------*\
|      Dialog Box Message Cracker:  OpenDlg_OnInitDialog.      |
\*------------------------------------------------------------*/
BOOL NEAR PASCAL
OpenDlg_OnInitDialog (HWND    hwnd,        // Dialog window handle.
                      HWND    hwndFocus,   // Control to get focus.
                      LPARAM  lParam)      // Init parameter.

    {
    HWND hCtl;

    // Initialize directory listing.
    lstrcpy (achWild, "*.*");
    DlgDirList (hwnd,
                achWild,
                IDD_DIRLIST,
                IDD_CURDIR,
                0xC010);

    // Initialize file listing.
```

```
        DlgDirList (hwnd,
                    achWild,
                    IDD_FILELIST,
                    IDD_CURDIR,
                    0);

        // Limit text length in edit control.
        hCtl = GetDlgItem (hwnd, IDD_NAME);
        SendMessage (hCtl,
                    EM_LIMITTEXT,
                    MAXFILENAMELEN,
                    0);

        // Put wild card into edit control.
        SendMessage (hCtl,
                    WM_SETTEXT,
                    0,
                    (LONG)(LPSTR)achWild);

        // Select text in edit control.
        SendMessage (hCtl,
                    EM_SETSEL,
                    0,
                    MAKELONG (0, MAXFILENAMELEN));

        return TRUE;
        }

/*----------------------------------------------------------------*\
|         Dialog Box Message Cracker:  OpenDlg_OnCommand.         |
\*----------------------------------------------------------------*/
VOID NEAR PASCAL
OpenDlg_OnCommand (HWND hwnd,          // Dialog window handle.
                   int  id,            // ID of dialog control.
                   HWND hwndCtl,       // hwnd of dialog control.
                   UINT codeNotify)    // Notification code.
    {
    BOOL    bWild;
    char    achBuff[MAXFILENAMELEN];
    HWND    hCtl;
    int     cc;
    int     iFile;
    int     iRet;
    OFSTRUCT of;
    PSTR    p;

    switch (id)
        {
        case IDD_OK:

            // Read file name from edit control.
            hCtl = GetDlgItem (hwnd, IDD_NAME);
            SendMessage (hCtl,
                        WM_GETTEXT,
```

```
                        MAXFILENAMELEN,
                        (LONG)(LPSTR)achBuff);

    //  Trim leading blanks from file name.
    p = achBuff;
    while (*p == ' ')
        p++;
    if (p != achBuff)
        lstrcpy (achBuff, p);

    //  Trim trailing blanks from file name.
    cc = lstrlen (achBuff);
    for (p = achBuff + cc - 1; *p == ' '; p--)
        *p = 0;

    //  Check for wild cards.
    bWild = FALSE;

    for (p = achBuff;*p != NULL; p++)
        {
        if (*p == '?' || *p == '*')
            {
            bWild = TRUE;
            break;
            }
        }

    //  If no wild cards, try to open it.
    if (!bWild)
        {
        // Is it a valid file name?
        iFile = OpenFile (achBuff,
                         &of,
                         OF_EXIST);

        //  If so, then we are done.
        if (iFile != -1)
            {
            lstrcpy (achOpenFile, achBuff);
            EndDialog (hwnd, TRUE);
            break;
            }
        else  //  If not, add wild card
            //   and continue.
            {
            p--;
            if (*p != '\\' && *p != '/')
                lstrcat (achBuff, "\\");
            lstrcat (achBuff, achWild);
            }
        }


    //  Rebuild list boxes.
    iRet = DlgDirList (hwnd,
                    achBuff,
```

```
                        IDD_DIRLIST,
                        IDD_CURDIR,
                        0xC010);

    //  Did DlgDirList report an error?
    if (!iRet)
        {
        MessageBox (hwnd,
                    achInvalid,
                    "Open-File",
                    MB_OK);
        }
    else
        {
        //  Initialize file list box.
        DlgDirList (hwnd,
                    achBuff,
                    IDD_FILELIST,
                    IDD_CURDIR,
                    0);

        //  Make local copy of wild card.
        lstrcpy (achWild, achBuff);

        //  Put wild card into edit control.
        hCtl = GetDlgItem (hwnd, IDD_NAME);
        SendMessage (hCtl,
                    WM_SETTEXT,
                    0,
                    (LONG)(LPSTR)achWild);
        }

    //  Select text in edit control.
    SendMessage (hCtl,
                EM_SETSEL,
                0,
                MAKELONG (0, MAXFILENAMELEN));

    //  Give keyboard to edit control.
    SetFocus (hCtl);
    break;

case IDD_CANCEL:
    EndDialog (hwnd, FALSE);
    break;

case IDD_NAME:
    if (codeNotify == EN_CHANGE)
        {
        //  Enable or disable push button
        //  based on whether edit control is
        //  empty or not.
        cc = (int)SendMessage (hwndCtl,
                        WM_GETTEXTLENGTH,
                        0, 0L);
```

```
                        hCtl = GetDlgItem (hwnd, IDD_OK);
                        EnableWindow (hCtl, cc);
                        }
                break;

        case IDD_FILELIST:
            if (codeNotify == LBN_SELCHANGE)
                {
                DlgDirSelect (hwnd,
                              achBuff,
                              IDD_FILELIST);

                hCtl = GetDlgItem (hwnd, IDD_NAME);
                SendMessage (hCtl,
                             WM_SETTEXT,
                             0,
                             (LONG)(LPSTR)achBuff);
                }

            if (codeNotify == LBN_DBLCLK)
                SendMessage (hwnd, WM_COMMAND, IDD_OK, 0L);
            break;

        case IDD_DIRLIST:
            if (codeNotify == LBN_SELCHANGE)
                {
                DlgDirSelect (hwnd,
                              achBuff,
                              IDD_DIRLIST);

                hCtl = GetDlgItem (hwnd, IDD_NAME);
                lstrcat (achBuff, achWild);
                SendMessage (hCtl,
                             WM_SETTEXT,
                             0,
                             (LONG)(LPSTR)achBuff);
                }

            if (codeNotify == LBN_DBLCLK)
                {
                DlgDirSelect (hwnd,
                              achBuff,
                              IDD_DIRLIST);
                DlgDirList (hwnd,
                            achBuff,
                            IDD_DIRLIST,
                            IDD_CURDIR,
                            0xC010);

                //  Initialize file listing.
                DlgDirList (hwnd,
                            achWild,
                            IDD_FILELIST,
                            IDD_CURDIR,
                            0);
```

```
                // Put wild card into edit control.
                hCtl = GetDlgItem (hwnd, IDD_NAME);
                SendMessage (hCtl,
                             WM_SETTEXT,
                             0,
                             (LONG)(LPSTR)achWild);

                // Select all text in edit control.
                SendMessage (hCtl,
                             EM_SETSEL,
                             0,
                             MAKELONG (0, MAXFILENAMELEN));

                // Give keyboard to edit control.
                SetFocus (hCtl);
                }
            break;
        }
    }
```

OPEN.DEF

```
NAME    OPEN

EXETYPE WINDOWS

DESCRIPTION 'File.Open Dialog  (c) 1992 By Paul Yao'

CODE    MOVEABLE PRELOAD
DATA    MOVEABLE MULTIPLE PRELOAD

HEAPSIZE    512
STACKSIZE   5120

SEGMENTS
    OPEN_TEXT MOVEABLE PRELOAD

EXPORTS
    OpenWndProc
    OpenDlgProc
```

OPEN.DLG

```
DLGINCLUDE RCDATA DISCARDABLE
BEGIN
    "OPENDLG.H\0"
END
```

```
IDD_OPEN DIALOG 36, 24, 207, 114
STYLE WS_POPUP | WS_CAPTION | WS_SYSMENU
CAPTION "Open"
BEGIN
    LTEXT           "File &Name:", -1, 8, 11, 39, 8, NOT WS_GROUP
    LTEXT           "&Files:", -1, 8, 29, 22, 8, NOT WS_GROUP
    LTEXT           "&Directories:", -1, 80, 45, 41, 8, NOT WS_GROUP
    LTEXT           "", IDD_CURDIR, 76, 24, 76, 8, NOT WS_GROUP
    EDITTEXT        IDD_NAME, 47, 10, 99, 13, ES_OEMCONVERT
    LISTBOX         IDD_FILELIST, 8, 43, 60, 65, LBS_SORT |
WS_VSCROLL |
                    WS_TABSTOP
    LISTBOX         IDD_DIRLIST, 80, 59, 63, 49, LBS_SORT |
WS_VSCROLL |
                    WS_TABSTOP
    DEFPUSHBUTTON   "Ok", IDD_OK, 156, 9, 40, 14
    PUSHBUTTON      "Cancel", IDD_CANCEL, 156, 32, 40, 14
END
```

OPEN.H

```
/*--------------------------------------------------------------*\
| Open.h  - Include file for Open.c.                             |
\*--------------------------------------------------------------*/

#define IDM_FILE_NEW      101
#define IDM_FILE_OPEN     102
#define IDM_FILE_SAVE     103
#define IDM_FILE_SAVEAS   104
#define IDM_FILE_PRINT    105
#define IDM_FILE_EXIT     106

#define IDM_EDIT_UNDO     201
#define IDM_EDIT_CUT      202
#define IDM_EDIT_COPY     203
#define IDM_EDIT_PASTE    204
#define IDM_EDIT_CLEAR    205
#define IDM_EDIT_DELETE   206

#define MAXFILENAMELEN     80
```

OPENDLG.H

```
#define IDD_OK        1
#define IDD_CANCEL    2
#define IDD_OPEN      11
#define IDD_CURDIR    201
#define IDD_DIRLIST   202
```

```
#define IDD_FILELIST   200
#define IDD_NAME       203
```

OPEN.LNK

```
Open.obj
Open.exe/align:16/map/nod/noe/CO
nul
mlibcew libw
Open.def
```

OPEN.MAK

```
# Directory search paths.

INCDIR = \WINDEV\INCLUDE

# Windows version to support
# Valid pairs include:
#     (0x0300, 30)
#     (0x0310, 31)

CLVER = WINVER=0x0300
RCVER = 30

# Compiler switches for applications.

CL_APP_SHIP_ALL = -AM -c -D$(CLVER) -Gsw -I$(INCDIR) -Ow -W3 -Zp
CL_APP_DEBG_ALL = -AM -c -D$(CLVER) -Gsw -I$(INCDIR) -Od -W3 -Zpi

CL_APP_SHIP_31  = -AM -c -G2s  -I$(INCDIR) -Ow -W3 -Zp
CL_APP_DEBG_31  = -AM -c -G2s  -I$(INCDIR) -Od -W3 -Zpi

# Compiler switches for DLLs.

CL_DLL_SHIP_ALL = -AMw -c -D$(CLVER) -Gsw -I$(INCDIR) -Ow -W3 -Zp
CL_DLL_DEBG_ALL = -AMw -c -D$(CLVER) -Gsw -I$(INCDIR) -Od -W3 -Zpi

CL_DLL_SHIP_31  = -AMw -c -G2s  -I$(INCDIR) -Ow -W3 -Zp
CL_DLL_DEBG_31  = -AMw -c -G2s  -I$(INCDIR) -Od -W3 -Zpi

# Make file primary target.

all: Open.exe

# Make file dependency targets.

Open.res: Open.rc Open.cur Open.dlg Opendlg.h Open.ico
    rc -r -i$(INCDIR) Open.rc
```

```
Open.obj: Open.c Open.h
    cl $(CL_APP_SHIP_ALL) Open.c

Open.exe: Open.obj Open.def Open.res
    link @Open.lnk
    rc -$(RCVER) Open.res

Open.exe: Open.res
    rc -$(RCVER) Open.res
```

OPEN.RC

```
#include <Windows.h>
#include "Open.h"
#include "OpenDlg.h"

snapshot icon Open.ico

hand  cursor Open.cur


#include "open.dlg"

1 MENU
    {
    POPUP "&File"
        {
        MENUITEM "&New",         IDM_FILE_NEW
        MENUITEM "&Open...",     IDM_FILE_OPEN
        MENUITEM "&Save",        IDM_FILE_SAVE
        MENUITEM "Save &As...",  IDM_FILE_SAVEAS
        MENUITEM SEPARATOR
        MENUITEM "&Print",       IDM_FILE_PRINT
        MENUITEM SEPARATOR
        MENUITEM "E&xit",        IDM_FILE_EXIT
        }
    POPUP "&Edit"
        {
        MENUITEM "&Undo\tCtrl+Z",   IDM_EDIT_UNDO
        MENUITEM SEPARATOR
        MENUITEM "Cu&t\tCtrl+X",    IDM_EDIT_CUT
        MENUITEM "&Copy\tCtrl+C",   IDM_EDIT_COPY
        MENUITEM "&Paste\tCtrl+V",  IDM_EDIT_PASTE
        MENUITEM SEPARATOR
        MENUITEM "Cl&ear",          IDM_EDIT_CLEAR
        MENUITEM "&Delete",         IDM_EDIT_DELETE
        }
    }
```

```
1 ACCELERATORS
    {
    ;  New Windows 3.1 clipboard accelerators.
    "Z",        IDM_EDIT_UNDO,    VIRTKEY, CONTROL
    "X",        IDM_EDIT_CUT,     VIRTKEY, CONTROL
    "C",        IDM_EDIT_COPY,    VIRTKEY, CONTROL
    "V",        IDM_EDIT_PASTE,   VIRTKEY, CONTROL

    ;  Maintain support for older clipboard accelerators.
    VK_BACK,    IDM_EDIT_UNDO,    VIRTKEY, ALT
    VK_DELETE,  IDM_EDIT_CUT,     VIRTKEY, SHIFT
    VK_INSERT,  IDM_EDIT_COPY,    VIRTKEY, CONTROL
    VK_INSERT,  IDM_EDIT_PASTE,   VIRTKEY, SHIFT
    }
```

The dialog box editor provides the best way to define a dialog box template since it allows you to visually arrange the layout of dialog box controls. It's often a good idea, however, to inspect the dialog box template that has been created, to make sure that the style flags are what you expect. For example, the dialog box editor includes the LBS_WANTKEYBOARDINPUT style when you create a listbox. However, this prevents the user from accessing the keyboard interface with a listbox. Therefore, you'll probably want to remove this style bit (or, from inside the dialog box editor, review the style bits in the listbox customizing dialog box and turn off the check box marked "Keyboard Input").

Also, pay attention to another style bit, the WS_TABSTOP style bit, that is necessary for the keyboard interface to a dialog box. When incorporated into the definition of a dialog box control, this style causes the dialog control to serve as a "bus-stop" when the user is striking the Tab key to browse through a dialog box.

The tabbing order of a dialog box is determined by the order in which controls are listed in the dialog box template. This is another reason to review the order created by the dialog box editor. It's a simple matter to cut and paste the dialog box template until you have defined a tabbing order that is right.

The creation of our open file dialog box starts with the creation of an instance thunk:

```
lpitOpenDlgProc = MakeProcInstance (OpenDlgProc, hInst);
```

As with the other dialog box examples in this chapter, this instance thunk is created during OPEN's initialization in the WinMain function. The dialog box itself is created when the user selects the Open... item on the File menu. This triggers the call to DialogBox that actually creates the dialog:

```
case IDM_OPEN:
    DialogBox (hInst,
        MAKEINTRESOURCE(IDD_OPEN),
        hwnd,
        lpitOpenDlgProc);
```

This creates a modal dialog box, using the OpenDlgProc routine in our program as the dialog box procedure. The dialog box procedure is a very long one, primarily because we need to handle all the different cases that arise when the user changes directories, changes the wild card for the files to display, or makes an error. Much of the work of this dialog box procedure is performed by the `DlgDirList` routine, which is defined:

```
int DlgDirList (hDlg, lpPath, nIDList, nIDStatic, wType)
```

- `hDlg` is a handle to the dialog box.

- `lpPath` is a long pointer to a character string for a directory path. It can consist of any portion of a fully qualified file path, including disk drive, directories, and wild card values.

- `nIDList` is the identifier of the listbox control to be filled with the files that match the file specification.

- `nIDStatic` is the identifier of a static text control to be used to display the current directory.

- `wType` holds flags that are used to determine the files to include in the listbox. It can be any combination of values ORed together from the following table:

Attribute Value	Description
0x0000	Read/write files with no other attributes.
0x0001	Files marked "read-only."
0x0002	Hidden files.
0x0004	System files.
0x0010	Subdirectories.
0x0020	Files that have the "archive" bit set.
0x4000	Drive letters.
0x8000	Exclude normal read/write files.

An additional attribute value requests that messages be transmitted as pull-model messages instead of push-model messages. That is, that the `PostMessage` routine be used instead of `SendMessage` to transmit the messages to the list box and the static control. This makes it easier for a program to intercept and manipulate the messages that are sent to these two controls:

Attribute Value	Description
0x2000	Transmit messages using `PostMessage` instead of `SendMessage`.

One of the truly convenient features of this routine is that it parses the path which it receives. This means that you only need to do a minimum amount of parsing. `DlgDirList` communicates with DOS to change the current disk drive, change the current directory, and display only the files that match the wild card specification. It even strips the disk and directory information from the path information, so that separating the wild card values from these other parts of the path is quite simple.

Whenever the user clicks in either of the two listboxes, this causes the file or directory name to be copied to the edit control. A filename is copied by itself, although a directory name will always have the wild card specification appended to the end of it. Checking for a mouse click involves watching for a WM_COMMAND message with an LBN_SELCHANGE notification code. Here, for example, is how a click in the file listbox is handled:

```
case IDD_FILELIST:
    if (wNotify == LBN_SELCHANGE)
            {
            DlgDirSelect (hdlg,
                        achBuff,
                        IDD_FILELIST);

            hCtl = GetDlgItem (hdlg, IDD_NAME);
            SendMessage (hCtl,
                        WM_SETTEXT,
                        0,
                        (LONG)(LPSTR)achBuff);
            }
```

DlgDirSelect conveniently reads the contents of a listbox. This code gets a handle to the edit control by calling GetDlgItem, and sends a WM_SETTEXT message to put the filename into the edit control.

Placing the filename into the edit control sets the stage for the handling of a double-click message. When the mouse double-clicks in a listbox, the second click has the effect of clicking on the Ok push button. This is why, in response to the LBN_DLBCLK notification from the files listbox, our dialog box procedure does very little except cause a jump to occur to the part of the dialog box procedure that handles a click on the Ok push button:

```
if (wNotify == LBN_DBLCLK)
    goto DoOK;
```

Responding to the Ok push button is the most complex part of the open file dialog box. The reason is not that it is so hard to select a file, but that the dialog box procedure must be prepared to handle error checking and also to allow the user to change the current disk, the current directory, and the wild card file specification. The first thing that our dialog box procedure does when the Ok button is pushed is to read the file name from the edit control:

```
case IDD_OK:
    // Read file name from edit control.
    DoOK:   hCtl = GetDlgItem (hdlg, IDD_NAME);
            SendMessage (hCtl,
                        WM_GETTEXT,
                        MAXFILENAMELEN,
                        (LONG)(LPSTR)achBuff);
```

Our dialog box procedure is very forgiving if the user entered leading or trailing blanks, as these are simply trimmed:

```
//  Trim leading blanks from file name.
p = achBuff;
while (*p == ' ')
    p++;
if (p != achBuff)
    lstrcpy (achBuff, p);

//  Trim trailing blanks from file name.
cc = lstrlen (achBuff);
for (p = achBuff + cc - 1; *p == ' '; p--)
    *p = 0;
```

A quick check is done for wild card by scanning the string for either the "?" or the "*" character. If one is not found, then we assume that the user has entered a valid filename. If this is the case, we try to open the file to test for its existence. If the file can be opened, then EndDialog is called to terminate the dialog box, as our work is over. If the file cannot be opened, then our dialog box procedure assumes that the user has entered the name of a directory instead of the name of a file.

```
//  Check for wild cards.
bWild = FALSE;
for (p = achBuff;*p != NULL; p++)
    {
    if (*p == '?' || *p == '*')
        {
        bWild = TRUE;
        break;
        }
    }

//  If no wild cards, try to open it.
if (!bWild)
    {
    // Is it a valid file name?
    iFile = OpenFile (achBuff,
                      &of,
                      OF_EXIST);

    //  If so, then we are done.
    if (iFile != -1)
        {
        lstrcpy (achOpenFile, achBuff);
        EndDialog (hdlg, TRUE);
        break;
        }
```

```
else  //  If not, add wild card and continue.
    {
    p--;
    if (*p != '\\' && *p != '/')
        lstrcat (achBuff, "\\");
    lstrcat (achBuff, achWild);
    }
}
```

Since we assume that the user has entered the name of a directory, we rebuild both dialog boxes by calling `DlgDirList` twice: once for the file listbox and once for the directories listbox. We start by setting up the directories listbox:

```
/*  Rebuild list boxes.                     */
iRet = DlgDirList (hdlg,
                        achBuff,
                        IDD_DIRLIST,
                        IDD_CURDIR,
                        0xC010);
```

If `DlgDirList` doesn't like what it finds, then we can assume that the user has entered an incorrect file specification. Perhaps a nonexistent disk drive was referenced, or a nonexistent directory name was entered. It might even be that that the wild card specification was somehow incorrect. Whatever the cause, a message box is displayed if `DlgDirList` didn't like what it saw. Otherwise, the reinitialization of the file listbox and the edit control is identical to what was done in response to the WM_INITIDIALOG message:

```
/*  Did DlgDirList report an error?         */
if (!iRet)
    {
    MessageBox (hdlg,
            achInvalid,
            "Open-File",
            MB_OK);
    }
else
    {
    /*  Initialize file list box.           */
    DlgDirList (hdlg,
            achBuff,
            IDD_FILELIST,
            IDD_CURDIR,
            0);

    /*  Make local copy of wild card.       */
    lstrcpy (achWild, achBuff);
```

```
/*  Put wild card into edit control.    */
hCtl = GetDlgItem (hdlg, IDD_NAME);
SendMessage (hCtl,
             WM_SETTEXT,
             0,
             (LONG)(LPSTR)achWild);
}
```

Whether or not there was an error, our dialog box procedure always leaves the keyboard focus in the edit control and makes sure that the characters in the edit control are selected. This makes it quite simple for the user to overwrite any unwanted values in the list box.

```
/*  Select text in edit control.        */
SendMessage (hCtl,
             EM_SETSEL,
             0,
             MAKELONG (0, MAXFILENAMELEN));

/*  Give keyboard to edit control.       */
SetFocus (hCtl);
break;
```

If you take a close look at our open file dialog box procedure, you'll notice that there is some room for improvement. In particular, we have not put any code into subroutines since this has the effect of making the code a little harder to read. However, if you want to make the code smaller, it should be a simple matter to reorganize the code into two or more smaller subroutines.

Another improvement that could be made to this routine has to do with the way in which the OpenFile routine works. Our program calls on this routine to check for the existence of a file. However, when this routine is called, it is provided just the name of the file that was entered in the edit control. The problem is that OpenFile will search through several directories if the file is not found in the current directory. While this may seem a minor point, it can slow down the check for a file, particularly if there are network directories in your search path. In spite of these two shortcomings, this open file dialog box should be complete enough and robust enough to be used in your applications.

## PART V

MESSAGE DRIVEN INPUT

15

Keyboard Input

In earlier chapters, we looked at the way a Windows program creates graphic output. The facilities available for graphics output can be considered quite high-level: Sophisticated drawing can be accomplished with a minimum of effort. In particular, this is the case if you consider how much code would be required to accomplish the same results without the help of GDI.

In this chapter and the next one, we will examine the way in which Windows handles *input*. In contrast to GDI's high-level output, the form in which input arrives can be regarded as very low-level. That is, keyboard input arrives in the form of individual keystroke messages, with two or three messages generated per key typed. The actions of the mouse are reported as a stream of messages that give a blow by blow account of the actions of this pointing device.

Specifically, this chapter discusses keyboard input, while the next chapter will describe mouse input.

How a Windows Program Receives Keyboard Input

Figure 15.1 shows all the pieces that play a role in handling keyboard input. The black lines represent data flow.

We'll start our study of keyboard input by tracing the flow of data from the keyboard, through the various software layers into a typical Windows program. Every Windows program has a `GetMessage` loop which is responsible for pulling all keyboard messages into a program. But that's only half the story; once raw keyboard data arrives in a

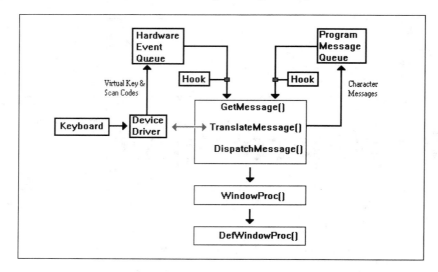

Figure 15.1   The flow of keyboard data

Windows program, a special Windows library routine must be called to cook the data to create truly useful character input. You've seen this library routine before, since it is a standard part of every `GetMessage` loop: `TranslateMessage`. While Windows provides an abundant set of messages to describe keyboard activity, you will find that you can concentrate your efforts on a subset of these messages, which we'll describe as we follow the path of the wily keyboard messages. Keyboard input starts in the hardware of the keyboard, so that's where we'll begin.

The Keyboard

Windows runs on IBM-compatible personal computers, so the range of keyboards you're likely to encounter is small. Nevertheless, since IBM introduced its first PC in 1981, the keyboard has changed. The first IBM PC had an 83-key keyboard. When IBM introduced a new keyboard with its PC/AT, it moved a few keys around and added the SysReq key for a total of 84 keys. With its current line of PS/2 computers, IBM has adopted yet another keyboard, the Enhanced 101/102-key keyboard. This keyboard has two added function keys, but most of the new keys were simply duplicates of keys already on the keyboard. With some minor variations, makers of IBM-compatible computers have adapted the same keyboard layout as IBM machines.

Although successive keyboards have moved a key here and added a key there, the basic operation of all keyboards has stayed the same. Every time you press or release a key, the keyboard hardware generates a one- or two-byte **scan code** that uniquely identifies the key. Every key produces two different scan codes, depending on whether the key is pressed or released. When you press a key, the value of the scan code is between 01H and 58H (for IBM-compatible keyboards). When you release the key, the value of the scan code is 80H higher. For example, when you press the letter Z, the keyboard generates a scan code of 2CH. When it is released, the keyboard generates a scan code of ACH (2CH + 80H).

From the keyboard's point of view, the two scan codes are the only meaningful information associated with a given key. The meaning of the scan code is interpreted by the software that receives the keyboard input. In our case, that means the Windows keyboard device driver. Consider the two scan codes from the previous example: 2CH and ACH. When the keyboard driver is told that a U.S. English keyboard is present, these codes are interpreted as the letter Z. But the same scan codes will be interpreted as the letter W if the keyboard driver is told that a French keyboard is present. From this example, you can see how international support is provided: The keyboard driver simply needs the correct scan-code to virtual key code and virtual key code to ASCII translation tables.

As keys are pressed and released, scan codes are sent via the keyboard cable to control circuitry on the system board of the computer. When the control circuitry senses that keyboard input is available, it generates a hardware interrupt 09H. When DOS is present, this interrupt results in a call to the ROM BIOS keyboard handler. But when Windows is present, another mechanism is put into place which meets the special requirements that Windows has for handling keyboard input. That mechanism is part of the Windows keyboard device driver, which we'll look at next.

The Windows Keyboard Device Driver

During Windows start up, the Windows keyboard driver installs an interrupt handler to receive keyboard scan codes. The interrupt handler is called any time a key is pressed or released. It reads scan values from the keyboard port and maps these onto a set of **virtual key** values that make up the **Windows virtual keyboard.**

The virtual keyboard defines a standard set of keys for all keyboards currently on the market. It also defines keys that don't correspond to any current keyboard to allow room for growth. Table 15.1 lists all of the keys in the virtual keyboard, along with the symbolic names as defined in Windows.h.

Once the keyboard driver has translated the scan code information into a virtual key code, it calls Windows. Windows puts both scan code and virtual key data into a special buffer called the **hardware event queue**. We briefly discussed the role of this buffer in Chapter 4, when we talked about the message loop. Let's return to this topic to see how it affects keyboard input.

The Hardware Event Queue

From the point of view of keyboard input, the hardware event queue is simply a type-ahead buffer. It can hold up to 120 hardware events, which means 60 characters worth of data, since two events are generated when a keyboard key is pressed and released. Even for the fastest typists, this should be enough to prevent data loss.

Table 15.1 The Windows Virtual Keys

(hex)	(dec)	Symbolic Name	Key Pressed (US English 101/102 Kbd)
1	1	VK_LBUTTON	
2	2	VK_RBUTTON	
3	3	VK_CANCEL	Ctrl-Break
4	4	VK_MBUTTON	
8	8	VK_BACK	Backspace
9	9	VK_TAB	Tab
C	12	VK_CLEAR	5 on Numeric keypad w/Num Lock OFF
D	13	VK_RETURN	Enter
10	16	VK_SHIFT	Shift
11	17	VK_CONTROL	Ctrl
12	18	VK_MENU	Alt
13	19	VK_PAUSE	Pause (or Ctrl-Num Lock)
14	20	VK_CAPITAL	Caps Lock
1B	27	VK_ESCAPE	Esc
20	32	VK_SPACE	Spacebar
21	33	VK_PRIOR	Page Up
22	34	VK_NEXT	Page Down
23	35	VK_END	End
24	36	VK_HOME	Home
25	37	VK_LEFT	Left Arrow
26	38	VK_UP	Up Arrow
27	39	VK_RIGHT	Right Arrow
28	40	VK_DOWN	Down Arrow
29	41	VK_SELECT	<unused>
2A	42	VK_PRINT	<unused>
2B	43	VK_EXECUTE	<unused>
2C	44	VK_SNAPSHOT	Print Screen
2D	45	VK_INSERT	Ins
2E	46	VK_DELETE	Del
2F	47	VK_HELP	<unused>
30–39	48–57	VK_0 to VK_9	0 to 9 above letter keys
41–5A	65–90	VK_A to VK_Z	A to Z
60	96	VK_NUMPAD0	0 on Numeric keypad w/Num Lock ON

(continued)

Table 15.1 The Windows Virtual Keys

(hex)	(dec)	Symbolic Name	Key Pressed (US English 101/102 Kbd)
61	97	VK_NUMPAD1	1 on Numeric keypad w/Num Lock ON
62	98	VK_NUMPAD2	2 on Numeric keypad w/Num Lock ON
63	99	VK_NUMPAD3	3 on Numeric keypad w/Num Lock ON
64	100	VK_NUMPAD4	4 on Numeric keypad w/Num Lock ON
65	101	VK_NUMPAD5	5 on Numeric keypad w/Num Lock ON
66	102	VK_NUMPAD6	6 on Numeric keypad w/Num Lock ON
67	103	VK_NUMPAD7	7 on Numeric keypad w/Num Lock ON
68	104	VK_NUMPAD8	8 on Numeric keypad w/Num Lock ON
69	105	VK_NUMPAD9	9 on Numeric keypad w/Num Lock ON
6A	106	VK_MULTIPLY	* on Numeric keypad
6B	107	VK_ADD	+ on Numeric keypad
6C	108	VK_SEPARATOR	\<unused\>
6D	109	VK_SUBTRACT	– on Numeric keypad
6E	110	VK_DECIMAL	. on Numeric keypad w/Num Lock ON
6F	111	VK_DIVIDE	/ on Numeric keypad
70	112	VK_F1	F1 function key
71	113	VK_F2	F2 function key
72	114	VK_F3	F3 function key
73	115	VK_F4	F4 function key
74	116	VK_F5	F5 function key
75	117	VK_F6	F6 function key
76	118	VK_F7	F7 function key
77	119	VK_F8	F8 function key
78	120	VK_F9	F9 function key
79	121	VK_F10	F10 function key
7A	122	VK_F11	F11 function key
7B	123	VK_F12	F12 function key
7C	124	VK_F13	
7D	125	VK_F14	
7E	126	VK_F15	
7F	127	VK_F16	
90	144	VK_NUMLOCK	Num Lock
91	145		Scroll Lock

(continued)

Table 15.1   The Windows Virtual Keys

(hex)	(dec)	Symbolic Name	Key Pressed (US English 101/102 Kbd)
The following code applies to US keyboards only			
BA	186		colon/semi-colon
BB	187		plus/equal
BC	188		less than/comma
BD	189		underscore/hyphen
BE	190		greater than/period
BF	191		question/slash
C0	192		tilde/back accent
DB	219		left squiggle brace/left square brace
DC	220		horizontal bar/backslash
DD	221		right squiggle brace/right square brace
DE	222		double quote/single quote

A type-ahead buffer is necessary because of the way that a Windows program retrieves keyboard input. As discussed in Chapter 4, Windows' multitasking is non-preemptive. That is, the operating system does not interrupt one program to allow another to run. Instead, programs interrupt themselves. This polite form of multitasking works because it is built into Windows' message delivery mechanism. All input to a program, including keyboard input, is delivered in the form of messages. Since Windows does not interrupt programs to deliver keyboard information, the data has to be stored someplace: That place is the hardware event queue. Otherwise, a fast typist might outpace a program's ability to retrieve keyboard input.

The contents of the hardware event queue are eventually delivered to a windows program in the form of two messages: WM_KEYDOWN and WM_KEYUP. These correspond to the two types of scan codes: key press and key release. As indicated by the diagram in Figure 15.1, a program gets these two messages from the hardware event queue by calling GetMessage.

However, the real meaning of keyboard messages comes from the values stored in one 2-byte integer value and one 4-byte integer value which make up a window procedure's wParam and lParam parameters. The format of these two fields is identical for both the WM_KEYDOWN and the WM_KEYUP messages.

wParam contains the virtual key code of the key that was pressed or released. The keyboard driver generates this value from the scan code received from the keyboard hardware. This is the most important field that Windows provides with these two messages. After all, the virtual key code represents how the keyboard driver views a keyboard event, taking into account the type of keyboard currently attached to the system.

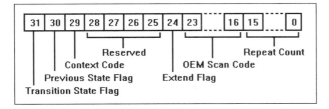

Figure 15.2 Six Fields of `lParam` for keystroke messages

The `lParam` parameter is divided into six fields, as shown in Figure 15.2. Let's review these fields one at a time.

Repeat Count. Built into the hardware of the keyboard is the ability to automatically repeat a single character if a key is held down: a feature that IBM calls **typematic**. To prevent such keys from overflowing the hardware event queue, Windows increments the repeat count when it finds that a new keyboard event is identical with the previous keyboard event in the queue. In so doing, Windows combines several WM_KEYDOWN messages into a single message.

A repeat count greater than 1 means that keyboard events are occurring faster than your program is able to process them. In such cases, a program can interpret each WM_KEYDOWN message as multiple messages, depending on the repeat value.

OEM Scan Code. This field contains the scan code value as it was sent from the keyboard. For most programs, the virtual key code is more useful, since it represents a device-independent code for a key stroke. Because the scan code represents a hardware-dependent value, you'll avoid this field in most cases. But sometimes it is necessary to use the scan code information to tell the difference, for example, between the left shift key and the right shift key. For certain keys, the keyboard driver uses the hardware scan code to translate the WM_KEYDOWN message into a WM_CHAR message. This is the case, for example, with keys in the numeric keypad.

Extend Flag. This field is actually an extension of the OEM Scan Code. In effect, it tells a program that the pressed key was one of the duplicate keys on IBM's extended keyboard. Like the Scan Code, the value of this field is device-dependent, so great care should be taken when using it.

Context Code. This flag is 1 if the Alt key is down; otherwise it has a value of 0.

Previous State Flag. This flag helps to identify messages generated by typematic action. It has a value of 1 if the previous state of the key was down, and a value of 0 if the previous state of the key was up.

Transition State Flag. This flag is 1 if the key is being released and 0 if the key is being pressed. It will always be 1 for WM_KEYUP and 0 for the WM_KEYDOWN message.

From these messages, a program receives both the raw keyboard scan codes and the half-cooked virtual key codes. As you'll see shortly, the most useful keyboard data arrive as fully-cooked character messages. However, there are some keystrokes that are

Table 15.2   Keystrokes Available Only with WM_KEYDOWN and WM_KEYUP

Keystroke	*Description*
F1–F9, F11–F16	Function Keys. The F10 function key is reserved for Windows' use as the Menu Select Hot Key.
Shift, Ctrl, Alt.	Shift Keys. The Alt key is a reserved system key and does not generate WM_KEYDOWN or WM_KEYUP unless the Ctrl key is down. Normally, it only generates WM_SYSKEYDOWN and WM_SYSKEYUP messages.
Caps Lock, Num Lock, and Scroll Lock.	Toggle Keys.
Print Screen	Reserved key for copying screen to clipboard (Print Screen alone), or for copying the active window to the clipboard (Alt + Print Screen). Windows eats the WM_KEYDOWN message, leaving WM_KEYUP.
Pause	Pause key.
Insert, Delete, Home, End, Page Up, Page Down.	Text editing keys. Although there are two of each of these keys on the 101/102 keyboard, each pair has only one virtual key code. However, they can be distinguished with the Extend flag.
Up, Left, Down, Right.	Direction Keys. Although there are eight keys in this set, like the text editing keys, the duplicate keys do not have a separate virtual key code. However, they can be distinguished with the Extend flag.

not available as character messages, since they do not represent characters but rather keyboard commands.

Table 15.2 shows a list of the keystrokes that can only be detected with the WM_KEY-DOWN and WM_KEYUP messages. The keys in this table do not produce ASCII characters, so they do not generate WM_CHAR messages. Therefore, if you are interested in detecting key strokes generated by these keys, you'll watch for the WM_KEYDOWN message. (In a moment, we'll discuss the WM_CHAR message, which provides ASCII character information.)

To detect one of these keys in a Windows program, you'll test the value of wParam against the virtual key values listed in Table 15.1. For example, here is code that checks for a key-down transition of the F1 function key:

```
WindowProc (HWND hwnd,      UINT msg,
            WPARAM wParam, LPARAM lParam)
   {
   switch (msg)
```

```
    {
case WM_KEYDOWN:
    if (wParam == VK_F1)
        /*  F1 Keydown. */
        ...
    break;
```

For programming the function keys, it is often easier to define an Accelerator.

Although it would involve a lot of work, it is possible to receive all the keyboard input that you might require using WM_KEYDOWN and WM_KEYUP messages. Notice, however, that to tell the difference between a capital letter and a lowercase letter would require you to know the state of the shift key in addition to detecting the keystroke message. There's no reason to do all that work, since Windows has a built-in facility that will do it for you. The routine that provides this service is a standard part of every message loop: TranslateMessage.

The GetMessage Loop

So far, we've traced the path taken by keyboard data: It starts in the keyboard, moves through the keyboard driver into the hardware event queue. From there, hardware events are retrieved when a program calls GetMessage, typically as part of a message loop like the one we've encountered in every Windows program thus far. The minimum standard message loop is as follows:

```
while (GetMessage (&msg, 0, 0, 0))
    {
    TranslateMessage (&msg);
    DispatchMessage (&msg);
    }
```

GetMessage reads messages from two places: the hardware event queue and a program's private message queue. For every message it retrieves, a call is made to TranslateMessage, which ignores every message except two: WM_KEYDOWN and WM_SYSKEYDOWN.

WM_SYSKEYDOWN is one of three **system keyboard messages**. The other two are WM_SYSKEYUP and WM_SYSCHAR. The behavior of these messages parallels the behavior of the three regular keyboard messages, but system keyboard messages are used primarily as part of the keyboard interface to menus. We'll look at another use of these messages when we discuss the window procedure in a short while.

The role of TranslateMessage is simple. It takes the virtual key data from the WM_KEYDOWN (or WM_SYSKEYDOWN) message and calls the keyboard device driver to convert the virtual key code into an ASCII code. For keys with no ASCII equivalent, no translation is done. For the rest, a WM_CHAR (or WM_SYSCHAR) message is generated and placed in the private message queue.

The sequence of messages that are created in response to hitting the "w" key, for example, is as follows:

Key	*wParam Contains*
WM_KEYDOWN	Virtual key W
WM_CHAR	ASCII code w
WM_KEYUP	Virtual key W

And when a capital letter is struck, the sequence of messages is even more involved. Here is the message traffic when the user types "W":

Key	*wParam Contains*
WM_KEYDOWN	Virtual key VK_SHIFT
WM_KEYDOWN	Virtual key W
WM_CHAR	ASCII code W
WM_KEYUP	Virtual key W
WM_KEYUP	Virtual key VK_SHIFT

On some non-English keyboards (French and German, to name two), special key combinations are used to create diacritical marks over vowels. For example, to type the words gâteau (the French word for "cake") and München (the German name for the city of Munich) on a French keyboard, you need to use special key combinations because there is no dedicated â or ü key.

These special keys are called **dead-keys**, since they are not expected to produce characters, but modify the keystroke that follows. In response to a WM_KEYDOWN (or WM_SYSKEYDOWN) for such keys, TranslateMessage generates WM_DEADCHAR (or WM_SYSDEADCHAR) messages. You can safely ignore these messages, since Windows will create the correct character message from the keystrokes that follow.

If you'd like to experiment with dead-key processing, you can install a different keyboard translation table using the Control Panel. Bring up the International Settings dialog box and select the country whose keyboard layout you want to use. If you bring up the French keyboard, you'll discover that the A and Q keys have been switched, as have the W and Z keys. The dead-key for the circumflex is located at the key marked "[," and the dead-key for the umlaut is shift-[.

The message sequence that is generated on a French keyboard to produce the letter â is as follows:

Key	*wParam Contains*
WM_KEYDOWN	Scan code for pressing circumflex key
WM_DEADCHAR	Dead Character message for circumflex key
WM_KEYUP	Scan code for releasing circumflex key

Key	*wParam Contains*
WM_KEYDOWN	Scan code for pressing 'a'
WM_CHAR	Character message for â
WM_KEYUP	Scan code for releasing 'a'

With the exception of the keys listed in Table 15.2, keyboard input will normally come from the WM_CHAR messages that are created by TranslateMessage. The resulting translation takes into account the state of the various shift keys, to provide upper- and lowercase letters, numbers, and punctuation marks. Since the ASCII character set includes a complete range of accented vowels, this mechanism also supports international keyboards.

After TranslateMessage generates the WM_CHAR (or WM_SYSCHAR) message, it returns control to the message loop. The DispatchMessage routine then pushes the WM_KEYDOWN or WM_SYSKEYDOWN message to the window procedure for processing.

Since the character message is placed on the program's message queue, it does not become available to the program until GetMessage is called to read a new message. At that time, the WM_CHAR (or WM_SYSCHAR) message is read in, ignored by TranslateMessage, and finally sent on to the window procedure by DispatchMessage. Although the key-down message causes the character message to be generated, the key-down message has already been processed by the time the window procedure sees the character message.

The window procedure parameters for the WM_CHAR message are similar to those for the other keyboard messages already discussed. That is, the lParam field in a character message contains the same six fields as the WM_KEYDOWN and WM_KEYUP messages.

The WM_CHAR message is different, however, in that the wParam parameter contains the ASCII code of the character whose key was pressed. It's the job of the window procedure to trap this message and read whatever character input is required.

To build bullet-proof processing for character input, you'll probably want to filter out the WM_CHAR messages which are created for keystrokes not ordinarily printed, including the tab, backspace, and return keys. The following table lists the WM_CHAR messages which require special processing apart from ASCII printable characters.

Keystroke	*ASCII VALUE* *(hex)*	*(dec)*	*Description*
Ctrl-A to Ctrl-G	1 – 7	1 – 7	Nonprintable characters.
Backspace	8	8	Backspace key (VK_BACK).
Ctrl-H	8	8	Surrogate backspace key (VK_BACK).
Tab	9	9	Tab key (VK_TAB).
Ctrl-I	9	9	Surrogate Tab key (VK_TAB).
Ctrl-J	A	10	Linefeed.

(continued)

	ASCII VALUE		
Keystroke	*(hex)*	*(dec)*	*Description*
Ctrl-K to Ctrl-L	B – C	11 – 12	Nonprintable characters.
Return	D	13	Return key (VK_RETURN).
Ctrl-M	D	13	Surrogate return key (VK_RETURN).
Ctrl-N to Ctrl-Z	E – 1A	15 – 26	Nonprintable characters.
Esc	1B	27	Escape key (VK_ESCAPE).

When an accelerator has been defined with a Ctrl + letter key combination, then no WM_CHAR is generated for that keystroke. (See discussion of accelerators in Chapter 11.)

The Window Procedure

Our journey with keyboard data finally results in keyboard messages in a window procedure. Although some minimal keyboard processing is done in the message loop, the window procedure handles the bulk of keyboard input processing.

Table 15.3 summarizes Windows' eight types of keyboard messages. You can safely ignore most of them, and concentrate your efforts on two messages: WM_CHAR for all character input, and WM_KEYDOWN for all non-character function key input. In the example program, KEYINPUT, these are the only messages we rely on to create a text-entry and editing window.

In certain situations, you may wish to process system keyboard messages. In particular, when the active window in the system is iconic, Windows substitutes the system keyboard messages (WM_SYSKEYDOWN, WM_SYSKEYUP, WM_SYSCHAR) in place of the regular keyboard messages. Since most programs are not interested in keyboard input when they are iconic, this convention helps avoid spurious input. If you *do* want to

Table 15.3 A Summary of Keyboard Messages

WM_KEYDOWN	Key pressed
WM_CHAR	Character input
WM_DEADCHAR	Dead-character
WM_KEYUP	Key released
WM_SYSKEYDOWN	System key pressed
WM_SYSCHAR	System character input
WM_SYSDEADCHAR	System dead-character
WM_SYSKEYUP	System key released

receive keyboard input in this situation, however, you'll need to pay attention to the system keyboard messages.

In general, however, you'll ignore system keyboard messages, which are primarily used by Windows for its own internal housekeeping purposes. Since some of this housekeeping is done in the default window procedure, you'll want to be sure that—like other unused messages—these messages are passed on.

The Default Window Procedure

Keyboard data ends its trip through the system in the default window procedure. This procedure ignores regular keyboard messages, so window procedures that don't use keyboard messages can safely pass them on.

The default window procedure plays an important role in handling the system keyboard messages. System keyboard messages are usually generated in place of regular keyboard messages when the Alt key is down. In particular, system keyboard messages provide keyboard access to menus.

For example, when a window has a system menu icon, the system menu will appear when you strike the Alt + spacebar keys. From our discussion of menus in Chapter 11, you know you can define your own menu hot keys to access popup menus with an Alt key + letter combination. These keystrokes are handled as system keyboard messages.

The default window procedure also plays a role in making certain keyboard combinations operate correctly. For example, you can quit an application by typing Alt-F4, go to the Task List by pressing Ctrl-Esc, and switch the active program with Alt-Tab. For these system hot keys to work properly, the default window procedure must get all system keyboard messages.

In our look at the path taken by keyboard events, there is one item that we have overlooked: hooks. Although the subject of hooks is outside the scope of this book, it is important for you to be aware of them because they can affect the path of keyboard input.

Hooks

A hook is a subroutine that is installed into Windows' message handling mechanism. Hooks allow you to monitor and trap certain types of messages. Figure 15.1 shows the relationship of hooks to the flow of keyboard data.

Windows has a total of seven different hooks, although our discussion will be limited to two of them: keyboard hooks and getmessage hooks. Hooks must operate on a systemwide basis. That is, if a program installs such a hook, it affects every program in the system.

The keyboard hook taps into the flow of keyboard messages coming out of the hardware event queue and provides a means of listening to all keyboard input in the system. Creating a keyboard hook in Windows is comparable to stealing the keyboard interrupt under DOS; it gives you complete control over the flow of keystroke messages (WM_KEYDOWN and WM_KEYUP) in the system.

One use of a keyboard hook is to watch for special "Hot Keys." For example, you might want to give a user the ability to call up your program at any time by simply typing the Alt-F12 key combination. You accomplish this by installing a keyboard hook when your program starts running. The hook lets all keyboard input pass until it encounters the desired keystroke. At that time, it lets Windows know that it wants the key for itself, which causes the key to be ignored by the rest of the system. The hook then notifies the program (perhaps via a message) that the hot key has been struck. At that time, it is up to the program to respond in a way that makes sense—perhaps that might mean opening a window to offer some service to the user.

The second type of hook that affects keyboard input is the getmessage hook. This hook is actually called by the `GetMessage` routine for every message that it receives before it gives the message to a program. The getmessage hook can do anything it wants to the message, including change any of the parameters or even the value of the message!

Since a getmessage hook has access to every message received by the `GetMessage` routine, it can be used for many different types of applications. For example, a hot-key could be implemented using a getmessage hook. Or, it could be used to detect mouse button messages on a given window—perhaps to prevent a user from accessing any other window until a password has been typed correctly. The getmessage hook can be used for any messages that `GetMessage` retrieves, including all keyboard and mouse messages as well as the `WM_PAINT` and `WM_TIMER` messages.

A Sample Program

To demonstrate the way a program can receive keyboard input, we have written KEY-INPUT. This program creates a simple single-line text entry window. Figure 15.3 shows a sample of the output created by this program.

KEYINPUT shows how the `WM_CHAR` and `WM_KEYDOWN` messages can be used to receive character input and perform some simple editing. The following cursor move-

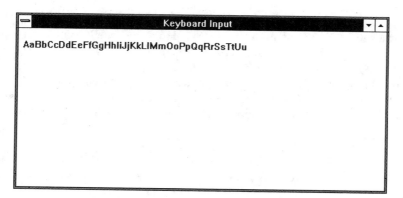

Figure 15.3 Output from KEYINPUT program

ment keys are recognized: Home, End, Left Arrow, and Right Arrow. In addition, the
Backspace and Delete keys can be used to erase characters.

KEYINPUT.C

```c
/*-------------------------------------------------------------*\
| KEYINPUT.C -- Character input program.                        |
\*-------------------------------------------------------------*/
#define STRICT
#include <Windows.H>


/*-------------------------------------------------------------*\
|                       Function Prototypes.                    |
\*-------------------------------------------------------------*/
LRESULT CALLBACK KeyInputWndProc (HWND, UINT, WPARAM, LPARAM);


/*-------------------------------------------------------------*\
|                       Global Variables.                       |
\*-------------------------------------------------------------*/
char achWndClass[] = "KeyInput:MAIN";
char achAppName[]  = "Keyboard Input";


/*-------------------------------------------------------------*\
|                  Main Function:  WinMain.                      |
\*-------------------------------------------------------------*/
int PASCAL
WinMain (HINSTANCE hInstance,        // Who am I?
         HINSTANCE hPrevInstance,    // Any older siblings?
         LPSTR     lpszCmdLine,      // Ptr to command line.
         int       cmdShow)          // How to open my window?
    {
    HWND      hwnd;
    MSG       msg;
    WNDCLASS  wndclass;

    if (!hPrevInstance)
        {
        wndclass.lpszClassName = achWndClass;
        wndclass.hInstance     = hInstance;
        wndclass.lpfnWndProc   = KeyInputWndProc;
        wndclass.hCursor       = LoadCursor (hInstance, "hand");
        wndclass.hIcon         = LoadIcon (hInstance,"snapshot");
        wndclass.lpszMenuName  = NULL;
        wndclass.hbrBackground = (HBRUSH)(COLOR_WINDOW+1);
        wndclass.style         = NULL;
        wndclass.cbClsExtra    = 0;
        wndclass.cbWndExtra    = 0;

        RegisterClass( &wndclass);
        }
```

```
hwnd = CreateWindowEx(0L,                        // Extra style.
                    achWndClass,                 // Class name.
                    achAppName,                  // Title.
                    WS_OVERLAPPEDWINDOW,         // Style bits.
                    CW_USEDEFAULT,               // x - default.
                    0,                           // y - default.
                    CW_USEDEFAULT,               // cx - default.
                    0,                           // cy - default.
                    NULL,                        // No parent.
                    NULL,                        // Class menu.
                    hInstance,                   // Creator.
                    NULL);                       // Params.
    ShowWindow (hwnd, cmdShow);

    while (GetMessage(&msg, 0, 0, 0))
        {
        TranslateMessage(&msg); // Convert KEYDOWNs to CHARs
        DispatchMessage(&msg);  // Transmit message to WndProc
        }
    return 0;
    }

/*--------------------------------------------------------------*\
|                 Window Procedure:  KeyInputWndProc.            |
\*--------------------------------------------------------------*/
LRESULT CALLBACK
KeyInputWndProc (HWND    hwnd,      // For whom is message sent?
                UINT    mMsg,      // What is exact message?
                WPARAM wParam,     // ...message details.
                LPARAM lParam)     // ...message details.
    {
#define BUFSIZE 40
    static unsigned char achInput[BUFSIZE]; //  Input array.
    static int  cc = 0;                     //  Character count.
    static int  icc = 0;                    //  Array index.
    static int  yLineHeight;
    static int  xLeftMargin;

    switch (mMsg)
        {
        case WM_CHAR:
            {
            int i;

            //  Backspace.
            if (wParam == VK_BACK)
                {
                if (icc == 0)
                    MessageBeep(0);
                else //  Remove a character.
                    {
                    icc--;
                    for (i=icc;i<cc;i++)
                        achInput[i]=achInput[i+1];
```

```
                    cc--;
                    InvalidateRect (hwnd, NULL, TRUE);
                    }
                break;
                }

        //  Filter out unwanted character codes.
        if (wParam <= VK_ESCAPE)
            {
            MessageBeep(0);   // Complain.
            break;
            }

        //  Complain if buffer is full.
        if (cc >= BUFSIZE)
            {
            MessageBeep (0);
            break;
            }

        //  Make room for a new character.
        for (i=cc;i>icc;i--)
            achInput[i]=achInput[i-1];

        //  Put new character in buffer.
        achInput[icc] = (unsigned char)wParam;

#if 1       //  Minimal updating (first case) vs.
        //  "Brute Force" (second case).

        {   //  New Code in Brackets.
        DWORD dw;
        HDC hdc;

        cc++;
        hdc = GetDC(hwnd);
        dw = GetTextExtent (hdc, &achInput[0], icc);
        TextOut (hdc,
                xLeftMargin+LOWORD(dw),
                yLineHeight,
                &achInput[icc],
                cc - icc);
        ReleaseDC (hwnd, hdc);
        }
        icc++;

#else
        icc++;
        cc++;
        InvalidateRect (hwnd, NULL, TRUE);
#endif
        }
        break;
```

```
        case WM_CREATE:
            {
            HDC hdc;
            TEXTMETRIC tm;

            hdc = GetDC (hwnd);
            GetTextMetrics (hdc, &tm);
            yLineHeight = tm.tmHeight + tm.tmExternalLeading;
            xLeftMargin = tm.tmAveCharWidth;
            ReleaseDC (hwnd, hdc);
            }
            break;

    case WM_DESTROY:
        PostQuitMessage(0);   // Handle application shutdown.
        break;

    case WM_KEYDOWN:
        switch (wParam)
            {
            case VK_DELETE:
                //  If end of buffer, complain.
                if (icc == cc)
                    MessageBeep(0);
                else  //  Remove a character.
                    {
                    int i;
                    for (i=icc;i<cc;i++)
                        achInput[i]=achInput[i+1];
                    cc--;
                    InvalidateRect (hwnd, NULL, TRUE);
                    }
                break;
            case VK_END:
                icc = cc;
                break;
            case VK_HOME:
                icc = 0;
                break;
            case VK_LEFT:
                if (icc > 0) icc--;
                else MessageBeep(0);
                break;
            case VK_RIGHT:
                if (icc < cc) icc++;
                else MessageBeep(0);
                break;
            }
        break;

    case WM_PAINT:
        {
        PAINTSTRUCT ps;

        BeginPaint (hwnd, &ps);
```

```
            TextOut (ps.hdc, xLeftMargin, yLineHeight,
                    achInput, cc);
            EndPaint (hwnd, &ps);
            }
            break;

        default:
            return(DefWindowProc(hwnd,mMsg,wParam,lParam));
            break;
        }
    return 0L;
    }
```

KEYINPUT.DEF

```
NAME    KEYINPUT

EXETYPE WINDOWS

DESCRIPTION 'Keyboard Input (c) 1992 By Paul Yao'

CODE    MOVEABLE PRELOAD
DATA    MOVEABLE MULTIPLE PRELOAD

HEAPSIZE    512
STACKSIZE   5120

SEGMENTS
    KEYINPUT_TEXT MOVEABLE PRELOAD

EXPORTS
    KeyInputWndProc
```

KEYINPUT.LNK

```
KeyInput.obj
KeyInput.exe/align:16/map/nod/noe/CO
nul
mlibcew libw
KeyInput.def
```

KEYINPUT.MAK

```
# Directory search paths.

INCDIR = \WINDEV\INCLUDE
```

```
# Windows version to support
# Valid pairs include:
#     (0x0300, 30)
#     (0x0310, 31)

CLVER = WINVER=0x0300
RCVER = 30


# Compiler switches for applications.

CL_APP_SHIP_ALL = -AM -c -D$(CLVER) -Gsw -I$(INCDIR) -Ow -W3 -Zp
CL_APP_DEBG_ALL = -AM -c -D$(CLVER) -Gsw -I$(INCDIR) -Od -W3 -Zpi

CL_APP_SHIP_31  = -AM -c -G2s  -I$(INCDIR) -Ow -W3 -Zp
CL_APP_DEBG_31  = -AM -c -G2s  -I$(INCDIR) -Od -W3 -Zpi


# Compiler switches for DLLs.

CL_DLL_SHIP_ALL = -AMw -c -D$(CLVER) -Gsw -I$(INCDIR) -Ow -W3 -Zp
CL_DLL_DEBG_ALL = -AMw -c -D$(CLVER) -Gsw -I$(INCDIR) -Od -W3 -Zpi

CL_DLL_SHIP_31  = -AMw -c -G2s  -I$(INCDIR) -Ow -W3 -Zp
CL_DLL_DEBG_31  = -AMw -c -G2s  -I$(INCDIR) -Od -W3 -Zpi


# Make file primary target.

all: KeyInput.exe

# Make file dependency targets.

KeyInput.res: KeyInput.rc KeyInput.cur KeyInput.ico
    rc -r -i$(INCDIR) KeyInput.rc

KeyInput.obj: KeyInput.c
    cl $(CL_APP_SHIP_ALL) KeyInput.c

KeyInput.exe: KeyInput.obj KeyInput.def KeyInput.res
    link @KeyInput.lnk
    rc -$(RCVER) KeyInput.res

KeyInput.exe: KeyInput.res
    rc -$(RCVER) KeyInput.res
```

KEYINPUT.RC

```
snapshot icon KeyInput.ico

hand   cursor KeyInput.cur
```

Like the other sample programs in this book, KEYINPUT was built on top of the minimum Windows program, introduced in Chapter 2. This program handles five different messages: WM_CHAR, WM_CREATE, WM_DESTROY, WM_KEYDOWN, and WM_PAINT. The window procedure is organized alphabetically by message name to help make the code easier to read. If you find this helps, you might wish to adopt this convention in your own programs.

As the WM_CHAR keyboard character messages occur, KEYINPUT accumulates the characters in a character array defined as

```
static unsigned char achInput[BUFSIZE];
```

The use of the *unsigned* character type is a good practice, which will help when working with the extended ASCII character set supported by Windows. It helps avoid the confusion that otherwise can occur with normal signed characters that use the high-order bit as a sign bit. Since Windows' extended ASCII uses this high-order bit for the characters between 128 and 255 (80h to ffh), this can cause unexpected results. Consider the following lines of code:

```
unsigned char chUnsigned;
char chSigned;

chUnsigned = 'â';   /*  In Windows' extended ASCII,  */
chSigned   = 'â';   /*    â  = e2h.                   */

if (chSigned == 'â')
    {
    /*  This will never be true.  */
    }

if (chUnsigned == 'â')
    {
    /*  This will always be true.  */
    }
```

The problem occurs because of the way various compilers interpret the numeric value of characters. Character values are converted into two-byte word values before a comparison is done. When this happens, the sign bit is extended to provide the correct word value. If you use unsigned char arrays, you will avoid this problem.

Getting back to our sample program, KEYINPUT has two variables that keep track of the contents of achInput: cc and icc. cc is the count of characters in the array, and icc is an index into the array, and functions as the insertion point when new characters are typed. KEYINPUT increments and decrements these two fields as characters are entered and deleted.

Every time a change is made to the values in the character array, KEYINPUT generates a WM_PAINT message by calling InvalidateRect:

```
InvalidateRect (hwnd, NULL, TRUE);
```

which tells Windows, in effect, that the entire window is damaged and should be completely erased and redrawn. This is a pretty radical step to take. It means that every time the user types a letter key, the entire window is redrawn. The same thing happens when a single letter is deleted. However, it guarantees that the contents of the window is always correct, since the WM_PAINT message reads the character array with the changes in place.

One way to improve this program involves eliminating the excessive drawing, which means replacing the calls to InvalidateRect with actions that change the display screen in the smallest possible way. This requires a little more work, but avoids the annoying blinking that occurs when characters are typed or erased. For example, here is how we could draw each new character (and the characters that follow in the array) when a new letter is typed:

```
/*  Put new character in buffer.  */
acInput[icc] = (unsigned char)wParam;

{  /*  New Code in Brackets.  */
DWORD dw;
HDC hdc;

cc++;
hdc = GetDC(hwnd);
dw = GetTextExtent (hdc, &acInput[0], icc);
TextOut (hdc,
      xLeftMargin+LOWORD(dw),
      yLineHeight,
      &acInput[icc],
      cc - icc);
ReleaseDC (hwnd, hdc);
}

icc++;
```

This code redraws from the current position to the end of the line. As characters are inserted or typed at the end of the line, characters to the left of the insertion point are left alone. Only characters to the right of the insertion point are redrawn.

Quite a few other improvements could be made to this program, but it is enough to give you the basic idea about how keyboard input can be collected and displayed. We'll come back to this program in a minute, to see how a **caret** can be used to highlight the current insertion point. Before that, we need to discuss some issues that are critical in correctly handling character data: character sets and other internationalization issues.

Character Sets and International Support

As keyboard data travels from the keyboard to your program, it undergoes a number of conversions: Keyboard data starts out as scan codes, which are converted by the device driver into virtual key information. And finally, virtual key codes are converted into ASCII character values to provide upper- and lowercase letters, numbers, and punctuation marks. Figure 15.4 shows Windows' ANSI Character Set.

	0-	1-	2-	3-	4-	5-	6-	7-	8-	9-	A-	B-	C-	D-	E-	F-
-0	|	|		0	@	P	`	p	|	|		°	À	Ð	à	ð
-1	|	|	!	1	A	Q	a	q	|	´	¡	±	Á	Ñ	á	ñ
-2	|	|	"	2	B	R	b	r	|	´	¢	²	Â	Ò	â	ò
-3	|	|	#	3	C	S	c	s	|	|	£	³	Ã	Ó	ã	ó
-4	|	|	$	4	D	T	d	t	|	|	¤	´	Ä	Ô	ä	ô
-5	|	|	%	5	E	U	e	u	|	|	¥	µ	Å	Õ	å	õ
-6	|	|	&	6	F	V	f	v	|	|	¦	¶	Æ	Ö	æ	ö
-7	|	|	'	7	G	W	g	w	|	|	§	·	Ç	×	ç	÷
-8	|	|	(	8	H	X	h	x	|	|	¨	¸	È	Ø	è	ø
-9	|	|	)	9	I	Y	i	y	|	|	©	¹	É	Ù	é	ù
-A	|	|	*	:	J	Z	j	z	|	|	ª	º	Ê	Ú	ê	ú
-B	|	|	+	;	K	[	k	{	|	|	«	»	Ë	Û	ë	û
-C	|	|	,	<	L	\	l	|	|	|	¬	¼	Ì	Ü	ì	ü
-D	|	|	-	=	M	]	m	}	|	|	-	½	Í	Ý	í	ý
-E	|	|	.	>	N	^	n	~	|	|	®	¾	Î	Þ	î	þ
-F	|	|	/	?	O	_	o	|	|	|	¯	¿	Ï	ß	ï	ÿ

ANSI Character Set - Code Page 1004

Figure 15.4 ANSI Character Set

What is a character set? It is a convention or a standard that helps avoid confusion. For example, according to the ANSI Character Set, the value 41h (65 decimal) stands for a capital A. Microsoft adopted the ANSI Character Set to allow the data created by a Windows program to be readable by other Windows programs, and interpreted correctly on different brands of computers and different brands of printers, as well as computers and peripherals in different countries. Windows uses the ANSI character set to interpret how a text character should be displayed, and provides a standard that allows file sharing between different Windows computers.

In addition to the ANSI character set, every Windows computer has a second character set used by DOS. For example, IBM-compatible computers manufactured for use in the United States have a character set that IBM calls code page 437. Figure 15.5 shows the characters in code page 437. This is the character set used by DOS programs for creating data files, and is the character set used by DOS for filenames.

For upper- and lowercase letters, numbers, and punctuation marks, this character set is identical to the Windows ANSI character set. Thus, if you are writing a Windows program for use only in the United States, you can mix and match data files between DOS and Windows programs with little chance for confusion. This will be true as long as your Windows and DOS programs use printable characters in the range 20h to 7eh (32 to 126 decimal).

For Windows programs to work on computers outside the United States, some effort is required on your part. In the first place, other code pages besides 437 are used on computers manufactured for different languages. For example, code page 860 substi-

OEM Character Set - Code Page 437

	0-	1-	2-	3-	4-	5-	6-	7-	8-	9-	A-	B-	C-	D-	E-	F-
-0		►		0	@	P	`	p	Ç	É	á	░	└	╨	α	≡
-1	☺	◄	!	1	A	Q	a	q	ü	æ	í	▒	┴	╤	ß	±
-2	☻	↕	"	2	B	R	b	r	é	Æ	ó	▓	┬	╥	Γ	≥
-3	♥	‼	#	3	C	S	c	s	â	ô	ú	│	├	╙	π	≤
-4	♦	¶	$	4	D	T	d	t	ä	ö	ñ	┤	─	╘	Σ	⌠
-5	♣	§	%	5	E	U	e	u	à	ò	Ñ	╡	┼	╒	σ	⌡
-6	♠	▬	&	6	F	V	f	v	å	û	ª	╢	╞	╓	µ	÷
-7	•	↨	'	7	G	W	g	w	ç	ù	º	╖	╟	╫	τ	≈
-8	◘	↑	(	8	H	X	h	x	ê	ÿ	¿	╕	╚	╪	Φ	°
-9	○	↓	)	9	I	Y	i	y	ë	Ö	⌐	╣	╔	┘	Θ	∙
-A	◙	→	*	:	J	Z	j	z	è	Ü	¬	║	╩	┌	Ω	·
-B	♂	←	+	;	K	[	k	{	ï	¢	½	╗	╦	█	δ	√
-C	♀	∟	,	<	L	\	l	|	î	£	¼	╝	╠	▄	∞	ⁿ
-D	♪	↔	-	=	M	]	m	}	ì	¥	¡	╜	═	▌	φ	²
-E	♫	▲	.	>	N	^	n	~	Ä	₧	«	╛	╬	▐	ε	■
-F	☼	▼	/	?	O	_	o	⌂	Å	ƒ	»	┐	╧	▀	∩	

Figure 15.5 DOS Character Set in the United States: Code Page 437

tutes 16 accented characters not available in code page 437 that are required for computers sold in Portugal. Code page 863 has 22 new accented and other special characters to meet the requirements of French Canada. And code page 865 has four characters that change the U.S. code page for use in creating Norwegian data files.

Therefore, every machine that runs Windows will have at least two character sets: Windows' ANSI character set (sometimes known as code page 1004), which has the most complete support for accented characters, and what Microsoft calls an OEM character set, which is the character set used by DOS to meet the language needs of different countries (code page 437).

When a DOS program is running in a window, Windows uses a font containing characters that match the OEM character set. In this way, the character set provides backwards compatibility between Windows and DOS. If you are writing a program to display a text file created by a DOS program, there is a stock font available that uses the OEM character set. You can access this font by saying:

```
hfontOEM = GetStockObject (OEM_FIXED_FONT);
SelectObject (hdc, hfontOEM);
```

Converting Between Character Sets

If a Windows program reads files written by DOS programs, the files must be converted from the OEM character set to Windows ANSI character set for the program to work properly on all non-U.S. machines. Conversely, if a Windows program writes to a file that a DOS program may read, the Windows program should convert from the ANSI character set to the native OEM character set expected by DOS programs in order to work outside the United States. Fortunately, some Windows library routines are available to do the conversion for you:

Routine	*Description*
AnsiToOem	Convert null-terminated ANSI string to DOS characters.
AnsiToOemBuff	Convert *n* ANSI characters to DOS characters.
OemToAnsi	Convert null-terminated DOS characters to ANSI.
OemToAnsiBuff	Convert *n* DOS characters to ANSI.

In addition to DOS data files, the DOS file system itself uses the OEM character set for filenames. However, if you use the OpenFile Windows library routine, your filenames are automatically converted to the OEM character set before DOS is called.

Upper- and Lowercase Conversion

Programmers in the United States who work with characters exclusively in the range 20h to 7eh (32 to 126 decimal) often play tricks to convert text to upper- or lowercase. In this range, the upper- and lowercase letters are 20h (32) apart, like those shown here:

Uppercase	*Ascii(hex)*	*(dec)*	*Lowercase*	*(hex)*	*(dec)*
A	41h	65	a	61h	97
B	42h	66	b	62h	98
C	43h	67	c	63h	99
.					
.					
Z	5ah	90	z	7ah	122

In this range, uppercase conversion is easy; here is code that does this for us:

```
for (i=0;i<cc;i++)
    {
    if (ach[i] >= 'a' && ach[i] <= 'z')
        ach[i] -= 32;
    }
```

Consider the following pairs of upper- and lowercase accented letters:

Uppercase	*Ascii(hex)*	*(dec)*	*Lowercase*	*(hex)*	*(dec)*
À	c0h	192	à	e0h	224
Ç	c7h	199	ç	e7h	231

Uppercase	Ascii(hex)	(dec)	Lowercase	(hex)	(dec)
È	c8h	200	è	e8h	232
Ï	cfh	207	ï	efh	239
Õ	d5h	213	õ	f5h	245
Û	dbh	219	û	fbh	251

If the array in our earlier example included any of the lowercase letters in this table, the case conversion would not have worked correctly. If you are writing a program to be sold outside the United States, you should use the following Windows library routines for upper- and lowercase conversion instead of writing your own.

Routine	Description
AnsiLower	Converts null-terminated string to lowercase.
AnsiLowerBuff	Converts *n* characters to lowercase.
AnsiUpper	Converts null-terminated string to uppercase.
AnsiUpperBuff	Converts *n* characters to uppercase.

To convert a null-terminated character string to all uppercase, you could pass a long pointer to `AnsiUpper`, as in

```
AnsiUpper (lpszConvert);
```

or, using `AnsiUpperBuff`, you could say:

```
i = lstrlen (lpszConvert);
AnsiUpperBuff (lpszConvert, i);
```

Another set of routines tests whether character information is upper- or lowercase, whether it is an alphabetic character, or whether it is alphanumeric:

Routine	Description
IsCharAlpha	Returns TRUE if character is an alphabetic character.
IsCharAlphaNumeric	Returns TRUE if character is either an alphabetic or numeric character.
IsCharLower	Returns TRUE if character is lowercase.
IsCharUpper	Returns TRUE if character is uppercase.

Sorting Character Strings

The existence of accented characters requires special handling when converting text strings to uppercase or to lowercase. The same is true when sorting character strings.

Programmers who perform a simple numeric sort of character strings will put words with accents out of order. For example, the following sort order results from a simple numeric sort:

cheese

chocolate

church

château

Of course, the problem is that the numeric value of the character â is e2h (226 decimal), which comes after "e" (65h or 101 decimal), "o" (6fh or 111 decimal), and "u" (75h or 117 decimal). Since this is the way that the C-runtime library routine, strcmp, works, this routine should be avoided if you want your product to work correctly outside the United States.

Putting château at the top of the list, where it belongs, requires that we call a Windows library routine to perform string comparison during our sort. Actually, there are two such routines: one that compares in a case-insensitive fashion, lstrcmpi, and one that compares in a case-sensitive fashion, lstrcmp.

String Tables

Windows has a facility, the **string table**, which helps in the effort to prepare a product for translation to another language—a process called **localization** by Microsoft. A string table allows you to put all the strings from a program in a central place: the resource file. When your programs need to access a string, it makes a call to Windows using a numeric index. In this way, all messages for the user are centralized in one place. The job of a translator is simplified, since there is only one file that must be converted to localize an entire application.

To create a string table, entries are made in the .RC resource file, like the following:

```
#include "myinclude"

STRINGTABLE
    {
    FILENOTFOUND, "File Not Found."
    HELPPROMPT, "For Help, Type F1."
    RECALCMESSAGE, "Recalculating."
    }
```

The file myinclude would contain definitions like the following:

```
#define FILENOTFOUND    101
#define HELPPROMPT      102
#define RECALCMESSAGE   103
```

which provide a unique, numeric ID for each string. When the time comes to use a string, a Windows library routine, `LoadString`, is called:

```
char acMessage[BUFSIZE];

LoadString (hInstance,        // instance handle
            FILENOTFOUND,     // string id value
            acMessage,        // character buffer
            BUFSIZE);         // buffer size
```

and the string can be displayed, perhaps using the `TextOut` routine.

There are other benefits to using string tables besides the international support issue. Objects in a string table are read-only data and, as such, Windows loads them when needed and purges them from memory when not needed. In other words, the benefit of string tables is that they are very efficient in terms of the memory used.

Entering Characters from the Numeric Keypad

You may be aware that when running DOS you can enter ASCII codes directly from the numeric keypad. Windows provides the same mechanism, which is supported by the Windows keyboard driver. You can actually enter characters from either the ANSI or OEM character sets.

To enter characters from the ANSI character set, with Num-Lock toggled on, hold down the Alt key and enter a zero followed by the decimal ASCII character code. To enter the letter À, for example, you hold Alt and type 0192.

You can enter characters from the OEM character set as well, although they will be mapped to the corresponding ANSI character set value. With the Num-Lock toggled on, hold down the Alt key and enter the decimal OEM character code. For example, to enter the letter á, you hold Alt and type 160.

Multitasking Issues

In addition to understanding the basics of handling keyboard input and dealing with different character sets, you must be aware of certain multitasking issues in order to make effective use of the keyboard. Because Windows is multitasking, there has to be a mechanism for sharing devices like the keyboard. There are two concepts that Windows uses to direct where keyboard input is sent: the **active window** and the **focus**.

When a program creates a window, the program decides whether the window is a **top-level window** or a child of another top-level window. Most programs create a single top-level window, which serves as the primary means of the user interaction with the program. One characteristic of top-level windows is that they appear on the Task List displayed in response to the Ctrl-Esc key combination. The Task List, shown in Figure 15.6, lets users select the top-level window that they wish to make active.

The active window, then, is simply the top-level window chosen by the user. Of course, there are other ways to make a window active besides selecting from the Task List. For example, a user could click with the mouse to make a window active, or hit the Alt-Tab key combination continuously to circulate among the top-level windows. The

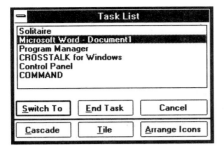

Figure 15.6 The Windows Task List

active window is always on top of every other top-level window in the system. This makes sense, because a particular window should be completely visible if the user has decided to work with it.

When a top-level window becomes active, Windows sends it a WM_ACTIVATE message with a nonzero value in wParam. In effect, this tells the window, that "the boss wants to see you. Now." Windows also sends a WM_NCACTIVATE message, which causes the window's caption bar to change colors so that the user has a visual clue to the active window. Like other non-client area messages, this one is handled by the default window procedure.

In response to a WM_ACTIVATE message, the default window procedure gives the active window the focus. Here is the actual code from DefWindowProc:

```
case WM_ACTIVATE:
    if (wParam)
        SetFocus (hWnd);
```

The focus is simply an indicator within Windows that identifies which window should get keyboard input. In effect, when a window has the focus, it has the keyboard. It alone will receive keyboard messages.

When a window receives the focus, Windows lets it know by sending it a message: WM_SETFOCUS. Before it does that, it sends a WM_KILLFOCUS message to the window that is losing the keyboard. By watching these two messages, a window procedure can keep track of whether it has control of the keyboard.

Why should a window care whether it has the keyboard? Won't it still get the proper keyboard messages? The answer is yes. But sometimes a window procedure will want to know when it has the focus, and will want to take special steps. One such case occurs when we wish to have a keyboard pointer, or **caret**, in a window. That is the next topic for discussion.

Creating a Keyboard Pointer: Carets

As a program receives keyboard input, it's quite common to display a keyboard pointer to let the user know where the next character will be entered. In most environments, this is called a **cursor**. But Windows uses the term cursor to refer to the mouse pointer, and instead uses the term caret to refer to a keyboard pointer.

A caret is a rectangular blinking bitmap that lets the user know several things. First of all, it indicates which window has the keyboard—that is, which window has the focus. Second, as we mentioned a moment ago, it shows the user the current position—the location where text (or some other object) will appear next.

While the most obvious use of a caret is to highlight a text entry point, that is certainly not the only use. For example, a caret can be used to indicate the "current object" in a drawing program, and is used in listboxes to show the user which item would be affected by keyboard input.

Windows has five routines for creating and maintaining the keyboard caret:

Routine Name	*Description*
CreateCaret	Creates a caret.
SetCaretPos	Positions the caret.
ShowCaret	Makes a caret visible.
DestroyCaret	Destroys a caret.

You might be tempted to create a caret at the beginning of your program and hold onto it until your program exits, but this won't give you the results you expect. The reason is that internally, Windows is only able to recognize one caret for the entire system. Thus, you cannot keep a caret for the life of your program. You can only keep it for as long as you have the focus. For this reason, do not create a caret like this:

```
/*  DO NOT DO THIS!  */
case WM_CREATE:  /* Window Creation Message.*/
    CreateCaret (hwnd, 0, xWidth, yHeight);
    break;

case WM_DESTROY:  /* Window Destruction Message.*/
    DestroyCaret ();
    break;
```

Instead, the proper way to create and destroy a caret is in response to the WM_SETFOCUS and WM_KILLFOCUS messages. Every time your window gains the keyboard focus, it will create a caret, and every time it loses the keyboard focus, it hides and destroys its caret. This might seem like a lot of trouble for a tiny, blinking bitmap; but this approach is necessary to properly maintain a caret in a Windows program.

```
/*  Correct Way to Create a Caret.  */
case WM_SETFOCUS:  /* You have the keyboard.*/
    CreateCaret (hwnd, 0, xWidth, yHeight0);
    break;

case WM_KILLFOCUS: /* You've lost the keyboard.*/
    DestroyCaret ();
    break;
```

The `CreateCaret` routine is defined as follows:

```
void CreateCaret (hWnd, hBitmap, nWidth, nHeight)
```

- `hWnd` is a handle to the window where the caret is to be located.
- `hBitmap` is a handle to a bitmap. It can be 0, 1, or a real bitmap handle.
- `nWidth` is the caret width.
- `nHeight` is the caret height.

The second field, `hBitmap`, is the key field that determines the shape and color of the caret. If it is set to zero, then the bitmap will be a black square `nWidth` by `nHeight`. If set to one, the bitmap is a gray square `nWidth` by `nHeight`. Otherwise, if it is a GDI bitmap, the caret takes on the shape of the bitmap.

When we create a caret, we'll want to make sure it is large enough to be visible. Since we're going to use the caret to highlight a text entry point, it makes sense to make the caret the same height as the text. Here is how to create a black caret to accomplish that:

```
...
case WM_CREATE:
    {
    HDC hdc;
    TEXTMETRIC tm;
    hdc = GetDC (hwnd);
    GetTextMetrics (hdc, &tm);
    cyHeight = tm.tmHeight;
    ReleaseDC (hwnd, hdc);
    }

case WM_SETFOCUS:
    CreateCaret (hwnd,
                0,     // default black caret
                0,     // default width
                cyHeight);
    ...
```

Here is how to create a gray caret that is the same size:

```
CreateCaret (hwnd,
            1,     // default gray caret
            0,     // default width
            cyHeight);
```

By selecting a width of zero, we let Windows use the default size. This will be the width of a window border, to make sure that the caret is visible.

We could also create a bitmap, draw onto it using GDI drawing routines, and use it as a caret. We're going to create a monochrome bitmap. The black portion of the bitmap will be ignored while the white portion will blink. Here is how to make a caret in the shape of an I-Beam. Notice that most of the work involves creating the bitmap and drawing onto it:

```
case WM_CREATE:
    {
    HBITMAP hbmOld;
    HDC hdc;
    HDC hdcBitmap;
    TEXTMETRIC tm;

    hdc = GetDC (hwnd);
    GetTextMetrics (hdc, &tm);
    yLineHeight = tm.tmHeight + tm.tmExternalLeading;
    ReleaseDC (hwnd, hdc);

    hdcBitmap = CreateCompatibleDC (hdc);
    hbm = CreateBitmap (xLeftMargin,
                        yLineHeight,
                        1, 1, NULL);
    hbmOld = SelectObject (hdcBitmap, hbm);

    /*  Blank out bitmap.  */
    SelectObject (hdcBitmap,
    GetStockObject (BLACK_BRUSH));
    Rectangle (hdcBitmap, 0, 0,
              xLeftMargin, yLineHeight);

    /*  Do actual drawing in white.  */
    SelectObject (hdcBitmap,
    GetStockObject (WHITE_PEN));
    MoveTo (hdcBitmap, 0, 0);
    LineTo (hdcBitmap, xLeftMargin+1, 0);
    MoveTo (hdcBitmap, xLeftMargin/2, 0);
    LineTo (hdcBitmap, xLeftMargin/2, yLineHeight-1);
    MoveTo (hdcBitmap, 0, yLineHeight-1);
    LineTo (hdcBitmap, xLeftMargin+1, yLineHeight-1);
    SelectObject (hdcBitmap, hbmOld);
    DeleteDC (hdcBitmap);

    }
    break;

case WM_DESTROY:
    DeleteObject (hbm);
    PostQuitMessage(0);
    break;

case WM_KILLFOCUS:
    HideCaret(hwnd);
    DestroyCaret();
    break;
```

```
case WM_SETFOCUS:
    {
    CreateCaret(hwnd,
                hbm,      // hBitmap
                0,        // xWidth
                0);       // yWidth
    SetCaretPos (x, y);
    ShowCaret(hwnd);
    }
```

Of course, this code fragment assumes that a bitmap handle has been allocated as a static object:

```
static HBITMAP hbm;
```

Let's look at an actual program that uses a caret. We've modified the KEYINPUT program so that it uses a caret. In addition to creating and deleting the caret properly, it also moves the caret in response to the cursor-movement keys on the keyboard. Here is our caret-handling program: CARET.

CARET.C

```
/*-------------------------------------------------------------*\
 | CARET.C -- Shows proper handling of a keyboard pointer.     |
 \*-------------------------------------------------------------*/
#define STRICT
#include <Windows.H>


/*-------------------------------------------------------------*\
 |                  Function Prototypes.                        |
 \*-------------------------------------------------------------*/
LRESULT CALLBACK CaretWndProc (HWND, UINT, WPARAM, LPARAM);
void NEAR PASCAL CaretSetCaretPos (HWND, int, char *, int *,
                                   int *, int);


/*-------------------------------------------------------------*\
 |                  Global Variables.                          |
 \*-------------------------------------------------------------*/
char achWndClass[] = "Caret:MAIN";
char achAppName[]  = "Caret Demo";


/*-------------------------------------------------------------*\
 |                  Main Function:  WinMain.                    |
 \*-------------------------------------------------------------*/
int PASCAL
WinMain (HINSTANCE hInstance,      // Who am I?
         HINSTANCE hPrevInstance, // Any older siblings?
         LPSTR     lpszCmdLine,   // Ptr to command line.
         int       cmdShow)       // How to open my window?
```

```
    {
HWND    hwnd;
MSG     msg;
WNDCLASS wndclass;

if (!hPrevInstance)
    {
    wndclass.lpszClassName = achWndClass;
    wndclass.hInstance     = hInstance;
    wndclass.lpfnWndProc   = CaretWndProc;
    wndclass.hCursor       = LoadCursor (hInstance, "hand");
    wndclass.hIcon         = LoadIcon (hInstance,"snapshot");
    wndclass.lpszMenuName  = NULL;
    wndclass.hbrBackground = (HBRUSH)(COLOR_WINDOW+1);
    wndclass.style         = NULL;
    wndclass.cbClsExtra    = 0;
    wndclass.cbWndExtra    = 0;

    RegisterClass( &wndclass);
    }

hwnd = CreateWindowEx(0L,               // Extra style.
                achWndClass,            // Class name.
                achAppName,             // Title.
                WS_OVERLAPPEDWINDOW,    // Style bits.
                CW_USEDEFAULT,          // x - default.
                0,                      // y - default.
                CW_USEDEFAULT,          // cx - default.
                0,                      // cy - default.
                NULL,                   // No parent.
                NULL,                   // Class menu.
                hInstance,              // Creator.
                NULL);                  // Params.
ShowWindow (hwnd, cmdShow);

while (GetMessage(&msg, 0, 0, 0))
    {
    TranslateMessage(&msg); // Convert KEYDOWNs to CHARs
    DispatchMessage(&msg);  // Transmit message to WndProc
    }
return 0;
    }


/*----------------------------------------------------------*\
|               Window Procedure:  CaretWndProc.             |
\*----------------------------------------------------------*/
LRESULT CALLBACK
CaretWndProc (HWND    hwnd,     // For whom is message sent?
            UINT    mMsg,       // What is exact message?
            WPARAM wParam,      // ...message details.
            LPARAM lParam)      // ...message details.
    {
#define BUFSIZE 40
    static unsigned char achInput[BUFSIZE]; //  Input array.
    static int  cc = 0;                     //  Character count.
```

```
      static int  icc = 0;                      //  Array index.
      static int  yLineHeight;
      static int  xLeftMargin;
      static int  xCaretPos, yCaretPos;

      switch (mMsg)
          {
          case WM_CHAR:
              {
              int i;

              //  Backspace.
              if (wParam == VK_BACK)
                  {
                  if (icc == 0)
                      MessageBeep(0);
                  else  //  Remove a character.
                      {
                      icc--;
                      CaretSetCaretPos (hwnd, icc, achInput,
                          &xCaretPos, &yCaretPos, xLeftMargin);

                      for (i=icc;i<cc;i++)
                          achInput[i]=achInput[i+1];
                      cc--;
                      InvalidateRect (hwnd, NULL, TRUE);
                      }
                  break;
                  }

              //  Filter out unwanted character codes.
              if (wParam <= VK_ESCAPE)
                  {
                  MessageBeep(0);  // Complain.
                  break;
                  }

              //  Complain if buffer is full.
              if (cc >= BUFSIZE)
                  {
                  MessageBeep (0);
                  break;
                  }

              //  Make room for a new character.
              for (i=cc;i>icc;i--)
                  achInput[i]=achInput[i-1];

              //  Put new character in buffer.
              achInput[icc] = (unsigned char)wParam;

#if 1         //  Minimal updating (first case) vs.
              //  "Brute Force" (second case.

              {  //  New Code in Brackets.
```

```
        DWORD dw;
        HDC hdc;

        HideCaret (hwnd);  // Must hide when drawing.

        cc++;
        hdc = GetDC(hwnd);
        dw = GetTextExtent (hdc, &achInput[0], icc);
        TextOut (hdc,
                    xLeftMargin+LOWORD(dw),
                    yLineHeight,
                    &achInput[icc],
                    cc - icc);
        ReleaseDC (hwnd, hdc);

        ShowCaret (hwnd);  // Restore caret visibility.
        }
        icc++;

#else
        icc++;
        cc++;
        InvalidateRect (hwnd, NULL, TRUE);
#endif
        CaretSetCaretPos (hwnd, icc, achInput,
            &xCaretPos, &yCaretPos, xLeftMargin);
        }
        break;

    case WM_CREATE:
        {
        HDC hdc;
        TEXTMETRIC tm;

        hdc = GetDC (hwnd);
        GetTextMetrics (hdc, &tm);
        yLineHeight = tm.tmHeight + tm.tmExternalLeading;
        xLeftMargin = tm.tmAveCharWidth;
        yCaretPos = yLineHeight;
        ReleaseDC (hwnd, hdc);
        }
        break;

    case WM_DESTROY:
        PostQuitMessage(0);  // Handle application shutdown.
        break;

    case WM_KEYDOWN:
        {
        BOOL bCaretMoved = FALSE;

        switch (wParam)
            {
            case VK_DELETE:
                //  If end of buffer, complain.
```

```
                    if (icc == cc)
                        MessageBeep (0);
                    else  //  Remove a character.
                        {
                        int i;
                        for (i=icc;i<cc;i++)
                            achInput[i]=achInput[i+1];
                        cc--;
                        InvalidateRect (hwnd, NULL, TRUE);
                        }
                    break;
                case VK_END:
                    icc = cc;
                    bCaretMoved = TRUE;
                    break;
                case VK_HOME:
                    icc = 0;
                    bCaretMoved = TRUE;
                    break;
                case VK_LEFT:
                    if (icc > 0)
                        {
                        icc--;
                        bCaretMoved = TRUE;
                        }
                    else
                        MessageBeep (0);
                    break;
                case VK_RIGHT:
                    if (icc < cc)
                        {
                        icc++;
                        bCaretMoved = TRUE;
                        }
                    else MessageBeep (0);
                    break;
                }
            if (bCaretMoved)
                {
                CaretSetCaretPos (hwnd, icc, achInput,
                    &xCaretPos, &yCaretPos, xLeftMargin);
                }
            }
        break;

    case WM_KILLFOCUS:
        HideCaret (hwnd);
        DestroyCaret ();
        break;

    case WM_PAINT:
        {
        PAINTSTRUCT ps;

        BeginPaint (hwnd, &ps);
```

```
            TextOut (ps.hdc, xLeftMargin, yLineHeight,
                    achInput, cc);
            EndPaint (hwnd, &ps);
            }
            break;

        case WM_SETFOCUS:
            CreateCaret(hwnd,
                        0,              // hBitmap
                        0,              // xWidth
                        yLineHeight);   // yWidth

            CaretSetCaretPos (hwnd, icc, achInput,
                &xCaretPos, &yCaretPos, xLeftMargin);
            ShowCaret (hwnd);
            break;

        default:
            return(DefWindowProc(hwnd,mMsg,wParam,lParam));
            break;
        }
    return 0L;
    }

/*-------------------------------------------------------------*\
|                Caret Movement: CaretSetCaretPos.              |
\*-------------------------------------------------------------*/
void NEAR PASCAL
CaretSetCaretPos (HWND hwnd,            // Window containing caret.
                  int icc,             // Character count.
                  char * achInput,     // Ptr to char string.
                  int *pxCaretPos,     // Ptr to Caret X position.
                  int *pyCaretPos,     // Ptr to Caret Y position.
                  int xLeftMargin)     // Pixel count of left margin.

    {
    DWORD dw;
    HDC hdc;

    hdc = GetDC (hwnd);
    dw = GetTextExtent (hdc, achInput, icc);
    ReleaseDC (hwnd, hdc);
    *pxCaretPos = LOWORD(dw) + xLeftMargin;
    SetCaretPos (*pxCaretPos, *pyCaretPos);
    }
```

CARET.DEF

```
NAME    CARET

EXETYPE WINDOWS

DESCRIPTION 'Caret Keyboard Pointer (c) 1992 By Paul Yao'
```

```
CODE     MOVEABLE PRELOAD
DATA     MOVEABLE MULTIPLE PRELOAD

HEAPSIZE     512
STACKSIZE    5120

SEGMENTS
    CARET_TEXT MOVEABLE PRELOAD

EXPORTS
    CaretWndProc
```

CARET.LNK

```
Caret.obj
Caret.exe/align:16/map/nod/noe/CO
nul
mlibcew libw
Caret.def
```

CARET.MAK

```
# Directory search paths.

INCDIR = \WINDEV\INCLUDE

# Windows version to support
# Valid pairs include:
#     (0x0300, 30)
#     (0x0310, 31)

CLVER = WINVER=0x0300
RCVER = 30

# Compiler switches for applications.

CL_APP_SHIP_ALL = -AM -c -D$(CLVER) -Gsw -I$(INCDIR) -Ow -W3 -Zp
CL_APP_DEBG_ALL = -AM -c -D$(CLVER) -Gsw -I$(INCDIR) -Od -W3 -Zpi

CL_APP_SHIP_31  = -AM -c -G2s  -I$(INCDIR) -Ow -W3 -Zp
CL_APP_DEBG_31  = -AM -c -G2s  -I$(INCDIR) -Od -W3 -Zpi

# Compiler switches for DLLs.

CL_DLL_SHIP_ALL = -AMw -c -D$(CLVER) -Gsw -I$(INCDIR) -Ow -W3 -Zp
CL_DLL_DEBG_ALL = -AMw -c -D$(CLVER) -Gsw -I$(INCDIR) -Od -W3 -Zpi

CL_DLL_SHIP_31  = -AMw -c -G2s  -I$(INCDIR) -Ow -W3 -Zp
CL_DLL_DEBG_31  = -AMw -c -G2s  -I$(INCDIR) -Od -W3 -Zpi
```

```
# Make file primary target.

all: Caret.exe

# Make file dependency targets.

Caret.res: Caret.rc Caret.cur Caret.ico
    rc -r -i$(INCDIR) Caret.rc

Caret.obj: Caret.c
    cl $(CL_APP_SHIP_ALL) Caret.c

Caret.exe: Caret.obj Caret.def Caret.res
    link @Caret.lnk
    rc -$(RCVER) Caret.res

Caret.exe: Caret.res
    rc -$(RCVER) Caret.res
```

CARET.RC

```
snapshot icon Caret.ico

hand   cursor Caret.cur
```

In this program, one subroutine does most of the work: `CaretSetCaretPos`. Any time the current position moves, this routine is called to adjust the location of the caret; in fact, this means any time the variable `icc` changes, because this points to the current character position in the array of characters.

Not a lot of additional code is required to support a caret. The only requirement is that the caret be created and destroyed at the proper time. Carets must be created in response to the `WM_SETFOCUS` message, because this message is sent to tell a window procedure that it owns the keyboard. Since the caret is a keyboard pointer, we create a caret in response to this message to let the user know the next input location. Because Windows only supports one caret in the system at a time, we hide and destroy our caret in response to the `WM_KILLFOCUS` message, which is sent to our window procedure to inform us that we have lost the keyboard. If a program then fails to destroy a caret, it will confuse the Window Manager, which may then leave an orphaned caret in your window. Avoiding this problem is easy: Create and destroy a caret in response to the proper messages.

This concludes our look at keyboard input and carets. You see now that keyboard input goes through a two-step conversion process: from scan code to virtual key and from virtual key to ASCII character code. This two-step process helps make Windows an international operating environment, and allows Windows programs to run unchanged around the world.

In the next chapter, we will discuss the other type of input device available to Windows programs: the mouse. Ideally, a Windows program will allow a user to switch between the mouse and the keyboard for all of its operations. Let's see what this involves.

16

Mouse Input

A mouse is a pointing device about the size of a deck of playing cards connected via cable to a computer. The first mouse was developed in the mid-1960s at the Stanford Research Institute (SRI). During the 1970s, the mouse played a key role in the computer research done at Xerox's Palo Alto Research Center (PARC). But the mouse didn't come into widespread use until the 1980s, with the advent and immense popularity of personal computers.

The mouse allows a user to quickly point to different objects and locations on the display screen. Objects can be picked up, moved, and directly manipulated with a versatility not possible with the keyboard alone. The advantage of the mouse over the keyboard is that pointing is a very natural, human action that we are capable of from a very young age. Pressing letter combinations on a keyboard is arguably a less natural way to communicate.

The mouse is a very important input device in Windows. Used alone, quite a bit of interaction is possible: programs can be started, windows moved, menu items selected and, in programs that allow it, data objects can be directly manipulated. As you begin to create Windows programs, you'll want to keep in mind the tremendous possibilities available through the simple act of pointing.

Although Windows and Windows applications make significant use of the mouse, not every Windows computer will have a mouse. Even on computers equipped with a mouse, there may be times when a particular user prefers to avoid it. Early in the development of Windows, this issue was raised by the developers of some popular software packages. In particular, the developers of DOS-based programs that relied primarily on keyboard input were concerned with the suitability of Windows for their programs. In response, Microsoft adopted the position that all available mouse functions should also be available with the keyboard. Ideally, programs should allow users to switch from one to the other at any time.

This approach is built into the way Windows handles menus. Consider the system menu. When you want to see the system menu, you can click the mouse on the system menu icon or strike the Alt + Spacebar keys. Once the system menu has made its appearance, you can select system menu commands using either the mouse or the keyboard. Using the mouse, you click on the desired menu item. Using the keyboard, there are two choices: You can use the arrow keys followed by the return key, or simply strike a letter key that matches an underlined letter in a menu item name. On the other hand, having seen the system menu, you might decide that you don't want to select any of its commands after all. Again, there is a keyboard approach and a mouse approach to dismissing the system menu. From the keyboard, you hit the Esc key. Using the mouse, simply click anywhere outside the system menu.

This flexibility allows the user to alternate between the two devices based on personal preference. We suggest that you take a similar approach while designing the user interface to your Windows programs. It will require some thought on your part to create a robust, flexible interface, but the increased *usability* of your program will most likely cause an increase in the *use* of your program.

If you have never worked with a mouse before, you might be skeptical about its usefulness as an input device. There's a story about a researcher at Xerox PARC, Larry Tesler, who used to think that way. He set up an experiment to prove that the mouse wasn't a very useful input device. He took people off the streets, and taught them to use a full-screen editor with cursor keys. After an hour or so, he would introduce the mouse as an alternative to the cursor keys. After playing with the mouse a little, most people ended up ignoring the cursor keys in favor of the mouse. The experiment backfired: Although he was trying to demonstrate that the mouse was an unsuitable input device, Tesler found that most users were more comfortable using the mouse instead of the keyboard to select input locations on a display screen.

Perhaps, like many programmers, you are primarily oriented toward keyboard input. If so, it might be worth your while to practice using the mouse. This will help you become a better Windows programmer, since it will help you to better understand the benefits that the mouse can provide to your users. To get you started, the next section discusses some of the common uses of the mouse in Windows.

The Uses of a Mouse

Let's start our discussion of the mouse from the point of view of the user, who asks the question: What is a mouse used for? If you're an experienced mouse user, you might wish to skip ahead a few pages to where our discussion of programming issues begins.

In use, the mouse rests on a flat surface like a desk top. It controls the movement of a tiny symbol, called a **cursor**, on the display screen. The cursor sometimes changes shape to emphasize the significance of a particular location on the screen. For example, some windows have a thick border for use in resizing the window. When positioned on top of such a border, the cursor changes into a two-headed arrow to let you know that resizing can take place.

A mouse may have one or more buttons. Although cursor location is important, it's actually the use of the buttons that triggers an action. There are several different uses of the mouse buttons that are common in the world of Windows, including clicking, double-clicking, clicking with a shift key, and dragging. We're going to discuss each of these briefly, to introduce the basic mouse actions, and to discuss some of the techniques that you'll see mentioned in this chapter. A more complete discussion of mouse interaction techniques can be found in the IBM publication *Systems Application Architecture, Common User Access: Advanced Interface Design Guide* (SC26-4582-0). This document describes a set of user-interface standards that have been adopted for Windows and OS/2 Presentation Manager programs. Microsoft includes another user-interface guide with the 3.1 version of the SDK, *The Windows Interface: An Application Design Guide*.

The first mouse action that we're going to describe is **Clicking**. Clicking involves pressing and releasing a mouse button without moving the mouse. A click is used to select objects and actions. For example, clicking causes menus to appear and is used to make scroll bars operate.

Double-clicking involves two clicking operations at the same location in a very short time interval. The default time interval is one-half second, but this can be changed using the Control Panel. While a single click makes a selection, a double-click means "do the default action." For example, a double-click on the system menu icon means "close this window." A double-click on a program icon in the Program Manager means "start this program." In general, a double-click should extend the action that was started by a single click.

Clicking with a shift key involves holding down one of the shift keys (Shift or Ctrl) while clicking a mouse button. The shift key modifies the mouse click in the same way that a shift key modifies a keyboard key. Shift key + A key, for example, gives us a capital A. The meaning of Shift + Click or Ctrl + Click will depend on the program. In general, though, Shift + Click is a request to extend a selection that was started with a single Click.

Dragging is a two-part mouse action that starts with clicking on an object to select it, then—with the mouse button still pressed—moving the mouse to cause the selected object to move. When the object has arrived at the desired location, the mouse button is released. Dragging is perhaps the hardest operation for new Windows users to master, since it combines mouse button action and mouse movement. It is also widely used. For example, in graphic programs, dragging allows a user to directly manipulate objects on the display screen. In the Windows interface itself, dragging is an important mouse action—it is used to move windows, select menu items, and operate scroll bars.

This brief introduction to mouse actions is not a substitute for your working with the Windows user interface and becoming comfortable with each of these techniques. If you are a regular Windows user, it will help make you a better Windows programmer. Now, let's investigate some of the issues that will help you program for the mouse. In the same way that we traced the path of keyboard data from the hardware into our program, we're going to follow the path mouse data takes in hopes of understanding how a Windows program can best make use of this device.

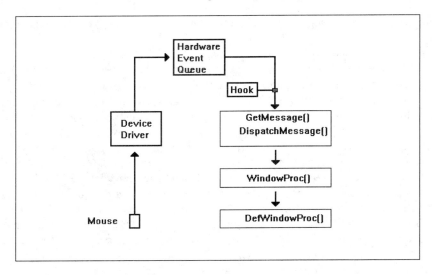

Figure 16.1 The flow of mouse data

How a Windows Program Receives Mouse Input

The path that mouse data takes is illustrated in Figure 16.1. In many respects, mouse data is much simpler than keyboard data, so this figure is correspondingly simpler than the flow of keyboard data diagram in the last chapter. Nevertheless, mouse input has some unique qualities, and understanding these qualities will help you use mouse input.

The Mouse

Although there are other pointing devices besides the mouse—pens, track balls, joy sticks, touch screens, and cats paws, to name a few—none have experienced the same popularity as the mouse. At present, a relatively small number of companies ship mice, including Hewlett-Packard, Logitech, Microsoft, and Mouse Systems. There aren't many differences among the mouses each company provides. Some have two buttons and others have three. Some detect movement by the motion of a rubber-coated steel ball, while others use optical detection methods. There is also little variety in the way different mice connect to the computer system. Some mice use a communication port, while others connect to a special bus adapter card, and still others connect to the system through the keyboard.

When a mouse reports its location, it does so in terms of movement along the X and Y axes. Like keyboard activity, mouse button actions are reported as button down and button up actions. When one of these events occurs, a signal is sent which results in a hardware interrupt being generated. The handling of the interrupt is the job of the next component to be discussed: the device driver.

Mouse Device Driver

When Windows starts up, the mouse driver loads itself and goes off in search of a mouse. When Windows asks, the device driver lets Windows know whether a mouse is present in the system. If it is, Windows calls the driver to provide an address of a procedure to be called to report mouse events. From that point on, the job of the device driver is simple: Whenever a mouse event occurs, the driver calls Windows to report mouse actions.

When Windows is notified of a mouse event, one of the first things it does is to check whether the mouse has moved. If it has, Windows calls the display driver to move the mouse cursor. In this way, the movement of the mouse cursor always occurs at interrupt time, and will preempt almost all other activities. However, this happens in the background, so you never need worry that it might disrupt the proper operation of your programs.

Like keyboard events, mouse events are not delivered to programs at interrupt time. The disruption that this would cause to Windows' nonpreemptive scheduling system would make writing Windows programs very difficult. Instead, mouse events are handled like keyboard events and placed into Windows' hardware event queue.

The Hardware Event Queue

Mouse events are written into the hardware event queue where they wait for delivery to the message loop of a program. As you know, the hardware event queue has room for 120 events. Although it is easy enough to keep ahead of most typists, you might be concerned that the queue can overflow if the mouse were to be quickly moved across the screen.

To circumvent this problem, Windows regards mouse movement in a very special way. Before a new mouse move event is written to the hardware event queue, a check is made to see if the previous hardware event was also reporting mouse movement. If so, the previous event is overwritten with the latest mouse move information. After all, when the user is moving the mouse, the destination is more important than every point traversed by the mouse.

The events in the hardware event queue don't yet belong to any particular program, until they are claimed by the `GetMessage` routine. This is necessary for the proper operation of the system. After all, one mouse message might cause a window to move or to close. This would change the way in which subsequent mouse messages are handled, since mouse input is based on mouse cursor location. That decision is made by the next link in the mouse handling chain: the `GetMessage` loop.

The GetMessage Loop

Every program has a `GetMessage` loop that serves as one of the gateways for messages to enter a program for processing. As discussed earlier, this message-passing mechanism also serves to keep Windows' multitasking system working properly.

When a program calls `GetMessage`, it opens the possibility that Windows may decide to put the program to sleep and wake up another program. This is precisely what happens when `GetMessage` finds that the hardware event queue contains a mouse event for another program. It puts the first program to sleep, and wakes up the second program. The second program can then return from its own call to `GetMessage`, where it has been sleeping, with a mouse message to process.

`GetMessage` decides which program should receive a mouse message by finding out which program owns the window where the mouse cursor resides. For now, though, let's set aside these multitasking issues and concentrate on the way `GetMessage` operates once it has decided that a specific program should receive a mouse message.

Even after `GetMessage` has found a mouse event for one of our windows, it still isn't ready to bring a message back to our program. The problem is simple: There are two types of mouse messages, depending on where the cursor is resting. Table 16.1 provides a list of the two types: client area and non-client area messages. The distinction is important, since Windows itself takes care of mouse messages in the *non-client area* of the window, and lets our program handle *client* area mouse messages.

Table 16.1 shows that Windows has messages for up to three mouse buttons, which are called the left, middle, and right buttons. Since some mice have only two buttons, few programs rely on the middle button for mouse input. In addition, Windows itself relies exclusively on the left button, and many programs follow this practice.

In case you are worried that this is unfair to users who prefer the right mouse button, Windows has a built-in solution. The Control Panel lets a user swap the left and right mouse buttons. When this is done, Windows automatically converts all right button messages into left button messages. Therefore, if a program uses only one mouse button, it can safely rely on left button messages and still satisfy users who prefer to use the right button.

To determine where the mouse cursor is resting in a window, and therefore what type of message is needed, the `GetMessage` routine sends a message to the window

Table 16.1 Windows Mouse Messages

Client Area Messages	*Non-Client Area Message*
WM_LBUTTONDOWN	WM_NCLBUTTONDOWN
WM_LBUTTONUP	WM_NCLBUTTONUP
WM_LBUTTONDBLCLK	WM_NCLBUTTONDBLCLK
WM_MBUTTONDOWN	WM_NCMBUTTONDOWN
WM_MBUTTONUP	WM_NCMBUTTONUP
WM_MBUTTONDBLCLK	WM_NCMBUTTONDBLCLK
WM_RBUTTONDOWN	WM_NCRBUTTONDOWN
WM_RBUTTONUP	WM_NCRBUTTONUP
WM_RBUTTONDBLCLK	WM_NCRBUTTONDBLCLK
WM_MOUSEMOVE	WM_NCMOUSEMOVE

procedure: WM_NCHITTEST. To understand how this works, we need to review Windows' message-passing mechanisms.

In Chapter 4, we introduced two types of message processing: push-model and pull-model processing. At the time, we said that the GetMessage routine takes care of pull-model processing to read hardware event information. Yet, to determine the location of the mouse cursor, GetMessage relies on push-model processing. In more familiar terms, the GetMessage routine calls your window procedure as if it were a subroutine.

It does so using a Windows library routine that we have not yet encountered: SendMessage. A window procedure cannot be called directly because of the way in which a window procedure is connected to Windows' push-model message mechanism. Instead, the SendMessage routine calls a window procedure for us. In other words, if you want to call a window procedure named MinWindowProc, you would never do this:

```
/*  Do not call a window procedure like this.  */
MinWindowProc (hwnd, msg, wValue, lValue);
```

Instead, you would use the SendMessage routine like this:

```
lRetVal = SendMessage (hwnd, msg, wValue, lValue);
```

This is exactly like a function call. The window procedure is called immediately, using the four parameters specified. Also, like a function call, we get back whatever return value the window procedure has decided to give us.

The return value is very important in the context of the WM_NCHITTEST message that GetMessage sends to our window procedure. This message asks the window procedure to identify where the mouse cursor is resting. Most programs pass this message on to the default window procedure, which studies the location of the mouse cursor, and provides a **hit-test code** as a return value. The hit-test codes are shown in Figure 16.2.

Most of the hit-test codes describe a location on the window border, like HTTOP and HTTOPLEFT. Others identify different non-client area objects like scroll bars and menus. One of the hit-test codes, HTCLIENT, refers to the window's client area. GetMessage uses the hit-test code to decide what type of mouse message to generate. When the hit-test code is equal to HTCLIENT, a client area message is generated; all other hit-test codes cause non-client area mouse messages to be generated.

Before GetMessage returns a mouse message to our program, there is yet one more thing that it does: It makes sure the shape of the mouse cursor is correct for the location of the mouse. To do this, it sends yet another message to our window procedure: WM_SETCURSOR. Like the WM_NCHITTEST message, most programs ignore this message and allow the default window procedure to do the right thing. The hit-test code is included with the message as the low word of the lParam parameter, so that the default window procedure knows how to correctly set the cursor shape. For example, the HTTOP hit-test code indicates that a two-headed arrow cursor is needed to show that window resizing is available, while the HTMENU code summons the normal arrow cursor.

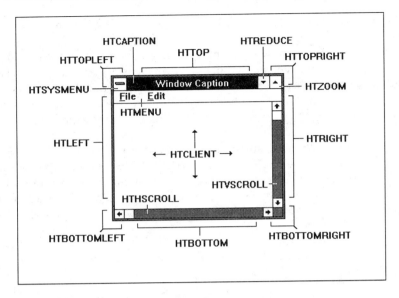

Figure 16.2   Windows hit-test codes

Figure 16.3 shows an example of SPY listening to mouse messages. This is typical mouse message traffic. With one exception, which we'll cover when we discuss *mouse capture*, the WM_NCHITTEST and WM_SETCURSOR messages always precede a

Figure 16.3   SPY listening to mouse messages

mouse message. The reason now should be evident: Windows must first find the location of the mouse cursor to know whether to generate a client area or a non-client area message. Once the location is known, Windows makes sure that the user knows by setting the mouse cursor to the correct shape.

When we discussed keyboard input, we mentioned that Windows allows for the installation of message hooks, which can be used to alter the flow of messages. While we aren't going to take the time now to describe how to install a hook, you should be aware that a WH_GETMESSAGE hook can alter the flow of any client area or non-client area mouse message. Once GetMessage is ready to bring a message into our program, it makes a call to the hook to see if any changes need to be made before the message itself is delivered to a program.

Once GetMessage has brought a mouse message into our program, the message is sent on to the correct window procedure by the DispatchMessage routine. From the point of view of our program, the window procedure is where all the action is. So, let's take a look at how a window procedure can handle mouse traffic.

The Window Procedure

Of the 20 mouse messages that exist in Windows, 10 are non-client area messages and can be safely ignored by a window procedure. After all, the non-client area of a window is maintained by Window's default handler, DefWindowProc. Among the 10 client area messages, one lets our program know the location of the mouse in our client area: WM_MOUSEMOVE. Of the other nine, three are for the left button, three for the middle button, and three for the right button. Since the processing for each set of messages is the same, and because most programs ignore the middle and right buttons, we're going to focus our attention on the left mouse button and its three messages: WM_LBUTTONDOWN, WM_LBUTTONUP, and WM_LBUTTONDBLCLK.

The WM_LBUTTONDOWN Message. When the user pushes the left mouse button with the cursor in our client area, our window procedure receives a WM_LBUTTONDOWN message. Besides telling us that a click has occurred in our client area, the two window procedure parameters, wParam and lParam, tell us quite a bit more about the message. Incidentally, the wParam and lParam values are the same for all client area mouse messages.

The lParam value in a mouse message contains the location of the mouse cursor, in client area coordinates (introduced in Chapter 6). This coordinate system places the origin in the upper-left corner of the client area, with one unit equal to one pixel. Figure 16.4 shows how client area coordinates flip the normal Cartesian coordinate system upside-down, with the Y axis positive going downward.

The X value is in the low word of lParam and the Y value is in the high word. One way to extract these values is to use the HIWORD and LOWORD macros, as shown here:

```
LRESULT CALLBACK WindowProc (...)
    {
    int xValue, yValue;

    switch (msg)
```

```
    {
case WM_LBUTTONDOWN:
    xValue = LOWORD(lParam);
    yValue = HIWORD(lParam);
    . . .
```

Often it's more convenient to store the location of the mouse in a variable of type POINT. POINT is defined in Windows.h as

```
typedef struct tagPOINT
    {
    int x;
    int y;
    } POINT;
```

so that it has a place for a pair of integer values, x and y. There's a special macro, MAKEPOINT, which converts lParam into a POINT value. Here is how it is used:

```
LRESULT CALLBACK WindowProc (...)
    {
    POINT pt;

    switch (msg)
        {
    case WM_LBUTTONDOWN:
        pt = MAKEPOINT (lParam);
        . . .
```

We can then conveniently refer to pt.x and pt.y as the coordinate pair that tells us where the user is pointing in our client area.

Figure 16.4 Client area coordinates

The wParam value in a mouse message is a set of flags that describes the state of all three mouse buttons as well as the state of the Shift key and the Ctrl key. Figure 16.5 shows the layout of these flags.

The value of a field is 1 if the corresponding mouse button or keyboard key is down; otherwise, the value is 0. To test whether a specific field is down, you can use the C language bitwise-AND operator, "&". Here is how to see if the shift key is down in response to a left-button down message:

```
LRESULT CALLBACK WindowProc (...)
    {

    switch (msg)
        {
        case WM_LBUTTONDOWN:
            if (wParam & MK_SHIFT)
                {
                /* Shift key is down.  */
                }
    ...
```

The WM_LBUTTONUP Message. This message signals that the left mouse button has been released. In many ways, this message is analogous to the WM_KEYUP keyboard message. While Windows programs rarely pay attention to the WM_KEYUP message when handling keyboard input, the WM_LBUTTONUP message, on the other hand, is quite important. If you are writing a program that uses the mouse to draw, for example, this message will tell you when to stop drawing. In the enhanced rectangle drawing program that you'll find later in this chapter, this message is used both to finish drawing rectangles and to finish the job when we drag a rectangle across the window.

The WM_LBUTTONDBLCLK Message. At the beginning of this chapter, we introduced double-clicking as a common user action. To be effective, a program that responds to a double-click should be careful that the double-click is an extension of a single click. The reason is that a single-click message will always be received before a double-click message.

Figure 16.5 Five fields of wParam for client area mouse messages

For a window to receive double-click messages, it must have been defined with a special class style: `CS_DBLCLKS`. Here is a code fragment showing how this is done:

```
wndclass.style = CS_DBLCLKS;
...
RegisterClass (&wndclass);
```

When a window has this bit set in its style definition, it changes how button-down messages are handled: A button down-message causes a timer to be started. This causes the system to incur some additional overhead. Even though this overhead is small, programs without plans to use double-click messages should avoid setting this style bit.

If a second button down message is received within a short (1/2 second) period of time, a double-click message is substituted for the second button down message. Here is the sequence of messages that will be sent when the user performs a double-click on the left mouse button:

Message	*Comment*
WM_LBUTTONDOWN	First button down message
WM_LBUTTONUP	
WM_LBUTTONDBLCLK	Replaces second button down message
WM_LBUTTONUP	

The WM_MOUSEMOVE Message. The final message to be examined is the mouse movement message. Since Windows has a built-in mechanism to prevent mouse move messages from overflowing the hardware event queue, the mouse movement messages that a program receives might only provide a sampling of all of the places that mouse visited. However, the sampling is sufficient for most programs to track the movement of this pointing device.

In a moment, we'll look at some sample programs that show the use of each of these mouse messages. But first, let's look at the last component that plays an important role in handling mouse messages, the default window procedure.

The Default Window Procedure

When we first introduced the default window procedure, we described it as the central reason that Windows programs behave in such a uniform manner. It provides all the basic, minimum processing that allows a common set of user actions to produce the same results from different Windows programs. Menus, scroll bars, and windows can all be accessed using the same set of user actions. This uniformity assumes, of course, that Windows programmers pass along all their "extra" messages. In the case of mouse messages, the default window procedure ignores the client area messages and instead relies on non-client area messages.

The default window procedure is also responsible for providing a common mouse and keyboard interface. It does this by translating input into a set of system commands, which show up as WM_SYSCOMMAND messages. Finally, the default window procedure handles the `WM_NCHITTEST` and `WM_SETCURSOR` messages which pave the way for almost all mouse messages.

When a mouse message gets to the default window procedure, it has arrived at its final destination. Starting at the mouse itself, mouse input follows a pretty direct route into a program. But, as we've seen, that route may cause Windows' multitasking switcher to stop feeding messages to one program and start feeding them to another. Finally, we've seen that half of the mouse messages that occur can be safely ignored—assuming we pass our ignored messages on to the default window procedure.

For all this mouse theory to be helpful to you in building Windows programs, it would help to see some practical examples. We will show you three such examples. The first program, CARET2, will show how a mouse click can be used in a text input window to move a caret. Our second program, RECT2, is a revision of the rectangle drawing program we first encountered in Chapter 9. We'll explore the application of GDI raster operations to create stretchable rectangles and draggable objects. Our final program, DYNACURS, creates a mouse cursor "on the fly." It echoes the mouse location, using the cursor, and in the process shows how to use a Windows library routine that is new with Windows 3.0: `CreateCursor`.

A Mouse Input Sample: Caret2

In the last chapter, we introduced a program that receives keyboard input. We then enhanced this program with a caret so the user could always see the current text entry position. Using the keyboard cursor keys, the user moves the caret to different positions in the text. Now that we've been discussing the use of the mouse, the time has come to enhance our program one more time so the mouse can be used to move the caret.

CARET2.C

```
/*-------------------------------------------------------------*\
| CARET2.C -- Shows keyboard input, caret handling and mouse   |
|             input.                                           |
\*-------------------------------------------------------------*/
#define STRICT
#include <Windows.H>


/*-------------------------------------------------------------*\
|                    Function Prototypes.                      |
\*-------------------------------------------------------------*/
LRESULT CALLBACK CaretWndProc (HWND, UINT, WPARAM, LPARAM);
void NEAR PASCAL CaretSetCaretPos (HWND, int, char *, int *,
                              int *, int);


/*-------------------------------------------------------------*\
|                    Global Variables.                        |
\*-------------------------------------------------------------*/
```

```
char achWndClass[] = "Caret:MAIN";
char achAppName[]  = "Caret and Mouse Input";

/*------------------------------------------------------------*\
|                   Main Function:  WinMain.                   |
\*------------------------------------------------------------*/
int PASCAL
WinMain (HINSTANCE hInstance,        // Who am I?
         HINSTANCE hPrevInstance,    // Any older siblings?
         LPSTR     lpszCmdLine,      // Ptr to command line.
         int       cmdShow)          // How to open my window?
    {
    HWND      hwnd;
    MSG       msg;
    WNDCLASS  wndclass;

    if (!hPrevInstance)
        {
        wndclass.lpszClassName = achWndClass;
        wndclass.hInstance     = hInstance;
        wndclass.lpfnWndProc   = CaretWndProc;
        wndclass.hCursor       = LoadCursor (hInstance, "hand");
        wndclass.hIcon         = LoadIcon (hInstance,"snapshot");
        wndclass.lpszMenuName  = NULL;
        wndclass.hbrBackground = (HBRUSH)(COLOR_WINDOW+1);
        wndclass.style         = NULL;
        wndclass.cbClsExtra    = 0;
        wndclass.cbWndExtra    = 0;

        RegisterClass( &wndclass);
        }

    hwnd = CreateWindowEx(0L,               // Extra style.
                       achWndClass,         // Class name.
                       achAppName,          // Title.
                       WS_OVERLAPPEDWINDOW, // Style bits.
                       CW_USEDEFAULT,       // x - default.
                       0,                   // y - default.
                       CW_USEDEFAULT,       // cx - default.
                       0,                   // cy - default.
                       NULL,                // No parent.
                       NULL,                // Class menu.
                       hInstance,           // Creator.
                       NULL);               // Params.
    ShowWindow (hwnd, cmdShow);

    while (GetMessage(&msg, 0, 0, 0))
        {
        TranslateMessage(&msg); // Convert KEYDOWNs to CHARs
        DispatchMessage(&msg);  // Transmit message to WndProc
        }
    return 0;
    }
```

```
/*-------------------------------------------------------------*\
|              Window Procedure:  CaretWndProc.               |
\*-------------------------------------------------------------*/
LRESULT CALLBACK
CaretWndProc (HWND    hwnd,      // For whom is message sent?
              UINT    mMsg,      // What is exact message?
              WPARAM  wParam,    // ...message details.
              LPARAM  lParam)    // ...message details.
    {
#define BUFSIZE 40
    static unsigned char achInput[BUFSIZE]; // Input array.
    static int  cc = 0;                     // Character count.
    static int  icc = 0;                    // Array index.
    static int  yLineHeight;
    static int  xLeftMargin;
    static int  xCaretPos, yCaretPos;
    static RECT rHit;

    switch (mMsg)
        {
        case WM_CHAR:
            {
            int i;

            //  Backspace.
            if (wParam == VK_BACK)
                {
                if (icc == 0)
                    MessageBeep(0);
                else  //  Remove a character.
                    {
                    icc--;
                    CaretSetCaretPos (hwnd, icc, achInput,
                        &xCaretPos, &yCaretPos, xLeftMargin);

                    for (i=icc;i<cc;i++)
                        achInput[i]=achInput[i+1];
                    cc--;
                    InvalidateRect (hwnd, NULL, TRUE);
                    }
                break;
                }

            //  Filter out unwanted character codes.
            if (wParam <= VK_ESCAPE)
                {
                MessageBeep(0);  // Complain.
                break;
                }

            //  Complain if buffer is full.
            if (cc >= BUFSIZE)
                {
```

```
                    MessageBeep (0);
                    break;
                    }

            // Make room for a new character.
            for (i=cc;i>icc;i--)
                    achInput[i]=achInput[i-1];

            // Put new character in buffer.
            achInput[icc] = (unsigned char)wParam;

#if 1       // Minimal updating (first case) vs.
            // "Brute Force" (second case.

            { // New Code in Brackets.
            DWORD dwExtent;
            HDC hdc;

            HideCaret (hwnd);  // Must hide when drawing.

            cc++;
            hdc = GetDC(hwnd);
            dwExtent = GetTextExtent (hdc, &achInput[0], icc);
            TextOut (hdc,
                    xLeftMargin+LOWORD(dwExtent),
                    yLineHeight,
                    &achInput[icc],
                    cc - icc);

            ReleaseDC (hwnd, hdc);

            ShowCaret (hwnd);  // Restore caret visibility.
            }
            icc++;

#else
            icc++;
            cc++;
            InvalidateRect (hwnd, NULL, TRUE);
#endif
            CaretSetCaretPos (hwnd, icc, achInput,
                &xCaretPos, &yCaretPos, xLeftMargin);
            }
            break;

        case WM_CREATE:
            {
            HDC hdc;
            TEXTMETRIC tm;

            hdc = GetDC (hwnd);
            GetTextMetrics (hdc, &tm);
            yLineHeight = tm.tmHeight + tm.tmExternalLeading;
            xLeftMargin = tm.tmAveCharWidth;
            yCaretPos = yLineHeight;
```

```
            ReleaseDC (hwnd, hdc);

            // Calculate hit rectangle.
            GetClientRect (hwnd, &rHit);
            rHit.top    = yLineHeight,
            rHit.bottom = rHit.top + yLineHeight;
            }
            break;

        case WM_DESTROY:
            PostQuitMessage(0);  // Handle application shutdown.
            break;

        case WM_KEYDOWN:
            {
            BOOL bCaretMoved = FALSE;

            switch (wParam)
                {
                case VK_DELETE:
                    //  If end of buffer, complain.
                    if (icc == cc)
                        MessageBeep(0);
                    else  //  Remove a character.
                        {
                        int i;
                        for (i=icc;i<cc;i++)
                            achInput[i]=achInput[i+1];
                        cc--;
                        InvalidateRect (hwnd, NULL, TRUE);
                        }
                    break;
                case VK_END:
                    icc = cc;
                    bCaretMoved = TRUE;
                    break;
                case VK_HOME:
                    icc = 0;
                    bCaretMoved = TRUE;
                    break;
                case VK_LEFT:
                    if (icc > 0)
                        {
                        icc--;
                        bCaretMoved = TRUE;
                        }
                    else
                        MessageBeep(0);
                    break;
                case VK_RIGHT:
                    if (icc < cc)
                        {
                        icc++;
                        bCaretMoved = TRUE;
                        }
```

```
                          else MessageBeep(0);
                          break;
                     }
            if (bCaretMoved)
                {
                CaretSetCaretPos (hwnd, icc, achInput,
                     &xCaretPos, &yCaretPos, xLeftMargin);
                }
            }
        break;

    case WM_KILLFOCUS:
        DestroyCaret();
        break;

    case WM_LBUTTONDOWN:
        {
        DWORD dw;
        HDC hdc;
        int i;
        int xTotWidth;
        int xPrevHalfWidth;
        int xNextHalfWidth;
        POINT pt;

        pt = MAKEPOINT (lParam);

        //  First check:  is it in our hit area?
        if (PtInRect(&rHit, pt))
            {
            hdc = GetDC (hwnd);
            xTotWidth = xLeftMargin;
            xPrevHalfWidth = xLeftMargin;

            icc = cc;  // Default = end of string.

            //  Next: loop through characters.
            for (i=0;i<cc;i++)
                {
                dw = GetTextExtent (hdc, &achInput[i], 1);
                xNextHalfWidth = LOWORD(dw)/2;
                if ((xTotWidth - xPrevHalfWidth) <= pt.x &&
                    (xTotWidth + xNextHalfWidth) >  pt.x)
                    {
                    //  A hit!  Set caret position.
                    icc = i;
                    break;
                    }
                xPrevHalfWidth = xNextHalfWidth;
                xTotWidth += LOWORD(dw);
                }

            //  Any mousing around in the hit rectangle
            //    will cause caret to move.
```

```
                    CaretSetCaretPos (hwnd, icc, achInput,
                        &xCaretPos, &yCaretPos, xLeftMargin);

                    ReleaseDC (hwnd, hdc);
                    }
                }
            break;

        case WM_PAINT:
            {
            PAINTSTRUCT ps;

            BeginPaint (hwnd, &ps);
            TextOut (ps.hdc, xLeftMargin, yLineHeight,
                    achInput, cc);

            EndPaint (hwnd, &ps);
            }
            break;

        case WM_SETFOCUS:
            CreateCaret(hwnd,
                        0,              // hBitmap
                        0,              // xWidth
                        yLineHeight);   // yWidth

            CaretSetCaretPos (hwnd, icc, achInput,
                &xCaretPos, &yCaretPos, xLeftMargin);
            ShowCaret (hwnd);
            break;

        default:
            return(DefWindowProc(hwnd,mMsg,wParam,lParam));
            break;
        }
    return 0L;
    }


/*------------------------------------------------------------*\
|            Caret Movement: CaretSetCaretPos.                 |
\*------------------------------------------------------------*/
void NEAR PASCAL
CaretSetCaretPos (HWND hwnd,            // Window containing caret.
                  int icc,             // Character count.
                  char * achInput,     // Ptr to char string.
                  int *pxCaretPos,     // Ptr to Caret X position.
                  int *pyCaretPos,     // Ptr to Caret Y position.
                  int xLeftMargin)     // Pixel count of left margin.
    {
    DWORD dwExtent;
    HDC hdc;

    hdc = GetDC (hwnd);
    dwExtent = GetTextExtent (hdc, achInput, icc);
```

```
    ReleaseDC (hwnd, hdc);
    *pxCaretPos = LOWORD(dwExtent) + xLeftMargin;
    SetCaretPos (*pxCaretPos, *pyCaretPos);
    }
```

CARET2.DEF

```
NAME    CARET2

EXETYPE WINDOWS

DESCRIPTION 'Caret and Mouse Input (c) 1992 By Paul Yao'

CODE    MOVEABLE PRELOAD
DATA    MOVEABLE MULTIPLE PRELOAD

HEAPSIZE    512
STACKSIZE   5120

SEGMENTS
    _TEXT_CARET2 MOVEABLE PRELOAD

EXPORTS
    CaretWndProc
```

CARET2.LNK

```
Caret2.obj
Caret2.exe/align:16/map/nod/noe/CO
nul
mlibcew libw
Caret2.def
```

CARET2.MAK

```
# Directory search paths.

INCDIR = \WINDEV\INCLUDE

# Windows version to support
# Valid pairs include:
#     (0x030, 30)
#     (0x031, 31)

CLVER = WINVER=0x030
```

```
RCVER = 30

# Compiler switches for applications.

CL_APP_SHIP_ALL = -AM -c -D$(CLVER) -Gsw -I$(INCDIR) -Ow -W3 -Zp
CL_APP_DEBG_ALL = -AM -c -D$(CLVER) -Gsw -I$(INCDIR) -Od -W3 -Zpi

CL_APP_SHIP_31  = -AM -c -G2s  -I$(INCDIR) -Ow -W3 -Zp
CL_APP_DEBG_31  = -AM -c -G2s  -I$(INCDIR) -Od -W3 -Zpi

# Compiler switches for DLLs.

CL_DLL_SHIP_ALL = -AMw -c -D$(CLVER) -Gsw -I$(INCDIR) -Ow -W3 -Zp
CL_DLL_DEBG_ALL = -AMw -c -D$(CLVER) -Gsw -I$(INCDIR) -Od -W3 -Zpi

CL_DLL_SHIP_31  = -AMw -c -G2s  -I$(INCDIR) -Ow -W3 -Zp
CL_DLL_DEBG_31  = -AMw -c -G2s  -I$(INCDIR) -Od -W3 -Zpi

# Make file primary target.

all: Caret2.exe

# Make file dependency targets.

Caret2.res: Caret2.rc Caret2.cur Caret2.ico
    rc -r -i$(INCDIR) Caret2.rc

Caret2.obj: Caret2.c
    cl $(CL_APP_SHIP_ALL) Caret2.c

Caret2.exe: Caret2.obj Caret2.def Caret2.res
    link @Caret2.lnk
    rc -$(RCVER) Caret2.res

Caret2.exe: Caret2.res
    rc -$(RCVER) Caret2.res
```

CARET2.RC

```
snapshot icon Caret2.ico

hand  cursor Caret2.cur
```

System Cursors

All of the programs discussed thus far have used the hand cursor created for the MIN program back in Chapter 2. Since CARET2 uses the mouse to point at text, we will take advantage of a predefined system cursor that is more suitable for working with text: the I-Beam cursor. This tall, skinny cursor is well suited for working in the narrow space between text characters.

IDC_ARROW	☖	**IDC_ICON**	■
IDC_IBEAM	I	**IDC_SIZENWSE**	⬉
IDC_WAIT	⧗	**IDC_SIZENESW**	⬈
IDC_CROSS	+	**IDC_SIZEWE**	↔
IDC_UPARROW	⇧	**IDC_SIZENS**	↕
IDC_SIZE	✛		

Figure 16.6 Windows predefined system cursors

Figure 16.6 shows Windows' eleven predefined system cursors. In many ways, these cursors are like the stock objects encountered in our discussion of GDI programming. To use a system cursor, you need a handle to the cursor. The LoadCursor routine does the job for us, and is defined as follows:

```
HCURSOR LoadCursor (hInstance, lpCursorName)
```

- hInstance is the instance handle of the module that owns the cursor, or NULL for a system cursor.

- lpCursorName is the name of the cursor in the resource file. Or, for system cursors, is one of the identifiers shown in Figure 16.6.

The easiest way to incorporate a system cursor into a program is to make the cursor part of the class definition during program initialization. This is just what we did to get the I-Beam cursor into CARET2. Here are the lines of code that attached this cursor to the window class of our program's main window:

```
wndclass.hCursor = LoadCursor (NULL, IDC_IBEAM);
...
RegisterClass( &wndclass);
```

Suppose our program was going to be busy for a moment or two and wanted to display the hourglass cursor to let the user know that an operation is going to take an extended amount of time. This is typical when saving a file, or performing another lengthy operation. It's a simple matter to change the cursor for a moment using the SetCursor routine. SetCursor takes a single parameter: a cursor handle. First, of course, we'll need to get a handle to the hourglass cursor. Here is code:

```
WindowProc (...)
    {
    static HCURSOR hcrWait;
```

```
switch(msg)
    {
    case WM_CREATE:
        hcrWait = LoadCursor (NULL, IDC_WAIT);
        ...
```

Here is how to change the cursor:

```
{
int hcrOld;

hcrOld = SetCursor (hcrWait);
...
/*  Lengthy operation.  */
...
SetCursor (hcrOld);
}
```

Another way to switch cursors involves responding to the WM_SETCURSOR message. This is useful when we want a cursor to show the user that we're working in a different mode. For example, a drawing program might use an I-Beam to show that text input is expected, and a Cross cursor to show that rectangle drawing is expected. Of course, we need to start by getting a handle to these two system cursors, which we do as follows:

```
WindowProc (...)
    {
    static HCURSOR hcrIBeam;
    static HCURSOR hcrCross;

    switch(msg)
        {
        case WM_CREATE:
            hcrIBeam = LoadCursor (NULL, IDC_IBEAM);
            hcrICross= LoadCursor (NULL, IDC_CROSS);
            ...
```

In response to the WM_SETCURSOR message, here is how we would set the cursor properly:

```
case WM_SETCURSOR:
    if (LOWORD(lParam) == HTCLIENT)
        {
        if (fType == TEXT)
            SetCursor (hcrIBeam);
        else
            SetCursor (hcrCross);
        }
    else
        DefWindowProc (hwnd, msg, wParam, lParam);
    break;
        ...
```

When processing the WM_SETCURSOR message, it is important to check the hit-test code that is passed in the low word of lParam. After all, we're only interested in client area mouse messages. All other messages should be passed on to the default window procedure.

Later in this chapter, we will investigate other alternatives for changing a program's cursor, including the creation of cursors "on the fly."

Hit-Testing

Besides using the I-Beam system cursor, the primary difference between CARET2 and CARET has to do with how the WM_LBUTTONDOWN message is handled. CARET ignores this message, and CARET2 uses it to detect where to place the mouse cursor.

Connecting mouse input to objects drawn on the display is called **hit-testing**. There are two Windows library routines for hit-testing: PtInRegion and PtInRect. Both routines tell you if a point lies inside a specified area. The PtInRect routine lets you define the area in terms of a simple rectangle, while PtInRegion lets the area be defined in terms of a region. As you may recall from our discussion of clipping in Chapter 6, a region is defined by a set of rectangles. Let's take a closer look at PtInRect, which is the routine used by CARET2.

The PtInRect routine is defined as follows:

```
BOOL PtInRect (lpRect, Point)
```

- lpRect is a long pointer to a RECT data structure containing the rectangle against which the hit-testing is performed.

- Point is a variable of type POINT. That is, it is an X and a Y value.

The return value is TRUE if the point is inside the rectangle; otherwise, it returns FALSE.

CARET2 uses the PtInRect routine to determine if the cursor is located within a hit rectangle. The hit rectangle is defined when the text is displayed, that is, in response to the WM_PAINT message. It makes sense to define the hit areas during the WM_PAINT message, since the coordinates of the output need to be calculated to handle the requirements of output. It's a simple matter to store these values so they can be useful for testing mouse input.

The PtInRect routine is only used for preliminary hit-testing to see if the cursor is located anywhere inside an imaginary rectangle that bounds the text and extends to the left and right borders of the window. But we need to do some more work to determine exactly where the cursor is resting to properly place the caret.

Actually, since a caret should always be placed between two characters, the real issue involves figuring out the letter break that lies closest to the cursor. CARET2 has it easy, since the caret position is defined in terms of character cells by the variable icc. CARET2 calculates the hit area by looping through the array of characters, achInput.

The key to understanding the character hit-test loop lies with three variables: xTotWidth, xPrevHalfWidth, and xNextHalfWidth, visually depicted in

Figure 16.7 Hit-testing characters in CARET2

Figure 16.7. Notice first of all that we're only interested in X values. The reason is simple: The PtInRect test has already determined that we're in the proper Y range. The value of xTotWidth is the total width of the text, including the margin. This means that xTotWidth is the distance from the left border measured in client area coordinates. The xPrevHalfWidth variable holds a value equal to one-half the width of the previous character. xNextHalfWidth holds a value of one-half the width of the next character. As we loop through the array of characters, hit-testing becomes simple: We test whether the point is between the beginning of the previous character and the end of the next character, as shown here:

```
if ((xTotWidth - xPrevHalfWidth) <= pt.x &&
    (xTotWidth + xNextHalfWidth) >  pt.x)
    {
    /*  A hit!  Set caret position.  */
    icc = i;
    break;
    }
```

Once a hit is made, it's a simple matter to set the current character position variable, icc, break out of the loop, and call our private caret moving routine, CaretSetCaretPos. Of course, this routine calls the Windows routine, SetCaretPos, to do the actual work.

CARET2 has shown a number of things: the use of predefined system cursors, and one approach to take in combining mouse input with text. Of course, part of the challenge in working with the system font is the fact that it is nonproportional. Hit-testing a fixed pitch font, after all, would be quite a bit easier. However, Windows gives you all the tools you need to make the hit-testing work.

There is certainly room for improvement in this program. For example, it would probably be more efficient to calculate the width of each character cell ahead of time. Once stored away, much of the hit-testing and caret movement becomes simpler. Of course, this improvement would have its trade-off in memory used.

Now let's look at our second sample program. This time, we've improved on the rectangle drawing program from Chapter 9.

Draggable Objects and Stretchable Rectangles

As the mouse cursor travels across the system display, it seems to perform a little magic. It can go anywhere on the display screen, yet it never causes any damage to any of the objects it walks over. In most cases, this magic is the result of software. A well-written device driver gives the illusion that the mouse cursor isn't part of the rest of the display. In other cases, the magic is part of the hardware. Some display adapters have a built-in ability to support cursors. Whichever approach is taken, the result is the same: The cursor never causes any damage to any objects on the display screen.

A similar effect is seen when a window is moved. If the user clicks on the caption bar of a window (or selects the Move item on the system menu), a dotted outline of the window lets the user see the proposed location for the window as it is moved. Thus, the user can preview the results of the move before actually committing to the move.

These same types of "floating images" can be very useful in a Windows program. They can be used to help the user reposition objects in a window. Since they don't damage other objects in the window, the user can arrange objects in different ways before committing to one arrangement or another.

These effects can be achieved using GDI **raster operation** (or ROP) codes. We first discussed the topic of ROP codes in Chapter 8. We did not provide a programming example then, however, since ROP codes are most easily understood in the context of the mouse.

As you may recall, a raster operation is a combination of one or more Boolean operations applied between a source, which might be a pen or a brush, and a destination. Some of the raster operations ignore the source and simply change the destination. In a moment, we're going to look at a sample program, RECT2, which uses the NOT operator to produce the effect of draggable and stretchable rectangles.

A draggable rectangle can be grabbed (using the mouse) and placed in a new position. Although our demonstration program uses rectangles, the principle is the same if you wish to drag any object that is drawn using GDI's pixel, line, or filled area routines. Figure 16.8 shows an example of a rectangle being dragged in our sample program. Notice how the outline of the rectangle is always visible, no matter what color is part of the background. Also, as it is moved, it doesn't damage the other rectangles. Both of these qualities are achieved using raster operations.

A stretchable rectangle is also drawn using raster operations. A stretchable rectangle lets you preview the rectangle as it is drawn. By providing this feedback, the rectangle drawing program makes it easy to avoid unwanted effects. Figure 16.9 shows how a stretchable rectangle helps position a rectangle as it is drawn. In the (b) panel, this preview capability helps us see that we've made a mistake, but it is one that is easily corrected before we commit to our final rectangle.

Like our first rectangle drawing program, RECT2 draws rectangles in response to mouse button activity. The first corner of a rectangle is selected by pressing the mouse button. The second, opposing corner is selected by releasing the mouse button. As the

Figure 16.8 A draggable rectangle

mouse is dragged from the first corner to the second corner, a stretchable rectangle outline is echoed to the user indicating where the final rectangle is to be placed. RECT2 has also been enhanced to allow the user to drag rectangles. The drag action is differentiated from a drawing operation by the use of the Shift key to accompany a button click.

Figure 16.9 A stretchable rectangle

RECT2.C

```
/*----------------------------------------------------------------*\
|   RECT2.C - Draws rectangles in response to mouse messages,  |
|             echoing a stretchable rubber rectangle.          |
|             A rectangle can be moved when it is clicked       |
|             with the SHIFT key depressed.                     |
\*----------------------------------------------------------------*/
#define STRICT
#include <Windows.H>


/*----------------------------------------------------------------*\
|                      Function Prototypes.                     |
\*----------------------------------------------------------------*/
LRESULT CALLBACK Rect2WndProc (HWND, UINT, WPARAM, LPARAM);
void NEAR PASCAL Rect2DrawNotRect (HWND, int, int, int, int);


/*----------------------------------------------------------------*\
|                      Global Variables.                       |
\*----------------------------------------------------------------*/
char achWndClass[] = "Rect2:MAIN";
char achAppName[]  = "Rectangles - Version 2";


/*----------------------------------------------------------------*\
|                  Main Function:  WinMain.                     |
\*----------------------------------------------------------------*/
int PASCAL
WinMain (HINSTANCE hInstance,       // Who am I?
         HINSTANCE hPrevInstance,   // Any older siblings?
         LPSTR     lpszCmdLine,     // Ptr to command line.
         int       cmdShow)         // How to open my window?
    {
    HWND     hwnd;
    MSG      msg;
    WNDCLASS wndclass;

    if (!hPrevInstance)
        {
        wndclass.lpszClassName = achWndClass;
        wndclass.hInstance     = hInstance;
        wndclass.lpfnWndProc   = Rect2WndProc;
        wndclass.hCursor       = LoadCursor (hInstance, "hand");
        wndclass.hIcon         = LoadIcon (hInstance,"snapshot");
        wndclass.lpszMenuName  = NULL;
        wndclass.hbrBackground = (HBRUSH)(COLOR_WINDOW+1);
        wndclass.style         = NULL;
        wndclass.cbClsExtra    = 0;
        wndclass.cbWndExtra    = 0;

        RegisterClass( &wndclass);
        }

    hwnd = CreateWindowEx(0L,                   // Extra style.
                    achWndClass,                // Class name.
```

```
                    achAppName,             // Title.
                    WS_OVERLAPPEDWINDOW,    // Style bits.
                    CW_USEDEFAULT,          // x - default.
                    0,                      // y - default.
                    CW_USEDEFAULT,          // cx - default.
                    0,                      // cy - default.
                    NULL,                   // No parent.
                    NULL,                   // Class menu.
                    hInstance,              // Creator.
                    NULL);                  // Params.
    ShowWindow (hwnd, cmdShow);

    while (GetMessage(&msg, 0, 0, 0))
        {
        TranslateMessage(&msg); // Convert KEYDOWNs to CHARs
        DispatchMessage(&msg);  // Transmit message to WndProc
        }
    return 0;
    }

/*------------------------------------------------------------*\
|                 Window Procedure:  Rect2WndProc.             |
\*------------------------------------------------------------*/
LRESULT CALLBACK
Rect2WndProc (HWND   hwnd,      // For whom is message sent?
              UINT   mMsg,      // What is exact message?
              WPARAM wParam,    // ...message details.
              LPARAM lParam)    // ...message details.
    {
#define MAXRECTS 50
    static BOOL   fCapture = FALSE;      // Capture flag
    static BOOL   fDrag    = FALSE;      // Dragging flag
    static int    cRects = 0;           // Rectangle count
    static int    iDrag  = -1;          // Current drag location
    static POINT  ptDrag;
    static RECT   rSave[MAXRECTS]; // Rectangle array

    switch (mMsg)
        {
        case WM_DESTROY:
            PostQuitMessage(0);  // Handle application shutdown.
            break;

        case WM_LBUTTONDOWN:
            {
            int  i;
            POINT pt;

            SetCapture (hwnd);
            fCapture = TRUE;

            pt = MAKEPOINT (lParam);

            // Record starting point.
            rSave[cRects].left = rSave[cRects].right  = pt.x;
```

```
                        rSave[cRects].top  = rSave[cRects].bottom = pt.y;

                    /*  If not dragging, exit.  */
                    if (!(MK_SHIFT & wParam))
                        break;

                    /*  Loop through all rectangles.  */
                    for (i=cRects-1;i>=0;i--)
                        {
                        /*  If hit test = TRUE, then start drag.  */
                        if (PtInRect (&rSave[i], pt))
                            {
                            ptDrag = pt;
                            fDrag = TRUE;
                            iDrag = i;
                            InvalidateRect (hwnd, &rSave[i], TRUE);
                            UpdateWindow (hwnd);
                            Rect2DrawNotRect (hwnd, rSave[iDrag].left,
                                                    rSave[iDrag].top,
                                                    rSave[iDrag].right,
                                                    rSave[iDrag].bottom);

                            break;
                            }
                        }
                    }
                break;

            case WM_LBUTTONUP:
                if (!fCapture)
                    break;

                ReleaseCapture ();
                fCapture = FALSE;

                if (fDrag)
                    {
                    Rect2DrawNotRect (hwnd, rSave[iDrag].left,
                                            rSave[iDrag].top,
                                            rSave[iDrag].right,
                                            rSave[iDrag].bottom);
                    InvalidateRect (hwnd, &rSave[iDrag], TRUE);

                    fDrag = FALSE;
                    iDrag = -1;
                    }
                else
                    {
                    int i;

                    Rect2DrawNotRect (hwnd, rSave[cRects].left,
                                            rSave[cRects].top,
                                            rSave[cRects].right,
                                            rSave[cRects].bottom);
```

```
          /*  Make sure order is correct: left < right.  */
          if (rSave[cRects].left > rSave[cRects].right)
             {
             i = rSave[cRects].left;
             rSave[cRects].left = rSave[cRects].right;
             rSave[cRects].right = i;
             }

          /*  Top should be less than bottom.  */
          if (rSave[cRects].top > rSave[cRects].bottom)
             {
             i = rSave[cRects].top;
             rSave[cRects].top = rSave[cRects].bottom;
             rSave[cRects].bottom = i;
             }

          InvalidateRect (hwnd, &rSave[cRects], TRUE);

          cRects++;
          if (cRects == MAXRECTS) cRects = 0;
          }
     break;

case WM_MOUSEMOVE:
     {
     POINT pt;

     if (!fCapture)
         break;

     pt = MAKEPOINT (lParam);

     if (fDrag)
         {
         /* Remove previous rectangle.  */
         Rect2DrawNotRect (hwnd, rSave[iDrag].left,
                                 rSave[iDrag].top,
                                 rSave[iDrag].right,
                                 rSave[iDrag].bottom);

         /*  Calculate relative movement.  */
         ptDrag.x = ptDrag.x - pt.x;  // X-offset
         ptDrag.y = ptDrag.y - pt.y;  // Y-offset

         rSave[iDrag].left   -= ptDrag.x;
         rSave[iDrag].top    -= ptDrag.y;
         rSave[iDrag].right  -= ptDrag.x;
         rSave[iDrag].bottom -= ptDrag.y;

         /*  Remember drag point for next time.  */
         ptDrag = pt;

         /* Draw next rectangle.  */
         Rect2DrawNotRect (hwnd, rSave[iDrag].left,
                                 rSave[iDrag].top,
```

```
                                                rSave[iDrag].right,
                                                rSave[iDrag].bottom);
                }
        else
                {
                /* Remove previous rectangle.  */
                Rect2DrawNotRect (hwnd, rSave[cRects].left,
                                        rSave[cRects].top,
                                        rSave[cRects].right,
                                        rSave[cRects].bottom);

                rSave[cRects].right  = pt.x;
                rSave[cRects].bottom = pt.y;

                /* Draw a new rectangle.  */
                Rect2DrawNotRect (hwnd, rSave[cRects].left,
                                        rSave[cRects].top,
                                        rSave[cRects].right,
                                        rSave[cRects].bottom);
                }
        }
        break;

    case WM_PAINT:
        {
        PAINTSTRUCT ps;
        int i;

        BeginPaint (hwnd, &ps);
        SelectObject (ps.hdc, GetStockObject (BLACK_BRUSH));

        for (i = 0; i < cRects ; i++ )
                {
                if (i == iDrag)
                        continue;
                Rectangle (ps.hdc, rSave[i].left,
                                   rSave[i].top,
                                   rSave[i].right,
                                   rSave[i].bottom);
                }

        EndPaint (hwnd, &ps);
        }
        break;

    default:
        return(DefWindowProc(hwnd,mMsg,wParam,lParam));
        break;
    }
    return 0L;
    }


/*-------------------------------------------------------------------*\
|            Rect2DrawNotRect: Draw a NOT Rectangle.                  |
\*-------------------------------------------------------------------*/
```

```
void NEAR PASCAL Rect2DrawNotRect (HWND hwnd, int x1, int y1,
                                   int x2, int y2)
    {
    HDC hdc;

    hdc = GetDC (hwnd);
    SelectObject (hdc, GetStockObject (NULL_BRUSH));
    SetROP2 (hdc, R2_NOT);
    Rectangle (hdc, x1, y1, x2, y2);
    ReleaseDC (hwnd, hdc);
    }
```

RECT2.DEF

```
NAME     RECT2

EXETYPE WINDOWS

DESCRIPTION 'Rectangle Drawing w/Mouse (c) 1992 By Paul Yao'

CODE     MOVEABLE PRELOAD
DATA     MOVEABLE MULTIPLE PRELOAD

HEAPSIZE     512
STACKSIZE    5120

SEGMENTS
    _TEXT_RECT2 MOVEABLE PRELOAD

EXPORTS
    Rect2WndProc
```

RECT2.LNK

```
Rect2.obj
Rect2.exe/align:16/map/nod/noe/CO
nul
mlibcew libw
Rect2.def
```

RECT2.MAK

```
# Directory search paths.

INCDIR = \WINDEV\INCLUDE
```

```
# Windows version to support
# Valid pairs include:
#     (0x0300, 30)
#     (0x0310, 31)

CLVER = WINVER=0x0300
RCVER = 30

# Compiler switches for applications.

CL_APP_SHIP_ALL = -AM -c -D$(CLVER) -Gsw -I$(INCDIR) -Ow -W3 -Zp
CL_APP_DEBG_ALL = -AM -c -D$(CLVER) -Gsw -I$(INCDIR) -Od -W3 -Zpi

CL_APP_SHIP_31  = -AM -c -G2s  -I$(INCDIR) -Ow -W3 -Zp
CL_APP_DEBG_31  = -AM -c -G2s  -I$(INCDIR) -Od -W3 -Zpi

# Compiler switches for DLLs.

CL_DLL_SHIP_ALL = -AMw -c -D$(CLVER) -Gsw -I$(INCDIR) -Ow -W3 -Zp
CL_DLL_DEBG_ALL = -AMw -c -D$(CLVER) -Gsw -I$(INCDIR) -Od -W3 -Zpi

CL_DLL_SHIP_31  = -AMw -c -G2s  -I$(INCDIR) -Ow -W3 -Zp
CL_DLL_DEBG_31  = -AMw -c -G2s  -I$(INCDIR) -Od -W3 -Zpi

# Make file primary target.

all: Rect2.exe

# Make file dependency targets.

Rect2.res: Rect2.rc Rect2.cur Rect2.ico
    rc -r -i$(INCDIR) Rect2.rc

Rect2.obj: Rect2.c
    cl $(CL_APP_SHIP_ALL) Rect2.c

Rect2.exe: Rect2.obj Rect2.def Rect2.res
    link @Rect2.lnk
    rc -$(RCVER) Rect2.res

Rect2.exe: Rect2.res
    rc -$(RCVER) Rect2.res
```

RECT2.RC

```
snapshot icon Rect2.ico

hand   cursor Rect2.cur
```

Dragging and Stretching

Any program that does dragging or stretching will be responding to three mouse messages: button down, mouse move, and button up. In response to the button down message, the window procedure does whatever initialization it needs to do to make the dragging or stretching work. The mouse move message means the mouse cursor has moved, and that the dragged or stretched object needs to be modified to reflect that movement. The simplest way to handle this is to erase the image of the object at the old location and create a copy of the object at the new location. The button up message means that no more movement is required, so dragging or stretching can be turned off and the object made permanent.

While movement is going on, the raster operations provide a convenient manner to quickly draw and erase the moveable/stretchable rectangles. The particular raster operation used is the one associated with the NOT operation, R2_NOT. A nice feature of this raster operation is that it virtually guarantees that the object you draw will appear. Every white pixel encountered will turn black and every black pixel encountered will turn white. Pixels with colors other than black and white will be changed to the logical inverse color. This produces some slightly unexpected results—like the fact that R2_NOT of Blue on a 16-color VGA adapter gives Yellow (instead of Orange). This is a limitation of the hardware, and a compromise to allow a reasonable set of colors to be available on this device.

In spite of this odd behavior with color, the second—and most important—advantage of the R2_NOT raster operation is that everything is easily reversible. Let's look at the two-color monochrome case to convince ourselves that this is true. The *first* time a figure (say a rectangle) is drawn, every white pixel turns black and every black pixel turns white. The *second* time the same figure is drawn, every white pixel turns black and every black pixel turns white. But after the figure is drawn the second time, the figure itself disappears. Put together, the two advantages of the R2_NOT raster operation are ideal for drawing draggable and stretchable rectangles.

In RECT2, the routine that draws all the R2_NOT rectangles is Rect2DrawNotRect. It calls GetDC for a DC that can draw anywhere in the client area. It selects the stock null brush into the DC, so that we only draw the outline of the rectangle. It sets the raster operation to R2_NOT by calling the SetROP2 routine, then draws a rectangle. The routine itself doesn't know (or care) whether it is drawing the first rectangle, to make one appear, or the second rectangle, to make it disappear.

A second issue raised by the RECT2 program is that of the mouse capture, which we're going to discuss next.

The Mouse Capture

Mouse messages are always sent to the window lying under the mouse cursor. In this way, the user is free to move the cursor to the desired program and start it with a mouse click. There are times, however, when it makes sense to restrict all mouse messages to one window. In particular, it is useful when some operation has started that must be completed in order to leave the program in a stable, known state. Rectangle dragging and stretching are two such times.

In RECT2, when the `WM_LBUTTONDOWN` message is received, the program gets set up to draw a new rectangle or to move an existing rectangle. The program expects to receive another message—a `WM_LBUTTONUP`—before things are returned to "normal." If a second `WM_LBUTTONDOWN` message is received before a `WM_LBUTTONUP` message, it will cause some confusion in the program and a mess in the window.

To make sure that our window gets the expected sequence of messages, the window procedure **captures** the mouse. This is done by making a call to `SetCapture`, which takes a single parameter: a window handle. A call is made to `SetCapture` in response to the `WM_LBUTTONDOWN` message, which guarantees that no other window will get a mouse message until the capture is released.

Releasing the capture is done by making a call to `ReleaseCapture`, which is a Windows library routine that takes no parameters. RECT2 calls `ReleaseCapture` in response to a `WM_LBUTTONUP` message, to allow other programs to receive mouse messages from the user.

In Chapter 7, we introduced the Windows sandwich in which the use of a system resource is sandwiched between two calls: The first call obtains the resource and the second call releases the resource. This is certainly an accurate description of the way the mouse capture is handled. In culinary terms:

The Windows Sandwich	*Applied to Mouse Capture*
Top Slice of Bread	`SetCapture` called at `WM_LBUTTONDOWN` time
Filling	Mouse events used during `WM_MOUSEMOVE`
Bottom Slice of Bread	`ReleaseCapture` called at `WM_LBUTTONUP` time

The final point to be made about the mouse capture is that the hit-testing and cursor setting messages are disabled when the mouse is captured. That is, you will not encounter the `WM_NCHITTEST` or `WM_SETCURSOR` messages when the mouse is captured. The hit-testing message, `WM_NCHITTEST`, after all, tests whether a client area or non-client area message should be sent; only client area messages are sent when the mouse is captured. The `WM_SETCURSOR` is not sent since Windows doesn't expect the cursor to change when one window has reserved all mouse input for itself.

At this point, we're going to turn our attention to the third sample program of this chapter. It creates a mouse cursor on the fly, a capability introduced with Windows 3.0.

Creating Dynamic Cursors

In Chapter 2, when we introduced the minimum Windows program, we created a custom cursor in the shape of a hand, using two tools: the Paintbrush program, which drew the basic outline of a hand, and the Image Editor, which we used to fine-tune the bits in the cursor. Once the cursor was created, it was saved to a file, MIN.CUR, which was referenced in the resource file for our minimum Windows program, MIN.RC.

While a static custom cursor like this will serve most of your needs, there may be times when you need to create a dynamic cursor. A dynamic cursor is created by a Windows program at execution time, instead of during program development time. One way to create a dynamic cursor is to create a GDI bitmap, then use GDI routines to draw the desired shape. This is the approach we will take. This simple description hides the fact that quite a bit of shuffling is required to create a custom cursor.

The DYNACURS Program

Our dynamic cursor program echoes the current mouse location. Figure 16.10 shows a sample of its output. The "hot-spot" of the cursor is in the upper-left corner, marked by a dot. The top number is the X-location of the cursor, and the bottom number is the Y-location.

One of the first things you notice when you run this program is the way the cursor seems to blink a lot. That is, as the mouse moves and the cursor changes, the dynamic cursor doesn't have the smooth quality associated with a normal cursor. The reason has to do with the fact that the background—the area "behind" the cursor—must be restored every time the cursor changes. While this would be a very annoying feature in a commercially released Windows product, it's only a minor flaw in a program that demonstrates the creation of dynamic cursors.

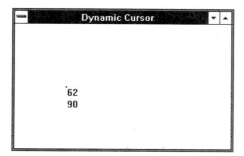

Figure 16.10 The cursor in DYNACURS echoes the mouse location

DYNACURS.C

```
/*------------------------------------------------------------*\
|   DYNACURS - Creates a dynamic cursor on the fly.            |
\*------------------------------------------------------------*/
#define STRICT
#include <Windows.H>
```

```
/*-------------------------------------------------------------*\
|                    Function Prototypes.                       |
\*-------------------------------------------------------------*/
LRESULT CALLBACK DynaCursWndProc (HWND, UINT, WPARAM, LPARAM);


/*-------------------------------------------------------------*\
|                     Global Variables.                         |
\*-------------------------------------------------------------*/
char achWndClass[] = "DynaCurs:MAIN";
char achAppName[]  = "Dynamic Cursor";


/*-------------------------------------------------------------*\
|                  Main Function:  WinMain.                     |
\*-------------------------------------------------------------*/
int PASCAL
WinMain (HINSTANCE hInstance,        // Who am I?
         HINSTANCE hPrevInstance,    // Any older siblings?
         LPSTR     lpszCmdLine,      // Ptr to command line.
         int       cmdShow)          // How to open my window?
    {
    HWND     hwnd;
    MSG      msg;
    WNDCLASS wndclass;

    if (!hPrevInstance)
        {
        wndclass.lpszClassName = achWndClass;
        wndclass.hInstance     = hInstance;
        wndclass.lpfnWndProc   = DynaCursWndProc;
        wndclass.hCursor       = NULL;
        wndclass.hIcon         = LoadIcon (hInstance,"snapshot");
        wndclass.lpszMenuName  = NULL;
        wndclass.hbrBackground = (HBRUSH)(COLOR_WINDOW+1);
        wndclass.style         = NULL;
        wndclass.cbClsExtra    = 0;
        wndclass.cbWndExtra    = 0;

        RegisterClass( &wndclass);
        }

    hwnd = CreateWindowEx(0L,               // Extra style.
                    achWndClass,            // Class name.
                    achAppName,             // Title.
                    WS_OVERLAPPEDWINDOW,    // Style bits.
                    CW_USEDEFAULT,          // x - default.
                    0,                      // y - default.
                    CW_USEDEFAULT,          // cx - default.
                    0,                      // cy - default.
                    NULL,                   // No parent.
                    NULL,                   // Class menu.
                    hInstance,              // Creator.
                    NULL);                  // Params.
    ShowWindow (hwnd, cmdShow);
```

```
      while (GetMessage(&msg, 0, 0, 0))
           {
           TranslateMessage(&msg); // Convert KEYDOWNs to CHARs
           DispatchMessage(&msg);  // Transmit message to WndProc
           }
      return 0;
      }

/*-------------------------------------------------------------*\
 |              Window Procedure: DynaCursWndProc.             |
\*-------------------------------------------------------------*/
LRESULT CALLBACK
DynaCursWndProc (HWND    hwnd,      // For whom is message sent?
                 UINT    mMsg,      // What is exact message?
                 WPARAM  wParam,    // ...message details.
                 LPARAM  lParam)    // ...message details.
      {
      static HCURSOR hcrPrev = 0;
      static HBITMAP hbm;
      static HBITMAP hbmOld;
      static HBRUSH  hbrWhite;
      static HBRUSH  hbrBlack;
      static HDC     hdcBitmap;
      static HGLOBAL hmemAND;
      static HGLOBAL hmemXOR;
      static int cbSize;
      static int cxCursor;
      static int cyCursor;

      switch (mMsg)
           {
           case WM_CREATE:
                {
                HDC hdc;

                //  Find out expected size of cursor.
                cxCursor = GetSystemMetrics (SM_CXCURSOR);
                cyCursor = GetSystemMetrics (SM_CYCURSOR);

                //  Create some scratch objects:

                        //  A bitmap.
                hbm = CreateBitmap (cxCursor,  // width
                                    cyCursor,  // height
                                    1,         // planes
                                    1,         // bits per pixel
                                    NULL);     // initial data

                        //  A DC for the bitmap.
                hdc = GetDC (hwnd);
                hdcBitmap = CreateCompatibleDC (hdc);
                ReleaseDC (hwnd, hdc);
```

```
                // Connect the bitmap to the DC.
        hbmOld = SelectObject (hdcBitmap, hbm);


                // Some memory scratch space.
        cbSize = (cxCursor/8) * cyCursor;
        hmemAND = GlobalAlloc (GMEM_MOVEABLE,    // flags
                                (DWORD)cbSize); // size

        hmemXOR = GlobalAlloc (GMEM_MOVEABLE,    // flags
                                (DWORD)cbSize); // size

            // Get GDI objects to use.
        hbrWhite = GetStockObject (WHITE_BRUSH);
        hbrBlack = GetStockObject (BLACK_BRUSH);

            // Error checking.
        if (hbm == NULL      || hdcBitmap == NULL ||
            hmemAND == NULL || hmemXOR == NULL   ||
            cxCursor%8 != NULL)
            {
            MessageBox (hwnd, "Unable to Initialize",
                        "Dynamic Cursor", MB_OK);
            DestroyWindow (hwnd);
            break;
            }
        }
        break;

    case WM_DESTROY:
        SelectObject (hdcBitmap, hbmOld);
        DeleteDC (hdcBitmap);
        DeleteObject (hbm);
        DestroyCursor(hcrPrev);
        GlobalFree (hmemAND);
        GlobalFree (hmemXOR);

        PostQuitMessage(0);  // Say good-bye Gracie.
        break;

    case WM_SETCURSOR:
        {
        char acLine1[8];
        char acLine2[8];
        HCURSOR    hcrTemp;
        HINSTANCE hInst;
        int   cc1;
        int   cc2;
        LPSTR lpAND;
        LPSTR lpXOR;
        POINT pt;

            // Ignore all non-client area messages.
        if (LOWORD(lParam) != HTCLIENT)
            goto DefaultExit;
```

```
// Set up AND Mask.
SelectObject (hdcBitmap, hbrWhite);
PatBlt (hdcBitmap, 0, 0, cxCursor, cyCursor,
        PATCOPY);

// Light up the hot-spot.
SetPixel (hdcBitmap, 0, 0, 0L);
SetPixel (hdcBitmap, 0, 1, 0L);
SetPixel (hdcBitmap, 1, 0, 0L);
SetPixel (hdcBitmap, 1, 1, 0L);

// Where is the mouse cursor?
GetCursorPos (&pt);
ScreenToClient (hwnd, &pt);

cc1 = wsprintf (acLine1,"%d", pt.x);
cc2 = wsprintf (acLine2,"%d", pt.y);

// Write coordinates onto bitmap.
TextOut (hdcBitmap, 3, 0, acLine1, cc1);
TextOut (hdcBitmap, 3, cyCursor/2, acLine2, cc2);

// Set up memory to grab bits.
lpAND = GlobalLock (hmemAND);
if (lpAND == NULL)
    goto DefaultExit;
GetBitmapBits (hbm, (DWORD)cbSize, lpAND);

// Set up XOR Mask.
SelectObject (hdcBitmap, hbrBlack);
PatBlt (hdcBitmap, 0, 0, cxCursor, cyCursor,
        PATCOPY);

// Set up memory to grab bits.
lpXOR = GlobalLock (hmemXOR);
if (lpXOR == NULL)
    goto DefaultExit;
GetBitmapBits (hbm, (DWORD)cbSize, lpXOR);

// Spin a cursor on the fly.
hInst  = (HINSTANCE)GetWindowWord (hwnd,
                                   GWW_HINSTANCE);
hcrTemp = CreateCursor (
    hInst,     // Instance which will own cursor
    0,         // X-hotspot
    0,         // Y-hotspot
    cxCursor,  // width
    cyCursor,  // height
    lpAND,     // AND bitmask
    lpXOR);    // XOR bitmask

GlobalUnlock (hmemAND);
GlobalUnlock (hmemXOR);
```

```
                SetCursor (hcrTemp);   // Select new cursor.

                //  Remove old cursor.
                if (hcrPrev != NULL)
                    DestroyCursor(hcrPrev);

                hcrPrev = hcrTemp;
                }
                break;

        default:
DefaultExit:
                return(DefWindowProc(hwnd,mMsg,wParam,lParam));
                break;
        }
    return 0L;
    }
```

DYNACURS.DEF

```
NAME    DYNACURS

EXETYPE WINDOWS

DESCRIPTION 'Dynamic Cursors (c) 1992 By Paul Yao'

CODE    MOVEABLE PRELOAD
DATA    MOVEABLE MULTIPLE PRELOAD

HEAPSIZE    512
STACKSIZE   5120

SEGMENTS
    _TEXT_DYNACURS MOVEABLE PRELOAD

EXPORTS
    DynaCursWndProc
```

DYNACURS.LNK

```
DynaCurs.obj
DynaCurs.exe/align:16/map/nod/noe/CO
nul
mlibcew libw
DynaCurs.def
```

DYNACURS.MAK

```
# Directory search paths.

INCDIR = \WINDEV\INCLUDE

# Windows version to support
# Valid pairs include:
#     (0x0300, 30)
#     (0x0310, 31)

CLVER = WINVER=0x0300
RCVER = 30

# Compiler switches for applications.

CL_APP_SHIP_ALL = -AM -c -D$(CLVER) -Gsw -I$(INCDIR) -Ow -W3 -Zp
CL_APP_DEBG_ALL = -AM -c -D$(CLVER) -Gsw -I$(INCDIR) -Od -W3 -Zpi

CL_APP_SHIP_31  = -AM -c -G2s  -I$(INCDIR) -Ow -W3 -Zp
CL_APP_DEBG_31  = -AM -c -G2s  -I$(INCDIR) -Od -W3 -Zpi

# Compiler switches for DLLs.

CL_DLL_SHIP_ALL = -AMw -c -D$(CLVER) -Gsw -I$(INCDIR) -Ow -W3 -Zp
CL_DLL_DEBG_ALL = -AMw -c -D$(CLVER) -Gsw -I$(INCDIR) -Od -W3 -Zpi

CL_DLL_SHIP_31  = -AMw -c -G2s  -I$(INCDIR) -Ow -W3 -Zp
CL_DLL_DEBG_31  = -AMw -c, -G2s  -I$(INCDIR) -Od -W3 -Zpi

# Make file primary target.

all: DynaCurs.exe

# Make file dependency targets.

DynaCurs.res: DynaCurs.rc DynaCurs.cur DynaCurs.ico
    rc -r -i$(INCDIR) DynaCurs.rc

DynaCurs.obj: DynaCurs.c
    cl $(CL_APP_SHIP_ALL) DynaCurs.c

DynaCurs.exe: DynaCurs.obj DynaCurs.def DynaCurs.res
    link @DynaCurs.lnk
    rc -$(RCVER) DynaCurs.res

DynaCurs.exe: DynaCurs.res
    rc -$(RCVER) DynaCurs.res
```

DYNACURS.RC

```
snapshot icon DynaCurs.ico
```

DYNACURS is interested in three messages: WM_CREATE, WM_DESTROY, and WM_SETCURSOR. In response to the WM_CREATE message, several objects that will be needed to support the cursor creation are created and initialized . This includes a monochrome memory bitmap, a device context to connect to the bitmap, and some dynamically allocated memory. The WM_SETCURSOR message triggers the dynamic cursor creation, which involves determining the mouse cursor location, calling GDI routines to write this location to the memory bitmaps, and then calling the CreateCursor routine to convert this data into a full-fledged cursor. In response to the third message, WM_DESTROY, DYNACURS cleans up and deallocates the objects created in response to the WM_CREATE message. To understand why these objects are needed, it will help to explore the insides of a cursor, so that you'll know what makes it tick.

How Cursors Work

A cursor is a data object consisting of two parts. Each part is a monochrome bitmap that is combined with the pixels of the display surface to create the cursor image. The first part is called the AND mask, to reflect the fact that the pixels of this bitmap are combined with the surface using the logical AND operation. The second part of the cursor is called the XOR mask, which again reflects the fact that a logical operation, XOR, is used to combine this bitmap with the display surface.

When the display driver draws a cursor, it starts by making a copy of the pixels already on the display surface. This ensures that the old image can be restored, and is key in maintaining the integrity of the image on the display surface. Once the copy has been made, the AND mask is applied to the surface, followed by the XOR mask. Through the magic of Boolean operations, this two-step process allows four different effects: black, white, display, and not-display. By "display," we mean that the cursor is transparent and allows the background to show through. By "not-display," we mean the pixels on the background are inverted. This is a rarely used combination, but it can provide some interesting effects. For example, the not-display effect might be used on a cursor in the shape of a magnifying glass to help suggest the fuzzy distortion of the lens surface. Table 16.2 has a truth table showing how pixels of the AND mask and XOR mask combine to create the four effects.

To create an all black cursor, you need to set both masks to black. An all white cursor would result from an all black AND mask and an all white XOR mask. DYNACURS creates black text on a transparent (display colored) background by combining an AND mask of black text on a white background with an all black XOR mask.

The routine that creates a dynamic cursor is CreateCursor, defined as

```
CreateCursor (hInstance, xHotSpot, yHotSpot, nWidth,
              hHeight, lpANDbitPlane, lpXORbitPlane);
```

Table 16.2 Truth Table for Cursor Creation

AND Mask	*XOR Mask*	*Cursor*
0 (Black)	0 (Black)	Black
0 (Black)	1 (White)	White
1 (White)	0 (Black)	Display
1 (White)	1 (White)	Not Display

- hInstance is the instance handle that was passed to our program as a parameter to WinMain. If you don't want to store this value in a global variable and if you have a window handle, you can call GetWindowWord like this to get the instance handle:

```
GetWindowWord (hwnd, GWW_HINSTANCE)
```

- xHotSpot is the X coordinate for the cursor hot-spot.

- yHotSpot is the Y coordinate for the cursor hot-spot.

- nWidth is the width in pixels of the cursor. If the size we provide doesn't match the size desired by the display driver, our cursor will be stretched (or shrunk). To make sure we have a match, we ask Windows to provide the size expected by the display driver. The following call provides the correct width value:

```
GetSystemMetrics (SM_CXCURSOR);
```

- nHeight is the height in pixels of the cursor. We set this value to match the size desired by the display driver by calling the following routine:

```
GetSystemMetrics (SM_CYCURSOR);
```

- lpANDbitPlane is a LPSTR (char far *) pointer to the bits that make up the AND mask.

- lpXORbitPlane is a LPSTR (char far *) pointer to the bits that make up the XOR mask.

Here is the call that DYNACURS makes to create the dynamic cursor:

```
hcr = CreateCursor (GetWindowWord (hwnd, GWW_HINSTANCE),
                    0,            // X-hotspot
                    0,            // Y-hotspot
                    cxCursor,     // width
                    cyCursor,     // height
                    lpAND,        // AND bitmask
                    lpXOR);       // XOR bitmask
```

Most of the work needed to create a custom cursor involves creating the two bit masks. Understanding what DYNACURS does to get these two bit masks requires an understanding of two topics, GDI Bitmaps and dynamic memory allocation.

Creating a GDI Bitmap

In our introduction to GDI in Chapter 6, we described a bitmap as a type of pseudo-device used primarily to store pictures. If you think of a bitmap as nothing more than a type of device, you will be half way to understanding how to use it. The other half involves understanding how to get a handle to a DC that will allow you to write on a bitmap. The following calls accomplish that:

```
hbm = CreateBitmap (cxCursor,  // width
                    cyCursor,  // height
                    1,         // planes
                    1,         // bits per pixel
                    NULL);     // initial data

hdc = GetDC (hwnd);
hdcBitmap = CreateCompatibleDC (hdc);
ReleaseDC (hwnd, hdc);

/*  Connect the bitmap to the DC.  */
hbmOld = SelectObject (hdcBitmap, hbm);
```

The first routine, `CreateBitmap`, requests GDI to allocate the memory that will be used to store the bits of our bitmap. The width and height values, `cxCursor` and `cyCursor`, come from Windows itself, which tells us, via the `GetSystemMetr-ics` routine, the size of the cursor that the current display driver expects to use:

```
/*  Find out expected size of cursor.  */
cxCursor = GetSystemMetrics (SM_CXCURSOR);
cyCursor = GetSystemMetrics (SM_CYCURSOR);
```

To build a cursor, we need a monochrome bitmap, which is the reason we set the number of planes to 1 and the bits per pixel to 1. The `CreateBitmap` routine returns a handle to a bitmap, of the type `HBITMAP`, which we store in the variable `hbm`.

By itself, a bitmap is just a block of memory. We need to create a connection to the memory, and also a set of drawing tools that will allow us to send output to the bitmap just as we send output to the display device. We need a device context. The simplest way to create a DC is to ask GDI to make a copy of an existing DC for us. This is accomplished with the following calls:

```
hdc = GetDC (hwnd);
hdcBitmap = CreateCompatibleDC (hdc);
ReleaseDC (hwnd, hdc);
```

We borrow and return a DC with a `GetDC`/`ReleaseDC` pair, and create a new DC with the call to `CreateCompatibleDC`. The value returned by `Create-CompatibleDC` is a handle to a DC. By itself, it has no connection to our bitmap (or any device, for that matter), so we need to create a connection. We do this by calling `SelectObject`:

```
hbmOld = SelectObject (hdcBitmap, hbm);
```

As you may recall, we use the `SelectObject` routine to install pens, brushes, and other drawing objects into a DC. The bitmap is more than just a drawing object—it is a full-fledged drawing surface, or, a *pseudo-device*. Once the bitmap and DC are connected, we draw to the bitmap by calling any GDI drawing routine and providing the DC handle as a parameter. When the bitmap is connected to the DC `SelectObject` provides, we save the value returned by `SelectObject` so we can later disconnect the bitmap from the DC. At cleanup time, this will make it easy to destroy both objects.

At this point, we've seen how to create a bitmap. Let's look at how DYNACURS uses the bitmap.

Using the GDI Bitmap

When DYNACURS receives a `WM_SETCURSOR` message, it draws into our bitmap to create the desired pixel patterns for the AND and XOR bit masks. The bits are then copied from the bitmap into two dynamically allocated pieces of memory, since `CreateCursor` does not read a bitmap directly. Instead, it reads the bit masks as blocks of memory. These bit masks are passed to `CreateCursor` via the two pointers that make up `CreateCursor`'s last two parameters.

The first bit mask set up is the AND mask. First, we set all the bits to white, using a routine called `PatBlt`. This GDI routine fills a rectangular area on a drawing surface using the currently selected brush. Here is the correct code:

```
SelectObject (hdcBitmap, hbrWhite);
PatBlt (hdcBitmap, 0, 0, cxCursor, cyCursor, PATCOPY);
```

Drawing the four pixel square hot-spot involves four calls to `SetPixel`:

```
SetPixel (hdcBitmap, 0, 0, 0L);
SetPixel (hdcBitmap, 0, 1, 0L);
SetPixel (hdcBitmap, 1, 0, 0L);
SetPixel (hdcBitmap, 1, 1, 0L);
```

DYNACURS then makes a call to `GetCursorPos`, which finds out the location of the mouse cursor in **screen coordinates**. Like client area coordinates, screen coordinates are pixel units. But they differ from client area coordinates in that the origin (0,0) is at the upper-left corner of the entire screen instead of the upper-left corner of the client area. To convert from one to the other, a call is made to `ScreenToClient`. Then, the coordinates are converted from integer values to a character string, and the two lines are written onto the bitmap:

```
GetCursorPos (&pt);
ScreenToClient (hwnd, &pt);

cc1 = wsprintf (acLine1,"%d", pt.x);
cc2 = wsprintf (acLine2,"%d", pt.y);

/*  Write coordinates onto bitmap.  */
TextOut (hdcBitmap, 3, 0, acLine1, cc1);
TextOut (hdcBitmap, 3, cyCursor/2, acLine2, cc2);
```

At this point, the bitmap contains the image we want to use for the AND mask on the cursor. But we have to ask GDI to make a copy of the bits in a form that `CreateCursor` will accept. This is the job of the `GetBitmapBits` routine, which is defined:

```
DWORD GetBitmapBits (hBitmap, dwCount, lpBits)
```

- `hBitmap` is a handle to a bitmap.
- `dwCount` is a `DWORD` value for the size of the storage area.
- `lpBits` is a char far * (`LPSTR`) flag that points to the data area to hold the bits.

The following line of code from DYNACURS copies the bits from the bitmap into a block of dynamically allocated memory, suitable for passing to `CreateCursor`:

```
GetBitmapBits (hbm, (DWORD)cbSize, lpAND);
```

The creation of the XOR bit mask is similar, but much simpler. The `PatBlt` routine is called to set every pixel in the bitmap to black. Once this is done, a call is made to `GetBitmapBits` to copy the bits from the bitmap to a piece of dynamically allocated memory. To fully understand how DYNACURS works, we need to explore further the allocation and use of dynamically allocated memory.

Dynamically Allocating Memory

Dynamically allocated memory is necessary because there is no way to anticipate the amount of memory required to hold the bits of a cursor. For example, here are the cursor sizes and memory requirements for some of today's popular display adapters:

Display Adapter	*Cusor Size*	*Memory Required*
CGA	32 x 16	64 bytes
EGA/VGA	32 x 32	128 bytes
8514/a	32 x 32	512 bytes

New display adapters may come along tomorrow that require larger blocks of memory to store the AND and XOR bit masks, so, to be safe, we depend upon dynamic memory allocation to provide the memory we need.

If you've done a lot of C language programming, you're probably familiar with `malloc`, the C-runtime library routine which dynamically allocates memory. For reasons we'll describe in Chapter 18, Windows programmers don't use this routine. Instead they will rely on two sets of memory allocating routines built into Windows. Here are the routines used by DYNACURS:

Routine Name	Description
GlobalAlloc	Allocates a block (segment) of memory.
GlobalLock	Locks the memory in place and provides a far pointer.
GlobalUnlock	Unlocks the memory to allow it to move.
GlobalFree	Deallocates a block of memory.

To determine the amount of memory that is required, we start by asking Windows for the cursor size required by the display adapter:

```
cxCursor = GetSystemMetrics (SM_CXCURSOR);
cyCursor = GetSystemMetrics (SM_CYCURSOR);
```

Since `cxCursor` is the width in pixels and `cyCursor` is the height in pixels, we can get the total size in bytes necessary to store this object by dividing `cxCursor` by eight and then multiplying by `cyCursor`, like this:

```
cbSize = (cxCursor/8) * cyCursor;
```

We allocate two blocks of memory: one for the AND mask and one for the XOR mask using the `GlobalAlloc` routine, as shown here:

```
hmemAND = GlobalAlloc (GMEM_MOVEABLE,   // flags
                       (DWORD)cbSize); // size
hmemXOR = GlobalAlloc (GMEM_MOVEABLE,   // flags
                       (DWORD)cbSize); // size
```

The `GMEM_MOVEABLE` flag tells Windows that it can move the object when we aren't using it. This is necessary because Windows runs in the real mode of the Intel-86 family of CPUs, which doesn't provide any hardware assistance to manage memory. So, Windows programs must manage memory in a way that cooperates with Windows and with other Windows programs. The `GMEM_MOVEABLE` flag offers a reasonable compromise between usefulness and cooperativeness. We'll explore the use of this and other flags more fully in Chapter 18.

`GlobalAlloc` returns a handle to the memory block, which serves to identify a block of memory, although it does not tell us where movable memory is located. To find that out, we must lock the memory down using the `GlobalLock` routine. This routine

returns a far pointer to the memory block, which is how we can access it. GlobalL-
ock is defined:

```
LPSTR GlobalLock (hMem)
```

- hMem is a handle to a global memory object, allocated with the GlobalAlloc
  routine.

Here are the lines of code from DYNACURS that lock the memory so it can be accessed.
Notice that we check the return value to make sure that we have retrieved a valid pointer.
This is a good habit to get into, since a NULL pointer can cause problems, depending on
Windows' operating mode. In real mode, it allows you to trash the interrupt vectors
located at the very low end of memory. In protected mode, it causes a protection
violation which results in the termination of your program. Neither alternative is attractive, but it is quick and easy to avoid these problems.

```
lpAND = GlobalLock (hmemAND);
if (lpAND == NULL) goto DefaultExit;

lpXOR = GlobalLock (hmemXOR);
if (lpXOR == NULL) goto DefaultExit;
```

After we are done using a block of dynamically allocated memory, we unlock the
memory objects by calling GlobalUnlock. The primary reason we do this is to allow
our programs to behave nicely when Windows is running in real mode:

```
GlobalUnlock (hmemAND);
GlobalUnlock (hmemXOR);
```

The final issue to be addressed is the freeing of our memory objects when
DYNACURS gets a WM_DESTROY message. That is the job of the GlobalFree
routine. Windows is smart enough to reclaim unused memory when a program exits, but
we think it's a good programming practice to clean up after yourself. After all, someone
may later use your code as part of a larger programming project, and not make sure that
you have cleaned up properly. Since GDI objects do not automatically get cleaned up,
you must make sure to destroy the GDI objects that you have created. Here is how
DYNACURS cleans up the memory, the leftover cursor, and GDI objects that it created:

```
...
case WM_DESTROY:
     SelectObject (hdcBitmap, hbmOld);
     DeleteDC (hdcBitmap);
     DeleteObject (hbm);
     DestroyCursor(hcr);
     GlobalFree (hmemAND);
     GlobalFree (hmemXOR);
     PostQuitMessage(0);  /*  Say good-bye Gracie.  */
     break;
```

While creating a dynamic cursor takes a lot of work, it provides a way to create
custom cursors at run time. You might create a cursor in the shape of a clock face or a

timer to count down a lengthy operation. You can even let users define their own private, custom cursors. Any cursor you create can be used as an icon as well, since the two user-interface objects share the exact same format.

We're going to step back a moment and look at a cursor created with the CreateCursor routine that doesn't involve GDI bitmaps or dynamically allocated memory. If you found the earlier example to be somewhat long and involved, this might help you appreciate exactly what is happening when a cursor is created on the fly.

A Simpler Dynamic Cursor

A simpler way to create a dynamic cursor involves figuring out the layout of the AND mask and XOR mask ahead of time by hand, and passing a pointer to these masks to the CreateCursor routine. A serious drawback to this approach is that it is very device-dependent. However, it illustrates the creation of a dynamic cursor in a somewhat simpler fashion that may help clarify exactly what was happening in our last example. Figure 16.11 shows our dynamic cursor, which is in the shape of a rocket.

Figure 16.11 Another dynamic cursor

Here is the window procedure of the program that created this:

```
/*-------------------------------------------------------------*\
|            Window Procedure:  MinWndProc.                     |
\*-------------------------------------------------------------*/
LRESULT  CALLBACK  MinWndProc  (HWND    hwnd,
                                UINT    wMsg,
                                WPARAM  wParam,
                                LPARAM  lParam)

    {
    static char acAND[] = {0xff, 0xff, 0xff, 0xff,   // Scan 1
                           0xff, 0xfe, 0x3f, 0xff,   // Scan 2
                           0xff, 0xfc, 0x1f, 0xff,   // Scan 3
                           0xff, 0xfc, 0x9f, 0xff,   // Scan 4
                           0xff, 0xf8, 0x8f, 0xff,   // Scan 5
                           0xff, 0xf9, 0xcf, 0xff,   // Scan 6
                           0xff, 0xf1, 0xc7, 0xff,   // Scan 7
```

```
                        0xff, 0xf3, 0xe7, 0xff,    // Scan 8
                        0xff, 0xe3, 0xe3, 0xff,    // Scan 9
                        0xff, 0xe7, 0xf3, 0xff,    // Scan 10
                        0xff, 0xc0, 0x01, 0xff,    // Scan 11
                        0xff, 0xcf, 0xf9, 0xff,    // Scan 12
                        0xff, 0xca, 0x89, 0xff,    // Scan 13
                        0xff, 0xca, 0x89, 0xff,    // Scan 14
                        0xff, 0xca, 0xb9, 0xff,    // Scan 15
                        0xff, 0xca, 0x89, 0xff,    // Scan 16
                        0xff, 0xca, 0x89, 0xff,    // Scan 17
                        0xff, 0xca, 0xe9, 0xff,    // Scan 18
                        0xff, 0xc8, 0x89, 0xff,    // Scan 19
                        0xff, 0xc8, 0x89, 0xff,    // Scan 20
                        0xff, 0xcf, 0xf9, 0xff,    // Scan 21
                        0xff, 0xcf, 0xf9, 0xff,    // Scan 22
                        0xff, 0xcf, 0xf9, 0xff,    // Scan 23
                        0xff, 0xcf, 0xf9, 0xff,    // Scan 24
                        0xfe, 0x00, 0x00, 0x3f,    // Scan 25
                        0xfe, 0x00, 0x00, 0x3f,    // Scan 26
                        0xfe, 0x4f, 0xf9, 0x3f,    // Scan 27
                        0xfe, 0x4d, 0x59, 0x3f,    // Scan 28
                        0xfe, 0x0d, 0x58, 0x3f,    // Scan 29
                        0xfe, 0x0d, 0x58, 0x3f,    // Scan 30
                        0xff, 0xfd, 0x5f, 0xff,    // Scan 31
                        0xff, 0xf1, 0xc7, 0xff};   // Scan 32

static char acXOR[] ={0, 0, 0, 0, 0, 0, 0, 0,
                      0, 0, 0, 0, 0, 0, 0, 0,
                      0, 0, 0, 0, 0, 0, 0, 0,
                      0, 0, 0, 0, 0, 0, 0, 0,
                      0, 0, 0, 0, 0, 0, 0, 0,
                      0, 0, 0, 0, 0, 0, 0, 0,
                      0, 0, 0, 0, 0, 0, 0, 0,
                      0, 0, 0, 0, 0, 0, 0, 0,
                      0, 0, 0, 0, 0, 0, 0, 0,
                      0, 0, 0, 0, 0, 0, 0, 0,
                      0, 0, 0, 0, 0, 0, 0, 0,
                      0, 0, 0, 0, 0, 0, 0, 0,
                      0, 0, 0, 0, 0, 0, 0, 0,
                      0, 0, 0, 0, 0, 0, 0, 0,
                      0, 0, 0, 0, 0, 0, 0, 0,
                      0, 0, 0, 0, 0, 0, 0, 0};

static HCURSOR hcr;

switch (wMsg)
    {
    case WM_CREATE:
        hcr = CreateCursor (
            GetWindowWord (hwnd, GWW_HINSTANCE),
```

```
                0,              // X-hotspot
                0,              // Y-hotspot
                32,             // width
                32,             // height
                acAND,          // AND bitmask
                acXOR);         // XOR bitmask
        break;

    case WM_DESTROY:
        PostQuitMessage(0);
        break;

    case WM_SETCURSOR:
        if (LOWORD(lParam) == HTCLIENT)
            SetCursor (hcr);
        else
            return(DefWindowProc(hwnd,wMsg,wParam,lParam));
        break;

    default:
        return(DefWindowProc(hwnd,wMsg,wParam,lParam));
        break;
    }
    return 0L;
    }
```

While this shows a simple way to create a dynamic cursor, there are several problems. First, the cursor is quite device-dependent. This cursor works properly with EGA and VGA display adapters, both of which use a 32x32 bit cursor, but will not work on devices which call for a different size. In addition, this is not a very dynamic cursor. You would be better off creating a regular static cursor. What this does do, we hope, is provide a simpler framework for understanding the way that dynamic cursor creation works.

This concludes our look at how a Windows program receives keyboard and mouse input from the user. In the next section, we'll be looking at operating systems considerations in a Windows program: memory management and dynamic linking.

PART VI

OPERATING SYSTEM CONSIDERATIONS

17

Memory, Part I: System Memory Management

To fully appreciate how Windows manages memory, you need to look at the hardware on which Windows runs: the Intel-86 family of CPUs. Among the members of this family are the 8086, 8088, 80186, 80188, 80286, 80386 (SX and DX), and the 80486 (SX and DX) microprocessors. Windows can run on all these processors because Intel designed each new CPU with an eye toward creating a migration path from the older processors. As advanced capabilities were introduced in new processors, doors were always left open to help migrate software from older chips.

From the start, Windows was built with the more advanced chips in mind. The architect of memory management in Windows 1.x was Steve Wood, a former Yale graduate student who started working for Microsoft in June of 1983. He laid the foundation for Windows' memory management, which he modeled after the Protected Mode of the Intel 286 processor. In those days, Microsoft was contemplating a successor to MS-DOS, and planned for Windows to run with the new operating system. Of course, today we know that two operating systems are competing to take over as king of the operating system hill: OS/2 and Windows NT. Both will run Windows 3.x applications—that is, applications written to the 16-Bit Windows API, also known as **WIN16**. In addition, Windows NT will provide a 32-bit superset of that API, known as the 32-Bit Windows API or **WIN32** for short.

Each subsequent version of Windows built on the original design to improve memory use. The architect of Windows' memory management for Windows 2.x and 3.x, David Weise, was also on the design team for the EMS 4.0 Memory Specification. This allowed him to build EMS support into Windows 2.x and to continue that support in Real Mode Windows 3.0.

In Windows 3.1, Microsoft has chosen to drop support for Real Mode. The reasons are quite practical: fewer than 3 percent of the users surveyed use Real Mode. In addition, it's very difficult to debug Real Mode applications. An executive at one software firm reportedly compared debugging Windows applications with "nailing jelly to a wall." The disappearance of Real Mode is a very positive step for Windows, and will simplify your development and testing efforts.

In this chapter, we will discuss all of Windows' operating modes: past, present, and future. First, we'll cover (the now defunct) Real Mode, because familiarity with it will help you understand some of Windows' memory management quirks (like the need to lock objects). Next, we'll discuss Windows 3.1's two operating modes, Standard Mode and Enhanced Mode. Finally, we'll touch on a future operating mode, known as **NT Mode**.

Our emphasis will be on Windows' memory, from the point of view of the *operating system*. In the next chapter, we'll continue the topic of memory management from the point of view of how *programs* manage memory. Let's start our discussion by getting down to bare metal: Let's start by looking at the processors.

The Intel-86 Family of Processors

Our discussion is limited to the processors representing the three memory modes in which Windows operates: the 8088, 80286, and 80386. These possess the most widely used chips and most significant advances in *capabilities* for this processor family. (This is not to say, of course, that the 80486—or the rumored future 80586—does *not* represent a significant advance.)

The Physical Address Space

An important aspect of any microprocessor is the maximum amount of accessible memory—that is, the size of its physical address space. One way to determine this is to count the number of memory address lines that connect the processor to system memory. That number raised to a power of 2 is the size of the address space. For example, the 8088 has 20 address lines, which translates into a 2^{20} or 1 megabyte (1,048,576 bytes) address space. With 24 address lines, the 80286 can address 2^{24} or 16 megabytes (16,777,216 bytes) of physical RAM. Finally, the 80386, with its 32 address lines, can use up to 2^{32} or 4 gigabytes (4,294,967,296 bytes) of system memory.

Every byte of memory in the system has its own unique physical address, starting at zero up to n-1 for a system with n bytes of memory. For example, the 8088 has a memory address range from 0 to 1,048,575. In this regard, the Intel-86 family of processors is like any other processor: The CPU uses the physical address to identify memory locations. Software, however, doesn't use a physical address; instead, logical addresses are translated by the CPU into a physical address. The Intel-86 processor family provides a logical address space that uses a segmented addressing scheme.

Segmented Memory

All members of the Intel-86 family use segmented memory addressing. If you are new to this processor family, it may help to think about addresses used for buildings in the physical world. The Prime Minister of Great Britain, for example, lives at Number 10 Downing Street; the President of the United States lives at 1600 Pennsylvania Avenue. A two-part *logical* address gives each program the freedom to divide its address space into many small "streets" or *segments*, each of which can hold from one to 65,535 "houses" or *bytes*. If we push the analogy further, this approach permits operating system software to give each program its own "city"—that is, its own private address space.

To programmers unaccustomed to the Intel-86 family of processors, segmented addressing can be both confusing and frustrating. For experienced MS-DOS and OS/2 programmers, segmented addressing will be very familiar, although you should pay attention to the particular way that Windows operates in this environment. A key benefit of segmented addressing is software migration. This architecture was first selected by Intel to allow software to migrate from the older 8-bit 8080 processor to the first member of the Intel-86 family, the 8086. The continued adoption of this addressing scheme has allowed MS-DOS to run on all members of the Intel-86 family when they run in Real Mode. It is also one reason that MS-DOS programs can run under the various Intel-86 based operating systems, like Microsoft Windows, OS/2, and UNIX. Finally, it gives properly written Windows programs a migration path from the earlier versions of Windows to the Protected Mode operation of Windows 3.x, and on to future versions.

From the point of view of software development, segmented addressing can help program debugging. A program can be divided into multiple code and data segments to create "fire-walls" between different parts of an application. Fire-walls prevent bad memory references in one part of an application from contaminating the data in another part of the application, thereby making programs easier to debug. In Protected Mode, the processor complains loudly when an invalid segment reference is made, or when a program tries to read or write beyond the end of a segment.

Finally, a benefit of segmented programs is that they provide the operating system with hints about the **working sets** of a program. These hints can result in improved performance and lower memory requirements. A working set is a division of a program that performs a task or a set of tasks for the user. Since Windows incorporates an overlay facility called **dynamic linking**, only *part* of a program has to be present in memory at any given moment. If each working set in a program is a cleanly defined set of code segments, memory use is optimized. In a low-memory situation, Windows discards code segments from the current working set *last*. In this way, a program with well-defined working sets—what Windows programmers call "well-tuned"—will have lower memory requirements than the same program that hasn't been tuned. The latter program will slow down in a low-memory situation, since Windows will have to continually re-read previously discarded code segments from disk: a situation called **disk-thrashing**.

Microsoft includes a swap-tuning utility with the Windows Software Development Kit to help determine the working sets of a program. The information generated by this facility will help you restructure your program to optimize code structure and memory use. The importance of tuning an application's working sets has inspired one developer, Chris Suver, to build a high-end application tuning tool called—appropriately enough—**The Segmentor**. Chris' company in Seattle, Washington is MicroQuill. If you're developing an application for which performance is important, you should look into this tool. In the next chapter, we'll discuss some of the mechanics of segmenting a Windows program.

Microsoft's 32-Bit Windows API, which should be available in 1992, will provide developers with access to the Windows API without having to worry about segmented addressing. When writing to this API, you'll have access to a non-segmented, "flat" 32-bit address space. Although no product with this API has officially started shipping, the Win32 API will see several incarnations: a thirty-two bit layer on top of existing Windows 3.1 (also known as Win32s), the native API for the new Windows NT operating system, and a future, MS-DOS based rendition of Windows with the complete Win32 API.

Since every member of the Intel-86 family uses a segmented addressing scheme, how can Win32, Windows NT, or *any* future version of Windows provide a flat, 32-bit address space? The younger members of this family—from the 80386 onward—have built in support for using 32-bit offsets. Therefore, when running Win32, a single segment will be set up to address the entire 32-bit address space. Even though segmented addressing will still be used by the processor, it can effectively be ignored by application software.

As of this writing, the 32-bit API is still a ways off. Until then, if you're interested in creating Windows applications, you have to work with the segmented, Win16 API. Let's take a closer look at the segmented physical to logical address translation process.

The Logical Address

While a CPU uses a *physical address* to read and write in physical memory, programmers use a higher level abstraction called a **logical address**. It's the job of the CPU to translate logical addresses into physical addresses to access locations in the physical address space. This is illustrated in Figure 17.1.

The translation process that takes place in the CPU might be very simple or very involved, depending on the current operating mode of the CPU. In *Real Mode*, for example, simple bit shifting and addition is involved. In the various *Protected Modes*, however, the CPU uses a lookup table to determine how to map a logical address into a physical address. This lookup table allows the operating system to move memory objects so it can minimize fragmentation of the physical address space. The operating system can even play tricks, like writing memory to disk to implement virtual memory. If you are familiar with the operation of OS/2 version 1.x, you know that its virtual memory manager writes segments to disk. Finally, the higher end 80386 and 80486 chips have special hardware that, when enabled, provides an additional level of indirection that divides memory into four K-byte pages. This paging mechanism is particularly useful in creating a very efficient virtual memory system, which is how the Windows memory manager implements virtual memory in 386-Enhanced Mode (also known as Enhanced Mode).

In a moment, we will look more closely at all of Windows' operating modes. But first, let's look at the pieces that make up a logical address. As we've said, every processor in the Intel-86 family uses a two-part logical address, made up of a **segment identifier** and an **offset**.

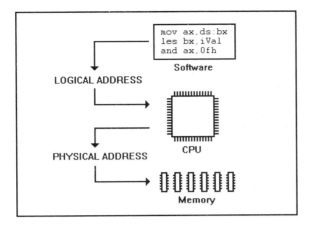

```
mov ax,ds:bx
les bx,iVal
and ax,0fh
```
Software

LOGICAL ADDRESS

CPU

PHYSICAL ADDRESS

Memory

Figure 17.1 The Translation of a logical address to a physical address

The role of the segment identifier is to identify a memory segment of interest. This 16-bit value is the "street name." In the logical-to-physical address translation process, it answers the question "where in the world is the segment?" The answer might be within the physical address space of the CPU, or, in a virtual memory system, swapped out to disk.

The offset indicates the distance from the start of the segment to the specific byte address with which we wish to work. It is the house number. Alternatively, think of a segment as an array and the offset as an array index. In any event, both segment identifier and offset are used together to address specific bytes in system memory.

With this introduction to the basics of memory addressing for the Intel-86 family, let's look at how the Intel-86 family supports all of Windows' operating modes: Real Mode, Standard Mode, Enhanced Mode, and NT Mode. To check the current mode, a user can look at the About box in the Program Manager. From a program, you can find this out by calling the GetWinFlags routine. Also, you can manually start the different modes (except NT mode) using one of the following switches on the Windows' command line, providing you have the proper hardware setup:

Mode	*Windows Command Line*	*Comment*
Real	C> win /r	Any Intel-86 processor with 640K of RAM (Windows 3.0 only).
Standard	C> win /2	Requires 80286 or 80386 CPU with 640K plus 192K extended memory and the HIMEM.SYS (or equivalent) driver.
Enhanced	C> win /3	Requires 80386 CPU with 640K plus 1 megabyte extended memory and the HIMEM.SYS (or equivalent) driver.

Figure 17.2   Real mode address calculation

Real Mode Operation

While all members of the Intel-86 family can operate efficiently in Real Mode, it is usually associated with the oldest members of this family, the 8086 and 8088. With 20 address lines, these chips have a one-megabyte address space. To maintain complete compatibility, the other processors adopt this same limit when operating in Real Mode.

Real Mode gets its name from the fact that a logical address directly translates to a *real* physical address. To convert a logical address to the physical address, the CPU starts by shifting the 16-bit segment value left by four bits to create a 20-bit value. To this, it adds the 16-bit offset. Figure 17.2 illustrates this process.

Because the segment value is shifted left by four bits, which effectively multiplies it by 16, the smallest segment in Real Mode is 16 bytes. Intel calls this a **paragraph**. Because of the way Windows operates in Real Mode, the granularity of segments is actually two paragraphs, or 32 bytes. The other modes adopt this granularity to enhance compatibility between the modes. Another way to visualize the logical-to-physical address conversion of Real Mode is shown in Figure 17.3.

The Real Mode Address Space

Since Windows runs as an extension to MS-DOS, it inherits the DOS environment. In memory terms, this means the one-megabyte address space of Real Mode, divided as depicted in Figure 17.4.

In this figure, the dotted lines in the 640K address space are meant to suggest that the size of each piece can vary. MS-DOS, its device drivers, and terminate-and-stay-resident (TSR) programs get first crack at the lowest end of memory. When Windows starts up, it requires a minimum of 200K or so for its device drivers, resident fonts, and the fixed code and data used by the Windows' core components: KERNEL, USER, and GDI. The space marked "application area" is used for both Windows programs and for the discardable parts of Windows over and above Windows' minimum working set.

The well-publicized "640K Limit" on MS-DOS applications results from the design of the DOS address space, which reserves the area between 640K and 1024K for system

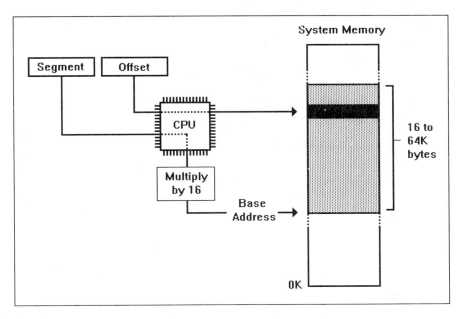

Figure 17.3 Logical-to-physical address conversion in Real Mode

uses: video adapter cards, ROM, and other uses. Since this memory area is occupied by hardware, Windows can't do anything to make it available for its own use, except in Real Mode, when it is used for EMS support.

On 80286 and 80386 CPUs, Windows gets an extra 64 Kbytes of memory from the **High Memory Area** (HMA), located just above the one-megabyte address line, when an XMS (eXtended Memory Specification) driver, such as HIMEM.SYS, is installed. This is the beginning of the extended memory area, usually only available in Protected Mode. This memory is available in Real Mode through tricks that an XMS driver plays.

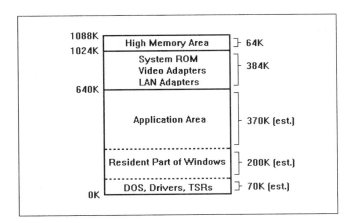

Figure 17.4 The real mode address space

Above the HMA, Real Mode Windows has other uses for extended memory. The SMARTDRV disk-caching device driver, for example, can be set up to optimize disk transfer operations. And the RAMDRIVE driver emulates a disk drive in RAM, for fast temporary files. In addition, the Windows Memory Manager uses extra extended memory to store code segments that would otherwise be discarded. Thus, if you are running in Real Mode, it's a good idea to leave about 256K or so of extended RAM unallocated. Windows will put this memory to good use to provide better performance.

In Real Mode, the amount of memory available to a Windows program varies from 300K to 450K, depending on the amount of space taken up by MS-DOS device drivers, and the availability of the high memory area. While this may seem a very small amount of memory, Windows' dynamic linking facility allows a program 10 times this size (or *larger*) to run. While such an arrangement might be sluggish, at least such a program *can* run. Hopefully, such a situation will encourage a hardware upgrade.

Real Mode and Windows

Prior to Windows 3.0, Windows ran exclusively in Real Mode, because the installed base of microcomputers—computers based on the Intel 8088 and 8086 CPUs—could only be run in Real Mode. Windows' memory manager was first built for Real Mode, but was designed with the Protected Modes of the higher-end chips in mind. The architecture of the Windows memory manager is a key factor in the ability of Windows 3.0 to operate in its various modes.

Real Mode addressing is fast and efficient, since there is very little overhead in translating logical addresses to physical addresses. To seasoned DOS programmers, it provides an open, accessible environment for programming. And it is—until you try creating a multitasking operating system.

An operating system manages and distributes resources. A resource might be processor time, disk space, or memory. The problem with Real Mode addressing is that it makes it very difficult for an operating system to manage memory. It's easy enough to allocate memory to a program—the operating system carves off a piece of system memory and assigns it to a program. But great care must be taken in the *way* memory is assigned. If a Real Mode operating system assigns memory by providing an address, it is almost impossible for the operating system to move that block of memory. And yet, memory movement is precisely what an operating system must do to avoid the problems associated with memory fragmentation. To circumvent this problem, Real Mode Windows uses a handle-based approach to allocating memory.

Movable Memory

When a block of memory is allocated, a program does not receive an addresss, but a handle that identifies the memory. Like the DC and window handles encountered previously, a memory handle has no meaning except to the subsystem that issued the handle. Like a claim check at a restaurant coat room, a memory handle gets traded for an address of the memory. The process of "trading-in" a handle is referred to as "locking" a memory object. When a memory object is locked, Windows provides a pointer to the memory. In addition, the memory manager increments the lock count. Windows refrains from moving objects which have a lock count greater than zero. All other times, the Windows Memory Manager is free to move and compact system memory to reduce fragmentation. In coat room terms, your hat and coat can be moved to another room or even to another floor when the main coat room gets too crowded.

A handle-based, movable memory system helps the Windows' memory manager to avoid memory loss due to fragmentation. But another mechanism is needed to deal with the problem of running out of physical memory: a situation sometimes referred to as "memory overcommit." In the world of mainframe computers, virtual memory systems solve this problem by copying portions of memory to disk. But this requires fast disks and, in the best of cases, hardware support for memory management. When Windows was first being created, neither was available on the hardware for which Windows was targeted.

The target computer for the first version of Windows was a 4.77 MHz 8088-based system with 256K of RAM and two floppy diskette drives. In those days (circa 1983), hard disks were rare, and even the lowly 80286-based IBM PC/AT had not yet been introduced. Given the low power of this target machine, even if the 8088 had any sophisticated memory management capabilities (which it doesn't), the two floppy drives of the target system could provide neither fast enough response nor sufficient capacity for a virtual memory system. Instead, Microsoft implemented what might be called a "poor man's" virtual memory system: dynamic linking. This facility depends on the second type of memory to be discussed: discardable memory.

Discardable Memory

To help ease the memory crunch, the Windows memory manager can do more than just move memory around. If it needs to, it can **discard** objects from memory. A discarded object is purged from the system and its location overwritten by whatever objects are allocated in its place. The most obvious type use of discardable memory is for code. In most cases, code is not modified, which means even if we throw away a code segment we can always recover it by re-reading the executable file.

Discardable, read-on-demand code is the basis of Windows' dynamic link mechanism. This very flexible mechanism allows programs to run in a smaller address space than would otherwise be required. In some ways, this mechanism has a lot in common with memory overlay facilities used by some MS-DOS programs, and by some older mainframe systems. The difference between Windows' dynamic linking and overlays is that dynamic linking is transparent to the application programmer. Overlays, on the other hand, typically must be designed with great care to avoid a deadlock—a situation in which the system must halt because it cannot read in the next overlay. Windows dynamic link mechanism does the work to ensure that deadlocks do not occur.

Resources are another type of object commonly placed into discardable memory objects. To the Windows Memory Manager, a resource is a block of read-only data. When needed, a resource is read from disk. Later, when system memory gets crowded, the Memory Manager can discard the resource to allow room for other objects.

Windows has several types of built-in resources. Some support the user interface—menu templates, dialog box templates, icons, and cursors. Others store GDI objects, like fonts and bitmaps. Beyond these, you can create custom resources for private data types. Like discardable code, discardable resources give the Windows memory manager the freedom to purge objects that might otherwise clog system memory.

Thus far, we've looked at two types of memory objects that can be allocated in Windows: movable and discardable. Both types allow a flexible, dynamic memory management system to be implemented on top of the relatively inflexible addressing of Real Mode. Windows supports a third type of memory—fixed memory—which application programmers should avoid. However, it is important for the well-being and overall efficient operation of certain parts of the system.

Fixed Memory

While movable and discardable memory objects are necessary for the Memory Manager to meet the demands of Windows' multitasking, there are situations requiring memory that won't be moved or discarded. For example, an interrupt-handler will require a fixed location since it must always be ready to receive an interrupt. For such uses, the Windows memory manager allows the allocation of fixed segments.

Programmers who wrote to Real Mode Windows had to avoid creating fixed memory objects. The risk was that system memory would get clogged. In the protected modes of Windows 3.1, quite a few things change. For one thing, the difference between fixed and moveable objects has disappeared. Both types of objects can move in the physical address space, yet their logical addresses remain unchanged. This is due to the magic of the protected mode CPU. At the same time, there are more options for immobilizing segments in the physical address space, and for tagging them as untouchable by the virtual memory manager's page swapper. We'll cover both types in the next chapter.

EMS and Real Mode Windows

Microsoft's second major revision of Windows, version 2.x, introduced support for EMS memory, which is memory made available according to the **expanded memory specification**. EMS describes a software interface for bank-switching memory to increase the total amount of memory that MS-DOS programs can access. Since Windows runs on top of DOS, Windows is able to take advantage of EMS. On the one hand, Windows programs can communicate directly with the expanded memory manager to allocate pages just like their MS-DOS counterparts. On the other hand, Real Mode Windows programs don't do anything special to benefit from the presence of EMS memory. Instead, the Windows Memory Manager does all the work behind the scenes to increase total available system memory.

EMS does not increase the size of the hardware address space. Instead, it switches extra memory into unused parts of the MS-DOS address space. In this way, EMS allows up to 32 additional megabytes of memory to be accessible in the MS-DOS address space. At first glance, this seems to be enough memory to satisfy the needs of *any* MS-DOS or Windows program. But the gobs of memory provided by EMS are not *simultaneously* accessible, which makes EMS only a limited solution to the memory crunch.

While you'll see references to EMS memory, it's primarily of interest to DOS programs. If you're interested in learning more about Windows' use of EMS memory, see the accompanying boxed discussion.

▼ **Windows' Use of EMS Memory**

EMS describes a bank-switching method for making more memory available in the Real Mode address space. It works by banking-in a section of memory into an otherwise unused portion of the Real Mode 1-megabyte address space. For example, in one configuration, a 64K memory window serves as the only access point for all of the memory on an EMS card. This memory window is called the **EMS page frame**. If a program wanted to access more than 64K of EMS memory at a time, it would have to decide which EMS pages to use and which pages to ignore. With its tiny memory window, EMS cannot be a general-purpose memory management solution, but there is no denying that it has helped ease the memory shortage of Real Mode systems. Figure 17.5 illustrates the relationship of the Real Mode address space to EMS memory pages.

Windows' use of EMS is transparent to Windows programs. When a Windows program starts running, the program receives a private EMS bank. The program is guaranteed to have private use of this memory, free from competition with other programs. As Windows' multitasking switcher lets other programs run, it communicates with the EMS memory manager to map the correct EMS bank into the EMS page frame. The net result is reduced competition for memory between different programs, more total available memory, and better overall performance. The improved performance comes from postponing low-memory situations, when code must be discarded and reread from disk.

When running in Real Mode, Windows 3.0 allocates EMS memory for programs in the same way that Windows 2.x did. In its other operating modes, Windows ignores EMS memory. That is, Windows does not use EMS memory for Windows programs in Standard Mode or Enhanced Mode, nor will it be used by NT Mode. These other modes have access to extended memory, which doesn't suffer the same shortcomings of EMS memory. Extended memory, after all, is accessible without bank-switching.

Under Windows 2.x, a program could ask Windows to step aside so the program can directly allocate and manage its own EMS memory. This capability is also available in Windows 3.0. Programs that wish to do this must have the -l switch set when the resource compiler is run (rc.exe) so the proper flag gets set in the program's executable file.

Figure 17.5   EMS lets real-mode programs peek at a larger address space

EMS support can be provided in several ways. Windows comes with an EMS driver called EMM386.SYS for systems with an 80386 processor. However, this is not required when running in Enhanced Mode, since this mode has built-in EMS support for both Windows programs and MS-DOS programs run under Windows. Another way in which EMS can be made available is with the use of a dedicated EMS card and at least a version 4.0 driver. Finally, EMS support can be provided using various software emulations.

Windows programs only benefit from the presence of EMS when running in Real Mode. In Real Mode, bank-switched memory increases the size of the total address space, but only one bank of memory is available at a time. In its other operating modes, Windows uses extended memory, which provides the same amount of extra memory *without* the need for bank-switching. For this reason, Windows 3.0 ignores EMS when running in either of the two Protected Modes. There is no question, however, that EMS support provided an important improvement for Windows 2.x, and that it can benefit users who need to run Windows 3.0 in Real Mode.

EMS is important because it represents the first time that Windows' memory management supported the concept of a private address space for application programs. A private address space helps protect applications from the misbehavior of other applications, since a private address space can only be accessed by its owner. In Windows 3.0 Protected Mode, the idea of a private address space is also starting to be implemented with the memory protection that is provided. Future versions of Windows will continue to enhance and enforce the concept of private address spaces to help protect programs from the problems arising when memory addressing errors occur. For the present, in both Standard Mode and Enhanced Mode, Windows takes advantage of the memory protection features of the 80286 and higher processors. Let's take a look at those two modes and the way they operate.

Standard and Enhanced Mode

As mentioned earlier, when Windows' memory management system was first being designed, it was with an eye toward someday moving Windows to the Protected Modes of the Intel-86 family. With Windows 3.0, this vision was realized in not one but *two* operating modes: Windows Standard Mode and Enhanced Mode. The future NT mode moves the Windows API away from the segmented addressing of the Intel-86 architecture into a portable, 32-bit API running on 32-bit (and greater) processors.

Standard Mode gives Windows the benefits of Protected Mode on the 80286 and 80386 processors. In this mode, Windows programs get a physical address space that breaks the one-megabyte boundary of Real Mode and can be as large as 16 megabytes. Unlike the bank-switched memory of EMS, in Protected Mode the additional memory is **extended memory**—that is, the memory is a directly addressable extension to the Real Mode address space. Protected Mode provides special memory management support that is not available in Real Mode. This support includes the enforcement of memory access rules that help preserve the integrity of each program, of each program's data, and of the system itself.

In Enhanced Mode, Windows gets all the benefits of Standard Mode, plus an even larger address space. When running in this mode, don't be alarmed when the Program Manager tells you that the system has more *free* memory than you have RAM installed in your system. During the development of Windows, someone complained about this problem in a bug report, and was told: *"Welcome to the world of virtual memory!"*

The virtual memory of Enhanced Mode is provided by a 386 control program, WIN386.EXE, which works with the memory paging support built into the 80386 processor. In Windows 3.0, the address space can grow up to four times the available physical memory. For example, five megabytes of physical memory can support a virtual address space of 20 megabytes. And 16 megabytes of RAM can support a 64-megabyte virtual memory address space. These examples assume, of course, that there is enough disk space for the swap file. This is the default setting in Windows 3.1 as well, although you can set a switch in SYSTEM.INI to use a different multiplier.

Protected Mode

The term *Protected Mode* refers to a state of the processor in which certain rules are enforced when memory is addressed. These rules minimize the risk that a program will overwrite—either accidentally or intentionally—memory that doesn't belong to it. A program that violates these rules is subject to a serious penalty: It is terminated.

This harsh treatment contrasts sharply with the way a similar action is treated in Real Mode. For example, it's quite common for a MS-DOS program to busy itself poking around the MS-DOS data areas, installing private interrupt handlers, and in general making itself at home. Since MS-DOS is a single-tasking system, such liberties are allowable because they don't interfere with the operation of other programs.

But Windows is a multitasking system, and even though programs can fiddle with any part of system memory in Real Mode Windows, this should be avoided. Programs should refrain from actions that might have adverse side effects for other programs. Such actions may cause a program to be incompatible with Protected Mode Windows.

And yet, an otherwise "well-behaved" program might mistakenly overwrite memory belonging to another program—or even memory that belongs to Windows itself. Without the memory protection of Protected Mode, such actions can lead to data corruption and even a system crash. Protected Mode provides increased system integrity because of its memory protection features.

Memory Addressing in Protected Mode

Memory addressing in Protected Mode uses a two-part segment address, just as in Real Mode. But in Protected Mode, the logical-to-physical addresss conversion is not simply a shift and add operation. Instead, the processor relies on special reference segments called **descriptor tables** that are created and maintained by the operating system. There are two types of descriptor tables: **Global Descriptor Tables** (GDT), and **Local Descriptor Tables** (LDT). (A third type of descriptor table, the **Interrupt Descriptor Table** or IDT, is used to hold interrupt vectors. Its use is beyond this discussion.)

Intel designed its Protected Mode with a lot of flexibility in the way that descriptor tables can be used by different operating systems. In general, a descriptor table contains an array of segment information records, known as **segment descriptors**. In Protected Mode, the "segment identifier" part of a memory address is referred to as a **segment selector**. A segment selector contains an index into a descriptor table. Here is what a segment descriptor contains:

Segment Descriptor Field	*80286 Size*	*80386 Size*
Segment Location (aka Base Address)	3 bytes	4 bytes
Segment Size (aka Segment Limit)	2 bytes	2 1/2 bytes
Flags	1 byte	1 1/2 bytes
Unused	2 bytes	0 bytes
Total:	8 bytes	8 bytes

When referencing memory, the CPU loads segment descriptor data into special registers. The CPU uses these registers to locate the physical segment, and to perform its various validation checks on memory accesses. If the memory reference is valid, the offset is added to the base address to produce the physical address needed by the memory addressing hardware. This process is illustrated in Figure 17.6.

Actually, only 13 of the 16 bits in a segment value are used as a descriptor table index. As shown in Figure 17.7, the other three bits are two additional fields that play an important part in the addressing scheme and protection mechanism of Protected Mode. Bit 2 is a flag that indicates which descriptor table to use.

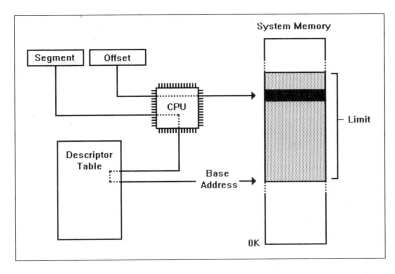

Figure 17.6 The segment value is an index into a descriptor table

Intel designed its Protected Mode addressing to be flexible enough for different types of operating systems. For example, each process in the system could be given its own LDT for its private consumption. At the same time, a single GDT accessible to any process could be created. Such a mechanism combines memory protection with the availability of a shared address space.

Bits 0 and 1 describe a segment's **privilege level**. These bits are set by operating system software to create and enforce a memory protection scheme having four privilege levels, 0 to 3, with 0 being the highest level reserved for the most trusted operating system software. In Windows, the DOS Protected Mode Interface (DPMI) code has the highest ring 0 privilege level.

The DPMI support code resides in one of two places. In Standard Mode, it resides in DOSX.EXE. In Enhanced Mode, the file WIN386.EXE provides DPMI support. DPMI provides access to memory above the 640K line. Memory in the range 640K to 1024K

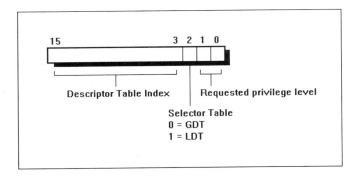

Figure 17.7 Structure of a protect mode selector

Figure 17.8   Windows' fatal error message

is known as **upper memory blocks** (UMB). The 64K from 1024K to 1088K is called the **high memory area** (HMA). Finally, memory allocated above the 1088K line is called **extended memory blocks** (EMBs).

In this architecture, memory protection is enforced in the following way. A memory error causes an exception to occur—that is, a CPU interrupt. In Windows, this results in the offending program being terminated with an error message like that shown in Figure 17.8. In the earliest, prerelease versions of Windows 3.0, this message contained the word "Trayf"—Yiddish for "Not Kosher," an apt description for an invalid memory reference.

Several types of errors cause this message to appear. For example, if a program tries to address memory using an invalid segment selector, the CPU catches the error and reports it to the operating system. Similarly, if a program tries to access memory beyond the end of a segment—that is, if the offset value is greater than the segment limit—the memory management hardware prevents the program from accessing memory that does not belong to it. It notifies the operating system that a program has violated the rules for the proper use of memory.

When such an error occurs and a debugger like CodeView is present, Windows refrains from displaying the error message. Instead, it passes control to the debugger. At that time, CodeView shows you where the error occurred. If it is within your program, CodeView shows you the source code line that caused the error. If it is not in your code—for example, if the error occurred in a device driver or in one of Windows' libraries—CodeView only shows you the machine instruction responsible for the error.

Windows Virtual Memory Support

All that we have said about Protected Mode operation applies equally to Standard Mode and Enhanced Mode. But there is an important capability that is only available in Enhanced Mode (and in the future NT Mode): support for virtual memory.

Virtual memory support works alongside the Protected Mode addressing mechanism. In other words, the segment value in an address is still used as an index into a descriptor table to determine the base address of a segment, and the offset is added to this base address to determine the exact bytes to be worked on.

The difference between regular Protected Mode and the virtual-memory Protected Mode on the 386 has to do with how this base offset address is interpreted. In regular

Figure 17.9 Virtual memory addressing

Protected Mode, it is interpreted as a physical memory address. In Enhanced Mode, the paging hardware of the Intel 80386 processor is enabled, allowing addresses to be treated as virtual memory addresses. Figure 17.9 illustrates how this translation is done.

This figure shows how the segment and offset values are decoded into an address in the virtual (or "linear") address space. This address space is divided into 4K pages, each of which resides in either physical memory or in a swapfile on disk. When a reference is made to a page that has been swapped to disk, a page fault is triggered. At such times, the virtual memory manager reads the desired page from the swap file. The instruction that triggered the page fault is then restarted so that paging is transparent to application software.

The virtual memory manager packs segments into the virtual address space as tightly as it can. In other words, as suggested in Figure 17.9, the beginning and end of a segment do not necessarily coincide with a page boundary. The net result is that the virtual memory manager avoids wasting even a single byte. The paging hardware behaves in a traditional manner, so that part of a segment can be on disk while another part is in physical memory. As you might expect, the portions in physical memory do not have any special relationship with each other. Instead, the virtual memory manager can relocate a page of memory anywhere that is convenient.

Even with virtual memory available, Windows still discards segments when it runs out of memory. However, discarding only occurs when the Windows Memory Manager has used up the virtual address space. In other words, Enhanced Mode prefers swapping to discarding. All other things being equal, it is more expensive to swap than to discard and re-read: Swapping involves two disk operations while a discard/re-read only involves one.

Why does Windows prefer to swap? Put simply, the best case swapping scenario outperforms the worst case discard and re-read scenario. The best case swapping scenario requires that a user install a permanent swap-file. This is not a difficult requirement, but gives a significant performance boost to swapping. Unlike with a temporary swap-file, the swapper bypasses the MS-DOS file system when reading or writing pages. In that case, a read and a write can almost outperform a single read that must traverse DOS.

The worst case discard and re-read scenario doesn't involve code segments. Instead, it involves TrueType fonts. The disk format for TrueType fonts is not bitmaps, but rather a low-level font-hinting machine language. To recreate a discarded font, the font engine must grind out character patterns one at a time. Since these fonts are so important to the device-independence of Windows, the Windows memory manager was tuned for them.

Our wish list for the Windows Memory Manager includes some way to indicate whether a discardable segment prefers to be discarded or swapped. That would allow better tuning of system memory usage. Our wish is complicated by the fact that Enhanced Mode has *two* memory managers at work: Support for the Windows API is provided by KRNL386.EXE, which manages dynamic linking, the global heap, and responds to application requests for memory. The second memory manager is contained in WIN386.EXE. It provides the virtual address space for the Windows global heap, and also manages the 8086 virtual machines that allow multiple MS-DOS applications to run. Getting the two to talk to each other is necessary to make our wish come true.

Windows NT Mode

The future of Windows is in 32-bit addressing. At least, that's how Microsoft is positioning three new enhancements to the Windows API. Put briefly—and roughly in the order of their scheduled release—these enhancements include: WIN32s ("s" stands for "subset"), Windows NT, and Windows 4.0. All will provide 32-bit addressing. Each fills a hole to help give Microsoft's Windows Architecture (as it's being called) a broad appeal. Let's look at each of these enhancements, one at a time.

Microsoft started shipping Windows 3.1 in April of 1992, but it doesn't support 32-bit addressing. The WIN32s dynamic link libraries, due for shipment a few months after Windows 3.1, adds 32-bit programming to the Windows 3.1 API. It will not, however, provide any new functionality beyond what is in Windows 3.1. You will, however, be able to write applications that ignore segmented memory and directly use 32-bit offsets. Underneath the 32-bit DLLs, calls to Windows are translated for the segmented addressing that Windows 3.1 and MS-DOS expect. The key benefit of Win32s is that it will allow you to write 32-bit applications today. In particular, you'll be able to ensure that such applications are source code compatible between Windows 3.1 and Windows NT.

The second 32-bit enhancement is a new operating system, Windows NT. Microsoft started working on NT in the fall of 1988. Originally, its name was OS/2 3.0, to reflect Microsoft's initial intent to build on and extend OS/2. After the phenomenal success of Windows 3.0, however, Microsoft changed its plans. It reengineered the new operating system to make a star of the 32-bit Windows API.

Microsoft was able to change course quickly because the core of the new operating system, known as the **NT Executive**, was built to support a variety of different APIs. For example, in addition to supporting 32-bit Windows applications, NT will run POSIX compliant applications. POSIX describes a portable, UNIX-like programming interface that has become an important standard. Windows NT, then, will run a wide range of applications: 32-bit Windows applications, POSIX applications, 16-bit Windows applications, and MS-DOS applications. It will even run character-based OS/2 applications, although not applications written to the OS/2 Presentation Manager API.

Unlike Win32s, which is essentially a thin layer over Windows 3.1, Windows NT will provide a greatly enhanced set of functionality. In number of function calls alone, Windows NT will stretch the 700 API of Windows 3.1 by about 400 to more than 1100 function calls. The list of new features is a long one. The user interface will provide true preemptive scheduling, so input to one application will never interfere with input to a second application. The 32-bit GDI will provide support for beziers, rotated and transparent bitmaps, paths, and rotated coordinate transformation. The core operating system functionality of the API will support threads, semaphores, memory-mapped files, virtual memory, and system-wide security. A key feature of Windows NT, in fact, is a security system that is robust enough to meet US government standards. NT will also have built-in network support, including named pipes and mailslots.

The third 32-bit enhancement to Windows involves a product called Windows 4.0. It will bring many (but not all) of the features of Windows NT to an MS-DOS based product. Although details are sketchy, it effectively means that the core components of MS-DOS based Windows will run in true 32-bit mode. Not only will they run applications written to the Win16 API, but will run Win32 applications with close to the full API as implemented in Windows NT.

After this quick peek into the future, it's time to cover an aspect of Windows that is important to the current product: How Windows selects memory segments for discarding.

How Windows Selects a Segment for Discarding

In all of its operating modes, Windows can purge code and data segments that are marked as *discardable* when it runs out of free memory. Understanding how Windows chooses to discard one segment over another will help you understand Windows' behavior in a low-memory situation. This, in turn, will help you write programs that can operate effectively when memory is scarce because many programs are running.

Windows discards segments on a *least recently used* (LRU) basis. When it needs to discard a segment, it picks a discardable segment that has resided in system memory the longest without being used. To determine the least recently used segment, Windows maintains a table of discardable segments known as the **LRU List**. Every discardable code and data segment has an entry on the LRU List.

Every one-quarter second, Windows scans an access flag associated with each discardable code segment in the system. If the segment has been accessed since the last time the flag was checked, the segment gets moved to the bottom of the LRU list. That is, it gets promoted to the most recently used position in the table. Once a segment has been promoted, the access flag is cleared so that it is ready to be tripped again if the segment is used again.

A drawback to this approach is that it isn't exact. In other words, it doesn't distinguish between a segment that was accessed 30 times and one that was accessed just once. It was chosen because it is fast.

The access flags for discardable code segments reside in different places depending on whether the system is running in Real or Protected Mode. In Real Mode, the Windows memory manager supports a data structure called a **module database** for every program and dynamic link library (we'll take a closer look at this data structure later in this chapter). The access flags are stored as an array of bytes in the module database, with one byte per discardable code segment.

In Protected Mode, the Intel-86 family provides support for an access flag in hardware. To be more precise, the access flag is a one-bit field in the descriptor table entry for each segment. The memory management hardware automatically sets this bit when a segment has been accessed. Windows checks this bit when it scans all discardable segments to update the LRU List.

Data segments are treated a little differently, but the idea is the same. Windows doesn't keep an access flag for data segments. Instead, the LRU List is automatically updated by the locking and unlocking mechanism used to access discardable data objects. After all, a segment must be locked to access it. Then, when it is unlocked, the segment gets automatically promoted to the bottom of the LRU List, to make it the most recently used segment.

You might find yourself working on an application that doesn't work well with the "least recently used" discarding algorithm. Consider, for example, a database program that walks a circular linked-list of data segments. As it makes the round of these segments, the very *next* segment that the program wants to use will also be the least recently used and, therefore, the one most likely to be discarded. In such cases, there are Windows library routines that can be used to directly modify the LRU tables: `GlobalLRU- Newest`, which makes a segment the least likely to be discarded, and `GlobalLRUOldest`, which makes a segment the most likely to be discarded.

The LRU mechanism is largely transparent to Windows programs running in Protected Mode. In Real Mode, if you run the SYMDEB debugger, you might run across a single machine instruction that is added to help update the LRU List. This instruction is embedded in a piece of dynamic link code called a **thunk**:

```
SAR  CS:[xxxx], 1
```

This *shift arithmetic right* instruction trips the access byte of a discardable code segment. Segments that are fixed or not present have a value of FFh. Segments that haven't been accessed since the last LRU timer tick have a value of 01h. This instruction leaves the FFh value unchanged, while it changes the value of 01h to 00h. The bytes that are modified by this instruction are scanned by Windows as it updates the LRU List.

Now let's take a look at the data objects that Windows itself allocates. In this chapter, we will focus on the data objects allocated by the Windows Kernel. In the next chapter, we'll look at the memory used by Windows' other two core components: USER.EXE and GDI.EXE, when we discuss application memory use.

The KERNEL's Private Memory Use

When Windows' three main components are doing work for Windows programs, they consume memory. For the most part, a Windows programmer doesn't have to know how this memory is consumed. But it can help if you're interested in knowing what makes Windows tick. Also, there are certain system limits that you will understand only when you know how Windows uses memory.

The KERNEL is responsible for dynamic linking, memory management, and bridging the gap between MS-DOS and Windows' multitasking nature. Although there are many tiny data structures tucked away throughout the system used by the KERNEL, our discussion will be limited to three of the most important: the Burgermaster, the task database, and the module databases. These objects are visible using the HEAPWALK utility when Windows is running in Real Mode, as shown in Figure 17.10. In Protected Mode, the Burgermaster goes away because its job is taken over by the Protected Mode descriptor tables, and other internal data structures.

The Burgermaster. The Burgermaster gets its name from a fast-food restaurant next door to the building where Windows was first developed. In those days, two phone numbers were programmed into the telephone auto-dialer at Microsoft; one was the number of the take-out service at Burgermaster. (The other was the number of the athletic club to which Microsoft employees were given memberships.) This object was named in honor of the restaurant, because the KERNEL development team ate lunch at Burgermaster almost every day.

The Burgermaster is the master memory handle table for movable and discardable objects in Windows. In other words, like the descriptor tables in Protected Mode, the Burgermaster maintains the physical addresses of movable memory objects. When a program needs to get the address of such a segment, it makes a call to one of several Windows library routines, which then look it up in the Burgermaster.

ADDRESS	HANDLE	SIZE	LCK	FLG	OWNER-NAME	OBJ-TYPE	ADD-INFO
0009D6A0		0			----- code fence -----		
000341F0	0066	1280			Burgermaster	Shared	
00025A10		384			Clock	Module DataBase	
00025B90		544			Clock	Task DataBase	
00029930	03E2	256			Clock	Resource	28678
00039150	03E6	5920			Clock	Data	
00053F90	039A	6048			Clock	Code 1	
0002F330		448			Comm	Module DataBase	
0002F4F0		1056			Comm	Code 2	
0002F910		768			Comm	Data	
00034AD0		224			Coure	Module DataBase	
0005B7F0	037A	3616	D		Coure	Resource	Font

Figure 17.10 HEAPWALK in Real Mode showing a snapshot of Windows' global heap

The Task Database. A Task Database (or TDB) is created for every instance of every program that runs in Windows. In our example, a single copy of CLOCK is running, so there is a single TDB. A TDB sits in a fixed segment and contains pointers to all of the things that make an instance of a program unique. Here is a partial list of some of the things stored in the TDB:

TDB Field	*Comment*
Array of Instance Thunks	Created by `MakeProcInstance` routine for use by dialog box procedures and other "call-back" procedures but *not* for window procedures.
Current MS-DOS Disk & Directory	On a task switch, Windows sets up the current disk and directory for the active program.
Handle to Application Message Queue	Keeps private messages that have been posted to a program (using the `PostMessage` routine).
Module Database Handle	Memory object that contains directory of objects in the module's .EXE or .DLL file.
Private Interrupt Vector Table	Contains the private interrupts that a program has installed. Only a small set can be installed, including interrupts 0, 2, 4, 6, 7. These deal with errors in arithmetic functions. Change by calling DOS Services interrupt 21h, function number 25h.
Pointer to MS-DOS Program Database	Also known as the MS-DOS Program Segment Prefix or PSP. Windows provides a copy of this data structure for each Windows program that runs. A program can get the address of this by calling `GetCurrentPDB`.
Task-Switch Save Area	Saves CPU registers between task switches.

This list is not complete, nor is this the order of the actual TDB. Microsoft has not documented the contents of the TDB, which means it may change in a future version. It's included here to give you an idea of the type of data saved by Windows for every instance of every program. For example, from the list you can see that Windows keeps track of the current disk and directory for each program. A program can freely change these and not be worried about any adverse effects on other programs. Also, in case you wondered where the application's private message queue lives, it lives in a segment referenced by the TDB. Notice that the TDB has a private interrupt vector table. If you want to trap the interrupts generated when certain arithmetic errors occur, you can install your own interrupt handler. For example, interrupt vector 0 is issued when a divided-by-zero error occurs. Programs that don't handle those interrupts themselves are terminated when such errors occur.

Windows always creates one TDB per instance of every program that runs. When an instance of a program terminates, the TDB is removed from memory. Knowing this, you should check that your Windows programs terminate properly. How? It's easy. Run HEAPWALK, and check that there are no unexpected objects labeled "Task Database" when you think your program should have terminated.

The Module Database. There is an entry in the TDB that points to another data object used by the KERNEL: the module database. The module database contains an abbreviated version of the header to an EXE file, known more simply as an EXE header. The module database is basically a directory of segments that can be read from an executable file. A utility included with the Microsoft C compiler, EXEHDR.EXE, lets you read this header.

Windows uses the module database whenever it needs to load anything from an executable file. This includes code, resources, and data. When we discuss dynamic linking in Chapter 19, you'll see that Windows sets up tiny code fragments called *thunks* to make dynamic linking work. In Real Mode, thunks allow code to be discarded and moved with a minimum of overhead.

Programs have module databases, but so do dynamic link libraries. If you run HEAP-WALK, you'll notice that KERNEL, USER, and GDI each have a module database. There is even a module database for fonts, which are dynamic link libraries with no code.

In this chapter, we have examined Windows' ability to take advantage of the memory capabilities of the entire family of Intel-86 processors. In the next chapter, we're going to look at application-specific memory use issues.

18

Memory, Part II: Application Memory Use

When a programmer thinks about packing a program's data into memory, it can be compared to what a traveler thinks about when packing for a trip. The first question is: "What bags do I take?" For a weekend, a small suitcase might do. For a two-week vacation, several suitcases might be needed. In the context of a program, the question is "What kinds of containers can a Windows program use to store data?"

In designing the approach that your programs will take in using memory, there are a number of basic issues to consider, such as allocation, visibility, lifetime, and overhead. As we look at the different types of memory available to a Windows program, we'll consider each of these issues, and weigh their importance. Table 18.1 summarizes these issues for the many types of memory available to a Windows application.

The issue of **allocation** involves *who* allocates a given piece of memory. The compiler allocates some memory for you, which is the case with static and automatic variables. In other cases, you must explicitly allocate memory. For example, to allocate memory using one of Windows' dynamic memory allocation packages, you call either `LocalAlloc` or `GlobalAlloc`. In some instances, memory allocation is a side-effect of creating certain types of system objects. For example, when you create a device context (DC) in GDI, objects are allocated in GDI's local heap space.

The issue of **visibility** has to do with who can see the memory. Some objects have a very limited visibility, such as automatic variables declared inside a function. Others have a visibility that is system wide, like GDI drawing objects and certain objects allocated from the global heap. Such objects can be shared between programs, but be careful to clean up these objects when you are done. Windows doesn't automatically clean them up for you.

Table 18.1 A Summary of Application Memory Use

Memory Type	Allocation	Visibility	Lifetime	Overhead
Static variables	C compiler	in a program	program	none
Automatic variables	C compiler	in a function	function	none
Local Heap	calls to LocalAlloc	in a program	program	4 or 6 bytes
Global Heap	calls to GlobalAlloc	program/system	program/system	24 bytes
Resources	Resource manager	program/system	owner	24 bytes
GDI Objects	GDI routines	system	system	varies
USER Objects	USER routines	system	owner	varies

The issue of **lifetime** describes how memory is reclaimed. With some objects, memory is reclaimed automatically when a program terminates. This is the case with static and automatic variables, as well as with objects allocated from the local heap. Other objects must be explicitly deallocated to free this memory for other uses. In general, it is a good programming practice to free memory when it is no longer needed, even if that memory will be automatically freed.

Finally, the issue of **overhead** describes what extra costs are associated with allocating a piece of memory beyond the actual used bytes. This issue is especially important when deciding how to use dynamic memory allocation—allocation from the local and global heaps. For example, every global memory object has an overhead of 24 bytes *minimum*. If you are in the habit of allocating hundreds of tiny (12-byte) objects, you'll want to think again before putting each into its own global memory object.

Let's begin by looking at each different type of available memory. We'll then discuss issues relating to the allocation of memory from the global heap—the most flexible and useful type of dynamic memory allocation. We'll examine how code structure affects memory use, then look at allocation from the local heap, the use of custom resources, and some tricks that will allow you to perform local heap allocation in a dynamically allocated segment. We'll provide you with a lot of sample code, so you can examine in detail the pieces required to make each type of memory work properly.

Overview of Application Memory Use

In the last chapter, we described how the Intel-86 family of processors uses a segmented addressing scheme. Since Windows is built on top of this architecture, Windows programmers should keep in mind that the segment is the fundamental unit of memory. This being the case, our discussion of memory is organized in terms of segments. We'll start with the default data segment, which holds three types of data objects: static variables, automatic variables, and the local heap.

Figure 18.1 HEAPWALK shows MIN's default data segment

Default Data Segment

Windows works best with programs having a *single* data segment. This is another way of saying that you should use the small or medium compiler models, since these memory models create a single data segment by default. (Note: some compilers, including the Borland C++ compiler, create a single data segment in large model. With such compilers, you can freely use large model as long as you are careful to avoid creating a second data segment.) A single data segment is best because of the way that Windows' dynamic linking mechanism works. It can fix up the data segment register when a Windows library routine calls a function in your program. This call-back mechanism is used for window procedures; therefore it is fundamental to Windows' operation. For each program, Windows internally stores only *one* data segment value.

Programs that *must* have more than one default data segment can do so—that is, you can use the compact, large, or huge compiler models, but your program is subject to certain restrictions. For one thing, Windows will only allow one instance of your program to run at a time. Also, a bug in Windows 3.0 causes the data segments to be fixed in the *physical* address space, which creates sandbars that can hinder optimal performance of Windows' memory management. If at all possible, build your Windows programs around a single default data segment, since doing otherwise can cause more grief than benefit.

In Figure 18.1, HEAPWALK shows the default data segment that belongs to MIN, the minimum Windows program we developed earlier in this book. In many respects, a program's default data segment is just another segment in the global heap: The Windows' loader allocates the segment from the global heap using the global heap allocation routine, `GlobalAlloc`. For details on Real Mode operation, see the accompanying boxed discussion.

▼ Real Mode and the Default Data Segment:

The default data segment is unique in some respects. For one thing, it is automatically **locked** whenever a message is delivered to your program. When we discuss global heap allocation, you'll see that programs must explicitly lock dynamically allocated data segment, but not the default data segment, which Windows locks for you. The default data segment is also special in that Windows is careful to set up the correct value in the DS (data segment) register when a message is delivered to a program. When we discuss dynamic linking in Chapter 19, you'll see how important this is. Every program and some dynamic link libraries will have a default data segment (dynamic link libraries aren't required to have a data segment). The dynamic link mechanism is set up to support this and to make sure that your program always has access to its required data.

As the gateway to many messages that are sent to your program, the GetMessage routine locks and unlocks your default data segment at the proper time. Also, when another program directly calls one of your window procedures with the SendMessage routine, your default data segment is also locked. Among the routines that *may* cause your data segment to become momentarily unlocked are the local heap allocation routines (LocalAlloc and LocalReAlloc) and the atom table allocation routines, since they call the local heap allocation routines. To avoid the problems that this can cause, avoid writing code like this:

```
LPSTR lp;
lp = &static_or_stack_object;
hMem = LocalAlloc (...);
//   After a call to LocalAlloc or LocalReAlloc,
//   previously constructed far pointers to
//   local data or to the stack may be invalid.
```

As the comment in the code suggests, if you construct a far pointer to any object in your default data segment, then call LocalAlloc or LocalReAlloc, the far pointer may be invalid. In fact, it will be invalid when your program is running in real mode and the default data segment has to be grown—and moved—to satisfy the allocation request. On the other hand, if you increment the lock count on your default data segment (by calling LockData), the segment will not move, although this may cause calls to LocalAlloc / LocalReAlloc to fail.

A program's data segment is divided into four or five parts: a header, static data area, stack, local heap, and an optional atom table. Figure 18.2 shows a typical program's data segment with each part labeled. For the sake of comparison, it's interesting to note that a dynamic link library's data segment may contain all of these same elements, except that DLLs ordinarily do not have a stack. Instead, DLLs use the stack of the programs that call the library routines. Figure 18.3 shows a typical DLL data segment. Let's look at each element in a typical program's data segment, starting with the segment header.

Default Data Segment Header. The header is a 16-byte area containing pointers used by the KERNEL to manage the local data segment. A Windows program should

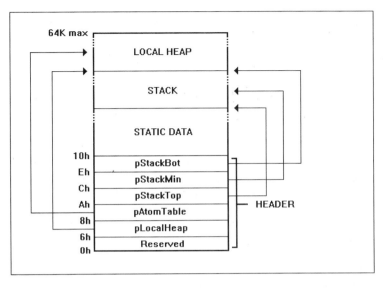

Figure 18.2 A typical program's local data segment

leave this area alone, since it is automatically allocated at compile/link time and managed by the KERNEL at runtime. When allocating a local heap on a dynamically allocated segment, however, you'll need to set aside the first 16 bytes for use by the KERNEL. We'll show how this is done later in this chapter. Other than that, our primary interest in this data area rests in what we can learn about Windows' management of a local data segment.

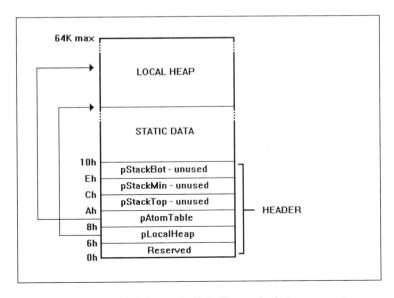

Figure 18.3 A typical dynamic link library's data segment

Of the five pointers in the segment header, the most important is the pointer to the local heap, `pLocalHeap`. It is used by the local heap management routines to find the local heap so it doesn't interfere with other data objects in the data segment. Your Windows program should not directly modify the local heap, but should instead call the various local heap routines.

Three of the pointers reference the stack: `pStackBot, pStackMin,` and `pStackTop`. When the debug version of Windows is installed, these three pointers are used to check for stack overflows. It's a good idea to test your Windows programs against this special version, since it will help you find errors that might otherwise go undetected.

The fifth and final pointer, `pAtomTable`, points to an atom table if a program has created one. Atom tables are created from memory allocated out of the local heap and are managed by the various atom management routines. Notice that the segment header doesn't have any pointer to the static data area. The compiler and the linker work together to define the static data area and generate the correct code to use it.

The Static Data Area. The static data area holds a program's "global" data. This includes all variables declared outside of functions, all variables declared with the `static` keyword, all static strings, and the static data allocated for use by various C library routines.

In the following code fragment, four different objects are allocated in the static data area, and five are not. Can you identify the static data objects?

```
char * pch = "String of Characters";
int   i;

LRESULT CALLBACK WndProc (HWND hwnd,
                          UINT wMsg,
                          WPARAM wParam,
                          LPARAM lParam)
    {
    static int iCount;
    long       lValue;
    ...
```

As you might expect, the two variables defined outside any function— `pch` and `i`—are allocated in the static data area. So is `iCount`, which uses the `static` keyword. This declaration, since it's inside the bounds of a function, limits the **scope** of this variable to the `WndProc` function. In other words, `iCount` is only visible to code *inside* this function. However, as a static object, it has a lifetime as long as the program itself, which means that it resides in the static data area.

The fourth object placed in the static area is the string: `"String of Charac-ters"`. Because strings can take up quite a bit of space, you can reduce the size of the static data area by putting all strings into a string resource. When a string is needed, it can be loaded and used. When not needed, string resources can be discarded from memory to reduce the overall demand for system memory.

The Stack. The stack is a dynamic data area managed for you through a high-level language like C. Stacks are so central to software that the Intel processors have a set of registers dedicated to the use and maintenance of the stack area. These include the `SS` (stack segment) register, and the BP (base pointer) and SP (stack pointer) offset registers. When the processor makes a function call, it automatically pushes a return address on the stack. When returning from a function call, the return address is retrieved from the stack as part of the way the RET machine instruction operates.

The C compiler and the processor store three things on the stack: local variables, arguments passed to called functions, and return addresses. As you may recall, the STACKSIZE statement in the module definition (.DEF) file defines the amount of space reserved for the stack, with a *minimum* stack size of 5120 bytes. You'll want to understand how your program uses this stack, so that you can allocate the proper amount of stack space.

Variables declared inside a function *without* the static keyword are local variables, such as lValue in the code fragment we looked at a moment ago. Space on the stack for local variables is allocated when a function is called, and freed when returning from a function. If you are writing a program that allocates a lot of local variables, you may wish to use a higher STACKSIZE value to reflect the additional needed memory. A higher stack size should also be requested for programs that do a lot of recursive calling, since local variables are allocated for *each* call made into functions. The accompanying boxed discussion provides some additional details on the use of the stack for the three basic stack objects.

 The accompanying figure shows the relationship of the three main types of stack objects: arguments, return address, and local variables.

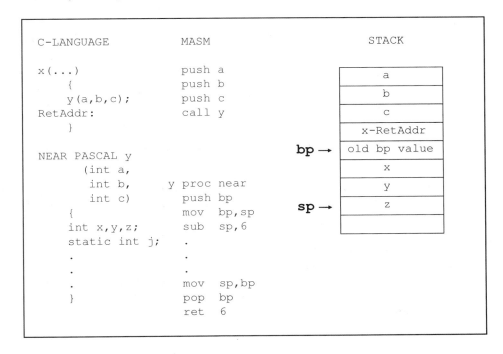

Also shown is the C-language call, and the resulting assembly language instructions that support this stack structure. The `push` instruction puts arguments on the stack for called functions. The `call` instruction places a return address on the stack, and passes control to the called function. Inside the called function, the compiler creates the code to adjust the base pointer, `BP`, and the stack pointer, `SP`, to access both the passed arguments and the local variables on the **stack frame**. Notice that the variable defined with the `static` keyword, j, is not allocated on the stack. Instead, as a static data object, it is allocated in the static data area.

The `BP`, or base-pointer, register is set up as the reference point for accessing arguments and local variables. If you run a debugger like Codeview, you can see the machine language references to arguments as positive offsets from `BP`. Here is an assembly language instruction that references the third passed argument in our example:

```
MOV   AX, [BP+04]
```

Local variables are referenced as negative offsets from `BP`. For example, here is how the third local variable might be accessed:

```
MOV   AX, [BP-06]
```

Because the `PASCAL` calling convention has been selected, the called function cleans up the stack. This is actually built into the return instruction, which is one reason that this calling convention creates smaller, faster code:

```
RET   6
```

If this seems somewhat esoteric and complex, don't worry too much—the details of stack management are mostly the concern of assembly language programmers and compiler writers. The compiler takes care of everything; you don't have to think about it. However, keep in mind the three uses of the stack, so that you can be sure to adjust your stack size when you write a Windows program that uses either a lot of local variables or deeply nested recursive calls.

The Debug Version of Windows and Stack Checking. Under ordinary circumstances, a stack overflow will go unnoticed, or it will result in mysterious and untraceable problems with your program. To prevent this problem, you must test your programs under very special circumstances, since the normal C stack checking is disabled under Windows. Here's what you need. First, you must compile your programs with stack checking *enabled*, which means compile *without* the -Gs switch. Next, you must have a special version of Windows, known as the **debug version**, installed on your system. The debug version of Windows is created by copying a set of dynamic link library files from the Windows software development kit into the system subdirectory (\windows\system).

This special set of DLLs performs additional error checking, including a check for a stack overflow. When running the debug version of Windows, you need to make a few special arrangements to receive the debugging messages. For details on what this involves, see the accompanying boxed discussion.

▼ **Getting Debug Messages**

The debug versions of the Windows libraries send messages to you by calling the `OutputDebugString` function in the Windows KERNEL. Think of this function as a radio transmitter: It provides the central place from which Windows sends out its signals. You need to make special provision to receive its messages—that is, you need some mechanism to function as the radio receiver.

You have several choices, each of which involves introducing a new hardware device or a new piece of software to catch the output of the KERNEL's debug string function. Your choices include: attaching an asynchronous terminal to your `COM1:` port, running a Windows compatible debugger, or using an application that relies on the ToolHelp library's ability to capture the output of `OutputDebugString`. Let's look at these one at a time.

Asynchronous Terminal. This hardware-only solution involves connecting a terminal, like the DEC VT-100, to your `COM1:` port. By default, the Windows KERNEL sends its output to the `AUX` device, which defaults to `COM1`. You must use a null-modem cable, and need to set up the communications parameters from the terminal as well as from the Windows Control Panel. This isn't the most elegant solution, but it can be convenient if you have extra terminals around your office.

Windows Compatible Debugger. A Windows compatible debugger, like Microsoft's Codeview or Borland's Turbo Debugger for Windows, will know how to redirect the debugging output to a debug window. Of course, you'll have to keep the debugger running whenever your system is running. But if you're already set up for a debugger, you can quickly and easily use it to receive the messages sent by the debug version of Windows.

Relying on ToolHelp. A third choice involves using the ToolHelp.DLL library that Microsoft ships with Windows 3.1. Among the many services provided by this library is the ability to define a call-back function for system notifications. One of these notifications is for calls made to `OutputDebugString`. If you have the Microsoft SDK, you should look at the DBWIN sample program. This program does everything you need to redirect debug output to a file, out the COM port, to a window, or to a monochrome display screen. This is the easiest solution of all—*provided* that you use the Microsoft SDK.

The Local Heap. Local heaps are one of two places from which programs can dynamically allocate memory (the other is the global heap). Local heaps operate within the bounds of a single segment. The standard application startup code installs a local heap in the default data segment. You can also use Windows' local heap allocation routines to subdivide a dynamically allocated segment into smaller pieces—a process we refer to as subsegment allocation. Of the samples in this chapter, LOCALMEM shows local heap allocation in the default data segment. SUBSEG shows how to set up and use local heaps in other segments.

Without requiring any special effort on your part, every program has one local heap which resides at the end of the default data segment. The initial size of the heap depends on the value defined in the module definition (.DEF) file with the HEAPSIZE statement. The heap can grow beyond this size, though. When it does, the segment containing the local heap will grow as well. A local heap can continue to grow until the segment containing it reaches a maximum size of 64K.

Programs allocate memory from a local heap using one of the twelve local heap management routines. You can easily identify these routines, since the name of each routine starts with the word "Local." For example, LocalAlloc allocates memory from a local heap. LocalFree releases the allocated memory. Table 18.2 provides a complete list of the local heap management routines. Later in this chapter, we'll take a closer look at local heap management, and provide more detail on the routines marked with a "*".

In the previous chapter, we described the primary attributes of objects (segments) in the global heap: moveable, discardable, and fixed. The local heap also supports these

Table 18.2 Windows Local Heap Management Routines

LocalAlloc *	Allocates memory from a local heap.
LocalCompact	Reorganizes a local heap.
LocalDiscard	Discards an unlocked, discardable object.
LocalFlags	Provides information about a specific memory object.
LocalFree *	Frees a local memory object.
LocalHandle	Provides the handle of a local memory object associated with a given memory address.
LocalInit *	Initializes a local heap.
LocalLock *	Increments the lock count on a local memory object, and returns its address.
LocalReAlloc *	Changes the size of a local memory object.
LocalShrink	Reorganizes a local heap and reduces the size of the heap (if possible) to the initial, starting size. If this routine is successful, it reduces the size of the data segment that contains the heap, so that the memory can be reclaimed by the global heap.
LocalSize	Returns the current size of a local memory object.
LocalUnlock *	Decrements the lock count on a local memory object.

three types. Moveable objects can be allocated to help minimize memory fragmentation, and discardable objects can be allocated to give the local memory manager the freedom to purge unneeded objects when memory is low. By comparison, the standard C library routines only allocate fixed objects and do not support moveable or discardable objects. In this way, the local memory manager provides quite a bit more sophistication than the C library's `malloc` routine in allocating and managing a heap space.

To support moveable and discardable memory objects, the local heap manager provides a **memory handle** when it allocates a local memory object. Like the handles encountered in the context of GDI objects, a memory handle is simply an identifier that can be traded in to access the real object. When a memory handle is passed to the `LocalLock` routine, a memory pointer is provided. As we'll see later, this means that code like the following is required to access a local memory object:

```
HANDLE hMem;
PSTR   pstr;

/*  Allocate a 15 byte moveable object.  */
hMem = LocalAlloc (LMEM_MOVEABLE, 15);

/*  Lock the object, getting a pointer.  */
pstr = LocalLock (hMem);

lstrcpy (pstr, "Hello World");

/*  Unlock the object.  */
LocalUnlock (hMem);
```

Let's continue our tour of program memory management by looking at the last item in the default data segment, the atom table.

Atom Tables. Optionally, a program can create an atom table in its local data segment. An atom table provides a way to store and retrieve variable-length character strings. When an atom is created, a handle is issued that uniquely identifies the string. At two bytes, a handle is a small, fixed-size value that can easily and conveniently be placed into fixed length data structures with a minimum of overhead. Atom tables are efficient, since duplicate requests create the same atom value. The USER module uses atoms to store the names of window classes, clipboard formats, and application-defined messages. You may also wish to use them to store variable-length strings.

In addition to the private atom table in local data segments, Windows provides a global atom table. Windows' Dynamic Data Exchange (DDE) protocol relies on the global atom table to pass the ASCII names of data topics between programs. Since DDE uses messages to relay requests for data, an atom provides a compact way to store the name of a desired data element in a very small space.

Dynamically Allocated Segments

Dynamically allocated segments provide the most flexible type of read/write memory for an application to use. Up to the limit of available system memory, you can have as many as you want, and each can be as large as 64K. In fact, you can allocate segments larger than 64K. The `_huge` keyboard lets the compiler know to generate the code required to handle crossing from one segment to another. Since huge pointers are quite a bit less efficient than near or far pointers, it's best to avoid them if possible; but when you have to access a block of data larger than 64K, they provide an easy method for doing so.

How many dynamically allocated segments *can* a program create? Assuming there is sufficient memory, the limits relate to the maximum size of the system handle table. In the last chapter, we described the Real Mode Burgermaster and the Protected Mode LDT, both of which can hold up to 8,192 entries, which makes this the limit for the number of segments (minus the few hundred that Windows and its drivers allocate). By the way, this is a *system-wide* limit and not a per process limit. Also, if you're working with the Standard Mode of Windows 3.0, you should know that, because it creates *two* selectors per segment, it has a limit of 4,096 segments.

Programs allocate and manage dynamic segments using Windows' global heap management routines. This is a set of 21 routines starting with the word "Global." `GlobaAlloc`, for example, allocates a segment and `GlobalFree` releases a segment. When you look for dynamically allocated segments using HEAPWALK, keep in mind version 3.0 labels such segments as "Task" and "Shared," as shown in figure 18.4. Version 3.1 uses the term "Private."

The SEGALLOC program later in this chapter demonstrates the use of the global heap management routines. For now, let's move on to discuss another type of data storage container: resources.

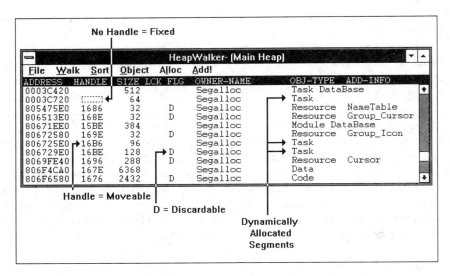

Figure 18.4 Dynamically allocated segment as seen by HEAPWALK

Resources

An important type of memory object often overlooked for its memory management qualities is the resource. A resource is a read-only data object that has been merged into a program's .EXE file by the resource compiler. When the data is needed, the resource manager reads it from disk and places it into a discardable memory object. When the memory manager needs to reclaim the memory for another use, a resource can typically be discarded or purged from system memory. The system's Resource Manager places each resource in a segment, which means—like dynamically allocated segments—a resource segment can be fixed, movable, or discardable. Since discardable resources are the most flexible, they are the most common.

Using HEAPWALK, it's easy to find the resource segments: They are labeled "Resource." HEAPWALK knows the difference between different types of resources, so it tells whether a specific object is a menu, dialog box template, cursor, icon, or whatever. In addition, if you double-click on a resource which contains a graphic image (such as an icon or a cursor), HEAPWALK displays the object for you. Figure 18.5 shows HEAPWALK listing several resources and displaying the image of one of GDI's cursors.

Table 18.3 provides a list of the different types of resources that Windows supports, along with the chapter in this book that discusses the use of each type. As you can see, resources play a key role in how certain data objects are packaged. Resources are used for user-interface objects, GDI objects, and space-saving objects like string-tables, and custom resources.

Figure 18.5 HEAPWALK lets you see resource-type objects

Table 18.3 Windows' Predefined Resources

Resource Type	Covered In Depth
Accelerator Table	Chapter 11
Bitmaps	
Cursors	Chapter 17
Custom Resources	Chapter 18
Dialog Box Templates	Chapter 14
Fonts	Chapter 10
Icons	
Menu Templates	Chapter 11
String Tables	Chapter 18

From the point of view of memory use, each resource resides in a separate segment. In other words, a program with one accelerator table, two menu templates, and four dialog box templates has seven different segments worth of resources. The advantage of having one segment per resource is that each can be independently loaded and discarded.

GDI Data Segment

Whenever a program creates a GDI object, space is allocated out of GDI's data segment or, more specifically, space is allocated from GDI's local heap. While there's no doubt that programs will need to use such objects, care should be taken to avoid creating too many of these types of objects. In addition, programs that create GDI drawing objects should be careful to destroy the objects when they are not needed. Otherwise, if GDI's heap gets full, it can prevent other programs from being able to run properly. Allocate only the minimum number of objects needed, and be sure to destroy objects when you are done using them.

Table 18.4 provides a list of GDI objects and the size that each takes from GDI's data segment. These sizes are subject to change; they are provided to help you get a sense for the demands that each object places on system memory. These sizes were determined using HEAPWALK, which can show the contents of GDI's data segment. Two of these objects reside in their own segment: fonts and bitmaps. Each has a corresponding local heap object which references the external segment.

If you'd like to see for yourself, you can run HEAPWALK and select the **Object.GDI LocalWalk** menu item. HEAPWALK opens a window showing the objects in GDI's local heap, like the window shown in Figure 18.6. It's interesting to note that GDI's data segment starts out relatively small. In this figure, it is 16 Kbytes—so there is room for growth to meet the demands made by applications for GDI drawing objects.

One other data area can get filled by the actions taken by programs, and should be monitored carefully: the USER library's data segment.

Table 18.4 Space Taken in GDI's Local Heap by Various GDI Drawing Objects

Object	Size
Brush	32 bytes
Bitmap	28–32 bytes
Font	40–44 bytes
Pen	28 bytes
Region	28 bytes to several Kbytes
Palette	28 bytes

USER Data Segment

Windows' USER module provides the support for Windows' user-interface objects. This includes windows, menus, dialog boxes, and accelerator tables. Unlike GDI objects, USER objects in general are not shared between programs. For this reason, when a Windows program terminates, USER can free the data objects that were created. Nonetheless, the wise Windows programmer makes frugal use of memory and will destroy objects when done using them.

Quite a few user-interface objects start out as resources, which have their own segments. In some cases, the resource data is copied into objects in Windows' local heap. That is the case, for example, with menus and dialog box data. Table 18.5 summarizes the user-interface objects which do, in fact, take up USER heap space.

Figure 18.6 HEAPWALK showing GDI's data segment

Table 18.5 Approximate Size of Various USER Data Objects

Object	Size
menus	20 bytes/ menu plus
	20 bytes/ menu item
window class	40–50 bytes
window	60–70 bytes

Unfortunately, HEAPWALK doesn't show the size of individual objects in USER's data segment as it does for GDI's data segment. So the estimates in this table were created by looking at the size of data structures in the Microsoft documentation and adding 50% for internal overhead. Of course, the exact size is not as important (since it can change from version to version) as the simple fact that your use of these objects takes up space which, at least for now, is in short supply. For example, if you define 10 window classes and create 100 windows of each class, you consume about 7500 bytes of USER heap space. Since USER's heap is also used by other programs, including the Program Manager and File Manager, you need to be careful not to create too many objects that may cause this heap space to fill up.

Two very useful types of application memory get allocated in USER's heap space: **class extra bytes** and **window extra bytes**. Each allows your program to connect private data with a Window Manager data object: Class extra bytes are connected with a window class, and window extra bytes are connected with individual windows. Windows does not give you a pointer to these kinds of data areas, but rather will read or write a small number of bytes for you. Here is a list of the routines that access window and class extra bytes:

Class Extra Bytes	*Window Extra Bytes*
SetClassWord	SetWindowWord
SetClassLong	SetWindowLong
GetClassWord	GetWindowWord
GetClassLong	GetWindowLong

Although both types have their uses, window extra bytes are the most common. They are useful because they provide an easy way to create a connection between a user-interface object—a window—and your application's data. In normal "C" programming, there is no provision for connecting data to the user interface. Instead, global variables are available throughout an application, and local variables only survive during the life of a particular function. Windows extra bytes, on the other hand, bridge the gap between the user interface and user data.

Since window extra bytes are allocated from USER's heap space, you'll want to limit yourself to a fairly small number. Personally, we like to use two or four window extra bytes. The debug version of Windows is a little more generous: It only complains if you allocate more than 40 extra bytes. With two window extra bytes, you can store a memory handle. Effectively, this would allow you to attach quite a bit of data to a single window. The most obvious use for extra bytes is for dialog box controls. They are also useful in other situations in which you are working with several windows, such as you do with the multiple document interface (MDI).

With this brief introduction to the different types of memory available to Windows applications, you have a reasonably complete picture of the choices you can make. Now let's examine the implementation details for using different types of memory. The rest of this chapter provides five code examples to help clarify how an application can use memory:

1. SEGALLOC   This sample program demonstrates how to use memory allocated out of the global heap. The accompanying discussion provides more details on the various global heap management routines.

2. MIN2   We will take a second look at the minimum Windows program to support a discussion of code structure and memory use. This program demonstrates how a Windows program can be divided into multiple code segments to improve memory use.

3. LOCALMEM   This program provides an example of using the local heap management routines to allocate objects from a program's default data segment. It also demonstrates the use of string tables.

4. SUBSEG   This program shows how the local heap management routines can be used with a segment that is dynamically allocated from the global heap. The program combines global heap management routines and local heap management routines.

5. CUSTRES   This program demonstrates the creation of a custom resource. A sine table is stored as a resource and used to calculate sine and cosine values, which are used to draw a circle.

Let's get started, then, with a look at using the global heap management routines.

Global Heap Allocation

When a program allocates memory from Windows' global heap, it allocates a segment. Fixed, moveable, or discardable segments can be allocated, depending on what a program needs. In general, though, programmers should keep in mind the words of John Pollock, who worked on Windows' first KERNEL and was the first Windows instructor for many programmers. He urged programmers to keep dynamically allocated segments "as *few* as possible, as *small* as possible, and as *discardable* as possible."

As Few as Possible. You'll want to keep your segments as *few* as possible because of the overhead of a segment. Segments are expensive. Each incurs 24 bytes of overhead: a 16-byte invisible header linking all segments together and an 8-byte entry in the BurgerMaster (for Real Mode) or in the local descriptor table (in Protected Mode).

Because of this high overhead, you'll want to *minimize* the number of segments you allocate. For example, with an overhead of 24 bytes, if you allocate a segment to hold a 24-byte data object, it really costs you 48 bytes. That's a lot like having a sales tax of 100 percent on everything you buy. Since this is a fixed cost, you can effectively lower your "memory-use tax" by putting many objects into a single segment. For example, if you put 2400 bytes of data into a single object, you have effectively lowered your taxes to a mere 1 percent. When you start to think about how to make the best use of dynamically allocated segments, think about using arrays of records instead of working with a linked list of segments. It will help you get your money's worth from the memory manager.

A second related issue to segment overhead is **granularity**. This refers to the actual size of memory that Windows carves out when you allocate a segment. Dynamically allocated segments have a granularity of 32 bytes or, in Real Mode memory terms, two paragraphs. (Recall that in real mode the smallest segment is 16 bytes, which Intel calls a paragraph. Even though Protected Mode allows for smaller segments, Windows doesn't.) To minimize differences between the different modes, both Standard Mode and Enhanced Mode inherit this granularity. Therefore, when you ask for 1 to 32 bytes, you'll get a 32-byte segment. If you ask for 33 bytes, Windows gives you a 64-byte segment.

If compatibility with Windows 3.0 is important, you should keep in mind that Windows 3.0 Standard Mode uses a slightly different scheme. In particular, granularity in this mode is on an odd paragraph boundary. In other words, if you ask for a segment between 1 and 16 bytes, you'll get a 16-byte segment (a 16-byte header at the beginning of the segment makes the total size 32 bytes, but you only have access starting at the 17th byte). If this puzzles you, just remember that applications which must run in Windows 3.0 should be tested in Standard Mode as vigorously as they are in Enhanced Mode. That should go a long way towards shaking out bugs that might result from a slightly different granularity scheme.

As Small as Possible. Keep your segments as small as possible, because Windows is a multitasking system, and allocated memory is not available for other Windows programs. This is particularly an issue in Real Mode, with its tiny, one-megabyte address space. But even in other modes, only allocate the amount of memory you need and no more.

One reason that John Pollock made this recommendation has to do with the way some MS-DOS programs behave. Since DOS is a single-tasking operating system, many DOS programs allocate all of system memory at startup. If a Windows program tried to do this, it could lock out other programs from the system.

Whether you are moving to Windows from MS-DOS or from some other programming environment, keep in mind that memory is a shared, and often a scarce, resource. Allocate what you need, when you need it. When you are done using a block of memory, free it so it is available to other Windows programs.

As Discardable as Possible. In the last chapter, we talked about the three types of memory objects: fixed, moveable, and discardable. To the Windows memory manager, fixed is the least flexible and therefore least desirable type of memory object, and discardable is the most desirable. But programmers new to Windows tend to see things just the opposite way: Fixed memory seems the most comfortable, discardable seems the most disastrous, and moveable only slightly less so. After all, what sane programmer wants to deal with data that keeps wiggling away or disappears completely?

John Pollock's recommendation to make memory as discardable as possible reflects the fact that memory should be treated as a scarce resource. Programs with moderate requirements for memory usually keep data in moveable data segments. After all, a moveable segment gives the memory manager the freedom to shuffle memory so it can minimize fragmentation.

Programs with a large or unlimited need for memory, like word processing programs or spreadsheet programs, require their own mechanism to transfer data between main system memory and disk. After all, even a virtual memory system can run out of memory. When Windows is without virtual memory in Standard Mode, such programs will run out of "real memory" sooner. Discardable memory provides a way for such programs to volunteer objects to be purged. When memory is plentiful, discardable objects don't have to be purged. But when memory is scarce, the memory manager can exercise its option to remove discardable objects.

Global Heap API

Table 18.6 shows all of Windows' global heap management routines. This table is set up to show how 12 of these routines must be paired together to create a sandwich construction (first introduced in Chapter 7). The other nine routines either act on a specific global memory object or on the global heap as a whole.

Table 18.6 Windows' Global Heap Management Routines

Top Slice	Bottom Slice	Description
GlobalAlloc	GlobalFree	Allocates a segment from the global heap.
GlobalCompact	na	Reorganizes the global heap to determine the largest block of available free memory.
GlobalDiscard	na	Purges an unlocked, discardable segment from memory.
GlobalDosAlloc	GlobalDosFree	Allocates a block of memory in the DOS address space, that is, below the one-megabyte line, so that a Windows program can share a data area with a DOS device driver.
GlobalFix	GlobalUnfix	Prevents an object from moving in the linear address space. Notice that this doesn't keep an object from being swapped to disk—only the GlobalPageLock routine can do that.
GlobalFlags	na	Retrieves the flags associated with a global memory object.
GlobalHandle	na	Provides the global handle associated with a specific segment address.
GlobalLock	GlobalUnlock	Retrieves the address of a global memory object. In Real Mode, it also increments the lock count to prevent it from moving in physical memory. In all modes, it prevents a discardable object from being discarded.

(continued)

Table 18.6 Windows' Global Heap Management Routines

Top Slice	Bottom Slice	Description
GlobalLRUNewest	na	Changes a segment's priority in the LRU discarding table to make it *least* likely to be discarded.
GlobalLRUOldest	na	Changes a segment's priority in the LRU discarding table to make it the *most* likely to be discarded.
GlobalNotify	na	Sets up a call-back procedure through which the global heap manager notifies a program *before* a segment is discarded. A program can implement a virtual memory management scheme using this routine, that will work in all Windows' different operating modes.
GlobalPageLock	GlobalPageUnlock	Fixes a segment's location in the linear address space, and also prevents the virtual memory pages from being swapped out to disk. This provides the maximum protection against any movement of a segment, which is required for certain types of device drivers. However, programs should avoid using this since overuse of page locking can be severely detrimental to overall system performance.
GlobalReAlloc	na	Changes the size of a segment on the global heap. Both locked and unlocked segments can be resized, although a special flag must be set if you want to allow a locked segment to move if it is necessary to satisfy the allocation request.
GlobalSize	na	Returns the size of a segment on the global heap.
GlobalWire	GlobalUnwire	In Real-Mode Windows, moves a segment to a very low memory position for segments that are going to be locked for an unusually long period of time. This measure helps avoid serious fragmentation that otherwise occurs when movable or discardable memory objects are left locked for longer periods of time than to process a single message.

For most uses, programs can get by with five routines: `GlobalAlloc`, `GlobalReAlloc`, `GlobalLock`, `GlobalUnlock`, and `GlobalFree`. We will take a close look at this set of routines, to provide you with enough information so you can start using them in your programming projects.

GlobalAlloc. The `GlobalAlloc` routine allocates memory from the global heap. It is defined as

```
HANDLE GlobalAlloc (wFlags, dwBytes)
```

- `wFlags` is a combination of one or more global memory allocation flags, discussed below.

- `dwBytes` is an unsigned long value for the number of bytes to allocate.

`GlobalAlloc` returns the handle that identifies the segment you've allocated. Be sure to *always* check the return value from this function, since there is no guarantee that your request can be satisfied. When an allocation request cannot be met, `GlobalAlloc` lets you know by returning a `NULL` handle.

The value of `wFlags` can be a combination of nine different flags, depending on the type of memory you wish to allocate (fixed, moveable, or discardable), whether the memory is going to be shared, and other considerations. Here are the nine flags:

Description	*Flag*
Fixed memory object	`GMEM_FIXED`
Moveable memory object	`GMEM_MOVEABLE`
Discardable memory object	`GMEM_DISCARDABLE	GMEM_MOVEABLE`
Initialize with zeros	`GMEM_ZEROINIT`
Segment will be shared	`GMEM_DDESHARE`
Do not compact	`GMEM_NOCOMPACT`
Do not discard	`GMEM_NODISCARD`
Tag a discardable segment so that a notification routine is called *before* the segment is discarded	`GMEM_NOTIFY`
Do not put in EMS memory	`GMEM_NOT_BANKED`

The first four sets of flags are the most important and useful. Most of the time, you'll start by deciding the disposition of your memory object: fixed, moveable, or discardable. Next, you'll decide whether to initialize the data area with zeros; then your job is done. The other flags have more specialized uses, which we'll review briefly to help you decide when one might be useful to you.

The second parameter, `dwBytes`, is the number of bytes to allocate. Since this is an unsigned long value, you'll often have to supply a type-cast if you have calculated the size of an object using regular integer values. For example, here is how to allocate a 200-byte, moveable segment:

```
hMem = GlobalAlloc (GMEM_MOVEABLE, (DWORD)200);
```

This routine accepts an unsigned long value for the size of a memory object because it supports memory objects larger than 64K. Since this is the limit on the size of a segment, Windows allocates objects larger than 64K by setting aside multiple segments to satisfy your memory request. To allocate objects larger than 64K, you'll have to do some special **segment arithmetic** to allow segment boundaries to be crossed correctly.

One approach to handling segment arithmetic is to rely on the built-in support provided by some C Compilers. Pointers to such objects are referred to as huge pointers. However, this approach involves taking on quite a bit of overhead for even the simplest pointer operations. A more efficient approach is to use the __AHINCR symbol provided by Windows, which you can add to a segment address yourself if a segment boundary has been crossed.

The remaining flags are used for special circumstances. For example, the GMEM_DDESHARE flag marks a segment to be shared between programs. The "DDE" in the flag name is the acronym for the **dynamic data exchange** (DDE), a data sharing protocol built on top of Windows' message passing system. This flag should be used when sharing data using either DDE or the Clipboard.

In Windows 3.0 and 3.1 this flag changes the way Windows handles cleanup of the segment so the segment can be used even after its creator terminates. By default, whenever a segment gets allocated—either by an application or by a dynamic link library—ownership is assigned to the current application. To be more specific, ownership is assigned to the *task database* of the current application. When the task database goes away—that is, when the application terminates—every associated segment automatically is freed.

The use of the GMEM_DDESHARE flag by an application causes ownership to be assigned to the application's module database. This allows an application to allocate a segment, and share the segment with other instances of itself that are running. As long as an instance of the application continues to run, Windows will refrain from automatically freeing the segment. Without this flag, such a segment would be freed when the instance which created it terminates.

Another important use of GMEM_DDESHARE occurs when a dynamic link library wishes to allocate a segment for its own use. Although it may not have been clear from the earlier discussion, only an application can own memory without this flag. Even if a DLL allocates a block of memory, it's considered an allocation on behalf of the application. When the application terminates, the memory is freed. Except, however, when a DLL uses this flag. In such cases, ownership is assigned to the DLL's module database. The segment itself will only be freed when the DLL itself terminates.

The GMEM_NOCOMPACT flag prevents the memory manager from reorganizing global memory to satisfy an allocation request. The GMEM_NODISCARD flag gives a similar restriction: It prevents the memory manager from discarding segments to satisfy an allocation request. These flags are useful for programs that want to avoid disturbing the global heap. For a program that is very sensitive to performance issues, memory movement is expensive. These flags tell the memory manager that memory should be allocated *only* if it can be done quickly from an existing free block.

The GMEM_NOTIFY flag is used for discardable segments to request the memory manager to notify you before it discards your segments. When the time comes to discard a segment, the memory manager calls a function that you have defined as a notification call-back function. The notification routine is assigned using the GlobalNotify routine. It is useful for implementing a virtual memory system that works in all of Windows' operating modes.

The final flag, GMEM_NOT_BANKED, is primarily for the use of optimizing device drivers for Real Mode when EMS memory is present. EMS was a very important addition to Windows 2.x; but with the advent of Protected Mode and the use of extended memory, EMS is something that will become less and less useful over time. Since Real Mode support has been discontinued with Windows 3.1, this flag is obsolete.

GlobalLock. This routine provides the address of a global segment, and increments the lock count for certain types of segments. It is defined as

```
LPSTR GlobalLock (hMem)
```

• hMem is a memory handle of a segment allocated with GlobalAlloc.

Programs call GlobalLock to get the address of a moveable or discardable segment. In addition, this routine increments the lock count for discardable objects to prevent them from being discarded. Using moveable or discardable segments requires a two-step process. The first step is to allocate the memory itself. The second step involves calling GlobalLock to retrieve a far pointer that can be used to access the memory. For example, here is how to allocate a moveable segment that can accommodate a 274-byte object, and lock it for use:

```
HANDLE hMem;
LPSTR lp;

hMem = GlobalAlloc (GMEM_MOVEABLE, (DWORD)274));
if (!hMem)
    goto ErrorExit1;

lp = GlobalLock (hMem);
if (!lp)
    goto ErrorExit2;
```

Notice the two sets of error checking in this code fragment. The first check makes sure that the allocation was successful. The second check is to make sure that the lock is successful.

There are two basic ways to deal with Windows' allocation and locking: lock for every use and lock once at allocation. Although it might seem strange to lock an object every time you use it, that was a rule that programmers for Real Mode Windows had to follow. Otherwise, sandbars are created in the system heap. Even today, with Windows

3.1, you'll use this method for discardable objects. When you wish to prevent a discardable segment from disappearing, you must lock it. Locking an object for every use also requires you to unlock it for every use. This requires another call, `GlobalUnlock`.

For non-discardable segments, you'll lock at allocation time and only unlock right before freeing. As you may recall from our discussion of the the Protected Mode architecture, a locked segment can still be moved in physical memory and can even be swapped to disk.

Microsoft has provided a number of macros in WindowsX.h. These combine together the locking and unlocking steps into a single line of code. To allocate and lock a segment, use the `GlobalAllocPtr` macro. This combines a call to `GlobalAlloc` and `GlobalLock`. Freeing a segment involves calling this macro's close cousin, `GlobalFreePtr`.

GlobalReAlloc. This routine changes the size of a memory object on the global heap, and is defined as

```
HANDLE GlobalReAlloc (hMem, dwBytes, wFlags)
```

- `hMem` is a memory handle, obtained by calling `GlobalAlloc`.

- `dwBytes` is an unsigned long value for the number of bytes to allocate, or zero if the `GMEM_MODIFY` flag is being used to change the memory disposition of a memory object.

- `wFlags` is one or more flags, or zero if the object is just changing sizes.

The `GlobalReAlloc` routine can be used to do two different things: change the size of a global memory object and change the memory disposition of a memory object. It takes all the same flags as the `GlobalAlloc` routine plus one new one: `GMEM_MODIFY`. This flag indicates when the memory disposition is being changed— for example, when a moveable object is being made discardable, or when a discardable object is being made moveable. Aside from this, the `GlobalReAlloc` routine can pretty much be treated as an extension of the `GlobalAlloc` routine. Here are some examples of its usage:

```
/*  Make an object moveable.  */
GlobalReAlloc (hMem, 0, GMEM_MODIFY | GMEM_MOVEABLE);

/*  Resize an object.  */
GlobalReAlloc (hMem, (DWORD)1843, 0);

/*  Resize an object, filling new area with zeroes. */
GlobalReAlloc (hMem, (DWORD)dwSize, GMEM_ZEROINIT);
```

GlobalUnlock. The `GlobalUnlock` routine decrements the lock count for certain types of segments, and is defined as

```
BOOL GlobalUnlock (hMem)
```

- `hMem` is a memory handle allocated with the `GlobalAlloc` routine.

This function reverses the effects of the `GlobalLock` function. For discardable segments, you'll pair this with a call to `GlobalLock` every time you use the object. With non-discardable segments, on the other hand, you'll only need to unlock right before you free the segment.

GlobalFree. The `GlobalFree` routine frees an unlocked global memory object that was allocated with the `GlobalAlloc` routine. It is defined as

```
HANDLE GlobalFree (hMem)
```

- `hMem` is a global memory handle allocated by calling `GlobalAlloc`.

`GlobalFree` releases the segment and all internally created data structures associated with a given memory handle. Even though Windows frees all memory segments when a program terminates, it's a good practice to explicitly free every object when you are done using it.

This in-depth introduction to Windows' global heap management routines has almost prepared us for a look at sample programs. But first, we will explore an issue that should give you another perspective on how memory is managed in Windows. Even if you never use any of these routines in any of your Windows programs, understanding where they might be useful will help you better understand Windows' memory management. We're referring to the various routines that coerce a global segment to reside in a fixed location.

Locked, Wired, Fixed, and Page Locked

In our discussion of Windows global heap management routines, we identified `GlobalLock` as the routine used by programs to **dereference** a handle to get a pointer. By dereference, we simply mean to convert into a pointer. `GlobalLock` has a second role: When needed, it keeps objects from moving. Because of the difference between Real and Protected Modes, the exact meaning of this depends on the current operating mode. For example, in Protected Mode, `GlobalLock` doesn't prevent a movable object from being relocated, or even from being swapped to disk. However, in Real Mode, which doesn't have special hardware memory management support, `GlobalLock` *does* prevent such objects from moving. In all modes, it prevents discardable objects from being purged. Windows supports three other ways to influence the movement of a memory segment besides locking. A segment can also be wired, fixed, or page locked. Let's explore the meaning of each of these.

Wired Segments. When a program asks Windows to allocate a segment from the global heap, Windows searches through its free list, which is a set of doubly-linked lists that can be walked from either end. When allocating a fixed or moveable object, the memory manager always starts at the low-memory end of the free list. When allocating a discardable object, the search starts at the high-memory end. As depicted in Figure 18.7, this tends to group fixed and moveable objects at the bottom of memory, and discardable objects at the top of memory.

In addition, when allocating a fixed object, the global memory manager works quite hard to move moveable objects so fixed objects can be as low as possible. This accentu-

Figure 18.7 The layout of the global heap

ates the layering of the global heap even more; so—ideally at least—all fixed objects will be allocated lower than any moveable object. With fixed objects at the bottom of memory, moveable objects in the middle, and discardable objects at the top, fragmentation among moveable objects can be minimized. In a low-memory situation, Windows can purge several discardable objects at once, freeing up space for other uses.

In general, a program can change a discardable object into a movable object, or a movable object into a fixed object. (However, you can't change an object from being discardable to being fixed or vice-versa. If you need to do this, you must use two separate calls.) Unfortunately, such changes can destroy the organization of the global heap. For temporary changes to a global object's disposition, use the `GlobalWire`/ `GlobalUnwire` pair of routines.

`GlobalWire` first *moves* a moveable or discardable object to a very low memory location, then locks it down. This allows such objects to be fixed, without the fragmentation that would otherwise occur if the `GlobalLock` routine were used, for example. When a wired object does not have to be fixed any more, the `GlobalUnwire` routine can be used to let it rejoin the ranks of moveable and discardable objects.

Fixed Segments. In Protected Modes Windows, a locked global memory object can still move. In fact, it can even be swapped to disk. As described in the preceding chapter, such movement is possible because of the hardware memory management built into Protected Mode. The LDT table, for example, allows a memory segment to move in physical memory without a change in its logical address.

Certain device drivers, however, don't operate on the logical address but instead they use the physical address. For their use, the global heap management routines include the `GlobalFix`/ `GlobalUnfix` pair. The `GlobalFix` routine forces a segment to remain at the same physical address. In the same way that programs shouldn't lock down segments for lengthy periods of time, segments should not be fixed for lengthy periods of time. This can cause fragmentation of the physical address space, which makes overall system memory management less efficient. But for device drivers and other uses that require a fixed physical addresss, the `GlobalFix` routine can be used. To counter the effect of `GlobalFix`, call `GlobalUnfix`.

Page-Locked Segments. Even though `GlobalFix` can prevent an object from moving in the physical address space, it can still be swapped to disk. The reason is that there are two memory managers at work: one that manages the linear, "virtual" address space, and another that supports this address space by moving blocks of memory—also known as "pages"—between RAM and disk. When a referenced page is not present, a page fault forces the virtual memory manager to fetch the required page.

While `GlobalFix` prevents an object from moving in the virtual address space, there are times when even more control is needed. In particular, for time-critical device drivers, it may be necessary to select certain segments and designate them as **page-locked**. A page-locked segment is the most securely attached segment provided by Windows. Such segments cannot move in the virtual address space, so their address stays the same. In addition, such segments cannot be swapped to disk; therefore, access time is always the best it can be. Even if you never write a device driver that requires page-locking, it's nice to know that Windows has this capability to allow time-critical operations, such as keyboard, communications, and mouse driver code, to be serviced as quickly as possible.

From earlier versions of Windows, some programmers have gotten into the habit of using a segment's lock-count to determine whether the segment needs to be unlocked. In Windows 3.x, with its sophisticated memory management, certain things have changed. If you are new to Windows programming, or if you are starting a new programming project, you don't need to worry about this practice. But if you are supporting older Windows code, be on the lookout for code using the lock count as a reference count.

> **HINT:** Avoid depending on using the lock count to determine whether `GlobalLock` has locked a segment. In both Protected Modes, `GlobalLock` does not affect the lock count of a moveable segment.

It's time to look closely at a sample Windows program that allocates memory from the global heap.

A Sample Program: SEGALLOC

This sample program allocates three different segments from the global heap and displays information about each one. Figure 18.8 shows the output from our program, SEGALLOC. As you can see, SEGALLOC allocates one fixed, one moveable, and one discardable segment. Also displayed are the bytes requested, the actual size of the allocated object, the handle, and the address of the segment.

If you compare the handle and the address for each type of memory, you'll notice that the segment selector is always equal to the memory handle plus one. This seems like a good shortcut to take, but don't do it! Your program is guaranteed to break in a future version of Windows in which this pattern may not be followed. Microsoft plans to continue enhancing Windows. If you rely on this particular quirk, your programs may stop working in a future version of Windows.

Description	Req/Actual	Handle -> Address
Fixed Object	50 / 64	128d -> 128d:0000
Moveable Memory	75 / 96	1296 -> 1295:0000
Discardable Segment	100 / 128	129e -> 129d:0000

Global Heap Allocation

Figure 18.8 SEGALLOC displays information about the segments it allocates

SEGALLOC.C

```
/*-----------------------------------------------------------*\
| SEGALLOC - Sample program showing global heap allocation in |
|            Microsoft Windows.                               |
\*-----------------------------------------------------------*/
#include <Windows.H>
#include <WindowsX.H>

#define STRSIZE 30
typedef struct tagSEGDATA
    {
    char  achDesc[STRSIZE];  /*  Description of data.  */
    DWORD dwAlloc;           /*  Amount asked for.     */
    DWORD dwActual;          /*  Actually allocated.   */
    WORD  wFlags;            /*  Allocation flags.     */
    } SEGDATA;

typedef SEGDATA FAR *LPSEGDATA;

#define COUNT       3

// Create WindowsX.H type of macro
#define GlobalSizePtr(lp) (GlobalSize((GlobalPtrHandle(lp))))


/*-----------------------------------------------------------*\
|                   Function Prototypes.                      |
\*-----------------------------------------------------------*/
LRESULT CALLBACK SegAllocWndProc (HWND, UINT, WPARAM, LPARAM);

/*-----------------------------------------------------------*\
|                   Global Variables.                         |
\*-----------------------------------------------------------*/
char achWndClass[] = "SegAlloc:MAIN";
char achAppName[]  = "Global Heap Allocation";

/*-----------------------------------------------------------*\
|                   Main Function:  WinMain.                  |
\*-----------------------------------------------------------*/
```

```
int PASCAL
WinMain (HINSTANCE hInstance,        // Who am I?
         HINSTANCE hPrevInstance,    // Any older siblings?
         LPSTR     lpszCmdLine,      // Ptr to command line.
         int       cmdShow)          // How to open my window?
    {
    HWND      hwnd;
    MSG       msg;
    WNDCLASS wndclass;

    if (!hPrevInstance)
        {
        wndclass.lpszClassName = achWndClass;
        wndclass.hInstance     = hInstance;
        wndclass.lpfnWndProc   = SegAllocWndProc;
        wndclass.hCursor       = LoadCursor (hInstance, "hand");
        wndclass.hIcon         = LoadIcon (hInstance,"snapshot");
        wndclass.lpszMenuName  = NULL;
        wndclass.hbrBackground = (HBRUSH)(COLOR_WINDOW+1);
        wndclass.style         = NULL;
        wndclass.cbClsExtra    = 0;
        wndclass.cbWndExtra    = 0;

        RegisterClass( &wndclass);
        }

    hwnd = CreateWindowEx(0L,                // Extra style.
                    achWndClass,             // Class name.
                    achAppName,              // Title.
                    WS_OVERLAPPEDWINDOW,     // Style bits.
                    CW_USEDEFAULT,           // x - default.
                    0,                       // y - default.
                    CW_USEDEFAULT,           // cx - default.
                    0,                       // cy - default.
                    NULL,                    // No parent.
                    NULL,                    // Class menu.
                    hInstance,               // Creator.
                    NULL);                   // Params.
    ShowWindow (hwnd, cmdShow);

    while (GetMessage(&msg, 0, 0, 0))
        {
        TranslateMessage(&msg); // Convert KEYDOWNs to CHARs
        DispatchMessage(&msg);  // Transmit message to WndProc
        }
    return 0;
    }

/*-------------------------------------------------------------*\
|             Window Procedure:  SegAllocWndProc.              |
\*-------------------------------------------------------------*/
LRESULT CALLBACK
SegAllocWndProc (HWND   hwnd,      // For whom is message sent?
                 UINT   mMsg,      // What is exact message?
                 WPARAM wParam,    // ...message details.
```

```
                        LPARAM lParam)    // ...message details.
        {
        static char Label1[] = "Description";
        static char Label2[] = "Req/Actual";
        static char Label3[] = "Handle  ->  Address";

        static int  cb1 = sizeof (Label1) - 1;
        static int  cb2 = sizeof (Label2) - 1;
        static int  cb3 = sizeof (Label3) - 1;

        static LPSEGDATA lpsd[COUNT];

        static SEGDATA sd[COUNT] =
            {
            "Fixed Object",                50, 0, GMEM_FIXED,
            "Moveable Memory",             75, 0, GMEM_MOVEABLE |
                                                  GMEM_ZEROINIT,
            "Discardable Segment",        100, 0, GMEM_DISCARDABLE |
                                                  GMEM_MOVEABLE,
            };
        static TEXTMETRIC tmSys;

        switch (mMsg)
            {
            case WM_CREATE:
                {
                HDC        hdc;
                int        i;
                LPSEGDATA lpsdTemp;

                for (i=0;i<COUNT;i++)
                    {
                    lpsdTemp =
                    lpsd[i]  = (LPSEGDATA)GlobalAllocPtr(
                                        sd[i].wFlags,
                                        sd[i].dwAlloc);

                    if (!lpsd)
                        goto ErrorExit;

                    lstrcpy (lpsdTemp->achDesc, sd[i].achDesc);
                    lpsdTemp->dwAlloc  = sd[i].dwAlloc;
                    lpsdTemp->dwActual = GlobalSizePtr (lpsd[i]);
                    lpsdTemp->wFlags   = sd[i].wFlags;
                    } /* [for] */

                hdc = GetDC (hwnd);
                GetTextMetrics (hdc, &tmSys);
                ReleaseDC (hwnd, hdc);
                break;
                }
        ErrorExit:
                MessageBox NULL,
                            "Not enough memory",
                            "SegAlloc", MB_OK);
                return -1L;
```

```
            break;

    case WM_DESTROY:
        {
        int i;

        for (i=0;i<COUNT;i++)
            GlobalFreePtr (lpsd[i]);
        }
        PostQuitMessage(0);   // Handle application shutdown.
        break;

    case WM_PAINT:
        {
        char buff[30];
        int i;
        int xText1;
        int xText2;
        int xText3;
        int yText;

        HGLOBAL      hmem;
        LPSEGDATA    lpsdTemp;
        PAINTSTRUCT  ps;

        BeginPaint (hwnd, &ps);

        /*  Calculate text positioning variables.          */
        xText1 = tmSys.tmAveCharWidth * 2;
        xText2 = xText1 + (STRSIZE * tmSys.tmAveCharWidth);
        xText3 = xText2 + ((cb2+5) * tmSys.tmAveCharWidth);
        yText = tmSys.tmHeight;

        /*  Print titles.                                   */
        TextOut (ps.hdc, xText1, yText, Label1, cb1);
        TextOut (ps.hdc, xText2, yText, Label2, cb2);
        TextOut (ps.hdc, xText3, yText, Label3, cb3);

        yText += tmSys.tmHeight * 2;

        for (i=0 ;i<COUNT ;i++)
            {

            lpsdTemp = lpsd[i];

            /*  Print description.                          */
            TextOut (ps.hdc, xText1, yText,
                    lpsdTemp->achDesc,
                    lstrlen(lpsdTemp->achDesc));

            /*  Print allocated vs actual size.             */
            wsprintf (buff, "%ld / %ld", lpsdTemp->dwAlloc,
                                        lpsdTemp->dwActual);
            TextOut (ps.hdc, xText2, yText,
                    buff, lstrlen (buff));
```

```
                        /*  Print handle and actual address.          */
                        hmem = (HGLOBAL)LOWORD(GlobalHandle(
                                            SELECTOROF(lpsdTemp)));
                        wsprintf (buff, "%04x  ->  %04x:%04x", hmem,
                                  HIWORD(lpsdTemp), LOWORD(lpsdTemp));
                        TextOut (ps.hdc, xText3, yText,
                                  buff, lstrlen (buff));

                        /*  Advance to next line.                      */
                        yText += tmSys.tmHeight + tmSys.tmExternalLeading;
                        }

                EndPaint (hwnd, &ps);
                }
                break;

        default:
                return(DefWindowProc(hwnd,mMsg,wParam,lParam));
                break;
        }
    return 0L;
    }
```

SEGALLOC.DEF

```
NAME    SEGALLOC

EXETYPE WINDOWS

DESCRIPTION 'Segment Allocation (c) 1992 By Paul Yao'

CODE    MOVEABLE PRELOAD
DATA    MOVEABLE MULTIPLE PRELOAD

HEAPSIZE    512
STACKSIZE   5120

SEGMENTS
    SEGALLOC_TEXT MOVEABLE PRELOAD

EXPORTS
    SegAllocWndProc
```

SEGALLOC.LNK

```
SegAlloc.obj
SegAlloc.exe/align:16/map/nod/noe/CO
nul
```

```
mlibcew libw
SegAlloc.def
```

SEGALLOC.MAK

```
# Directory search paths.

INCDIR = \WINDEV\INCLUDE

# Windows version to support
# Valid pairs include:
#     (0x0300, 30)
#     (0x0310, 31)

CLVER = WINVER=0x0300
RCVER = 30

# Compiler switches for applications.

CL_APP_SHIP_ALL = -AM -c -D$(CLVER) -Gsw -I$(INCDIR) -Ow -W3 -Zp
CL_APP_DEBG_ALL = -AM -c -D$(CLVER) -Gsw -I$(INCDIR) -Od -W3 -Zpi

CL_APP_SHIP_31  = -AM -c -G2s  -I$(INCDIR) -Ow -W3 -Zp
CL_APP_DEBG_31  = -AM -c -G2s  -I$(INCDIR) -Od -W3 -Zpi

# Compiler switches for DLLs.

CL_DLL_SHIP_ALL = -AMw -c -D$(CLVER) -Gsw -I$(INCDIR) -Ow -W3 -Zp
CL_DLL_DEBG_ALL = -AMw -c -D$(CLVER) -Gsw -I$(INCDIR) -Od -W3 -Zpi

CL_DLL_SHIP_31  = -AMw -c -G2s  -I$(INCDIR) -Ow -W3 -Zp
CL_DLL_DEBG_31  = -AMw -c -G2s  -I$(INCDIR) -Od -W3 -Zpi

# Make file primary target.

all: SegAlloc.exe

# Make file dependency targets.

SegAlloc.res: SegAlloc.rc SegAlloc.cur SegAlloc.ico
    rc -r -i$(INCDIR) SegAlloc.rc

SegAlloc.obj: SegAlloc.c
    cl $(CL_APP_SHIP_ALL) SegAlloc.c

SegAlloc.exe: SegAlloc.obj SegAlloc.def SegAlloc.res
    link @SegAlloc.lnk
    rc -$(RCVER) SegAlloc.res

SegAlloc.exe: SegAlloc.res
    rc -$(RCVER) SegAlloc.res
```

SEGALLOC.RC

```
snapshot icon SegAlloc.ico

hand   cursor SegAlloc.cur
```

Perhaps the most important aspect of this code involves the error checking performed when a global memory object is allocated. It is important to check the return value when you allocate, because there is no guarantee that you will get the memory you have requested. Even if you get the requested memory, you must guard against the possibility that a memory handle will become invalid. In a large program with many different pieces, it's always possible that a memory handle can get overwritten or inadvertently freed.

Another important aspect of global heap allocation has to do with the length of time that a memory object is left locked. Although the rule under Real Mode was to lock an object only when it was in use, in Windows 3.1 this rule only applies to discardable objects. If you are responsible for maintaining older code, and if you determine that you're only going to run in Protected Mode, you may wish to rewrite your code using the `GlobalAllocPtr` macro, as used in SEGALLOC.

Our next sample program looks at the relationship between the structure of a program's code and good memory usage. The recommendation that a program be divided into multiple, small code segments goes against the grain of many MS-DOS programmers. But since DOS is a single-tasking system, with no built-in support for dynamic overlays, DOS programmers can get away with creating monolithic programs with large code segments. Efficient operation under Windows, on the other hand, requires a different approach.

Code Structure and Memory Use

Although most of the material in this chapter deals with the data used by a program, an equally important issue is the memory used by a program's code. Because of the magic of dynamic linking, Windows can run with only part of a program loaded into memory at any given time. Dynamic linking gives you all the benefits of a sophisticated overlay manager, without requiring you to carefully design each overlay.

While care is not *required* in putting together the different overlay working sets that make up a program, some effort is required to get the best performance in a low-memory situation. Even in Protected Mode, when there are megabytes and megabytes of memory, a program can encounter a low-memory situation when there are lots of other programs running. To help you create programs that run well in low memory situations, we're going to provide two basic recommendations: one easy and one requiring a little more effort. The approach you take will depend on the size of your program, and the need to perform well in low-memory situations.

The simple approach involves dividing your program into multiple, small (4K or so) code segments. When working with the Microsoft C Compiler, this requires that you first divide your code between multiple source files. But beyond that, you must make entries into your program's module definition (.DEF) file. This is necessary because the linker (LINK.EXE) will try to pack smaller code segments into larger code segments. However, by restructuring your application, you'll be able to define your own PRE-LOAD segments, so the Windows loader can be sure to load the minimum required set of segments to make your program's start-up perform quickly.

The second approach that you can take to improve your program's performance in low-memory situations involves running **swap-tuner** to test the memory activity associated with your program. One such tool is the Segmentor, created by MicroQuill of Seattle, Washington. The Segmentor records all memory loading and discarding activity. This information is used to calculate the optimal **working sets** of your program. A working set is defined as the groupings of code segments required to perform a specific task or set of tasks. The swap-tuner helps you see the actual memory activity of your program, so you can adjust the code that each code segment contains to minimize thrashing—the need to re-read many different segments from disk in order to accomplish a specific task. The Segmentor simplifies this process by automating the placement of functions into segments.

A Sample Segmented Program

We're going to start with a simple example of a segmented program. This is hardly going to be a "realistic example," since we're just going to divide our minimum Windows program, MIN, into three segments. However, our experience shows that some of the trouble with segmenting applications stems from little quirks in the development tools. Therefore, this example will show you how to overcome these quirks to successfully divide a program into multiple code segments.

We're going to call this program MIN2, although you can call it "Son of Min," if you'd like. To start, the Microsoft C Compiler requires the code from each segment to be in a different source file. MIN2 has two source files: MIN2.C and MIN2INIT.C.

MIN2.C

```
/*-------------------------------------------------------------*\
| MIN2.C  A Minimum Windows Program that demonstrates the      |
|         principles of segmenting code in an application.     |
\*-------------------------------------------------------------*/
#define STRICT
#include <Windows.H>


/*-------------------------------------------------------------*\
|                    Function Prototypes.                      |
\*-------------------------------------------------------------*/
LRESULT CALLBACK Min2WndProc (HWND, UINT, WPARAM, LPARAM);
VOID FAR PASCAL Min2Init (HINSTANCE, HINSTANCE, int);


/*-------------------------------------------------------------*\
|                    Global Variables.                         |
\*-------------------------------------------------------------*/
char achWndClass[] = "MIN2:MAIN";
```

```c
char achAppName[]  = "Minimum";

/*-------------------------------------------------------------*\
 |                   Main Function:  WinMain.                   |
 \*-------------------------------------------------------------*/
int PASCAL
WinMain (HINSTANCE hInstance,        // Who am I?
         HINSTANCE hPrevInstance,    // Any older siblings?
         LPSTR     lpszCmdLine,      // Ptr to command line.
         int       cmdShow)          // How to open my window?
    {
    MSG     msg;

    // Register class & create window.
    Min2Init (hInstance, hPrevInstance, cmdShow);

    while (GetMessage(&msg, 0, 0, 0))
        {
        TranslateMessage(&msg); // Convert KEYDOWNs to CHARs
        DispatchMessage(&msg);  // Transmit message to WndProc
        }
    return 0;
    }


/*-------------------------------------------------------------*\
 |              Window Procedure:  Min2WndProc.                |
 \*-------------------------------------------------------------*/
LRESULT CALLBACK
Min2WndProc (HWND    hwnd,      // For whom is message sent?
             UINT    mMsg,      // What is exact message?
             WPARAM  wParam,    // ...message details.
             LPARAM  lParam)    // ...message details.
    {
    switch (mMsg)
        {
        case WM_DESTROY:
            PostQuitMessage(0);  // Handle application shutdown.
            break;

        default:
            return(DefWindowProc(hwnd,mMsg,wParam,lParam));
            break;
        }
    return 0L;
    }
```

MIN2INIT.C

```c
/*-------------------------------------------------------------*\
 |   Min2Init.C - Initialization routine for MIN2.             |
 \*-------------------------------------------------------------*/
#define STRICT
```

```
#include <Windows.H>

/*-------------------------------------------------------------*\
|                    Function Prototypes.                       |
\*-------------------------------------------------------------*/
LRESULT CALLBACK Min2WndProc (HWND, UINT, WPARAM, LPARAM);
VOID FAR PASCAL Min2Init (HINSTANCE, HINSTANCE, int);

/*-------------------------------------------------------------*\
|                     Global Variables.                        |
\*-------------------------------------------------------------*/
extern char achWndClass[];
extern char achAppName[];

/*-------------------------------------------------------------*\
|            Application Initialization:  Min2Init.            |
\*-------------------------------------------------------------*/
VOID FAR PASCAL Min2Init (HINSTANCE hInstance,
                          HINSTANCE hPrevInstance,
                          int cmdShow)
    {
    HWND     hwnd;
    WNDCLASS wndclass;

    if (!hPrevInstance)
        {
        wndclass.lpszClassName  = achWndClass;
        wndclass.hInstance      = hInstance;
        wndclass.lpfnWndProc    = Min2WndProc;
        wndclass.hCursor        = LoadCursor (hInstance, "hand");
        wndclass.hIcon          = LoadIcon (hInstance,"snapshot");
        wndclass.lpszMenuName   = NULL;
        wndclass.hbrBackground  = (HBRUSH)(COLOR_WINDOW+1);
        wndclass.style          = NULL;
        wndclass.cbClsExtra     = 0;
        wndclass.cbWndExtra     = 0;

        RegisterClass( &wndclass);
        }

    hwnd = CreateWindowEx(0L,                 // Extra style.
                    achWndClass,              // Class name.
                    achAppName,               // Title.
                    WS_OVERLAPPEDWINDOW,      // Style bits.
                    CW_USEDEFAULT,            // x - default.
                    0,                        // y - default.
                    CW_USEDEFAULT,            // cx - default.
                    0,                        // cy - default.
                    NULL,                     // No parent.
                    NULL,                     // Class menu.
                    hInstance,                // Creator.
                    NULL);                    // Params.
    ShowWindow (hwnd, cmdShow);

    }
```

MIN2.DEF

```
NAME    MIN2

EXETYPE WINDOWS

DESCRIPTION 'Minimum Windows Program (c) 1992 By Paul Yao'

CODE    MOVEABLE PRELOAD
DATA    MOVEABLE MULTIPLE PRELOAD

HEAPSIZE    512
STACKSIZE   5120

SEGMENTS
    MIN_TEXT        MOVEABLE PRELOAD
    MIN2INIT_TEXT   MOVEABLE PRELOAD DISCARDABLE
    _TEXT           MOVEABLE PRELOAD

EXPORTS
    Min2WndProc
```

MIN2.LNK

```
Min2.obj + Min2Init.obj
Min2.exe/align:16/map/nod/noe/CO
Min2.map/map
mlibcew libw
Min2.def
```

MIN2.MAK

```
# Directory search paths.

INCDIR = \WINDEV\INCLUDE

# Windows version to support
# Valid pairs include:
#     (0x0300, 30)
#     (0x0310, 31)

CLVER = WINVER=0x0300
RCVER = 30

# Compiler switches for applications.

CL_APP_SHIP_ALL = -AM -c -D$(CLVER) -Gsw -I$(INCDIR) -Ow -W3 -Zp
CL_APP_DEBG_ALL = -AM -c -D$(CLVER) -Gsw -I$(INCDIR) -Od -W3 -Zpi
```

```
CL_APP_SHIP_31  = -AM -c -G2s  -I$(INCDIR) -Ow -W3 -Zp
CL_APP_DEBG_31  = -AM -c -G2s  -I$(INCDIR) -Od -W3 -Zpi

# Compiler switches for DLLs.

CL_DLL_SHIP_ALL = -AMw -c -D$(CLVER) -Gsw -I$(INCDIR) -Ow -W3 -Zp
CL_DLL_DEBG_ALL = -AMw -c -D$(CLVER) -Gsw -I$(INCDIR) -Od -W3 -Zpi

CL_DLL_SHIP_31  = -AMw -c -G2s  -I$(INCDIR) -Ow -W3 -Zp
CL_DLL_DEBG_31  = -AMw -c -G2s  -I$(INCDIR) -Od -W3 -Zpi

# Make file primary target.

all: Min2.exe

# Make file dependency targets.

Min2.res: Min2.rc Min2.cur Min2.ico
    rc -r -i$(INCDIR) Min2.rc

Min2.obj: Min2.c
    cl $(CL_APP_SHIP_ALL) Min2.c

Min2Init.obj: Min2Init.c
    cl $(CL_APP_SHIP_ALL) Min2Init.c

Min2.exe: Min2.obj Min2Init.obj Min2.def Min2.res
    link @Min2.lnk
    rc -$(RCVER) Min2.res

Min2.exe: Min2.res
    rc -$(RCVER) Min2.res
```

MIN2.RC

```
snapshot icon Min2.ico

hand   cursor Min2.cur
```

Even though this program has only two source files, there are actually three code segments. The third code segment contains a program's start-up code and other support routines that are automatically linked in at program creation time. These items reside in a segment named _TEXT. The names of the other segments are created by the C compiler using the filename plus _TEXT. For example, the source file MIN2.C creates a code segment with the name MIN2_TEXT.

Each segment of our program is listed in the module definition file under the SEG-MENTS keyword. Getting a large application to start quickly involves making a decision about which segments to mark as PRELOAD. Assuming that you're able to isolate all the required initialization code into a few preload segments, you'll get the best startup time possible.

Notice the use of the four keywords in MIN2's module definition file: PRELOAD, MOVEABLE, DISCARDABLE, and LOADONCALL. As the names suggest, each keyword gives a memory attribute to a segment. While the FIXED keyword can also be used, it should be avoided. There is a bug in version 3.0 of Windows that makes such segments fixed and page-locked. While this will be corrected in a future version, you should avoid this keyword for now. While the use of this keyword is suitable for device drivers, it is not suitable for application programs because of the constraints its use puts on the global heap manager.

The next step to tuning MIN2 involves running it through the swap-tuner. This would allow us to see when segments are loaded and discarded. Of course, there are only a few routines in the two segments that make up MIN2. In a larger program, the swap-tuner would help to restructure a program to improve the performance in a low-memory situation.

The results of swap tuning can seem paradoxical at times. For example, to make the best use of memory, it may be necessary to duplicate certain routines that are used in several different places. Instead of centralizing the "helper" routines in a program, it may make sense to create multiple copies of each, with a local copy in the code segments where the service is needed. Another alternative involves proving each function with its own code segment. Of course, the trade-off here is that far calls are quite a bit more expensive than near calls.

We hope this introduction to the effect of code structure on memory use will help you start thinking about code in a different way. Code structure *can* affect the performance of a Windows program, just as surely as the structure of a program's data will affect its performance. It's time to look at our next sample program, which provides an example of using the local heap automatically provided as part of every program's default data segment.

Local Heap Allocation

Let's take a look at Windows' local heap allocation routines. Table 18.7 lists all of the routines provided for local heap management. We're going to focus our attention on six of them: LocalInit, LocalAlloc, LocalLock, LocalReAlloc, LocalUnlock, and LocalFree.

LocalInit. The LocalInit routine initializes a local heap. LocalInit takes three parameters:

```
BOOL LocalInit (wSegment, pStart, pEnd)
```

- wSegment is the segment address of the heap to be initialized; or, if it is zero, the data segment referenced by the DS register is initialized.

- pStart is the beginning offset of the heap in the segment.

- pEnd is the offset of the end of the heap in the segment; *or*, if pStart is zero, then pEnd is the size of the heap, and a heap is created at the *end* of the designated segment.

Table 18.7 Windows Local Heap Management Routines

LocalAlloc	Allocates memory from a local heap.
LocalCompact	Reorganizes a local heap.
LocalDiscard	Discards an unlocked, discardable object.
LocalFlags	Provides information about a specific memory object.
LocalFree	Frees a local memory object.
LocalHandle	Provides the handle of a local memory object associated with a given memory address.
LocalInit	Initializes a local heap.
LocalLock	Increments the lock count on a local memory object, and returns its address.
LocalReAlloc	Changes the size of a local memory object.
LocalShrink	Reorganizes a local heap and reduces the size of the heap (if possible) to the initial, starting size. If this routine is successful, it reduces the size of the data segment that contains the heap, so that the memory can be reclaimed by the global heap.
LocalSize	Returns the current size of a local memory object.
LocalUnlock	Decrements the lock count on a local memory object.

LocalInit installs the necessary data structures required to support local heap allocation in a segment. Windows programs do not need to initialize their default data segment, since LocalInit is called automatically. However, LocalInit *can* be called to set up a local heap in another segment. As we'll detail later in this chapter, this allows you to have access to as many local heaps as you need.

Unlike application programs, Windows dynamic link libraries must explicitly call LocalInit in order to have a local heap.

LocalAlloc. The LocalAlloc routine allocates memory from a local heap. It is defined as

```
HANDLE LocalAlloc (wFlags, wBytes)
```

- wFlags is a combination of one or more local memory allocation flags, discussed below.

- wBytes is an unsigned integer value of the size of the object to allocate.

LocalAlloc returns a handle that identifies the object you've allocated. Be sure that you *always* check the return value, since there is never a guarantee that you'll get the memory you requested. A NULL handle is returned when a memory allocation request fails.

The value of `wFlags` can be a combination of five flags, depending on the type of memory object you wish to allocate (fixed, moveable, or discardable), whether to avoid disturbing the heap, and whether to initialize with zeros. This table lists your choices:

Description	*Flags*
Fixed memory object	`LMEM_FIXED`
Moveable memory object	`LMEM_MOVEABLE`
Discardable memory object	`LMEM_MOVEABLE	LMEM_DISCARDABLE`
Do not compact or discard	`LMEM_NOCOMPACT`
Initialize with zeros	`LMEM_ZEROINIT`

As this table suggests, if you wish to allocate a discardable object, you use *both* the moveable and the discardable flag. This makes sense, since a discardable object must also be moveable. The `LMEM_NOCOMPACT` flag tells the local memory manager that your need for memory can be satisfied some other way, and that if there isn't an available free block, no moving or discarding should be done to satisfy the memory allocation. When you wish to use more than one flag, you combine them using the OR operator " | ". For example, to allocate a five-byte moveable object that is initialized with zeros, you say:

```
hMem = LocalAlloc (LMEM_MOVEABLE | LMEM_ZEROINIT, 5);
```

Be careful to avoid the `LMEM_NODISCARD` flag, which is mentioned in the Microsoft documentation, but doesn't seem to have the effect to prevent discarding that the documentation says it should. It seems to have no effect at all.

`LocalAlloc` returns a memory handle. For moveable and discardable memory objects, you obtain a pointer by calling the `LocalLock` routine, which we'll discuss shortly. For fixed objects, the handle itself is a pointer. In this way, `LocalAlloc` can be used in exactly the same manner as the C library's `malloc`. In other words, here is how to allocate and use a fixed memory object:

```
char * pch;
pch =(char *)LocalAlloc (LMEM_FIXED|LMEM_ZEROINIT, 15);
lstrcpy (pch, "Hello World");
```

For the sake of clarity, this code uses the normal C type, `char *`, instead of the more precise Windows type, `PSTR`. You may have already noticed that this code casts the return value from `LocalAlloc`, which prevents the compiler from complaining about assigning a `HANDLE` value (`unsigned int`) to a pointer. We know it's correct. The cast tells the compiler to save its error messages for real problems.

LocalLock. The `LocalLock` routine increments the lock count on a local memory object, and returns its address.

```
PSTR LocalLock (hMem)
```

- `hMem` is a handle to a memory object, returned by a call to `LocalAlloc`.

Programs call `LocalLock` to get the address of a moveable or discardable object. At the same time, this routine makes sure that the object won't get moved or discarded so the address will be valid until a call is made to `LocalUnlock`. In general, it's a good idea to keep all objects unlocked until the precise time that they are needed. This gives the local heap manager the freedom to move memory as needed to optimize the use of the local heap.

According to the prototype in Windows.H, `LocalLock` returns a near pointer to a character string. However, this doesn't mean that only character values can be placed into a memory object. You put the return value from `LocalLock` into any type of pointer, to provide you with a convenient way to access any type of dynamically allocated data. The following example makes it easy to store an array of integers into a local memory object:

```
int * pi;

pi = (int near * )LocalLock (hmem);
if (pi)
        {
        pi[0] = 1;
        pi[1] = 2;
        LocalUnlock (hmem);
        }
else
        {
        /* Error.  */
        }
```

It's very important to check the return value from `LocalLock`, as we've done in this example. A null pointer indicates that the lock has failed. Several things could make this happen. If we are trying to lock a discardable object, it's possible that the object has been discarded or the memory handle has been accidentally overwritten. Whatever the cause, you don't want to write using a null pointer. You will overwrite the memory locations at the bottom of your data segment, which means the data area that is used to maintain your data segment.

LocalReAlloc. The `LocalReAlloc` routine changes the size of a local memory object. `LocalReAlloc` is defined as

```
HANDLE LocalReAlloc (hMem, wBytes, wFlags)
```

- hMem is a memory handle returned by the `LocalAlloc` routine.

- wBytes is the new size. When you make an object smaller, it truncates (and loses) the data from the end of the object. When you make an object larger, it preserves the previous contents of the object.

- wFlags is a combination of one or more local allocation flags.

`LocalReAlloc` returns a HANDLE, which is one of three values. If the reallocation fails, the return value is NULL. For moveable and discardable objects, if the allocation is successful, the return value is the same handle value that was passed into the routine. For fixed objects, the handle may be the same or may be different, depending on whether the object must be moved to satisfy the allocation request.

To understand why, recall from our earlier discussion that the handle to a fixed memory object is actually a pointer to the object itself. If the object must be moved to satisfy a memory allocation request, it follows that the pointer must change as well. To prevent the local memory manager from mysteriously moving a fixed object, a fixed object will only be moved by the `LocalReAlloc` call if the `LMEM_MOVEABLE` flag is specified. For example, here is how to reallocate a fixed memory object, allowing it to move:

```
/*  Enlarge a fixed object, and let it move.        */
hNew = LocalReAlloc (hOld,
                     cbSize,          /* New size.    */
                     LMEM_MOVEABLE);/* Ok to move.   */
if (!hNew)
      {
      /*  Error.  */
      }
else
      hOld = hNew;
```

The `LMEM_MOVEABLE` flag has another use. This flag allows a moveable or discardable memory object that is *locked* to be moved if needed to satisfy an allocation request. In most cases, you'll only change the size of a moveable or discardable memory object when it is unlocked. At such times, the memory manager is free to relocate the object. But, if you wish to make a locked object larger, you'll need to include the `LMEM_MOVEABLE` flag in case the object must be moved.

If you want to change the *size* of a local memory object and *not* its memory disposition (fixed, moveable, discardable), you can set `wFlags` to zero, or use the `LMEM_ZEROINIT` flag to ask for a larger object with the newly allocated space zero initialized. For example, even though the `wFlags` field is set to zero in this example, it doesn't change the memory disposition—only the size:

```
h = LocalReAlloc (hMem,
                  28,    //  New size.
                  0);    //  Ignore flags.
```

To change the memory disposition of a memory object, use the `LMEM_MODIFY` flag. You can't change the disposition of a fixed memory object. However, you *can* make a moveable object discardable, or make a discardable object into a moveable object. To make a moveable object discardable, you say:

```
LocalReAlloc (hMem,
              0,                    // Ignore the size.
              LMEM_MODIFY   |       // Just change flags.
              LMEM_MOVEABLE |
              LMEM_DISCARDABLE);
```

and to make a discardable object moveable, you say:

```
LocalReAlloc (hMem,
              0,                    // Ignore the size.
              LMEM_MODIFY |         // Just change flags.
              LMEM_MOVEABLE);
```

When you change the memory disposition like this, the reallocation size is ignored. In these examples, even though we request a reallocation size of zero, the LMEM_MODIFY flag has precedence; so we can safely use a value of zero, to avoid having to figure out the current size of the object and pass it in to LocalReAlloc.

LocalUnlock. The LocalUnlock routine decrements the lock count on a local memory object.

```
BOOL LocalUnlock (hMem)
```

• hMem is a local memory handle, as provided by LocalAlloc.

The LocalUnlock routine is the second slice to a Windows sandwich. To give the local memory manager the greatest freedom to manage the local heap, you should lock memory objects for only the briefest period of time. For example, to store character values that a program receives from a WM_CHAR message, you would say:

```
...
case WM_CHAR:
    pch = LocalLock(hmem);
    pch[iNextChar] = (unsigned char) wParam;
    LocalUnlock (hmem);
    break;
...
```

In this case, the memory object identified by the handle hmem is only kept locked for as long as it takes to copy a character into the memory object.

LocalFree. The LocalFree routine frees a local memory object.

```
HANDLE LocalFree (hMem)
```

• hMem is a memory handle returned by LocalAlloc.

Any time a dynamic memory object is allocated, it consumes memory that cannot be used for other purposes. Therefore, care should be taken to free memory that is not needed. The LocalFree routine is provided for this purpose.

Of course, Windows has *some* safeguards to keep memory from going away permanently. For example, when a program terminates, all of the dynamic memory that it allocated is automatically freed. This helps prevent the global heap from becoming congested with unnecessary blocks of memory that programs forgot to free. In spite of this, Windows programmers should always free memory that is no longer needed.

LOCALMEM: A Sample Heap Allocation Program

Let's look at a sample Windows program showing some basic techniques in dealing with local memory. This program actually shows how to use two different types of

Figure 18.9 Sample program showing local heap allocation

application memory: the local heap and string resources. This program reads in a list of cities that are saved as string resources. These are stored in movable memory objects allocated from the local heap. Figure 18.9 shows the program running.

LOCALMEM.C

```
/*-----------------------------------------------------------*\
|   LOCALMEM.C - Demonstration of local memory allocation,    |
|                and the use of string tables.                |
\*-----------------------------------------------------------*/
#define STRICT
#include <Windows.H>
#include "localmem.h"


/*-----------------------------------------------------------*\
|                    Function Prototypes.                      |
\*-----------------------------------------------------------*/
LRESULT CALLBACK LocalMemWndProc (HWND, UINT, WPARAM, LPARAM);
BOOL NEAR PASCAL LocalCreate (HWND hwnd);
VOID NEAR PASCAL LocalPaint (HWND hwnd);


/*-----------------------------------------------------------*\
|                    Global Variables.                        |
\*-----------------------------------------------------------*/
char   achWndClass[] = "LocalMem:MAIN";
HANDLE hInst;
HANDLE ahCities;
PSTR   pchTitle;
PSTR   pchNoMem;
TEXTMETRIC tmSys;


/*-----------------------------------------------------------*\
|                  Main Function:  WinMain.                    |
\*-----------------------------------------------------------*/
```

```
int PASCAL
WinMain (HINSTANCE hInstance,      // Who am I?
         HINSTANCE hPrevInstance, // Any older siblings?
         LPSTR     lpszCmdLine,   // Ptr to command line.
         int       cmdShow)       // How to open my window?
    {
    HWND     hwnd;
    int      ccSize;
    MSG      msg;
    WNDCLASS wndclass;

    if (!hPrevInstance)
        {
        wndclass.lpszClassName = achWndClass;
        wndclass.hInstance     = hInstance;
        wndclass.lpfnWndProc   = LocalMemWndProc;
        wndclass.hCursor       = LoadCursor (hInstance, "hand");
        wndclass.hIcon         = LoadIcon (hInstance,"snapshot");
        wndclass.lpszMenuName  = NULL;
        wndclass.hbrBackground = (HBRUSH)(COLOR_WINDOW+1);
        wndclass.style         = NULL;
        wndclass.cbClsExtra    = 0;
        wndclass.cbWndExtra    = 0;

        RegisterClass( &wndclass);
        }

    hInst = hInstance;

    /*  Load application title from string table.          */
    pchTitle = (PSTR)LocalAlloc (LMEM_FIXED, MAXSTRLEN);
    if (!pchTitle) goto ErrExit;  /* Fail?  Exit program.      */

    ccSize = LoadString (hInst, IDS_TITLE, pchTitle, MAXSTRLEN);
    LocalReAlloc ((HANDLE)pchTitle, ccSize+1, 0);


    /*  Load 'out of memory' message from string table.      */
    pchNoMem = (PSTR)LocalAlloc (LMEM_FIXED, MAXSTRLEN);
    if (!pchNoMem) goto ErrExit;  /* Fail?  Exit program.      */

    ccSize = LoadString (hInst, IDS_NOMEM, pchNoMem, MAXSTRLEN);
    LocalReAlloc ((HANDLE)pchNoMem, ccSize+1, 0);


    hwnd = CreateWindowEx(0L,                 // Extra style.
                      achWndClass,        // Class name.
                      pchTitle,           // Title.
                      WS_OVERLAPPEDWINDOW, // Style bits.
                      CW_USEDEFAULT,      // x - default.
                      0,                  // y - default.
                      CW_USEDEFAULT,      // cx - default.
                      0,                  // cy - default.
                      NULL,               // No parent.
                      NULL,               // Class menu.
```

```
                                hInstance,              // Creator.
                                NULL);                  // Params.
            ShowWindow (hwnd, cmdShow);

            while (GetMessage(&msg, 0, 0, 0))
                {
                TranslateMessage(&msg); // Convert KEYDOWNs to CHARs
                DispatchMessage(&msg);  // Transmit message to WndProc
                }

    ErrExit:
        return 0;
        }

    /*------------------------------------------------------------*\
    |           Window Procedure:  LocalMemWndProc.              |
    \*------------------------------------------------------------*/
    LRESULT CALLBACK
    LocalMemWndProc (HWND    hwnd,      // For whom is message sent?
                     UINT    mMsg,      // What is exact message?
                     WPARAM  wParam,    // ...message details.
                     LPARAM  lParam)    // ...message details.
        {
        switch (mMsg)
            {
            case WM_CREATE:
                if (!LocalCreate(hwnd))
                    {
                    MessageBox (GetFocus(), pchNoMem,
                                pchTitle, MB_OK);
                    DestroyWindow (hwnd);
                    }
                break;

            case WM_DESTROY:
                PostQuitMessage(0);  // Handle application shutdown.
                break;

            case WM_PAINT:
                LocalPaint (hwnd);
                break;

            default:
                return(DefWindowProc(hwnd,mMsg,wParam,lParam));
                break;
            }
        return 0L;
        }

    /*------------------------------------------------------------*\
    |           LocalCreate - Process WM_CREATE messages.        |
    \*------------------------------------------------------------*/
    BOOL NEAR PASCAL LocalCreate (HWND hwnd)
        {
        HDC     hdc;
        int     i;
```

```
int      cbSize;
PHANDLE pah;
PSTR     pstr;

/*  Allocate and lock memory for array of handles.         */
ahCities = LocalAlloc (LHND, sizeof(HANDLE) * CITYCOUNT);
pah = (PHANDLE)LocalLock (ahCities);

/*  Error checking:  if lock fails, exit.                  */
if (!pah)
    goto ErrExit1;

/* Loop to read city names.                                */
for (i=0;i<CITYCOUNT ;i++)
    {
    /*  Allocate and lock memory.                          */
    pah[i] = LocalAlloc (LMEM_MOVEABLE, MAXSTRLEN);
    pstr = LocalLock (pah[i]);

    /*  If lock fails, exit.                               */
    if (!pstr)
        goto ErrExit2;

    /*  Copy string into dynamic memory object.           */
    cbSize = LoadString (hInst, i+IDS_CITY, pstr, MAXSTRLEN);

    /*  Unlock and resize memory to exact string size.    */
    LocalUnlock (pah[i]);
    LocalReAlloc (pah[i], cbSize+1, 0);

    } /* [for i] */

LocalUnlock (ahCities);

hdc = GetDC (hwnd);
GetTextMetrics (hdc, &tmSys);     /*  Save for later.      */
ReleaseDC (hwnd, hdc);

return TRUE;   /*  All went well.  Indicate sucess.        */

ErrExit2:

/*  Out of memory.  Free everything.                       */
for (i--;i>=0;i--)
    LocalFree (pah[i]);
LocalUnlock (ahCities);
LocalFree(ahCities);

ErrExit1:
return FALSE;  /*  Unable to complete - indicate failure.  */
}


/*------------------------------------------------------------*\
|              LocalPaint - Process WM_PAINT messages.         |
\*------------------------------------------------------------*/
```

```
VOID NEAR PASCAL LocalPaint (HWND hwnd)
    {
    int i;
    int xText;
    int yText;
    int xTabPosition;
    PAINTSTRUCT ps;
    PHANDLE pah;
    PSTR    pstr;
    RECT    r;

    BeginPaint (hwnd, &ps);

    /*  Initialize values for writing lines of text.         */
    xText = tmSys.tmAveCharWidth * 4;
    yText = tmSys.tmHeight * 2;
    GetClientRect (hwnd, &r);
    xTabPosition = r.right/2;

    /*  Lock array of handles.  If fail, exit.               */
    pah = (PHANDLE)LocalLock (ahCities);
    if (!pah)
        goto ErrExit;

    for (i=0;i<CITYCOUNT;i++)
        {
        pstr = LocalLock (pah[i]);
        TabbedTextOut (ps.hdc,
                       xText,
                       yText,
                       pstr,
                       lstrlen(pstr),
                       1,
                       &xTabPosition,
                       0);

        LocalUnlock (pah[i]);

        /*  Increment for next line.                        */
        yText += tmSys.tmHeight + tmSys.tmExternalLeading;
        }
    LocalUnlock (ahCities);

ErrExit:
    EndPaint (hwnd, &ps);
    }
```

LOCALMEM.H

```
/*-------------------------------------------------------------*\
|  LOCALMEM.H - Symbolic constants for use by LOCALMEM.       |
\*-------------------------------------------------------------*/
```

```
#define IDS_TITLE   1
#define IDS_NOMEM   2
#define IDS_CITY    3
#define MAXSTRLEN  80
#define CITYCOUNT  10
```

LOCALMEM.DEF

```
NAME    LOCALMEM

EXETYPE WINDOWS

DESCRIPTION 'Local Heap Allocation (c) 1992 By Paul Yao'

CODE    MOVEABLE PRELOAD
DATA    MOVEABLE MULTIPLE PRELOAD

HEAPSIZE    512
STACKSIZE   5120

SEGMENTS
    LOCALMEM_TEXT MOVEABLE PRELOAD

EXPORTS
    LocalMemWndProc
```

LOCALMEM.LNK

```
LocalMem.obj
LocalMem.exe/align:16/map/nod/noe/CO
nul
mlibcew libw
LocalMem.def
```

LOCALMEM.MAK

```
# Directory search paths.

INCDIR = \WINDEV\INCLUDE

# Windows version to support
# Valid pairs include:
#     (0x0300, 30)
#     (0x0310, 31)

CLVER = WINVER=0x0300
```

```
RCVER = 30

# Compiler switches for applications.

CL_APP_SHIP_ALL = -AM -c -D$(CLVER) -Gsw -I$(INCDIR) -Ow -W3 -Zp
CL_APP_DEBG_ALL = -AM -c -D$(CLVER) -Gsw -I$(INCDIR) -Od -W3 -Zpi

CL_APP_SHIP_31  = -AM -c -G2s  -I$(INCDIR) -Ow -W3 -Zp
CL_APP_DEBG_31  = -AM -c -G2s  -I$(INCDIR) -Od -W3 -Zpi

# Compiler switches for DLLs.

CL_DLL_SHIP_ALL = -AMw -c -D$(CLVER) -Gsw -I$(INCDIR) -Ow -W3 -Zp
CL_DLL_DEBG_ALL = -AMw -c -D$(CLVER) -Gsw -I$(INCDIR) -Od -W3 -Zpi

CL_DLL_SHIP_31  = -AMw -c -G2s  -I$(INCDIR) -Ow -W3 -Zp
CL_DLL_DEBG_31  = -AMw -c -G2s  -I$(INCDIR) -Od -W3 -Zpi

# Make file primary target.

all: LocalMem.exe

# Make file dependency targets.

LocalMem.res: LocalMem.rc LocalMem.cur LocalMem.ico
    rc -r -i$(INCDIR) LocalMem.rc

LocalMem.obj: LocalMem.c
    cl $(CL_APP_SHIP_ALL) LocalMem.c

LocalMem.exe: LocalMem.obj LocalMem.def LocalMem.res
    link @LocalMem.lnk
    rc -$(RCVER) LocalMem.res

LocalMem.exe: LocalMem.res
    rc -$(RCVER) LocalMem.res
```

LOCALMEM.RC

```
#include "LocalMem.H"


snapshot icon LocalMem.ico

hand  cursor LocalMem.cur

stringtable
  {
  IDS_TITLE, "Local Memory Allocation"
  IDS_NOMEM, "Unable to Initialize Program - Out of Memory"
  IDS_CITY   "The World's Largest Cities (pop. in thous.)"
  IDS_CITY+1, " ";
```

```
    IDS_CITY+2, "Tokyo-Yokohama, Japan\t25,434"
    IDS_CITY+3, "Mexico City, Mexico\t16,901"
    IDS_CITY+4, "Sao Paolo, Brazil\t14,911"
    IDS_CITY+5, "New York, U.S.\t14,598"
    IDS_CITY+6, "Seoul, South Korea\t13,665"
    IDS_CITY+7, "Osaka-Koba-Kyoto, Japan\t13,562"
    IDS_CITY+8, "Buenos Aires, Argentina\t10,750"
    IDS_CITY+9, "Calcutta, India\t10,462"
    }
```

Most of the action in LOCALMEM occurs in response to two messages: WM_CRE-ATE and WM_PAINT. Memory is allocated and string tables read in response to WM_CREATE. All of this is displayed when the WM_PAINT message is received.

If there is one issue in local memory management that is more critical than any other, it is error checking. In order for a Windows program to be robust and error free, it must respond properly to failed memory allocation requests. The point is simple: Not every allocation request can be satisfied. When an allocation fails, a program must be ready to take corrective action to avoid losing data.

For this reason, every dynamic allocation request in LOCALMEM is followed by a check for a valid memory handle. For example:

```
/*  Load application title from string table.       */
pchTitle = (PSTR)LocalAlloc (LMEM_FIXED, MAXSTRLEN);
if (!pchTitle) goto ErrExit; /* Fail?  Exit program. */
```

Since a fixed memory object is being allocated, the handle is a pointer to a character string. In the terms of Windows.h definitions, PSTR is the same as char near *. If LocalAlloc fails, it returns a null value. On receipt of a null, this code jumps to the error handling portion of the function. While advocates of structured programming may dislike the use of goto statements, they provide an excellent method for error handling when a memory allocation request fails. In WIN32, you'll use **structured exception handling** instead of goto's to deal with such errors.

If the above lines of code are successful, the LoadString routine is called to copy a string from a string table resource into the allocated memory. The object is then shrunk so that it is just large enough to hold the number of characters that LoadString reports as having been copied.

```
ccSize = LoadString (hInst, IDS_TITLE, pchTitle, MAXSTRLEN);
LocalReAlloc ((HANDLE)pchTitle, ccSize+1, 0);
```

The LoadString routine is defined as follows:

```
LoadString (hInstance, wID, lpBuffer, nBufferMax)
```

- hInstance is an instance handle.

- wID is an integer identifier of the string to be retrieved.

- lpBuffer is a long pointer to a character string buffer.

- nBufferMax is the maximum number of characters to copy to lpBuffer.

Later in this chapter, we will discuss some of the memory implications of using resources. In brief, resources provide a great deal of flexibility in moving read-only data out of a program's data segment and onto disk. As they are needed, resources—like the strings from the string table resource—can be read into memory and accessed. Resources provide another type of data container that should be considered as part of a Windows program's total memory management picture. For now, let's get back to LOCALMEM.

Another approach to error checking involves testing only the return value of `LocalLock` and not `LocalAlloc`. Here is an example:

```
/*  Allocate and lock memory.                          */
pah[i] = LocalAlloc (LMEM_MOVEABLE, MAXSTRLEN);
pstr = LocalLock (pah[i]);

/*  If lock fails, exit.                                */
if (!pstr)
    goto ErrExit2;
```

In this case, a single line of error checking does the work that might otherwise require two checks: for a valid pointer *as well as* a valid memory handle. Programmers are often eager to omit error checking, but this is unwise. After all, an "invalid" pointer is still usable from the point of view of the C programming language: It points to the bottom of the data segment, which is where the segment header lives. A single write to the right byte in this area can cause otherwise robust programs to come crashing down.

A program can have more than one local heap. This capability is often overlooked by Windows programmers. The primary reason is probably the lack of a well-documented approach, plus the need to write some assembly language code. If you are using Microsoft's C Compiler, version 6.0, you may know that it has support for embedded assembly language. We're going to take advantage of this capability to show you how a program can create as many local heaps as it wishes. Each local heap resides in its own dynamically allocated segment, which the local heap manager will grow until it reaches a maximum of 64K.

Local Heap Allocation in a Dynamically Allocated Segment

As you know, there are two dynamic memory allocation packages in Windows: local heap allocation and global memory allocation. By default, every Windows program has a local heap. The heap is created by a routine called `InitApp`, which is not documented anywhere but is part of the standard (but hidden) startup sequence of every program. The advantage of the local heap is that the overhead for objects is fairly low and, with an alignment of four bytes, wastage is at a minimum. The only problem with the default local heap, however, is that it is too small for many uses. At most, depending on the size of your stack and static data, a default local heap might be 30–50K.

The problem of size can be solved by using the global heap. The global heap, after all, is the sum total of the address space in the system. On systems with an 80386, this means disk space in addition to physical RAM. The problem with the global heap, however, is that the overhead per object is very high. And, at 32 bytes, the granularity of segments is too high to be used for very small objects. Only large objects, or arrays of small objects, are suitable for storage in objects allocated from the global heap.

To get the benefits of both local and global heap management routines, it's possible to create a local heap in a dynamically allocated global segment. From this heap, small objects can be allocated that can efficiently share the segment with the other objects, all managed by the local heap manager. Doing this requires a little sleight of hand and a little assembly language programming, but the results can be well worth the effort.

The first thing to think about is the fact that the first 16 bytes of the segment are reserved. The local heap manager uses various bytes in this area for its own purposes. If you use this space for something else, you risk overwriting the pointers into your local heap. So, whatever you do, make sure the first 16 bytes are initialized to zero.

The second issue is the initialization of the local heap. This is easily done with the `LocalInit` routine. Here is one way to initialize a local heap in a dynamically allocated segment:

```
HANDLE hMem;
int    pStart, pEnd;
LPSTR lp;
WORD  wSeg;

hMem = GlobalAlloc (GMEM_MOVEABLE|GMEM_ZEROINIT, 4096L);
if (!hMem)
     goto ErrorOut;

lp = GlobalLock (hMem);
wSeg = HIWORD (lp);

pStart = 16;
pEnd   = (int)GlobalSize (hMem)-1;
LocalInit (wSeg, pStart, pEnd);
GlobalUnlock(hMem);
GlobalUnlock (hMem);
```

Notice that two calls to `GlobalUnlock` are required. One counteracts our own call to `GlobalLock`—it's the second slice in a code sandwich. The second call to `GlobalUnlock` is required because `LocalInit` leaves a segment locked. Without this second call, the data segment would remain locked in memory. This would prevent the segment from growing, and would create a memory sandbar in the global heap.

Even though we asked for a 4096-byte segment, different operating modes align on different segment boundaries, so we call `GlobalSize` to make sure we know the exact size of the segment. `pStart` is set to 16 to make room for the header. `pEnd` is set to the offset of the last byte in the segment, which is the segment size minus one.

Incidentally, a slightly shorter way to do the same thing involves setting `pStart` to zero and setting `pEnd` to the actual *size* of the local heap. Here's the code to accomplish that:

```
pEnd    = (int)GlobalSize (hMem)-16;
LocalInit (wSeg, 0, pEnd);
```

In this case, notice that we're subtracting 16 from the size of the segment rather than just one. The reason is simple: We must set aside the first 16 bytes for the segment header.

Accessing the local heap requires a little assembly language programming. We're going to cheat a little, and use a capability of Microsoft's C Compiler, version 6.0, that lets us embed assembler into C code. If your compiler doesn't support this, you will have to write stand-alone assembly language subroutines. We can call any local heap management routine. The only difference is that before and after each call, we must change the value in the DS register to hold the address of our local heap. Here's how to do it:

```
LPSTR lp;
HANDLE hmem;
WORD  wHeapDS;   /*  Must be a stack variable!  */

lp = GlobalLock (hmem);   /* Where local heap lives. */
wHeapDS = HIWORD (lp);

_asm{
      push DS

      mov   AX, wHeapDS
      mov   DS, AX

      }

hmem = LocalAlloc (LMEM_MOVEABLE, 16);

_asm{
      pop   DS
      }

GlobalUnlock (hmem);
```

While it may look rather complex and bizarre, this approach allows a Windows program to derive the benefits of both memory management packages, and to overcome some of the drawbacks of each.

Of course, to use a memory object, you must call two lock routines: one for the segment and one for the local heap object. To keep either of these data areas from becoming too fragmented, you will probably want to unlock at both levels. There are compromises, of course. For example, a program might make all local heap objects *fixed*, which removes the need to do the second lock. For the most effective use, it probably makes sense to build a small subroutine library to manage the two-level allocation scheme. This might be as simple as creating 32-bit handles, with half for the local handle and half for the global handle. That, in fact, is the approach taken by our sample program. Or, a subroutine package could issue its own, private 16-bit handles to use in finding the right segment and the right local memory object. There are several approaches to take; this brief introduction has provided information to help you find one that will work for you.

If you're like many programmers, all this theoretical discussion and bits of code are not as interesting as a full-blown working program that demonstrates how to put the theory into practice. So, without further ado, here is our sample program: SUBSEG.

SUBSEG: A Combined Local/Global Heap Allocation Program

SUBSEG demonstrates how to perform subsegment allocation in a dynamically allocated segment. We borrow the term "subsegment allocation" from the world of OS/2, since it seems to be more suggestive of what we are doing than the term "local allocation." To help you get the most from this example, we have written a set of subsegment allocation routines that mirror the format of the routines in Windows' standard memory allocation routines. In other words, we've written a routine called `SubAlloc` which takes all the same parameters as the `LocalAlloc` routine. Four other routines provide the basic allocation services to get you started in writing a complete suballocation library. There is one additional function, `SubInitialize`, which allocates a segment from the global heap and initializes the segment to hold a local heap.

SUBSEG is adapted from SEGALLOC, which is the segment allocation sample we presented earlier in this chapter. SUBSEG displays information about the allocated data objects. To convince you that it works as advertised, it reads this information from the data object itself. Figure 18.10 shows SUBSEG running. If you compare this program to the SEGALLOC program, one thing you may notice is that the overhead of objects is much lower in this program. That is because segments allocated from the global heap are aligned on 32-byte boundaries, whereas objects allocated from a local heap are allocated on four-byte boundaries. The wastage due to "rounding" is much less in local heaps.

```
            Sub-Segment Allocation                   ▼ ▲

  Description           Req/Actual      Handle -> Address

  Object # 1 - Fixed        50 / 52     0a1e:0050 -> 0a1d:0050
  Object # 2 - Moveable     75 / 78     0a1e:008a -> 0a1d:0fa6
  Object # 3 - Discardable  100 / 102   0a1e:008e -> 0a1d:0f3a
```

Figure 18.10 SUBSEG shows information about the objects it allocates

SUBSEG.C

```
/*-------------------------------------------------------------*\
|   SUBSEG - Sample program showing global heap allocation     |
|            in Microsoft Windows.                             |
\*-------------------------------------------------------------*/
#include <Windows.H>

typedef DWORD HANDLE32;

/*-------------------------------------------------------------*\
|                    Function Prototypes.                      |
\*-------------------------------------------------------------*/
long FAR  PASCAL SubsegWndProc (HWND, WORD, WORD, LONG);

BOOL     FAR PASCAL SubInitialize(VOID);
HANDLE32 FAR PASCAL SubAlloc(WORD, WORD);
HANDLE32 FAR PASCAL SubFree(HANDLE32);
LPSTR    FAR PASCAL SubLock(HANDLE32);
WORD     FAR PASCAL SubSize(HANDLE32);
BOOL     FAR PASCAL SubUnlock(HANDLE32);


/*-------------------------------------------------------------*\
|                  Main Function:  WinMain.                     |
\*-------------------------------------------------------------*/
int PASCAL
WinMain (HINSTANCE hInstance,        // Who am I?
         HINSTANCE hPrevInstance,    // Any older siblings?
         LPSTR     lpszCmdLine,      // Ptr to command line.
         int       cmdShow)          // How to open my window?
    {
    HWND    hwnd;
    MSG     msg;
    WNDCLASS wndclass;

    if (!hPrevInstance)
        {
        wndclass.lpszClassName = "Subseg:MAIN";
        wndclass.hInstance     = hInstance;
        wndclass.lpfnWndProc   = SubsegWndProc;
        wndclass.hCursor       = LoadCursor (hInstance, "hand");
        wndclass.hIcon         = LoadIcon (hInstance,"snapshot");
        wndclass.lpszMenuName  = NULL;
        wndclass.hbrBackground = COLOR_WINDOW+1;
        wndclass.style         = NULL;
        wndclass.cbClsExtra    = 0;
        wndclass.cbWndExtra    = 0;

        RegisterClass( &wndclass);
        }

    hwnd = CreateWindow("Subseg:MAIN",        /* Class name.  */
                                              /* Title.       */
                        "Sub-Segment Allocation",
```

```
                     WS_OVERLAPPEDWINDOW,    /* Style bits.   */
                     CW_USEDEFAULT,          /* x - default.  */
                     0,                      /* y - default.  */
                     CW_USEDEFAULT,          /* cx - default. */
                     0,                      /* cy - default. */
                     NULL,                   /* No parent.    */
                     NULL,                   /* Class menu.   */
                     hInstance,              /* Creator       */
                     NULL);                  /* Params.       */

    ShowWindow (hwnd, cmdShow);

    while (GetMessage(&msg, 0, 0, 0))
        {
        TranslateMessage(&msg);             /*  Keyboard input.      */
        DispatchMessage(&msg);
        }
    return 0;
    }

#define STRSIZE 30
typedef struct tagSEGDATA
    {
    char  achDesc[STRSIZE];  /* Description of data.  */
    DWORD dwAlloc;           /* Amount asked for.     */
    DWORD dwActual;          /* Actually allocated.   */
    WORD  wFlags;            /* Allocation flags.     */
    } SEGDATA;

typedef SEGDATA FAR *LPSEGDATA;

#define COUNT      3


/*-------------------------------------------------------------*\
|               Window Procedure:  SubsegWndProc.               |
\*-------------------------------------------------------------*/
LRESULT CALLBACK
SubsegWndProc (HWND   hwnd,      // For whom is message sent?
               UINT   mMsg,      // What is exact message?
               WPARAM wParam,    // ...message details.
               LPARAM lParam)    // ...message details.
    {
    static char Label1[] = "Description";
    static char Label2[] = "Req/Actual";
    static char Label3[] = "Handle  ->  Address";

    static int  cb1 = sizeof (Label1) - 1;
    static int  cb2 = sizeof (Label2) - 1;
    static int  cb3 = sizeof (Label3) - 1;

    static HANDLE32 h[COUNT];
    static SEGDATA sd[COUNT] =
        {
        "Object # 1 - Fixed",          50, 0, LMEM_FIXED,
```

```
                "Object # 2 - Moveable",      75, 0, LMEM_MOVEABLE |
                                                     LMEM_ZEROINIT,
                "Object # 3 - Discardable", 100, 0, LMEM_DISCARDABLE |
                                                     LMEM_MOVEABLE,
            };
    static TEXTMETRIC tmSys;

    switch (mMsg)
        {
        case WM_CREATE:
            {
            HDC hdc;
            int i;
            LPSEGDATA lpsd;

            if (!SubInitialize())
                goto ErrorExit;

            for (i=0;i<COUNT;i++)
                {
                h[i] = SubAlloc(sd[i].wFlags,
                                (WORD)sd[i].dwAlloc);
                if (!h[i])
                    goto ErrorExit;

                lpsd = (LPSEGDATA)SubLock (h[i]);
                if (!lpsd)
                    goto ErrorExit;

                lstrcpy (lpsd->achDesc, sd[i].achDesc);
                lpsd->dwAlloc = sd[i].dwAlloc;
                lpsd->dwActual = SubSize (h[i]);
                lpsd->wFlags = sd[i].wFlags;
                SubUnlock (h[i]);
                } /* [for] */

            hdc = GetDC (hwnd);
            GetTextMetrics (hdc, &tmSys);
            ReleaseDC (hwnd, hdc);
            break;

    ErrorExit:
            MessageBox (GetFocus(), "Not enough memory",
                        "Subseg", MB_OK);
            DestroyWindow (hwnd);
            }
            break;

        case WM_DESTROY:
            PostQuitMessage(0);
            break;

        case WM_PAINT:
            {
            char buff[30];
```

```
int i;
int xText1;
int xText2;
int xText3;
int yText;

LPSEGDATA lpsd;
PAINTSTRUCT ps;

BeginPaint (hwnd, &ps);

/*  Calculate text positioning variables.        */
xText1 = tmSys.tmAveCharWidth * 2;
xText2 = xText1 + (STRSIZE * tmSys.tmAveCharWidth);
xText3 = xText2 + ((cb2+5) * tmSys.tmAveCharWidth);
yText = tmSys.tmHeight;

/*  Print titles.                                 */
TextOut (ps.hdc, xText1, yText, Label1, cb1);
TextOut (ps.hdc, xText2, yText, Label2, cb2);
TextOut (ps.hdc, xText3, yText, Label3, cb3);

yText += tmSys.tmHeight * 2;

for (i=0;i<COUNT;i++)
    {
    lpsd = (LPSEGDATA)SubLock (h[i]);

    /*  Print description.                         */
    TextOut (ps.hdc, xText1, yText,
             lpsd->achDesc, lstrlen(lpsd->achDesc));

    /*  Print allocated vs actual size.            */
    wsprintf (buff, "%ld / %ld", lpsd->dwAlloc,
                                 lpsd->dwActual);
    TextOut (ps.hdc, xText2, yText,
             buff, lstrlen (buff));

    /*  Print handle and actual address.           */
    wsprintf (buff, "%04x:%04x  ->  %04x:%04x",
              HIWORD(h[i]), LOWORD(h[i]),
              HIWORD(lpsd), LOWORD(lpsd));
    TextOut (ps.hdc, xText3, yText,
             buff, lstrlen (buff));

    SubUnlock (h[i]);

    /*  Advance to next line.                      */
    yText += tmSys.tmHeight + tmSys.tmExternalLeading;
    }

EndPaint (hwnd, &ps);
}
break;
```

```
      default:
          return(DefWindowProc(hwnd,mMsg,wParam,lParam));
          break;
      }
   return 0L;
   }
```

SUBMEM.C

```
/*----------------------------------------------------------------*\
 |   SUB.C  -  Subsegment allocation routines, for creating       |
 |             local heaps in dynamically allocated segments.     |
 \*----------------------------------------------------------------*/
#include <Windows.H>

typedef DWORD HANDLE32;

/*----------------------------------------------------------------*\
 |                    Static Data Definitions.                    |
 \*----------------------------------------------------------------*/
HANDLE hSegment;

/*----------------------------------------------------------------*\
 |   SubInitialize - Call first to allocate a segment from the    |
 |                   global heap.                                 |
 \*----------------------------------------------------------------*/
BOOL    FAR PASCAL SubInitialize(VOID)
   {
   BOOL  bRetVal;
   LPSTR lp;
   WORD  wSeg;
   WORD  wSize;

   hSegment = GlobalAlloc (GMEM_MOVEABLE | GMEM_ZEROINIT,
                           4096);
   if (!hSegment)
      return FALSE;

   lp = GlobalLock (hSegment);
   if (!lp)
      return FALSE;

   wSeg = HIWORD (lp);
   wSize = (WORD)GlobalSize (hSegment) - 16;

   bRetVal = LocalInit (wSeg, 0, wSize);

   GlobalUnlock (hSegment);
   GlobalUnlock (hSegment);  /*  Undo LocalInit's GlobalLock. */

   return bRetVal;
   }
```

```
/*-------------------------------------------------------------*\
|   SubAlloc - Allocate a subsegment.                         |
|                                                             |
|   Input:  wFlags = local heap allocation flags.            |
|           wBytes = number of bytes to allocate.            |
|                                                             |
|   Returns:  A 4-byte "handle", put together as:            |
|               HIWORD = Handle to global segment.            |
|               LOWORD = Handle to local object.              |
\*-------------------------------------------------------------*/
HANDLE32 FAR PASCAL SubAlloc(WORD wFlags, WORD wBytes)
    {
    HANDLE hMem;
    LPSTR lp;
    WORD  wSeg;

    lp = GlobalLock (hSegment);
    if (!lp)
        return 0L;

    wSeg = HIWORD (lp);

    _asm { push    ds
           mov     ax, wSeg
           mov     ds, ax    }

    hMem = LocalAlloc (wFlags, wBytes);

    _asm { pop     ds }

    GlobalUnlock (hSegment);

    if (!hMem)
        return 0L;
    else
        return MAKELONG (hMem, hSegment);
    }


/*-------------------------------------------------------------*\
|   SubFree - Free a subsegment.                              |
|                                                             |
|   Input:  A 4-byte "handle", put together as:              |
|               HIWORD = Handle to global segment.            |
|               LOWORD = Handle to local object.              |
|                                                             |
|   Returns:  The original handle, if successful.  Otherwise, |
|               returns NULL.                                  |
\*-------------------------------------------------------------*/
HANDLE32 FAR PASCAL SubFree(HANDLE32 hSubMem)
    {
    HANDLE hSeg;
    HANDLE hMem;
    LPSTR lp;
    WORD  wSeg;
```

```
    hSeg = HIWORD (hSubMem);
    hMem = LOWORD (hSubMem);

    lp = GlobalLock (hSeg);
    if (!lp)
        return 0L;

    wSeg = HIWORD (lp);

    _asm { push    ds
           mov     ax, wSeg
           mov     ds, ax   }

    hMem = LocalFree (hMem);

    _asm { pop     ds }

    GlobalUnlock (hSeg);

    if (!hMem)
        return 0L;
    else
        return MAKELONG (hMem, hSeg);
    }

/*-----------------------------------------------------------------*\
|  SubLock - Lock a subsegment and the segment it lives in.        |
|                                                                  |
|  Input:  A 4-byte "handle", put together as:                    |
|          HIWORD = Handle to global segment.                     |
|          LOWORD = Handle to local object.                       |
|                                                                  |
|  Returns: A far pointer to the object.                          |
\*-----------------------------------------------------------------*/
LPSTR    FAR PASCAL SubLock(HANDLE32 hSubMem)
    {
    HANDLE hSeg;
    HANDLE hMem;
    LPSTR lp;
    PSTR  p;
    WORD  wSeg;

    hSeg = HIWORD (hSubMem);
    hMem = LOWORD (hSubMem);

    lp = GlobalLock (hSeg);
    if (!lp)
        return 0L;

    wSeg = HIWORD (lp);

    _asm { push    ds
           mov     ax, wSeg
           mov     ds, ax   }
```

```
    p = LocalLock (hMem);

    _asm { pop     ds }

    /*  No Matching GlobalUnlock -- leave segment locked      */
    /*  for caller to use.  We'll unlock twice in SubUnlock.  */

    if (!p)
        return (LPSTR)0;
    else
        return (LPSTR)MAKELONG (p, wSeg);
    }

/*-----------------------------------------------------------*\
|  SubSize - Returns the size of a subsegment.                |
|                                                             |
|  Input:  A 4-byte "handle", put together as:                |
|             HIWORD = Handle to global segment.              |
|             LOWORD = Handle to local object.                |
|                                                             |
|  Returns: a WORD value with the subsegment size, or zero    |
|           if the handle is invalid.                         |
\*-----------------------------------------------------------*/
WORD    FAR PASCAL SubSize(HANDLE32 hSubMem)
    {
    HANDLE hSeg;
    HANDLE hMem;
    LPSTR lp;
    WORD  wSeg;
    WORD  wSize;

    hSeg = HIWORD (hSubMem);
    hMem = LOWORD (hSubMem);

    lp = GlobalLock (hSeg);
    if (!lp)
        return 0;

    wSeg = HIWORD (lp);

    _asm { push    ds
           mov     ax, wSeg
           mov     ds, ax    }

    wSize = LocalSize (hMem);

    _asm { pop     ds }

    GlobalUnlock (hSeg);

    return wSize;
    }
```

```
/*------------------------------------------------------------*\
|   SubUnlock - Unlock a subsegment, and the segment it lives  |
|               in.                                            |
|   Input:  A 4-byte "handle", put together as:               |
|               HIWORD = Handle to global segment.            |
|               LOWORD = Handle to local object.              |
|                                                              |
|   Returns: The LocalUnlock return value, which is zero if    |
|            the block's reference count was decreased to      |
|            zero, otherwise it is non-zero.                   |
\*------------------------------------------------------------*/
BOOL     FAR PASCAL SubUnlock(HANDLE32 hSubMem)
    {
    BOOL    bRetVal;
    HANDLE  hSeg;
    HANDLE  hMem;
    LPSTR   lp;
    WORD    wSeg;

    hSeg = HIWORD (hSubMem);
    hMem = LOWORD (hSubMem);

    lp = GlobalLock (hSeg);
    if (!lp)
        return 0L;

    wSeg = HIWORD (lp);

    _asm { push    ds
           mov     ax, wSeg
           mov     ds, ax   }

    bRetVal = LocalUnlock (hMem);

    _asm { pop     ds }

    GlobalUnlock (hSeg);
    GlobalUnlock (hSeg);

    return bRetVal;
    }
```

SUBSEG.DEF

```
NAME    SUBSEG

EXETYPE WINDOWS

DESCRIPTION 'Sub-Segment Allocation (c) 1992 By Paul Yao'

CODE    MOVEABLE PRELOAD
DATA    MOVEABLE MULTIPLE PRELOAD
```

```
HEAPSIZE      512
STACKSIZE     5120

SEGMENTS
    SUBSEG_TEXT MOVEABLE PRELOAD
    SUBMEM_TEXT MOVEABLE DISCARDABLE

EXPORTS
    SubsegWndProc
```

SUBSEG.LNK

```
SubSeg.obj + SubMem.obj
SubSeg.exe/align:16/map/nod/noe/CO
SubSeg.map/map
mlibcew libw
SubSeg.def
```

SUBSEG.MAK

```
# Directory search paths.

INCDIR = \WINDEV\INCLUDE

# Windows version to support
# Valid pairs include:
#      (0x0300, 30)
#      (0x0310, 31)

CLVER = WINVER=0x0300
RCVER = 30

# Compiler switches for applications.

CL_APP_SHIP_ALL = -AM -c -D$(CLVER) -Gsw -I$(INCDIR) -Ow -W3 -Zp
CL_APP_DEBG_ALL = -AM -c -D$(CLVER) -Gsw -I$(INCDIR) -Od -W3 -Zpi

CL_APP_SHIP_31  = -AM -c -G2s  -I$(INCDIR) -Ow -W3 -Zp
CL_APP_DEBG_31  = -AM -c -G2s  -I$(INCDIR) -Od -W3 -Zpi

# Compiler switches for DLLs.

CL_DLL_SHIP_ALL = -AMw -c -D$(CLVER) -Gsw -I$(INCDIR) -Ow -W3 -Zp
CL_DLL_DEBG_ALL = -AMw -c -D$(CLVER) -Gsw -I$(INCDIR) -Od -W3 -Zpi

CL_DLL_SHIP_31  = -AMw -c -G2s  -I$(INCDIR) -Ow -W3 -Zp
CL_DLL_DEBG_31  = -AMw -c -G2s  -I$(INCDIR) -Od -W3 -Zpi
```

```
# Make file primary target.

all: SubSeg.exe

# Make file dependency targets.

SubSeg.res: SubSeg.rc SubSeg.cur SubSeg.ico
    rc -r -i$(INCDIR) SubSeg.rc

SubSeg.obj: SubSeg.c
    cl $(CL_APP_SHIP_ALL) SubSeg.c

SubMem.obj: SubMem.c
    cl $(CL_APP_SHIP_ALL) SubMem.c

SubSeg.exe: SubSeg.obj SubMem.obj SubSeg.def SubSeg.res
    link @SubSeg.lnk
    rc -$(RCVER) SubSeg.res

SubSeg.exe: SubSeg.res
    rc -$(RCVER) SubSeg.res
```

SUBSEG.RC

```
snapshot icon subseg.ico

hand   cursor subseg.cur
```

The first thing you may notice about this program is that very little is different from the SEGALLOC program from which it was derived. This is intentional, since the allocation routines that we have created are meant to exactly mirror both the local and global heap management routines. So, the SubAlloc routine takes the place of GlobalAlloc or LocalAlloc, and the SubLock routine takes the place of GlobalLock or LocalLock. However, when you look at the code to the subsegment routines, you'll find that calls are made to *both* local and global heap management routines.

There is also an important difference in the handle that SubAlloc returns. Instead of the normal 16-bit handle, it returns a 32-bit handle. This is really two handles in one: The high-word contains the handle of the segment, and the low-word contains the handle of the local heap object. This allows the routines to be extended to support several local heaps in several different segments. The only requirement is that LocalInit be called to initialize each segment. This program only uses one segment for the sake of simplicity.

Another limitation of this program is that the segment that contains the local heap is never freed. While this may be reasonable for a tiny sample program, it is clearly a case of "do as I say, and not as I do." In other words, please be sure to free any memory you allocate, unlock any memory you lock, and in general undo whatever needs undoing to free any resource you use.

Let's move on to our next and final sample program, which creates a custom resource.

Custom Resources

Although Windows provides built-in support for several different types of resources, you may wish to create your own custom resource types. This lets you take advantage of the built-in memory management features of resources, with a minimum of effort on your part. The best candidates for custom resources are data objects that won't change. Our example will show a resource that will be used to calculate sine and cosine values. This table allows a calculation of an integer sine value, which is simply a sine value multiplied by 10,000. The advantage of using a lookup table is that it is faster than calculating "on the fly." In addition, since the low-end members of the Intel-86 family (80386 and earlier) do not have built-in floating point support, you'll get faster overall performance if you limit your calculations to integer arithmetic. It may interest you to know that this factor influenced Microsoft enough to build Windows without *any* use of floating point arithmetic.

We will write two routines that will provide sine and cosine values for an angle entered in degrees. Roughly speaking, then, with two functions and 360 degrees, 720 different values are required for our lookup table. However, we will take advantage of the symmetry of this table to play a few tricks, do a little folding and rotating, and produce the same results with a single table of 90 sine values. To see how we pull this off, read on!

First, it is necessary to create a table of values. There are many ways to do this, but the most straightforward involves writing a small C program that calculates our sine values and writes them as ASCII text to a data file. Why ASCII text? We're going to show you a trick that will allow you to build complex binary data objects from ASCII text files. The only tools required are the macro assembler (MASM), the linker, and a special converter called EXE2BIN.EXE which comes with MS-DOS. Here are the program files used to create our table of sine values:

SINE.C

```
/*------------------------------------------------------------*\
|   SINE.C - Creates a .ASM data file containing sine values   |
|            from 0 to 90 degrees.  This file is suitable      |
|            for creating a custom Windows resource.           |
\*------------------------------------------------------------*/

#include "stdio.h"
#include "math.h"

char achFileHeader[] =
     ";\n"
     "; Sine/Cosine Data Table\n"
     ";\n"
     ";\n"
     "; Table of Sine values from 0 to 90 degrees\n"
     ";\n"
     "SINDATA segment public\n";
```

```
char achFileFooter[] =
    "\n"
    "SINDATA ends\n"
    "END\n";


main()
    {
    double dbPI  = 3.1415926536;
    double dbRad;
    FILE    * fp;
    int     iAngle;
    int     iSin;

    if (!(fp = fopen("sinedata.asm", "w")))
        {
        printf("Can't create sinedata.asm.\n");
        exit(1);
        }

    fprintf (fp, achFileHeader);
    fprintf (fp, "DW ");

    for (iAngle = 0; iAngle <= 90; iAngle++)
        {
        dbRad = (((double)iAngle) * dbPI) / 180.0;
        iSin = sin(dbRad) * 10000.0 + 0.5;
        fprintf(fp, " %5d", iSin);

        if (iAngle % 8 == 7)
            fprintf (fp, "\nDW ");
        else if (iAngle != 90)
            fprintf (fp, ",");
        }

    fprintf(fp, achFileFooter);

    fclose(fp);
    }
```

SINE.MAK

```
sine.obj: sine.c
    cl -c sine.c

sine.exe: sine.obj
    link sine;

sinedata.asm: sine.exe
    sine
```

```
sinedata.bin: sinedata.asm
    masm sinedata.asm, sinedata.obj;
    link sinedata, sinedata.exe;
    exe2bin sinedata.exe
```

The data file created by this program is essentially a MASM language file, containing the data definitions suitable for use as a data segment. But we're not going to write any MASM code to support it. Instead, we will let MASM convert the data definitions into binary format. Here is the MASM file that is created, SINEDATA.ASM:

```
;Sine/Cosine Data Table
;
;
;Table of Sine values from 0 to 90 degrees
;
SINDATA segment public
DW       0,    175,    349,    523,    698,    872,   1045,   1219
DW    1392,   1564,   1736,   1908,   2079,   2250,   2419,   2588
DW    2756,   2924,   3090,   3256,   3420,   3584,   3746,   3907
DW    4067,   4226,   4384,   4540,   4695,   4848,   5000,   5150
DW    5299,   5446,   5592,   5736,   5878,   6018,   6157,   6293
DW    6428,   6561,   6691,   6820,   6947,   7071,   7193,   7314
DW    7431,   7547,   7660,   7771,   7880,   7986,   8090,   8192
DW    8290,   8387,   8480,   8572,   8660,   8746,   8829,   8910
DW    8988,   9063,   9135,   9205,   9272,   9336,   9397,   9455
DW    9511,   9563,   9613,   9659,   9703,   9744,   9781,   9816
DW    9848,   9877,   9903,   9925,   9945,   9962,   9976,   9986
DW    9994,   9998,  10000
SINDATA ends
END
```

After this data file has been run through the macro assembler and the linker, the result is an .EXE file that is almost ready to run as a MS-DOS program. Well, it's not really ready, since it doesn't have any code; it's just an executable file with a data segment. To isolate the data into a pure binary object, we run the EXE2BIN program. This program is ordinarily used to create .COM files from .EXE files. COM files are simply memory images that can be loaded and run "as is." Since that's exactly what we want—a pure, binary image—EXE2BIN does the trick to create our sine table resource.

To test that the sine and cosine functions are providing accurate values, our sample program, CUSTRES, connects 359 points together to draw a circle with a radius of 100 pixels. The drawing appears in Figure 18.11. While this is quite a bit slower, and rougher than you would expect from calling GDI's `Ellipse` routine, it demonstrates quite nicely that the sine and cosine values that we generate at least *look* right in the range 0 to 360 degrees.

Here is the code for our custom resource program, CUSTRES.EXE, that used the sine table information to calculate sines and cosines used to actually draw the circle shown in the figure.

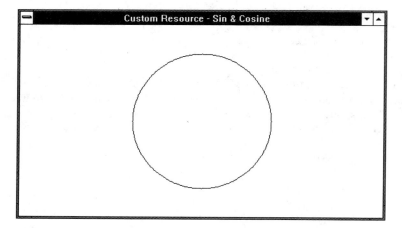

Figure 18.11 Circle drawn by CUSTRES

CUSTRES.C

```
/*----------------------------------------------------------------*\
 | CUSTRES.C - Creating a custom resource in Windows.  This       |
 |             program creates a resource that contains a         |
 |             sine table.  This table is used for the            |
 |             calculation of sines and cosines for any           |
 |             degree value entered.                              |
 \*----------------------------------------------------------------*/
#define STRICT
#include <Windows.H>
#include "custres.h"


/*----------------------------------------------------------------*\
 |                    Function Prototypes.                        |
 \*----------------------------------------------------------------*/
LRESULT CALLBACK CustResWndProc (HWND, UINT, WPARAM, LPARAM);
int NEAR PASCAL intSine (int iValue);
int NEAR PASCAL intCos (int iValue);


/*----------------------------------------------------------------*\
 |                    Global Variables.                          |
 \*----------------------------------------------------------------*/
char achWndClass[] = "CustRes:MAIN";
char achAppName[]  = "Custom Resource - Sine and Cosine";

HANDLE hInst;
HANDLE hresSineData;


/*----------------------------------------------------------------*\
 |                    Main Function:  WinMain.                    |
 \*----------------------------------------------------------------*/
```

```
int PASCAL
WinMain (HINSTANCE hInstance,      // Who am I?
         HINSTANCE hPrevInstance, // Any older siblings?
         LPSTR     lpszCmdLine,    // Ptr to command line.
         int       cmdShow)        // How to open my window?
    {
    HWND      hwnd;
    MSG       msg;
    WNDCLASS wndclass;

    if (!hPrevInstance)
        {
        wndclass.lpszClassName = achWndClass;
        wndclass.hInstance     = hInstance;
        wndclass.lpfnWndProc   = CustResWndProc;
        wndclass.hCursor       = LoadCursor (hInstance, "hand");
        wndclass.hIcon         = LoadIcon (hInstance,"snapshot");
        wndclass.lpszMenuName  = NULL;
        wndclass.hbrBackground = (HBRUSH)(COLOR_WINDOW+1);
        wndclass.style         = CS_HREDRAW | CS_VREDRAW;
        wndclass.cbClsExtra    = 0;
        wndclass.cbWndExtra    = 0;

        RegisterClass( &wndclass);
        }

    hInst = hInstance;

    hwnd = CreateWindowEx(0L,                  // Extra style.
                     achWndClass,              // Class name.
                     achAppName,               // Title.
                     WS_OVERLAPPEDWINDOW,      // Style bits.
                     CW_USEDEFAULT,            // x - default.
                     0,                        // y - default.
                     CW_USEDEFAULT,            // cx - default.
                     0,                        // cy - default.
                     NULL,                     // No parent.
                     NULL,                     // Class menu.
                     hInstance,                // Creator.
                     NULL);                    // Params.
    ShowWindow (hwnd, cmdShow);

    while (GetMessage(&msg, 0, 0, 0))
        {
        TranslateMessage(&msg); // Convert KEYDOWNs to CHARs
        DispatchMessage(&msg);  // Transmit message to WndProc
        }
    return 0;
    }

/*-------------------------------------------------------------*\
 |              Window Procedure:  CustResWndProc.            |
 \*-------------------------------------------------------------*/
```

```
LRESULT CALLBACK
CustResWndProc (HWND    hwnd,       // For whom is message sent?
                UINT    mMsg,       // What is exact message?
                WPARAM  wParam,     // ...message details.
                LPARAM  lParam)     // ...message details.
    {
    switch (mMsg)
        {
        case WM_CREATE:
            {
            HANDLE hRes;
            hRes = FindResource (hInst,
                    MAKEINTRESOURCE(SINE),     /* Name.  */
                    MAKEINTRESOURCE(TABLE));   /* Type.  */
            hresSineData = LoadResource (hInst, hRes);
            }
            break;

        case WM_DESTROY:
            FreeResource (hresSineData);
            PostQuitMessage(0);  // Handle application shutdown.
            break;

        case WM_PAINT:
            {
            int i;
            int x, y;
            PAINTSTRUCT ps;
            RECT r;

            BeginPaint (hwnd, &ps);
            GetClientRect (hwnd, &r);
            SetViewportOrg (ps.hdc, r.right/2, r.bottom/2);

            x = intCos (0)/100;
            y = intSine (0)/100;
            MoveTo (ps.hdc, x, y);

            for (i=0;i<=360;i++)
                {
                x = intCos (i)/100;
                y = intSine (i)/100;
                LineTo (ps.hdc, x, y);
                }

            EndPaint (hwnd, &ps);
            }
            break;

        default:
            return(DefWindowProc(hwnd,mMsg,wParam,lParam));
            break;
        }
    return 0L;
    }
```

```
/*------------------------------------------------------------*\
| intSine - Calculates an integer sine value in units equal   |
|           to 10,000th for any degree entered, using a       |
|           value derived from a custom Sine resource.        |
\*------------------------------------------------------------*/
int NEAR PASCAL intSine (int iValue)
    {
    int iSign;

    int FAR * fpSine;

    fpSine = (int FAR *)LockResource (hresSineData);
    if (fpSine == NULL)
        return (0);

    while (iValue < 0)   iValue +=360;
    while (iValue > 360) iValue -=360;

    iSign = 1;

    if (iValue > 90 && iValue <=180)
        {
        iValue = 180 - iValue;
        }
    else if (iValue > 180 && iValue <= 270)
        {
        iSign = -1;
        iValue = iValue - 180;
        }
    else if (iValue > 270 && iValue <= 360)
        {
        iSign = -1;
        iValue = 360 - iValue;
        }

    /*  Adjust pointer to correct table entry.  */
    fpSine += iValue;

    iSign = *fpSine * iSign;
    UnlockResource (hresSineData);

    return (iSign);
    }


/*------------------------------------------------------------*\
|  intCos  -  Calculates an integer cosine value in units     |
|             equal to 10,000th for any degree entered, using |
|             a value derived from a custom sine resource.    |
\*------------------------------------------------------------*/
int NEAR PASCAL intCos (int iValue)
    {
    return (intSine (iValue-90));
    }
```

CUSTRES.DEF

```
NAME       CUSTRES

EXETYPE WINDOWS

DESCRIPTION 'Custom Resource (c) 1992 By Paul Yao'

CODE       MOVEABLE PRELOAD
DATA       MOVEABLE MULTIPLE PRELOAD

HEAPSIZE     512
STACKSIZE    5120

SEGMENTS
    CUSTRES_TEXT MOVEABLE PRELOAD

EXPORTS
    CustResWndProc
```

CUSTRES.H

```
/*-------------------------------------------------------------*\
|   CUSTRES.H - Include file for custom resource demo program.  |
\*-------------------------------------------------------------*/

#define TABLE  100    /*  Custom resource type value.          */
#define SINE   100    /*  ID of particular custom resource.    */
```

CUSTRES.LNK

```
CustRes.obj
CustRes.exe/align:16/map/nod/noe/CO
nul
mlibcew libw
CustRes.def
```

CUSTRES.MAK

```
# Directory search paths.

INCDIR = \WINDEV\INCLUDE

# Windows version to support
```

```
# Valid pairs include:
#     (0x0300, 30)
#     (0x0310, 31)

CLVER = WINVER=0x0300
RCVER = 30

# Compiler switches for applications.

CL_APP_SHIP_ALL = -AM -c -D$(CLVER) -Gsw -I$(INCDIR) -Ow -W3 -Zp
CL_APP_DEBG_ALL = -AM -c -D$(CLVER) -Gsw -I$(INCDIR) -Od -W3 -Zpi

CL_APP_SHIP_31  = -AM -c -G2s  -I$(INCDIR) -Ow -W3 -Zp
CL_APP_DEBG_31  = -AM -c -G2s  -I$(INCDIR) -Od -W3 -Zpi

# Compiler switches for DLLs.

CL_DLL_SHIP_ALL = -AMw -c -D$(CLVER) -Gsw -I$(INCDIR) -Ow -W3 -Zp
CL_DLL_DEBG_ALL = -AMw -c -D$(CLVER) -Gsw -I$(INCDIR) -Od -W3 -Zpi

CL_DLL_SHIP_31  = -AMw -c -G2s  -I$(INCDIR) -Ow -W3 -Zp
CL_DLL_DEBG_31  = -AMw -c -G2s  -I$(INCDIR) -Od -W3 -Zpi

# Make file primary target.

all: CustRes.exe

# Make file dependency targets.

CustRes.res: CustRes.rc CustRes.cur CustRes.ico
    rc -r -i$(INCDIR) CustRes.rc

CustRes.obj: CustRes.c
    cl $(CL_APP_DEBG_ALL) CustRes.c

CustRes.exe: CustRes.obj CustRes.def CustRes.res
    link @CustRes.lnk
    rc -$(RCVER) CustRes.res

CustRes.exe: CustRes.res
    rc -$(RCVER) CustRes.res
```

CUSTRES.RC

```
#include "CustRes.H"

snapshot icon CustRes.ico

hand   cursor CustRes.cur

SINE TABLE sinedata.bin DISCARDABLE
```

CUSTRES does all its work during three messages: `WM_CREATE`, `WM_PAINT`, and `WM_DESTROY`. All of the sine and cosine information is provided in two routines: `intSin` and `intCos`. The second function actually cheats: Since a cosine is always 90 degrees out of phase with a sine, the `intCos` function subtracts 90 degrees from the actual angle and calls the `intSin` function—just a little trigonometric sleight of hand to make Mom proud.

To use a custom function, you must call three routines: `FindResource`, `LoadResource`, and `LockResource`. In response to the `WM_CREATE` message, the first two are called. The result is a memory handle that is stored in `hresSinData`. The `FindResource` searches for the reference to a resource in the module database, which, as we mentioned earlier, is simply an abbreviated memory image of the module's file header. `FindResource` takes three parameters:

```
FindResource (hInstance, lpName, lpType)
```

- `hInstance` is an instance handle.

- `lpName` is a long pointer to a character string with the resource name.

- `lpType` is a long pointer to a character string with the resource type.

Even though `lpName` and `lpType` are pointers to character strings, this is not the most efficient way to identify a resource. The simple reason is that a string comparison is more expensive than an integer comparison. For this reason, we use a macro, `MAKEINTRESOURCE`, which lets us define integers and use them in place of a character string. Here are the two integers we defined in CUSTRES:

```
#define  TABLE   100  /*  Custom resource type.   */
#define  SINE    100  /*  ID of sine table.       */
```

which we use in the call to `FindResource`, as follows:

```
hRes = FindResource (hInst,
                MAKEINTRESOURCE(SIN),     /* Name. */
                MAKEINTRESOURCE(TABLE));   /* Type. */
```

The `MAKEINTRESOURCE` macro creates a pseudo-pointer, with zero for a segment identifier and the integer value for the offset value. It casts this value as an `LPSTR`, which is how this routine is defined, so the C compiler doesn't complain. When the `FindResource` routine sees this value, it does not treat it as a pointer (this would be a fatal error!). Instead, it uses the two-byte integer value to find the resource definition. It can find it, because the resource file, CUSTRES.RC, has the following line:

```
SINE   TABLE   sinedata.bin DISCARDABLE
```

This causes the data in the resource file, sinedata.bin, to be copied entirely into CUSTRES.EXE at compile/link time. This means that CUSTRES is a stand-alone program and doesn't need the original resource data file to be present at run time.

Once `FindResource` has identified the specific resource that we are interested in, it provides a resource identifier: a handle that must be provided to the `LoadResource` routine. `LoadResource` is the next routine called, and it is defined as

```
LoadResource (hInstance, hresInfo)
```

- `hInstance` is the instance handle.

- `hresInfo` is the handle returned by the `FindResource` routine.

In spite of its name, `LoadResource` does *not* cause the resource to be loaded into memory. Instead, it allocates a memory object from the global heap with a size of zero. This doesn't actually cause any memory to be allocated, but does cause a global memory handle to be assigned for our use. `LoadResource` provides this memory handle as a return value, which CUSTRES stores in `hresSinData`.

The routine that actually causes a resource to be loaded into memory is `LockResource`. But CUSTRES doesn't call this routine until it actually needs to use the data in the sine table. By postponing the loading of such a memory object, CUSTRES helps minimize the demand it makes on system memory. `LockResource` does several things: It loads the resource into memory, locks it in place, and returns a pointer to the data. `LockResource` is defined as

```
LPSTR LockResource (hResData)
```

- `hResData` is the handle returned by the `LoadResource` function.

`LockResource` returns a long pointer to a string. If you're not storing characters in a resource, it's a simple matter to define the desired string and cast the results of `LockResource` to the right thing.

Here is how CUSTRES handles its need for a pointer to integer data:

```
int FAR * fpSin;

fpSin = (int FAR *)LockResource (hresSinData);
if (fpSin == NULL)
    return (0);
```

As mentioned elsewhere, casting the return value to routines like `LockResource` keeps the compiler complaining about an alleged type-mismatch. We know better, and we let the compiler know it. Also, we check the return value from `LockResource`, in case it wasn't able to load the resource into memory.

The `LockResource` routine should never be discussed alone, but always in the context of an `UnlockResource`, with which it creates a *Windows sandwich*. We discussed this code construction earlier as a way to organize the use of a shared resource. In this case, the resource is memory. Calls to `LockResource` must be paired with calls to `UnlockResource`. The first loads the resource and ties it down in memory. The second unties the resource, allowing it to be moved in memory or even discarded, if the memory manager sees fit to do so. In CUSTRES, the `intSin` function uses these two routines to bracket its use of the sine data, creating a Windows sandwich, which ensures that the object is locked when we need it, and unlocked when we don't. The `UnlockResource` function is defined as

```
BOOL UnlockResource (hResData)
```

- `hResData` is the handle returned by the `LoadResource` function.

The final routine that plays a role in the handling of the custom resource is `FreeResource`. This frees all the memory associated with our custom resource. `FreeResource` is defined as

```
FreeResource (hResData)
```

- `hResData` is the handle returned by the `LoadResource` function.

This routine is called in response to the `WM_DESTROY` message, to deallocate the sine data memory. In this program, we don't actually need to call `FreeResource`, since the resource will be freed when our program terminates. However, it is a good programming practice that will help your code survive future programmers who fix, update, modify, and in other ways use your code in their projects.

It's worth noting that this program draws pixel coordinates using the default `MM_TEXT` mapping mode. In Chapter 20, when we discuss coordinate mapping, you'll see that there are better ways to make sure you can get a round circle. The only reason the circle you saw in Figure 18.11 was perfectly round is that the screen shot was taken on a device with a 1:1 aspect ratio, a VGA. We give you a brief preview of coordinate mapping, though, by moving the drawing origin from the upper-left corner to the very middle of the window:

```
GetClientRect (hwnd, &r);
SetViewportOrg (ps.hdc, r.right/2, r.bottom/2);
```

A complete look at the issues relating to coordinate transformations are provided in Chapter 20.

From our discussion, you can see that Windows provides many choices in how a program uses memory for its code and data. Understanding these choices will help you tune your program to work optimally in all of Windows operating modes, and for compatibility with future versions of Windows.

19

Dynamic Linking

In all its operating modes—Real, Standard, and Enhanced—Windows uses dynamic linking. Dynamic linking is several things rolled into one. First of all, it is a memory management technique that allows code to be loaded from disk on demand. Dynamic linking allows code to be discarded to free memory for other uses. When running in Protected Mode, Windows' dynamic linking depends on the built-in memory management features of the Intel-86 family of CPUs to trigger the loading process. When running in Real Mode, even without the hardware support, Windows is able to provide dynamic linking that is just as efficient as its Protected Mode counterpart with a mechanism implemented entirely in software.

Second, dynamic linking provides a way to connect subroutine libraries to programs at *run time*. This contrasts sharply with static linking, in which routines from a subroutine library are copied to a program's executable file at program *creation time*. For example, if a Windows program uses the `memset` C-runtime routine, a copy of the routine is stored in the program's .EXE file. This is **static linking**. For the program to be able to access a new version of the `memset` routine (if it were made smaller, faster, more bug-free, or whatever), the program file must be recreated. Thus, a statically linked routine doesn't allow automatic upgrades when library functions are improved. But dynamic linking does, since the functions in a dynamic link library are not copied to a program's executable file at program creation time, but are linked to the program at run time. This is why, for example, Windows programs can run unchanged in Windows NT and in OS/2 2.0.

Third, dynamic linking provides an efficient mechanism for sharing code and data between application programs. For example, a single copy of the code for the subroutines in Windows graphic library, GDI.EXE, is shareable among all the different Windows programs that wish to use them. When your program runs alongside Aldus PageMaker, for example, both programs use the same copy of the TextOut routine. The net result is a much lower demand on system memory. An example of *data* sharing occurs whenever text appears on a display screen. GDI fonts are implemented in dynamic link libraries, which means that they are shared by whichever programs wish to use them. Even with many programs accessing a font, only a single copy of the font data is present in the system.

The most obvious examples of dynamic linking occur between Windows programs and the main Windows dynamic link libraries: KERNEL.EXE (or KRNL286.EXE for Standard Mode, KRNL386.EXE for 386-Enhanced Mode), USER.EXE, and GDI.EXE. When a Windows program is running, it relies on dynamic linking to make the proper connections to the various Windows library routines. Dynamic links are also created between the three main Windows dynamic link libraries and Windows' device drivers. For example, when GDI accesses a printer, it dynamically links to a printer driver. Dynamic linking makes it easy to upgrade or replace different parts of Windows—fonts, device drivers, or even the main libraries themselves.

The Dynamic Linking Mechanism

Let's take a moment to look at the nuts and bolts of Windows' dynamic linking mechanism. Although Microsoft has dropped support for Real Mode with Windows 3.1, we're going to describe the software-only dynamic linking mechanism of Real Mode Windows. If nothing else, it stands as a testimony to the amazing things that can be accomplished in software.

Even though dynamic linking occurs without requiring you to know how it works, there are several reasons why it is helpful to understand the mechanism itself. First of all, you might not be convinced that you can build programs that are bigger than your address space on a microcomputer. Even if you're comfortable with this idea, you might be concerned that the mechanism isn't efficient or has unexpected side-effects. You might want to know if you can build your own dynamic link libraries; understanding the mechanism can help you decide when they are appropriate and when they are not. Or you might just be the kind of person who wants to know how things really work. Whatever your motivation, we think you'll find that—in all its operating modes—Windows' dynamic link mechanism is a fast, efficient, and very elegant approach to the problems of managing the dynamic loading and linking of code.

The architect of Windows' dynamic link mechanism is Steve Wood, who joined Microsoft in 1983. While a graduate student at Yale University, Steve had been involved with some systems programming projects on DEC-20 computers. One project involved the creation of a mechanism to share library code between different processes. This was accomplished by mapping the address space of different processes into the same physical address space. The net result was a reduction in required memory to support shared code.

This sounds a lot like dynamic linking. The difference is that, when he started to work on building the dynamic link mechanism, Steve and the other members of the first KERNEL team were working on a machine with minimal capabilities. The target machine for the first version of Windows, after all, only offered a 4.77 MhZ Intel 8088 CPU, two floppy disk drivers, and 256K of RAM. Dynamic linking could only require a minimum of overhead and had to be a software-only solution to a problem that had been solved elsewhere using dedicated hardware.

With a minimum amount of memory, the solution was to make much of the system reside in code segments that could be discarded. After all, if code resided on disk instead of in memory, there would be more room for applications to do their work. The trick was to figure out how to bring a code segment into memory. It became quickly apparent that a whole new set of tools would have to be forged in order to get dynamic linking to work properly.

For example, a new linker had to be built to support the new .EXE file format required to support dynamic linking. A new program loader had to be built to accommodate the fact that not all segments would necessarily be present when a program was running. Finally, a new compiler had to be built to generate code that would seamlessly connect programs and dynamic link libraries together in a working system. The first Windows development team discovered quite quickly that one of the challenges to working with new tools was determining when a bug was caused by the tools and when it was caused by your own code.

The program loader built into the first version of Windows served as the foundation on which all later loaders were built. To describe its operation, we need to look at how code segments are dynamically loaded and routines linked for discardable, movable, and fixed code segments. We'll start with the hardest case: discardable code.

Dynamic Linking and Discardable Code Segments

When you are building a dynamic link mechanism like the one Windows uses, the hardest aspect of dealing with discardable code segments is the fact that you never know when a code segment is present in memory. Without the hardware memory magic of Protected Mode, Real Mode Windows creates a tiny code stub for every FAR routine in programs and dynamic link libraries. These code stubs are called **loader thunks** or **call thunks** and reside in the module database.

Consider the case of a program using GDI's `Rectangle` routine which, for this example, we'll suppose is in a discardable code segment. We'll call our program DRAWRECT. Before this program starts running, Windows will already have created a module database for GDI. Inside GDI's module database, there is one call thunk for every FAR routine in GDI, including `Rectangle`. Figure 19.1 depicts GDI's module database in memory. In Real Mode, a call thunk for routines in discardable segments has one of two states: an interrupt to the loader, as depicted in Figure 19.1, or a jump to the routine in memory, depicted in Figure 19.3.

When the first instance of DRAWRECT starts running, the Windows loader starts the load process by creating DRAWRECT's module database. The module database is used to resolve calls *into* DRAWRECT; therefore, it is not interesting to us in the context of

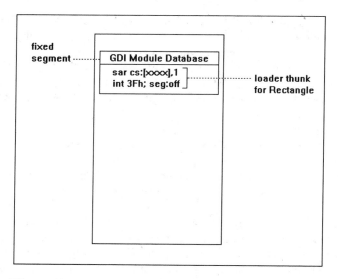

Figure 19.1 Memory before the dynamic link

linking DRAWRECT to GDI's `Rectangle` routine. However, DRAWRECT's module database *is* needed to locate DRAWRECT's entry point. After loading all of DRAWRECT's preload segments, control is passed to this entry point.

The dynamic link from DRAWRECT to GDI's `Rectangle` routine occurs when Windows loads a code segment which actually calls `Rectangle`. Appended to the end of such a code segment is a **relocation table**, which contains the fix-up information needed to create the first half of a dynamic link.

There are basically two types of relocation table entries: internal references and external references. The internal references define far calls to routines inside DRAWRECT. Part of dynamic linking, then, involves creating connections between a newly loaded code segment and other code segments in the same program or dynamic link library.

The external references define calls to dynamic link library routines, such as GDI's `Rectangle`. When DRAWRECT's code segment is loaded into memory, the far call to the `Rectangle` routine is fixed up to the address of the `Rectangle` routine's alias—that is, to the call thunk—in GDI's module database, as depicted in Figure 19.2.

When the Windows loader has finished creating all of the fix-ups described in the segment's relocation table, it frees the memory associated with the relocation table. When the relocation information is needed again, it will be re-read from disk along with the code segment.

When a code segment is loaded into memory, it is patched once for every far call in the segment, including far calls to internal as well as external routines. This means simply that the code in the newly loaded code segment has been modified so that every far call points to *something*. In the Windows programs that you write, you'll want to keep your code segments small and the number of far calls to a minimum because of the overhead incurred when a code segment is loaded into memory.

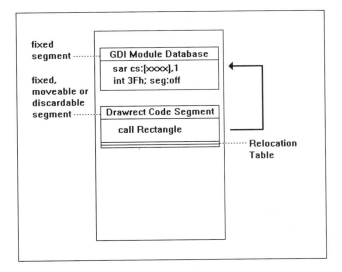

Figure 19.2 DRAWRECT fix-up to GDI's module database

Getting back to our example program, an interesting aspect of the dynamic link is that, even though DRAWRECT's code segment has been fixed up to call into GDI's module database, the code segment that actually holds the `Rectangle` routine does not have to be present in memory. As you'll see in a moment, when the code segment is not present, code in `Rectangle`'s call thunk causes the code segment containing `Rectangle` to actually be loaded into memory.

The next step in the dynamic link process occurs when DRAWRECT actually calls `Rectangle`. Of course, it calls into the call thunk in the module database. The call thunk, a tiny code stub, will have one of two states, depending on whether `Rectangle` is open for business or out to lunch. Let's assume that it is out to lunch, to see how the call thunk responds. In such cases, the call thunk will have code that looks like the following:

```
                         ; -->> "Out-To-Lunch"
    SAR   CS:[00B4h],1    ; update access flag
    INT   3Fh            ; Call to the Windows' loader
    DB    seg            ; Code segment number
    DW    off            ; Offset to Rectangle routine
```

When DRAWRECT calls into this piece of code, it triggers a software interrupt which calls the Windows loader, interrupt 3F. The Windows loader reads the next three bytes of information, which contain the segment number (from 1 to 255) and the offset into the code segment (0 to 65535). Since there is only a single byte for the segment number, the total number of discardable segments in an .EXE or .DLL file is 255 (segment zero is reserved for return thunks, to be covered later). This limitation is intrinsic to the format of the EXE file itself. However, you can create a dynamic link library that allows a program to easily overcome this limitation.

Once the Windows loader has read the necessary code segment from disk, it modifies the module database so that the thunk associated with the `Rectangle` routine has machine instructions represented by the following assembly language:

```
                        ; -->> "Open For Business"
SAR   CS:[00B4h],1     ; Update access flag
JMP   Rectangle
```

Fix-ups are performed not only for the `Rectangle` routine's call thunk, but also for the thunks of all *other* far routines residing in `Rectangle`'s code segment. If `Rectangle` makes far calls to other code segments, those calls are fixed up along with any other far calls *from* `Rectangle`'s code segment. In other words, both inward bound and outward bound far calls are patched. Once the code segment has been loaded into memory and the module database fixed up, the dynamic link is complete. The `Rectangle` routine can retrieve its parameters off the stack and do its job. The complete dynamic link, from DRAWRECT through GDI's module database and into `Rectangle`, is depicted in Figure 19.3.

All calls to `Rectangle` are fixed up to call `Rectangle`'s alias in the module database, which serves as a kind of switchboard operator for this routine. Notice that the Windows memory manager can move `Rectangle`'s segment at any time. When it does so, it does not have to patch every program's code segment that calls `Rectangle`. Instead, it simply patches `Rectangle`'s call thunk (and the call thunk of other far routines that might be in the same code segment). The code segment can also be discarded from memory at any time. When this occurs, the dynamic linker simply fixes up the call thunks with an `INT 3F` instruction to call the Windows loader to restore the code segment into memory. Of course, fix-ups are not free. But the dynamic link mech-

Figure 19.3   Final fix-up from GDI's module database to Rectangle's code segment

anism allows a code segment to be removed from memory, and reloaded later to give the greatest flexibility in how memory is used.

Dynamic Linking and Fixed Code Segments

Once you understand how a dynamic link to a discardable code segment is created, you'll see that dynamic links to fixed code segments are even simpler. Dynamic links to fixed code segments are not routed through a call thunk, but instead link a caller directly to the called routine. One reason for this is that fixed code segments are always treated as preload segments; therefore, they are always resident in memory and never move.

Consider a program that calls GDI's `TextOut` routine, which we'll assume for the moment is in a fixed code segment. For this example, we'll name our program DOTEXT, which calls `TextOut`. As before, when GDI is first brought into memory, the Windows loader creates GDI's module database. Once this is done, the loader reads all fixed code segments into memory. Figure 19.4 shows the state of two objects that are in memory after GDI has been loaded: the module database and the fixed code segment containing `TextOut`.

Since the fixed code segment is loaded when GDI starts running, it will never need a loader thunk. However, to locate the routine itself, the module database lists the address of far routines. The loader will require this information when it loads DOTEXT into memory. At that time, a dynamic link is created that directly connects DOTEXT to `TextOut`, as depicted in Figure 19.5. Unlike the fix-up to a movable or discardable segment, the fix-up to a *fixed* code segment always goes directly from the caller to the called routine.

In Protected Mode, the memory management hardware can move memory objects without changing the logical address. For this reason, all dynamic link fix-ups in Pro-

Figure 19.4 GDI immediately after loading

Figure 19.5 Direct fix-up from DOTEXT to TextOut

tected Mode are treated like the dynamic link we just described. In other words, all fix-ups in Protected Mode are treated as if every code segment were fixed. Far calls are patched up by the Windows loader to directly connect a caller to the called routine. This is true for movable segments as well as discardable segments.

Since Protected Mode doesn't have call thunks in the module database, you might wonder how discardable code segments are reloaded. In Real Mode, as you'll recall, the loader thunk in the module database triggers a code segment reload:

```
SAR   CS:[00B4h],1    ; Update access flag
INT   3Fh             ; Call to the Windows' loader
DB    seg             ; Code segment number
DW    off             ; Offset to Rectangle routine
```

In Protected Mode, when an absent code segment is called, a segment fault occurs. As our discussion of Protected Mode operation in Chapter 17 revealed, every segment identifier contains an index into a Protected Mode descriptor table. Among the information kept in these tables is a flag that lets the system know whether a segment is actually present in memory. When it is not present, the segment fault—which is simply a software interrupt—notifies the memory manager that it must load the missing segment. Windows' memory manager loads the code segment into memory, then causes the instruction that triggered the segment fault to be restarted. In this way, the memory management hardware that operates in Protected Mode is able to operate in a manner that is transparent to application software.

Other Real Mode Dynamic Linking Considerations

In Protected Mode, the dynamic link mechanism is greatly simplified by the hardware memory management provided by the various Intel processors. Segments can be moved around in physical memory without invalidating the logical address used by programs. Discarded code segments can be automatically reloaded when a *segment not present* interrupt occurs.

In Real Mode, Windows has to play a number of tricks to achieve the same flexibility that comes for free in Protected Mode. Two of these tricks are **stack patching** and the use of **return thunks**. To help you appreciate the work that Real Mode Windows had to do, we're going to describe these mechanisms in more detail.

Stack Patching. Stack patching involves walking the stack of a program and updating references made to code segments that have moved. Earlier, we mentioned that the only thing that had to happen when a code segment was moved was to update the references to the routine in a module database. This is true most of the time. But if the address of a routine is referenced as a return address on the stack, that reference must also be fixed up.

Whenever a function is called—inside a dynamic link library or inside a regular program—a return address is placed on the stack. This address identifies the location of the machine instruction that is to be executed next when we return from the function. When a code segment referenced on the stack moves, Windows must walk the stack and patch the return address so that calls can correctly find their way back to the calling function. Windows patches the stack for every instance of every program running in the system.

Because Windows can patch stacks, it is free to move any code segment at any time. This gives the Windows memory manager the freedom to move any movable code segment at any time, and allows Real Mode Windows to have the same flexibility of Protected Mode Windows—which is critical, given the greater memory constraints of Real Mode operation.

Return Thunks. In the same way that stack patching allows code segments to be *moved*, return thunks allow code segments to be *discarded*. In our discussion of dynamic linking, we mentioned that a code segment could be discarded at any time, as long as the module database was updated to call the Windows loader the next time a function in the segment was called.

When Windows discards a code segment that is referenced as a return address on the stack, the stack is patched. The stack patching operation involves walking the stack of all programs, looking for a reference to the discarded code segment. Since the stack cannot be patched with the address of a discarded code segment, which has no address, it is instead patched to return to a tiny code stub called a **return thunk**. A return thunk is similar to a call thunk, except that after loading the necessary code segment, it provides a bridge for a return instruction instead of a call instruction. After the segment has been loaded, execution continues at the return address on the stack before the segment was discarded. Here is an example of a return thunk:

```
INT   3Fh        ; Call to the Windows' loader.
DB    0          ; Zero segment = return thunk.
DW               ; seg:IP packed into 20 bits.
DB               ; Handle to data segment packed into 12 bits.
```

A return thunk looks a lot like a loader thunk, except that an invalid segment number is given: zero. This flags the INT 3F loader, identifying it as a return thunk. In this case, it knows that the three bytes that follow contain all the data it needs to continue, although things are packed a little tightly. For one thing, the segment number and the code segment offset are crammed into 20 bits. This is possible since the code segment number will be a number between 0 and 255, which means it only takes one byte. That leaves 16 bits for the offset. A handle to the data segment is stored in the return thunk, since the data segment itself may have moved while memory was being jostled around. When the return thunk is run, the data segment is patched to reflect the new location of the data segment. All of this allows Windows to survive even a very low memory situation, since *any* code segment in the entire system (except the currently executing one) can be discarded if more memory is needed.

Thus far, our discussion of dynamic linking has focused on *code*, and how code can be loaded, moved, and discarded in all of Windows' operating modes. Windows takes advantage of the features of Protected Mode, when they are available, but also adapts to the constraints and limitation of Real Mode with no change in overall system capabilities. Now we will examine the impact of dynamic linking on *data*. Windows allows every program and dynamic link library to create a default data segment, and it provides several mechanisms to make sure that every program and dynamic link library is always able to access its default data.

Dynamic Linking and Module Data Segments

When you write a stand-alone application in most operating systems, you may use functions from various static link libraries. When you do, these blend invisibly into your program so that it is almost impossible to distinguish the machine instructions created by *your* code from the machine instructions associated with library routines. If a static library routine needs to store global variables to maintain state information, the linker blends the library's global variables with your program's global variables.

When working with dynamic link libraries, the distinction between your program and the library code is more evident. For example, dynamic link libraries have their own separate executable files. GDI.EXE, for example, is the dynamic link library file where GDI routines live. The file maintains a separate existence from the programs that use the library routines.

Dynamic link libraries also have their own data segment that allow them to keep global variables separate from the data areas of the programs using its routines. You can convince yourself of this by running the HEAPWALK utility and looking for the objects marked as "Data" owned by the USER and GDI libraries, as well as various device driver DLLs. In Figure 19.6, the data segments of the USER and the WINOLDAP dynamic link libraries are highlighted. (WINOLDAP creates a shell around MS-DOS programs when they are running under Windows.)

A Windows library makes certain functions available to Windows programs. These functions serve as a doorway into the capabilities and features of the dynamic link libraries. Such functions are given a very special flag to enable Windows to help the DLL access its proper data segment. The flag marks a function as **exported**. Windows

```
┌──────────────────────────────────────────────────────────────────┐
│ ▬           HeapWalker- (Main Heap)                         ▼  ▲  │
├──────────────────────────────────────────────────────────────────┤
│ File  Walk  Sort  Object  Alloc  Add!                             │
├──────────────────────────────────────────────────────────────────┤
│SELECTOR HANDLE   SIZE LCK FLG  OWNER-NAME   OBJ-TYPE  ADD-INFO   ▲│
│0007ABE0  04BE    1280     D    User         Code                 ■│
│0007B0E0  04B6    8768     D    User         Code                  │
│0007E5C0  0256      32     D    User         Resource  Group_Cursor│
│000826E0  05C6    2080     D    User         Code                  │
│00083E80  05EE    2944     D    User         Code                  │
│00085FC0  054E    2336     D    User         Code                  │
│0008BAA0  05FE   29952 1        User         Data                  │
│0009C500  05AE    9728     D    User         Code                  │
│8051D660  055E    9152     D    User         Code                  │
│00035EE0          512           Winoldap     Task DataBase         │
│000360E0          992           Winoldap     Data                  │
│000365C0  094E      64 1        Winoldap     Code                  │
│00037740  09BE      32     D    Winoldap     Resource  NameTable   │
│0005A300  09EE      32     D    Winoldap     Resource  String      │
│0005D500  09F6      32     D    Winoldap     Resource  String      │
│0005D620  09CE      64     D    Winoldap     Resource  Group_Icon  │
│0005D660  09FE      32     D    Winoldap     Resource  String      │
│0005D740  0A06      32     D    Winoldap     Resource  String     ▼│
└──────────────────────────────────────────────────────────────────┘
```

Figure 19.6 HEAPWALK with data segments of USER and WINOLDAP highlighted

modifies the first three bytes of every exported library function to set up the library's data segment, using code like this:

```
MOV   AX, DGROUP       ; Get data segment address
PUSH  DS               ; Save caller's DS
MOV   DS, AX           ; Install in DS register
```

When the library's data segment moves, Windows updates the value of DGROUP for all exported routines in the library. This causes the data segment register to be correctly set whenever a program calls into one of the exported "doorway" functions. Here is the complete set of assembly language instructions used to set up the data segment of an exported far routine in a dynamic link library:

```
MOV   AX, DGROUP       ; Get data segment address
INC   BP
PUSH  BP
MOV   BP, SP
PUSH  DS               ; Save caller's DS
MOV   DS, AX
```

Earlier, when we described some of the tricks that Real Mode Windows must play, we said that it must sometimes walk and patch the stack when a code segment has moved or been discarded. The PUSH BP and MOV BP, SP instructions are how the compiler ordinarily saves the old BP value and initializes it for the private use of the current function. This effectively creates a linked list of stack frames that simplify stack walking. The INC BP instruction is only used for far calls to help the memory manager to distinguish between a near and far call. At certain times, a Windows library routine will call functions within a Windows program. Such routines are referred to as **call-back functions**. Until now, we have discussed two types of call-back functions: window procedures and dialog box procedures. Other types include enumeration procedures and subclass procedures. Just like a window procedure, and the special "doorway" functions in a dynamic link library, all call-back procedures must be *exported*. There are two ways to export a procedure: You can place an entry into the module definition file, like this:

```
EXPORTS
    MinWindowProc
```

Or, if you are using the Microsoft C Compiler, version 5.1 or later, you can use the **_exports** directive as shown here:

```
LRESULT CALLBACK _exports
MinWindowProc (HWND hwnd,
               UINT wMsg,
               WPARAM wParam,
               LPARAM lParam)
```

It is very important to export a procedure that Windows calls, because the data segment register will be set up for one of Windows dynamic link libraries (USER or GDI), when Windows calls you. By exporting the call-back procedures, you put in place part of a mechanism that sets the DS register up properly so you can access your program's data segment.

Another part of the mechanism involves the way the prolog and epilog codes are generated by the compiler at the beginning and end of each far function. Here is the prolog generated by the Microsoft C Compiler when you specify the -Gw compiler switch:

```
PUSH DS        ; Put DS value into
POP  AX        ; the AX register.
NOP            ; Place holder
INC  BP        ; stack-walking preparation
PUSH BP        ; set up regular stack frame
MOV  BP, SP    ; set up regular stack frame
PUSH DS        ; save caller's DS
MOV  DS, AX    ; install our own DS
```

At first glance, it looks as if this routine does a lot of work for nothing. But this somewhat complicated piece of code makes sure that every far call saves a copy of the caller's data segment on the stack. Why? This allows Windows to patch the address of *data segments* that are moved at the same time that it patches code segment addresses. Anytime any code or data segment moves, Windows has no problem patching references to it.

At the moment a code segment is loaded into memory, the Windows loader checks for exported functions. For each one it finds, it modifies the function prolog. Windows replaces the PUSH DS, POP AX instructions with three NOP (no operation) instructions, as shown here:

```
NOP
NOP
NOP
```

```
INC   BP          ; stack-walking preparation
PUSH  BP          ; set up regular stack frame
MOV   BP, SP      ; set up regular stack frame
PUSH  DS          ; save caller's DS
MOV   DS, AX      ; install our own DS
```

This allows an exported function to receive its data segment value in the AX register. But wait—how does the data segment value get into the AX register? That depends on the type of call-back function: window procedures use one mechanism and all other call-back functions use another.

A window procedure receives its data segment fix-up value as part of Windows' message delivery mechanism. When you call CreateWindow (or CreateWindowEx) to create a window, you pass an instance handle that identifies the data segment to be associated with the window. The message delivery mechanism places this value in the AX register for use by the window procedure's prolog.

All other call-back functions must use another mechanism that requires a little work on your part, but ensures that the AX register will be set up properly with the address of the data segment. The mechanism is called an **Instance Thunk**.

The Instance Thunk

The dynamic link mechanism allows the code from different **modules**—executable programs and dynamic link libraries—to be linked together efficiently at run time. Every module can have its own data segment, which allows programs and dynamic link libraries to store global variables needed to do their work. The rule about data fix-ups is that *a data segment* (DS) fix-up is required every time a module boundary is crossed. We have already described how this is done for dynamic link libraries and for window procedures in applications. The third type of data segment fix-up must be setup and managed by a Windows program.

Here is a list of the different call-back procedures that can be created in Windows. As you can see, call-backs play many different roles in Windows. A call-back provides a way for Windows to deliver information to a Windows program in a fairly efficient manner.

Call-Back Function	*Description*
Dialog box procedure	Used to initialize and maintain a dialog box.
Enumeration procedure	When a program wants to query Windows, an enumeration procedure is often used. Windows calls the enumeration procedure once for each object. Enumerated objects include windows, fonts, GDI drawing objects, and clipboard formats.
Hook	Allows a program to eavesdrop and change message traffic in the system. A keyboard hook, for example, lets a program respond to any "hot key" even if the program isn't currently active.

Call-Back Function	Description
Memory discarding notification procedure	`GlobalNotify` lets a program set up a call-back procedure that is called before the Windows memory manager discards a memory object.
Sub-class procedure	Provides a means of eavesdropping in and modifying the message traffic for a particular window.
Timer	A timer procedure allows a program to specify an alternative method for receiving timer notifications other than by a `WM_TIMER` message.

An important issue to keep in mind is that an instance thunk is only required if a call-back resides in an application. For call-backs in DLLs, instance thunks are not needed.

An instance thunk is a very small piece of code. Here is an example of one:

```
MOV   AX, DSvalue
JMP   DialogBoxProc
```

If the routine, `DialogBoxProc`, resided in a fixed code segment, this fix-up would jump directly to the code itself. Figure 19.7 shows the relationship of the different pieces to one another, and the flow of control through an instance thunk for all Protected Mode and for fixed code segments in Real Mode.

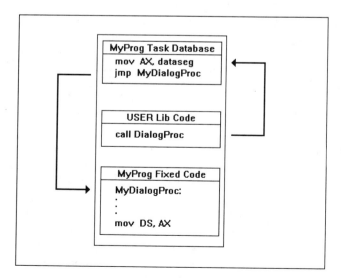

Figure 19.7 An Instance Thunk and a fixed code segment

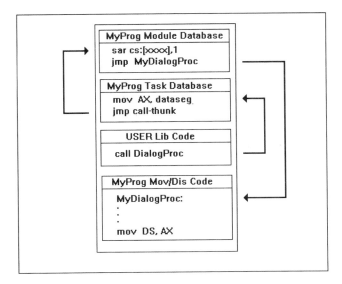

Figure 19.8 An Instance Thunk and a movable or discardable code segment

There is another case worth looking at briefly, since it helps to bring the complexity of Real Mode operation into perspective. Earlier, we mentioned that in Real Mode, calls into moveable and discardable code segments are always routed through a module database call thunk. When you add an instance thunk, you get an arrangement like that depicted in Figure 19.8. First, control passes to the instance thunk to put the data segment value into AX. Next, the Real Mode dynamic linker passes control to a call thunk, which either loads an absent segment or passes control to the called function.

Notice that the call gets routed through both the task database and the module database of the program. In the task database, the instance thunk puts the value of the program's data segment into the AX register. If the data segment moves, the memory manager walks through all the active thunks in the task database to insure that these thunks stay current. From the task database, a jump is made into the module database. It arrives at the loader thunk that we described earlier. After all, this is the mechanism that allows a code sement to be discarded or moved in real mode. And finally, control arrives at our call-back procedure. Of course, as we saw in the earlier code fragments, one of the first instructions in the call-back procedure will establish the data segment address by copying the value in the AX register into the DS register.

A program creates an instance thunk by calling the **MakeProcInstance** routine, which we have seen already in our discussion of dialog boxes in Chapter 14. This routine takes as one of its parameters a procedure address—which, in real-mode operation, is the address of a module database call thunk for functions that reside in movable or discardable segments. It returns an instance thunk, which can then be provided as the address of a far procedure for those Windows library routines which require the address of call-back procedures.

Clean Up Before You Go Home

We have described three different sets of entries that can be made into far functions: exported library entries, unexported program entries, and exported program entries. The first reflects how the Windows loader sets up a dynamic link library's data segment. The second is simply what the C Compiler creates to allow the other two entries to work properly. The third is for call-back functions like window procedures and dialog box procedures.

Although there are three different entries for far functions, all far functions in Windows clean up the stack in the same way, with the following instructions:

```
MOV  SP, BP    ; restore caller's stack frame
POP  DS        ; restore caller's DS
POP  BP        ; reset caller's stack frame
DEC  BP        ; Undo stack walking flag
RETF 0002      ; far return
```

In other words, the caller's data segment value—the DS register—is restored. While it was on the stack, the memory manager may have modified it to reflect a new location for a data segment. The caller's stack frame is restored by the POP BP instruction, then BP is decremented. Finally, a return instruction sends control back to the caller.

Windows 3.1 Dynamic Linking Improvements

It's worth noting that the data side of dynamic linking has been made a lot simpler in Windows 3.1. To make Windows more robust, Microsoft implemented a number of changes, small and large. Among the changes was a new approach to handling call-back functions. In Windows 3.0, a program that forgot to export a function or to call MakeProcInstance ran the risk of overwriting the data areas of either GDI or USER.

To fix this problem, Windows 3.1 modifies the DS, ES, and AX registers with the current contents of the stack segment register before it calls into your code. After all, most applications have a default data segment like the one shown in Chapter 17: The stack is embedded as part of the default data segment. Put another way, SS == DS. Since this is the case, Windows' fixup to the segment registers accomplishes two goals: First, it makes it less likely that an application will overwrite one of Windows' private data areas. Second, it makes it unnecessary for an application to call Make-ProcInstance or to **export** functions. You can leave these out of your Windows **application** code, provided that (a) your application will *only* run in Windows 3.1 or greater, and (b) your application doesn't play any strange tricks with the SS or DS registers. Note, however, that you'll still need to export functions in **dynamic link libraries**. The reason is simple: Most DLLs have their own automatic data segment, but use the stack of the calling application. In other words, they run in an SS !=DS configuration.

As you've seen, dynamic linking has both a code and a data aspect. The code aspect allows a program to be linked to library code at run time instead of at link time. This has allowed programs written for a previous version of Windows to run (almost) effortlessly in Windows 3. The data aspect of dynamic linking is invisible to a program for its window procedures, and involves a call to `MakeProcInstance` for all other call-back procedures. While the data side of dynamic linking is not as transparent as the code side, both parts work together with relatively little effort on your part.

Dynamic linking is a robust, flexible mechanism that helped the earliest versions of Windows run in Real Mode with acceptable performance. For the present, it continues to operate in Windows 3.1. For the future, it will continue as an important operating system mechanism in operating systems like OS/2 and Windows NT.

## PART VII

MORE TOPICS IN GDI PROGRAMMING

20

Coordinate Transformation and Scrolling

The creation and use of graphical output is a vast subject area about which much has been written and much will continue to be written. This chapter and the next return to the subject of graphics to ensure that we have covered the basics you'll need to know to build a full-blown Windows application.

In this chapter, we cover two topics: coordinate transformation and scrolling. Coordinate transformation has to do with GDI's facilities for using other coordinates besides the pixel-based client area coordinates that we have used thus far. Scrolling is the process by which a program whose data does not fit in a window can make that data available to users. The user-interface portion of scrolling is, of course, scroll bars. But making the best use of the programming interface involves understanding the help that Windows gives you when you scroll pixels on the display.

Coordinate Transformation

Coordinate transformation refers to the way GDI interprets the drawing coordinates that you provide to describe the location and shape of geometric figures and text. Until now, we haven't used coordinate transformations, but have used only pixel coordinates. However, GDI does not restrict you to pixel coordinates. For example, you can tell GDI to interpret drawing coordinates in inches or millimeters, or you can define your own coordinate system to scale—for example, 10 units per pixel, one unit per 18 pixels, or whatever arbitrary scaling factors you wish to apply.

Table 20.1 GDI Mapping Modes

Mapping Mode Name	One Logical Unit	Inches	Millimeters
MM_TEXT	1 pixel	-	-
MM_HIMETRIC	0.01 mm	0.000394	0.01
MM_TWIPS	1/1440 inches	0.000694	0.0176
MM_HIENGLISH	0.001 inches	0.001	0.0254
MM_LOMETRIC	0.1 mm	0.00394	0.1
MM_LOENGLISH	0.01 inches	0.01	0.254
MM_ISOTROPIC	} Scaling based on ratio between two DC		
MM_ANISOTROPIC	} attribute values: window extent and viewport extent		

Like many of GDI's other features, coordinate transformations are controlled by making changes to the drawing attributes in a DC. Here is a list of the DC attributes that play a part in coordinate transformation:

Attribute	*Description*
Mapping mode	Determines the units. See Table 20.1.
Viewport extent	Pixel units for scaling in MM_ANISOTROPIC and MM_ISOTROPIC mapping modes.
Viewport origin	Pixel units for coordinate translation.
Window extent	Real world units for scaling in MM_ANISOTROPIC and MM_ISOTROPIC mapping modes.
Window origin	Real world units for coordinate translation.

In the world of graphics programming, there are three types of coordinate transformation: **translation**, **scaling**, and **rotation**. GDI supports translation and scaling, but has no built-in support for rotation. This does not mean that a program cannot rotate a drawing, but doing so requires a program to calculate the rotated coordinate values itself.

As depicted in Figure 20.1(b), translation involves sliding an image to a new location. This is sometimes referred to as **scrolling** or **panning**. Translation by itself does not change the size of a picture, nor does it cause the picture to appear at a different angle; translation just changes the picture's location. In terms of how the coordinates are interpreted, translating involves one or more of the following operations: adding or subtracting an X-translation value to x-coordinates, and adding or subtracting a Y-translation value to y-coordinates.

Figure 20.1(c) shows an example of scaling. Scaling, also referred to as **zooming**, causes a picture to change size. When **uniform scaling** takes place, the changes to the

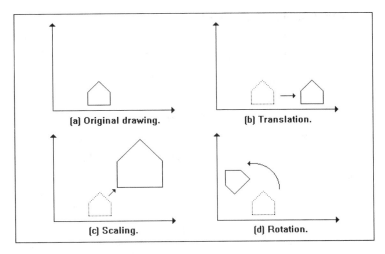

**Figure 20.1 Coordinate transformation: (a) the original drawing;
(b) translation; (c) scaling; and (d) rotation.**

x-coordinates are proportional to the changes to the y-coordinates. **Differential scaling**, on the other hand, means that the scaling factor for x-coordinates is different from the scaling factor applied to the y-coordinates. In addition to changing the *size* of a picture, scaling also changes the distance from the origin. In other words, a coordinate transformation that causes scaling also causes translation (sliding) either toward or away from the origin.

Just as translations can be seen in terms of adding or subtracting values to coordinates, scaling can be seen in multiplication terms. Indeed, it's pretty common to hear people describe scaling in terms of a multiplier, since scaling involves multiplying by a scaling factor. Something might be twice as large as something else, or only half as large.

Figure 20.1(d) shows an example of a rotated picture. GDI does not provide any rotation for you, but for the sake of completeness we'll explore what rotation involves in the world of graphics programming. Rotation is usually described in terms of rotation around a point. The simplest rotation uses the origin (0,0) as the rotation point. The illustration shows this type of rotation, in which the picture seems to behave like a constellation in the sky: Although it has traveled some distance, the angle of the image itself doesn't seem to have rotated very much. On the other hand, if we place the rotation point somewhere in the middle of an object, it rotates around the rotation point like a phonograph record rotates on a turntable.

GDI's eight mapping modes can be divided into four categories: device, fully constrained, partially constrained, and fully unconstrained. The mapping modes in each category are listed in Table 20.2. To determine the active mapping mode in a DC, you call `GetMapMode`, which is defined:

```
int GetMapMode (hDC)
```

- `hDC` is a handle to a device context.

Table 20.2 Categories of Mapping Modes

Category	Mapping Modes	One Unit Equals
Device	MM_TEXT	One pixel.
Fully constrained	MM_HIMETRIC	One-hundredth of a millimeter.
	MM_TWIPS	Approx. 1/1440 of a point.
	MM_HIENGLISH	One-thousandth of an inch.
	MM_LOMETRIC	One-tenth of a millimeter.
	MM_LOENGLISH	One-hundredth of an inch.
Partially constrained	MM_ISOTROPIC	Arbitrary units, but uniform scaling is applied to X and Y, which means that X units and Y units are identical.
Fully unconstrained	MM_ANISOTROPIC	Arbitrary units. Differential scaling is allowed; X and Y can be independently scaled.

Setting a mapping mode requires a call to `SetMapMode`, which is defined:

```
int SetMapMode (hDC, nMapMode)
```

- `hDC` is a handle to a device context.
- `nMapMode` is one of the mapping modes from Table 20.2.

Let's look at each of the categories in turn, starting with the device mapping mode.

Device Mapping Mode

There is only one mapping mode in this category, `MM_TEXT`. As you may recall, this is the default mapping mode and is the only one we have been using in this book. In this mapping mode, one unit equals 1 pixel, in both the X and the Y direction.

This mapping mode is the most accurate. When you are writing applications in which you must have pixel-perfect drawing, you may wish to limit yourself to this mapping mode. It is also the most portable mapping mode. If you are writing code that you plan to port to other environments (like the Apple Macintosh and the various X-Window systems), you will probably want to limit yourself to this mapping mode, since pixel-based coordinates are available in all GUI systems. The OS/2 Presentation Manager, on the other hand, incorporates all of Windows' coordinate transformations and more. If you port your Windows applications to this environment, you can use any of GDI's mapping modes with wild abandon.

Since drawing units are pixels, this mapping mode doesn't support scaling. But it does support translation—that is, scrolling. In GDI, translation is defined in terms of where the origin is located. There are two GDI routines that change the origin:

`SetViewportOrg` and `SetWindowOrg`. `SetWindowOrg` defines a translation *before* the scaling, and `SetViewportOrg` defines a translation to be applied *after* scaling. As you'll see, this latter routine always refers to pixels, so it is the one we use in our translation of MM_TEXT coordinates. `SetViewportOrg` is defined:

```
DWORD SetViewportOrg (hDC, X, Y)
```

- hDC is a handle to a device context.
- X is the x-coordinate of the new origin.
- Y is the y-coordinate of the new origin.

When drawing on the display, the following code sets the origin in the middle of a window's client area. Figure 20.2 provides a more graphic depiction of the new location of the origin.

```
RECT r;
...
GetClientRect (hwnd, &r);
SetViewportOrg (hdc, r.right/2, r.bottom/2);
...
```

To set the origin in the middle of the page on a printer, here is what we could say:

```
int cxWidth;
int cyHeight;
...
cxWidth  = GetDevicecaps (hdcPrinter, HORZSIZE);
cyHeight = GetDevicecaps (hdcPrinter, VERTSIZE);
SetViewportOrg (hdcPrinter, cxWidth/2, cyHeight/2);
...
```

`hdcPrinter` is a handle to a printer DC. We're getting a little ahead of ourselves here, since we haven't yet discussed the creation of a printer DC. However, a printer DC is a lot like a display DC; both provide a set of drawing attributes and a connection to

Figure 20.2 The origin in the center of the client area, in device coordinates

their respective devices. As you probably guessed, the two calls to `GetDeviceCaps` provide the width and height of a printed page.

A potential problem with the `MM_TEXT` mapping mode is that you may inadvertently create device-*dependent* code. For example, you may decide that some graphic object should be 100 pixels wide by 100 pixels tall. After all, if you developed your program on a VGA display, you'd find that this size creates an image that occupies a little more than one square inch. While you might be satisfied with the image on a VGA display, the object would change sizes when drawn on a different device. For example, on a 300-dots-per-inch laser printer, the same drawing occupies an area one-tenth as big.

There are several solutions to this problem. You can call `GetSystemMetrics` to determine the size of various objects on the display screen. For example, in Chapter 13, we used this method to determine how big to make a top-level window. Of course, this routine can only be used to determine the size of objects on the display screen; it doesn't tell us how to size objects on other devices.

If you are dealing with text, you can call `GetTextMetrics` to retrieve text measurement information and use these values to place text in a device-independent manner. We first used this in Chapter 10, when we discussed drawing text. You may also recall that dialog box coordinates are defined in terms of system font metrics, which allows them to achieve a large degree of device independence.

You'll want to consider a third solution if you plan to work with different sizes and styles of text: **logical inches**. A logical inch is defined in terms of an (x,y) pair. To retrieve the values for the logical inches on a device, call `GetDeviceCaps`, which gives applications access to the capability bits and metrics for a device. This routine is defined:

```
int GetDeviceCaps (hDC, nIndex)
```

- `hDC` is a handle to a device context.

- `nIndex` specifies the value to be returned. `LOGPIXELSX` provides the number of pixels in a logical inch in the X direction, and `LOGPIXELSY` provides the number of pixels in a logical inch in the Y direction.

To retrieve the number of pixels per logical inch along both the X and Y axes, you say:

```
int cxInch, cyInch;

cxInch = GetDeviceCaps (hdc, LOGPIXELSX);
cyInch = GetDeviceCaps (hdc, LOGPIXELSY);
```

A logical inch is a fudge factor for scaling fonts on display screens. Its primary purpose is to improve the readability of fonts on displays. The range of font sizes used for **text type**—the type that makes up the main body of printed documents—varies from eight to twelve points (a point is approximately 1/72 of an inch). Since a primary use of the display screen is to preview text copy before it is sent to the printer, this fudge factor simplifies the process of emulating the printed page on a display screen—a capability sometimes called "what you see is what you get," or WYSIWYG, output.

On lower resolution devices, if fonts were scaled according to a ruler inch, eight-point type would be unreadable. Consider, for example, a CGA display, which has 28 pixels per Y-axis ruler inch. An eight-point font on this device would only be (8 x 28) / 72 or about 3 pixels high. Even on an EGA display, with its 51 pixels per Y-axis ruler inch, an eight-point font would only be (8 x 51) / 72 or six pixels high. Depending on the display device, a logical inch may be anywhere between 25 and 70 percent larger than a ruler inch.

Programs that depend heavily on different sizes of text can use a logical inch for both text and graphics. In this case, such a program can use the MM_TEXT mapping mode and still achieve a very high level of device independence. Of course, this requires that you do all of the scaling yourself. An alternative is to use GDI's mapping modes, which map directly to ruler inches on both the display screen and printers. We are referring, of course, to the fully constrained mapping modes, to be discussed next.

Fully Constrained Mapping Modes

GDI's fully constrained mapping modes are referred to as "fully constrained" because each limits you to a single scaling factor. Depending on the mode you choose, these mapping modes allow you to draw using inch, millimeter, or printer's point coordinates. The scaling of each is fixed, then, to various "real world" measuring units.

To understand this set of mapping modes, you need to understand the way GDI does arithmetic. GDI uses integer arithmetic exclusively for all its calculations, instead of floating-point coordinates which are, in some respects, more suitable coordinates. The problem with floating-point arithmetic is that the Intel-86 family of processors has no built-in floating-point support. Accurate floating-point arithmetic would require quite a bit of work, all of which would have to be done in software. For reasons of performance, then, GDI limits itself to integer arithmetic. What's more, it uses only 16-bit short integers instead of the more accurate, but slower, 32-bit integer arithmetic.

To overcome the implicit loss of precision from integer arithmetic, the fully constrained mapping modes are scaled so that units are not whole inches, millimeters, and points. Instead, units are equal to a fixed fraction of inches, millimeters, and printer's points. For example, when you use the MM_HIMETRIC mapping mode, each unit is equal to 0.01 millimeter. To draw an object that is a millimeter long in this mapping mode, you specify 100 units. In the MM_HIENGLISH mapping mode, which uses units equal to .001 inch, you need to specify 1000 units when drawing an object that is one inch. To give you a better idea of the relationship between the units used by these mapping modes, Figure 20.3 shows a set of 100-unit squares. For comparison sake, we've included a square whose sides are a logical inch. The last square does not have sides that are 100 units; instead—since this figure was drawn on a VGA display—the sides are 96 pixels each. The obvious difference between the logical inch square and the MM_LOENGLISH object, which is a ruler inch on each side, demonstrates the discrepancy between a logical inch and a ruler inch.

When working with these mapping modes, you must take into account the fact that the direction taken by the Y axis is different from the direction in the MM_TEXT mapping mode. In the default text mapping mode, Y coordinates increase moving down the

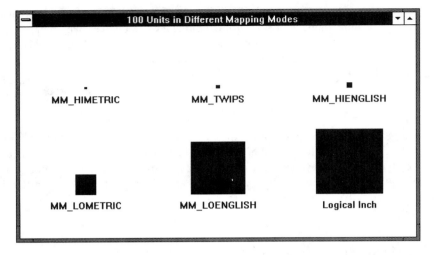

Figure 20.3 Squares drawn with the fully constrained mapping modes and with a logical inch

screen (or printed page). However, in all of the fully constrained mapping modes, Y coordinates increase when moving *up* the screen. In this way, these mapping modes mimic the approach taken by the Cartesian coordinate system. Figure 20.4 depicts this graphically.

When you call either `BeginPaint` or `GetDC` to borrow a display DC from the Window Manager (a topic we first introduced in Chapter 6), the DC has its origin (0,0) in the upper-left corner of the window. As you'll see in the next chapter, when you call `CreateDC` to obtain a DC to draw on a printer, the DC has its origin in the upper-left corner of the drawing surface. This means that if you use draw with any of these mapping modes and use positive Y coordinates, your drawing will not appear. So, if you wish to use positive Y coordinates, one of the first things you should do is to move the

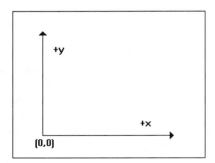

Figure 20.4 Fully constrained coordinates and the Y-axis

origin to a new location. From our earlier discussion, you may recall that the `SetViewportOrg` routine can do this for us.

For example, the following code moves the origin to the lower-left corner of a window, sets the mapping mode to `MM_LOENGLISH`, then draws a rectangle which is one inch by three inches:

```
RECT r;
...
SetMapMode (hdc, MM_LOENGLISH);

GetClientRect (hwnd, &r);
SetViewportOrg (hdc, 0, r.bottom);

Rectangle (hdc, 0, 0, 100, 300);
...
```

Or, if you are drawing on a printer, here is how you can place the origin at the bottom-left corner of the printed page:

```
int cyHeight;
...
cyHeight = GetDevicecaps (hdcPrinter, VERTSIZE);
SetViewportOrg (hdcPrinter, 0, cyHeight);
...
```

The `SetViewportOrg` routine moves the origin using pixel coordinates. Therefore, if you want to move it anywhere else on a drawing surface, you call this routine and specify the new pixel location for the origin.

One convenient aspect of the fully constrained mapping modes is that units in the X direction and units in the Y direction are set equal. This is particularly important on devices that do not have an **aspect ratio** of 1:1, like the CGA and EGA displays and certain types of printers. An aspect ratio describes the ratio between the distance moved in Y to achieve an equal movement in X. For example, CGA displays have a 2-to-1 aspect ratio, and EGA displays have a 1.33-to-1 aspect ratio. These mapping modes provide one way to compensate for this type of discrepancy by scaling coordinates so that X and Y units are effectively equal. This makes sense, of course, since we expect one vertical inch to have the same length as one horizontal inch.

Let's take a look at a sample program that makes use of two of these mapping modes. Our program, RULERS, draws a pair of rulers—one horizontal and one vertical—to help introduce the fully constrained mapping modes.

A Sample Program: RULERS

Our sample program, RULERS, draws two-inch rulers on the left and bottom of its client area. Figure 20.5 shows the output produced by this program. As you can see, the rulers are subdivided into eighths of an inch, with a medium-size tick to mark the half-inches, and a long mark for the inches. Here is the code that produced this output.

Figure 20.5   The two rulers drawn by RULERS

RULERS.C

```
/*------------------------------------------------------------*\
| RULERS.C - Draw a ruler to show coordinates transformation. |
\*------------------------------------------------------------*/
#define STRICT
#include <Windows.H>

#define SMALLTICK   (4)
#define MEDIUMTICK (15)
#define LARGETICK  (25)


/*------------------------------------------------------------*\
|                   Function Prototypes.                       |
\*------------------------------------------------------------*/
LRESULT CALLBACK RulersWndProc (HWND, UINT, WPARAM, LPARAM);
void NEAR PASCAL RulersInstallCoords (HDC, HWND);
void NEAR PASCAL RulersDrawVertRuler(HDC);
void NEAR PASCAL RulersDrawHorzRuler(HDC);


/*------------------------------------------------------------*\
|                    Global Variables.                         |
\*------------------------------------------------------------*/
char achWndClass[] = "Rulers:MAIN";
char achAppName[]  = "Rulers";


/*------------------------------------------------------------*\
|                 Main Function:  WinMain.                     |
\*------------------------------------------------------------*/
int PASCAL
```

```
WinMain (HINSTANCE hInstance,        // Who am I?
         HINSTANCE hPrevInstance,    // Any older siblings?
         LPSTR     lpszCmdLine,      // Ptr to command line.
         int       cmdShow)          // How to open my window?
    {
    HWND     hwnd;
    MSG      msg;
    WNDCLASS wndclass;

    if (!hPrevInstance)
        {
        wndclass.lpszClassName = achWndClass;
        wndclass.hInstance     = hInstance;
        wndclass.lpfnWndProc   = RulersWndProc;
        wndclass.hCursor       = LoadCursor (hInstance, "hand");
        wndclass.hIcon         = LoadIcon (hInstance,"snapshot");
        wndclass.lpszMenuName  = NULL;
        wndclass.hbrBackground = (HBRUSH)(COLOR_WINDOW+1);
        wndclass.style         = CS_HREDRAW | CS_VREDRAW;
        wndclass.cbClsExtra    = 0;
        wndclass.cbWndExtra    = 0;

        RegisterClass( &wndclass);
        }

    hwnd = CreateWindowEx(0L,                  // Extra style.
                          achWndClass,         // Class name.
                          achAppName,          // Title.
                          WS_OVERLAPPEDWINDOW, // Style bits.
                          CW_USEDEFAULT,       // x - default.
                          0,                   // y - default.
                          CW_USEDEFAULT,       // cx - default.
                          0,                   // cy - default.
                          NULL,                // No parent.
                          NULL,                // Class menu.
                          hInstance,           // Creator.
                          NULL);               // Params.
    ShowWindow (hwnd, cmdShow);

    while (GetMessage(&msg, 0, 0, 0))
        {
        TranslateMessage(&msg); // Convert KEYDOWNs to CHARs
        DispatchMessage(&msg);  // Transmit message to WndProc
        }
    return 0;
    }

/*------------------------------------------------------------*\
|               Window Procedure:  RulersWndProc.              |
\*------------------------------------------------------------*/
LRESULT CALLBACK
RulersWndProc (HWND   hwnd,    // For whom is message sent?
               UINT   mMsg,    // What is exact message?
               WPARAM wParam,  // ...message details.
               LPARAM lParam)  // ...message details.
```

```
{
static char achTitle[80];
static int  fCapture = FALSE;

switch (mMsg)
    {
    case WM_DESTROY:
        PostQuitMessage(0);  // Handle application shutdown.
        break;

    case WM_MOUSEMOVE:
        if (!fCapture)
            break;
        /*  Fall through to WM_LBUTTONDOWN.                   */

    case WM_LBUTTONDOWN:
        {
        char ach[80];
        HDC hdc;
        POINT pt1, pt2;

        /*  Get current location in device and logical      */
        /*  coordinates.                                     */
        pt1 = pt2 = MAKEPOINT (lParam);
        hdc = GetDC (hwnd);
        RulersInstallCoords (hdc, hwnd);
        DPtoLP (hdc, &pt2, 1);
        ReleaseDC (hwnd, hdc);

        /*  Do button down specific init.                    */
        if (mMsg == WM_LBUTTONDOWN)
            {
            GetWindowText (hwnd, achTitle, 80);
            SetCapture (hwnd);
            fCapture = TRUE;
            }

        /*  Display location in window title bar.            */
        wsprintf (ach, "Device = (%d,%d), Logical = (%d,%d)",
                pt1.x, pt1.y, pt2.x, pt2.y);
        SetWindowText (hwnd, ach);

        }
        break;

    case WM_LBUTTONUP:
        if (fCapture)
            {
            ReleaseCapture();
            SetWindowText (hwnd, achTitle);
            fCapture = FALSE;
            }
        break;
```

```
        case WM_PAINT:
            {
            PAINTSTRUCT ps;

            BeginPaint (hwnd, &ps);
            RulersInstallCoords (ps.hdc, hwnd);

            /*  Draw horizontal ruler.                        */
            RulersDrawHorzRuler(ps.hdc);

            /*  Draw vertical ruler.                          */
            RulersDrawVertRuler(ps.hdc);

            EndPaint (hwnd, &ps);
            }
            break;

        default:
            return(DefWindowProc(hwnd,mMsg,wParam,lParam));
            break;
        }
    return 0L;
    }


/*-------------------------------------------------------------*\
| RulersInstallCoords:  Install coordinate transformation.    |
\*-------------------------------------------------------------*/
void NEAR PASCAL RulersInstallCoords (HDC hdc, HWND hwnd)
    {
    RECT r;

    SetMapMode (hdc, MM_LOENGLISH);

    /*  Move pixel origin to bottom of window.                */
    GetClientRect (hwnd, &r);
    SetViewportOrg (hdc, 0, r.bottom);

    /*  Move real-world origin 1/2 inch up & 1/2 inch right.  */
    SetWindowOrg (hdc, -50, -50);
    }




/*-------------------------------------------------------------*\
|         RulersDrawVertRuler: Draw vertical ruler.           |
\*-------------------------------------------------------------*/
void NEAR PASCAL RulersDrawVertRuler(HDC hdc)
    {
    char ach[5];
    int i;
    int x, y;
```

```
                /*  Draw main axis of ruler.                      */
                MoveTo (hdc, 0, 0);
                LineTo (hdc, 0, 500);

                /*  Draw tick marks for ruler.                    */
                for (i=0;i<=5000 ; i+=125)
                    {
                    /*  Width of regular ticks.                   */
                    x = -SMALLTICK;

                    /*  Width of half-inch ticks.                 */
                    if (i%500 == 0) x = -MEDIUMTICK;

                    /*  Width of whole-inch ticks.                */
                    if (i%1000 == 0) x = -LARGETICK;

                    y = (i+5)/10;
                    MoveTo (hdc, x, y);
                    LineTo (hdc, 0, y);
                    }

                /*  Draw labels for inches.                       */
                SetTextAlign (hdc, TA_BOTTOM | TA_RIGHT);
                SetBkMode (hdc, TRANSPARENT);
                for (y=0;y<=500;y+=100)
                    {
                    wsprintf (ach, "%d", y/100);
                    TextOut (hdc, -(2*SMALLTICK), y, ach, lstrlen(ach));
                    }
                }

    /*-------------------------------------------------------------*\
    |          RulersDrawHorzRuler: Draw horizontal ruler.          |
    \*-------------------------------------------------------------*/
    void NEAR PASCAL RulersDrawHorzRuler(HDC hdc)
        {
        char ach[5];
        int i;
        int x, y;

        /*  Draw main axis of ruler.                      */
        MoveTo (hdc, 0, 0);
        LineTo (hdc, 800, 0);

        /*  Draw tick marks for ruler.                    */
        for (i=0;i<=8000 ; i+=125)
            {
            x = (i+5)/10;
            /*  Height of regular ticks.                  */
            y = -SMALLTICK;

            /*  Width of half-inch ticks.                 */
            if (i%500 == 0) y = -MEDIUMTICK;

            /*  Width of whole-inch ticks.                */
```

```
        if (i%1000 == 0) y = -LARGETICK;

        MoveTo (hdc, x, y);
        LineTo (hdc, x, 0);
        }

    /*  Draw labels for inches.                             */
    SetTextAlign (hdc, TA_TOP | TA_LEFT);
    SetBkMode (hdc, TRANSPARENT);
    for (x=0;x<=800;x+=100)
        {
        wsprintf (ach, "%d", x/100);
        TextOut (hdc,
                 x+SMALLTICK,
                 -SMALLTICK,
                 ach,
                 lstrlen(ach));
        }
    }
```

RULERS.DEF

```
NAME    RULERS

EXETYPE WINDOWS

DESCRIPTION 'Draws a Ruler (c) 1992 By Paul Yao'

CODE    MOVEABLE PRELOAD
DATA    MOVEABLE MULTIPLE PRELOAD

HEAPSIZE    512
STACKSIZE   5120

SEGMENTS
    RULERS_TEXT MOVEABLE PRELOAD

EXPORTS
    RulersWndProc
```

RULERS.LNK

```
Rulers.obj
Rulers.exe/align:16/map/nod/noe/CO
nul
mlibcew libw
Rulers.def
```

RULERS.MAK

```
# Directory search paths.

INCDIR = \WINDEV\INCLUDE

# Windows version to support
# Valid pairs include:
#     (0x0300, 30)
#     (0x0310, 31)

CLVER = WINVER=0x0300
RCVER = 30

# Compiler switches for applications.

CL_APP_SHIP_ALL = -AM -c -D$(CLVER) -Gsw -I$(INCDIR) -Ow -W3 -Zp
CL_APP_DEBG_ALL = -AM -c -D$(CLVER) -Gsw -I$(INCDIR) -Od -W3 -Zpi

CL_APP_SHIP_31  = -AM -c -G2s  -I$(INCDIR) -Ow -W3 -Zp
CL_APP_DEBG_31  = -AM -c -G2s  -I$(INCDIR) -Od -W3 -Zpi

# Compiler switches for DLLs.

CL_DLL_SHIP_ALL = -AMw -c -D$(CLVER) -Gsw -I$(INCDIR) -Ow -W3 -Zp
CL_DLL_DEBG_ALL = -AMw -c -D$(CLVER) -Gsw -I$(INCDIR) -Od -W3 -Zpi

CL_DLL_SHIP_31  = -AMw -c -G2s  -I$(INCDIR) -Ow -W3 -Zp
CL_DLL_DEBG_31  = -AMw -c -G2s  -I$(INCDIR) -Od -W3 -Zpi

# Make file primary target.

all: Rulers.exe

# Make file dependency targets.

Rulers.res: Rulers.rc Rulers.cur Rulers.ico
    rc -r -i$(INCDIR) Rulers.rc

Rulers.obj: Rulers.c
    cl $(CL_APP_SHIP_ALL) Rulers.c

Rulers.exe: Rulers.obj Rulers.def Rulers.res
    link @Rulers.lnk
    rc -$(RCVER) Rulers.res

Rulers.exe: Rulers.res
    rc -$(RCVER) Rulers.res
```

RULERS.RC

```
snapshot icon Rulers.ico

hand  cursor Rulers.cur
```

Figure 20.6 RULERS echoing the mouse location

Perhaps the first thing worth mentioning in RULERS is a built-in debugging feature that should help you when working with any mapping mode or doing any coordinate transformation. We are referring to a feature of RULERS that echoes the location of the mouse in the title bar whenever the left button is clicked. Coordinates are provided in both device and logical coordinates. Figure 20.6 shows an example of this feature in action.

This debugging aid helps determine the exact conversion taking place. It is particularly useful when you first begin working with mapping modes, since it is easy to request a coordinate conversion that sends your drawing hundreds of miles away from your drawing surface, or shrinks your drawing until it is only one-quarter of a pixel wide.

When a window procedure receives a mouse message, the reported location is always in client area coordinates. You may recall that these are pixel units whose origin is at the upper-left corner of the window's client area. To convert from client area coordinates to logical coordinates, you call DPtoLP. This GDI routine converts one or more points from device to logical units, and is defined:

```
BOOL DPtoLP (hDC, lpPoints, nCount)
```

- hDC is a handle to a DC whose drawing attributes have been modified to reflect the desired coordinate conversion.

- lpPoints is a long pointer to an array of type POINT.

- nCount is an integer value for the number of points to be converted.

In response to either a WM_MOUSEMOVE or a WM_LBUTTONDOWN message, RULERS retrieves the location of the mouse from the lParam parameter and converts the pair of (x,y) coordinates to logical coordinates with the following code:

```
/*  Get current location in device and logical    */
/*  coordinates.                                   */
pt1 = pt2 = MAKEPOINT (lParam);
hdc = GetDC (hwnd);
RulersInstallCoords (hdc, hwnd);
DPtoLP (hdc, &pt2, 1);
ReleaseDC (hwnd, hdc);
```

The routine `RulersInstallCoords`, one of RULERS' routines, sets up the necessary coordinate transformations. Our program also calls this routine in response to the `WM_PAINT` message, so that our painting and our mouse-location echoing both use the same conversion. We'll look at this routine in a moment.

Displaying the device and logical coordinate values in the title bar of the window involves a call to `SetWindowText`. But first, another Windows library routine, `wsprintf`, formats the values into a character string:

```
// Display location in window title bar.
wsprintf (ach, "Device = (%d,%d), Logical = (%d,%d)",
          pt1.x, pt1.y, pt2.x, pt2.y);
SetWindowText (hwnd, ach);
```

RULERS uses the `MM_ENGLISH` mapping mode. Requesting this mapping mode is as easy as calling the `SetMapMode` routine, which sets up the desired *scaling* with one unit equaling .01 inch. But that's not the only coordinate tranformation used by RULERS. As shown in the code below, it also calls the `SetViewportOrg` and `SetWindowOrg` routines to install two translations to put the origin at the exact location we wish to use. Here is the `RulersInstallCoords` routine, which sets up the coordinate transformation used by RULERS:

```
void NEAR PASCAL RulersInstallCoords (HDC hdc, HWND hwnd)
{
    RECT r;

    SetMapMode (hdc, MM_LOENGLISH);

    /*  Move pixel origin to bottom of window.         */
    GetClientRect (hwnd, &r);
    SetViewportOrg (hdc, 0, r.bottom);

    /*  Move origin 1/2 inch up & 1/2 inch right.      */
    SetWindowOrg (hdc, -50, -50);
}
```

Both `SetViewportOrg` and `SetWindowOrg` perform translations, which always involve addition or subtraction. When translating between device and logical coordinates, the viewport coordinate refers to the pixel units that are added or subtracted. The window coordinate refers to the logical units (in this case, 1/100th of an inch) that are added or subtracted. However, when the numbers are combined, one thing remains constant: The device and logical coordinate systems always place their origin at the same location, and all scaling radiates out from the origin.

All the fully constrained mapping modes let you draw with a predefined scaling factor to represent real world measurements. There are times, however, when you don't want a fixed scaling factor. For example, you may wish to set your own arbitrary scaling factor to make a graph fill a window, or, you may wish to use a coordinate transformation to simplify the drawing of text. For each of these applications, the fully unconstrained mapping mode, which we're going to discuss next, will provide the capabilites needed.

Fully Unconstrained Mapping Mode

In contrast to the fully constrained mapping modes which provide a set of fixed factors for scaling, the fully unconstrained mapping mode, `MM_ANISOTROPIC`, lets you define any arbitrary scaling that suits you. This mapping mode lets you set scaling factors that eliminate all restrictions to allow X and Y units to be scaled independently.

Defining your own set of scaling factors requires you to call two routines: `SetViewportExt` and `SetWindowExt`. `SetViewportExt`, which defines the pixels to be used in a ratio for scaling, is defined:

```
DWORD SetViewportExt (hDC, X, Y)
```

- `hDC` is a handle to a DC.

- `X` defines one-half of a ratio for scaling in the X direction. The other half of the ratio is defined by the `SetWindowExt` routine.

- `Y` defines one-half of a ratio for scaling in the Y direction. The other half of the ratio is defined by the `SetWindowExt` routine.

`SetWindowExt`, which defines the "real-world" units for a scaling ratio, is defined similarly:

```
DWORD SetWindowExt (hDC, X, Y)
```

- `hDC` is a handle to a DC.

- `X` defines one-half of a ratio for scaling in the X direction. The other half of the ratio is defined by the `SetViewportExt` routine.

- `Y` defines one-half of a ratio for scaling in the Y direction. The other half of the ratio is defined by the `SetViewportExt` routine.

The key to understanding the scaling is to recognize that each of these routines provides one-half of the needed elements that define a ratio. Of course, to use this mapping mode, we must first call `SetMapMode`:

```
SetMapMode (hdc, MM_ANISOTROPIC);
SetWindowOrg (hdc, 2, 2);
SetViewportOrg (hdc, 1, 1);
```

The scaling set up by this code converts two logical units to one device unit. With that scaling in place, the following code draws a rectangle with fifty pixels on each side:

```
MoveTo (hdc, 0, 0);
LineTo (hdc, 0, 100);
LineTo (hdc, 100, 100);
LineTo (hdc, 100, 0);
LineTo (hdc, 0, 0);
```

Perhaps the best way to understand the Anisotropic mapping mode is in terms of a sample program. Let's take a look at POPCHART, which draws a graph using this mapping mode.

A Sample Program: POPCHART

Figure 20.7 shows three instances of POPCHART. This program draws a graph of the U.S. population for the years 1940 –1990. Notice how the client area of each instance is completely filled by the chart. One feature of the Anisotropic mapping mode is that it stretches or shrinks graphic objects to fill the available device drawing area. In a graph

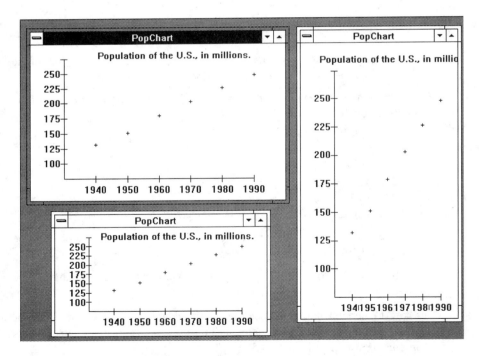

Figure 20.7 ANISOTROPIC mapping mode lets a graph fill the available area

like this, we are less concerned about the proportions of the drawing than we are about filling the available space.

Here is the code to POPCHART:

POPCHART.C

```
/*-------------------------------------------------------------*\
|  POPCHART.C  -  Population Chart showing use of the          |
|                 Anisotropic mapping mode.                    |
\*-------------------------------------------------------------*/
#define STRICT
#include <Windows.H>

#define NUM_X_VALUES 6
#define X_START 100
#define X_STEP  100
#define X_ORIGIN  0

#define NUM_Y_VALUES 7
#define Y_START 100
#define Y_STEP    25
#define Y_ORIGIN 75

#define FLIP_Y_AXIS -1


/*-------------------------------------------------------------*\
|                    Function Prototypes.                      |
\*-------------------------------------------------------------*/
LRESULT CALLBACK PopChartWndProc (HWND, UINT, WPARAM, LPARAM);
VOID NEAR PASCAL DrawMarker (HDC hdc, int x, int y);

VOID NEAR PASCAL PopInitMapping(HWND hwnd, HDC hdc);
VOID NEAR PASCAL PopDrawAxis (HDC hdc);
VOID NEAR PASCAL PopDrawLabels (HDC hdc);

/*-------------------------------------------------------------*\
|                    Global Variables.                        |
\*-------------------------------------------------------------*/
char achWndClass[] = "PopChart:MAIN";
char achAppName[]  = "PopChart";

char *acY_Labels[] = { "100", "125", "150", "175",
                       "200", "225", "250"};

char *acX_Labels[] = { "1940", "1950", "1960", "1970",
                       "1980", "1990"};

int  popData[] = { 132, 151, 179, 203, 226, 248 };
```

```
/*-------------------------------------------------------------*\
 |                  Main Function:  WinMain.                    |
 \*-------------------------------------------------------------*/
int PASCAL
WinMain (HINSTANCE hInstance,       // Who am I?
         HINSTANCE hPrevInstance,   // Any older siblings?
         LPSTR     lpszCmdLine,     // Ptr to command line.
         int       cmdShow)         // How to open my window?
    {
    HWND      hwnd;
    MSG       msg;
    WNDCLASS  wndclass;

    if (!hPrevInstance)
        {
        wndclass.lpszClassName = achWndClass;
        wndclass.hInstance     = hInstance;
        wndclass.lpfnWndProc   = PopChartWndProc;
        wndclass.hCursor       = LoadCursor (hInstance, "hand");
        wndclass.hIcon         = LoadIcon (hInstance,"snapshot");
        wndclass.lpszMenuName  = NULL;
        wndclass.hbrBackground = (HBRUSH)(COLOR_WINDOW+1);
        wndclass.style         = CS_HREDRAW | CS_VREDRAW;
        wndclass.cbClsExtra    = 0;
        wndclass.cbWndExtra    = 0;

        RegisterClass( &wndclass);
        }

    hwnd = CreateWindowEx(0L,                  // Extra style.
                    achWndClass,               // Class name.
                    achAppName,                // Title.
                    WS_OVERLAPPEDWINDOW,       // Style bits.
                    CW_USEDEFAULT,             // x - default.
                    0,                         // y - default.
                    CW_USEDEFAULT,             // cx - default.
                    0,                         // cy - default.
                    NULL,                      // No parent.
                    NULL,                      // Class menu.
                    hInstance,                 // Creator.
                    NULL);                     // Params.
    ShowWindow (hwnd, cmdShow);

    while (GetMessage(&msg, 0, 0, 0))
        {
        TranslateMessage(&msg); // Convert KEYDOWNs to CHARs
        DispatchMessage(&msg);  // Transmit message to WndProc
        }
    return 0;
    }


/*-------------------------------------------------------------*\
 |             Window Procedure:  PopChartWndProc.             |
 \*-------------------------------------------------------------*/
LRESULT CALLBACK
```

```
PopChartWndProc (HWND     hwnd,      // For whom is message sent?
                 UINT     mMsg,      // What is exact message?
                 WPARAM   wParam,    // ...message details.
                 LPARAM   lParam)    // ...message details.
    {
    switch (mMsg)
        {
        case WM_DESTROY:
            PostQuitMessage(0);  // Handle application shutdown.
            break;

        case WM_PAINT:
            {
            int i;
            PAINTSTRUCT ps;

            BeginPaint (hwnd, &ps);
            PopInitMapping(hwnd, ps.hdc);
            PopDrawAxis (ps.hdc);
            PopDrawLabels (ps.hdc);

            /*  Loop through data drawing markers.           */
            for (i=0; i<NUM_X_VALUES; i++)
                DrawMarker (ps.hdc, (i+1)*100, popData[i]);

            EndPaint (hwnd, &ps);
            }
            break;

        default:
            return(DefWindowProc(hwnd,mMsg,wParam,lParam));
            break;
        }
    return 0L;
    }

/*------------------------------------------------------------*\
|                       PopInitMapping                         |
\*------------------------------------------------------------*/
VOID NEAR PASCAL PopInitMapping(HWND hwnd, HDC hdc)
    {
    RECT  r;
    DWORD dwLen;
    int   xAdjust;
    int   yAdjust;

    dwLen = GetTextExtent (hdc, acY_Labels[0],
                           lstrlen(acY_Labels[0]));
    yAdjust = HIWORD(dwLen) * 2;
    xAdjust = LOWORD(dwLen) * 2;

    SetMapMode (hdc, MM_ANISOTROPIC);
    GetClientRect (hwnd, &r);
    r.bottom = r.bottom - yAdjust;
    r.right  = r.right - xAdjust;
```

```
    SetViewportExt (hdc, r.right, r.bottom);
    SetWindowExt (hdc, 700, FLIP_Y_AXIS * 225);
    SetViewportOrg (hdc, xAdjust, r.bottom);
    SetWindowOrg (hdc, 0, 75);
    }


/*------------------------------------------------------------*\
|                        PopDrawAxis                           |
\*------------------------------------------------------------*/
VOID NEAR PASCAL PopDrawAxis (HDC hdc)
    {
    DWORD dw;
    int    iIndex;
    int    xHalf;
    int    yThird;

    /* Draw axis.  */
    MoveTo (hdc, 0, 275);
    LineTo (hdc, 0, 75);
    LineTo (hdc, 600, 75);

    /* Draw relative to current font.  */
    dw = GetTextExtent (hdc, "X", 1);
    xHalf = LOWORD (dw) /2;
    yThird = HIWORD (dw) /3;

    /* Draw Y Axis Tick Marks.  */
    for (iIndex = Y_START;
         iIndex < Y_START + ((NUM_Y_VALUES+1) * Y_STEP);
         iIndex+= Y_STEP)
        {
        MoveTo (hdc, X_ORIGIN - xHalf, iIndex);
        LineTo (hdc, X_ORIGIN + xHalf, iIndex);
        }

    /* Draw X Axis Tick Marks.  */
    for (iIndex = X_START;
         iIndex < X_START + NUM_X_VALUES * X_STEP;
         iIndex+= X_STEP)
        {
        MoveTo (hdc, iIndex, Y_ORIGIN - yThird);
        LineTo (hdc, iIndex, Y_ORIGIN + yThird) ;
        }
    }


/*------------------------------------------------------------*\
|                       PopDrawLabels                          |
\*------------------------------------------------------------*/
VOID NEAR PASCAL PopDrawLabels (HDC hdc)
    {
    DWORD dw;
    int    iIndex;
```

```
    int   iCnt;
    int   xHalf;
    int   yHalf;

    /* Graph Title.  */
    SetTextAlign (hdc, TA_TOP | TA_CENTER);
    TextOut (hdc, 350, 290, "Population of the U.S., in millions.",
                  lstrlen ("Population of the U.S., in millions."));

    /* Draw relative to current font.  */
    dw = GetTextExtent (hdc, "X", 1);
    xHalf = LOWORD (dw) /2;
    yHalf = HIWORD (dw) /2;

    /* Y Axis Labels.  */
    SetTextAlign (hdc, TA_TOP | TA_RIGHT);
    for (iIndex = Y_START, iCnt=0;
         iIndex < Y_START + (NUM_Y_VALUES * Y_STEP);
         iIndex+= Y_STEP, iCnt++)
        {
        TextOut (hdc,
                 X_ORIGIN - xHalf,
                 iIndex + yHalf,
                 acY_Labels[iCnt],
                 lstrlen (acY_Labels[iCnt]));
        }

    /* X Axis Labels.  */
    SetTextAlign (hdc, TA_TOP | TA_CENTER);
    for (iIndex = X_START, iCnt = 0;
         iIndex < X_START + NUM_X_VALUES * X_STEP;
         iIndex+= X_STEP, iCnt++)
        {
        TextOut (hdc,
                 iIndex,
                 Y_ORIGIN - yHalf,
                 acX_Labels[iCnt],
                 lstrlen (acX_Labels[iCnt]));
        }
    }


/*-------------------------------------------------------------*\
|                           DrawMarker                          |
\*-------------------------------------------------------------*/
#define MARKERSIZE 2
VOID NEAR PASCAL DrawMarker (HDC hdc, int x, int y)
    {
    int i;
    int iDC;
    POINT pt;

    /* Convert point to device coordinates.  */
    pt.x = x; pt.y = y;
```

```
LPtoDP (hdc, &pt, 1);
x = pt.x; y = pt.y;

iDC = SaveDC (hdc);

/* Restore Device Coordinate Mapping.  */
SetMapMode (hdc, MM_TEXT);
SetViewportExt (hdc, 1, 1);
SetWindowExt (hdc, 1, 1);
SetViewportOrg (hdc, 0, 0);
SetWindowOrg (hdc, 0, 0);

SetROP2 (hdc, R2_NOT);
SetPixel (hdc, x, y, RGB (0, 0, 0));

for (i=1;i<=MARKERSIZE; i++)
    {
    SetPixel (hdc, x+i, y, RGB(0,0,0) );
    SetPixel (hdc, x-i, y, RGB(0,0,0) );
    SetPixel (hdc, x, y+i, RGB(0,0,0) );
    SetPixel (hdc, x, y-i, RGB(0,0,0) );
    }

RestoreDC (hdc, iDC);
}
```

POPCHART.DEF

```
NAME    POPCHART

EXETYPE WINDOWS

DESCRIPTION 'Population Chart (c) 1992 By Paul Yao'

CODE    MOVEABLE PRELOAD
DATA    MOVEABLE MULTIPLE PRELOAD

HEAPSIZE    512
STACKSIZE   5120

SEGMENTS
    POPCHART_TEXT MOVEABLE PRELOAD

EXPORTS
    PopChartWndProc
```

POPCHART.LNK

```
PopChart.obj
PopChart.exe/align:16/map/nod/noe/CO
```

```
nul
mlibcew libw
PopChart.def
```

POPCHART.MAK

```
# Directory search paths.

INCDIR = \WINDEV\INCLUDE

# Windows version to support
# Valid pairs include:
#     (0x0300, 30)
#     (0x0310, 31)

CLVER = WINVER=0x0300
RCVER = 30

# Compiler switches for applications.

CL_APP_SHIP_ALL = -AM -c -D$(CLVER) -Gsw -I$(INCDIR) -Ow -W3 -Zp
CL_APP_DEBG_ALL = -AM -c -D$(CLVER) -Gsw -I$(INCDIR) -Od -W3 -Zpi

CL_APP_SHIP_31  = -AM -c -G2s  -I$(INCDIR) -Ow -W3 -Zp
CL_APP_DEBG_31  = -AM -c -G2s  -I$(INCDIR) -Od -W3 -Zpi

# Compiler switches for DLLs.

CL_DLL_SHIP_ALL = -AMw -c -D$(CLVER) -Gsw -I$(INCDIR) -Ow -W3 -Zp
CL_DLL_DEBG_ALL = -AMw -c -D$(CLVER) -Gsw -I$(INCDIR) -Od -W3 -Zpi

CL_DLL_SHIP_31  = -AMw -c -G2s  -I$(INCDIR) -Ow -W3 -Zp
CL_DLL_DEBG_31  = -AMw -c -G2s  -I$(INCDIR) -Od -W3 -Zpi

# Make file primary target.

all: PopChart.exe

# Make file dependency targets.

PopChart.res: PopChart.rc PopChart.cur PopChart.ico
    rc -r -i$(INCDIR) PopChart.rc

PopChart.obj: PopChart.c
    cl $(CL_APP_SHIP_ALL) PopChart.c

PopChart.exe: PopChart.obj PopChart.def PopChart.res
    link @PopChart.lnk
    rc -$(RCVER) PopChart.res

PopChart.exe: PopChart.res
    rc -$(RCVER) PopChart.res
```

POPCHART.RC

```
snapshot icon PopChart.ico

hand   cursor PopChart.cur
```

The crux of this program lies in the way the mapping mode is set, which is the job of the `PopInitMapping` routine. This routine begins by determining the width and height of one of the text labels by calling `GetTextExtent`. The width and height are in pixels, which we're going to use to adjust the mapping so there is room for the text labels on the left side and the bottom of the drawing:

```
dwLen = GetTextExtent (hdc, acY_Labels[0],
                           lstrlen(acY_Labels[0]));
yAdjust = HIWORD(dwLen) * 2;
xAdjust = LOWORD(dwLen) * 2;
```

After POPCHART retrieves the size information, it sets up the mapping mode by calling `SetMapMode`:

```
SetMapMode (hdc, MM_ANISOTROPIC);
```

Anisotropic scaling has two halves: real-world or "logical" units (referred to as the "window") and pixel units (referred to as the "viewport"). POPCHART starts by setting the range of the logical units, which is the range of the values used by POPCHART in its calls to GDI:

```
SetWindowExt (hdc, 700, FLIP_Y_AXIS * 225);
```

In the X direction, the selection of the value 700 is purely arbitrary. It allows us to plot six years' worth of points, spaced evenly between areas that are 100 logical units wide. The same results would have appeared had we used the value 7, which would create evenly spaced areas, each one logical unit wide.

The value of `FLIP_Y_AXIS` is -1. As the name suggests, this causes the Y axis to flip. This is necessary because, by default, the direction of the Y axis in the Anisotropic mapping mode is the same as that of the `MM_TEXT` mapping mode: Y increases as we move down.

In the Y direction, we select 225 since this is the range of population values that we wish to graph (from 75 million to 300 million). Even though the scale on the graph only reads from 100 to 250, the extra space is used for aesthetics and to allow enough room on the top of the graph to draw the title.

Setting the other half of the Anisotropic scaling ratio, the number of pixels against which to scale, involves calling `SetViewportExt`. The X and Y extents passed to this routine are essentially the width and height of the client area minus an adjustment for the text labels that we plan to display:

```
GetClientRect (hwnd, &r);
r.bottom = r.bottom - yAdjust;
```

```
r.right  = r.right - xAdjust;
SetViewportExt (hdc, r.right, r.bottom);
```

The final step taken to set up the coordinate mapping involves moving the origin. As you saw earlier, this can be either a one- or two-step process, since we can change the location of the origin both in terms of pixel coordinates and in terms of logical coordinates. POPCHART does both. To move the origin to a specific location in its window's client area, POPCHART calls:

```
SetViewportOrg (hdc, xAdjust, r.bottom);
```

The call to `SetViewportOrg` moves the origin to a spot where the two axes meet on our chart. Next, POPCHART calls `SetWindowOrg` to move the origin below the bottom of the client area:

```
SetWindowOrg (hdc, 0, 75);
```

In the X direction, the value 0 is chosen; then we advance 100 per year. Of course, we could have set this to 1930 and used the value of the year as a graphic point. The value of 75 for the Y value sets 75 million as the lowest population figure in which we are interested.

Perhaps the most challenging aspect of the Anisotropic mapping mode is that it is so flexible. In fact, you could even say that it is *too* flexible. For any particular application, there are undoubtedly several different approaches to take in setting up a logical coordinate system. Perhaps the key lies in keeping things simple and creating logical coordinate systems that allow you to use your own application's convenient coordinates.

Before we leave the Anisotropic mapping mode, it's worth mentioning a way that this mapping mode can simplify the handling of text output. It underscores the usefulness of this mapping mode, which allows the creation of any arbitrary scaling.

Text and the Anisotropic Mapping Mode

It would be easy to dismiss mapping modes as something useful only for graphic images. However, since GDI treats text as graphic information, there must be a way to take advantage of the mapping modes to make text easier to work with. Although there are many possibilites, here is one with widespread uses.

Since the anisotropic mapping mode allows you to create arbitrary scaling, it is possible to build a set of coordinates that revolves around the metrics of text. For example, here is a code fragment that sets the pixel coordinates for the Y axis so that one logical unit is equal to the height of one text line:

```
case WM_PAINT:
    {
    int cyLineHeight;
    PAINTSTRUCT ps;
    TEXTMETRIC tm;

    BeginPaint (hwnd, &ps);
```

```
    SetMapMode (ps.hdc, MM_ANISOTROPIC);

    GetTextMetrics (ps.hdc, &tm);
    cyLineHeight = tm.tmHeight + tm.tmExternalLeading;
    SetViewportExt (ps.hdc, 1, cyLineHeight);

    TextOut (ps.hdc, 10, 0, "Line 0", 6);
    TextOut (ps.hdc, 10, 1, "Line 1", 6);
    TextOut (ps.hdc, 10, 2, "Line 2", 6);
    TextOut (ps.hdc, 10, 3, "Line 3", 6);
    TextOut (ps.hdc, 10, 4, "Line 4", 6);
    TextOut (ps.hdc, 10, 5, "Line 5", 6);
    TextOut (ps.hdc, 10, 6, "Line 6", 6);
    TextOut (ps.hdc, 10, 7, "Line 7", 6);
    TextOut (ps.hdc, 10, 8, "Line 8", 6);

    EndPaint (hwnd, &ps);
    }
    break;
```

Each unit in the Y direction is equal to the height of one line. In effect, each logical unit in the Y direction is equal to the line number. The output produced by this code fragment is shown in Figure 20.8.

When working with a fixed pitch font, you can go one step further and use the Anisotropic mapping mode to allow you to output text using coordinates that are simply character row and column values. Here is the code which does that:

```
case WM_PAINT:
    {
    int cyLineHeight;
    int cxCharWidth;
    PAINTSTRUCT ps;
    TEXTMETRIC tm;

    BeginPaint (hwnd, &ps);
    SetMapMode (ps.hdc, MM_ANISOTROPIC);

    GetTextMetrics (ps.hdc, &tm);
    cyLineHeight = tm.tmHeight + tm.tmExternalLeading;
    cxCharWidth  = tm.tmAveCharWidth;
    SetViewportExt (ps.hdc, cxCharWidth, cyLineHeight);
    ...
```

If you have worked with character-oriented windows, and if you don't mind limiting yourself to working with a fixed-pitch font, we think you'll find this coordinate mapping to be very useful.

We have one more mapping mode, which combines some of the features of the fully constrained mapping modes and the fully unconstrained mapping modes, yet to cover.

Figure 20.8 Lines of text drawn with the Anisotropic Mapping Mode

The next topic to be covered is that of the partially constrained mapping mode, the Isotropic Mapping Mode.

Partially Constrained Mapping Mode

The Isotropic Mapping Mode is referred to as "partially constrained" because it enforces uniform scaling—X and Y units must be equal—which makes it similar to the fully constrained mapping modes. However, the choice of units is up to you. In this respect, the Isotropic Mapping Mode is like the fully *unconstrained* mapping mode. Let's look at what this mapping mode involves.

Since the Isotropic mapping mode lets you decide on a scaling factor, you call the same two routines used to set up scaling in the Anisotropic Mapping Mode: `SetViewportExt` and `SetWindowExt`. However, when a scaling factor has been selected, GDI modifies the viewport extent to enforce the uniform scaling of this mapping mode. The viewport extent will be modified in one of two ways: either the X value will be reduced or the Y value will be reduced.

Recall that the Viewport refers to the number of pixels on which to draw. Thus, this mapping mode guarantees that the drawing you request will fit inside the desired pixels. In addition, since this mapping mode maintains uniform scaling, it is often referred to as *shape-preserving*. In other words, perfectly round figures will always appear perfectly round. If you wish to avoid the stretching and shrinking of the Anisotropic mapping mode, but still wish to select your own coordinates, then the Isotropic mapping mode is for you.

Figure 20.9 shows how the isotropic mapping mode retains the shape of figures—in this case, a circle. Notice that when the client area is irregularly shaped, quite a bit of it is wasted. At the same time, however, we are able to see our circle completely, regardless of the shape or size of the client area. Since the picture adjusts itself to the size of the client area, the user can adjust the scaling as desired by simply changing the size of

Figure 20.9 Isotropic mode is shape retaining

the window. Here is the code for the WM_PAINT message of the program that created
the circle:

```
case WM_PAINT:
    {
    HANDLE      hbrHatch;
    PAINTSTRUCT ps;
    RECT r;

    BeginPaint (hwnd, &ps);

    //  Install isotropic mapping mode.
    SetMapMode (ps.hdc, MM_ISOTROPIC);

    //  Set up logical coordinates for 200 x 200.
    SetWindowExt (ps.hdc, 200, 200);

    //  Set viewport to enclose entire client area.
    GetClientRect (hwnd, &r);
    SetViewportExt (ps.hdc, r.right, r.bottom);

    //  Move origin into center of client area.
    SetViewportOrg (ps.hdc, r.right/2, r.bottom/2);
```

```
//  Create a hatch brush for drawing.
hbrHatch = CreateHatchBrush (HS_CROSS, RGB (0,0,0));
SelectObject (ps.hdc, hbrHatch);<

//  Draw a circle.
Ellipse (ps.hdc, -100, -100, 100, 100);
EndPaint (hwnd, &ps);

//  Destroy hatch brush.
DeleteObject (hbrHatch);
}
```

As this code fragment illustrates, you should always set the window extent first before setting the viewport extent. The reason is that, in the isotropic mapping mode, GDI modifies the viewport extent to create the desired fit whenever either of the extents is changed. If you change the viewport extent *first*, then GDI may modify it to suit whatever window extent is present, thus changing the desired scaling that you are actually requesting.

Our discussion of GDI's mapping modes and coordinate transformations has gotten us ready to explore another topic: **scrolling**. Programs generally make scrolling available whenever a data object is too large to fit inside a window. The presence of scroll bars suggests to the user that this may be the case. However, scroll bars by themselves do not make scrolling happen. Instead, a program must be modified to respond to messages sent by the scroll bar. In addition, the WM_PAINT processing performed by a program must be synchronized with scrolling. Let's take a look at what this involves.

Scrolling

From the point of view of the user, scrolling solves the problem that arises when an object to be displayed extends beyond the window in which it is displayed. Scrolling can be used for wading through a very large spreadsheet or word processing document, for browsing database records, or for any operation in which only part of a data collection is visible.

Scrolling is controlled by **scroll bars**. There are two types of scroll bars: horizontal and vertical. A window can have one or both types to control scrolling. David Durant, a long-time Windows programming guru, describes a scroll bar as a visual representation of three numbers: a minimum value, a maximum value, and a current value that must lie between the minimum and the maximum.

The minimum value is represented when the **scroll thumb** rests on the top of a vertical scroll bar (or to the left of a horizontal scroll bar). The maximum value is represented when the scroll thumb rests on the bottom of a vertical scroll bar (or on the right of a horizontal scroll bar). The current position is represented by the relative position of the scroll thumb between the two. On some systems, like the OS/2 Presentation Manager, a fourth number is represented by the relative size of the scroll thumb. This indicates the relative amount of the document that is, in fact, visible. This last feature is not part of Windows, however, which instead has a fixed-size scroll thumb.

Figure 20.10 The wParam values for scroll bar messages

To add a scroll bar to a window, you specify additional style bits in the call to `CreateWindow`: `WS_VSCROLL` for a vertical scroll bar or `WS_HSCROLL` for a horizontal scroll bar. Once scroll bars have been added to a window, user actions on the scroll bar are translated into messages. Horizontal scroll bars send `WM_HSCROLL` messages, and vertical scroll bars send `WM_VSCROLL` messages. Each message is accompanied by a value in the `wParam` parameter indicating the portion of the scroll bar on which the user has clicked. The values are shown in Figure 20.10 as the symbolic constants defined in Windows.h.

When the user interacts with most parts of the scroll bar, a single message is of interest. However, when the user drags the scroll thumb directly, two types of messages are generated: one during the dragging (scroll message with `wParam` `=SB_THUMBTRACK`) and one when the dragging is completed (scroll message with `wParam = SB_THUMBPOSITION`). The simplest way to handle this is to ignore the messages sent during the dragging and respond only to the dragging-complete message. But programs can scroll during the dragging messages, to give the user immediate feedback about the effect of the scrolling operation.

A Sample Program: SCROLL

Figure 20.11 shows the output of our sample program, SCROLL. You may remember this program from Chapter 10, when we introduced the `TabbedTextOut` routine. SCROLL only uses a vertical scroll bar, but demonstrates the principles of scrolling that can be applied to horizontal scrolling. In addition to a scroll bar, which receives mouse input for scrolling, SCROLL also incorporates keyboard input in the scrolling process.

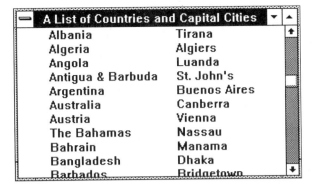

Figure 20.11 The output produced by the SCROLL program

Here is the source code to SCROLL:

SCROLL.C

```
/*-------------------------------------------------------------*\
|   SCROLL.C  -  Scrolling text.                                |
\*-------------------------------------------------------------*/
#define STRICT
#include <Windows.H>

#define COUNT 19


/*-------------------------------------------------------------*\
|                      Function Prototypes.                     |
\*-------------------------------------------------------------*/
LRESULT CALLBACK ScrollWndProc (HWND, UINT, WPARAM, LPARAM);


/*-------------------------------------------------------------*\
|                       Global Variables.                      |
\*-------------------------------------------------------------*/
char achWndClass[] = "Scroll:MAIN";
char achAppName[]  = "A List of Countries and Capital Cities";
char *apch[]= {"Country \tCapital",
               "--------------- \t----------",
               "Afghanistan \tKabul",
               "Albania \tTirana",
               "Algeria \tAlgiers",
               "Angola \tLuanda",
               "Antigua & Barbuda \tSt. John's",
               "Argentina \tBuenos Aires",
               "Australia \tCanberra",
```

```
                       "Austria \tVienna",
                       "The Bahamas \tNassau",
                       "Bahrain \tManama",
                       "Bangladesh \tDhaka",
                       "Barbados \tBridgetown",
                       "Belgium \tBrussels",
                       "Belize \tBelmopan",
                       "Benin \tPorto-Novo",
                       "Bhutan \tThimphu",
                       "Bolivia \tLa Paz"};

/*-------------------------------------------------------------*\
|                  Main Function:  WinMain.                     |
\*-------------------------------------------------------------*/
int PASCAL
WinMain (HINSTANCE hInstance,        // Who am I?
         HINSTANCE hPrevInstance,    // Any older siblings?
         LPSTR     lpszCmdLine,      // Ptr to command line.
         int       cmdShow)          // How to open my window?
    {
    HWND      hwnd;
    MSG       msg;
    WNDCLASS  wndclass;

    if (!hPrevInstance)
        {
        wndclass.lpszClassName = achWndClass;
        wndclass.hInstance     = hInstance;
        wndclass.lpfnWndProc   = ScrollWndProc;
        wndclass.hCursor       = LoadCursor (hInstance, "hand");
        wndclass.hIcon         = LoadIcon (hInstance,"snapshot");
        wndclass.lpszMenuName  = NULL;
        wndclass.hbrBackground = (HBRUSH)(COLOR_WINDOW+1);
        wndclass.style         = CS_HREDRAW | CS_VREDRAW;
        wndclass.cbClsExtra    = 0;
        wndclass.cbWndExtra    = 0;

        RegisterClass( &wndclass);
        }

    hwnd = CreateWindowEx(0L,                    // Extra style.
                    achWndClass,                 // Class name.
                    achAppName,                  // Title.
                    WS_OVERLAPPEDWINDOW,         // Style bits.
                    CW_USEDEFAULT,               // x - default.
                    0,                           // y - default.
                    CW_USEDEFAULT,               // cx - default.
                    0,                           // cy - default.
                    NULL,                        // No parent.
                    NULL,                        // Class menu.
                    hInstance,                   // Creator.
                    NULL);                       // Params.
    ShowWindow (hwnd, cmdShow);
```

```
    while (GetMessage(&msg, 0, 0, 0))
        {
        TranslateMessage(&msg); // Convert KEYDOWNs to CHARs
        DispatchMessage(&msg);  // Transmit message to WndProc
        }
    return 0;
    }

/*-----------------------------------------------------------*\
 |              Window Procedure:  ScrollWndProc.            |
\*-----------------------------------------------------------*/
LRESULT CALLBACK
ScrollWndProc (HWND    hwnd,    // For whom is message sent?
               UINT    mMsg,    // What is exact message?
               WPARAM  wParam,  // ...message details.
               LPARAM  lParam)  // ...message details.
    {
    static int yScrollMin;
    static int yScrollCurrent;
    static int yScrollMax;

    static int xLeftMargin;
    static int xTab;
    static int xTabOrigin;
    static int cyLineHeight;
    static int cLines;

    switch (mMsg)
        {
        case WM_CREATE:
            {
            HDC hdc;
            TEXTMETRIC tm;

            /*  Init TabbedTextOut values.                  */
            hdc = GetDC (hwnd);
            GetTextMetrics (hdc, &tm);
            ReleaseDC (hwnd, hdc);
            xTab  = 20 * tm.tmAveCharWidth;
            xTabOrigin = 3 * tm.tmAveCharWidth;
            cyLineHeight = tm.tmHeight + tm.tmExternalLeading;
            xLeftMargin = tm.tmAveCharWidth * 2;

            /*  Init values needed for scrolling.           */
            yScrollMin = 0;
            yScrollCurrent = 0;
            cLines = COUNT;
            SetScrollRange (hwnd, SB_VERT, 0, 0, FALSE);
            }
            break;

        case WM_DESTROY:
            PostQuitMessage(0);  // Handle application shutdown.
            break;
```

```
case WM_KEYDOWN:
    {
    WORD wScroll;
    LONG lPosition;

    wScroll = -1;
    lPosition = 0L;

    switch (wParam)
        {
        case VK_PRIOR:
            wScroll = SB_PAGEUP;
            break;
        case VK_NEXT:
            wScroll = SB_PAGEDOWN;
            break;
        case VK_UP:
            wScroll = SB_LINEUP;
            break;
        case VK_DOWN:
            wScroll = SB_LINEDOWN;
            break;
        case VK_HOME:
            wScroll = SB_THUMBPOSITION;
            lPosition = (LONG)yScrollMin;
            break;
        case VK_END:
            wScroll = SB_THUMBPOSITION;
            lPosition = (LONG)yScrollMax;
            break;
        }

    if (wScroll != -1)
        SendMessage (hwnd, WM_VSCROLL, wScroll,
                        lPosition);
    }
    break;

case WM_PAINT:
    {
    int yText;
    PAINTSTRUCT ps;

    BeginPaint (hwnd, &ps);

    /*  Init coordinate mapping so that 1 unit in     */
    /*  direction = 1 line.                           */
    SetMapMode (ps.hdc, MM_ANISOTROPIC);
    SetViewportExt (ps.hdc, 1, cyLineHeight);
    SetViewportOrg (ps.hdc, xLeftMargin,0);
    SetWindowOrg (ps.hdc, 0, yScrollCurrent);

    for (yText = 0; yText<COUNT; yText++)
        {
        TabbedTextOut (ps.hdc,
```

```
                            xTabOrigin,
                            yText,
                            apch[yText],
                            lstrlen(apch[yText]),
                            1,
                            &xTab,
                            xTabOrigin);
        }

    EndPaint (hwnd, &ps);
    }
    break;

case WM_SIZE:
    {
    int cyClient;

    /*  Reset scroll bar range.                       */
    cyClient = HIWORD (lParam);
    yScrollMax = max(cLines-cyClient/cyLineHeight, 0);

    SetScrollRange (hwnd, SB_VERT,
                    yScrollMin, yScrollMax, FALSE);

    /*  Update current scroll bar position.           */
    yScrollCurrent = min (yScrollCurrent, yScrollMax);

    /*  Update the scroll bar.                         */
    SetScrollPos (hwnd, SB_VERT, yScrollCurrent, TRUE);
    }
    break;

case WM_VSCROLL:
    {
    int yNewLine;
    int cyScroll;

    /* Determine the number of lines to scroll.       */
    switch (wParam)
        {
        case SB_PAGEDOWN:
            yNewLine = yScrollCurrent + 4;
            break;
        case SB_PAGEUP:
            yNewLine = yScrollCurrent - 4;
            break;
        case SB_LINEDOWN:
            yNewLine = yScrollCurrent + 1;
            break;
        case SB_LINEUP:
            yNewLine = yScrollCurrent - 1;
            break;
        case SB_THUMBPOSITION:
            yNewLine = LOWORD(lParam);
            break;
```

```
                default:
                    yNewLine = yScrollCurrent;
                }

            /*  Make sure we are still in range.            */
            yNewLine = max (0, yNewLine);
            yNewLine = min (yScrollMax, yNewLine);
            if (yNewLine == yScrollCurrent)
                break;

            /*  Update the scroll bar.                       */
            SetScrollPos (hwnd, SB_VERT, yNewLine, TRUE);

            /*  Move the pixels.  A WM_PAINT message is also */
            /*  generated to repair the 'uncovered' part of  */
            /*  the client area.                             */
            cyScroll = (yScrollCurrent-yNewLine)*cyLineHeight;
            ScrollWindow (hwnd, 0, cyScroll, NULL, NULL);
            yScrollCurrent = yNewLine;
            }
            break;

        default:
            return(DefWindowProc(hwnd,mMsg,wParam,lParam));
            break;
        }
    return 0L;
    }
```

SCROLL.DEF

```
NAME    SCROLL

EXETYPE WINDOWS

DESCRIPTION 'Scrolling Text (c) 1992 By Paul Yao'

CODE    MOVEABLE PRELOAD
DATA    MOVEABLE MULTIPLE PRELOAD

HEAPSIZE    512
STACKSIZE   5120

SEGMENTS
    SCROLL_TEXT MOVEABLE PRELOAD

EXPORTS
    ScrollWndProc
```

SCROLL.LNK

```
Scroll.obj
Scroll.exe/align:16/map/nod/noe/CO
nul
mlibcew libw
Scroll.def
```

SCROLL.MAK

```
# Directory search paths.

INCDIR = \WINDEV\INCLUDE

# Windows version to support
# Valid pairs include:
#     (0x0300, 30)
#     (0x0310, 31)

CLVER = WINVER=0x0300
RCVER = 30

# Compiler switches for applications.

CL_APP_SHIP_ALL = -AM -c -D$(CLVER) -Gsw -I$(INCDIR) -Ow -W3 -Zp
CL_APP_DEBG_ALL = -AM -c -D$(CLVER) -Gsw -I$(INCDIR) -Od -W3 -Zpi

CL_APP_SHIP_31  = -AM -c -G2s  -I$(INCDIR) -Ow -W3 -Zp
CL_APP_DEBG_31  = -AM -c -G2s  -I$(INCDIR) -Od -W3 -Zpi

# Compiler switches for DLLs.

CL_DLL_SHIP_ALL = -AMw -c -D$(CLVER) -Gsw -I$(INCDIR) -Ow -W3 -Zp
CL_DLL_DEBG_ALL = -AMw -c -D$(CLVER) -Gsw -I$(INCDIR) -Od -W3 -Zpi

CL_DLL_SHIP_31  = -AMw -c -G2s  -I$(INCDIR) -Ow -W3 -Zp
CL_DLL_DEBG_31  = -AMw -c -G2s  -I$(INCDIR) -Od -W3 -Zpi

# Make file primary target.

all: Scroll.exe

# Make file dependency targets.

Scroll.res: Scroll.rc Scroll.cur Scroll.ico
    rc -r -i$(INCDIR) Scroll.rc
```

```
Scroll.obj: Scroll.c
    cl $(CL_APP_SHIP_ALL) Scroll.c

Scroll.exe: Scroll.obj Scroll.def Scroll.res
    link @Scroll.lnk
    rc -$(RCVER) Scroll.res

Scroll.exe: Scroll.res
    rc -$(RCVER) Scroll.res
```

SCROLL.RC

```
snapshot icon Scroll.ico

hand   cursor Scroll.cur
```

SCROLL defines three numbers to keep track of the three values used by the scroll bar:

```
static int yscrollMin;
static int yScrollCurrent;
static int yScrollMax;
```

In SCROLL, the scroll bar numbers represent line numbers for the displayed text. yScrollMin is the number of the lowest text line and is set to zero. yScrollCurrent stores the line number of the line to be displayed at the top of the window. yScrollMax indicates the highest line number that can be displayed at the top of the window. This may or may not be equal to the number of lines (cLines), depending on the size of the client area. SCROLL calibrates its scroll bar using yScrollMin and yScrollMax by calling the SetScrollRange routine. SetScrollRange is defined:

```
void SetScrollRange(hWnd, nBar, nMinPos, nMaxPos, bRedraw)
```

- hWnd is a window handle of the window containing the scroll bar.
- nBar is an integer indicating the scroll bar of interest. It is either SB_CTL, SB_HORZ, or SB_VERT.
- nMinPos is an integer value to be represented by the low end of the scroll bar.
- nMaxPos is an integer value to be represented by the high end of the scroll bar.
- bRedraw is a Boolean value that indicates whether the scroll bar should be redrawn to reflect the change.

SCROLL sets the range of its scroll bar with the following call:

```
SetScrollRange (hwnd, SB_VERT, yScrollMin, yScrollMax, FALSE);
```

The scroll range needs to be set twice: at window creation time in response to the WM_CREATE message and when the size of the window changes, which means in response to the `WM_SIZE` message. The range changes to reflect the number of lines that are not visible. When all text lines are visible, the scroll bar is removed. This happens whenever the minimum and maximum range values are set to zero. SCROLL is set up so that `yScrollMin` and `yScrollMax` are both set to zero whenever the client area is large enough to view the entire block of text; so the removal of the scroll bar occurs automatically.

As the user interacts with the scroll bar, scroll messages are sent to SCROLL's window procedure. As these messages are received, SCROLL calculates the line to be placed at the top of the window. For the `SB_LINEUP` and `SB_LINEDOWN` messages, this means adding or subtracting a single line. For `SB_PAGEUP` and `SB_PAGEDOWN`, it involves adding or subtracting four lines. It is customary for programs to scroll one screen's worth of data for the page up and page down messages. However, since SCROLL is working with a fairly short list, it only scrolls four lines when a page up or a page down scroll message is received.

```
// Determine the number of lines to scroll.
switch (wParam)
    {
    case SB_PAGEDOWN:
        yNewLine = yScrollCurrent + 4;
        break;
    case SB_PAGEUP:<
        yNewLine = yScrollCurrent - 4;
        break;
    case SB_LINEDOWN:
        yNewLine = yScrollCurrent + 1;
        break;
    case SB_LINEUP:
        yNewLine = yScrollCurrent - 1;
        break;
    case SB_THUMBPOSITION:
        yNewLine = LOWORD(lParam);
        break;
    default:
        yNewLine = yScrollCurrent;
    }
```

To ensure that the top and the bottom of the display area is respected, a check is made to see if the new line value is in range:

```
//  Make sure we are still in range.
yNewLine = max (0, yNewLine);
yNewLine = min (yScrollMax, yNewLine);
```

At that point, SCROLL updates the display to reflect the new arrangement of text lines. This involves a call to `ScrollWindow`:

```
cyScroll = (yScrollCurrent-yNewLine)*cyLineHeight;
ScrollWindow (hwnd, 0, cyScroll, NULL, NULL);
```

`ScrollWindow` is a fairly involved routine that does several things at once. First, it calls the `BitBlt` routine to move a rectangle of pixels on the display to a new location. Next, it calculates the area that has been "exposed" by the call to `BitBlt` and generates a `WM_PAINT` message so that the image in the window can be properly repaired. A third capability of `ScrollWindow` is that it can accept a clipping rectangle in which to restrict the scrolling operation. `ScrollWindow` is defined:

```
void ScrollWindow (hWnd, X, Y, lpRect, lpClipRect)
```

- `hWnd` is a handle to the window whose bits are to be scrolled.
- `X` indicates the number of device units in which to scroll in the X direction.
- `Y` indicates the number of device units in which to scroll in the Y direction.
- `lpRect` is a long pointer to a structure of type `RECT`, which identifies the rectangle of pixels to be scrolled, or `NULL` to scroll the entire client area.
- `lpClipRect` is a long pointer to a structure of type `RECT`, which identifies a clipping rectangle to be used to restrict the scrolling operation.

The last thing that SCROLL does in response to a scroll message is to update the location of the scroll bar thumb. This is accomplished with a call to `SetScrollPos`. `SetScrollPos` is defined:

```
int SetScrollPos (hWnd, nBar, nPos, bRedraw)
```

- `hWnd` is a window handle to the window containing the scroll bar.
- `nBar` is an integer which indicates the scroll bar of interest. It is either `SB_CTL`, `SB_HORZ`, or `SB_VERT`.
- `nPos` indicates the new scroll thumb position, based on the minimum and maximum values defined in the call to `SetScrollRange`.
- `bRedraw` is a Boolean value which indicates whether the scroll bar should be redrawn to reflect the change.

SCROLL simply moves the scroll thumb to the line number of the topmost line in the display. Since this is the value represented by `yScrollCurrent`, here is how SCROLL sets the position of its scroll thumb:

```
SetScrollPos (hwnd, SB_VERT, yScrollCurrent, TRUE);
```

The call to `ScrollWindow` causes a `WM_PAINT` message to be generated. However, the entire window is not updated, but rather `ScrollWindow` only declares the unscrolled pixels in a window to be damaged. In this way, the `WM_PAINT` message only repairs the part of the window that actually needs to be redrawn.

21

Printing

This chapter will focus on issues related to creating output on a printer or other hard-copy device. Windows solves some of the problems with which programmers have had to grapple under traditional programming environments. For example, Windows programmers don't have to hassle with device-specific control codes. Instead, the GDI calls that draw on displays also draw on printers. A printer driver helps GDI to convert GDI calls into the device-specific data stream needed to create graphic output on a specific printer.

GDI's device-independent drawing helps set the stage for duplicating on the printer the images on a display screen. This capability is sometimes called WYSIWYG, an acronym for "what you see is what you get." In the last chapter, we covered GDI's coordinate transformations. These go a long way toward helping create WYSIWYG output, particularly when geometric figures are drawn. WYSIWYG for text requires a little more work, since the output generated for printer fonts must be simulated using the display fonts. One approach to tackling this issue involves using only **TrueType** fonts, which can be generated both for displays and for printers.

We will start this chapter by looking at the user-interface end of printing. We'll provide a sample program, PRSETUP, which demonstrates the creation of a standard set of printer setup and configuration dialog boxes. Then we'll discuss the creation of a printer DC, which is the first ingredient needed to print. Finally, we'll cover the use of the `Escape` function and the creation of a printer abort function, which will serve to introduce our second sample program, PRINT.

Like many of the other areas we have covered, this discussion of printing will begin by addressing what the user expects to see, focusing first on user-interface issues.

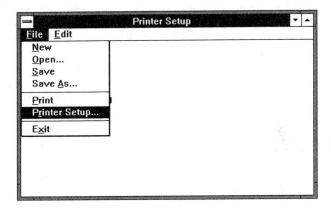

Figure 21.1 The Printer Setup... menu item

The User Interface to Printing

In Chapter 11, we introduced the standard File and Edit menus used in Windows programs. In particular, the "Print" menu option on the File menu is of interest to us because it initiates printing. Another menu item, not on our standard menu, "Printer Setup...", calls up a dialog box to allow the user to configure a printer. Figure 21.1 depicts this menu item in a revised File menu.

As you might expect from the ellipsis (...), selecting "Printer Setup..." causes a dialog box to appear. A typical Printer Setup dialog box is shown in Figure 21.2. A list box displays the installed printers, along with the name of the port to which each is attached. Allowing the user to select from the available printers requires you to create and maintain a dialog like the one in the figure. In a moment, we'll show you the code required to

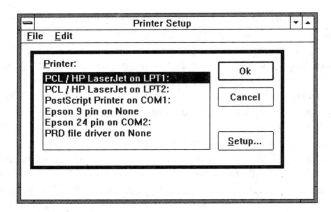

Figure 21.2 The "Printer Setup..." dialog box

Figure 21.3   An example of a printer device driver's setup dialog box

support this dialog, and another dialog box that is used for device-specific configuration information.

As Figure 21.2 shows, a standard part of a Printer Setup dialog box is a push button marked "Setup...". When the user pushes this button, a dialog box that allows the user to configure the currently selected printer is displayed. The specific dialog box that appears depends on the selected printer.

An example of a configuration dialog box is shown in Figure 21.3. This dialog box is created by the HP Laserjet printer driver, HPPCL.DRV. Although you don't have to worry about the contents of this dialog box, your program is responsible for calling the printer driver when a configuration dialog box like this is to be displayed.

Prior to the release of Windows 3, the role of a configuration dialog box was to change a printer's default settings. In those days, printer drivers wrote all changes to one place: the system-wide configuration file, WIN.INI. This created some annoying problems for users, in particular when a user needs to work with a different configuration for different types of print jobs.

Consider, for example, a user who uses landscape mode to print spreadsheets and portrait mode to print word-processing documents. To print spreadsheets, the printer configuration dialog box must be called to request the landscape mode. Later, when the user prints word-processing documents, the printer configuration dialog must again be summoned to switch to portrait mode. Earlier versions of Windows did not provide any way for a program to connect a particular printer configuration to a document.

Windows 3 introduces several solutions to this problem. An application can instruct a printer driver to use a private configuration file instead of WIN.INI for configuration information. A private configuration file avoids interference with other applications. An application can go one step further and retrieve a memory image of the configuration

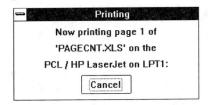

Figure 21.4 An abort print job dialog box

information. This can be written inside a data file to connect printer configuration data directly to a specific spreadsheet, word-processing document, or other application-specific data.

A final user-interface issue is that users expect to be able to abort a print job after it has begun. This can take several forms: Some applications display a dialog box with a "Cancel" push button that can be clicked to abort a print job. Figure 21.4 shows an example of such a dialog box. Other applications allow the user to strike the Esc key to terminate printing. Whichever approach you decide to take, programs should always provide the user with a way to abort a print job after it has been started.

Let's look at a sample program that displays the printer setup and configuration dialog boxes we looked at in Figures 21.2 and 21.3.

Printer Setup and Configuration

Printers are fundamentally a different type of device from display screens. For one thing, several different printers can be connected to one computer, but only one display screen can be used at any time. After a display adapter and its associated driver have been set up, there is no facility for changing the configuration of the display adapter while Windows is running. Instead, for example, a change from one resolution to another requires the user to run the Setup program and restart Windows. With a printer, however, quite a few configuration changes can be made: Output can appear in portrait or landscape mode, and it can be made to appear on letter-size or legal-size paper. While displays generally run in a single configuration, printers are able to run in many. Another difference is that a page of printed output can be ejected from a printer, while there is no comparable notion on a display screen.

To help clarify the basic ways to deal with these differences, our discussion of printing is divided into two parts. First, we'll describe how a program can set up and configure a printer. Then we'll present a fairly involved setup sample program, PRSETUP, which shows all the details needed to set up a printer so it can take advantage of the new features of Windows 3. The second half of this chapter details the use of printer escape calls to control print jobs, and the pagination of printer output. We'll describe what is needed to create an abort function and abort dialog box, for use when the user changes his mind and cancels a print job. Our sample program, PRINT, demonstrates the basics needed to create text and graphic output on a printer.

Printer Configuration and the Device Context

Just as you need a DC to draw on the display screen, a DC is also needed to send output to a printer. Getting a printer DC requires calling `CreateDC`. When we first discussed DCs in Chapter 6, we said that a DC represents a connection to a particular device. In the context of printers, this means a connection to a specific printer's device driver and the port to which the printer is connected. These make up two of the four parameters to `CreateDC`, which is defined:

```
HDC CreateDC (lpDriver, lpPrinter, lpPort, lpInit)
```

- `lpDriver` is a long pointer to a character string containing the DOS filename of a printer driver file, without an extension. For example, HPPCL identifies the HPPCL.DRV driver used for HP Laserjet printers.

- `lpPrinter` is a long pointer to a character string containing a printer description. For example, "PCL / HP Laserjet."

- `lpPort` is a long pointer to a character string containing a port name, such as LPT1 or COM1. It can also be the name of a file, when writing printer output to disk.

- `lpInit` is a long pointer to printer configuration data. If NULL, then the default configuration from WIN.INI is used.

`CreateDC` creates a DC for a specific printer connected to a specific port. When we cover the actual creation of printer output, we'll discuss this routine in more detail. For now, though, it is sufficient to say that printer setup and configuration revolves around providing the four parameters to `CreateDC`.

The Role of the WIN.INI File

When a printer is installed in Windows, an entry is made in the system configuration file, WIN.INI. There are two types of entries: One describes the default printer; the other describes all of the printers installed in the system at a given point in time. As you may recall, the configuration file stores strings that can be retrieved using two key words: an application name and a key name. The default printer is defined under the application name "windows" and the key name "device." For example, here is a sample WIN.INI entry for a default printer:

```
[windows]
device=PCL / HP LaserJet,HPPCL,LPT1:
```

To the right of the equal sign is the device name, the device driver, and the port.

To retrieve strings from WIN.INI, you call `GetProfileString`. This routine takes an application name and key name, and returns the string on the right of the equal sign. `GetProfileString` is defined:

```
int GetProfileString (lpApp, lpKey, lpDefault, lpReturn, cbSize)
```

- `lpApp` is a long pointer to a character string containing an application name.

- `lpKey` is a long pointer to a character string containing a key name.

- `lpDefault` is a long pointer to a character string containing the default string to be returned if the desired application/keyname pair is not found.

- `lpReturn` is a long pointer to a character buffer for the returned string.

- `cbSize` is an integer defining the size of the buffer.

A character buffer is defined:

```
char achBuffer[80];
```

This code copies the default printer information into the buffer:

```
cch = GetProfileString ("windows", "device", NULL, achBuffer,
80);
```

The creation of a DC for the default printer requires you to parse the needed values from the character buffer. Here is a routine that does all the work, calls `CreateDC`, and returns a handle to a printer DC:

```
HDC PASCAL GetDefPrinterDC (void)
    {
    char ach[80];
    HDC  hdc;
    int  cch;
    int  i;
    PSTR pDriver;
    PSTR pPort;
    PSTR pPrinter;

    cch = GetProfileString ("windows", "device", NULL, ach, 80);
    pDriver = pPrinter = &ach[0];
    for (i=0; i<cch; i++, pDriver++)
        {
        if (*pDriver == ',')
            {
            *pDriver = '\0';
            pDriver++;
            i++;
            break;
            }
        }

    for (pPort=pDriver; i<cch; i++, pPort++)
        {
        if (*pPort == ',')
            {
```

```
        *pPort = '\0';
        pPort++;
        break;
        }
    }

hdc = CreateDC (pDriver, pPrinter, pPort, NULL);
return (hdc);
}
```

This routine provides a DC for the default printer, using its default settings. It provides you with enough to start experimenting with sending output to the printer. If that is your primary goal, we suggest that you skip ahead to the second half of this chapter, which starts on page 721. The next few pages, and the code sample that follows, address the role of an application in the selection of a printer and in the configuration of the selected printer.

If you are in the process of creating a full-blown Windows application, you may wish to give the user a choice of system printers. Lacking this, users can always go to the Control Panel to change the default printer and its configuration. But there is much to be said for providing users with a convenient solution inside the application itself, which is how most of the desktop applications that ship with Windows operate.

To find out which printers are installed, retrieve the list from Windows' system configuration file, WIN.INI. Windows' Control Panel creates a list under the application name "device." The key name for each item in the list is, in fact, the name of the printer as supplied by each device driver. Here is an example of WIN.INI entries for installed printers:

```
[devices]
PCL / HP LaserJet=HPPCL,LPT1:,LPT2:
PostScript Printer=PSCRIPT,COM1:
Epson 9 pin=EPSON9,None
Epson 24 pin=EPSON24,COM2:
PRD file driver=D:\WINDOWS\APPS\WINWORD\PRDDRV.DRV,None
```

To retrieve the key names from a list like this, call `GetProfileString` with a NULL key name. The returned string contains all the key names in the list, each null terminated. For example, here is how to retrieve a list of the default printer key names:

```
char achBuff[256];

cch = GetProfileString ("devices", NULL, NULL, achBuff, 256);
```

This string can then be parsed and the results used in subsequent calls to `GetProfileString` to retrieve the rest of the information about the installed printers.

The next step in the configuration of a printer involves calling the device driver to request that it display a configuration dialog box. Although it takes care of creating and maintaining the dialog box, you'll need to find the driver, get the address of the driver's configuration function, and call the driver to make the whole operation work.

Configuring a Printer

After you have selected a printer from the Printer Setup dialog box, you may wish to configure the printer. If so, push the button marked "Setup..." In response, your program loads the device driver and calls its configuration function. At that point, the device driver takes over as it creates one or more modal dialog boxes through which it interacts with the user.

There are two configuration entry points for printer drivers: One is for drivers written for version 3.0 of Windows and later, and the other is for older, version 2.x drivers. When the time comes to call up a configuration dialog box, your program should first check for the Windows 3 configuration entry point. If this isn't available, then use the version 2.x entry point. In a moment, we'll discuss the ways that the Windows 3 configuration entry point provides a wider range of services even though the dialog box appears the same. The Windows 3 entry point is named `ExtDeviceMode`, and the Windows 2.x entry point is `DeviceMode`.

Accessing these two functions first requires the driver to be loaded into memory. Since a printer driver is a dynamic link library, calling `LoadLibrary` does the trick. `LoadLibrary` takes a single parameter: the name of the library to load. Here, for example, is how to load the HPPCL.DRV driver:

```
HANDLE hDriver;

hDriver = LoadLibrary ("HPPCL.DRV");
if (hDriver < 32)
    {
    /*  Error.  */
    }
else
    {
    /*  Ok.  */
    }
```

As suggested by this code, `LoadLibrary` returns a handle that identifies the library. If the return value is less than 32, it means an error has occurred. A program may respond by displaying a dialog box to let the user know that a problem has been encountered. If the library has already been loaded into memory, the library's reference count is incremented and `LoadLibrary` returns a handle to the library.

Once you have a valid handle to a library, you next search for a configuration function. This is the job of the `GetProcAddress` routine. `GetProcAddress` searches the module database for a function in a dynamic link library, or in an application. This routine is defined:

```
FARPROC GetProcAddress (hModule, lpProcName)
```

- `hModule` is a module handle that identifies an application or a dynamic link library. For a dynamic link library, it is the return value from **LoadLibrary**.

- `lpProcName` identifies the function either as an ASCII text string or as a numeric ordinal value.

Windows 2.x Configuration Function

To retrieve the address of an old-style configuration function, start by creating two new data types for the function address:

```
typedef WORD FAR PASCAL FNOLDDEVMODE( HWND, HANDLE, LPSTR, LPSTR);
typedef FNOLDDEVMODE FAR * LPFNOLDDEVMODE;
```

These data types will recognize and enforce the function prototype for the printer configuration function to minimize the possibility of type-mismatch errors when calling the function.

Next, define a variable of type LPFNOLDDEVMODE, as shown here:

```
LPFNOLDDEVMODE lpfnProc;
```

Retrieving the address of the Windows 2.x configuration function involves calling GetProcAddress as follows:

```
lpfnProc = GetProcAddress (hDriver, "DeviceMode");
```

This works because the DeviceMode function is named in the EXPORTS section of every printer driver's module definition file. The entry looks something like this:

```
EXPORTS
    DeviceMode @ 13
```

You may recall that applications export several types of functions, including window procedures and dialog box procedures. These call-back procedures are exported to make them available to modules outside our program. In the same way, when a printer driver exports its configuration function, it allows us to call GetProcAddress and to call into the function itself.

The number in the EXPORTS statement after the @ symbol identifies a unique number called an **ordinal identifier**. GetProcAddress allows you to retrieve a function by its ordinal identifier; therefore, we could retrieve the Windows 2.x printer configuration address by saying:

```
lpfnProc = GetProcAddress (hDriver, MAKEINTRESOURCE(13));
```

The MAKEINTRESOURCE macro creates a data object that looks like a long pointer to a character string, from the C compiler's point of view. This is necessary because of the way that GetProcAddress is prototyped. Inside the four-byte value, however, the segment identifier is zero, which is always an invalid value. The number 13 is put in the offset part of the pointer; from there it is read and used by GetProcAddress. This uses less memory than the example we saw a moment ago, because an integer takes less space than a character string. Also, this results in a faster lookup of the address, since ordinal values are always in memory, but string references live in a discardable resource called a **nonresident name table**, which must be loaded from disk to dereference the string.

Once you have the address of the function, calling the function is simple. The variable containing the function address can be treated like a regular function name. Here is an example of calling a printer configuration function located at address `lpfnProc`:

```
lpfnProc (hwnd, hDriver, achPrinter, achPort);
```

Some C programmers prefer to treat the function address like other pointers and call the function like this:

```
(*lpfnProc)(hwnd, hDriver, achPrinter, achPort);
```

Both work. The old-style device mode function is defined:

```
void DeviceMode (hWnd, hModule, lpPrinter, lpPort)
```

- `hWnd` is a window handle. The printer driver uses this handle to identify the parent of its modal dialog box. Since this function is normally called from within a dialog box procedure, this value is often a handle to your Printer Setup dialog box.

- `hModule` is a module handle for the printer driver. This is the value returned by **LoadLibrary**.

- `lpPrinter` is a long pointer to a character string for the printer name, such as "PCL / HP Laserjet."

- `lpPort` is a long pointer to a character string containing the port to which the printer is attached, such as "LPT1" or "COM1," or the DOS filename when writing to a file. Whichever is used, this must be the same as the value passed in the **CreateDC** call.

When a program calls the old-style device mode function, the printer driver takes over. It reads the current setup from WIN.INI and lets the user modify the printer configuration. The user can Cancel at any time, or save the changes by pressing the OK button. Once saved, the changes become the default printer settings, which apply to all applications the user wishes to print.

The Windows 3 configuration solves this problem in several ways. First, programs can have private configuration files. A program can even get a copy of a printer's configuration information and save it, so that each data file can have its own printer configuration information. Let's look at what is involved in the Windows 3 printer configuration function.

Windows 3 Configuration Function

Microsoft provides an include file with the Windows SDK that will help access a Windows 3 printer configuration function: PRINT.H. The first thing to do when accessing the configuration function is to get its address: Two data types are defined in this file, which serve as the data type for the function address:

```
typedef WORD FAR PASCAL FNDEVMODE(HWND, HANDLE, LPDEVMODE,
                                  LPSTR, LPSTR,LPDEVMODE,
                                  LPSTR, WORD);

typedef FNDEVMODE FAR * LPFNDEVMODE;
```

Retrieving the function address proceeds in the same fashion as for the Windows 2.x configuration function. When the printer driver has been brought into memory by the LoadLibrary function, we next call GetProcAddress to retrieve the address of ExtDeviceMode, which is the Windows 3 configuration function:

```
LPFNDEVMODE lpfnMode;

lpfnExtDeviceMode = GetProcAddress (hDriver, "ExtDeviceMode");
```

Like the Windows 2.x configuration function, this function is listed in the module definition file of a printer driver with a statement like:

```
EXPORTS
    ExtDeviceMode @ 90
```

This means that the ExtDeviceMode function can be retrieved using an ordinal reference like this:

```
lpfnExtDeviceMode = GetProcAddress (hDriver,
                                    MAKEINTRESOURCE (90));
```

Once we have the address of the ExtDeviceMode function, we can proceed to call it. First, however, let's look at how this function is defined. From there, you'll see that several options exist for how this function can be used. ExtDeviceMode is defined:

```
int ExtDeviceMode (hWnd, hDriver, lpDM, lpPrinter,
                   lpPort, lpInitDM, lpProfile, wMode)
```

- hWnd is a window handle used by the printer driver as the parent of its modal dialog box.

- hDriver is a handle to the printer driver, as returned by **LoadLibrary**.

- lpDM is a long pointer to an output buffer. When the DM_COPY mode is selected in the last parameter, the printer driver writes to this buffer a copy of the DEVMODE data for the new printer configuration.

- lpPrinter is a long pointer to a character string for a printer name, such as "PCL / HP Laserjet."

- lpPort is a long pointer to a character string for the port to which the printer is attached, or to a filename when output is being sent to disk.

- lpInitDM is a long point to an input buffer. When the DM_MODIFY mode is selected in the last parameter, the printer driver expects to find a copy of its DEVMODE data, which it uses to initialize the configuration dialog box.

- lpProfile is a long pointer to a character string. When the DM_UPDATE mode is selected in the last parameter, the printer driver updates a configuration file. If lpProfile is NULL, then WIN.INI is updated. Otherwise, the lpProfile is the name of the configuration file to be updated.

- wMode is a WORD field that can contain one or more of the following style bits, ORed together:

DM_COPY instructs the printer driver to copy the printer configuration data to the buffer referenced by lpDM.

DM_MODIFY instructs the printer driver to read the initial configuration information from the buffer referenced by lpInitDM.

DM_PROMPT instructs the printer to display a dialog box.

DM_UPDATE instructs the printer driver to modify the default settings in a configuration file. The exact configuration file to update depends on the value of lpProfile. If it is NULL, then WIN.INI is updated. Otherwise, the file referenced by lpProfile is updated.

Zero (0) instructs the printer driver simply to return the size of the buffer that is required to hold the printer configuration information.

Perhaps the most important field in this function is the last one, wMode. It provides a road map for the printer driver, describing exactly what the application program needs. Let's look at several ways in which function can be called.

First of all, if an application only wants to imitate the behavior of a Windows 2.x configuration function, it would need two flags: DM_PROMPT causes the dialog box to appear and DM_UPDATE (with lpProfile set to NULL) causes WIN.INI to be updated. But the Windows 2.x way of doing things causes applications to interfere with each other. There must be a better way.

A simple way to keep applications from disrupting each other involves using a private configuration file. An application can create such a file to store other configuration information as well, such as program options selected by the user. To get ExtDeviceMode to write a copy of its configuration information into MYPROFILE.INI, here is how it would be called:

```
lpfnExtDeviceMode (hWnd,          /*  Parent window.  */
                   hDriver,       /*  Driver handle.  */
                   NULL,          /*  Output data.  */
                   lpPrinter,     /*  Printer name.  */
                   lpPort,        /*  Port.  */
                   NULL,          /*  Input data.  */
                   "MYPROFILE",/*  Profile file.  */
                   DM_PROMPT |    /*  Mode  */
                   DM_UPDATE);
```

Another approach involves asking the printer driver to copy its configuration information into a buffer that you create. This data will consist of two parts. The first half corresponds to the DEVMODE data structure, defined in Windows.H as

```
typedef struct _devicemode {
    char dmDeviceName[CCHDEVICENAME];
    WORD dmSpecVersion;
    WORD dmDriverVersion;
```

```
        WORD dmSize;
        WORD dmDriverExtra;
        DWORD dmFields;
        short dmOrientation;
        short dmPaperSize;
        short dmPaperLength;
        short dmPaperWidth;
        short dmScale;
        short dmCopies;
        short dmDefaultSource;
        short dmPrintQuality;
        short dmColor;
        short dmDuplex;
    } DEVMODE;
```

The second half is made up of printer-specific information, whose contents are known only to the printer driver itself. Even without knowing the meaning of this part of the data structure, your program can make a copy of the data, perhaps storing it along with a word-processing document, spreadsheet, or whatever other data files your application creates.

Saving the configuration information requires at least two calls to ExtDeviceMode. The first retrieves the size of the configuration data. This allows your program to allocate the necessary buffer. The second call involves either the DM_COPY flag, to retrieve a copy of the default configuration information, or the DM_PROMPT flag, to request a dialog box to retrieve the user's printing preferences. Here is an example of some code that retrieves the size of the data block, allocates some memory, then calls the driver to create a dialog box:

```
HANDLE hmem;
int cbSize;
PSTR pDevModeOutput;

/*  Retrieve size of configuration data block.      */
cbSize = lpfnExtDeviceMode (NULL, hDriver, NULL,
                            lpPrinter, lpPort, NULL,
                            NULL, NULL);
hmem = LocalAlloc (LMEM_MOVEABLE, cbSize);
pDevModeOutput = LocalLock (hmem);
if (p == 0)
    goto ErrorExit;

/*  Get configuration block from user.             */
lpfnExtDeviceMode (hWnd, hDriver, pDevModeOutput,
                   lpPrinter, lpPort, NULL, NULL,
                   DM_PROMPT);
```

Later on, the printer configuration data is passed to CreateDC as its last parameter. The printer driver uses the configuration information at DC creation time to make sure that the DC reflects the configuration selected by the user.

Next, we're going to look at a sample program, PRSETUP, which shows how to deal with both types of printer configuration calls. Even though PRSETUP doesn't actually print, its sheer size gives you an idea of the amount of effort required to let the user configure the printer.

A Sample Program: PRSETUP

Figure 21.5 shows the output of PRSETUP. This program lets the user configure the printer, then displays the printer name, port, and driver name, as well as the size of the buffer needed to hold the printer configuration information.

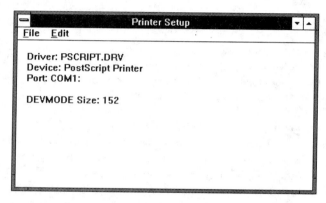

Figure 21.5 PRSETUP

Here is the source code to our program:

PRSETUP.C

```
/*------------------------------------------------------------*\
|  PrSetup.C -- Demo showing dialog box to setup printer.      |
\*------------------------------------------------------------*/
#define STRICT
#include <Windows.H>
#include <Print.H>

#include "PrSetup.h"
#include "setupdlg.h"


/*------------------------------------------------------------*\
|                     Function Prototypes.                     |
\*------------------------------------------------------------*/
LRESULT CALLBACK    PrSetupWndProc (HWND, UINT, WPARAM, LPARAM);
BOOL    CALLBACK    PrSetupDialog  (HWND, UINT, WPARAM, LPARAM);
```

```
BOOL    NEAR PASCAL PrSetupInit (HWND);
int     NEAR PASCAL PrsetupParseLB (HWND, PSTR, PSTR, PSTR);
int     NEAR PASCAL PrSetupCallDriver (HWND);
HLOCAL  NEAR PASCAL PrSetupGetDefPrinter (PSTR, PSTR, PSTR, int);

/*------------------------------------------------------------*\
 |                      Global Variables.                     |
\*------------------------------------------------------------*/
char      achWndClass[] = "PrSetup:MAIN";
char      achAppName[]  = "Printer Setup";

char      achPrinter[32];
char      achDriver[MAXDRIVERNAME];
char      achPort[20];
HLOCAL    hmemDM;
int       cbDM;
int       cbDMTemp;

HINSTANCE hInst;
FARPROC   lpitPrSetupDialog;

/*------------------------------------------------------------*\
 |              Main Function:  WinMain.                      |
\*------------------------------------------------------------*/
int PASCAL
WinMain (HINSTANCE hInstance,       // Who am I?
         HINSTANCE hPrevInstance,   // Any older siblings?
         LPSTR     lpszCmdLine,     // Ptr to command line.
         int       cmdShow)         // How to open my window?
    {
    HWND    hwnd;
    MSG     msg;
    WNDCLASS wndclass;

    if (!hPrevInstance)
        {
        wndclass.lpszClassName = achWndClass;
        wndclass.hInstance     = hInstance;
        wndclass.lpfnWndProc   = PrSetupWndProc;
        wndclass.hCursor       = LoadCursor (hInstance, "hand");
        wndclass.hIcon         = LoadIcon (hInstance, "snapshot");
        wndclass.lpszMenuName  = "#1";
        wndclass.hbrBackground = (HBRUSH)(COLOR_WINDOW+1);
        wndclass.style         = NULL;
        wndclass.cbClsExtra    = 0;
        wndclass.cbWndExtra    = 0;

        RegisterClass( &wndclass);
        }

    hInst = hInstance;

    hwnd = CreateWindowEx(0L,                // Extra style.
                        achWndClass,         // Class name.
                        achAppName,          // Title.
```

```
                            WS_OVERLAPPEDWINDOW,    // Style bits.
                            CW_USEDEFAULT,          // x -- default.
                            0,                      // y -- default.
                            CW_USEDEFAULT,          // cx -- default.
                            0,                      // cy -- default.
                            NULL,                   // No parent.
                            NULL,                   // Class menu.
                            hInstance,              // Creator.
                            NULL);                  // Params.
        ShowWindow (hwnd, cmdShow);

        lpitPrSetupDialog = MakeProcInstance ((FARPROC)PrSetupDialog,
                                              hInst);

        while (GetMessage(&msg, 0, 0, 0))
            {
            TranslateMessage(&msg); // Convert KEYDOWNs to CHARs
            DispatchMessage(&msg);  // Transmit message to WndProc
            }

        FreeProcInstance (lpitPrSetupDialog);

        return 0;
        }

/*-------------------------------------------------------------*\
|              Window Procedure:  PrSetupWndProc.               |
\*-------------------------------------------------------------*/
LRESULT CALLBACK
PrSetupWndProc (HWND    hwnd,    // For whom is message sent?
                UINT    mMsg,    // What is exact message?
                WPARAM  wParam,  // ...message details.
                LPARAM  lParam)  // ...message details.
    {
    static int cyLineHeight;
    static int cxCharWidth;

    switch (mMsg)
        {
        case WM_COMMAND:
            {
            char buffer[80];

            switch (wParam)
                {
                case IDM_EXIT:
                    DestroyWindow (hwnd);
                    break;

                case IDM_PRINT_SETUP:
                    DialogBox (hInst,
                            MAKEINTRESOURCE (IDD_PRSETUP),
                            hwnd,
                            (DLGPROC)lpitPrSetupDialog);
```

```
                    InvalidateRect (hwnd, NULL, TRUE);
                    break;

            default:
                wsprintf (buffer, "Command = %d", wParam);
                MessageBox (hwnd, buffer, "WM_COMMAND", MB_OK);
                break;
        }
    }
    break;

case WM_CREATE:
    {
    HDC hdc;
    TEXTMETRIC tm;
    hdc = GetDC (hwnd);
    GetTextMetrics (hdc, &tm);
    ReleaseDC (hwnd, hdc);
    cyLineHeight = tm.tmHeight;
    cxCharWidth  = tm.tmAveCharWidth;
    }
    break;

case WM_DESTROY:
    PostQuitMessage(0);  // Handle application shutdown.
    break;

case WM_PAINT:
    {
    char ach[80];
    int x, y;
    int cb;
    PAINTSTRUCT ps;

    BeginPaint (hwnd, &ps);
    x = cxCharWidth * 2;
    y = cyLineHeight;

    cb = wsprintf (ach, "Driver: %s", (LPSTR)achDriver);
    TextOut (ps.hdc, x, y, ach, cb);
    y += cyLineHeight;

    cb = wsprintf (ach, "Device: %s" (LPSTR)achPrinter);
    TextOut (ps.hdc, x, y, ach, cb);
    y += cyLineHeight;

    cb = wsprintf (ach, "Port: %s", (LPSTR)achPort);
    TextOut (ps.hdc, x, y, ach, cb);
    y += cyLineHeight;

    y += cyLineHeight;
    cb = wsprintf (ach, "DEVMODE Size: %d", cbDM);
    TextOut (ps.hdc, x, y, ach, cb);
```

```
            EndPaint    (hwnd, &ps);
            }
        break;

    default:
        return(DefWindowProc(hwnd,mMsg,wParam,lParam));
        break;
    }
return 0L;
}

/*-------------------------------------------------------------*\
|          Setup Dialog Box Procedure:  PrSetupDialog.          |
\*-------------------------------------------------------------*/
BOOL FAR  PASCAL
PrSetupDialog  (HWND   hdlg,
                UINT   wMsg,
                WPARAM wParam,
                LPARAM lParam)
    {
    switch (wMsg)
        {
        case WM_INITDIALOG:
            if (!PrSetupInit (hdlg))
                {
                MessageBox (hdlg,
                            "Out of memory.",
                            "PrSetup",
                            MB_OK);
                EndDialog (hdlg, TRUE);
                }
            return TRUE;
            break;

        case WM_COMMAND:
            {
            int     iRet;
            HCURSOR hcr;

            switch (wParam)
                {
                case IDD_OK:
                    /*  Change cursor to the hourglass.       */
                    hcr = LoadCursor (NULL, IDC_WAIT);
                    SetCursor (hcr);

                    /*  Retrieve and parse list box string    */
                    /*  for printer name, driver name, and port. */
                    iRet = PrsetupParseLB (hdlg, achPrinter,
                                           achPort, achDriver);

                    if (iRet == -1)
                        goto ErrorExit;

                    /*  Free old printer data block.          */
```

```
                            if (hmemDM  != 0)
                                LocalFree (hmemDM);

                            /*  Get new printer data block.              */
                            hmemDM = PrSetupGetDefPrinter (
                                            achPrinter,
                                            achPort,
                                            achDriver,
                                            0);

                            /*  Update size info for data block.         */
                            cbDM = cbDMTemp;

                            EndDialog (hdlg, TRUE);
                            break;

                        case IDD_CANCEL:
                            EndDialog (hdlg, TRUE);
                            break;

                        case IDD_SETUP:
                            iRet = PrSetupCallDriver (hdlg);
                            if (iRet == -1)
                                goto ErrorExit;
                            break;
                        }
                    return TRUE;
                    }
                break;

            default:
                return FALSE;
            }
        return FALSE;

ErrorExit:
    MessageBox (hdlg, "Cannot Access Specified Driver",
                "PrSetup", MB_OK);
    return FALSE;
    }

/*-------------------------------------------------------------*\
|          Process WM_INITDIALOG for PrSetupDialog.             |
\*-------------------------------------------------------------*/
BOOL NEAR PASCAL
PrSetupInit (HWND hdlg)
    {
    char    achDefault[SIZETEMPBUFF];
    char    ach[SIZETEMPBUFF];
    HGLOBAL hMem;
    HWND    hwndList;
    int     cch;
    int     cchNext;
    int     ichSearch;
    int     i;
```

```
int     ich;
int     j;
LPSTR   lpKey;
WORD    wIndex;


hMem = GlobalAlloc (GMEM_MOVEABLE, MAXKEYBUFFER);
lpKey = GlobalLock (hMem);
if (!lpKey)
    return FALSE;

/*  Get names of all printers installed in the system.    */
j = GetProfileString ("devices",
                        NULL,
                        NULL,
                        lpKey,
                        MAXKEYBUFFER);

hwndList = GetDlgItem (hdlg, IDD_PRINTERS);

/* Loop through key names, adding printer/port to listbox. */
for (i=0;i<j;i += cchNext)
    {
    lstrcpy (ach, &lpKey[i]);
    cchNext = lstrlen (&lpKey[i]);

    lstrcat (ach, "on");
    cchNext += 4;

    cch = GetProfileString ("devices",
                        &lpKey[i],
                        NULL,
                        &ach[cchNext],
                        SIZETEMPBUFF -- cchNext);

    /*  Set cch to NULL character at end of ach.           */
    cch += cchNext;

    /*  Skip past device driver name (ie. "HPPCL")         */
    for (ich=cchNext; ich < cch; ich++)
        {
        if (ach[ich] == ',')
            {
            ich++;
            break;
            }
        }

    /*  At this point, ach[ich]->first device, ie. "LPT1" */

    /*  Loop through each device that driver uses.         */
    for (ichSearch = ich; ichSearch <= cch; ichSearch++)
        {
```

```
        /*  If we hit a comma, or the end of the string... */
        if (ach[ichSearch] == ',' || ichSearch == cch)
            {
            ach[ichSearch] = 0;
            lstrcpy (&ach[cchNext], &ach[ich]);

            /*  Add string to list box.                   */
            SendMessage (hwndList, LB_ADDSTRING, 0,
                        (LONG)(LPSTR)ach);
            ich = ichSearch+1;
            }
        }

    cchNext = lstrlen (&lpKey[i]) + 1;
    }

/*  Get default printer info, either the name we kept    */
/*  or, if we don't have a printer name, from WIN.INI.   */
if (lstrlen (achPrinter) > 0)
    {
    lstrcpy (ach, achPrinter);
    lstrcat (ach, ",,");
    lstrcat (ach, achPort);
    cch = lstrlen (ach);
    }
else
    {
    /*  Get default printer information.                 */
    cch = GetProfileString ("windows",
                            "device",
                            NULL,
                            ach,
                            SIZETEMPBUFF);
    }

/*  Copy printer description.                            */
for (i=0;i < cch && ach[i] != ','; i++)
    achDefault[i] = ach[i];

j = i+1;
lstrcpy(&achDefault[i], "on");
i += 4;

/*  Skip driver name.                                    */
while (j<cch && ach[j] != ',')
    j++;

/*  Copy port name.                                      */
lstrcpy (&achDefault[i], &ach[j+1]);

/*  Search for default printer.                          */
wIndex = (WORD)SendMessage (hwndList, LB_FINDSTRING,
                        0xffff, (LONG)(LPSTR)achDefault);
```

```
    /*  If found, highlight default printer in list box.        */
    if (wIndex != LB_ERR)
        SendMessage (hwndList, LB_SETCURSEL, wIndex, 0L);

    GlobalUnlock (hMem);
    GlobalFree (hMem);

    return TRUE;
    }

/*-------------------------------------------------------------*\
|     PrsetupParseLB:  Parse string returned from listbox.    |
\*-------------------------------------------------------------*/
int   NEAR PASCAL
PrsetupParseLB (HWND hdlg,
               PSTR achPrinter,
               PSTR achPort,
               PSTR achDriver)
    {
    char    ach[SIZETEMPBUFF];
    char    achDriverTemp[MAXDRIVERNAME];
    char    achPrinterTemp[32];
    char    achPortTemp[20];
    HWND    hCtl;
    int     cch;
    int     i;
    OFSTRUCT of;

    /*  Get list box string.                                   */
    hCtl = GetDlgItem (hdlg, IDD_PRINTERS);
    i = (int)SendMessage (hCtl, LB_GETCURSEL, 0, 0L);
    i = (int)SendMessage (hCtl, LB_GETTEXT, i, (LONG)(LPSTR)ach);

    while (ach[i] != ' ')
        i--;

    lstrcpy (achPortTemp, &ach[i+1]);

    /*  Assumes that format of list box string is:             */
    /*                                                         */
    /*      <printer description> on <port>                    */
    /*                                                         */
    /*  We skip over "on", by moving back three spaces.        */
    i-= 3;
    ach[i] = 0;

    lstrcpy (achPrinterTemp, ach);

    cch = GetProfileString ("devices",
                            achPrinterTemp,
                            NULL,
                            ach,
                            SIZETEMPBUFF);
```

```
    if (cch == 0)
        return 0;

    /*  Get driver file name.                                    */
    for (i=0; i<cch && i<MAXDRIVERNAME;i++)
        {
        if (ach[i] == ',')
            {
            achDriverTemp[i]=0;
            break;
            }
        achDriverTemp[i] = ach[i];
        }

    /*  Search for period '.' to see if we have an extension.  */
    for (;i!=0;i--)
        {
        if (achDriverTemp[i] == '.')
            break;
        }

    /*  If not, let's add an extension of .DRV               */
    if (i == 0)
        lstrcat (achDriverTemp, ".DRV");

    /*  If cannot find driver file, then fail.               */
    i = OpenFile (achDriverTemp, &of, OF_EXIST | OF_READ);
    if (i == -1)
        return -1;

    lstrcpy (achDriver, achDriverTemp);
    lstrcpy (achPrinter, achPrinterTemp);
    lstrcpy (achPort, achPortTemp);
    return 1;
    }

/*-------------------------------------------------------------*\
|    PrSetupGetDefPrinter -- Get printer default setup info.    |
\*-------------------------------------------------------------*/
HLOCAL NEAR PASCAL
PrSetupGetDefPrinter (PSTR pPrinter,
                      PSTR pPort,
                      PSTR pDriver,
                      int  cbData)
    {
    HLOCAL      hmem;
    HINSTANCE   hDriver;
    LPFNDEVMODE lpfnMode;
    PDEVMODE    pdm;

    hmem = 0;

    hDriver = LoadLibrary (pDriver);
```

```
    if (hDriver == 0) goto Exit;
    lpfnMode = GetProcAddress ((HINSTANCE)hDriver, (LPCSTR) "ExtDeviceMode");
    if (lpfnMode == 0)  goto Exit;

    /*  If it wasn't passed to us, query data size.             */
    if (cbData == 0)
        {
        cbData = lpfnMode (NULL,
                           hDriver,
                           NULL,
                           pPrinter,
                           pPort,
                           NULL,
                           NULL,
                           0);
        cbDMTemp = cbData;
        }

    hmem = LocalAlloc (LHND, cbData);
    pdm = (PDEVMODE)LocalLock (hmem);
    if (hmem == 0)
        goto Exit;


    /*  Get default printer setup information.                  */
    lpfnMode (NULL,
              hDriver,
              pdm,
              pPrinter,
              pPort,
              NULL,
              "WIN.INI",
              DM_COPY);                      /*  Return settings.     */

Exit:
    if (hmem)
       LocalUnlock (hmem);
    if (hDriver)
        FreeLibrary (hDriver);
    return hmem;
    }



/*------------------------------------------------------------*\
|         Process Setup... push button for PrSetupDialog.      |
\*------------------------------------------------------------*/
int  NEAR PASCAL
PrSetupCallDriver (HWND hdlg)
    {
    char           achDriverT[MAXDRIVERNAME];
    char           achPrinterT[32];
    char           achPortT[20];
    HINSTANCE      hDriver = 0;
    HLOCAL         hmemDmNew = 0;
```

```
HLOCAL          hmemDmOld;
HCURSOR         hcr;
int             cbData;
int             i;
LPFNDEVMODE     lpfnMode;
LPFNOLDDEVMODE  lpfnOldMode;
PDEVMODE        pdmOld;
PDEVMODE        pdmNew;

/*  Change cursor to the hourglass.                        */
hcr = LoadCursor (NULL, IDC_WAIT);
SetCursor (hcr);

/*  Get printer, port, and driver info.                    */
i = PrsetupParseLB (hdlg, achPrinterT, achPortT, achDriverT);
if (i==-1)
    return -1;

/*  Load printer driver based on driver file name read     */
/*  from WIN.INI.                                          */
hDriver = LoadLibrary (achDriverT);
if (hDriver == 0) goto ErrorExit;

/*  Check for Win3 setup function.                         */
lpfnMode = GetProcAddress (hDriver, PROC_EXTDEVICEMODE);
if (lpfnMode == 0)  goto OldDriver;

/*  Query size of printer setup data.                      */
cbData = lpfnMode (NULL,
                   hDriver,
                   NULL,
                   achPrinterT,
                   achPortT,
                   NULL,
                   NULL,
                   0);

/*  If we don't have a printer data block, or its size     */
/*  is different from existing data block, get a new one.  */
if (hmemDM == 0 || cbData != cbDM)
    goto CreateNew;

/*  Check that existing printer data block is for the      */
/*  currently selected printer.  If not, get a new one.    */
pdmOld = (PDEVMODE) LocalLock (hmemDM);
if (pdmOld == 0)  goto ErrorExit;
if (lstrcmpi ((LPSTR)pdmOld, achPrinterT) == 0)
    {
    /*  We have a valid printer data block for currently   */
    /*  selected printer.  Give it to printer driver for   */
    /*  initial values for dialog box.                     */
    hmemDmOld = 0;
    goto GetUserData;
    }
```

```
        else
            LocalUnlock(hmemDM);

        /*  Allocate a block of memory for the default data.       */
    CreateNew:
        hmemDmOld = PrSetupGetDefPrinter (achPrinterT,
                                          achPortT,
                                          achDriverT,
                                          cbData);

        pdmOld = (PDEVMODE)LocalLock (hmemDmOld);
        if (pdmOld == 0) goto ErrorExit;

        /*  Allocate a block to receive new printer data block      */
        /*  that printer driver will return from setup dialog.      */
    GetUserData:
        hmemDmNew = LocalAlloc (LHND, cbData);
        pdmNew = (PDEVMODE)LocalLock (hmemDmNew);
        if (pdmNew == 0)
            goto ErrorExit;

        /*  Call printer initialization function to put up dialog   */
        /*  and allow user to change default printer settings.      */
        i = lpfnMode (hdlg,
                      hDriver,
                      pdmNew,
                      achPrinterT,
                      achPortT,
                      pdmOld,
                      "WIN.INI",
                      DM_MODIFY |
                      DM_UPDATE |
                      DM_PROMPT |
                      DM_COPY);

        /*  Clean up scratch memory, if we allocated it.            */
        if (hmemDmOld == 0)
            LocalUnlock (hmemDM);
        else
            {
            LocalUnlock (hmemDmOld);
            LocalFree (hmemDmOld);
            }

        LocalUnlock (hmemDmNew);
        LocalFree   (hmemDmNew);

        FreeLibrary (hDriver);

        return 1;


        /*  Here if the ExtDeviceMode function wasn't found, and    */
        /*  we need to ask for the DeviceMode function, which       */
        /*  indicates we have an old, pre-Win3 printer driver.      */
    OldDriver:
```

```
    lpfnOldMode = GetProcAddress (hDriver, PROC_OLDDEVICEMODE);
    if (lpfnOldMode == 0)
        goto ErrorExit;

    /*  Display dialog box to get new printer settings.       */
    lpfnOldMode (hdlg,
                 hDriver,
                 achPrinterT,
                 achPortT);

    /*  We're done, and setup worked.                         */
    FreeLibrary (hDriver);
    return 1;

    /*  We're done, but setup didn't work.                    */
ErrorExit:
    if (hDriver)
        FreeLibrary (hDriver);

    if (hmemDmNew)
        {
        LocalUnlock (hmemDmNew);
        LocalFree (hmemDmNew);
        }
    MessageBox (hdlg,
                "Error in Printer Setup",
                "PrSetup",
                MB_OK);

    return 0;
    }
```

PRSETUP.DEF

```
NAME    PRSETUP

EXETYPE WINDOWS

DESCRIPTION 'Printer Setup (c) 1992 By Paul Yao'

CODE    MOVEABLE PRELOAD
DATA    MOVEABLE MULTIPLE PRELOAD

HEAPSIZE    512
STACKSIZE   5120

SEGMENTS
    PRSETUP_TEXT MOVEABLE PRELOAD

EXPORTS
    PrSetupWndProc
    PrSetupDialog
```

PRSETUP.H

```
/*-----------------------------------------------------------*\
|   PrSetup.h -- Include file for PrSetup.c.                  |
\*-----------------------------------------------------------*/

#define IDM_NEW           1
#define IDM_OPEN          2
#define IDM_SAVE          3
#define IDM_SAVEAS        4
#define IDM_PRINT         5
#define IDM_PRINT_SETUP 6
#define IDM_EXIT          7

#define IDM_UNDO          8
#define IDM_CUT           9
#define IDM_COPY         10
#define IDM_PASTE        11
#define IDM_CLEAR        12
#define IDM_DELETE       13


#define MAXKEYBUFFER    300
#define SIZETEMPBUFF     80
#define MAXDRIVERNAME    80

typedef WORD FAR PASCAL FNOLDDEVMODE(HWND, HANDLE, LPSTR, LPSTR);
typedef FNOLDDEVMODE FAR * LPFNOLDDEVMODE;
```

PRSETUP.LNK

```
PrSetup.obj
PrSetup.exe/align:16/map/nod/noe/CO
nul
mlibcew libw
PrSetup.def
```

PRSETUP.MAK

```
# Directory search paths.

INCDIR = \WINDEV\INCLUDE

# Windows version to support
# Valid pairs include:
#     (0x0300, 30)
#     (0x0310, 31)
```

```
CLVER = WINVER=0x0300
RCVER = 30

# Compiler switches for applications.

CL_APP_SHIP_ALL = -AM -c -D$(CLVER) -Gsw -I$(INCDIR) -Ow -W3 -Zp
CL_APP_DEBG_ALL = -AM -c -D$(CLVER) -Gsw -I$(INCDIR) -Od -W3 -Zpi

CL_APP_SHIP_31  = -AM -c -G2s  -I$(INCDIR) -Ow -W3 -Zp
CL_APP_DEBG_31  = -AM -c -G2s  -I$(INCDIR) -Od -W3 -Zpi

# Compiler switches for DLLs.

CL_DLL_SHIP_ALL = -AMw -c -D$(CLVER) -Gsw -I$(INCDIR) -Ow -W3 -Zp
CL_DLL_DEBG_ALL = -AMw -c -D$(CLVER) -Gsw -I$(INCDIR) -Od -W3 -Zpi

CL_DLL_SHIP_31  = -AMw -c -G2s  -I$(INCDIR) -Ow -W3 -Zp
CL_DLL_DEBG_31  = -AMw -c -G2s  -I$(INCDIR) -Od -W3 -Zpi

# Make file primary target.

all: PrSetup.exe

# Make file dependency targets.

PrSetup.res: PrSetup.rc PrSetup.cur PrSetup.ico
    rc -r -i$(INCDIR) PrSetup.rc

PrSetup.obj: PrSetup.c
    cl $(CL_APP_SHIP_ALL) PrSetup.c

PrSetup.exe: PrSetup.obj PrSetup.def PrSetup.res
    link @PrSetup.lnk
    rc -$(RCVER) PrSetup.res

PrSetup.exe: PrSetup.res
    rc -$(RCVER) PrSetup.res
```

PRSETUP.RC

```
#include <Windows.h>
#include "PrSetup.h"
#include "setupdlg.h"

snapshot icon PrSetup.ico

hand   cursor PrSetup.cur

#include "setup.dlg"
```

```
1 MENU
    {
    POPUP "&File"
        {
        MENUITEM "&New",                    IDM_NEW
        MENUITEM "&Open...",                IDM_OPEN
        MENUITEM "&Save",                   IDM_SAVE
        MENUITEM "Save &As...",             IDM_SAVEAS
        MENUITEM SEPARATOR
        MENUITEM "&Print",                  IDM_PRINT
        MENUITEM "P&rinter Setup...",       IDM_PRINT_SETUP
        MENUITEM SEPARATOR
        MENUITEM "E&xit",                   IDM_EXIT
        }
    POPUP "&Edit"
        {
        MENUITEM "&Undo\tAlt+Backspace", IDM_UNDO
        MENUITEM SEPARATOR
        MENUITEM "Cu&t\tShift+Del",         IDM_CUT
        MENUITEM "&Copy\tCtrl+Ins",         IDM_COPY
        MENUITEM "&Paste\tShift+Ins",       IDM_PASTE
        MENUITEM SEPARATOR
        MENUITEM "Cl&ear",    IDM_CLEAR
        MENUITEM "&Delete",   IDM_DELETE
        }
    }
```

SETUP.DLG

```
IDD_PRSETUP DIALOG LOADONCALL MOVEABLE DISCARDABLE
                8, 8, 177, 82
STYLE WS_DLGFRAME | WS_POPUP
BEGIN
    CONTROL "&Printer:", IDD_TEXT1, "static",
        SS_LEFT | WS_CHILD, 7, 3, 28, 8
    CONTROL "", IDD_PRINTERS, "listbox",
        LBS_NOTIFY | WS_BORDER | WS_VSCROLL |
        WS_TABSTOP | WS_CHILD, 7, 14, 119, 57
    CONTROL "Ok", IDD_OK, "button",
        BS_DEFPUSHBUTTON | WS_TABSTOP | WS_CHILD,
        132, 6, 40, 14
    CONTROL "Cancel", IDD_CANCEL, "button",
        BS_PUSHBUTTON | WS_TABSTOP | WS_CHILD,
        132, 25, 40, 14
    CONTROL "&Setup...", IDD_SETUP, "button",
        BS_PUSHBUTTON | WS_TABSTOP | WS_CHILD,
        132, 57, 40, 14
END
```

SETUPDLG.H

```
#define IDD_OK          1
#define IDD_CANCEL      2
#define IDD_PRSETUP     5
#define IDD_TEXT1       101
#define IDD_SETUP       102
#define IDD_PRINTERS    103
```

Although there is a lot of code in PRSETUP, the important thing to keep in mind is that its entire purpose is to retrieve *four* data items, which are the four parameters to CreateDC: the driver name, the device name, the port (or filename), and driver initialization data. This last item is only available for drivers that have been updated for Windows 3 and which support the ExtDeviceMode function. For drivers that don't support this function, only the first three items are available.

Next, we're going to look at the steps involved in printing. The sample program will not have all the bells and whistles of PRSETUP, but rather prints on the default printer using default printer settings. You may find this the easiest approach to take as you begin to explore printing under Windows. Let's take a look, then, at what is needed to get output to appear on a printer.

Sending Output to the Printer

As mentioned earlier, sending output to the printer requires a printer device context. This provides a connection to a printer, a complete set of GDI drawing tools, and access to GDI's drawing routines. Creating a printer DC is a job for the CreateDC routine, which we covered earlier.

A few more steps are required to create printer output than were required for display output. For one thing, when outputting to the printer, programs must notify GDI about the beginning and end of a **printer job**, which is defined as a group of pages to be output in sequential order. A program also must notify GDI when it has finished writing to one page and is ready to begin a new page. All of these tasks are accomplished by a call to the Escape routine, which is our first topic of discussion.

A key concept in the world of Windows programming revolves around the idea that the user should be able to stop almost any process even after it has begun. This is certainly true of printing, since print jobs can be quite time consuming. Built into the printing process is the ability to define a message loop call-back procedure that allows the user to interact with other programs while a print job is in progress. It also allows the user to interact with a special Abort Print dialog box which will be described shortly. But first, let's take a look at the Escape function.

Controlling Printer Output: The Escape Function

Once you have gotten a handle to a printer DC, you're almost ready to draw on a printer. But first, you need to know about the `Escape` function. This GDI routine is used almost exclusively to communicate with printers and plotters (an exception is the `GETCOLORTABLE` escape, supported by certain non-palette-supporting displays). `Escape` is defined:

```
int Escape (hDC, nEscape, nCount, lpDataIn, lpDataOut)
```

- `hDC` is a handle to a DC.
- `nEscape` is an integer that identifies the escape subfunction to be performed.
- `nCount` is an integer that specifies the number of bytes in the input buffer referenced by the `lpDataIn` parameter.
- `lpDataIn` is a long pointer to a buffer that certain escape subfunctions use for input data.
- `lpDataOut` is a long pointer to a buffer that certain escape subfunctions use for output data.

There are 65 escape subfunctions defined in Windows.h. Some of these ask for information from the device driver. For example, the `GETPHYSPAGESIZE` subfunction returns the width and height of a printed page. Others give an application access to printer capabilities that aren't available in GDI. For example, the `BEGIN_PATH` and `END_PATH` escapes let a program create complex line drawings using the support for paths built into Postscript printers.

The following list of escape codes make up the minimum set required by every printer driver:

Escape Subfunction	*Description*
`ABORTDOC`	Abort a print job.
`ENDDOC`	Marks the end of a print job.
`NEWFRAME`	Marks the end of page in the current print job.
`QUERYESCSUPPORT`	Determine whether an escape subfunction is supported.
`SETABORTPROC`	Define a call-back procedure to connect printing with a message loop.
`STARTDOC`	Begin a print job.

To signal the beginning of a print job, a program sends the `STARTDOC` escape. When this escape is sent, the `nCount` parameter of the `Escape` function contains the length of the job name, and the `lpDataIn` field points to a character string for the job name itself. Here is an example:

```
cb = lstrlen (achJobName);
err = Escape (hdcPrinter, STARTDOC, cb, achJobName, NULL);
if (err == -1) goto Exit;
```

If `Escape` returns a value of -1, that means an error has occurred and printing cannot continue.

After the `STARTDOC` escape call, a program starts to output the first page of the document by making GDI drawing calls to the DC. These calls are collected until the program sends the `NEWFRAME` escape code, which signals the end of a page. This escape takes no other parameters to the `Escape` function:

```
err = Escape (hdcPrinter, NEWFRAME, NULL, NULL, NULL);
```

This continues until all the pages have been sent to the printer, at which time a program indicates the end of a print job by sending the `ENDDOC` escape code. This signals the end of the print job, after which a program can destroy the printer DC or start another print job. The `ENDDOC` escape takes no additional parameters to `Escape`:

```
err = Escape (hdcPrinter, ENDDOC, NULL, NULL, NULL);
```

At any time during the print job, a program can cancel a print job by sending an `ABORTDOC` escape code. When it is sent, this escape code takes the place of the `ENDDOC` escape:

```
err = Escape (hdcPrinter, ENDDOC, NULL, NULL, NULL);
```

Another way for a print job to be terminated involves a print abort function, which is defined with the `SETABORTPROC` escape code. This escape code, and the code required to support an Abort dialog box, are the next topic of our discussion.

Printing, Multitasking, and the Abort Function

Since Windows is a *nonpreemptive* multitasking system, it does not interrupt one program to allow another to run. Instead, programs must interrupt themselves. The driving force behind the operation of this system is the hunger of each application for messages. A program is dependent on messages to run properly, yet Windows will give a program only one message to process at a time. The multitasking system continues to work because programs continually poll for messages. At such time, Windows may decide to switch away from one program to allow another one to run.

This works well as long as programs continue to ask for messages. But the multitasking system breaks down when a program has a large processing task to do, such as printing a large document. In recognition of this problem, Microsoft provides a facility to allow the printing process to connect to the message system so that some degree of multitasking can occur even when a print job is in progress.

This facility is referred to as an **abort function**, although perhaps a better term would be a printing message loop. In any case, a primary role of this function is to allow user input to be delivered to a program so that it can cancel a print job in progress. The abort function is a call-back procedure that you provide in your program. The function itself is defined:

```
BOOL FAR PASCAL AbortFunc (HDC hdc, short code)
```

GDI periodically calls this routine to retrieve whatever messages might be in the print queue. At that time, hdc is the handle to the printer device context. The value of code indicates whether an error has occurred. It can have one of two values: zero if no error has occurred, and SP_OUTOFDISK when disk space is unavailable for spooling.

Here is a sample abort function:

```
BOOL FAR PASCAL AbortLoop (HDC hdc, short code)
   {
   MSG msg;

   while (PeekMessage (&msg, 0, 0, 0, PM_REMOVE))
      {
      TranslateMessage(&msg);
      DispatchMessage(&msg);
      }

   return TRUE;
   }
```

This looks a lot like the message loop of every Windows program. The PeekMessage routine is similar to GetMessage, except that it returns a value of FALSE when there are no more messages to be processed. The Abort function can be used to abort a print job simply by returning a value of FALSE. The code in this example returns a value of TRUE, which causes GDI to continue printing.

Since GDI calls the abort function, you will probably want to create an instance thunk by calling MakeProcInstance. This routine is used to set up the data segment register for dialog box procedures. It provides the same service for the abort function. To use it, you start by defining a variable of type FARPROC:

```
FARPROC lpitAbort;
```

This variable will hold the return value for MakeProcInstance. Here is how we might set up an instance thunk for the subroutine we saw earlier:

```
lpitAbort = MakeProcInstance (AbortLoop,hInstance);
```

Also, be sure to list your abort function EXPORTS section of your program's module definition (DEF) file.

To install the abort function when printing, you pass GDI a SETABORTPROC escape code, like this:

```
Escape (hdcPrinter, SETABORTPROC, NULL, (LPSTR)lpitAbort, NULL)
```

Once this has been done, GDI will periodically call into your function to let some messages flow through the system, so that the printing process does not too severely impact Windows' multitasking.

Next, we will examine a sample program which prints out some text and some graphic information onto the printer.

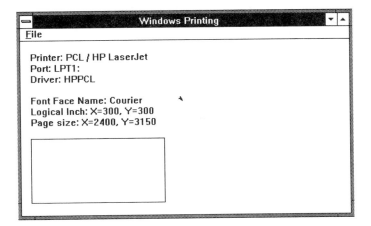

Figure 21.6 PRINT's display

A Sample Program: PRINT

Our next sample program, PRINT, puts together the two printing topics we have just finished discussing: the `Escape` call and the Abort function. Figure 21.6 shows PRINT's display, which also happens to be the output sent to the printer.

Here is the code to PRINT:

PRINT.C

```
/*------------------------------------------------------------*\
|   Print.C -- Demonstrates printing in Windows.              |
\*------------------------------------------------------------*/
#define STRICT
#include <Windows.H>
#include "Print.H"
#include "Abortdlg.H"


/*------------------------------------------------------------*\
|                     Function Prototypes.                     |
\*------------------------------------------------------------*/
LRESULT CALLBACK PrintWndProc (HWND, UINT, WPARAM, LPARAM);
BOOL    CALLBACK PrintAbortDlg (HWND, UINT, WPARAM, LPARAM);
void NEAR PASCAL PrintOutput (HDC hdc);
void NEAR PASCAL PrintPrint(HWND);
BOOL FAR  PASCAL PrintAbortMsg (HDC, short);
HDC  NEAR PASCAL GetDefPrinterDC (void);
```

```
/*-------------------------------------------------------------*\
|                      Global Variables.                        |
\*-------------------------------------------------------------*/
char achWndClass[] = "Print:MAIN";
char achAppName[]  = "Windows Printing";

BOOL bContinue;         /*  Abort printing flag.                */

char achDriver[80];     /*  Name of printer driver.            */
char achPrinter[32];    /*  Name of printer.                   */
char achPort[12];       /*  Name of port.                      */
char achFont[32];       /*  Printer font face name.            */
char achJobName[] = "Text and Rectangle Print Job.";

FARPROC lpitAbortDlg;   /*  Abort dialog instance thunk.       */
FARPROC lpitAbort;      /*  Abort message loop.                */

HANDLE hInst;           /*  Instance handle.                   */
HDC   hdcPrinter;       /*  Printer DC.                        */
HWND  hdlgAbort;        /*  Window handle of abort dlg box.    */

int   cxPrinterInch;    /*  Printer logical inch.              */
int   cyPrinterInch;    /*  Printer logical inch.              */

int   cxPageSize;       /*  Printer page size.                 */
int   cyPageSize;       /*  Printer page size.                 */


/*-------------------------------------------------------------*\
|                 Main Function:  WinMain.                      |
\*-------------------------------------------------------------*/
int PASCAL
WinMain (HINSTANCE hInstance,       // Who am I?
         HINSTANCE hPrevInstance,   // Any older siblings?
         LPSTR     lpszCmdLine,     // Ptr to command line.
         int       cmdShow)         // How to open my window?
   {
   HWND     hwnd;
   MSG      msg;
   WNDCLASS wndclass;

   if (!hPrevInstance)
       {
       wndclass.lpszClassName = achWndClass;
       wndclass.hInstance     = hInstance;
       wndclass.lpfnWndProc   = PrintWndProc;
       wndclass.hCursor       = LoadCursor (hInstance, "hand");
       wndclass.hIcon         = LoadIcon (hInstance, "snapshot");
       wndclass.lpszMenuName  = "#1";
       wndclass.hbrBackground = (HBRUSH)(COLOR_WINDOW+1);
       wndclass.style         = NULL;
       wndclass.cbClsExtra    = 0;
       wndclass.cbWndExtra    = 0;

       RegisterClass( &wndclass);
       }
```

```
    hInst = hInstance;

    hwnd = CreateWindowEx(0L,                     // Extra style.
                    achWndClass,                  // Class name.
                    achAppName,                   // Title.
                    WS_OVERLAPPEDWINDOW,          // Style bits.
                    CW_USEDEFAULT,                // x -- default.
                    0,                            // y -- default.
                    CW_USEDEFAULT,                // cx -- default.
                    0,                            // cy -- default.
                    NULL,                         // No parent.
                    NULL,                         // Class menu.
                    hInstance,                    // Creator.
                    NULL);                        // Params.
    ShowWindow (hwnd, cmdShow);

    lpitAbortDlg = MakeProcInstance ((FARPROC)PrintAbortDlg,
                                     hInstance);
    lpitAbort    = MakeProcInstance ((FARPROC)PrintAbortMsg,
                                     hInstance);

    while (GetMessage(&msg, 0, 0, 0))
        {
        TranslateMessage(&msg); // Convert KEYDOWNs to CHARs
        DispatchMessage(&msg);  // Transmit message to WndProc
        }

    FreeProcInstance (lpitAbortDlg);
    FreeProcInstance (lpitAbort);
    return 0;
    }

/*------------------------------------------------------------*\
|                 Window Procedure:  PrintWndProc.            |
\*------------------------------------------------------------*/
LRESULT CALLBACK
PrintWndProc (HWND    hwnd,     // For whom is message sent?
              UINT    mMsg,     // What is exact message?
              WPARAM  wParam,   // ...message details.
              LPARAM  lParam)   // ...message details.
    {
    static int cyLine;
    static int cxChar;

    switch (mMsg)
        {
        case WM_CREATE:
            {
            HDC         hdc;
            TEXTMETRIC  tm;

            hdcPrinter = GetDefPrinterDC();
            if (hdcPrinter == 0)
                {
```

```
                  MessageBox (hwnd,
                          "Unable to create Printer DC.",
                          "Print", MB_OK);
                  return -1L;
                  }

          /*  Get printer info.                              */
          GetTextFace (hdcPrinter, 32, achFont);
          cxPrinterInch =
                  GetDeviceCaps (hdcPrinter, LOGPIXELSX);
          cyPrinterInch =
                  GetDeviceCaps (hdcPrinter, LOGPIXELSY);

          cxPageSize = GetDeviceCaps (hdcPrinter, HORZRES);
          cyPageSize = GetDeviceCaps (hdcPrinter, VERTRES);

          /*  Get display text metric info.                  */
          hdc = GetDC (hwnd);
          GetTextMetrics (hdc, &tm);
          cyLine = tm.tmHeight + tm.tmExternalLeading;
          cxChar = tm.tmAveCharWidth;
          ReleaseDC (hwnd, hdc);
          }
          break;

  case WM_COMMAND:
      switch (wParam)
          {
          case IDM_PRINT:
              PrintPrint(hwnd);
              break;
          case IDM_EXIT:
              DestroyWindow (hwnd);
              break;
          default:
              MessageBox (hwnd,
                      "Command Not Supported.",
                      "Print", MB_OK);
          }
      break;

  case WM_DESTROY:
      DeleteDC (hdcPrinter);
      PostQuitMessage(0);  // Handle application shutdown.
      break;

  case WM_PAINT:
      {
      PAINTSTRUCT ps;

      BeginPaint (hwnd, &ps);

      PrintOutput (ps.hdc);

      EndPaint (hwnd, &ps);
```

```
                }
              break;

          default:
              return(DefWindowProc(hwnd,mMsg,wParam,lParam));
              break;
          }
      return 0L;
      }

/*----------------------------------------------------------*\
|  GetDefPrinterDC:  Retrieve DC handle for default printer.  |
\*----------------------------------------------------------*/
HDC NEAR PASCAL GetDefPrinterDC (void)
    {
    char ach[80];
    HDC  hdc;
    int  cch;
    int  i;
    PSTR pDriver;
    PSTR pPort;
    PSTR pPrinter;

    cch = GetProfileString ("windows", "device", NULL, ach, 80);
    pDriver = pPrinter = &ach[0];
    for (i=0; i<cch; i++, pDriver++)
        {
        if (*pDriver == ',')
            {
            *pDriver = '\0';
            pDriver++;
            i++;
            break;
            }
        }

    for (pPort=pDriver; i<cch; i++, pPort++)
        {
        if (*pPort == ',')
            {
            *pPort = '\0';
            pPort++;
            break;
            }
        }

    lstrcpy (achDriver, pDriver);
    lstrcpy (achPrinter, pPrinter);
    lstrcpy (achPort, pPort);

    hdc = CreateDC (pDriver, pPrinter, pPort, NULL);
    return (hdc);
    }
```

```
/*----------------------------------------------------------*\
|       PrintOutput:  Output to display screen or printer.     |
\*----------------------------------------------------------*/
void NEAR PASCAL PrintOutput (HDC hdc)
    {
    char        achBuff[120];
    int         cb;
    int         cxInch;
    int         cyInch;
    int         cyLine;
    int         X, Y;
    TEXTMETRIC  tm;

    /*  Get text measurement information.                  */
    GetTextMetrics (hdc, &tm);
    X = tm.tmAveCharWidth * 2;
    Y = cyLine = tm.tmHeight + tm.tmExternalLeading;

    /*  Get local device logical inch.                     */
    cxInch = GetDeviceCaps (hdc, LOGPIXELSX);
    cyInch = GetDeviceCaps (hdc, LOGPIXELSY);

    /*  Display printer name.                              */
    cb = wsprintf (achBuff, "Printer: %s",
                    (LPSTR)achPrinter);
    TextOut (hdc, X, Y, achBuff, cb);
    Y += cyLine;

    /*  Display port name.                                 */
    cb = wsprintf (achBuff, "Port: %s",
                    (LPSTR)achPort);
    TextOut (hdc, X, Y, achBuff, cb);
    Y += cyLine;

    /*  Display driver name.                               */
    cb = wsprintf (achBuff, "Driver: %s",
                    (LPSTR)achDriver);
    TextOut (hdc, X, Y, achBuff, cb);
    Y += cyLine * 2;

    /*  Display default printer face name.                 */
    cb = wsprintf (achBuff, "Font Face Name: %s",
                    (LPSTR)achFont);
    TextOut (hdc, X, Y, achBuff, cb);
    Y += cyLine;

    /*  Display size of logical inch.                      */
    cb = wsprintf (achBuff, "Logical Inch: X=%d, Y=%d",
                    cxPrinterInch, cyPrinterInch);
    TextOut (hdc, X, Y, achBuff, cb);
    Y += cyLine;

    /*  Display size of printed page in pixels.            */
    cb = wsprintf (achBuff, "Page size: X=%d, Y=%d",
                    cxPageSize, cyPageSize);
```

```
        TextOut (hdc, X, Y, achBuff, cb);
        Y += cyLine * 2;

        /*  Draw a rectangle.                                      */
        Rectangle (hdc, X, Y, X + ( 2*cxInch), Y + cyInch);


        }

/*--------------------------------------------------------------*\
|     PrintPrint:  Print to the printer.                         |
\*--------------------------------------------------------------*/
void NEAR PASCAL PrintPrint(HWND hwnd)
    {
    int   cb;
    int   err;

    /*  Set print continue flag.                                   */
    bContinue = TRUE;
    Escape (hdcPrinter, SETABORTPROC, NULL,
            (LPSTR)lpitAbort, NULL);

    /*  Create abort print dialog box.                             */
    hdlgAbort = CreateDialog (hInst, "#1", hwnd,
                              (DLGPROC)lpitAbortDlg);

    /*  Disable parent.                                            */
    EnableWindow (hwnd, FALSE);

    /*  Send STARTDOC escape.                                      */
    cb = lstrlen (achJobName);
    err = Escape (hdcPrinter, STARTDOC, cb, achJobName, NULL);
    if (err < 0) goto Exit;

    /*  Send output to printer.                                    */
    PrintOutput (hdcPrinter);

    /*  Signal next page, or abort printing.                       */
    if (bContinue)
        {
        err = Escape (hdcPrinter, NEWFRAME, NULL, NULL, NULL);
        if (err < 0) goto Exit;
        }
    else
        Escape (hdcPrinter, ABORTDOC, NULL, NULL, NULL);

    /*  Send ENDDOC escape.                                        */
    err = Escape (hdcPrinter, ENDDOC, NULL, NULL, NULL);

Exit:
    /*  Enable parent.                                             */
    EnableWindow (hwnd, TRUE);

    /*  Remove abort dialog box.                                   */
    DestroyWindow (hdlgAbort);
```

```
        if (bContinue && err < 0)
            MessageBox (hwnd, "Unable to print", "Print", MB_OK);
    }


/*------------------------------------------------------------*\
|    PrintAbortDlg:  Abort Print dialog box procedure.       |
\*------------------------------------------------------------*/
BOOL FAR  PASCAL PrintAbortDlg (HWND hdlg,    WORD wMsg,
                                    WORD wParam, LONG lParam)
    {
    switch (wMsg)
        {
        case WM_INITDIALOG:
            {
            char ach[50];

            /*  Initialize static text controls.            */
            SetDlgItemText (hdlg, IDD_JOBNAME, achJobName);
            lstrcpy (ach, achPrinter);
            lstrcat (ach, "on");
            lstrcat (ach, achPort);
            SetDlgItemText (hdlg, IDD_PRINTER, ach);
            }
            break;

        /*  User has pushed 'Cancel' button.  Abort printing. */
        case WM_COMMAND:
            bContinue = FALSE;
            return TRUE;

        default:
            return FALSE;
        }
    }


/*------------------------------------------------------------*\
| PrintAbortMsg:  Message loop to monitor abort print dialog.|
\*------------------------------------------------------------*/
BOOL FAR PASCAL PrintAbortMsg (HDC hdc, short code)
    {
    MSG msg;

    while (bContinue && PeekMessage (&msg, 0, 0, 0, PM_REMOVE))
        {
        if (!IsDialogMessage (hdlgAbort, &msg))
            {
            TranslateMessage(&msg);
            DispatchMessage(&msg);
            }
        }

    return bContinue;
    }
```

PRINT.DEF

```
NAME    PRINT

EXETYPE WINDOWS

DESCRIPTION 'Windows Printing (c) 1992 By Paul Yao'

CODE    MOVEABLE DISCARDABLE PRELOAD
DATA    MOVEABLE MULTIPLE PRELOAD

HEAPSIZE    512
STACKSIZE   5120

SEGMENTS
    PRINT_TEXT MOVEABLE PRELOAD

EXPORTS
    PrintWndProc
    PrintAbortDlg
    PrintAbortMsg
```

PRINT.H

```
/*-------------------------------------------------------------*\
|   Print.H -- Include file for Print.c.                        |
\*-------------------------------------------------------------*/

#define IDM_NEW      100
#define IDM_OPEN     101
#define IDM_SAVE     102
#define IDM_SAVEAS   103
#define IDM_PRINT    104
#define IDM_EXIT     105
```

PRINT.LNK

```
Print.obj
Print.exe/align:16/map/nod/noe/CO
nul
mlibcew libw
Print.def
```

PRINT.MAK

```
# Directory search paths.

INCDIR = \WINDEV\INCLUDE

# Windows version to support
# Valid pairs include:
#     (0x0300, 30)
#     (0x0310, 31)

CLVER = WINVER=0x0300
RCVER = 30

# Compiler switches for applications.

CL_APP_SHIP_ALL = -AM -c -D$(CLVER) -Gsw -I$(INCDIR) -Ow -W3 -Zp
CL_APP_DEBG_ALL = -AM -c -D$(CLVER) -Gsw -I$(INCDIR) -Od -W3 -Zpi

CL_APP_SHIP_31  = -AM -c -G2s  -I$(INCDIR) -Ow -W3 -Zp
CL_APP_DEBG_31  = -AM -c -G2s  -I$(INCDIR) -Od -W3 -Zpi

# Compiler switches for DLLs.

CL_DLL_SHIP_ALL = -AMw -c -D$(CLVER) -Gsw -I$(INCDIR) -Ow -W3 -Zp
CL_DLL_DEBG_ALL = -AMw -c -D$(CLVER) -Gsw -I$(INCDIR) -Od -W3 -Zpi

CL_DLL_SHIP_31  = -AMw -c -G2s  -I$(INCDIR) -Ow -W3 -Zp
CL_DLL_DEBG_31  = -AMw -c -G2s  -I$(INCDIR) -Od -W3 -Zpi

# Make file primary target.

all: Print.exe

# Make file dependency targets.

Print.res: Print.rc Print.cur Print.ico
    rc -r -i$(INCDIR) Print.rc

Print.obj: Print.c Print.h
    cl $(CL_APP_SHIP_ALL) Print.c

Print.exe: Print.obj Print.def Print.res
    link @Print.lnk
    rc -$(RCVER) Print.res

Print.exe: Print.res
    rc -$(RCVER) Print.res
```

PRINT.RC

```
#include <Windows.H>
#include "Print.H"
#include "Abortdlg.H"

#include "Abort.dlg"

snapshot icon Print.ico

hand   cursor Print.cur


1 MENU
    {
    POPUP "&File"
        {
        MENUITEM "&New",          IDM_NEW
        MENUITEM "&Open...",       IDM_OPEN
        MENUITEM "&Save"          IDM_SAVE
        MENUITEM "Save &As...",  IDM_SAVEAS
        MENUITEM SEPARATOR
        MENUITEM "&Print",        IDM_PRINT
        MENUITEM SEPARATOR
        MENUITEM "E&xit",         IDM_EXIT
        }
    }
```

ABORT.DLG

```
1 DIALOG LOADONCALL MOVEABLE DISCARDABLE 33, 32, 158, 67
CAPTION "Escape -- Printing"
STYLE WS_BORDER | WS_CAPTION | WS_DLGFRAME | WS_SYSMENU |
     WS_VISIBLE | WS_POPUP
BEGIN
    CONTROL "", IDD_JOBNAME, "static",
            SS_CENTER | WS_CHILD, 0, 10, 158, 8
    CONTROL "", IDD_PRINTER, "static",
            SS_CENTER | WS_CHILD, 0, 25, 158, 8
    CONTROL "Cancel", IDD_CANCEL, "button",
            BS_DEFPUSHBUTTON | WS_TABSTOP | WS_CHILD,
            60, 43, 43, 14
END
```

ABORTDLG.H

```
#define IDD_CANCEL    2
#define IDD_JOBNAME   100
#define IDD_PRINTER   101
```

As shown in Figure 21.7, PRINT creates a modeless dialog box that allows the user to cancel the print job by clicking on the Cancel push button, or by striking the Esc key.

The presence of a modeless dialog box means that the message loop in the Abort function must be changed to include a call to `IsDialogMessage`. As you may recall from our discussion of dialog boxes in Chapter 14, this routine enables the keyboard interface to a modeless dialog box.

The guts of the printing that PRINT performs is found in the routine named `PrintPrint`. It shows the use of the various escape codes and error handling when printing fails.

In response to the `WM_DESTROY` message, PRINT eliminates the printer DC by calling GDI's `DeleteDC` function. This insures that the memory used by the DC is available for other applications.

Figure 21.7 PRINT's abort dialog box

Appendix A

A Taxonomy of Messages

The Eight Types of Messages

Type	Description
Hardware	Mouse, Keyboard, Pen, and Timer Input.
Window Maintenance	Notification, Request for action, Query.
User-Interface Maintenance	Menu, mouse pointer, scroll bar, dialog boxes, MDI.
Termination	Application or system shutdown.
Private	Dialog box controls: edit, button, list box, combobox.
System Resource Notification	Color Changes, fonts, spooler, device modes.
Data Sharing	Clipboard and Dynamic Data Exchange (DDE).
Internal System	Undocumented Messages.

Hardware Messages

Mouse Messages: In a window's client area

WM_LBUTTONDBLCLK	Left button double-click.
WM_LBUTTONDOWN	Left button down.
WM_LBUTTONUP	Left button up.
WM_MBUTTONDBLCLK	Middle button double-click.
WM_MBUTTONDOWN	Middle button down.
WM_MBUTTONUP	Middle button up.
WM_MOUSEMOVE	Mouse move.
WM_RBUTTONDBLCLK	Right button double-click.
WM_RBUTTONDOWN	Right button down.
WM_RBUTTONUP	Right button up.

Mouse Messages: In a window's non-client area

WM_NCLBUTTONDBLCLK	Left button double-click.
WM_NCLBUTTONDOWN	Left button down.
WM_NCLBUTTONUP	Left button up.
WM_NCMBUTTONDBLCLK	Middle button double-click.
WM_NCMBUTTONDOWN	Middle button down.
WM_NCMBUTTONUP	Middle button up.
WM_NCMOUSEMOVE	Mouse move.
WM_NCRBUTTONDBLCLK	Right button double-click.
WM_NCRBUTTONDOWN	Right button down.
WM_NCRBUTTONUP	Right button up.

Keyboard Messages

WM_CHAR	Character input.
WM_DEADCHAR	Dead-character (umlaut, accent, etc.).
WM_KEYDOWN	Key has been depressed.
WM_KEYUP	Key has been released.
WM_SYSCHAR	System character input.
WM_SYSDEADCHAR	System dead-character.
WM_SYSKEYDOWN	System key has been depressed.
WM_SYSKEYUP	System key has been released.

Pen Messages (only systems with Pen for Windows installed)

WM_GLOBALRCCHANGE	The global recognition context has changed.
WM_HEDITCTL	Private message for the handwriting edit controls.

Pen Messages (only systems with Pen for Windows installed)

WM_HOOKRCRESULT	Message reporting the results of the handwriting recognition hook.
WM_RCRESULT	Message from the handwriting recognizer with the results of a recognition.
WM_SKB	Message used by on-screen keyboard.

Timer Message

WM_TIMER	Timer has gone off.

Window Maintenance Messages

Window Messages: Notification

WM_ACTIVATE	Window is active.
WM_ACTIVATEAPP	Application is active.
WM_CREATE	Window has been created.
WM_DESTROY	Window has been destroyed.
WM_ENABLE	Input to the window has been enabled.
WM_KILLFOCUS	Window has lost keyboard control.
WM_MOUSEACTIVATE	Notifies a window that it is going to become active because of a mouse click.
WM_MOVE	Window has been moved.
WM_PARENTNOTIFY	The child of a window has been created, destroyed, or been clicked by the mouse.
WM_SETFOCUS	Window has gained keyboard control.
WM_SIZE	Window's client area has changed size.
WM_WINDOWPOSCHANGING	Window is about to be moved, resized, or relocated in the system's Z-ordering.
WM_WINDOWPOSCHANGED	Window has just been moved, resized, or relocated in the system's Z-ordering.

Window Messages: Request for Action

WM_CANCELMODE	Send to inform a window to cancel any internal modes, such as mouse capture. The default window procedure responds to this message by finishing any modal scroll bar or menu activity.
WM_CLOSE	Close (destroy) window.
WM_ERASEBKGND	Erase background.
WM_ICONERASEBKGND	Erase background of iconic window.
WM_NCACTIVATE	Change title bar to show active state.

Window Messages: Request for Action

WM_NCCREATE	Create non-client area data.
WM_NCDESTROY	Destroy non-client area data.
WM_NCPAINT	Redraw non-client area.
WM_PAINT	Redraw client area.
WM_SETREDRAW	Inhibit redrawing of window.
WM_SETTEXT	Change window text.
WM_SHOWWINDOW	Change window visibility.

Window Messages: Query

WM_GETMINMAXINFO	What is min/max sizes for window?
WM_GETTEXT	What is the window text?
WM_GETTEXTLENGTH	What is the length of the window text?
WM_NCCALCSIZE	How big should the client area be?
WM_QUERYDRAGICON	Send to a minimized window which doesn't have a class icon to retrieve the icon to display for the window.
WM_QUERYNEWPALETTE	Do you have a new palette?
WM_QUERYOPEN	Can iconic window be opened?

User Interface Messages

Dialog Box and Dialog Box Control Messages

WM_CHARTOITEM	Listbox w/ LBS_WANTKEYBOARDINPUT style has received a WM_CHAR message.
WM_COMMAND	Dialog box control is sending a notification code to its parent.
WM_COMPAREITEM	Sent to the parent of an owner-draw dialog box control, asking to compare two items for the purpose of sorting.
WM_CTLCOLOR	Control asking for colors to be set.
WM_DELETEITEM	Notification to an owner-draw listbox or an owner-draw combobox that an item has been deleted.
WM_DRAWITEM	Request to the parent of an owner-draw control, or owner-draw menu, to draw.
WM_GETDLGCODE	Query control: want keyboard input?
WM_GETFONT	Query control: what font are you using?
WM_INITDIALOG	Initialize dialog.
WM_MEASUREITEM	Request to the parent of an owner-draw control or an owner-draw item to provide the dimensions of the item that is going to be drawn.
WM_SETFONT	Request to control: use this font.

Dialog Box and Dialog Box Control Messages

`WM_VKEYTOITEM`	Listbox w/ `LBS_WANTKEYBOARDINPUT` style has received a `WM_KEYDOWN` message.

Drag and Drop API Messages

`WM_DROPFILES`	Notifies an application that the user has dropped a file. This message is only sent if the application is registered as a draw and drop recipient.

Menu Messages

`WM_COMMAND`	Menu item has been selected.
`WM_INITMENU`	Initialize menu bar menu.
`WM_INITMENUPOPUP`	Initialize popup menu.
`WM_MENUCHAR`	Mneumonic key used to select menu.
`WM_MENUSELECT`	User is browsing through menus.

Mouse Pointer Messages

`WM_NCHITTEST`	Query: where is mouse on the window?
`WM_SETCURSOR`	Request: Change pointer to correct shape.

Multiple Document Interface Messages

`WM_CHILDACTIVATE`	Notifies a parent window that a child is active.
`WM_MDIACTIVATE`	Notifies an MDI child window that it is either gaining or losing activation.
`WM_MDICASCADE`	Request to arrange the open MDI child windows in a cascading, stair-step fashion.
`WM_MDICREATE`	Requests an MDI client window to create an MDI child window.
`WM_MDIDESTROY`	Requests to an MDI client window to destroy an MDI child window.
`WM_MDIGETACTIVE`	Query an MDI client window for the currently active MDI child window.
`WM_MDIICONARRANGE`	Request to arrange the iconic MDI child windows in an orderly fashion.
`WM_MDIMAXIMIZE`	Request to maximize, or zoom, an MDI child window so that it occupies all of its parent's client area.
`WM_MDINEXT`	Request to activate the next MDI child window.
`WM_MDIRESTORE`	Request to restore an MDI child window to its previous state—iconic, normal, or zoomed.
`WM_MDISETMENU`	Adjusts the menu on an MDI frame window.

Multiple Document Interface Messages

WM_MDITILE   Request to arrange the open MDI child windows in a tiled fashion in the MDI parent's client window.

Scroll Bar Messages

WM_HSCROLL   Horizontal scroll bar has been clicked.

WM_VSCROLL   Vertical scroll bar has been clicked.

System Commands: System Menu, Min/Max Buttons, Titlebar, etc.

WM_SYSCOMMAND   A system command has been selected.

Termination Messages

Application and System Termination

WM_QUIT   Request that a program should terminate.

WM_QUERYENDSESSION   Queries whether application will allow system to shutdown.

WM_ENDSESSION   Notification of results of shutdown query.

Private Messages

Button Control Messages

BM_GETCHECK   Query whether a button is checked or not.

BM_GETSTATE   Query state of a button.

BM_SETCHECK   Toggles a radio button or a check box.

BM_SETSTATE   Toggles the highlighting in a radio button or check box.

BM_SETSTYLE   Changes the style of an existing button.

Combo Box Control Message

CB_ADDSTRING   Adds a string to the list box of a combo box.

CB_DELETESTRING   Removes a string from the list box of a combo box.

CB_DIR   Adds a list of files from the current directory to the list box of a combo box.

CB_FINDSTRING   Searches the list box in a combo box for a string.

CB_GETCOUNT   Queries the number of items in the list box of a combo box.

CB_GETCURSEL   Queries the index of the currently selected item in the list box of a combo box.

Combo Box Control Message

CB_GETEDITSEL	Queries the selected text in the edit control of a combo box.
CB_GETITEMDATA	Queries the item identifier from the list box of a combo box.
CB_GETLBTEXT	Queries a string from the list box of a combo box.
CB_GETLBTEXTLEN	Queries the length of a string in the list box of a combo box.
CB_INSERTSTRING	Inserts a string into the list box of a combo box.
CB_LIMITTEXT	Sets the maximum number of characters that may be entered into the edit control of a combo box.
CB_RESETCONTENT	Removes all items from the list box of a combo box.
CB_SELECTSTRING	Creates a selection in the list box of a combo box.
CB_SETCURSEL	Sets the current selection in the list box of a combo box, and places the text into the edit or static control.
CB_SETEDITSEL	Selects a range of characters in the edit control of a combo box.
CB_SETITEMDATA	Sets the identifier for an item in a combo box.
CB_SHOWDROPDOWN	Shows or hides the drop down list box of a combo box.

Dialog Box Messages

DM_GETDEFID	Queries the ID of the default push button in a dialog box.
DM_SETDEFID	Sets the default push button in a dialog box.

Edit Control

EM_CANUNDO	Queries the ability of an edit control to undo a previous edit.
EM_EMPTYUNDOBUFFER	Instructs an edit control to clear its undo buffer.
EM_FMTLINES	Instructs an edit control on how to handle end of line characters.
EM_GETHANDLE	Queries an edit control created with the DS_LOCALEDIT style for the handle of the object allocated from the local heap.
EM_GETLINE	Retrieves a line of text from an edit control.
EM_GETLINECOUNT	Queries the number of lines of text in an edit control.
EM_GETMODIFY	Queries an edit control to determine if the user has entered or changed any text.
EM_GETRECT	Queries an edit control for its display rectangle, which is either its client area or a subset as set by the EM_SETRECT message.

Edit Control

EM_GETSEL	Queries the characters that are included in the current selection.
EM_LIMITTEXT	Sets a limit to the number of characters that may be entered.
EM_LINEFROMCHAR	Finds the first line that contains a specific character.
EM_LINEINDEX	Queries the number of lines that have been scrolled in a multi-line edit control.
EM_LINELENGTH	Queries the length of a line in an edit control.
EM_LINESCROLL	Scrolls a multi-line edit control.
EM_REPLACESEL	Overwrites the current selection with new text.
EM_SETHANDLE	For edit controls with the DS_LOCALEDIT style, this message instructs the edit control to use a new local memory object for its data.
EM_SETMODIFY	Sets the modify flag for an edit control.
EM_SETPASSWORDCHAR	Sets the character to be displayed when a password is entered in an ES_PASSWORD style edit control.
EM_SETRECT	Sets the display rectangle for a multi-line edit control and causes an immediate repaint to occur.
EM_SETRECTNP	Sets the display rectangle for a multi-line edit control, and postpones painting until later.
EM_SETSEL	Defines a range of characters to display as selected.
EM_SETTABSTOPS	Sets the tab-stops in a multi-line edit control.
EM_SETWORDBREAK	Defines a call-back function to be used for word-break processing in a multi-line edit control.
EM_UNDO	Instructs an edit control to undo the last edit.

Listbox Control

LB_ADDSTRING	Inserts a string into a list box.
LB_DELETESTRING	Removes a string for a list box.
LB_DIR	Adds a list of files from the current directory to a list box.
LB_FINDSTRING	Searches a list box for a string.
LB_GETCOUNT	Queries the number of items in a list box.
LB_GETCURSEL	Queries the index of the currently selected item in a list box.
LB_GETHORIZONTALEXTENT	Queries the width in pixels that can be scrolled for a list box with horizontal scroll bars.
LB_GETITEMDATA	Queries the item identifier from a list box.
LB_GETITEMRECT	Queries the dimensions of a rectangle that bounds a list box item.

Listbox Control

LB_GETSEL	Queries the selection state of a specific list box item.
LB_GETSELCOUNT	Queries the total number of items that are selected in a list box.
LB_GETSELITEMS	Queries the indices of the selected items in a list box.
LB_GETTEXT	Queries the text of a list box item.
LB_GETTEXTLEN	Queries the text length of a list box item.
LB_GETTOPINDEX	Queries the index of the item currently displayed at the top of a list box.
LB_INSERTSTRING	Adds a string to a list box.
LB_RESETCONTENT	Removes all items from a list box.
LB_SELECTSTRING	Selects an item in a list box.
LB_SELITEMRANGE	Selects a range of items in a multi-selection list box.
LB_SETCOLUMNWIDTH	Sets the column width of multi-column list box.
LB_SETCURSEL	Sets the current selection in a list box.
LB_SETHORIZONTALEXTENT	Sets the horizontal scrolling range of a list box.
LB_SETITEMDATA	Replaces an owner-draw item in a list box.
LB_SETSEL	Highlights a string in a multiple selection list box.
LB_SETTABSTOPS	Sets the tab stop of a list box that was created with the LBS_USETABSTOPS style.
LB_SETTOPINDEX	Scrolls a list box to place a specific item at the top of the list box.

System Resource Notification Messages

System Resources Notification Messages

WM_COMMNOTIFY	An event has occurred with a communication's device.
WM_COMPACTING	Notification that system memory is low, and that the Memory Manager is trying to free up some memory.
WM_DEVMODECHANGE	Printer setup has changed.
WM_ENTERIDLE	A menu or modal dialog box has entered an idle state.
WM_FONTCHANGE	Installed fonts in the system have changed.
WM_PALETTECHANGED	Hardware color palette has changed.
WM_PALETTEISCHANGING	Notification that the hardware palette is going to change.
WM_POWER	Sent to notify applications that the system is either entering or leaving power-down suspended mode. This message is used to support the battery-saving feature on battery-powered computers.
WM_QUERYNEWPALETTE	Notifies an application that it can install a new logical palette.

System Resources Notification Messages

WM_QUEUESYNC	Notifies a CBT application of the start and end of journal playback operations.
WM_SPOOLERSTATUS	Job has been removed from spooler queue.
WM_SYSCOLORCHANGE	One or more system colors has changed.
WM_SYSTEMERROR	Sent by the Windows KERNEL when a critical system has occured during task or DLL startup or termination.
WM_TIMECHANGE	System time has changed.
WM_WININICHANGE	Initialization file, WIN.INI, changed.

Data Sharing Messages

Clipboard Messages

WM_ASKCBFORMATNAME	Asks for the name of a Clipboard format.
WM_CHANGECBCHAIN	Notification of a change in the viewing chain.
WM_CLEAR	Delete the currently selected item.
WM_COPY	Copy the currently selected item to the clipboard.
WM_CUT	Delete the currently selected item and place it on the clipboard.
WM_DESTROYCLIPBOARD	Clipboard contents are being destroyed.
WM_DRAWCLIPBOARD	Clipboard contents have changed.
WM_HSCROLLCLIPBOARD	Horizonal scrolling of owner-draw clipboard item.
WM_PASTE	Copy the current contents of the clipboard to the current location.
WM_PAINTCLIPBOARD	Requests drawing of an owner draw clipboard item.
WM_RENDERALLFORMATS	Request to provide the data for all clipboard formats that have been promised.
WM_RENDERFORMAT	Request to provide data for a single clipboard format that has been promised.
WM_UNDO	Undo previous action.
WM_SIZECLIPBOARD	Notification to the owner of owner draw clipboard data that the size of the Clipboard viewer window has changed.
WM_VSCROLLCLIPBOARD	Vertical scrolling of an owner draw clipboard item.

Dynamic Data Exchange (DDE) Messages

WM_DDE_ACK	Acknowledgement.
WM_DDE_ADVISE	Request from a DDE client to establish a permanent data link.
WM_DDE_DATA	Send a data item from a DDE server to a DDE client.

Dynamic Data Exchange (DDE) Messages

WM_DDE_EXECUTE	Request a DDE server to execute a series of commands.
WM_DDE_INITIATE	Logon to a DDE server.
WM_DDE_POKE	Request by a client for a server to update a specific data item.
WM_DDE_REQUEST	One-time request by a DDE client for a piece of information.
WM_DDE_TERMINATE	Logoff from a DDE server.
WM_DDE_UNADVISE	Terminate a permanent data link that was initiated with the WM_DDE_ADVISE message.

Appendix B

The Default Window Procedure

For your convenience, here is a listing of the default window procedure that Microsoft provided in the Windows software development kit. To see the latest revision of this code, please refer to the sample source diskettes which Microsoft provides as part of the SDK. And here is a list of the messages to which DefWindowProc responds:

WM_NCACTIVATE
WM_NCHITTEST
WM_NCCALCSIZE
WM_NCLBUTTONDOWN
WM_NCMOUSEMOVE
WM_NCLBUTTONUP
WM_NCLBUTTONDBLCLK
WM_CANCELMODE
WM_NCCREATE
WM_NCDESTROY
WM_NCPAINT
WM_SETTEXT
WM_GETTEXT
WM_GETTEXTLENGTH
WM_CLOSE
WM_PAINT
WM_PAINTICON
WM_ICONERASEBKGNE

WM_ERASEBKGND
WM_QUERYOPEN
WM_QUERYENDSESSION
WM_SYSCOMMAND
WM_SYSKEYDOWN
WM_KEYUP
WM_SYSKEYUP
WM_SYSCHAR
WM_CHARTOITEM
WM_VKEYTOITEM
WM_ACTIVATE
WM_SETREDRAW
WM_SHOWWINDOW
WM_CTLCOLOR
WM_SETCURSOR
WM_MOUSEACTIVATE
WM_DRAWITEM

```
/*------------------------------------------------------------*/
/*                                                            */
/*   DefWindowProc() -                                        */
/*                                                            */
/*------------------------------------------------------------*/

LONG FAR PASCAL DefWindowProc(hwnd, message, wParam, lParam)

register HWND  hwnd;
         WORD  message;
register WORD  wParam;
         LONG  lParam;

{
  int          i;
  HDC          hdc;
  PAINTSTRUCT  ps;
  HICON        hIcon;
  RECT         rc;
  HANDLE       hCurs;
  HBRUSH       hbr;
  HWND         hwndT;

  if (!CheckHwnd(hwnd))
     return((DWORD)FALSE);

  switch (message)
     {
       case WM_NCACTIVATE:
         if (wParam != 0)
           SetWF(hwnd, WFFRAMEON);
         else
           ClrWF(hwnd, WFFRAMEON);

         if (TestWF(hwnd, WFVISIBLE) && !TestWF(hwnd,
                                                WFNONCPAINT))
            {
              hdc = GetWindowDC(hwnd);
              DrawCaption(hwnd, hdc, TRUE, TestWF(hwnd,
                                              WFFRAMEON));
              InternalReleaseDC(hdc);
              if (TestWF(hwnd,WFMINIMIZED))
                RedrawIconTitle(hwnd);
            }
         return(TRUE);

       case WM_NCHITTEST:
         return(FindNCHit(hwnd, lParam));

       case WM_NCCALCSIZE:
         CalcClientRect(hwnd, (LPRECT)lParam);
         break;

       case WM_NCLBUTTONDOWN:
         {
```

```
WORD      cmd;
RECT      rcWindow;
RECT      rcCapt;
RECT      rcInvert;
RECT      rcWindowSave;

cmd = 0;

switch(wParam)
  {
    case HTZOOM:
    case HTREDUCE:
      GetWindowRect(hwnd, (LPRECT)&rcWindow);
      CopyRect((LPRECT)&rcWindowSave, (LPRECT)&rcWindow);

      if (TestWF(hwnd, WFSIZEBOX))
        InflateRect((LPRECT)&rcWindow,
                    -cxSzBorderPlus1, -cySzBorderPlus1);
      else
        InflateRect((LPRECT)&rcWindow,
                    -cxBorder, -cyBorder);

      rcCapt.right = rcWindow.right + cxBorder;
      rcCapt.left = rcWindow.right - oemInfo.bmReduce.cx-
                    cxBorder;

      if (wParam == HTREDUCE)
        cmd = SC_MINIMIZE;
      else if (TestWF(hwnd, WFMAXIMIZED))
        cmd = SC_RESTORE;
      else
        cmd = SC_MAXIMIZE;

      if (wParam == HTREDUCE && TestWF(hwnd, WFMAXBOX))
        OffsetRect((LPRECT)&rcCapt,
                   -oemInfo.bmReduce.cx, 0);
      rcCapt.top = rcWindow.top;
      rcCapt.bottom = rcCapt.top + cyCaption;

      CopyRect((LPRECT)&rcInvert, (LPRECT)&rcCapt);
      InflateRect((LPRECT)&rcInvert,
                  -cxBorder, -cyBorder);

      rcInvert.right += cxBorder;
      rcInvert.left += cxBorder;

      /* Converting to window coordinates. */
      OffsetRect((LPRECT)&rcInvert,
                 -(rcWindowSave.left + cxBorder),
                 -(rcWindowSave.top + cyBorder));
      /* Wait for the BUTTONUP message and see if cursor
       *  is still in the Minimize or Maximize box.
       *
       * NOTE: rcInvert is in window coords, rcCapt is
       * in screen coords
```

```
             */
             if (!DepressTitleButton(hwnd, rcCapt,
                                       rcInvert, wParam))
               cmd = 0;

             break;

          default:
             if (wParam >= HTSIZEFIRST && wParam <= HTSIZELAST)
               /* Change HT into a MV command. */
               cmd = SC_SIZE +
                     (wParam - HTSIZEFIRST + MVSIZEFIRST);
       }

   if (cmd != 0)
     {
        /* For SysCommands on system menu,
         * don't do if menu item is disabled.
         */
        if (TestWF(hwnd, WFSYSMENU))
          {
          /* don't check old app child windows
           */
          if (LOWORD(GetExpWinVer(hwnd->hInstance)) >= VER
             || !TestwndChild(hwnd))
            {
              SetSysMenu(hwnd);
              if (GetMenuState(GetSysMenuHandle(hwnd),
                            cmd & 0xFFF0,
                            MF_BYCOMMAND)
                & (MF_DISABLED | MF_GRAYED))
                break;
            }
          }
        SendMessage(hwnd, WM_SYSCOMMAND, cmd, lParam);
        break;
     }
   /*** FALL THRU ***/
}

case WM_NCMOUSEMOVE:
case WM_NCLBUTTONUP:
case WM_NCLBUTTONDBLCLK:
  HandleNCMouseGuys(hwnd, message, wParam, lParam);
  break;

case WM_CANCELMODE:
  if (hwndCapture == hwnd && pfnSB != NULL)
    EndScroll(hwnd, TRUE);

    if (fMenu && hwndMenu == hwnd)
      EndMenu();

  /* If the capture is still set, just release at
   * this point.  Can put other End functions in later.
```

```
    */
  if (hwnd == hwndCapture)
    ReleaseCapture();
  break;

case WM_NCCREATE:
  if (TestWF(hwnd, (WFHSCROLL | WFVSCROLL)))
    if (InitPwSB(hwnd) == NULL)
      return((LONG)FALSE);

  return((LONG)DefSetText(hwnd,
               ((LPCREATESTRUCT)lParam)->lpszName));
case WM_NCDESTROY:
  if (hwnd->hName)
      hwnd->hName = TextFree(hwnd->hName);
  break;

case WM_NCPAINT:
  /* Force the drawing of the menu. */
  SetWF(hwnd, WFMENUDRAW);
  DrawWindowFrame(hwnd, (HRGN)wParam);
  ClrWF(hwnd, WFMENUDRAW);
  break;

case WM_SETTEXT:
  DefSetText(hwnd, (LPSTR)lParam);
  if (TestWF(hwnd, WFVISIBLE))
    {
      if (TestWF(hwnd,WFMINIMIZED))
        {
          ShowIconTitle(hwnd,FALSE);
          ShowIconTitle(hwnd,TRUE);
        }
      else if (TestWF(hwnd, WFBORDERMASK) ==
              (BYTE)LOBYTE(WFCAPTION))
        {
          hdc = GetWindowDC(hwnd);
          DrawCaption(hwnd,
                      hdc,
                      FALSE,
                      TestWF(hwnd, WFFRAMEON));
          InternalReleaseDC(hdc);
        }
    }
  break;

 case WM_GETTEXT:
   if (wParam)
     {
       if (hwnd->hName)
         return (DWORD)TextCopy(hwnd->hName,
                                (LPSTR)lParam,
                                wParam);

       /* else Null terminate the text buffer since
```

```
                       * there is no text.
                       */
                      ((LPSTR)lParam)[0] = NULL;
                      }
                 return (0L);


             case WM_GETTEXTLENGTH:
               if (hwnd->hName)
                   return(lstrlen(TextPointer(hwnd->hName)));

                 /* else */
                 return(0L);

             case WM_CLOSE:
               DestroyWindow(hwnd);
               break;

             case WM_PAINT:
               BeginPaint(hwnd, (LPPAINTSTRUCT)&ps);
               EndPaint(hwnd, (LPPAINTSTRUCT)&ps);
               break;

             case WM_PAINTICON:
               /* Draw the icon through the window DC if app used
                * own DC. If own DC is used the mapping mode may
                * not be MM_TEXT.
                */
               BeginPaint(hwnd, (LPPAINTSTRUCT)&ps);
               if (TestCF(hwnd, CFOWNDC) || TestCF(hwnd, CFCLASSDC))
                 {
                    /* If owndc, do the end paint now so that the
                     * erasebackgrounds/validate regions go through
                     * properly. Then we get a clean window dc to
                     * draw the icon into.
                     */
                    InternalEndPaint(hwnd, (LPPAINTSTRUCT)&ps, TRUE);
                    hdc = GetWindowDC(hwnd);
                 }
               else
                 {
                    hdc = ps.hdc;
                 }
               /* wParam is TRUE to draw icon, FALSE to ignore paint. */
               if (wParam)
                 {
                    hIcon = (HICON)(PCLS)(hwnd->pcls)->hIcon;
                    GetClientRect(hwnd, (LPRECT)&rc);

                    rc.left = (rc.right - rgwSysMet[SM_CXICON]) >> 1;
                    rc.top = (rc.bottom - rgwSysMet[SM_CYICON]) >> 1;

                    DrawIcon(hdc, rc.left, rc.top, hIcon);
                 }
```

```
      /* Delete the update region. */
        if (TestCF(hwnd, CFOWNDC) || TestCF(hwnd, CFCLASSDC))
          {
            InternalReleaseDC(hdc);
            /* ValidateRect(hwnd, NULL); */
          }
        else
            InternalEndPaint(hwnd, (LPPAINTSTRUCT)&ps, TRUE);
      break;

    case WM_ICONERASEBKGND:
      /* Erase the icon through the window DC if app used
       * own DC. If own DC is used the mapping mode may not
       * be MM_TEXT.
       */
      if (TestCF(hwnd, CFOWNDC) || TestCF(hwnd, CFCLASSDC))
        hdc = GetWindowDC(hwnd);
      else
        hdc = (HDC)wParam;

      if (TestWF(hwnd, WFCHILD))     /* for MDI child icons */
        {
          if ((hbr = GetBackBrush(hwnd->hwndParent)) == NULL)
            {
              /* No brush, punt. */
              goto AbortIconEraseBkGnd;
            }
          else
              goto ICantBelieveIUsedAGoToStatement;
        }

      if (hbmWallpaper)
        {
          /* Since desktop bitmaps are done on a wm_paint
           * message (and not erasebkgnd), we need to call
           * the paint proc with our dc.
           */
          PaintDesktop(hdc);
          /* SendMessage(hwndDesktop,WM_ERASEBKGND,hdc,0L); */
        }
      else
        {
          hbr = sysClrObjects.hbrDesktop;
ICantBelieveIUsedAGoToStatement:
          FillWindow(hwnd->hwndParent,hwnd,hdc,hbr);
        }

AbortIconEraseBkGnd:
        if (TestCF(hwnd, CFOWNDC) || TestCF(hwnd, CFCLASSDC))
          InternalReleaseDC(hdc);

      return((LONG)TRUE);

    case WM_ERASEBKGND:
```

```
      if ((hbr = GetBackBrush(hwnd)) != NULL)
        {
          FillWindow(hwnd, hwnd, (HDC)wParam, hbr);
          return((LONG)TRUE);
        }
      break;

    case WM_QUERYOPEN:
    case WM_QUERYENDSESSION:
      return((LONG)TRUE);

    case WM_SYSCOMMAND:
      SysCommand(hwnd, wParam, lParam);
      break;

    case WM_KEYDOWN:
      if (wParam == VK_F10)
        fF10Status = TRUE;
      break;
    case WM_SYSKEYDOWN:
      /* Is the ALT key down? */
      if (HIWORD(lParam) & SYS_ALTERNATE)
        {
          /* Toggle the fMenuStatus iff this is NOT a
           * repeat KEYDOWN message;  Only if the prev key
           * state was 0, then this is the first KEYDOWN
           * message and then we consider toggling menu
           * status.
           */
          if((HIWORD(lParam) & SYS_PREVKEYSTATE) == 0)
            {
              /* Don't have to lock hwndActive because it's
               * processing this key.
               */
              if ((wParam == VK_MENU) && (!fMenuStatus))
                fMenuStatus = TRUE;
              else
                fMenuStatus = FALSE;
            }

          fF10Status = FALSE;

          DWP_ProcessVirtKey(wParam);
        }
      else
        {
          if (wParam == VK_F10)
            fF10Status = TRUE;
          else
            {
              if (wParam == VK_ESCAPE)
                {
                  if(GetKeyState(VK_SHIFT) < 0)
                    SendMessage(hwnd,
                                WM_SYSCOMMAND,
```

```
                                SC_KEYMENU,
                                (DWORD)MENUSYSMENU);
                    }
                }
            }
        break;

case WM_KEYUP:
case WM_SYSKEYUP:
    /* Press and release F10 or ALT.
     * Send this only to top-level windows, otherwise MDI
     * gets confused.  The fix in which DefMDIChildProc()
     * passed up the message was insufficient in case
     * a child window of the MDI child had the focus.
     */
    if ((wParam == VK_MENU && (fMenuStatus == TRUE)) ||
        (wParam == VK_F10 && fF10Status) )
        SendMessage(GetTopLevelWindow(hwnd),
                    WM_SYSCOMMAND,
                    SC_KEYMENU,
                    (DWORD)0);

    fF10Status = fMenuStatus = FALSE;
    break;

case WM_SYSCHAR:
    /* If syskey is down and we have a char... */
    fMenuStatus = FALSE;
    if ((HIWORD(lParam) & SYS_ALTERNATE) && wParam)
        {
            if (wParam == VK_TAB || wParam == VK_ESCAPE)
                break;

            /* Send ALT-SPACE only to top-level windows. */
            if ((wParam == MENUSYSMENU) && (TestwndChild(hwnd)))
                SendMessage(hwnd->hwndParent,
                            message,
                            wParam,
                            lParam);
            else
                SendMessage(hwnd,
                            WM_SYSCOMMAND,
                            SC_KEYMENU,
                            (DWORD)wParam);
        }
    else
        /* Ctrl-Esc produces a WM_SYSCHAR,
         * But should not beep;
         */
        if (wParam != VK_ESCAPE)
            MessageBeep(0);
    break;

case WM_CHARTOITEM:
case WM_VKEYTOITEM:
```

```
         /* Do default processing for keystrokes into
          * owner draw listboxes.
          */
         return(-1);

     case WM_ACTIVATE:
       if (wParam)
         SetFocus(hwnd);
       break;

     case WM_SETREDRAW:
       DWP_SetRedraw(hwnd, wParam);
       break;

     case WM_SHOWWINDOW:
       /* Non null descriptor implies popup hide or show. */
       /* We should check whether it is a popup window
        * or Owned window
        */
       if (LOWORD(lParam) != 0 &&
          (TestwndPopup(hwnd) || hwnd -> hwndOwner))
         {
           /* IF NOT(showing, invisible, and not set as hidden)
            * AND NOT(hiding and not visible)
            */
           if (!(wParam != 0 && !TestWF(hwnd, WFVISIBLE) &&
                !TestWF(hwnd, WFHIDDENPOPUP)) &&
                !(wParam == 0 && !TestWF(hwnd, WFVISIBLE)))
             {
               /* Are we showing? */
               if (wParam)
                 /* Yes, clear the hidden popup flag. */
                 ClrWF(hwnd, WFHIDDENPOPUP);
               else
                 /* No, Set the hidden popup flag. */
                 SetWF(hwnd, WFHIDDENPOPUP);

               ShowWindow(hwnd,
                   (wParam ? SHOW_OPENNOACTIVATE : HIDE_WINDOW));
             }
         }
       break;

     case WM_CTLCOLOR:
       if (HIWORD(lParam) != CTLCOLOR_SCROLLBAR)
         {
           SetBkColor((HDC)wParam, sysColors.clrWindow);
           SetTextColor((HDC)wParam, sysColors.clrWindowText);
           hbr = sysClrObjects.hbrWindow;
         }
       else
         {
           SetBkColor((HDC)wParam, 0x00ffffff);
           SetTextColor((HDC)wParam, (LONG)0x00000000);
           hbr = sysClrObjects.hbrScrollbar;
```

```
        UnrealizeObject(hbr);
      }

    return((DWORD)hbr);

case WM_SETCURSOR:
  /* wParam  == hwnd that cursor is over
   * lParamL == Hit test area code (result of WM_NCHITTEST)
   * lParamH == Mouse message number
   */
  if (HIWORD(lParam) != 0 &&
      LOWORD(lParam) >= HTSIZEFIRST &&
      LOWORD(lParam) <= HTSIZELAST)
    {
      SetCursor(rghCursor[LOWORD(lParam)
                 - HTSIZEFIRST + MVSIZEFIRST]);
      break;
    }

  if ((hwndT = GetChildParent(hwnd)) != NULL &&
      (BOOL)SendMessage(hwndT,
                        WM_SETCURSOR,
                        wParam,
                        lParam))
    return((LONG)TRUE);
  if (HIWORD(lParam) == 0)
    {
      hCurs = hCursNormal;
      SetCursor(hCurs);
    }
  else
    {
      switch (LOWORD(lParam))
        {
        case HTCLIENT:
          if (((HWND)wParam)->pcls->hCursor != NULL)
            SetCursor(((HWND)wParam)->pcls->hCursor);
          break;

        case HTERROR:
          switch (HIWORD(lParam))
            {
            case WM_LBUTTONDOWN:
              if ((hwndT = DWP_GetEnabledPopup(hwnd)) !=
                   NULL)
                {
                  if (hwndT != hwndDesktop->hwndChild)
                    {
                      SetWindowPos(hwnd, NULL,
                                   0, 0, 0, 0,
                                   SWP_NOMOVE |
                                   SWP_NOSIZE |
                                   SWP_NOACTIVATE);
                      SetActiveWindow(hwndT);
                      break;
```

```
                           }
                       }

                       /*** FALL THRU ***/

                   case WM_RBUTTONDOWN:
                   case WM_MBUTTONDOWN:
                     MessageBeep(0);
                     break;
                   }
                   /*** FALL THRU ***/

               default:
                   SetCursor(hCursNormal);
               }
           }

       return((LONG)FALSE);

     case WM_MOUSEACTIVATE:
       if ((hwndT = GetChildParent(hwnd)) != NULL &&
           (i = (int)SendMessage(hwndT,
                               WM_MOUSEACTIVATE,
                               wParam,
                               lParam)) !=  0)
           return((LONG)i);

       /* Moving, sizing or minimizing?
        * Activate AFTER we take action.
        */
       if (LOWORD(lParam) == HTCAPTION)
         return((LONG)MA_NOACTIVATE);
       else
         return((LONG)MA_ACTIVATE);

     case WM_DRAWITEM:
         if (((LPDRAWITEMSTRUCT)lParam)->CtlType == ODT_LISTBOX)
           LBDefaultListboxDrawItem((LPDRAWITEMSTRUCT)lParam);
         break;

   }

  return(0L);
}
```

Appendix C

Glossary of Terms

__AHINCR__   This is a global symbol that can be used by an application program to increment the segment selector to address memory objects that occupy more than a single segment.

32-Bit Addressing   This refers to the capability in the Intel 80386 and later CPUs to use 32-bit offset to address memory. This allows the creation of memory segments that are as large as one megabyte. When running in 386-Enhanced Mode, Windows uses this type of addressing internally, but does not make it directly available to application programs. However, Microsoft does provide support for 32-bit addressing in a dynamic link library that is included with the Windows software development kit called WINMEM32.

Accelerator   See Keyboard Accelerator.

Active Window   The Active window is a top-level window belonging to the active application. The active application is the application given the highest priority by the user. When a user clicks the mouse on any window owned by an application, selects one of the application's top-level windows from Windows' Task List, or selects the application using keystroke combinations, then the application becomes active. The caption and border of the active application change color to indicate their state to the user. In addition, the windows of the active application are positioned on top of the windows belonging to other applications.

ANSI   American National Standards Institute.

ANSI Character Set   A standard that defines how character glyphs, or images, are stored as numeric character codes. According to the ANSI standard, the values 0 to 31 (1Fh) are reserved for control codes, the values 32 (20h) to 127 (7Fh) are for a standard set of printed characters, and the values 128 (80h) to 255 (FFh) define a range in which vendors can define their own character sequences. The IBM family of personal computers define a set of code pages that use upper range for line-drawing character, Greek letters, and accented characters. Windows defines a more

763

complete set of accented characters that allows Windows programs to more easily be written for support in non-English-speaking countries.

ASCII   American Standard Code for Information Interchange.

Application Message Queue   When a Windows application is running, Windows allocates a buffer that is used to store the messages that are posted (using the **PostMessage** routine) to a program. The messages wait in the queue until a program makes a call to **GetMessage** or to **PeekMessage**. By default, a message queue can hold up to 8 messages. Programs that need a larger message queue can request this by calling **SetMessageQueue**.

Aspect Ratio   The aspect ratio describes the ratio between the height of a pixel and its width. Another way to think about it is in terms of the relative "squareness" of pixels on a device. CGA displays have an aspect ratio of 2 to 1; EGA displays have a ratio of 1.33 to 1; VGA displays have an aspect ratio of 1 to 1.

Background Color   The background color is a DC attribute that is used for drawing text, styled (non-solid) lines, and hatched brushes. It is controlled by the setting of the background mode, another DC attribute.

Background Mode   The background mode is a toggle switch controlling whether the background color is used or not. When set to OPAQUE, the background color is turned on. Setting the background mode to TRANSPARENT turns off the background color.

BitBlt   An acronym for "BIT-boundary BLock Transfer." This GDI function copies rectangular patterns of bits from one location to another. The most obvious use of BitBlt is for moving windows on the display screen. But BitBlts are also used to make menus appear and disappear quickly. Application programs commonly use the BitBlt function to move images stored in bitmaps to an output device like the display screen or a printer. A program can also copy an image from a display screen to a bitmap.

Bitmap   Bitmaps are one of two pseudo-devices that GDI uses to store pictures (the other type is a metafile). Bitmaps use RAM to store rectangular picture images. Bitmaps are created by requesting GDI to allocate the RAM for the picture storage.

Once allocated, a bitmap provides an invisible drawing surface on which a program can draw by calling any of the GDI drawing routines. Bitmaps are also a type of resource that allow a program to store a graphic image inside its executable file. The third type of bitmaps are device-independent bitmaps (DIBs), which provide a device-independent way to store color information.

Brush   A brush is a GDI drawing object used to fill areas. There are three types of brushes: solid, pattern, and hatched. Every DC contains a brush that is used for area filling when on of the filled figure routines is called (**Rectangle**, **Ellipse**, **Polygon**, etc.). Another function which makes use of the brush is the **BitBlt** routine, which can use the brush in the destination DC to alter the effect of the bit-blt operation.

Call-back Functions   A call-back function provides a way for Windows to communicate with a program by calling it directly into a program subroutine.

Call thunk   A call thunk is a tiny piece of code that is used by Windows in real mode as a bridge to far functions in a moveable or discardable code segment.

Capture   see Mouse Capture.

Caret   A caret is a user interface object that serves as a keyboard pointer, in much the same way that the cursor serves as a mouse pointer. A caret is a blinking bitmap that notifies the user of the window that has the keyboard focus, and also provides feedback on the location of the current position in a window.

Casting   Refers to the ability of the C compiler to convert one data type into another data type. In the following example, a variable of type int, i, is set equal to the value of a long variable, lValue:

```
long lValue;
int i;

lValue = 1245;
i = (int)lValue
```

Casting overrides the default conversion that the compiler provides, and avoids the warning messages that compilers often generate in such situations. Nevertheless, Windows programmers can omit certain types of casting which were required for older versions of the C compiler. For example, in response to the WM_PAINT message, here is an outdated but still commonly encountered construction:

```
PAINTSTRUCT ps;

BeginPaint
(hwnd,(LPPAINTSTRUCT)&ps);
.
.
EndPaint
(hwnd,(LPPAINTSTRUCT)&ps);
```

While it is harmless enough in this example, explicit casting is not required and can hide certain types of problems. For example, if the programmer had omitted the "&" in the previous example, the compiler would not be able to see the error because of the casting:

```
PAINTSTRUCT ps;
BeginPaint
(hwnd,(LPPAINTSTRUCT)ps);
```

CDECL Calling Convention   The CDECL calling convention describes the way that parameters are passed on the stack to a subroutine (right to left), and also assigned the calling routine with the responsibility for clearing parameters from the stack. The CDECL calling convention allows routines to be defined with a variable number of parameters, with the disadvantage of creating slightly larger and slower code than the alternative PASCAL calling convention.

Class   see Window Class.

Class Database   Refers to the collection of window classes that have been registered in the system with **RegisterClass**.

Client Area Coordinates   describe a coordinate system that has its origin (0,0) at the upper-left corner of a window. Client area coordinate units are equal to pixels.

Clipping Region   A clipping region defines a closed area used for clipping. Inside the clipping region, drawing is allowed. Outside the clipping region, drawing is not allowed. Clipping regions in Windows are always described in terms of rectangles or groups of rectangles.

Clipping   Clipping describes the behavior of GDI drawing routines in the way they recognize arbitrary borders that are defined. Clipping is de-

fined in terms of closed areas: Inside the clipping region, drawing is allowed. Outside the clipping region, no drawing is allowed.

Clipboard   The Clipboard provides user-operated data sharing services between programs. Items on the Edit menu ordinarily serve as the primary user interface for the Clipboard, and provide Cut, Copy, and Paste options. In addition, a standard set of accelerator keys has been defined for Clipboard commands.

Code Page   A code page defines a character set. The code page determines the set of glyphs, or character images, that will be used to draw a particular character. For example, code page 437 is the standard character set for the United States version of the IBM-PC.

Common User Access (CUA)   Refers to the element of IBM's Systems Application Architecture (SAA) that covers the standards that have been developed for the user interfaces part of application and system software.

Compiler Memory Model   Refers to the set of defaults that the compiler sets for addressing both code and data.

Coordinate Transformation   A coordinate transformation refers to the way that drawing coordinates are interpreted in a graphics output environment. The three basic types of coordinate transformation include translation, scaling, and rotation. In Windows, GDI's coordinate transformations are limited to translation and scaling.

Cursor   A cursor is a bitmap that moves in response to the movement of a mouse.

Debug Version of Windows   Describes Windows when running with special copies of the KERNEL.EXE (KRNL286.EXE, KRNL386.EXE), USER.EXE and GDI.EXE dynamic link libraries.

Default Window Procedure   A Windows library routine that processes non-client area messages, system commands, system keystrokes, and other messages that window procedures do not process.

Desktop Window   Refers to the window that covers the entire display screen and sits behind every other window in the system.

Device Capability Bits   Refers to a set of flags that are provided by a GDI display or printer driver to describe the native capabilities of the device. GDI uses these flags to determine whether to send a high-level drawing request directly to a device driver, or to simulate the request in software and send the device driver a series of low-level drawing requests.

Device Context (DC)   A data structure created and maintained by GDI in support of device independent drawing operations on displays, printers, metafiles, and bitmaps. A device context is three things rolled into one: It is a toolbox containing a set of drawing attributes or drawing tools, it is a connection to a specific device, and it is a permission slip that allows a program to draw on a device.

Device Independent Bitmap (DIB)   A device-independent bitmap provides a standard format for storing color bitmap information. DIBs come in four formats: one-bit per pixel (monochrome), four bits per pixel (16 color), eight bits per pixel (256 color) and 24 bits per pixel (16 million colors).

Dialog Box   A dialog box is a window, inside of which are other windows that are commonly referred to as dialog box controls. A dialog box is typically used to gather additional information from the user required to complete a command.

Dialog Box Control   A dialog box control is a window that rests inside a dialog box and provides a specific set of services. Among the window classes that have been defined for dialog box controls are button, combo box, edit, listbox, scroll bar, and static.

Dialog Box Coordinates   Dialog box coordinates provide a device-independent way to specify the layout of a dialog box. Dialog box units are relative to the system font, or to whatever font has been defined for the dialog box.

Dialog Box Editor   The dialog box editor is a graphic layout tool for designing the look of a dialog box and the style of each dialog box controls. Microsoft provides the dialog box editor as part of its Software Development Kit (SDK).

Disabled Window   A disabled window is one that is prevented from receiving mouse and keyboard input. For example, the parent window of a modal dialog box is disabled.

Discardable Memory   A discardable memory object is one that, when unlocked, can be purged from memory by the memory manager when available system memory is otherwise unavailable. Windows uses a least recently used algorithm to determine the segment to discard next.

Drawing Attribute   A drawing attribute is a setting or a drawing object inside a device context that can change the appearance of the output produced by different GDI drawing routines. Some examples of drawing attributes include pens, brushes, fonts, mapping mode, and text color.

Dynamic Data Exchange (DDE)   A data exchange mechanism that is built on top of Windows' message passing mechanism. A DDE interaction is called a conversation. There are always two participants in a DDE conversation, one called the client and the other called the server. There are several types of DDE converations: ongoing data exchange, one-time data exchange, command execution, and poke of data back into the server's database.

Dynamic Link Library   A dynamic link library is a file containing code or data that can be shared by different application programs at runtime. For example, the core components that make up Windows itself are a collection of dynamic link libraries and include KERNEL.EXE, USER.EXE and GDI.EXE, as well as a set of device drivers. Fonts are an example of dynamic link libraries that contain no code, but only data to be shared between programs.

Dynamic Linking   Dynamic linking refers to the process by which different code and data of different modules—application programs and dynamic link libraries—are connected at run time.

Event-driven   Event-driven software is structured to process external events that do not necessarily occur in a sequential manner. Traditionally, interrupt-handling code in an operating system or in a device driver has been the primary domain of event driven software. But the development of personal computers and interactive software has made this a concern of application programmers. Graphical User Interfaces (GUIs) provide a programming environment which assists in the creation of event driven application software.

Expanded Memory Specification (EMS) The expanded memory specification refers to a protocol that was first introduced in 1984 by Lotus, Intel, and Microsoft to ease the memory crunch that was caused by the 640K memory limitation of real-mode operation. Windows 1.x used EMS memory to cache DOS applications that were dormant; Windows 2.x provided enhanced EMS support to Windows applications that increased the address space of each application in a manner that was transparent to the application programmer. Windows 3.x continues EMS support, although Windows itself only uses EMS in real mode. In the other modes of operation, a Windows program can access EMS memory, but Windows itself does not use EMS because of the greater flexibility that is available with extended memory.

Extended Memory Extended memory refers to the memory that is not ordinarily accessible from real mode, but requires protect-mode operation. Extended memory allows the address space of a machine to go beyond the one-megabyte boundary of real mode and to access up to 16 megabytes with an 80286 processor and up to 4 gigabytes with an 80386 processor.

Extended Memory Specification (XMS) The extended memory specification defines an interface for using the memory areas above the 640K line. This includes the upper memory blocks (UMBs) between 640 and 1024K, the high-memory area (HMA) from 1024 to 1088K, and the extended memory blocks (EMBs) above the 1088K line.

File Manager One of the desktop accessories that Microsoft has bundled with Windows 3.0.

Fixed Memory A fixed memory object is one whose logical address does not change. However, in protect mode, the physical address of a fixed memory block can change unless the memory has been fixed, which is done by calling **GlobalFix**. In addtion, in 386 Enhanced Mode, a fixed memory object can also be paged to disk unless it has been page-locked, which is accomplished by calling **GlobalPageLock**.

Focus see Keyboard Focus.

Font also see Logical Font.

Function Prototype Function prototypes provide a means by which the C Compiler can perform some automatic error checking, including check for proper use of the return value and the correct number and type of parameters. Here is an example of a function prototype taken from Window.h:

```
BOOL FAR PASCAL TextOut
(HDC, int, int, LPSTR, int);
```

Global Descriptor Table (GDT) A global descriptor table is one of two data areas used by the Intel 80286 and higher CPUs in protect mode. A global descriptor table allows the CPU to convert segment identifier values (also known as segment selectors) into the physical addresses of segments. Intel designed the GDT to provide a shared data area accessible from all processes. However, Windows does not use a GDT for any of its memory management, but uses the other data area, the local descriptor table (LDT) instead.

Global Heap The global heap refers to the total memory available to Windows itself, to Windows applications, and to other components like device drivers.

Global Memory Object A global memory object is an object allocated from the global heap. In Intel memory architecture terms, a global memory object is a segment.

Granularity In the context of memory allocation, granularity refers to the increments by which memory is actually allocated. The global heap manager uses a granularity of 32 bytes. The local heap manager uses a granularity of 4 bytes.

Graphic Device Interface (GDI) GDI is Windows' device-independent graphics output library.

Graphical User Interface (GUI) Refers to a type of operating system or operating environment that displays output on a bitmapped graphical display screen. Another characteristic of GUI systems is that they are event-driven, which means a different programming model is necessary besides the traditional, sequence oriented programming model that was originally developed for batch oriented systems. Microsoft Windows is an example of a GUI system. Other examples include the Apple Macintosh, the OS/2 Presentation Manager, which was jointly developed by IBM and Microsoft, and Digital Research Corporation's GEM. The various X-Windows systems deserve to be in this last as well, and they include the Open System Foundation's Motif, and Sun Microsystem's Open Look and Digital Equipment Corporation's DEC-Windows.

GUI   an acronym for Graphical User Interface.

Handle   A handle is a 16-bit, unsigned integer that identifies an object. In most cases, the meaning of a handle is only known to the subroutine library that issued the handle. A program can modify an object by providing the handle to the subroutine library, which then acts on the objects on behalf of the program.

Hardware Event Queue   A buffer maintained by Windows to hold keyboard and mouse events that are waiting to be retrieved by application programs.

High Memory Area (HMA)   The high memory area refers to the 64 K-bytes located immediately above the one-megabyte address line on 80286 and 80386 processors. Intel designed this space as the first 64K of extended memory, which was not meant to be part of the real mode address space. However, an XMS (eXtended Memory Specification) driver, like HIMEM.SYS, is able to trick the 80286 and higher chips into allowing access into this data area.

Hit-Test Code   Refers to a code returned by the default window procedure in reponse to the WM_NCHITTEST message, which identifies the area of a window where the mouse is located. Hit-test codes are used to help the window manager to install the correct mouse cursor.

Hook   A hook is a subroutine that is called by Windows' message handling mechanism to allow the monitoring and modification of message traffic in the system. Hooks are installed on a system-wide basis, and therefore care should be taken when using them to avoid disrupting the normal operation of other programs, and to avoid slowing the system down.

Hungarian naming   Hungarian naming is a convention for creating variable and function names that provide a quick way to compose short but useful identifiers.

Huge Memory Object   A huge memory object is a memory object in the global heap that is larger than 64K. Windows allocates huge memory objects by allocating two or more segments. To access the second and subsequent segments, huge pointer arithmetic is required. This involves updating the segment portion of the address as well as the offset portion. The segment portion is modified by changing the segment value using the __AHINCR update value. This value is added to the segment address to access the next segment in a huge object segment chain.

Icon   An icon is a graphic symbol that serves to remind the user of the presence of a program, file, or data object that is presently closed, but available for future access.

Import Library   An import library provides the linker with information about the exported entry points of a dynamic link library. An import library allows the linker to create a relocation record in a program's .EXE file so that Windows' dynamic link mechanism can provide the required fix-up to the calling code at program execution time.

Instance   An instance of a program refers to a copy of a program in memory. Windows allows several copies of a single program to run simultaneously. Each instance has its own, private data segment, but shares code and resource segments with every other instance of the program.

Instance Thunk   An instance thunk is a tiny piece of code that is created in a program's task database (TDB) to assist in the fix-up of the data segment for an exported call-back function. An instance thunk is created by **MakeProcInstance**, and freed by **FreeProcInstance**. With the exception of window procedures, every call-back procedure requires an instance thunk. This includes dialog box procedure, enumeration procedures, notification procedures, and certain subclass procedures. No instance thunk is required for any of these procedures when they reside in the code segment of a dynamic link library.

Interrupt Descriptor Table   An interrupt descriptor table (IDT) is a lookup table used by the higher end Intel-86 chips (80286 and above) in protect mode to hold an array of interrupts.

Keyboard Accelerator   A keyboard accelerator provides a means to define key-strokes that are interpreted as commands. Keyboard accelerators mimic menu selection messages, to minimize special processing that would otherwise be required to support a program's command keys.

Keyboard Focus   The keyboard focus tells Windows the window that should receive keyboard input. When a program receives the keyboard focus, it is notified with a WM_SETFOCUS message. When it loses the focus, it is notified with a WM_KILLFOCUS message.

Keyboard Scan Code   A keyboard scan code is a numeric value sent from the keyboard hardware as a notification that a key was pressed, released, or is being held down. Application programs do not ordinarily handle scan codes, since they represent a hardware dependent key code. In Windows, scan codes undergo two translation before they appear in a program as ASCII characters. The first translation is from scan code to virtual key codes. The second translation is from virtual key codes to ASCII characters.

KERNEL   The KERNEL is one of the three core components of Windows, and is responsible for memory management, dynamic linking, resources, atom tables, module managment, interface to DOS, and other operating system services that are available to Windows programs.

Load On Call segment   A load on call segment is a code or resource segment that is loaded into memory when it is referenced.

Local Descriptor Table (LDT)   A local descriptor table is one of two data areas used by the Intel 80286 and higher CPUs in protect mode. A local descriptor table allows the CPU to convert segment identifier values (also known as segment selectors) into the physical addresses of segments. Intel designed the LDT to provide a process with a private address space. In Windows 3.0, a single LDT is used by all application programs. However, a future version of Windows will provide one LDT per application program.

Local Heap   Refers to the heap that is created in a module's default data segment. The automatic startup code automatically initializes the local heap of an application program by calling the **LocalInit** routine. Dynamic link libraries that wish to use a local heap must explicitly call **LocalInit** themselves.

Logical Drawing Object   A logical drawing object is a GDI description of a pen, brush, font, or color. It provides a device-independent way to describe the drawing attributes that are installed in a DC.

Logical Font   A logical font is a description of a font that GDI's font mapper uses to select a font for drawing text. A logical font description can be created using the LOGFONT data structure.

Logical Pen   A logical pen describes the color, width, and style of lines requested by a program.

Mapping Mode   A mapping mode is a DC drawing attribute that describes how drawing coordinates that are given to GDI drawing routines are interpreted. For example, the default mapping mode, MM_TEXT, interprets coordinates as pixels. The other mapping modes can be used to scale coordinates into fractions of an inch, fractions of a centimeter, or scale to arbitrary ratios.

Marker   A marker is a graphic primitive that is guaranteed to be centered on the specified location. Although GDI itself does not directly implement markers, it is a simple matter to build a set of marker subroutines that draw using GDI drawing routines. See Chapter 7.

Message   A message is a 16-bit, unsigned value that notifies a window procedure that an event of interest has occurred. Windows' predefined messages are identified in Windows.H with symbolic constants whose names start with a WM_ prefix. For example, the WM_CREATE message is sent to a window procedure to notify it that a window of that class has been created.

Metafile   A metafile is a pseudo-device that GDI can create for the purpose of storing graphic images. A GDI metafile is a data structure containing a list of calls to be made to GDI routines to reconstruct a picture, along with the parameters to provide those calls.

Module   A module is a specific type of entity in Windows, which reflects the way that code and data is organized on disk. Windows recognizes two types of modules: executable application (.EXE) program files, and dynamic link libraries, which can have an extension of .EXE, .DRV, .DLL, or .FON, to name just a few.

Module Database   A module database is a memory resident image of the file header of an application program or a dynamic link library. The Windows loader uses the module database to load code and resources from disk when they are needed.

Module Definition File   An ASCII text file that contains program definition and memory use information. A module definition file normally has an extension of .DEF. At program creation time, the module definition file is given to the linker as part of the bulding of a .EXE or .DLL file.

Mouse Capture   Ordinarily, mouse messages are sent to the window lying under the mouse cursor. However, a program can restrict the flow of mouse messages to a single window by setting the mouse capture. This is done by calling **SetCapture**. To free mouse messages, a program calls **ReleaseCapture**.

Moveable Memory   Moveable memory objects are an artifact of real mode Windows. In real mode, a moveable object will only move when it is not locked by a program. In protect mode, segments can move at any time, since the physical address is hidden from application software. The protect mode memory management hardware converts logical addresses—which is how application software references memory—into physical addresses by means of a descriptor table. The Windows memory manager can move objects in physical memory without changing their logical addresses, which means that in protect mode, memory movement is transparent to application softare.

Multiple Document Interface   or MDI, describes a user-interface standard that opens a new window for each new file or document that is opened in a program.

Nonpreemptive Scheduling   Describes the way that a multitasking system schedules programs to run. In a nonpreemptively scheduled system, the operating system does not interrupt programs

OEM Character Set   Refers to the set of characters native to a machine. For IBM-compatible computers built for sale in United States, this means code page 437.

Page Locking   Page locking refers to a process by which memory in 386-Enhanced Mode is prevented from being swapped to disk. This is accomplished by calling the **GlobalPageLock**

routine and is primarily intended for the use of time-critical device drivers that must stay memory resident.

Paragraph   When the Intel-86 processors operate in real mode, a paragraph is the smallest memory unit that can be allocated. A paragraph is 16 bytes. Windows' memory manager allocates segments in two-paragraph increments, which means the granularity of the global memory manager is 32 bytes.

Paintbrush   One of the desktop accessories that is included with Windows 3.0.

Palette (PAL)   A palette provides two services: It describes the colors that are stored in a device-independent bitmap (DIB), and it allows a program to request changes to the physical palette of display devices that support palettes.

PASCAL Calling Convention   The PASCAL calling convention describes the way that parameters are passed on the stack to a subroutine (left to right), and also assigns the called routine with the responsibility for cleaning the parameters from the stack. Routines that are defined as PASCAL must have a fixed number of parameters, but this results in slightly smaller and faster code than the alternative CDECL calling convention.

Pen   A pen is a DC attribute that describes the color, style, and width of lines. See Logical Pen.

Preemptive Scheduling   Describes the way that a multitasking system schedules programs to run. In a preemptively scheduled system, the operating system will interrupt one program to allow another one to run.

Preload Segments   A code or resource segment that is marked as preload is moved into memory before a program starts running.

Private Window Class   A private window class is reserved for the use of a single program. In contrast are global window classes, which are available for use by any program in the system.

Process Database (PDB)   A data structure created by Windows to maintain DOS related per-process data. Windows adds its own elements to this data structure.

Profiler   see Swap Kernel.

Program Manager   Refers to the main program window in Windows 3.0.

Program Segment Prefix (PSP) see Process Database.

Protect Mode Protect mode refers to an operating mode of Intel 80286 chips and later. Protect mode is characterized by an addressing scheme that prevents programs from illegal access to un-owned memory areas. On the 80286, protect mode operation allows a physical address space of 16 megabytes. On the 80386 and 80486, protect mode allows access to a 4 gigabyte address space.

Pull-Model Processing Refers to a style of interaction between the operating system and application software. Pull-model processing places the application software in the active role, in which it polls the system for available input. This is the traditional way that interactive application software has been written, and is how Windows' handles mouse and keyboard input. Also, messages that are transmitted to a window procedure using the PostMessage routine are delivered in a pull-model manner, that is, via the GetMessage or PeekMessage routines. See also push-model processing.

Push-Model Processing Refers to a style of interaction between the operating system and application software. Push-model processing places the operating system software in the active role, in which it calls subroutines in the application software to perform the necessary tasks. Most of the non-hardware related messages in Windows are delivered in a push-model manner. For example, when a program calls the CreateWindow routine to create a window, a WM_CREATE message is pushed into the window procedure of the newly created window. Messages that are transmitted to a window procedure using the **SendMessage** routine are delivered in a push-model manner, which bypasses the pull-model **Get-Message** routine, and calls a window procedure directly.

Raster Operation A raster operation is a logical operation or combination of logical operations that describe how two or more inputs combine to produce a given output. One type of raster operation is the ROP2 codes, which are a DC attribute that describe how pixels, lines, and areas combine with a drawing surface. Another type of raster operation, sometimes known as ROP3 codes, are provided as parameters to the BitBlt and PatBlt

functions, to describe how a source bitmap, a destination bitmap, and a brush are to combine.

Return Thunks A return thunk is a tiny piece of code that real mode Windows uses to bridge a function return when the code segment containing the calling routine is discarded from memory.

Resource A resource is a read-only data object that is bound into an executable file at program creation time. From a memory management point of view, resources can be discarded and reread when needed. From the point of view of the Windows user interface, resources define dialog boxes, menus, cursors, icons, bitmaps, to name just a few.

Real Mode Real Mode refers to an operating mode of the Intel-86 family of processors. Real mode is characterized by a one-megabyte address space. Programs have access to the real, physical address of memory, which is how the mode gets its name.

Scan Code see Keyboard Scan Code.

Scanner A graphic scanner reads a graphic image on paper and converts it into a digital form suitable for creating GDI bitmaps.

Segment Selector When the Intel-86 family of processors are running in protect mode, a segment identifier is referred to as a segment selector. Part of a segment selector is an index into a table of descriptors in either an LDT (local descriptor table) or a GDT (global descriptor table), from which is read the physical location of a memory segment.

Segmented Addressing The Intel-86 family of CPUs address memory using a segmented addressing scheme. Segmented addressing requires two pieces in a memory address: a segment identifier and an offset.

Software Development Kit (SDK) The Windows Software Development Kit is a product that Microsoft provides for the purpose of assisting software developers to create Windows programs.

Software Migration Kit (SMK) The Software Migration Kit is a product that Microsoft provides to assist software developers in porting Windows programs to run in OS/2, version 1.2 and later.

Stack Patching Stack patching refers to the process by which the real mode Windows Kernel updates stack references to code segments that have moved or been discarded.

Standard Mode   Refers to an operating mode of Windows in which protect mode addressing is enabled to allow Windows to take advantage of features of the Intel family of processors that are available on the 80286 and higher CPUs.

Swap Kernel   The swap kernel is a special version of the Windows kernel that runs in real mode only and provides information about the segment loading and discarding of a program. It can be used to fine tune the segment working sets of a program to minimize the program's required memory.

Systems Application Architecture (SAA)   A collection of standards created by IBM to provide software consistency that extends from personal computers to mini-computers on up to mainframes. Aspects of application software that will be affected include the user interface, and application programming interface (API). The user interface standards are described in a standard that is part of SAA and is called Common User Access (CUA).

Task Database (TDB)   A task database is a memory object created by the Window scheduler to keep track of the things that are owned by a task. This includes file handles, the current MS-DOS disk and directory, information about a task's private interrupts, and a pointer to the DOS program database, also known as a program segment prefix (PSP).

Text Alignment   The text alignment is a DC attribute that describes the placement of a line of text relative to a control point.

Text Color   The text color is a DC attribute that describes the color for drawing text. Only pure, undithered colors are actually used for text, which means that GDI maps the requested color into the closest available device color.

Thunk   A thunk is a tiny piece of code that serves as a dynamic code link (in real mode Windows)

Tiled Windows   Tiled windows refers to the placement of windows so that no two windows overlap. Windows 1.x had built-in support for automatic tiling. This support was removed in versions 2.0 and later.

Top-Level Window   A top-level window is an overlapping window (WS_OVERLAP) or a popup window (WS_POPUP) which has no parent. All top-level windows are referenced in Windows' Task List that appears in response to the Ctrl + Esc key combination.

Unexpected Application Error (UAE)   A n error that causes an application to terminate. Some of the causes of unexpected application errors include general protection faults, unexpected paging fault, and unexpected interrupt.

Viewport Origin   The viewport origin is a DC attribute that defines the coordinate translation to take place after the scaling for the various GDI mapping modes.

Viewport Extent   The viewport extent is a DC attribute that provides a pair of X and Y values that are used to define the ratios for GDI's isotropic and anisotropic mapping modes.

Virtual Key Code   A virtual key code is a value that represents keystroke information as raw keyboard input. Raw keyboard input does not distinguish, for example, between upper and lower-case letters, and does not take into account the state of shift keys like Ctrl, Shift, and Alt. Nor do virtual key codes take into account the state of the various keyboard toggle keys, like Num Lock, Caps Lock, or Scroll Lock. Virtual key codes represent an intermediate step between scan code information, which is hardware-dependent keyboard input, and ASCII characters, which are device-independent representations of ASCII characters.

Window Class   A window class is a template for creating a window. Window classes are created by calling RegisterClass and supplying a pointer to a WNDCLASS structure with the class definition information.

Window Extent   The window extent is a DC attribute that provides a pair of X and Y values that are used to define the ratios for GDI's isotropic and anisotropic mapping modes.

Window Origin   The window origin is a DC attribute that defines the translation that is to take place in the world coordinate space before the scaling transformation of any of GDI's mapping modes.

Window Procedure   A function associated with a window class that processes the messages associated with a given window.

Windows Sandwich   A window sandwich describes a code construction made up of three parts: two slices of bread and some filling in between. The top slice of bread borrows a system resource, the filling uses the resource, and the bottom slice of bread returns the resource to the owner.

Appendix D

Contents of a Device Context

Drawing Attribute	Default Value	Lines	Filled Areas	Text	Raster	Comments
Background Color	White	X	X	X		styled pen, hatch brush
Background Mode	OPAQUE	X	X	X		On/Off switch
Brush Handle	White Brush		X		X	Filled areas
Brush Origin	(0 , 0)		X		X	hatch & dithered brushes
Clipping Region Handle	Entire Surface	X	X	X	X	
Color Palette Handle	Default Palette	X	X	X		
Current Pen Position	(0 , 0)	X				For LineTo routine
Drawing Mode	R2_COPYPEN	X	X			Boolean mixing
Font Handle	System Font			X		
Intercharacter Spacing	0			X		
Mapping Mode	MM_TEXT	X	X	X	X	One unit = 1 pixel
Pen Handle	Black Pen	X	X			

Drawing Attribute	Default Value	Lines	Filled Areas	Text	Raster	Comments
Polygon-Filling Mode	Alternate		x			For Polygon routine
Stretching Mode	Black on White				x	For StretchBlt routine
Text Alignment	Left & Top			x		
Text Color	Black			x		
Viewport Extent	(1 , 1)	x	x	x	x	Coordinate mapping
Viewport Origin	(0 , 0)	x	x	x	x	Coordinate mapping
Window Extent	(1 , 1)	x	x	x	x	Coordinate mapping
Window Origin	(0 , 0)	x	x	x	x	Coordinate mapping

Appendix E

ANSI and OEM Character Sets

	0-	1-	2-	3-	4-	5-	6-	7-	8-	9-	A-	B-	C-	D-	E-	F-
-0	I	I		0	@	P	`	p	I	I		°	À	Ð	à	ð
-1	I	I	!	1	A	Q	a	q	I	´	¡	±	Á	Ñ	á	ñ
-2	I	I	"	2	B	R	b	r	I	´	¢	²	Â	Ò	â	ò
-3	I	I	#	3	C	S	c	s	I	I	£	³	Ã	Ó	ã	ó
-4	I	I	$	4	D	T	d	t	I	I	¤	´	Ä	Ô	ä	ô
-5	I	I	%	5	E	U	e	u	I	I	¥	µ	Å	Õ	å	õ
-6	I	I	&	6	F	V	f	v	I	I	¦	¶	Æ	Ö	æ	ö
-7	I	I	'	7	G	W	g	w	I	I	§	·	Ç	×	ç	÷
-8	I	I	(	8	H	X	h	x	I	I	¨	¸	È	Ø	è	ø
-9	I	I	)	9	I	Y	i	y	I	I	©	¹	É	Ù	é	ù
-A	I	I	*	:	J	Z	j	z	I	I	ª	º	Ê	Ú	ê	ú
-B	I	I	+	;	K	[	k	{	I	I	«	»	Ë	Û	ë	û
-C	I	I	,	<	L	\	l	|	I	I	¬	¼	Ì	Ü	ì	ü
-D	I	I	-	=	M	]	m	}	I	I		½	Í	Ý	í	ý
-E	I	I	.	>	N	^	n	~	I	I	®	¾	Î	Þ	î	þ
-F	I	I	/	?	O	_	o	I	I	I	¯	¿	Ï	ß	ï	ÿ

Figure E.1   ANSI Character Set (Code Page 1004)

Figure E.2 OEM Character Set (Code Page 437)

Appendix F

The Windows Virtual Key Codes

(hex)	(dec)	Symbolic Name	Key Pressed (US English 101/102 Kbd)
1	1	VK_LBUTTON	
2	2	VK_RBUTTON	
3	3	VK_CANCEL	Ctrl-Break
4	4	VK_MBUTTON	
8	8	VK_BACK	Backspace
9	9	VK_TAB	Tab
C	12	VK_CLEAR	5 on Numeric keypad w/Num Lock OFF
D	13	VK_RETURN	Enter
10	16	VK_SHIFT	Shift
11	17	VK_CONTROL	Ctrl
12	18	VK_MENU	Alt
13	19	VK_PAUSE	Pause (or Ctrl-Num Lock)
14	20	VK_CAPITAL	Caps Lock
1B	27	VK_ESCAPE	Esc
20	32	VK_SPACE	Spacebar

(hex)	*(dec)*	*Symbolic Name*	*Key Pressed (US English 101/102 Kbd)*
21	33	VK_PRIOR	Page Up
22	34	VK_NEXT	Page Down
23	35	VK_END	End
24	36	VK_HOME	Home
25	37	VK_LEFT	Left Arrow
26	38	VK_UP	Up Arrow
27	39	VK_RIGHT	Right Arrow
28	40	VK_DOWN	Down Arrow
29	41	VK_SELECT	<unused>
2A	42	VK_PRINT	<unused>
2B	43	VK_EXECUTE	<unused>
2C	44	VK_SNAPSHOT	Print Screen
2D	45	VK_INSERT	Ins
2E	46	VK_DELETE	Del
2F	47	VK_HELP	<unused>
30-39	48-57	VK_0 to VK_9	0 to 9 above letter keys
41-5A	65-90	VK_A to VK_Z	A to Z
60	96	VK_NUMPAD0	0 on Numeric keypad w/Num Lock ON
61	97	VK_NUMPAD1	1 on Numeric keypad w/Num Lock ON
62	98	VK_NUMPAD2	2 on Numeric keypad w/Num Lock ON
63	99	VK_NUMPAD3	3 on Numeric keypad w/Num Lock ON
64	100	VK_NUMPAD4	4 on Numeric keypad w/Num Lock ON
65	101	VK_NUMPAD5	5 on Numeric keypad w/Num Lock ON
66	102	VK_NUMPAD6	6 on Numeric keypad w/Num Lock ON
67	103	VK_NUMPAD7	7 on Numeric keypad w/Num Lock ON
68	104	VK_NUMPAD8	8 on Numeric keypad w/Num Lock ON
69	105	VK_NUMPAD9	9 on Numeric keypad w/Num Lock ON
6A	106	VK_MULTIPLY	* on Numeric keypad
6B	107	VK_ADD	+ on Numeric keypad
6C	108	VK_SEPARATOR	<unused>
6D	109	VK_SUBTRACT	- on Numeric keypad
6E	110	VK_DECIMAL	. on Numeric keypad w/Num Lock ON
6F	111	VK_DIVIDE	/ on Numeric keypad
70	112	VK_F1	F1 function key
71	113	VK_F2	F2 function key

(hex)	*(dec)*	*Symbolic Name*	*Key Pressed (US English 101/102 Kbd)*
72	114	VK_F3	F3 function key
73	115	VK_F4	F4 function key
74	116	VK_F5	F5 function key
75	117	VK_F6	F6 function key
76	118	VK_F7	F7 function key
77	119	VK_F8	F8 function key
78	120	VK_F9	F9 function key
79	121	VK_F10	F10 function key
7A	122	VK_F11	F11 function key
7B	123	VK_F12	F12 function key
7C	124	VK_F13	
7D	125	VK_F14	
7E	126	VK_F15	
7F	127	VK_F16	
90	144	VK_NUMLOCK	Num Lock
91	145		Scroll Lock

The following code apply to US keyboards only

BA	186		colon/semi-colon
BB	187		plus/equal
BC	188		less than/comma
BD	189		underscore/hyphen
BE	190		greater than/period
BF	191		question/slash
C0	192		tilde/back accent
DB	219		left squiggle brace/left square brace
DC	220		horizontal bar/backslash
DD	221		right squiggle brace/right square brace
DE	222		double quote/single quote

Appendix G

Windows 3.1 Allocation and Cleanup Routines

Resource	Allocation Routine	Cleanup Routine	Deletion Required?
Accelerators	LoadAccelerators	n/a	No
Atoms	GlobalAddAtom	GlobalFreeAtom	Yes
Bitmap	CreateBitmap	DeleteObject	Yes **
	CreateBitmapIndirect	DeleteObject	Yes **
	CreateCompatibleBitmap	DeleteObject	Yes **
	CreateDIBitmap	DeleteObject	Yes **
	CreateDiscardableBitmap	DeleteObject	Yes **
	LoadBitmap	DeleteObject	Yes **
Brush	CreateBrushIndirect	DeleteObject	Yes
	CreateDIBPatternBrush	DeleteObject	Yes
	CreateHatchBrush	DeleteObject	Yes
	CreatePatternBrush	DeleteObject	Yes
	CreateSolidBrush	DeleteObject	Yes

Note: Reprinted by permission of the publisher from Paul Yao, "Careful Windows Resource Allocation and Cleanup Improves Application Hygiene," *Microsoft Systems Journal* Sep/Oct. 1991.

Resource	Allocation Routine	Cleanup Routine	Deletion Required?
Caret	CreateCaret	DestroyCaret	No +
Clipboard	OpenClipboard	CloseClipboard	Yes
Comm Port	OpenComm	CloseComm	Yes
Cursor	CopyCursor	DestroyCursor	Yes
	CreateCursor	DestroyCursor	Yes
	LoadCursor	n/a	No
DC	CreateDC	DeleteDC	Yes
	CreateCompatibleDC	DeleteDC	Yes ***
	GetDC	ReleaseDC	Yes
	GetWindowDC	ReleaseDC	Yes
	BeginPaint	EndPaint	Yes
Dialog Box	CreateDialog	DestroyWindow	No
	CreateDialogIndirect	DestroyWindow	No
	CreateDialogIndirectParam	DestroyWindow	No
	CreateDialogParam	DestroyWindow	No
File	OpenFile	_lclose	No
Fonts	CreateFont	DeleteObject	Yes
	CreateFontIndirect	DeleteObject	Yes
	AddFontResource	RemoveFontResource	Yes
GDI Stock Objects	GetStockObject	n/a	No ++
Hook	SetWindowsHook	UnhookWindowsHook	Yes
	SetWindowsHookEx	UnhookWindowsHookEx	Yes
Information Context	CreateIC	DeleteDC	Yes
Icon	CopyIcon	DestroyIcon	Yes
	CreateIcon	DestroyIcon	Yes
	LoadIcon	n/a	No
Library	LoadLibrary	FreeLibrary	Yes
Memory	AllocDStoCSAlias	FreeSelector	Yes
	AllocSelector	FreeSelector	Yes
	GlobalAlloc	GlobalFree	No
	GlobalFix	GlobalUnfix	No
	GlobalLock	GlobalUnlock	No
	GlobalPageLock	GlobalPageUnlock	No
	GlobalWire	GlobalUnwire	No
	LocalAlloc	LocalFree	No

Resource	Allocation Routine	Cleanup Routine	Deletion Required?
	`LocalLock`	`LocalUnlock`	No
Menu	`CreateMenu`	`DestroyMenu`	No *
	`CreatePopupMenu`	`DestroyMenu`	No *
	`LoadMenu`	`DestroyMenu`	No *
	`LoadMenuIndirect`	`DestroyMenu`	No *
	`GetSystemMenu`	`n/a`	No
Metafile	`CreateMetaFile`	`DeleteMetaFile`	Yes
Palette	`CreatePalette`	`DeleteObject`	Yes
Pen	`CreatePen`	`DeleteObject`	Yes
	`CreatePenIndirect`	`DeleteObject`	Yes
Regions	`CreateEllipticRgn`	`DeleteObject`	Yes
	`CreateEllipticRgnIndirect`	`DeleteObject`	Yes
	`CreatePolygonRgn`	`DeleteObject`	Yes
	`CreatePolyPolygonRgn`	`DeleteObject`	Yes
	`CreateRectRgn`	`DeleteObject`	Yes
	`CreateRectRgnIndirect`	`DeleteObject`	Yes
	`CreateRoundRectRgn`	`DeleteObject`	Yes
Resource	`FindResource`	`n/a`	No
	`LoadResource`	`FreeResource`	No
	`LockResource`	`UnlockResource`	No
Sound	`OpenSound`	`CloseSound`	Yes
String	`LoadString`	`n/a`	No
Thunk	`MakeProcInstance`	`FreeProcInstance`	No
Timer	`SetTimer`	`Killtimer`	No
Window	`CreateWindow`	`DestroyWindow`	No
	`CreateWindowEx`	`DestroyWindow`	No

* Menus not connected to any window must be freed before an application exits.

** Bitmaps must be disconnected from DCs before being freed.

*** DCs must be disconnected from bitmaps before being freed.

\+ If a bitmap is specified for the CARET, it must be freed.

\+\+ Calls to `DeleteObject` do not harm stock objects.

Index